Life-Course Criminology

Contemporary and Classic Readings

ALEX PIQUERO
Northeastern University,
College of Criminal Justice

PAUL MAZEROLLE
The University of Queensland,
Department of Sociology, Anthropology,
and Archeology

WADSWORTH
™
THOMSON LEARNING

Australia • Canada • Mexico • Singapore • Spain
United Kingdom • United States

WADSWORTH
TM
THOMSON LEARNING

Executive Editor, Criminal Justice: *Sabra Horne*
Development Editor: *Terri Edwards*
Assistant Editor: *Ann Tsai*
Editorial Assistant: *Cortney Bruggink*
Marketing Manager: *Jennifer Somerville*
Signing Representative: *Nicole Foran*
Project Editor: *Jennie Redwitz*
Print Buyer: *Karen Hunt*

Permissions Editor: *Bob Kauser*
Production Service: *Gustafson Graphics*
Copy Editor: *Alan DeNiro*
Illustrator: *Luis R. Martinez*
Cover Designer: *Bill Reuter*
Cover Printer: *Webcom, Ltd.*
Compositor: *Gustafson Graphics*
Printer: *Webcom, Ltd.*

Printed in Canada
2 3 4 5 6 7 04 03 02 01

For permission to use material from this text, contact us by
Web: http://www.thomsonrights.com
Fax: 1-800-730-2215
Phone: 1-800-730-2214

For information about our products, contact us:
Thomson Learning Academic Resource Center
1-800-423-0563
http://www.wadsworth.com

Wadsworth/Thomson Learning
10 Davis Drive
Belmont, CA 94002-3098
USA

International Headquarters
Thomson Learning
International Division
290 Harbor Drive, 2nd Floor
Stamford, CT 06902-7477
USA

UK/Europe/Middle East/South Africa
Thomson Learning
Berkshire House
168-173 High Holborn
London WC1V 7AA
United Kingdom

Asia
Thomson Learning
60 Albert Street, #15-01
Albert Complex
Singapore 189969

Canada
Nelson Thomson Learning
1120 Birchmount Road
Toronto, Ontario M1K 5G4
Canada

Library of Congress Cataloging-in-Publication Data

Life-course criminology: contemporary and classic
readings / [edited by]
Alex Piquero and Paul Mazerolle.
    p. cm. — (The Wadsworth series in criminological
    theory)
  Includes bibliographical references and index.
  ISBN 0-534-57492-0
    1. Criminology. 2. Developmental psychology.
    3. Life cycle, Human.
I. Piquero, Alexis Russell. II. Mazerolle, Paul.
III. Contemporary issues in crime and justice series.

HV6030 .L53 2000
364—dc21   00-042299

Contents

Foreword

ROBERT J. SAMPSON

Criminology has always been an exciting field of study. Indeed, fundamental questions such as why individuals violate norms, the origins of social order, official reactions to deviance, and the sources of violence have long fascinated scholars. In my opinion, the field has recently become even more vibrant with the explosion of life-course research, or, as my colleague John Laub and I have dubbed it, "life-course criminology" (Reading 10). This framework is perhaps best introduced by considering the questions *it* asks. They include, why and when do most juvenile delinquents stop offending? What factors explain "desistance"? Are some delinquents destined to become persistent criminals in adulthood? Is there, in fact, such a thing as a "life-course persistent" offender? Is the age-crime curve invariant across social conditions? What explains the stability of offending? Are there "turning points" that deflect previously criminal trajectories? Criminology is abuzz with attempts to answer such questions.

VARIABILITY IN CRIME
OVER THE LIFE COURSE

The life course has been conceptualized as trajectories and transitions through the age-differentiated life span (Elder, Reading 1). A trajectory is a pathway or line of development through life in such areas as work, marriage, parenthood, and criminal behavior ("criminal career"?). Trajectories refer to longer-term patterns and sequences of behavior, whereas transitions are marked by specific life events (e.g., first job or the onset of crime) that are embedded in trajectories and evolve over shorter time spans. The interlocking nature of trajectories and transitions may generate turning points or a change in life-course pattern. Therefore, a hallmark of life-course studies is the dual focus on the connection between childhood or adolescent experiences and adulthood outcomes (*continuity*) along with the potential for transitions or turning points to modify life-course trajectories (*change*).

The motivation for applying the life-course perspective to criminology can be appreciated by considering practice-as-usual. Criminologists have traditionally addressed the causes of crime by studying why some individuals and not others commit crimes, leading to between-individual comparisons and a well-known list of correlated attributes (sex, race, personality, family background, and so on). Although this research tradition is obviously important, a different way of approaching the problem is found in life-course criminology. Consistent with a dynamic process, longitudinal research has revealed an apparent paradox: although adult criminality is nearly always preceded by antisocial behavior in childhood, most antisocial children do not become criminals as adults. There is far more heterogeneity in criminal behavior over time than individual-difference theories (typical in psychology) or structural-causation theories (typical in sociology) allow. Variability is near ubiquitous.

There is marked variability in adult outcomes even among serious and persistent juvenile delinquents. For example, in Reading 14 we find that the standard chestnuts measuring family background—such as poverty, parental criminality, and child supervision—do not predict trajectories of adult offending among formerly incarcerated delinquents. Allegedly stable personality characteristics fare no better; measures of childhood extroversion, egocentricity, aggressiveness, difficult temperament, and tantrums all fail to distinguish persistent offenders from desisters. Looking forward from youth thus reveals both successes and failures, including troubled adolescents who desist. Yet apropos the paradox noted earlier, looking back over the careers of adult criminals exaggerates the picture of stability.

In short, the message of life-course criminology seems to be that static background variables are surprisingly weak when it comes to the *prospective* explanation of *trajectories* of crime over the course of individual lives. My own view is that within-individual changes in criminality are not somehow "called forth" from the distant past but are mediated by proximate and time-varying social processes, transitions (life events), and turning points. It follows that theories limited to time-stable factors are incapable of unpacking the zigzagging and temporally variable patterns characteristic of criminal offending. Studying variation within individuals over the full life course requires not only new methodologies, but also new theories that reconcile the social-interactional and changing features of the self with stable individual differences.

It is against this background that Piquero and Mazerolle's edited volume enters the scene. They have done all criminologists a great service by bringing together in one volume a state-of-the-art collection of contemporary readings. In the chapters to follow, readers will engage a number of debates on stability and change, criminal careers, the role of early onset, aging versus cohort effects, methods for the measurement of trajectories, state dependence versus heterogeneity, turning points, the idea of life-course persistent versus adolescent-limited offenders, interactional theory, when in the life course interventions are most effective, and much more. These debates are exciting not only because of the fundamental nature of the questions raised, but also because of the sharpness of some of the disagreements and the interdisciplinary quality of the research. In this regard I do not wish to claim that life-course criminology is of a uniform mind, or to claim a hegemonic status for particular theories. For example, while I personally happen to hold a more sociological view of the life course, I am fascinated by the possibilities for biological, psychological, and economic perspectives (see, e.g., Moffitt, Reading 5).

Moreover, as the reader will see, Piquero and Mazerolle have selected a number of seminal papers that vigorously question the very premise of life-course criminology. To take the most prominent example, Michael Gottfredson and Travis Hirschi have posited a direct effect of age on crime that would seem to deny the need for longitudinal inquiry. This provocative idea is an important part of modern criminology; fortunately, Piquero and Mazerolle had the wisdom to include two articles by these authors that critique both the criminal careers and life-course paradigms (Reading 4; Reading 9). In other areas as well, readers are given the opportunity to engage the full spectrum of debate over the nature and explanation of intraindividual and interindividual variability in criminal behavior.

Rather than taking up more space, I encourage getting on with it. I am confident that students of criminology—from the novice to the senior scholar—will find in the following pages a life-course feast that will satisfy most any intellectual appetite.

Introduction

ecent research and theory in the social sciences has embraced a life-course
perspective for better understanding the complexity of human behavior.
The life course has been defined as, "the interweave of age-graded trajectories, such as work careers and family pathways, that are subject to changing
conditions and future options, and to short-term transitions ranging from leaving school to retirement" (Elder, 1994, p. 5). Applying the life-course perspective
to the study of criminal behavior allows for an understanding of the initiation,
continuation, and termination of offending behavior across the lifespan (LeBlanc
& Loeber, 1998). The life-course perspective presents unique opportunities for
developing a comprehensive understanding of criminal behavior.

Several criminological controversies are included within the life-course
perspective. Perhaps the most prominent is the debate over the age-crime relationship. Little disagreement exists over the shape of the aggregate age-crime
curve—a unimodal distribution peaking in adolescence and declining in adulthood. However, disagreement arises over the interpretation of this relationship.
Some criminologists, for example, argue that the age-crime curve is similar for
all offenders, whereas other criminologists assert that meaningful differences
are found within the curve, suggesting that different types of offenders, with
distinctive etiologies and developmental courses, exist. This is just one example
of a criminological controversy that cuts across different strands of empirical
research and available theory on offending behavior. It is just one of the issues
that will be examined in this reader on *Life-Course Criminology: Contemporary
and Classic Readings.*

In this book we highlight the major works that illuminate theory and empirical research on crime and the life course. The reader of these works should develop an understanding of the foundation for the study of crime over the life course, as well as of the prominent theories and research in this area, and the many challenges associated with life-course research. Although this book does not include many of the articles that have emerged out of this research tradition, our purpose is to document the *central* theoretical and empirical contributions that inform this area of criminological inquiry, and to provide the reader with essential background material on current controversies in the field.

There are eight sections of the book. The first section introduces the conceptual and methodological aspects of the life-course perspective. The second section examines the interrelationship between age, crime, and criminal careers. The third section examines recent life-course theories of criminal behavior. The fourth section of the book includes empirical tests of recent life-course theories discussed in section three. The fifth section contrasts the utility of developmental versus static theories of criminal behavior. The sixth section presents a series of articles examining persistence in criminal behavior. The seventh section examines desistance from criminal behavior. The final section includes evaluations of intervention programs aimed at reducing criminal behavior over the life course.

SECTION I:

THE LIFE-COURSE PERSPECTIVE

According to Sampson and Laub (1993), two concepts underlie the analysis of life-course dynamics. The first is the concept of a trajectory, or the pathway of development over the life course marked by a sequence of transitions. Trajectories have at least three dimensions: entrance, success, and timing (Thornberry, 1997). The *entrance dimension* recognizes that everyone does not enter particular developmental trajectories. Some people commit crime, although others do not; some people have a job, although others do not; some people get married, although others do not. The *success dimension* recognizes the variation in the content and context of developmental trajectories across persons. For example, some people have successful marriages and jobs, although others do not. Finally, the *timing* of particular events along the trajectory can be significant in altering one's developmental course of offending. In other words, as Thornberry (1997) recognizes, events along the life course are age-graded; the timing of certain salient life events can differentially impact one's developmental trajectory at different stages along the life course. Having a child as an adult can alter one's criminal trajectory in a positive way, but this same event occurring during midadolescence (a so-called "off-age" event) can have more deleterious effects, leading to further embeddedness in a criminal or antisocial trajectory (Thornberry, 1997).

The second concept is that of a transition, or the life events (i.e., first criminal act, first job, etc.) embedded within a trajectory. Elder (1985) refers to transitions as "changes in state that are more or less abrupt" (pp. 31–32). Transitions over an individual's life tend to be consequential in terms of an individual's position in the life course, and transitions occurring throughout the life-span may either strengthen emerging patterns of behavior or alter, redirect, or change developmental trajectories (Rutter and Rutter, 1993). Analyses of life-course dynamics, therefore, focus on the *context* of the transition. In other words, life-course analyses "focus on the duration, timing, and ordering of major life events and their consequences for later life development" (Sampson & Laub, 1993, p. 8).

Strongly related to the study of trajectories and transitions is the concept of a turning point, or a significant change in the direction of one's developmental course (Elder, 1985). Turning points may lead to abrupt or gradual changes in one's developmental course. Elder and his colleagues (1991) suggest that for some people, turning points can produce radical turnarounds or changes in life history that separate the past from the future. Sampson and Laub (1997; see also Pickles and Rutter, 1991) assert, however, that for the majority of people, turning points are more gradual and incremental.

In sum, the life-course perspective identifies such concepts as trajectories, transitions, and turning points as important aspects for understanding crime over the life span. The life-course perspective seeks to link the social meanings of age throughout the life course, the intergenerational transmission of social patterns, and the effects of social history and social structure to the study of human behavior over time (Elder, 1992). Part of the appeal of this approach rests with its dynamic perspective in understanding how criminal behavior develops over time and how it is impacted systemically by age-graded events occurring throughout the life course. As Gerald Patterson (1993) observes, the life-course perspective "implies that changes in social behavior are related to age in an orderly way" (p. 911).

There are two articles in this section that introduce the life-course perspective and illustrate how it can be applied to the study of criminal behavior.

SECTION II: AGE,
CRIME, AND CRIMINAL CAREERS

Two events shape the current knowledge of the criminal-career perspective used for understanding criminal behavior. The first is the long-standing observation of the age-crime relationship, dating back to the work of Belgium statistician Adolph Quetelet in 1831. Criminologists have come to recognize the aggregate age-crime relationship as one of the few "facts" in criminology (Hirschi & Gottfredson, 1983, 1995); crime peaks in the late adolescent years and declines through adulthood. Controversy has emerged in recent years over the interpretation and generalizability of this relationship. Blumstein, Cohen,

Roth, and Visher (1986) and Blumstein, Cohen, and Farrington (1988) assert that variation exists beneath the curve in that some offenders desist, some persist, and some become frequent offenders, even through adulthood. Sociologists Gottfredson and Hirschi (1988, 1990) have been most vocal in their criticism of this viewpoint, arguing instead for the general invariance of the age-crime curve across persons, time periods, and crime types.

Interpreting the age-crime relationship is still controversial. Developing a firm understanding of the relationship between age and crime represents one of the fundamental aspects of the criminal career approach. How one interprets and comes to understand the relationship between age and crime shapes the current understanding of criminal careers.

A second event shaping our understanding of criminal careers comes from the seminal birth cohort studies conducted by Wolfgang, Sellin, and Figlio (1972), and Tracy, Wolfgang, and Figlio (1990) in Philadelphia. The original cohort, which followed 9,945 Philadelphia males, yielded two important conclusions. First, a substantial portion of the cohort had at least one official police contact. Second, a small number of individuals (6% of the cohort) were responsible for a large portion of the police contacts (52%). These general findings have been replicated in other longitudinal studies in different parts of the world (Farrington, 1994; see also Stattin, Magnusson, and Reichel, 1989; Tracy et al., 1990; Shannon, 1988). Wolfgang's research, as well as additional research examining longitudinal sequences of offending over time, is significant for its theoretical, empirical, and public policy implications. This research also highlights the importance of examining different dimensions of offending behavior over the life span.

The report by the National Academy of Sciences (Blumstein et al., 1986) is credited with renewing an emphasis on the study of criminal careers and crime over the life course. The NAS report reviewed the state of empirical knowledge of how criminal careers are shaped over time. The panel defined a criminal career as "the longitudinal sequence of crimes committed by an individual offender" (Blumstein et al., 1986, p. 12). Embedded within this sequence of criminal activity are four dimensions of the criminal career. The first dimension is *participation*, or the distinction between those who engage in crime and those who do not. The second dimension of the criminal career is *frequency*, or the rate of criminal activity among active offenders. The frequency dimension, commonly denoted by the Greek letter lambda (λ), is believed to be the most significant of all criminal career dimensions (Blumstein et al., 1986). The third aspect of the criminal career is the *seriousness* of the offense committed. The final dimension is *career length*, the length of time the offender is active. *Desistance*, or the cessation of the criminal career, is embedded within this fourth dimension. The NAS report suggests that partitioning criminal activity into distinct dimensions facilitates the analysis of "offending development" over time (Blumstein et al., 1986, p. 2). A logical extension of this position is that the characteristics associated with one criminal career dimension may not necessarily be the same as the characteristics associated with other dimensions (Farrington, Lambert, & West, 1998).

In this section of the reader, there are two studies examining varying aspects of the criminal career perspective, as well as the age-crime relationship.

SECTION III: LIFE-COURSE
THEORIES OF CRIMINAL BEHAVIOR

Life-course theories of criminal behavior have emerged in recent years offering useful and challenging statements about the causes of criminal behavior. Life-course theories are easily compared with more traditional theories of criminal behavior that have tended to be "static" in their descriptions of criminal behavior. Static theories, by definition, do not explicitly incorporate developmental components into their explanations of criminal behavior. Discussion of the progression and escalation of criminal behavior is often absent from static theories. Static theories tend to be time bounded, with little appreciation for how events shape offending behavior over time, even after offending has begun.

By contrast, life-course theories of criminal behavior are developmental or dynamic in their descriptions of offending behavior. Dynamic theories recognize various dimensions of offending behavior throughout the life course (e.g., onset, persistence, escalation, etc.). They recognize the developmental progression of behavior, the reciprocal consequences of offending behavior, as well as how events through the life course systematically shape the likelihood of criminal persistence or desistance. Life-course theories differ from most traditional theories of criminal behavior because they embrace a wider lens in explaining offending behavior.

There are advantages in using life-course theories to explain criminal behavior (Thornberry, 1997). Life-course theories take a broader view of offending behavior over time. In this regard, life-course theories are able to better understand how criminal behavior changes systematically over time; they are also able to integrate changes in various aspects of people's lives to changes in their criminal outcomes. Additionally, life-course theories allow for an appreciation of how criminal behavior is reciprocally related to the context of people's lives and, in so doing, has consequences for their likelihood of future criminal behavior. Life-course theories, with their dynamic and interactive focus, can better capture the richness of human lives and the pathways of offending behavior over the life course.

It is also sometimes useful to think of life-course theories as offering a contrast to general theories of criminal behavior, although this is not always the case. Some of the more recent life-course theories have identified distinct explanations for different "typologies" of offenders. Terrie Moffitt (1993) offered perhaps the most influential of these theories.

Moffitt's dual taxonomic theory of offending behavior recognizes that there are two groups of offenders, adolescent-limited and life-course persisters.

Adolescent-limited offenders engage in delinquent acts during adolescence (and sometimes into early adulthood) as a function of their frustration from desiring and not being able to legitimately attain adult privileges, resources, and responsibilities. Given this situation, adolescent-limited offenders become influenced by the delinquent activity of their peers. Through a process of social mimicry and observational learning, adolescent-limited offenders become involved in delinquent behavior. Importantly, however, change is likely for this group of offenders because as maturation occurs, adult roles become available. In short, conformity becomes a logical choice for adolescent-limited offenders as they adapt to the changing contingencies in their immediate environment.

By contrast, the antisocial activity of life-course persisters has its origins in the interaction between neuropsychological deficits, poverty, and disadvantaged familial environments. Subtle trait differences present at birth combine with deficits in parental management practices to increase the development of impulsive interactional styles. In concert with ongoing failures in academic pursuits, opportunities for these individuals to practice prosocial behavior and pursue healthy adult lifestyles become severely limited (Moffitt, 1997). Life-course-persistent offenders are antisocial in their conduct as children, become involved in delinquency at an early age, and progress into more serious forms of crime over time. For this group of offenders, desisting from criminal activity is unlikely due to the consequences of cumulative continuity, criminal embeddedness, and their persistent antisocial dispositions.

This section presents two life-course theories of offending behavior. Readers will observe that most life-course theories actually build on more traditional theories in criminology, including social learning and social control theories. Life-course extensions of these approaches incorporate the developmental and dynamic components required for understanding criminal behavior over the life span.

SECTION IV: EMPIRICAL TESTS
OF LIFE-COURSE THEORIES

Life-course theories have generated a substantial amount of empirical research on offending behavior. One of the methods for evaluating the validity of any theory is its ability to "fit the facts." Although some theories may seem logical and appear to offer clear explanations of offending behavior their usefulness will ultimately be determined by their empirical support.

Research on life-course theories has made use of a variety of samples, methodological designs, and measures of criminal behavior. Researchers have studied samples of grade school, high school, and college students, as well as offenders, to understand the development and cessation of criminal behavior across different types of individuals. In addition, researchers have focused on the offending patterns of different subgroups stratified on race and gender. A comprehensive understanding of crime over the life course requires theoretical assessments using alternative analytic techniques across different types of samples. Such efforts reveal the specific conditions under which these theories predict and explain offending behavior over the life course.

This section presents empirical tests of the life-course theories of Moffitt, and Sampson and Laub. While other studies exist, these articles have been selected as fairly representative of recent and comprehensive empirical tests of life-course theories. Additionally, these studies utilize different types of samples and methodological techniques to assess key predictions derived from the theories.

SECTION V: DEVELOPMENTAL VERSUS STATIC THEORIES: CURRENT DEBATES

Developmental theories offer dynamic explanations of offending behavior. These explanations encourage the use of longitudinal research designs to examine the unfolding or developmental processes related to criminal activity over time. Developmental theories differ markedly from static theories. Many static theories identify the causes of criminal behavior early in the life course, such as childhood. Moreover, many of these theories recognize that events occurring throughout the life course, such as getting married, do not alter criminal trajectories. Many static explanations contend that stable individual characteristics, established early and remaining relatively stable, account for crime at different points through the life span. As a consequence, static theories reject longitudinal designs in favor of cross-sectional studies.

This section presents an important exchange between sociologists Michael Gottfredson and Travis Hirschi (1995) and Robert Sampson and John Laub (1995). Gottfredson and Hirschi offer comprehensive arguments against embracing life-course theories of criminal behavior. Their observations are analytically sophisticated and challenging for life-course theories. Sampson and Laub, two of the most prominent life-course scholars in criminology, counter the arguments put forth by Gottfredson and Hirschi.

SECTION VI: UNDERSTANDING PERSISTENCE IN CRIMINAL BEHAVIOR

Past research finds that antisocial behavior has considerable cross-situational and temporal stability (Huessmann, Eron, Lefkowitz, & Walder, 1984). Indeed, one of the more widely known empirical regularities among crime researchers is that the best predictor of future criminal activity is prior criminal activity (Nagin & Paternoster, 1991). In other words, there appears to be much stability in offending behavior over the life course. Differences exist, however, among scholars in interpreting how and why past offending behavior is related to future offending. For example, some scholars (Gottfredson and Hirschi, 1990) attribute this to a process of self-selection whereby individuals who were "rotten apples" as kids are likely to be "rotten apples" as adults (Paternoster, Dean, Piquero, Mazerolle, & Brame, 1997; see also Robins, 1978). Referred to as *persistent heterogeneity,* this argument suggests that once established, relative differences in criminal propensity become stable throughout the life course. By implication, this position holds that past offending has no material impact on the likelihood of future offending. It simply is another manifestation of an underlying criminal propensity.

A competing viewpoint recognizes that the positive relationship between past and future offending behavior reflects a state-dependent process. Past offending actually has consequences for the likelihood of future offending. These consequences might involve labeling processes, or perhaps further embeddedness into a criminal trajectory. The larger point to consider is that crime has negative, criminogenic consequences for the future.

Two articles are presented in this section that examine different aspects of persistence or stability in criminal offending.

SECTION VII: DESISTANCE
FROM CRIMINAL BEHAVIOR

Desistance, the cessation of criminal activity, represents a relatively under-explored area within the life-course perspective (Loeber & Stouthamer-Loeber, 1998). In part, this is due to the numerous definitional and methodological challenges that confront research on criminal desistance. Desistance has been conceptualized as the complete or absolute stopping of criminal behavior and, alternatively, as the gradual cessation of criminal activity (Laub, Nagin, & Sampson, 1998). One of the main methodological challenges for researchers rests in deciding, in an operational sense, at what point desistance has occurred. With the knowledge that criminal careers are likely to start and stop throughout the life course (Blumstein et al., 1986; see also Horney, Osgood, & Marshall, 1995; Nagin & Land, 1993), periods of intermittence (Barnett, Blumstein, & Farrington, 1989) are likely to be misinterpreted as desistance. Moreover, in an extreme sense, a pure study of desistance may need to observe offending behavior over the entire life span. In sum, an understanding of what desistance is, what it looks like, and how it is to be measured, is central for future research on crime over the life course (Bushway, Piquero, Mazerolle, Broidy, & Cauffman, 2000).

With respect to research on desistance, available evidence reveals that salient life events (e.g., changes in marital status, employment status, or peer group structure, etc.) can produce meaningful changes in criminal behavior (Farrington & West, 1995; Laub, Nagin, & Sampson, 1998; Warr, 1998). Much remains to be learned, however, about these relationships, and differentiating the influence of self-selection from true desistance processes remains an important area of inquiry (Hirschi & Gottfredson, 1995).

In this section, two articles are presented that illustrate the complexity of current research on desistance from criminal behavior.

SECTION VIII: INTERVENTIONS TO REDUCE CRIME OVER THE LIFE COURSE

The life-course perspective offers a new way of thinking about crime reduction programs (Laub et al., 1995). Life-course approaches not only consider the developmental processes involved with crime; they also recognize that interventions aimed at reducing crime and delinquency must be age-graded. For interventions to be most effective, they should focus on specific developmental periods to identify key areas for intervention that are likely to reduce offending across different stages of the life course. Many intervention programs have been aimed at the adolescent years; however, interventions for adult offenders need to consider the context of that developmental period.

Although it is true that embracing a life-course perspective requires consideration of age-graded interventions over the life course, early childhood intervention programs have only recently become popular and emphasized. Early childhood is increasingly viewed as the crucial time period for preventing future manifestations of antisocial behavior. Additionally, intervening early in the life span creates opportunities to improve other outcomes, such as academic performance.

Of critical importance for early intervention efforts is recognition of the criminogenic processes and events within the family (Hirschi, 1995; see also Patterson, 1980). Recent "family based" intervention efforts include parent-training programs to provide parents with information and support in improving their parental management skills. Additionally, other programs focus directly at improving the health of children and newborn babies. A focus on improving child health represents an important attempt at redirecting "at-risk" children from future problems involving crime and delinquency.

To be sure, early intervention efforts are not the only areas worthy of investment. For example, a number of other interventions have been aimed at strengthening individuals' social ties to school, community, employment, and interpersonal relationships. Such social ties are expected to contribute to an individual's investment in social capital (Coleman, 1990). In sum, reducing crime over the life course will require an investment in a number of different intervention efforts that have been shown to be effective across various stages of the life span.

In this section, two articles that describe evaluations of parent training and nurse-home visitation programs are presented.

CONCLUSION

The life-course perspective offers a comprehensive approach to the study of criminal behavior (Giele and Elder, Jr., 1998). This approach considers the multitude of influences that shape offending behavior across different time periods and contexts. Not only is the life-course perspective valuable for better understanding offending behavior, it provides numerous options for designing and implementing effective intervention programs.

There exist a host of methodological challenges for future research on crime over the life course (Bryk & Raudenbush, 1992; see also Bushway, Brame, & Paternoster, 1999; Hsiao, 1986; Nagin, 1999; Nagin & Land, 1993; Osgood & Rowe, 1994). For example, identifying the most appropriate analytical designs to employ, either quantitative or qualitative approaches, represents an important consideration. Useful information has been gathered from quantitative procedures (Nagin & Farrington, 1992; Paternoster et al., 1997; Piquero et al., 2000), but at the same time information capturing the richness and complexity of human behavior can perhaps be better ascertained through qualitative approaches (Sampson & Laub, 1993; see also Sommers, Baskin, & Fagan, 1994). Ultimately, a comprehensive understanding of crime over the life course will benefit from the integration of both quantitative and qualitative analytic strategies (Laub & Sampson, 1998).

Additionally, measurement issues present ongoing challenges against developing a comprehensive understanding of crime over the life course. Concerns over which types of measures to employ (e.g., self-report versus official data), and the implications of choosing one over the other, are paramount (Lauritsen, 1998). Further, considerations of which type of criminal activity to measure—serious predatory offending, trivial events (trespassing), white-collar offending, or domestic violence—present challenges to researchers. At present, the majority of research on crime and the life course focuses on serious offending behavior drawn from either self-reports or official police and/or court records. There appears to be a bias toward focusing on serious offending behavior, with relatively little attention given to linking these types of crimes with, for example, domestic violence or other non-index offenses (though see Feld and Straus, 1989). There are good reasons for integrating self-reports with official offending indices as well as expanding the scope of criminal activity for examining the full range of offending behavior throughout the life span. Ultimately a more complex, richer understanding of crime throughout the life course will be achieved when methodological challenges are addressed and overcome. Once this occurs, we will be better able to assess available theories of offending behavior as well as the dynamics of offending processes that help us to better understand crime over the life course.

The collection of articles contained herein cover a broad range of areas that are of interest to the criminological community. These readings also illustrate many of the theories and explanations as well as cutting-edge research that will lead to the development of a comprehensive understanding of criminal behavior over the life course.

REFERENCES

Barnett, A., Blumstein, A., & Farrington, D. (1989). A prospective test of a criminal career model. *Criminology, 27*, 373–385.

Blumstein, A., Cohen, J., & Farrington, D. P. (1988). Criminal career research: Its value for criminology. *Criminology, 26*, 1–35.

Blumstein, A., Cohen, J., Roth, J. A. & Visher, C. A. (1986). *Criminal careers and career criminals.* Washington, DC: National Academy Press.

Bryk, A., & Raudenbush, S. (1992). *Hierarchical linear models.* Newbury Park, CA: Sage.

Bushway, S., Brame, R., & Paternoster, R. (1999). Assessing stability and change in criminal offending: A comparison of random effects, semiparametric, and fixed effects modeling strategies. *Journal of Quantitative Criminology, 15*, 23–62.

Bushway, S., Piquero, A. R., Mazerolle, P., Broidy, L., & Cauffman, E. (2000). A developmental framework for empirical research on desistance. Unpublished manuscript.

Coleman, J. S. (1990). *Foundations of social theory.* Cambridge, MA: Harvard University Press.

Elder, G. H., Jr. (1985). Perspectives on the life-course. In G. H. Elder (Ed.). *Life-course dynamics.* Ithaca, NY: Cornell University Press.

Elder, G. H., Jr. (1992). The life-course. In E. F. Borgatta and M. L. Borgatta (Eds.). *The Encyclopedia of Sociology* (Vol. 3). New York: Macmillan.

Elder, G. H., Jr. (1994). Time, human agency, and social change: Perspectives on the life course. *Social Psychology Quarterly, 57*, (1), 4–15.

Elder, G. H., Jr., Gimbel, C., & Ivie, R. (1991). Turning points in life: The case of military service and war. *Military Psychology, 3*, 215–231.

Farrington, D. P. (1994). Human development and criminal careers. In M. Maguire, R. Morgan, and R. Reiner (Eds.). *The Oxford Handbook of Criminology.* Oxford: Oxford University Press.

Farrington, D. P., Lambert, S., & West, D. J. (1998). Criminal careers of two generations of family members in the Cambridge Study in Delinquent Development. *Studies on Crime and Crime Prevention, 7*(1), 1–22.

Farrington, D. P., & West, D. J. (1995). Effects of marriage, separation, and children on offending by adult males. In Z. S. Blau and J. Hagan (Eds.). *Current Perspectives on Aging and the Life Cycle* (Vol. 4). Greenwich, CT: JAI Press.

Feld, S. L., & Straus, M. A. (1989). Escalation and desistance of wife assault in marriage. *Criminology, 27*, (1), 141.

Giele, J., & Elder, G. H., Jr. (1998). *Methods of life course research: Qualitative and quantitative approaches.* Newbury Park, CA: Sage.

Gottfredson, M., & Hirschi, T. (1988). Science, public policy, and the career paradigm. *Criminology, 26*, 37–55.

Gottfredson, M., & Hirschi, T. (1990). *A General Theory of Crime.* Stanford, CA: Stanford University Press.

Hirschi, T. (1995). The family. In J. Q. Wilson & J. Petersilia (Eds.). *Crime.* San Francisco: ICS Press.

Hirschi, T., & Gottfredson, M. (1983). Age and the explanation of crime. *American Journal of Sociology, 89*, 552–584.

Hirschi, T., & Gottfredson, M. (1995). Control theory and the life-course perspective. *Studies on Crime and Crime Prevention, 4*(2): 131–142.

Horney, J., Osgood, D. W., & Marshall, I. H. (1995). Variability in crime and local life circumstances. *American Sociological Review, 60*(5), 655–673.

Hsiao, C. (1986). *Analysis of Panel Data.* Cambridge: Cambridge University Press.

Huessmann, L. R., Eron, L. D., Lefkowitz, M. M., & Walder, L. O. (1984). Stability of aggression over time and generations. *Developmental Psychology, 20*, 1120–1134.

Laub, J. H., Nagin, D. S., & Sampson, R. J. (1998). Trajectories of change in criminal offending: Good marriages and the desistance process. *American Sociological Review, 63,* 225–238.

Laub, J. H. & Sampson, R. J. (1998). Integrating quantitative and qualitative data. In J. Z. Giele & G. H. Elder, Jr. (Eds.). *Methods of Life-Course Research.* Thousand Oaks, CA: Sage.

Laub, J. H., Sampson, R. J., Corbett, R. P., Jr., & Smith, J. S. (1995). The public policy implications of a life-course perspective on crime. In H. D. Barlow (Ed.). *Crime and Public Policy.* Boulder, CO: Westview.

Lauritsen, J. (1998). Age and crime: Assessing the limits of self-report data. *Social Forces, 77,* 127–155.

LeBlanc, M., & Loeber, R. (1998). Developmental criminology updated. In M. Tonry (Ed.). *Crime and justice. A review of research.* Chicago: University of Chicago Press.

Loeber, R., & Stouthamer-Loeber, M. (1998). Development of juvenile aggression and violence. *American Psychologist, 53*(2), 242–259.

Moffitt, T. E. (1993). Adolescence-limited and life-course-persistent antisocial behavior: A developmental taxonomy. *Psychological Review, 100,* 674–701.

Moffitt, T. E. (1997). Adolescence-limited and life-course-persistent offending: A complimentary pair of developmental theories. In T. P. Thornberry (Ed.). *Developmental theories of crime and delinquency: Advances in criminological theory.* New Brunswick, NJ: Transaction.

Nagin, D. S. (1999). Analyzing developmental trajectories: A semi-parametric, group-based approach. *Psychological Methods, 4*(2), 139–157.

Nagin, D. S., & Farrington, D. P. (1992). The stability of criminal potential from childhood to adulthood. *Criminology, 30*(2), 235–260.

Nagin, D. S., & Land, K. C. (1993). Age, criminal careers, and population heterogeneity: Specification and estimation of a nonparametric mixed Poisson model. *Criminology, 31,* 327–359.

Nagin, D. S., & Paternoster, R. (1991). On the relationship of past and future participation in delinquency. *Criminology, 29,* 163–190.

Osgood, D. W., & Rowe, D. C. (1994). Bridging criminal careers, theory and policy through latent variable models of individual offending. *Criminology, 32,* 517–554.

Paternoster, R., Dean, C., Piquero, A., Mazerolle, P., & Brame, R. (1997). Continuity and change in offending careers. *Journal of Quantitative Criminology, 13*(3), 231–266.

Patterson, G. R. (1980). Children who steal. In T. Hirschi & M. Gottfredson (Eds.). *Understanding Crime.* Beverly Hills, CA: Sage.

Patterson, G. R. (1993). Orderly change in a stable world: The antisocial trait as a chimera. *Journal of Consulting and Clinical Psychology, 61*(6), 911–919.

Pickles, A., & Rutter, M. (1991). Statistical and conceptual models of "turning points" in developmental processes. In D. Magnusson, L. Bergman, G. Rudinger, & B. Torestad (Eds.). *Problems and methods in longitudinal research: Stability and change.* Cambridge: Cambridge University Press.

Piquero, A. R., Blumstein, A., Brame, R., Haapanen, R., Mulvey, E. P., & Nagin, D. S. (2000). Assessing the impact of exposure time and incapacitation on longitudinal trajectories of criminal offending. *Journal of Adolescent Research,* forthcoming.

Quetelet, A. (1831). *Research on the propensity for crime at different ages.* Cincinnati, OH: Anderson.

Robins, L. (1978). Sturdy childhood predictors of adult antisocial behavior: Replications from longitudinal studies. *Psychological Medicine, 8,* 611–622.

Rutter, M., & Rutter, M. (1993). *Developing minds: Challenge and continuity across the life-span.* New York: Basic Books.

Sampson, R. J., & Laub, J. H. (1993). *Crime in the Making.* Cambridge, MA: Harvard University Press.

Sampson, R. J., & Laub, J. H. (1995). Understanding variability in lives through time: Contributions of life-course criminology. *Studies on Crime and Crime Prevention, 4*(2), 143–158.

Sampson, R. J., & Laub, J. H. (1997). A life-course theory of cumulative disadvantage and the stability of delinquency. In T. P. Thornberry (Ed.). *Developmental theories of crime and delinquency: Advances in criminological theory.* New Brunswick, NJ: Transaction.

Shannon, L. (1988). *Criminal career continuity: Its social context.* New York: Human Sciences Press.

Sommers, I., Baskin, D. R., & Fagan, J. (1994). Getting out of the life: Crime desistance by female street offenders. *Deviant Behavior, 15,* 125–149.

Stattin, H., Magnusson, D., & Reichel, H. (1989). Criminal activity at different ages: A study based on a Swedish longitudinal research population. *British Journal of Criminology, 29,* 368–385.

Thornberry, T. P. (1997). Introduction: Some advantages of developmental and life-course perspectives for the study of crime and delinquency. In T. P. Thornberry (Ed.). *Developmental theories of crime and delinquency: Advances in criminological theory.* New Brunswick, NJ: Transaction Publishers.

Tracy, P., Wolfgang, M., & Figlio, R. (1990). *Delinquency careers in two birth cohorts.* New York: Plenum.

Warr, M. 1998. Life-course transitions and desistance from crime. *Criminology, 36*(2), 183–216.

Wolfgang, M., Figlio, R., & Sellin, T. (1972). *Delinquency in a birth cohort.* Chicago: University of Chicago Press.

ACKNOWLEDGMENTS

We wish to thank a number of individuals who provided us with support and feedback during the production of this reader. These people include Sabra Horne, Robert Sampson, John Laub, Tim Brezina, Chester Britt, and Francis Cullen. Additionally, we wish to thank our spouses, Nicole Leeper Piquero and Lorraine Mazerolle for their continued support of our work. Finally, we'd like to thank the reviewers of this edition: Timothy Brezina, Tulane University; Chester Britt, Pennsylvania State University; Daniel Dotter, Grambling State University; Gerald R. Garrett, University of Massachusetts, Boston; John H. Laub, University of Maryland; Daniel Nagin, Carnegie Mellon University; Cyrus S. Stewart, Michigan State University.

SECTION I

The Life-Course
Perspective

The life-course perspective has emerged as a powerful influence for the study of criminal behavior. Drawn largely from recent developments in sociology and psychology, the life-course approach presents new opportunities for examining criminal behavior over time, as well as for investigating critical life events; the interaction between individuals and their social environments in connection with life events (e.g., their timing, interpretation, etc.); and the pathways, transitions, and turning points enacted over the life course. The two articles in this section introduce the life-course approach to the study of criminal behavior.

The first paper in this section, written by sociologist Glen Elder, identifies various themes drawn from a life-course perspective of human development. He describes the historical development of the approach and the substantive aspects of the life-course perspective. Also, Elder discusses both conceptual and methodological considerations of the life-course approach. Although the author does not discuss the life-course perspective from a criminological standpoint, the application to the study of crime is straightforward. The major components of the perspective—the interplay of human lives and historical context, the timing of life-course events and roles, the concept of linked lives through social integration, and the role of human agency in decision making—can all be applied to the study of criminal behavior. In fact, such an approach illustrates opportunities for better understanding the dynamic components of criminal activity and the pathways into and out of crime enacted over time.

Few criminologists have done more to promote the application of the life-course perspective to the study of criminal behavior than Robert Sampson and John Laub. Their paper in this section provides an important overview of how the life-course perspective can improve the manner in which criminologists study and ultimately understand criminal behavior. They recognize the importance of behavioral trajectories and how transitions through life are age-graded. They see the importance, moreover, of social institutions such as schools, workplaces, and families in shaping behavioral trajectories over time. Finally, Sampson and Laub identify four major areas in which the study of crime can be improved by embracing the life-course perspective: using prospective, longitudinal research designs; capturing the precise sequencing and impact of life events on behavioral trajectories; moving away from narrow, legal definitions of crime to consider alternative forms of antisocial behavior; and embracing alternative methodologies to study crime, including qualitative and quantitative approaches. In sum, Sampson and Laub present a number of compelling reasons for embracing a life-course perspective for the study of criminal behavior.

The articles comprising this introductory section present a comprehensive overview of the life-course perspective and illustrate the potential for fostering a better understanding of criminal behavior.

SUGGESTED READINGS

Clausen, J. (1991). Adolescent competence and the shaping of the life course (marriage, family, and the life course). *American Journal of Sociology, 96,* 805–842.

Cline, H. F. (1980). Criminal behavior over the life span. In O. G. Brim, Jr., & J. Kagan (Eds.), *Constancy and change in human development.* Cambridge: Cambridge University Press.

Hagan, J., & Palloni, A. (1988). Crimes as social events in the life course:

Reconceiving a criminological controversy. *Criminology, 26,* 87–100.

LeBlanc, M. & Loeber, R. (1998). Developmental criminology updated. In M. Tonry (Ed.), *Crime and justice: An annual review of research* (Vol. 23). Chicago: University of Chicago Press.

Sampson, R., & Laub, J. (1993). *Crime in the making.* Cambridge, MA: Harvard University Press.

1

Time, Human Agency, and Social Change

Perspectives on the Life Course*

GLEN H. ELDER, JR.

ABSTRACT   The life course has emerged over the past 30 years as a major research paradigm. Distinctive themes include the relation between human lives and a changing society, the timing of lives, linked or interdependent lives, and human agency. Two lines of research converged in the formation of this paradigm during the 1960s; one was associated with an older "social relationship" tradition that featured intergenerational studies, and the other with more contemporary thinking about age. The emergence of a life course paradigm has been coupled with a notable decline in socialization as a research framework and with its incorporation by other theories. Also, the field has seen an expanding interest in how social change alters people's lives, an enduring perspective of sociological social psychology.

T he study of human lives has become a lively enterprise over the past quarter-century, extending across substantive and diverse boundaries in the social and behavioral sciences. With this change has come an appreciation for "the long way" of thinking about human personality and its social pathways in changing societies. Developmentalists have gained more sensitivity to the interlocking nature of human lives and generations, as well as an informed awareness of individuals as choice makers and agents of their own lives.

SOURCE: *Social Psychology Quarterly,* Vol. 57, No. 1, pp. 4–15. Reprinted by permission of the American Sociological Assn.

*This paper was presented as the Cooley-Mead Lecture to the Social Psychology Section at the 1993 annual meeting of the American Sociological Association, held in Miami Beach. It is based on a program of research on the life course within the Carolina Consortium on Human Development and the Carolina Population Center. I am indebted to a great many colleagues who read and critiqued the paper in manuscript form, but my debt is especially large to John Clausen's and Urie Bronfenbrenner's mentoring across the years. I also acknowledge support by the National Institute of Mental Health (MH 41327, MH 43270, and MH 48165), a contract with the U.S. Army Research Institute, a grant from the Department of Veterans Affairs Merit Review Program, research support from the John D. and Catherine T. MacArthur Foundation Program for Successful Adolescent Development among Youth in High-Risk Settings, and a Research Scientist Award (MH 00567).

To grasp the dramatic surge of life studies, consider for a moment where we were 30 years ago. Mills's (1959, p. 149) provocative work, *The Sociological Imagination,* had just proposed an orienting concept in the behavioral sciences—in his words, "the study of biography, of history, and of the problems of their intersection within social structure." The concept of life course, however, as we know it today (Elder, 1992a; but see Cain, 1964), was not to be found in the scholarly literature. It did not appear in sociological or psychological theory or in the coursework of our leading graduate programs. I left graduate studies without any exposure to, or understanding of, the life course as field of inquiry, theory, or method.

Today we find that life course thinking has diffused across disciplinary boundaries and speciality areas within particular disciplines (Featherman, 1983). Application of the perspective in sociology extends across the subfields of population, social stratification, complex organizations, family, criminology, and medical sociology, among others. Beyond sociology, life course studies appear in social history (Elder, Modell, & Parke, 1993; Modell, 1989), developmental psychology (Bronfenbrenner, 1979), and gerontology, where Streib and Binstock (1990, p. 1) refer to the "tremendous increase in attention paid to the adult life course (and sometimes the full life course) context in which persons age."

What, then, is distinctive about the life course in contemporary social science—as concept, theoretical orientation, and field of inquiry?

THE LIFE COURSE:

AN EMERGING PARADIGM

The life course represents a major change in how we think about and study human lives. In this sense, it is an emerging paradigm. Broadly speaking, the change is part of a general conceptual trend that has made time, context, and process more salient dimensions of theory and analysis. This development has various theoretical strands including the macro world of age stratification (Elder, 1975; Riley, Johnson, & Foner, 1972), cultural and intergenerational models (Kertzer & Keith, 1984), and developmental life span psychology (Baltes, 1987). My perspective tends to stress the social forces that shape the life course and its developmental consequences.

Overall the life course can be viewed as a multilevel phenomenon, ranging from structured pathways through social institutions and organizations to the social trajectories of individuals and their developmental pathways. Though social psychological theories generally exist on one level or another, much of life course study crosses levels, as in the relation between historical change and life experience (Elder, 1974). Less is known about the effect of personality and life patterns on social structures (Turner, 1988).

In concept, the life course generally refers to the interweave of age-graded trajectories, such as work careers and family pathways, that are subject to changing conditions and future options, and to short-term transitions ranging from leaving school to retirement (Elder, 1985). Transitions are always embedded in trajectories that give them distinctive form and meaning. In terms of theory, the life course has defined a common field of inquiry by providing a framework that guides research on matters of problem identification and conceptual development. These problems have much to do with the impact of changing societies on developing lives.

Unlike the focus of single careers, so widely studied in the past, the life course perspective offers a framework for exploring the dynamics of multiple, interdependent pathways, an increasingly popular research topic (Eckenrode & Gore, 1990; Moen, Dempster-McClain, & Williams, 1992). Consider the relation between marriage and parenthood. A poor marriage diminishes the quality of birth experiences for women, and new parental responsibilities can diminish the mutuality and companionship of the marriage itself (Cowan & Cowan, 1992). Economic pressures accelerate this negative process.

With an eye to the full life course, analysis is sensitive to the consequences of early transitions for later experiences and events. Indeed, we now see that the implications of early adult choices extend even into the later years of retirement and old age (Clausen, 1993), from the adequacy of economic resources to adaptive skills and activities. The later years of aging cannot be understood in depth without knowledge of the prior life course. Role histories clearly matter for health (Elder, Shanahan, & Clipp, 1994) and for adaptations along the lifeline.

The implication of early choices and pursuits brings up a core premise of life course study: developmental processes and outcomes are shaped by the social trajectories that people follow, as through advancement and demotion. Causal influences flow in the other direction as well. Acting-out tendencies, for example, restrict the availability of certain options, such as a stable job. Theoretically informed panel studies (Caspi & Bem, 1990) are beginning increasingly to document the mechanisms of reciprocal influence between social and developmental trajectories.

Central Themes of a Paradigm

This is not the place for a detailed review of theoretical distinctions, but four themes deserve special note as central to the life course paradigm: the interplay of human lives and historical times, the timing of lives, linked or interdependent lives, and human agency in choice making.

Growing awareness of the link between human lives and their historical times has underscored the multiple levels, social embeddedness, and the dynamic features of the life course. Issues of timing, linked lives, and human agency identify key mechanisms by which environmental change and pathways influence the course and the substance of human lives. To explore this observation, I begin by considering the relation between lives and times in greater detail.

Lives and Historical Times   Especially in rapidly changing societies, differences in birth year expose individuals to different historical worlds, with their constraints and options. Individual life courses may well reflect these different times. Historical effects on the life course take the form of a cohort effect in which social change differentiates the life patterns of successive cohorts, such as older and younger women before World War II. History also takes the form of a period effect when the effect of change is relatively uniform across successive birth cohorts. Birth year and cohort membership, however, are merely a proxy for exposure to historical change.

Direct study of such change and its effects on the life course is required to identify the explanatory mechanisms. In inquiring about the personal implications of historical change, long-term as well as short-term, the analyst necessarily addresses the process by which the effects are expressed. Among the most important social changes for American children in the twentieth century, for example, historians have identified the long-term growth of mass media and public education as well as the short-term fluctuations of the economy (Elder et al., 1993). As a rule, any personal implications would be contingent on what people bring to the change process as well as on the nature and severity of the change itself.

The Timing of Lives   The social meanings of age deserve special mention because they have brought a temporal, age-graded perspective to social roles and events. Social timing refers to the incidence, duration, and sequence of roles, and to relevant expectations and beliefs based on age. Thus marriages may be relatively early or late according to demographic patterns and age norms. Similar observations apply to the birth of children. Some events are timely in relation to age norms, or may be ill-timed and particularly costly; teenage childbearing is an example.

Social timing also applies to the scheduling of multiple trajectories and to their synchrony or asynchrony. Young couples may schedule family and work events to minimize time and energy pressure. Disparities between social and biological timing frequently occur during the early years of development. Differences in rates of physical maturation generate early and late maturers in an age group. Turkewitz and Devenny (1993, p. xii) concede that an understanding of such differences is essential for theories that view development "as the outcome of interactions between a changing organism and changing context."

The timing of the life course events and roles tells much about the goodness of fit between lives and work careers. In World War II, for example, some men entered the services at a young age with no family or work responsibilities, whereas entrants in their thirties typically experienced the full brunt of social disruption on their subsequent health (Elder et al., 1994). This finding illustrates the importance of life stage at points of social change. According to the life stage principle, the personal impact of any change depends on where people are in their lives at the time of the change.

Linked Lives   No principle of life course study is more central than the notion of interdependent lives. Human lives are typically embedded in social relationships with kin and friends across the life span. Social regulation and support occur in part through these relationships. Processes of this kind are expressed across the life cycle of socialization, behavioral exchange, and generational succession. The misfortune and the opportunity of adult children, as well as their personal problems, become intergenerational.

> Failed marriages and careers frequently lead adult sons and daughters back to the parental households and have profound implications for the parents' life and plans on their later years. Conversely, economic setbacks and divorce among the parents to adolescents may impede their transition to adulthood by postponing leaving home, undertaking higher education or employment and marriage. Each generation is bound to fateful decisions and events in the other's life course (Elder, 1985, p. 40).

More generally, the principle of linked lives refers to the interaction between the individual's social worlds over the life span—family, friends, and coworkers. To a considerable extent, macrohistorical change is experienced by individuals through such worlds (Elder & O'Rand, 1995). A childhood in the Great Depression often meant hard times, whereas children of World War II frequently experienced employed but absent parents.

Human Agency   Concepts of the actor and of human agency have always been prominent in life history studies (see Thomas & Znaniecki, 1918–1920), and they are also prominent in the new wave of life course studies that relate individuals to the broader social context. Within the constraints of their world, people are planful and make choices among options that construct their life course (Clausen, 1993). Individual differences clearly matter in this research, particularly as they interact with changing environments to produce behavioral outcomes (Elder & O'Rand, 1995). Selection processes have become increasingly important in understanding life course development and aging.

  More generally, theoretical trends in the social sciences favor a constructionist view of individuals in shaping development and the life course. Examples include the cognitive revolution and Bandura's (1986, 1997) pioneering research on personal efficacy, greater knowledge of genetic influences on the selection of environments (Plomin & Dunn, 1991; Scarr & McCartney, 1983), and the extension of life studies beyond the early years.

  As defined by these central themes, the life course paradigm consists of well-established conceptual distinctions (e.g., linked lives), some new or reworked concepts (e.g., the timing of lives, lives and times), and theoretical integrations or syntheses. One important integration with particular relevance to the work I have done is summed up in terms of a merger between two approaches to the life course—generation—and age-based models.

  The generation-based model views individual lives in terms of the reproductive life cycle of intergenerational processes and socialization. Insofar as they focus on the life course, two- and three-generation studies tend to address these processes (Rossi & Rossi, 1990). Research examples extend back to Thomas and Znaniecki's (1918–1920) classic study on the immigration of Polish peasants to large cities in Europe and the United States. Kingsley Davis (1940) also followed this approach in his comparative and historical study of parent-youth conflict. The generation model contributed to the popularity of socialization research in the 1960s and at the same time, to an intergenerational approach in studies of social change.

An age-based model emerged from the 1960s in a theory of age stratification by Matilda Riley and her associates (Riley et al., 1972; Riley, Waring, & Foner, 1988), which relates age cohorts to social structures over the life span. By placing people in birth cohorts that permit analyses of historical effects, the theory advanced a view of age-graded life patterns embedded in cultures, institutions, and social structures, and responsive to social change. Norman Ryder (1965) also contributed to this theory through his writings on a cohort approach to social change and the life course. Another pioneer, Bernice Neugarten (Neugarten & Datan, 1973), fashioned a social psychology of age grading across the life course, including a concept of normative timetables. Contemporary studies of life transitions and their timing (Hogan, 1981; Model, 1989) owe much to Neugarten's original work.

The generation approach proved to be inadequate for two salient issues in the 1960s—the study of historical influence and adult development. Generational status did not match the historical precision of a birth cohort, and offered very little help in charting the adult life course. A concept of age grading proved to be essential.

For some of these reasons I drew on both models—generation and age—in developing a study of California children who grew up in the Great Depression (Elder, 1974). This became an intergenerational and longitudinal study that focused on a birth cohort of children and their life course to the middle years. The basic model traced the effects of the economic collapse through family deprivation and intergenerational processes to the lives of the children and their age-graded life course. Later in this essay I provide more details on how this integration occurred.

Over the years since I undertook this project, a large number of studies have combined the generation and the age perspectives. They include Hareven's (1982) historical study of the family and the life course in the textile community of Manchester, Rossi and Rossi's (1990) three-generation study of the relation between individual aging and kin-defined relationships across the life course, and Moen's two-generation study of women (Moen et al., 1992). Burton and Bengtson (1985) document the value of this conceptual integration by noting the consequences of a disparity between age and generational status among black mothers of teenagers who had just borne a child: most of the mothers refused to accept a grandmother's child care burden.

Up to this point I have mentioned primarily conceptual developments, but these occurred in relation to other advances such as the unparalleled growth of longitudinal samples from the 1960s to the present. Valuable data also came from retrospective life histories, as collected by life calendars (Freedman et al., 1988). This growth spurred the initiation of longitudinal studies and an expansion of their archives (Young, Savela, & Phelps, 1991), as well as the development of statistical operations to fit the analytic requirements of event sequences.

The life course paradigm today is rooted primarily in developments that occurred largely during the 1960s; yet any glance at the record suggests that at that time, human socialization occupied a more paradigmatic role in guiding social psychological research. In the following section I argue that today the field of socialization has been absorbed in other frameworks, including that of the life course.

From Socialization to the Life Course

Social and demographic changes after World War II focused attention on the rising influences of peers and prompted concern about the presumed decline of effective family socialization. By the end of the 1950s, studies by Bronfenbrenner (1961) and Coleman (1961) had explored the relative influence of parents and of peers. This research emphasis continued through the 1960s, coupled with studies of political, deviant, and adult socialization (Brim & Wheeler, 1966; Sears, 1990). By the end of the decade the field of socialization research and theory had its own handbook (Goslin, 1969), with more specialized volumes planned for the 1970s.

Despite this apparent vigor, socialization studies declined in all areas, even in the lively realm of politics (Sears, 1990). Midway through the 1980s, the field of political socialization bore an uncomfortable resemblance, as one observer put it (Merelman, 1986, p. 279), to "the twitchings of a still-quickened corpse." Life course studies gained momentum over these years, with some attention to matters of socialization, but the growth seemed to come at the expense of socialization research.

Looking back over this era, one is tempted to ask "Whatever happened to the study of socialization?" The decline of socialization as a research paradigm has numerous explanations, though one simple point seems to be compelling: the framework became increasingly less adequate for questions that concerned life span continuity and change. For example, all problem children do not become problem adults (Robins, 1966), but how does this occur? Such diversity could not be explained with the behavioral-learning presuppositions of the socialization approach.

The issue of human diversity increased during the 1960s as the scope of study expanded through adolescence to the adult years. As a result, socialization theory became more transactional in concept, with greater emphasis on human agency, but still it failed to provide useful answers to questions of this kind. More attention to age grading, turning points, and social control was needed (Sampson & Laub, 1993), along with an appreciation for the role of coping skills and human agency in selecting environments.

These limitations, among other factors, prompted a shift in framework among sociologists from socialization to the life course in the 1970s. Many of the leading investigators of socialization, including John Clausen, Orville Brim, and Alan Kerckhoff, became students of the life course. At the same time, more inclusive, multifaceted theories or models emerged, in which socialization was merely one element. In this category I would place theories of social mobility (Kerckhoff, 1976), social structure and personality (Kohn, [1969] 1977, 1989; Kohn & Schooler, 1983), and age stratification (Riley et al., 1972). Collectively these theories address processes of socialization as well as those of status allocation, career management, psychosocial adaptation, task experience, and decision making.

One of the most vivid examples of this change in social psychology comes from the Social Science Research Council (SSRC). Committees of the SSRC are typically organized around cutting-edge topics. In 1960 one such committee was appointed on the topic of socialization and social structure; John Clausen served as chairman. In 1977 another committee was appointed on the theme of life course perspectives on human development; Matilda Riley served as the chair. The socialization committee was charged with examining theories, data resources, and methodological issues in "research on the interrelationships of social structure, socialization processes, and personality" (Clausen, 1968, p. vii). The committee lasted five years and produced numerous publications, including a volume titled *Socialization and Society* (Clausen, 1968).

Over the next 25 years, key members of the socialization committee provided leadership in the life course field. In the early 1970s, for example, Orville Brim organized and chaired an SSRC committee on the middle years, and in 1977 became a member of a newly organized committee on the life course. Brewster Smith (1977), a distinguished social psychologist in psychology, also made the shift from the socialization to the life course committee. Careers and aging had become a central problem for John Clausen in the 1970s; this work led to *American Lives* (1993), his major empirical study of the life course. Another member of the socialization committee, Alex Inkeles, continued to pursue issues of socialization and personality through the 1970s (Inkeles & Smith, 1974), but he did so in the context of modernization.

Brim's career illustrates most vividly the shift from socialization to the life course. In the late 1950s his research agenda included studies of child socialization, particularly family roles (Brim, 1957). In the 1960s, an increase in the proportion of aging Americans gave fresh visibility to development across the adult years. Brim broke new ground in this area by addressing the neglected topic of adult socialization (Brim & Wheeler, 1966). In doing so, he discovered that a socialization perspective failed to illuminate many fundamental aspects of adult development, such as how lives and careers are managed.

Eventually this work led Brim to an interest in the middle years; he focused on life course issues rather than on processes of socialization. In 1980, with Jerome Kagan, he explored questions about life span continuity and change (Brim & Kagan, 1980). Chapters in their volume examined issues of continuity and change in competence, deviant behavior, and cohort influences. Evidence of substantial behavioral change between early childhood and late adult life raised doubts about the strategic value of studying early socialization.

In these brief paragraphs I have argued that the demise of socialization as a major research paradigm had much to do with its limitations in addressing questions that focused increasingly on problems of life span continuity and change. An understanding of these problems requires knowledge that extends beyond socialization to selection processes and human agency, social support and coping strategies under stress, and the task experiences of employment and household. Today more than in the past, socialization is part of other research paradigms, especially that of the life course.

Launching a Life Course Study in the 1960s

At a time of changing paradigms, newly established studies are likely to reflect both old and new ideas. Consider the life course framework that prevailed during the late 1960s and early 1970s. Key elements were in place at the time, but the approach was not always interpreted as a life course perspective within the social sciences. Indeed, *Children of the Great Depression* (Elder, 1974) expresses this ambiguity through the dual themes of socialization and life course.

Initially I viewed the study in the familiar tradition of social structure and personality (Elder, 1973). Modes of family socialization through parental authority, affection, and example provided a set of cross-level links. From another perspective, however, framed by drastic social change, human lives, and age grading, the study centered on lives in a rapidly changing world. The family and its adaptations became a way of linking severe economic decline to the experience and development of adolescents in the 1930s.

This project began in the fall of 1962, when I arrived at the Institute of Human Development at Berkeley for a half-time research appointment with John Clausen. My assignment was to develop codes for uncoded materials in the longitudinal data archive of the Oakland Growth Study. The approximately 185 members of this study were born in 1920 and 1921. They and their parents provided data from 1931 through the 1930s, and most of the study members were followed up to their sixties.

In developing appropriate codes, I could not disregard the dramatic changefulness of families and lives throughout the Great Depression. But what could I use to represent the change? Useful concepts of family and individual change were scarce at that time. For example, conventional measures of socio-economic status were not relevant to families that were responding constantly to a fast-changing economic situation. Eventually, notions of the family economy and its multiple actors became a way to conceptualize families as a socioeconomic process.

Drawing on studies of Depression-era households (e.g., Bakke, 1940), I found that adaptations to drastic income loss (e.g., cutting back on expenses, altering authority roles) formed a way of thinking about the process by which families could enhance their prospects for recovery or survival by altering family structures. W. I. Thomas's (1909) model of family response to crisis (regarding the relation between claims and resources) proved useful in developing an account of the mechanisms of family adaptation. For example, a loss of control over desired outcomes resulting from economic decline can motivate a family's efforts to regain control, possibly by reducing consumption and sending additional workers into the labor force.

Another major challenge, in addition to family change, concerned ways of thinking about the lives of family members. Concepts of the singular career were available in the literature (Barley, 1989); notions of life history, life planning, and life organization could be found in *The Polish Peasant* (Thomas & Znaniecki, 1918–1920). The Depression crisis, however, called for analysis of the relation *between* trajectories—between family and work, for example; Wilensky's (1961) notion of interlocking life cycles proved especially convincing on this point.

I also needed to know the ages of parents and children when hard times arrived. Ryder's (1965) essay on cohorts made clear that the meaning of social change depended on one's age status. As I began coding life records according to the age and the sequence of events and transitions, the social and developmental meanings of age acquired theoretical importance. With the inclusion of age distinctions in my approach, I began to join the two research traditions—generation and age.

Some Oakland families lost heavily in the economic collapse; others were largely spared. By taking advantage of this natural experiment, the study devised a comparative design involving relatively nondeprived and deprived families in the middle and working classes of 1929. In each social stratum, the analysis traced the effects of economic hardship through family crises and adaptations to the children's middle years.

I placed the Oakland cohort in historical context by comparing it with a younger cohort of Americans (the Berkeley Guidance sample) who were born just before the 1930s (Elder, 1979). The younger Berkeley boys experienced the greatest risk of an impaired future, extending into the middle years. In these ways I joined the initial Depression studies of social change to a study of human lives and development.

A concern about the pattern and content of lives in changing societies is perhaps the most distinctive theme of the new life studies. All other emerging themes—timing, lives linked across the life span, the role of human agency in shaping the life course—are connected to this concern in one way or another. The connection between lives and times also represents one of the defining and enduring features of sociological social psychology, beginning with the Chicago school of sociology. In conclusion I turn briefly to this theme and to issues regarding transhistorical knowledge.

JOINING HUMAN LIVES
WITH THEIR TIMES

In an essay titled "The Province of Social Psychology," published around the turn of the century, W. I. Thomas (1905) advocated studies that would examine "the crises or incidents in group-life which interrupt the flow of habit and give rise to changed conditions of consciousness and practice" (p. 445). At that time we did not know that he would carry out the pioneering study of this kind with Florian Znaniecki. Thomas himself (Baker, 1973, p. 246) experienced a social transformation as he made his way from the isolated foothills of Virginia to the University of Chicago, a journey that made him feel as if he had "lived in three centuries."

Thomas's advocacy for such studies extended to the 1930s, and work of this type continued in the post-Depression years. *The American Soldier* (Stouffer et al., 1949) and Inkele's (1955) Soviet study are notable examples. Yet a conceptual logic for relating lives to times was not developed until the 1960s, whose intellectual and social milieu included an aging population, the discontinuities of civil strife and rapid social change, and the emergence of a new social history.

From this era of renewed consciousness on matters of social change came historical studies of men's work lives (Thernstrom, 1964) and family life (Hareven, 1982), of modernization and individual modernity (Inkeles & Smith, 1974), and of Americans who grew up in the Great Depression and World War II (Elder, 1974, 1979). This social science was clearly attentive to social change in human experience and mentality.

Ironically, these developments coincided with an influential critique of the ahistorical character of psychological social psychology. In "Social Psychology as History," Kenneth Gergen (1973, p. 319) documents the impact of behavioral science on society, challenged the goal of transhistorical laws in social psychology, and concluded that "social psychological research is primarily the systematic study of contemporary history." Gergen's views are consonant with an intellectual movement (see Gergen & Davis, 1985) that depicts human psychology as a historically bounded enterprise.

In 1973 Gergen made no reference to the relevant literature of sociological social psychology. His message had little to offer sociologists who were engaged in studies relating social history to individual lives (also see Gergen & Gergen, 1984). In this realm at least, the two social psychologies, sociological and psychological (House, 1977), had little in common.

In other respects, however, Gergen's critique brings to mind the intellectual constraints and barriers that arise from what Robert Merton (1959, p. xv) once called "pseudofacts." False or misguided statements about reality sometimes become pseudofacts. In the social and behavioral sciences they tend to produce "pseudoproblems which cannot be solved because matters are not as they purport to be."

In Gergen's judgment, for example, historical change raises serious doubt about the prospects for developing empirical generalizations across historical time. By disclaiming the possibility of transhistorical generalization, his critique discourages attempts to test such generalizations, thereby inviting a self-fulfilling prophecy. Of course, the boundaries of generalization are uncertain for any study. Historically based studies can proceed only by testing their outer limits.

Consider a replication of *Children of the Great Depression* (Elder, 1974; also see Elder, 1979) in rural as well as urban studies of the 1980s and 1990s. Two decades after launching the Depression studies, I joined a research team (headed by Rand Conger) at Ames, Iowa, on a panel study of 451 rural families in the great farm crisis of the 1980s (Conger & Elder, 1994; Elder, 1992b; Elder et al., 1992). Land values suddenly had fallen by half, pushing countless families into extraordinary levels of debt. On leading economic indicators, this decline proved to be more severe than any crisis since the Great Depression.

Each study family in the eight-county region of north central Iowa, included two parents, a seventh-grade pupil, and a near sibling. Beginning in 1989, the annual data collections included questionnaires and videotaped family sessions. Data also were obtained from local, state, and federal statistical records.

We were concerned about families' adaptations to such drastic change and about pathways to alternative economic options. The Iowa study drew on the basic model of the Depression study, which focused on family interactive processes with an eye to the larger picture of economic decline and its consequences for parents and children.

The model from *Children of the Great Depression* (Elder, 1974) that guided work in the Iowa study specified three sets of links between hard times in the family and children's experiences; household economy, family relations, and strains. The family—its structures and processes—became a link between the macroscopic events of economic decline and the micro world of children.

In theory and in reality, severe income loss shifted the household economy toward labor-intensive operations involving more productive roles for the children and a greater burden for the mother. Family deprivation also altered relationships within the family, increasing the mother's centrality as the authority and the affectionate figure. Finally, heavy income loss magnified the risk of family discord, disorganization, and demoralization. Empirical findings from the Oakland study fully document these interrelated family processes as links; we obtained corresponding results from analyses of children in a younger birth cohort, members of the Berkeley Guidance Study (Elder, 1979).

In view of the differences between these urban Depression studies and the rural Iowa project, there was little reason to expect similar results. Even so, we tested the generalization issue on the Iowa study by setting up a causal model that resembled the model used in the Depression research (see Figure 1.1).

The first part of the model assumes that low income, unstable work, and income loss have consequences for marital discord and for parents' emotional distress by increasing economic pressures—the tangible pressures of running out of money and the adjustments of cutting back. Unlike our approach in the Depression studies, we assigned causal priority to changes in the household

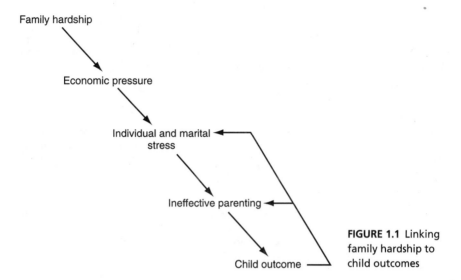

FIGURE 1.1 Linking family hardship to child outcomes

economy and regarded them as both harming family relations and creating social strain.

Marital discord and individual distress link economic pressure with ineffective parenting. The latter variable connects marital and individual distress with child outcomes. Here it is assumed that marital conflict and the parents' emotional distress have consequences for children by undermining the quality of the parents' behavior. When played out over time, behavioral outcomes have feedback effects on the interaction processes—for example, from child to parent. Our findings generally support this theoretical formulation.

Consider a study of Iowa boys who were in the seventh grade in 1989 (Conger et al., 1992). Using both observational and family member's reports, the study found that objective family hardship (measured by per capita income, debt-to-assist ratio, instability of work, and reported income loss) increased the risk of a depressed mood among mothers and fathers through perceived economic pressures. Depressed feelings heightened the likelihood of conflict in marriage, and consequently increased the risk of disrupted and nonnurturing behavior by both parents. These behaviors, in turn, undermined the boys' self-confidence, peer acceptance, and school performance. A similar process has been observed for girls (Conger et al., 1993).

Empirical tests of this mediational model have produced results that generally resemble the findings of the Depression studies, with the major exception of mothers. In the Iowa research, as noted above, the mother's emotional distress represents a strong link between economic pressure and marital discord. By comparison, mothers in the Depression studies were less prominent as a social and emotional link between hard times and the child's developmental experiences. Plausible explanations for this difference include historical trends in women's social roles, especially in the workplace. Women in the 1930s were far less deeply involved in the financial support and management of their families than are Iowa women in the 1990s.

In Iowa households under economic pressure, boys and girls also assumed more responsibilities, such as chores in the home, work on the farm, and paid jobs in the rural communities. As in the Great Depression, mounting economic pressures made the children's contributions more valuable. This process was most evident in farm families that embraced most fully the collective ethic of required helpfulness—family members' responsiveness to the collective welfare of the family. Farm boys' contributions in particular were valued by their parents. The more farm boys earned from work and the sale of their animals, the more positive were their parents' evaluations. By comparison, parental judgments of working sons in nonfarm households were more often negative, perhaps reflecting the individualistic nature of work and earnings in these communities.

These studies of economically deprived families in different times and places identify both transhistorical variations and continuities. The Great Depression and more contemporary studies, both rural and urban (Elder et al., 1993; Liem & Liem, 1990; McLeod & Shanahan, 1993), depict remarkable similarities in the family process whereby economic downturns influence children's developmental course and future. These similarities also extend to the productive roles of children in hard-pressed families. Also worth noting are the differences, such as the variable role of the mother in deprived households.

By testing analytic models of family adaptations in situations that vary in time and place, we are beginning to construct general theories that relate human lives to their changing worlds.

CONCLUSION

Over the past 30 years, sociological social psychology has experienced dramatic changes in prominent theories and lines of empirical research. Few changes document this observation more vividly than the emergence of life course studies as a field of inquiry and a research paradigm. This new development has been attended by renewed emphasis on formerly undeveloped themes in social psychology, from temporality and human agency to social change and contextual variations.

At midcentury the term *life course* was not part of our vocabulary in theory or research, and problems of aging from birth to death had yet to arouse substantial interest among social scientists. Instead problems of child and adolescent socialization occupied center stage, governing theoretical advances and research. Today these problems typically are embedded in more general theories, such as age stratification and social mobility, and have taken a back seat to contemporary issues of life course and human development.

The early wave of life course studies, headed by the work of Thomas and Znaniecki, focused on the family context and the processes of lives—kinship ties, social transmission, intergenerational relations, the life cycle in which one generation reproduces another, and generational status. In the 1960s this family perspective was supplemented by studies of age and the life course, producing a framework that featured paradigmatic themes such as lives and times, the timing of lives, linked lives, and human agency.

Thomas's favored concept—that of social psychology, as the study of macro social change in people's lives, —is being realized with increasing frequency by contemporary studies of the life course. The pace of change has suggested to some observers that social psychological knowledge is circumscribed by the particular times, but in fact this knowledge calls for studies of change processes that extend across time and place. Within the boundaries of current knowledge, for example, the effect of economic decline in children's lives tends to follow a similar course across time and place in twentieth-century America.

The challenge for social psychology as we near the end of the twentieth century is to locate people in relation to the massive social changes under way, such as the collapse of the Soviet Union, mass migration, and German reunification. Greater understanding of these changes in developmental processes will enable us to explain why life journeys reflect their historical times. In the words of Everett Hughes (1971, p. 124), "some people come to the age of work when there is no work, others when there are wars. . . . Such joining of a man's life with events, large and small, are his unique career, and give him many of his personal problems."

REFERENCES

Baker, Paul J., ed. 1973. "The Life Histories of W.I. Thomas and Robert E. Park," *American Journal of Sociology* 79:246–50.

Bakke, E. Wright. 1940. *Citizens without Work: A Study of the Effects of Unemployment upon the Workers' Social Relations and Practices,* New Haven: Yale University Press.

Baltes, Paul B. 1987. "Theoretical Propositions of Life-Span Developmental Psychology: On the Dynamics between Growth and Decline," *Developmental Psychology* 23:611–26.

Bandura, Albert. 1986. *Social Foundations of Thought and Action: A Social Cognitive Theory,* New York: Prentice-Hall.

———. 1997. *Self-Efficacy: The Exercise of Personal Control,* New York: Springer.

Barley, Stephen R. 1989. "Careers, Identities, and Institutions: The Legacy of the Chicago School of Sociology." Pp. 41–65 in *Handbook of Career Theory,* edited by M.B. Arthur, D.T. Hall, and B.S. Lawrence. New York: Cambridge University Press.

Brim, Orville G., Jr. 1957. "The Parent-Child Relations as a Social System: 1. Parent and Child Roles." *Child Development* 28(9):343–63.

Brim, Orville G., Jr. and J. Kagen, eds. 1980. *Constancy and Change in Human Development.* Cambridge, MA: Harvard University Press.

Brim, Orville G., Jr., and Stanton Wheeler. 1966. *Socialization after Childhood: Two Essays.* New York: Wiley.

Bronfenbrenner, Urie. 1961. "Some Familial Antecedents of Responsibility and Leadership in Adolescents." Pp. 239–71 in *Leadership and Interpersonal Behavior,* edited by L. Petrullo and B.M. Bass. New York: Holt.

———. 1979. *The Ecology of Human Development.* Cambridge, MA: Harvard University Press.

Burton, Linda M. and Vern L. Bengtson. 1985. "Black Grandmothers: Issues of Timing and Continuity of Roles." Pp. 61–77 in *Grandparenthood,* edited by V.L. Bengtson and J.F. Robertson, Beverly Hills: Sage.

Cain, Leonard. 1964. "The Life Course and Social Change." Pp. 272–309 in *Handbook of Modern Sociology,* edited by R.E.L. Faris. Chicago: Rand McNally.

Caspi, Avshalom and Daryl J. Bem. 1990. "Personality Continuity and Change across the Life Course." Pp. 549–75 in *Handbook of Personality,* edited by L.A. Pervin. New York: Guilford.

Clausen, John A., ed. 1968. *Socialization and Society.* Boston: Little, Brown.

———. 1993. *American Lives.* New York: Free Press.

Coleman, James S. 1961. *The Adolescent Society.* New York: Free Press.

———. 1988. "Social Capital in the Creation of Human Capital." *American Journal of Sociology* 94:S94–S120.

Conger, Rand D., Katherine J. Conger, Glen H. Elder Jr., Frederick O. Lorenz, Ronald L. Simons, and Les B. Whitbeck. 1993. "Family Economic Stress and Adjustment of Early Adolescent Girls." *Developmental Psychology* 29(2):206–19.

Conger, Rand D. and Glen H. Elder Jr. 1994. *Families in Troubled Times: Adapting to Change in Rural America.* Chicago, Aldine.

Conger, Rand D., Glen H. Elder Jr., Frederick O. Lorenz, Ronald L. Simons, and Les B. Whitbeck. 1992. "A Family Process Model of Economic Hardship and Adjustment of Early Adolescent Boys." *Child Development* 63:526–41.

Cowan, Carolyn P. and P.G. Cowan. 1992. *When Partners Become Parents: The Big Life Change for Couples.* New York: Basic Books.

Davis, Kingsley. 1940. "The Sociology of Parent-Youth Conflict." *American Sociological Review* 7:523–35.

Eckenrode, John and Susan Gore, eds. 1990. *Stress between Work and Family.* New York: Plenum.

Elder, Glen H., Jr., ed. 1973. *Linking Social Structure and Personality.* Beverly Hills: Sage.

———. 1974. *Children of the Great Depression: Social Change in Life Experiences.* Chicago: University of Chicago Press.

———. 1975. "Age Differentiation and the Life Course." *Annual Review of Sociology* 1:165–90.

———. 1979. "Historical Change in Life Patterns and Personality." Pp. 117–59 in *Life-Span Development and Behavior,* edited by Paul Baltes and Orville Brim Jr. New York: Academic Press.

———. 1985. "Perspectives on the Life Course." Pp. 23–49 in *Life Course Dynamics,* edited by Glen H. Elder Jr., Ithaca: Cornell University Press.

———. 1992a. "Life Course." Pp. 1120–30 in *Encyclopedia of Sociology,* edited by E. Borgatta and M. Borgatta. New York: Macmillan.

———. 1992b. "Children of the Farm Crisis." Paper presented at meetings of the Society for Research on Adolescence, Washington, DC.

Elder, Glen H., Jr. and Avshalom Caspi. 1990. "Studying Lives in a Changing Society: Sociological and Personological Explorations." Pp. 201–47 in *Studying Persons and Lives,* edited by A.I. Rabin, R.A. Zucker, and S. Frank. New York: Springer.

Elder, Glen H., Jr., Rand D. Conger, Michael Foster, and Monika Ardelt. 1992. "Families under Economic Pressure." *Journal of Family Issues* 31(1):5–37.

Elder, Glen H., Jr., Jacqueline Eccles, Monika Ardelt, and Sarah Lord. 1993. "Inner City Parents under Economic Pressure: Perspectives on the Strategies of Parenting. Presented at the biennial meeting of the Society for Research on Child Development, New Orleans.

Elder, Glen H., Jr., John Modell, and Ross Parke, eds. 1993. *Children in Time and Place: Developmental and Historical Insights.* New York: Cambridge University Press.

Elder, Glen H., Jr. and Angela O'Rand. 1995. "Adult Lives in a Changing Society." In *Sociological Perspectives on Social Psychology,* edited by J.S. House, K. Cook, and G. Fine. New York: Allyn & Bacon.

Elder, Glen H., Jr., Michael J. Shanahan, and Elizabeth C. Clipp. 1994. "When War Comes to Men's Lives: Life Course Patterns in Family, Work, and Health." *Psychology and Aging.* 9:5–16.

Featherman, David L. 1983. "The Life-Span Perspectives in Social Science Research." Pp. 1–57 in *Life-Span Development and Behavior,* edited by Paul B. Baltes and Orville G. Brim, Jr. New York: Academic.

Freedman, Deborah, Arland Thornton, Donald Camburn, Duane Alwin, and Linda Young-DeMarco. 1988. "The Life History Calendar: A Technique for Collecting Retrospective Data." *Sociological Methodology* 18:37–68.

Gergen, Kenneth J. 1973. "Social Psychology as History." *Journal of Personality and Social Psychology* 26:309–20.

Gergen, Kenneth J. and Keith E. Davis. 1985. *The Social Construction of the Person.* New York: Springer-Verlag.

Gergen, Kenneth J. and Mary M. Gergen, eds. 1984. *Historical Social Psychology.* Hillsdale, NJ: Erlbaum.

Goslin, D.A., ed. 1969. *Handbook of Socialization Theory and Research.* Chicago: Rand McNally.

Hareven, Tamara K. 1982. *Family Time and Industrial Time.* New York: Cambridge University Press.

Hogan, Dennis P. 1981. *Transitions and Social Change: The Early Lives of American Man.* New York: Academic Press.

House, James S. 1977. "The Three Faces of Social Psychology," *Sociometry* 40:161–77.

Hughes, Everett. 1971. *The Sociological Eye: Selected Papers on Work, Self and the Study of Society.* Vol. 1. Chicago: Aldine.

Inkeles, Alex. 1955. "Social Change and Social Character: The Role of

Parental Mediation." *Journal of Social Issues* 11:12–21.

Inkeles, Alex and James Smith. 1974. *Becoming Modern.* Cambridge, MA: Harvard University Press.

Kerckhoff, Alan C. 1976. "The Status Attainment Process: Socialization or Allocation?" *Social Forces* 55:368–81.

Kertzer, David I. and Jennie Keith, eds. 1984. *Age and Anthropologist Theory.* Ithaca: Cornell University Press.

Kohn, Melvin L. (1969) 1977. *Class and Conformity: A Study in Values.* Homewood, IL: Dorsey.

———. 1989. "Social Structure and Personality: A quintessentially Sociological Approach to Social Psychology." *Social Forces* 68:26–33.

Kohn, Melvin L. and Carmi Schooler. 1983. *Work and Personality: An Inquiry into the Impact of Stratification.* Norwood, NJ: Ablex.

Liem, Joan Huser, and G. Ramsey Liem. 1990. "Understanding the Individual and Family Effects of Unemployment." Pp. 175–204 in *Stress between Work and Family,* edited by J. Eckenrode and S. Gore. New York: Plenum.

McLeod, Jane D. and Michael J. Shanahan. 1993. "Poverty, Parenting, and Children's Mental Health." *American Sociological Review* 58:351–66.

Merelman, Richard. 1986. "Revitalizing Political Socialization." Pp. 279–319 in *Political Psychology: Contemporary Problems and Issues,* edited by M.G. Hermann, San Francisco: Jossey-Bass.

Merton, Robert K. 1959. "Notes on Problem Finding in Sociology." Pp. ix–xxxiv in *Sociology Today: Problems and Perspectives,* edited by R.K. Merton, L. Broom, and L.S. Cottrell Jr. New York: Basic Books.

Modell, John. 1989. *Into One's Own: From Youth to Adulthood in the United States 1920–1975.* Berkeley University of California Press.

Mills, C. Wright. 1959. *The Sociological Imagination.* New York: Oxford University Press.

Moen, Phyllis, Donna Dempster-McClain, and Robin M. Williams Jr. 1992. "Successful Aging: A Life-Course Perspective on Women's Multiple Roles and Health." *American Journal of Sociology* 97: 1612–38.

Neugarten, Bernice L. and N. Datan. 1973. "Sociological Perspectives on the Life Cycle." Pp. 53–69 in *Life-Span Developmental Psychology: Personality and Socialization,* edited by P.B. Baltes and K. W. Schaie. New York: Academic Press.

Plomin, Robert and Judy Dunn. 1991. *Separate Lives.* New York: Basic Books.

Riley, Matilda White, Marilyn E. Johnson, and Anne Foner, eds. 1972. *Aging and Society: A Sociology of Age Stratification.* Vol. 3. New York: Russell Sage Foundation.

Riley, Matilda White, Joan Waring, and Anne Foner. 1988. "The Sociology of Age." Pp. 243–290 in *The Handbook of Sociology,* edited by N. Smelser and R. Burt. Newbury Park, CA: Sage.

Robins, Lee. 1966. *Deviant Children Grown Up.* Baltimore: Williams and Wilkins.

Rossi, Alice S. and Peter H. Rossi. 1990. *Of Human Bonding.* New York: Aldine.

Ryder, Norman B. 1965. "The Cohort as a Concept in the Study of Social Change." *American Sociological Review* 30:843–61.

Sampson, Robert J. and John H. Laub. 1993. *Crime in the Making: Pathways and Turning Points through Life.* Cambridge, MA: Harvard University Press.

Scarr, Sandra and Kathleen McCartney. 1983. "How People Make Their Own Environments: A Theory of Genotype-Environment Effects." *Child Development* 54:424–35.

Sears, David O. 1990. "Whither Political Socialization Research? The Question of Persistence." Pp. 69–97 in *Political Socialization, Citizenship Education, and Democracy,* edited by O. Ichilov. New York: Teachers College Press.

Smith, Brewster M. 1977. "A Dialectical Social Psychology? Comments on a Symposium." *Personality and Social Psychology Bulletin* 3:719–24.

Stouffer, Samuel A., E.A. Suchman, L.C. DeVinney, S.A. Star, and R.A. Williams. 1949. *The American Soldier: Adjustment during Army Life.* Vols. 1 and 2. Princeton: Princeton University Press.

Streib, Gordon F. and Robert H. Binstock. 1990. "Aging and the Social Sciences: Changes in the Field." Pp. 1–15 in *Handbook of Aging and the Social Sciences,* edited by R.H. Binstock and L.K. George. New York: Academic Press.

Thernstrom, Stephan. 1964. *Poverty and Progress: Social Mobility in a Nineteenth Century City.* Cambridge, MA: Harvard University Press.

Thomas, William I. 1905. "The Province of Social Psychology." *American Journal of Sociology* 10:445–55.

———. 1909. *Sourcebook for Social Origins.* Boston: Badger.

Thomas, William I. and Florian Znaniecki. 1918–20. *The Polish Peasant in Europe and America.* Vols. 1–2. Urbana: University of Illinois Press.

Turkewitz, Gerald and Darlynne A. Devenny, ed. 1993. *Developmental Time and Timing.* Hillsdale, NJ: Erlbaum.

Turner, Ralph H. 1998. "Personality in Society: Social Psychology's Contribution to Sociology." *Social Psychology Quarterly* 51:1–10.

Wilensky, Harold L. 1961. "Orderly Careers and Social Participation in the Middle Mass." *American Sociological Review* 24:836–45.

Young, Coleman H., K.L. Savela, and E. Phelps. 1991. *Inventory of Longitudinal Studies in the Social Sciences.* Newbury Park, CA: Sage.

2

Crime and Deviance
in the Life Course

ROBERT J. SAMPSON
JOHN H. LAUB

ABSTRACT Criminological research has emphasized the strong relationship between age and crime, with involvement in most crimes peaking in
adolescence and then declining. However, there is also evidence of the
early onset of delinquency and of the stability of criminal and deviant
behavior over the life course. In this essay we reconcile these findings by
synthesizing and integrating longitudinal research on childhood antisocial
behavior, adolescent delinquency, and adult crime with theory and
research on the life course. Consistent with a life-course perspective, we
focus on continuities and discontinuities in deviant behavior over time and
on the social influences of age-graded transitions and salient life events.
Furthermore, we critically assess the implications of stability and change
for longitudinal research. We conclude with an emerging research agenda
for studying the relationship of crime and deviance with a broad range of
social phenomena (e.g. occupational attainment, opportunity structures,
marital attachment) over the life course.

INTRODUCTION

Accepted wisdom holds that crime is committed disproportionately by
adolescents. According to data from the United States and other industrialized countries, property and violent crime rise rapidly in the
teenage years to a peak at about ages 16 and 18, respectively, with a decline
thereafter until old age (Hirschi & Gottfredson, 1983; Farrington, 1986;
Flanagan & Maguire, 1990). The overrepresentation of youth in crime has
been demonstrated using multiple sources of measurement—whether official
arrest reports (Federal Bureau of Investigation, 1990), self-reports of offending (Rowe & Tittle, 1977), or victim reports of the ages of offenders
(Hindelang, 1981). It is thus generally accepted that, in the aggregate, age-
specific crime rates peak in the late teenage years and then decline with age.

SOURCE: *Annual Review of Sociology,* Vol. 18, pp. 63–84. Reprinted with permission
from the *Annual Review of Sociology,* Vol. 18. © 1992, by Annual Reviews.

The age-crime curve has had a profound impact on the organization and content of sociological studies of crime by channeling research to a focus on adolescents. As a result sociological criminology has traditionally neglected the theoretical significance of childhood characteristics and the link between early childhood behaviors and later adult outcomes (see Robins, 1966; Caspi et al., 1989; McCord, 1979; Farrington, 1989; Gottfredson & Hirschi, 1990; Loeber & LeBlanc, 1990; Sampson & Laub, 1990). Although criminal behavior does peak in the teenage years, evidence reviewed below indicates an early onset of delinquency as well as continuity of criminal behavior over the life course. By concentrating on the teenage years, sociological perspectives on crime have thus failed to address the life-span implications of childhood behavior.

At the same time, criminologists have not devoted much attention to the other end of the spectrum—desistance from crime and the transitions from criminal to noncriminal behavior in adulthood (Cusson & Pinsonneault, 1986; Shover, 1985; Gartner & Piliavin, 1988). As Rutter (1988a:3) argues, we know little about "escape from the risk process" and whether predictors of desistance are unique or simply the opposite of criminogenic factors. Therefore, not only has the early life course been neglected, but so has the relevance of social transitions in young adulthood and the factors explaining desistance from crime as people age.

In this paper we confront these issues by bringing both childhood and adulthood back into the criminological picture of age and crime. To accomplish this goal we synthesize and integrate the research literature on the life course and crime. As described below, the life-course perspective highlights continuities and discontinuities in behavior over time and the social influences of age-graded transitions and life events. Hence, the life course is concerned not only with early childhood experiences but also with salient events and socialization in adulthood. To the extent that the adult life course does explain variation in adult crime unaccounted for by childhood development, change must be considered part of the explanatory framework in criminology, along with the stability of early individual differences.

The life-course perspective also bears on recent controversies that have embroiled criminology. While all agree that the issue of age and crime is important, conflicting views have emerged on the implications of age for the study of crime and deviance. Hirschi and Gottfredson (1983) argue that the age-crime curve is invariant over different times, places, crime types, and demographic subgroups. Moreover, they believe that age has a direct effect on crime that cannot be explained by social factors, that the causes of crime are the same at every age, and hence that longitudinal research is not needed to study the causes of crime (see also Gottfredson & Hirschi, 1987, 1988, 1990). By contrast, Farrington (1986) argues that the age-crime curve reflects variations in prevalence rather than incidence and that incidence does not vary consistently with age. He also presents evidence to suggest that the relation between age and crime varies over time and by offense type, location, and gender. Blumstein and Cohen (1979) argue further that individual crime rates are constant during a criminal career, implying that arrest rates do not always decrease with age for all offenders (see also Blumstein et al., 1988).

Accordingly, even fundamental "facts" about the age-crime relationship and their implications for research design are subject to much debate. This predicament provides yet another motivation to link the study of age and crime to the life-course perspective. Indeed, the data on age and crime lend themselves naturally to a concern with how criminal behavior changes as individuals pass through different stages of the life course. By integrating knowledge on crime with age-graded transitions in the life course, our review attempts to shed further light on the age-crime debate.

This paper is organized in the following manner. Before assessing the criminological literature directly, we first highlight major ideas in life-course research and theory. In subsequent sections we then examine the research on continuity (stability) and discontinuities (change) in crime over the life course. In the final sections, we outline a research agenda on age and crime that stems from a reconceptualization of stability and change.

THE LIFE COURSE PERSPECTIVE

The life course has been defined as "pathways through the age differentiated life span," where age differentiation "is manifested in expectations and options that impinge on decision processes and the course of events that give shape to life stages, transitions, and turning points" (Elder, 1985:17). Similarly, Caspi et al. (1990:15) conceive of the life course as a "sequence of culturally defined age-graded roles and social transitions that are enacted over time." Age-graded transitions are embedded in social institutions and are subject to historical change (Elder, 1975, 1991).

Two central concepts underlie the analysis of life-course dynamics. A trajectory is a pathway or line of development over the life span such as worklife, marriage, parenthood, self-esteem, and criminal behavior. Trajectories refer to long-term patterns and sequences of behavior. Transitions are marked by specific life events (e.g. first job or first marriage) that are embedded in trajectories and evolve over shorter time spans—"changes in state that are more or less abrupt" (Elder, 1985:31–32). Some transitions are age-graded and some are not; hence, what is often assumed to be important is the normative timing and sequencing of changes in roles, statuses, or other socially defined positions along some consensual dimension (Jessor et al., 1991). For example, Hogan (1980) emphasizes the duration of time (spells) between a change in state and the ordering of events, such as first job or first marriage, on occupational status and earnings in adulthood. Caspi et al. (1990:25) argue that delays in social transitions (e.g. being "off-time") produce conflicting obligations that enhance later difficulties (see also Rindfuss et al., 1987). As a result, life-course analyses are often characterized by a focus on the duration, timing, and ordering of major life events and their consequences for later social development.

The interlocking nature of trajectories and transitions may generate turning points or a change in the life course (Elder, 1985:32). Adaptation to life events is crucial because the same event or transition followed by different adaptations can lead to different trajectories (Elder, 1985:35). The long-term view embodied by the life-course focus on trajectories implies a strong connection between childhood events and experiences in adulthood. However, the simultaneous shorter-term view also implies that transitions or turning points can modify life trajectories—they can "redirect paths." Social institutions and triggering life events that may modify trajectories include school, work, the military, marriage, and parenthood (see e.g. Elder, 1986; Rutter et al., 1990; Sampson & Laub, 1990).

In addition to the study of trajectories of change and the continuity between childhood behavior and later adulthood outcomes, the life-course framework encompasses at least three other themes: (i) a concern with the social meanings of age throughout the life course, (ii) intergenerational transmission of social patterns, and (iii) the effects of macrolevel events (e.g. Great Depression, World War II) and structural location (e.g. class and gender) on individual life histories (see Elder, 1974, 1985). As Elder (1991) notes, a major objective of the study of the life course is to link social history and social structure to the unfolding of human lives. To address these themes individual lives are studied through time, with particular attention devoted to aging, cohort effects, historical context, and the social influence of age-graded transitions. Naturally, prospective longitudinal research designs form the heart of life-course research.

Of all the themes emphasized in life-course research, the extent of stability and change in both behavior and personality attributes over time is perhaps the most complex. Stability versus change in behavior is also one of the most hotly debated and controversial issues in the social sciences (Brim & Kagan, 1980a; Dannefer, 1984; Baltes & Nesselroade, 1984). Given its pivotal role we thus turn to an assessment of the research literature as it bears on stability and change in criminal behavior. Although personality development is obviously an important topic (see Block, 1971; Caspi, 1987), space considerations demand that we focus primarily on behavior. As we shall see, the research literature contains evidence for both continuity and change in deviant behavior over the life course.

STABILITY OF CRIME AND DEVIANCE

Unlike sociological criminology, the field of developmental psychology has long been concerned with the continuity of maladaptive behaviors (Brim & Kagan, 1980a; Caspi & Bern, 1990). As such, a large portion of the longitudinal evidence on stability comes from psychologists and others who study "antisocial behavior" generally, where the legal concept of crime may or may not be a component. An example is the study of aggression in psychology (Olweus, 1979). In exploring this research tradition, our purpose is to highlight the extent to which deviant childhood behaviors have important ramifications, whether criminal or noncriminal, in later adult life.

Our point of departure is the widely reported claim that individual differences in antisocial behavior are stable across the life course (Olweus, 1979; Caspi et al., 1987; Loeber, 1982; Robins, 1966; Huesmann et al., 1984; Gottfredson & Hirschi, 1990; Jessor et al., 1977, 1991). The stability of crime and antisocial behavior over time is often defined as homotypic continuity, which refers to the continuity of similar behaviors or phenotypic attributes over time (Caspi & Bem, 1990:553). For example, in an influential study of the aggressiveness of 600 subjects, their parents, and their children over a 22-year period, Huesmann et al. (1984) found that early aggressiveness predicted later aggression and criminal violence. They concluded that "aggression can be viewed as a persistent trait that . . . possesses substantial cross-situational constancy" (1984:1120). An earlier study by Robins (1966) also found a high level of stability in crime and aggression over time.

More generally, Olweus's (1979) comprehensive review of over 16 studies on aggressive behavior revealed "substantial" stability—the correlation between early aggressive behavior and later criminality averaged .68 for the studies reviewed (1979:854–55). Loeber (1982) completed a similar review of the extant literature in many disciplines and concluded that a "consensus" has been reached in favor of the stability hypothesis: "children who initially display high rates of antisocial behavior are more likely to persist in this behavior than children who initially show lower rates of antisocial behavior" (1982:1433). Recent empirical studies documenting stability in criminal and deviant behavior across time include West and Farrington (1977), Wolfgang et al. (1987), Shannon (1988), Elliott et al. (1985), and Jessor et al. (1991).

Although more comprehensive, these findings are not new. Over 50 years ago the Gluecks found that virtually all of the 510 reformatory inmates in their study of criminal careers "had experience in serious antisocial conduct" (Glueck & Glueck, 1930:142). Their data also confirmed "the early genesis of antisocial careers" (1930:143). In addition, the Gluecks' follow-up of 1000 males originally studied in *Unraveling Juvenile Delinquency* (1950) revealed remarkable continuities. As they argued in *Delinquents and Non-Delinquents in Perspective:* "while the majority of boys originally included in the non-delinquent control group continued, down the years, to remain essentially law-abiding, the greatest majority of those originally included in the delinquent group continued to commit all sorts of crimes in the 17–25 age-span" (1968: 170). Findings regarding behavioral or homotypic continuity are thus supported by a rich body of empirical research that spans several decades (for more extensive discussion see Robins, 1966, 1978; West & Farrington, 1977; Gottfredson & Hirschi, 1990). In fact, much as the Gluecks reported earlier, Robins (1978) summarized results from her studies of four male cohorts by stating that "adult antisocial behavior virtually requires childhood antisocial behavior" (1978:611).

Perhaps more intriguing, the linkage between childhood misbehavior and adult outcomes is found across life domains that go well beyond the legal concept of crime. This phenomenon is usually defined as heterotypic continuity—continuity of an inferred genotypic attribute presumed to underlie diverse phenotypic behaviors (Caspi & Bem, 1990:553). For instance, a specific behavior in childhood might not be predictive of the exact same behavior in later adulthood but might still be associated with behaviors that are conceptually consistent with that earlier behavior (Caspi & Moffitt, 1991:4). Although not always criminal per se, adult behaviors falling in this category might include excessive drinking, traffic violations, marital conflict or abuse, and harsh discipline of children. Gottfredson and Hirschi (1990:91) invoke a similar idea when they refer to adult behaviors "analogous" to crime such as accidents, smoking, and sexual promiscuity.

Evidence for the behavioral coherence implied by heterotypic continuity is found in the Huesmann et al. (1984) study, where they report that aggression in childhood was related not just to adult crime but to spouse abuse, drunk driving, moving violations, and severe punishment of offspring. Other studies reporting a similar coalescence of deviant and criminal acts over time include West and Farrington (1977), Robins (1966), and Jessor et al. (1991). It is interesting that the findings of heterotypic continuity generated largely by psychologists are quite consistent with criminological research, showing little or no specialization in crime as people age (Wolfgang et al., 1972; Blumstein et al., 1986; Elliott et al., 1989; Osgood et al., 1988).

Invoking another dimension of heterotypic continuity, Caspi (1987) has argued that personality characteristics in childhood (e.g. ill tempered behavior) will not only appear across time but will be manifested in a number of diverse situations. Specifically, Caspi (1987:1211) found that the tendency toward explosive, undercontrolled behavior in childhood was recreated over time, especially in problems with subordination (e.g. in education, military, and work settings) and in situations that required negotiating interpersonal conflicts (e.g. marriage and parenting). For example, children who display temper tantrums in childhood are more likely to abort their involvement with education, which in turn is related to a wide range of adult outcomes such as unemployment, job instability, and low income. In *Deviant Children Grown Up,* Lee Robins also found strong relations between childhood antisocial behavior and adult employment status, occupational status, job stability, income, and mobility (1966:95–102). Robins went so far as to conclude that "antisocial behavior [in childhood] predicts class status more efficiently than class status predicts antisocial behavior" (1966:305). In a similar vein, Sampson and Laub's (1990) reanalysis of longitudinal data from the Gluecks' archives found that childhood antisocial behavior strongly predicted not just adult criminality but outcomes as diverse as joblessness, divorce, welfare dependence, and educational failure—independent of childhood economic status and IQ.

Implications for Social Theories of Crime

There is ample evidence that antisocial behavior is relatively stable across stages of the life course, regardless of traditional sociological variables like stratification. As Caspi and Moffitt (1991:2) conclude, robust continuities in antisocial behavior have been revealed over the past 50 years in different nations (e.g. Canada, England, Finland, New Zealand, Sweden, and the

United States) and with multiple methods of assessment (e.g. official records, teacher ratings, parent reports, and peer nominations of aggressive behavior). These replications across time and space yield an impressive generalization that is rare in the social sciences.

Antisocial behavior in childhood also predicts a wide range of troublesome adult outcomes, supporting Hagan and Palloni's (1988) observation that delinquent and criminal events "are linked into life trajectories of broader significance, whether those trajectories are criminal or noncriminal in form" (1988: 90, see also Hagan, 1991). Because most research by criminologists has focused either on the teenage years or adult behavior limited to crime, this idea has not been well integrated into the criminological literature.

As a result of this dual neglect, sociological approaches to crime have been vulnerable to attack for not coming to grips with the implications of behavioral stability. Not surprisingly, developmental psychologists have long seized on stability to argue for the primacy of early childhood and the irrelevance of the adult life course. But even recent social theories of crime take much the same tack, denying that adult life-course transitions can have any real effect on adult criminal behavior. For example, Gottfredson and Hirschi (1990:238) argue that ordinary life events (e.g. jobs, getting married, becoming a parent) have little effect on criminal behavior because crime rates decline with age "whether or not these events occur." They go on to argue that the life-course assumption that such events are important neglects its own evidence on the stability of personal characteristics (1990:237, see also Gottfredson & Hirschi, 1987). And, since crime emerges early in the life course, traditional sociological variables (e.g. peers, labor market, marriage) are again presumed impotent. The reasoning is that since crime emerges before sociological variables appear, the latter cannot be important, even in modifying known trajectories.

A dominant viewpoint in criminology is therefore that stability in crime over the life course is generated by population heterogeneity in an underlying criminal propensity that is established early in life and remains stable over time (Wilson & Herrnstein, 1985; Gottfredson & Hirschi, 1990; Nagin & Paternoster, 1991). Precisely because individual differences in the predisposition to commit crime emerge early and are stable, childhood and adult crime will be positively correlated. The hypothesized causes of early propensity cover a number of factors, including lack of self control (Gottfredson & Hirschi, 1990), parental criminality (Farrington et al., 1975), impulsivity (Wilson & Herrnstein, 1985), and even heredity (Rowe & Osgood, 1984). Although primarily methodological in nature, the heterogeneity argument has import for theoretical understanding, implying that the correlation between past and future delinquency is not causal. Rather, the correlation is spurious because of the heterogeneity of the population in its propensity to crime.

It is clear that traditional approaches to stability leave little room for the relevance of sociological theories of age-graded transitions. As it turns out, however, whether the glass of stability appears half empty or half full seems to result at least as much from theoretical predilections as from empirical reality. Moreover, not only are there important discontinuities in crime that need to be explained, a reconsideration of the evidence suggests that stability itself may be explained by sociological influences over the life course. To assess these alternative conceptions we first review the evidence on change, followed by a revisionist look at the explanation of stability.

CHANGE AND THE ADULT LIFE COURSE

In an important paper Dannefer (1984) sharply critiques existing models of adult development, drawn primarily from the fields of biology and psychology, for their exclusive "ontogenetic" focus and their failure to recognize the "profoundly interactive nature of self-society relations" and the "variability of social environments" (1984:100). He further argues that "the contributions of sociological research and theory provide the basis for understanding human development as socially organized and socially produced, not only by what happens in early life, but also by the effects of social structure, social interaction, and their effects on life chances throughout the life course" (1984:106). Is there evidence in the criminological literature to support Dannefer's (1984) general observations regarding change over the life course and the importance of social structure and interaction?

We begin to answer this question with a seeming paradox—while studies reviewed earlier do show that antisocial behavior in children is one of the best predictors of antisocial behavior in adults, "most antisocial children do not become antisocial as adults" (Gove, 1985:123). Robins (1978) found identical results in her review of four longitudinal studies, stating that most antisocial children do not become antisocial adults (1978:611). A follow-up of the Cambridge-Somerville Youth study found that "a majority of adult criminals had no history as juvenile delinquents" (McCord, 1980:158). Cline (1980:665) states that although there is "more constancy than change . . . there is sufficient change in all. the data to preclude simple conclusions concerning criminal career progressions." He concludes that there is far more heterogeneity in criminal behavior than previous work has suggested, and that many juvenile offenders do not become career offenders (Cline, 1980:669–70). Loeber and LeBlanc make a similar point: "Against the backdrop of continuity, studies also show large within-individual changes in offending, a point understressed by Gottfredson & Hirschi" (1990:390).

Caspi and Moffitt's (1991) review reaches a similar conclusion when they discover large variations in the stability of antisocial behavior over time. In particular, antisocial behavior appears to be highly stable and consistent only in a relatively small number of males whose behavior problems are quite extreme. Loeber's (1982) review also found that extremes in antisocial conduct were linked to the magnitude of stability. Moffitt (1993) builds on this information to argue that stability is a trait among those she terms "life-course persistent" delinquents. In other words, whereas change is the norm for most adolescents, stability characterizes those at the tail of the antisocial-conduct distribution.

This conceptualization points to the dangers of relying on measures of central tendency that mask divergent subgroups.

Moffitt's (1993) review further suggests that social factors may work to modify childhood trajectories for the majority of youth who are not "life-course-persistent." In support of this idea recent criminological research suggests that salient life events influence behavior and modify trajectories—a key thesis of the life course model. A follow-up of 200 Borstal boys found that marriage led to "increasing social stability" (Gibbens, 1984:61). Knight et al. (1977) discovered that while marriage did not reduce criminality, it reduced antisocial behavior such as drinking and drug use (see also Osborn & West, 1979; West, l982; Rand, 1987). Osborn (1980) examined the effect of leaving London on delinquency and found that subjects who moved had a lower risk of reoffending when compared with a similar group who stayed in London (see also West, 1982). Rand (1987) found mixed results of going into the armed forces on later offending, but for some subgroups criminal behavior declined after serving in the military. And, there is some evidence that episodes of unemployment lead to higher crime rates (Farrington et al., 1986).

In the context of personality characteristics, Caspi (1987) found that although the tendency toward explosive, under-controlled behavior in childhood was evident in adulthood, "invariant action patterns did not emerge across the age-graded life course" (1987:1211). Similarly, using a prospective longitudinal design to study poverty, Long and Vaillant (1984) found both discontinuity and continuity across three generations of subjects. The transmission of "underclass" or dependent life styles was not inevitable or even very likely, refuting the hypothesis that the chances of escape from poverty are minimal. "The transmission of disorganization and alienation that seems inevitable when a disadvantaged cohort is studied retrospectively appears to be the exception rather than the norm in a prospective study that locates the successes as well as the failures" (Long & Vaillant, 1984:344).

This is an important methodological point that applies to the stability of crime. Looking back over the careers of adult criminals exaggerates the prevalence of stability. Looking forward from youth reveals the successes and failures, including antisocial adolescents who go on to be normal functioning adults. This is the paradox noted earlier—adult criminality seems to be always preceded by childhood misconduct, but most conduct-disordered children do not become antisocial or criminal adults (Robins, 1978).

Two recent studies of crime support a dual concern with stability and change, using a prospective approach to life histories. First, Rutter et al. (1990) analyzed follow-up data from two groups of youth. One was a sample of youth institutionalized in group homes because of family dysfunctions (e.g. parental criminality, abuse, desertion). The other was a quasi-random sample of the population of noninstitutionalized individuals of the same age living in inner-city London. Both groups were thus similar in composition but varied on childhood adversity. Consistent with the stability literature, Rutter et al. (1990) found that the high-risk institutionalized youth went on to experience a diversity of troublesome outcomes in adulthood, including crime. By comparison, the control group was relatively well adjusted in later life.

Yet Rutter et al. (1990) found in both groups considerable heterogeneity in outcomes that was associated with later adult experiences. In particular, marital support in early adult life provided a protective mechanism that inhibited deviance. Positive school experience among females was another factor that promoted desistance from crime, especially indirectly through its effect on planning and stable marriage choices. These results maintained despite controls for numerous measures of childhood deviance (1990:152), leading Rutter et al. to rule out individual self-selection bias as an explanation (cf. Nagin & Paternoster, 1991). As they concluded: "the data showed substantial heterogeneity in outcomes, indicating the need to account for major discontinuities as well as continuities in development. In that connection marital support from a nondeviant spouse stood out as a factor associated with a powerful protective effect" (1990:152). Adult transitions in the life course can thus "modify the effect of adversities experienced in childhood" (Rutter et al., 1990:152). They also pointed out a key reason why change is possible—because the chain of stability "relied on multiple links, each one dependent on the presence of some particular set of features, there were many opportunities for the chain of adversity to be broken" (Rutter et al., 1990:137).

In a second study along similar lines, Sampson and Laub (1990) theorized that social ties to the adult institutions of informal social control (e.g. family, community, work) influence criminal behavior over the life course despite delinquent and antisocial background. Their organizing principle derived from the central idea of social control theory—crime and deviance result when an individual's bond to society is weak or broken. Their theoretical model focused on the transition to adulthood and, in turn, the new role demands from higher education, full-time employment, military service, and marriage. Unlike much life-course research, however, Sampson and Laub (1990) emphasized the quality or strength of social ties more than the occurrence or timing of discrete life events (cf. Hogan, 1978; Loeber & LeBlanc, 1990:430–32). For example, while Gottfredson and Hirschi (1990:140–41) argue that marriage per se does not increase social control, a strong attachment to one's spouse and close emotional ties increase the social bond between individuals and, all else equal, should lead to a reduction in criminal behavior (cf. Shover, 1985:94). Similarly, employment alone does not increase social control. It is employment coupled with job stability, job commitment, and ties to work that should increase social control and, all else equal, lead to a reduction in criminal behavior. It was thus the social capital in the institutional relationship that was hypothesized to dictate the salience of informal social control at the individual level.

Sampson and Laub's theory of informal social control found support in an analysis of the natural histories of two groups of boys that differed dramatically in childhood antisocial behavior. More specifically, they reexamined the life histories originally gathered by Glueck and Glueck (1968) of 500 delinquents and 500 control subjects matched on age, IQ, SES, and ethnicity and followed from ages 14 to 32. Consistent with the Gluecks' earlier reports, the results showed marked differences in adolescent delinquency that were relatively stable over the life course. For example, as adults the former delinquents were much more likely to be arrested and report excessive drinking compared with the control-group men (1990:615).

Consistent with a theory of adult development and informal social control, however, Sampson and Laub (1990:616–24) found that job stability and marital attachment in adulthood were significantly related to changes in adult crime—the stronger the adult ties to work and family, the less crime and deviance among both delinquents and controls. The results were consistent over a wide variety of outcome measures, control variables for childhood antisocial behavior, and analytical techniques, and the effect estimates were largely invariant across the two groups that varied on childhood delinquency. Hence, much like Rutter et al. (1990), the Sampson and Laub study suggests that social ties embedded in adult transitions (e.g. marital attachment, job stability) explain variations in crime unaccounted for by childhood deviance.

RETHINKING STABILITY AND CHANGE

Taken as a whole, the foregoing review suggests that conclusions about the inevitability of antisocial continuities have either been overstated or misinterpreted. In terms of the former, stability coefficients are far from perfect and leave considerable room for the emergence of discontinuities. In retrospect, criminologists should have been forewarned about making sweeping generalizations of stability in light of the lengthy history of prediction that shows childhood variables to be quite modest prognostic devices. Known as the false positive problem, childhood prediction scales invariably result in the substantial over-prediction of future criminality (Loeber & Stouthamer-Loeber, 1987; Farrington & Tarling, 1985). Likewise, prediction attempts often fail to identify accurately those who will become criminal even though past behavior suggests otherwise (false negatives).

In probably the best recent study on this topic, White et al. (1990:521) document that, consistent with past research, "early antisocial behavior is the best predictor of later antisocial behavior." Nevertheless, their data clearly show the limitations of relying only on childhood information to understand behavior over time. As White et al. (1990:521) argue, a high false positive rate precludes the use of early antisocial behavior alone as a predictor of later crime. They go on to note the general inaccuracy of specific predictions and how the heterogeneous nature of delinquency in later adolescence (and by implication, adulthood) thwarts accurate prediction.

The prediction literature again reinforces the need to look at both stability and change, and hence the futility of either/or conceptions of human development. Namely, while there is longitudinal consistency, research has established large variations in later adolescent and adult criminal behavior that are not simply accounted for by childhood propensities. Furthermore, these changes in adult criminality appear to be structured by social transitions and adult life events in the life course (Rutter et al., 1990; Sampson & Laub, 1990), underscoring the utility of a life-course perspective.

Equally important, however, is the fact that the conception of stability traditionally used in criminology is quite narrow and has been frequently misinterpreted. Rank-order correlations and other measures of stability refer to the consistency of between-individual differences over time and consequently rely on an aggregate picture of relative standing. As Huesmann et al. (1984) note, what remains stable over time is the aggressiveness of an individual relative to the population (1984:1131). Stability coefficients do not measure the consistency or heterogeneity of individual behaviors over time (i.e. individual change). Consider Gottfredson and Hirschi's (1990) argument that "If there is continuity over the life course in criminal activity, it is unnecessary to follow people over time" (1990:230). The continuity to which they refer is relative stability, which does not mean that individuals remain constant in their behavior over time. In conjunction with a conceptualization of the adult life course as a probabilistic linkage or chain of events and transitions (Rutter et al., 1990), it becomes clearer how change is possible—if not likely—despite the stability of relative rank orderings. The following sections elaborate on the implications for the study of crime of a revised conceptualization of both change and stability.

Assessing Individual Change

A promising direction for future research is the analysis of individual pathways of crime and deviance. That is, rather than relying on stability coefficients or aggregate age-crime curves, an alternative conception of change is to map individual trajectories embedded in the life course. One approach entails grouping subjects according to their individual patterns of change. In his study *Lives Through Time,* Block (1971) compared "changers and nonchangers" with respect to personality. He then developed a more detailed typology that permitted an assessment of personality change over time. Similarly, Crouter and McHale (1990) recently developed a three-fold typology of parental monitoring whereby children were grouped by important individual differences in development. Block (1971) and Crouter and McHale (1990:20–21) argue that such individual trajectories are the best way to assess developmental change and its antecedents, concomitants, and consequences.

A similar strategy is to use growth curves that measure the direction and amount of systematic change in behavior over multiple time points (Jessor et al., 1991; Rogosa, 1988; Rogosa et al., 1982). Like criminology, longitudinal research in the behavioral sciences at large has focused almost exclusively on the consistency of individual differences over time rather than the consistency of individual behavior. But as Rogosa (1988:172) argues, research questions about growth and development "center on the systematic change in an attribute over time, and thus the individual growth curves are the natural foundation for modeling the longitudinal data." Similarly, Caspi and Bem (1990:569) argue that when the term "change" appears in the literature, it frequently refers to the absence of continuity. Caspi and Bem call for the development of theory to begin to account for "systematic" change as opposed to the mere absence of continuity. Accounting for developmental trajectories in crime and deviance will help to distinguish between true systematic change fostered by life transitions and the absence of continuity.

Focusing on growth curves and systematic change parallels Farrington's (1988) argument that criminology has neglected the study of changes within individuals in favor of between-individual analyses. As one example, it is quite common to study whether unemployed persons have higher crime rates than the employed. It is rare that we investigate whether an individual moving from employment to a state of unemployment increases criminal activities, a methodology where each person acts as his or her own control (Farrington, 1988:180). Only by studying both individual change trajectories and between-individual differences in stability are we likely to resolve some of the current controversies on age and crime. This seems especially true with respect to Gottfredson and Hirschi's claim that the causes of crime are the same at each age, a claim rooted in prior between-individual analyses (1990:123–144).

In short, the conceptualization, measurement, and analysis of change have not had the same attention as stability. Given this imbalance, a focus on change ought to take center stage in future research, alongside stability. This orientation recognizes that the two concepts are not mutually exclusive as is often thought (Jessor, 1983). To the contrary, intra-individual change and inter-individual differences in intra-individual change are both concerns of developmental study and are uniquely reserved to research that is longitudinal in design and that undertakes repeated measurements and analysis of the same individuals over time (Jessor et al., 1991:VII–l). Rather than being irreconcilable, continuity and change "are best seen as two aspects of a single dialectical process in which even major transformations of individuality emerge consequentially from the interaction of prior characteristics and circumstances" (Jessor et al., 1991:VII-2).

Explaining Continuity

Perhaps ironically, even the stability of individual differences in crime over time is amenable to a sociological life-course perspective. This point is often overlooked because the mere empirical documentation of stability has begged the important theoretical question of why continuity exists. In particular, given the negative consequences that much antisocial behavior generates, why should it persist? Is "early propensity" the only conceptual tool we need to understand stability over time? Efforts to understand the structural and interactional processes underlying stability over the life course have been given rather short shrift, primarily because research on stability and continuities in deviant behavior has stopped at the point of prediction. Recent thinking has attempted to move beyond mere prediction in an effort to address issues of explanation.

One explanation consistent with a life-course perspective is that the relationship of past to future crime is generated by state dependence. This hypothesis implies that committing a crime has a genuine behavioral influence on the probability of committing future crimes. In other words, crime itself—whether directly or indirectly—causally modifies the future probability of engaging in crime (Nagin & Paternoster, 1991:166). In this regard Caspi (1987) has argued that antisocial children replicate their antisocial behavior in a variety of adult realms in large part because of the differing reactions that antisocial behavior brings forth. Maladaptive behaviors are "found in interactional styles that are sustained both by the progressive accumulation of their own consequences (cumulative continuity) and by evoking maintaining responses from others during reciprocal social interaction (interactional continuity)" (Caspi et al., 1987:313, emphasis added). As an example of the latter, interactional continuity might be sustained when the child with temper tantrums provokes angry and hostile reactions in parents and teachers, which in turn feed back to trigger further antisocial behavior by the child.

Extending the idea of cumulative continuity, Moffitt (1993) argues that social reactions to delinquency generate negative consequences that further diminish life chances. Official labeling, incarceration, school failure, and other negative life events associated with delinquency may lead to the "closing of doors" as far as opportunities go. Official mechanisms of delinquency control may thus interfere with successful adult development through the cumulative continuity of lost opportunity, above and beyond that generated by early propensity to antisocial conduct and what Caspi et al. (1987) refer to as interactional continuity.

The notion of cumulative continuity is consistent with the original contentions of labeling theory that reactions to primary deviance may create problems of adjustment that foster additional crime in the form of secondary deviance (Lemert, 1951). A good example is the negative effects of arrest and incarceration on future employment chances (Bondeson, 1989). Here the connection between official childhood misbehavior and adult outcomes may be accounted for in large part by the structural disadvantages and diminished life chances accorded institutionalized and stigmatized youth. Institutionalization may also weaken informal social bonds to school, friends, and family, in turn enhancing the risk of future crime (see e.g. Wheeler, 1961). The stigma of conviction may even extend across generations, explaining the effects of parental conviction on sons' delinquency regardless of family background and early propensity to crime (Hagan & Palloni, 1990).

Clearly, then, the idea that official labels, incarceration experiences, and rejection by institutions of informal social control are criminogenic is a classic state-dependence interpretation of the link between past and future crime. Parenthetically, it should be noted that state dependence effects do not have to be positive. Deterrence theory suggests that reactions by the criminal justice system (e.g. arrest, imprisonment) have a deterrent effect on future offending (Nagin & Paternoster, 1991). Either way, the essential point according to the state dependence argument is that the relationship between past and future crime is causal in nature.

As noted earlier, traditional accounts of continuity rest on population heterogeneity in an underlying propensity for crime that is established early in life and remains stable over time (see Nagin & Paternoster, 1991). From this alternative viewpoint the diverse outcomes correlated with childhood antisocial behavior are all expressions of the same underlying trait. However, population heterogeneity is still consistent with the life-course framework because the changing manifestations of the same construct over time are structured by social opportunities to commit crime, differential reactions by the criminal justice system, and constraints imposed by aging (Shover, 1985:77–125; Gottfredson & Hirschi, 1990:177–178). The observed stability in crime and deviance may even be underestimated by the failure to conceptualize life-course transitions in social opportunities. For example, in asking whether crime declines with age, we do not know whether adults are disproportionately involved in crimes typically not counted in official statistics, especially white collar offenses (see Braithwaite, 1989:46). It is conceivable that while street crime declines with age, white collar offending and other "hidden" deviance (family violence, alcohol abuse) take up the slack (see also Moffitt, 1991). This concern highlights the need to link age and crime with the life-course framework by explicating how age-graded transitions (e.g. work and family careers) create both opportunities for crime and differential probabilities of detection and labeling by official agents of social control.

It is fair to say, then, that even if individual propensity remains relatively constant, explanations of continuity across the life course require that we account for the structure of social opportunities and the differing labels attached to behaviors as people age. Moreover, it is also important to recognize that ecological constancy (e.g. community constraints) and continuities in the interpersonal environment may underlie individual-level stability. Indeed, behavioral patterns may show stability simply because the contextual environment remains stable. Although further discussion of environmental stability is beyond the scope of our review, the key point is that behavioral stability does not necessarily imply causal forces operating solely at the level of the individual. Therefore, whether derived from heterogeneity among individuals in an early propensity that manifests itself differently across time, state dependence fostered by social reactions to crime and interactional styles, or constancy in ecological context, the fact remains that explanations of stability are inextricably tied to a sociological perspective on the life-course.

FURTHER RESEARCH NEEDS

Advances in knowledge on crime and delinquency over the life course require not only rethinking what we mean by stability and change, but a fresh infusion of data we can use to address key limitations of past research. The first step is to counterbalance the dominance in criminological research of cross-sectional designs, and, to a lesser extent, short-term panel studies. Indeed, there have been surprisingly few longitudinal data sets that prospectively follow individuals over extended periods of the life course (see also Farrington, 1979; Blumstein et al., 1986; Tonry et al., 1991). Combined with the tendency of researchers to analyze longitudinal data cross-sectionally, it is understandable that information gleaned from the typical panel study in criminology often simply reaffirms the results of cross-sectional research. But, rather than dismissing longitudinal research as Gottfredson and Hirschi (1987, 1990) advocate, we believe a more productive strategy is to collect or analyze longitudinal data in ways that permit proper inferences on individual trajectories of stability and change (Rutter, 1988a; Rogosa, 1988). Note that the need for fresh data does not necessarily imply new and potentially expensive data (cf. Tonry et al., 1991), for there are excellent data archives capable of sustaining research on the life course in different historical and macrolevel contexts (see e.g. Elder, 1974; McCord, 1979; Vaillant, 1983; Caspi et al., 1987; Featherman et al., 1984; Elliott et al., 1989; Sampson & Laub, 1990).

Second, longitudinal studies of crime have often failed to measure the timing and sequencing of changes in salient life events over the life course. In fact, longitudinal data sets in criminology frequently focus on unchanging demographic characteristics that have little bearing on theories of the life course (see Tonry et al., 1991; Blumstein et al., 1986). To establish influences on individual development one must account not only for background factors but the changing nature of important life events (e.g. work, family, and military ties), especially during the late adolescence to young adulthood transition. Quantitative measurement of the timing, duration, and ordering of life transitions has the further advantage of permitting substantive applications of event-history analyses (see Featherman & Lerner, 1985), growth curve trajectories (Rogosa et al., 1982), and recent methods for detecting resemblance in career sequence data (Abbott & Hyrack, 1990).

A third limitation of prior research in criminology is the narrow focus on legally defined categories of crime. As we have documented, one of the staples of developmental research is the heterotypic continuity of antisocial behaviors. Consequently there is a need to measure a wide spectrum of behaviors both legal and illegal that are relevant to the study of crime. This strategy permits addressing the question of whether there are individuals for whom antisocial behavior, regardless of the actual sphere in which the activity occurs, does not decline with age (e.g. absenteeism at work as an adult might be conceptualized as the theoretical equivalent of truancy in childhood). Other life-domains ripe for inquiry include occupational mobility, educational attainment, poverty, physical health, mental health, and homelessness, especially as they interact with class of origin. For example, Hagan's (1991) recent research suggests that the effect of adolescent deviance on adult stratification outcomes is contingent on social class background (see also Jessor et al., 1991). More generally, we need to broaden our conceptualization to investigate the impact of childhood delinquency and structural location on a wide range of non-crime outcomes that nonetheless have significance for adult development.

A fourth and related limitation is that explanations of the age-crime curve have focused mostly on official accounts of crime. Reliance on arrest data may exaggerate age differences and stability—the former because of differential recording by age and the latter because official reaction may "close doors" in ways that reinforce tendencies to later crime. One interpretation of continuity offered above relied on state dependence, whereby official labeling in adolescence mortgages the future in terms of employment, marriage, and other social bonds, in turn leading to increased criminality as an adult. The continuity between official juvenile crime and adult outcomes may thus reflect much more than simple propensities in childhood (Hagan & Palloni, 1990). Societal reactions to crime may also interact with age (Gartner & Piliavin, 1988:302; Shover, 1985). Research should thus examine the extent to which labeling, particularly formal labeling by the criminal justice system, affects life-course development relating to crime and non-crime outcomes.

Fifth, the research questions demand that data collection efforts include qualitative as well as quantitative data on variables and persons (Magnusson & Bergman, 1990; Cairns, 1986). Qualitative data derived from systematic open-ended questions or narrative life histories can help uncover underlying social processes of stability and change. They can also help to confirm the results derived from quantitative analyses. Using prospective natural histories, we further need to identify subjective transitions in the life course independently of behavioral transitions in understanding desistance from crime (Gartner & Piliavin, 1988:302). For example, Sampson and Laub (1990) and Rutter et al. (1990) provide evidence that the assumption of social roles and the subsequent effects of informal social controls around these roles may help account for the age-crime relation. Qualitative data would be especially useful here because social transitions (e.g. marriage, parenthood, work) probably do not have the same meaning for everyone (Rutter, 1989:20). Our point is not that one approach is better than the other; rather, both are needed to understand development in the life course.

Finally, in implementing all the above strategies we need research that better "unpacks" the meaning of age. Rutter (1989) argues that in order to understand age changes in behavior, chronological age must be broken down into its component parts. Without this separation, "age is devoid of meaning" (1989:3). According to Rutter (1989), from a developmental perspective age reflects at least four components: cognitive level, biological maturity, duration of experience, and types of experiences. Separating these and other components of age (e.g. biological vs chronological age) surely will help to resolve conflicts over the direct and indirect effects of age on crime.

CONCLUSION

The traditional hostility among sociologists toward research establishing early childhood differences in delinquency and antisocial behavior that remain stable over time is unwarranted. Not only can stability be studied sociologically, its flip side is change, and the latter appears to be systematically structured by adult bonds to social institutions. The unique advantage of a sociological perspective on the life course is that it brings the formative period of childhood back into the picture yet recognizes that individuals can change through interaction with key social institutions as they age. With improvements in measurement and conceptualization, the prospects appear bright for future research to uncover the interlocking trajectories of crime, deviance, and human development.

Acknowledgments

We would like to thank Avshalom Caspi, John Hagan, Richard Jessor, and Terrie Moffitt for their helpful comments on an earlier draft.

LITERATURE CITED

Abbott, A., Hrycak, A. 1990. Measuring resemblance in sequence data: An optimal matching analysis of musicians' careers. *Am. J. Sociol.* 96:144–85

Baltes, P., Nesselroade, J. 1984. Paradigm lost and paradigm regained: Critique of Dannefer's portrayal of life-span developmental psychology. *Am. Sociol. Rev.* 49: 841–46

Block, J. 1971. *Lives Through Time.* Berkeley: Bancroft

Blumstein, A., Cohen, J. 1979. Estimation of individual crime rates from arrest records. *J. Crim. Law Criminol.* 70:561–85

Blumstein, A., Cohen, J., Roth, J., Visher, C., eds. 1986. *Criminal Careers and "Career Criminals".* Washington, DC: Natl. Acad. Sci.

Blumstein, A., Cohen, J., Farrington, D. 1988. Criminal career research: Its value for criminology. *Criminology* 26:1–35

Bondeson, U. 1989. *Prisoners in Prison Societies.* New Brunswick: Transaction

Braithwaite, J. 1989. *Crime, Shame, and Reintegration.* Cambridge: Cambridge Univ. Press

Brim, O., Kagan, J. 1980a. Constancy and change: A view of the issues. See Brim & Kagan 1980b, pp. 1–25

Brim, O., Kagan, J., eds. 1980b. *Constancy and Change in Human Development.* Cambridge: Harvard Univ. Press

Cairns, R. B. 1986. Phenomena lost: Issues in the study of development. In *The Individual Subject and Scientific Psychology,* ed. J. Valsiner, pp. 97–111. New York: Plenum

Caspi, A. 1987. Personality in the life course. *J. Pers. Soc. Psychol.* 53:1203–13

Caspi, A. Elder, G. H. Jr., Bem, D. 1987. Moving against the world: Life-course patterns of explosive children. *Dev. Psychol.* 23:308–13

Caspi, A., Bem, D., Elder, G. H. Jr. 1989. Continuities and consequences of interactional styles across the life course. *J. Pers.* 57:375–406

Caspi, A., Bem, D. 1990. Personality continuity and change across the life course. In *Handbook of Personality: Theory and Research,* ed. L. A. Pervin, pp. 549–75. New York: Guilford

Caspi, A., Elder, G. H. Jr., Herbener, E. 1990. Childhood personality and the prediction of life-course patterns. See Robins & Rutter 1990, pp. 13–35

Caspi, A., Moffitt, T. 1995. The continuity of maladaptive behavior: From description to understanding in the study of antisocial behavior. In *Manual of Developmental Psychopathology,* ed. D. Cicchetti, D. Cohen, pp. 472–511. New York: Wiley

Cline, H. F. 1980. Criminal behavior over the life span. See Brim & Kagan 1980b, pp. 641–74

Crouter, A., McHale, S. 1990. Family processes in single- and dual-earner contexts: Themes from the Penn State Family Relationships Project. *Conf. Paper, Bridging Levels of Analysis in the Study of Women's Lives Across Three Longitudinal Data Sets,* Woods Hole, Mass.

Cusson, M., Pinsonneault, P. 1986. The decision to give up crime. In *The Reasoning Criminal: Rational Choice Perspectives of Offending,* ed. D. B. Cornish, R. V. Clarke, pp. 72–82. New York: Springer-Verlag

Dannefer, D. 1984. Adult development and social theory: a paradigmatic reappraisal. *Am. Sociol. Rev.* 49:100–6

Elder, G. H. Jr. 1974. *Children of the Great Depression.* Chicago: Univ. Chicago Press

Elder, G. H. Jr. 1975. Age differentiation and the life course. *Annu. Rev. Sociol.* 1:165–90

Elder, G. H. Jr. 1985. Perspectives on the life course. In *Life Course Dynamics,* ed. G. H. Elder Jr., pp. 23–49. Ithaca: Cornell Univ. Press

Elder, G. H. Jr. 1986. Military times and turning points in men's lives. *Dev. Psychol.* 22:233–45

Elder, G. H. Jr. 1992. The life course. In *The Encyclopedia of Sociology,* ed. E. F. Borgatta, M. L. Borgatta, vol. 3, pp. 1120–1130. New York: MacMillan

Elliott, D., Huizinga, D., Ageton, S. 1985. *Explaining Delinquency and Drug Use.* Beverly Hills: Sage.

Elliott, D., Huizinga, D., Menard, S. 1989. *Multiple Problem Youth: Delinquency, Substance Use, and Mental Health Problems.* New York: Springer-Verlag

Farrington, D. 1979. Longitudinal research on crime and delinquency. In *Crime and Justice,* ed. N. Morris, M. Tonry, 1:289–348. Chicago: Univ. Chicago Press

Farrington, D. 1986. Age and crime. In *Crime and Justice,* ed. N. Morris, M. Tonry, 7:189–250. Chicago: Univ. Chicago Press

Farrington, D. 1988. Studying changes within individuals: The causes of offending. See Rutter 1988b, pp. 158–83

Farrington, D. 1989. Later adult life outcomes of offenders and nonoffenders. In *Children at Risk: Assessment, Longitudinal Research, and Intervention,* ed. M. Brambring, F. Losel, H. Skowronek, pp. 220–44. New York: Walter de Gruyter

Farrington, D., Gallagher, B., Morley, L., Ledger, R. J. St., West, D. 1986. Unemployment school leaving and crime. *Br. J. Criminol.* 26:355–56

Farrington, D., Gundry, G., West, D. 1975. The familial transmission of criminality. *Med. Sci. Law* 15:177–86

Farrington, D., Tarling, R., eds. 1985. *Prediction in Criminology,* Albany: State Univ. NY Press

Featherman, D., Hogan, D., Sorenson, A. 1984. Entry in adulthood: Profiles of young men in the 1950s. In *Life-Span Development and Behavior,* ed. P. Baltes, O. Brim Jr., 6:160–203. Orlando: Academic Press

Featherman, D., Lerner, R. 1985. Ontogensis and sociogenesis: Problematics for theory and research about development and socialization across the lifespan. *Am. Sociol. Rev.* 50:659–76

Federal Bureau of Investigation. 1990. *Age-Specific Arrest Rates and Race-Specific Arrest Rates for Selected Offenses.* Washington, DC: US Dep. Justice

Flanagan, T., Maguire, K., eds. 1990. *Sourcebook of Criminal Justice Statistics - 1989.* Washington, DC: US Govt. Print. Off.

Gartner, R., Piliavin, I. 1988. The aging offender and the aged offender. In *Life-Span Development and Behavior,* ed. P. B. Baltes, D. L. Featherman, R. M. Lerner, 9:287–315. Hillside, NH: Erlbaum

Gibbens, T. C. N. 1984. Borstal boys after 25 years. *Br. J. Criminol.* 24:49–62

Glueck, S., Glueck, E. 1930. *500 Criminal Careers.* New York: Knopf

Glueck, S., Glueck, E. 1950. *Unraveling Juvenile Delinquency.* New York: Commonwealth Fund

Glueck, S., Glueck, E. 1968. *Delinquents and Nondelinquents in Perpsective*. Cambridge: Harvard Univ. Press

Gottfredson, M., Hirschi, T. 1987. The methodological adequacy of longitudinal research on crime. *Criminology* 25:581–614

Gottfredson, M., Hirschi, T. 1988. Science, public policy, and the career paradigm. *Criminology* 26:37–55

Gottfredson, M., Hirschi, T. 1990. *A General Theory of Crime*. Stanford: Stanford Univ. Press

Gove, W. R. 1985. The effect of age and gender on deviant behiavor: A biopsychosocial perspective. In *Gender and the Life Course*, ed. A. S. Rossi, pp. 115–44. New York: Aldine

Hagan, J. 1991. Destiny and drift: Subcultural preferences, status attainments, and the risks and rewards of youth. *Am. Sociol. Rev.* 56:567–82

Hagan, J., Palloni, A. 1988. Crimes as social events in the life course: Reconceiving a criminological controversy. *Criminology* 26:87–100

Hagan, J., Palloni, A. 1990. The social reproduction of a criminal class in working-class London, circa 1950–1980. *Am. J. Sociol.* 96:265–99

Hindelang, M. J. 1981. Variations in sex-race-age-specific incidence rates of offending. *Am. Sociol. Rev.* 46:461–74

Hirschi, T., Gottfredson, M. 1983. Age and the explanation of crime. *Am. J. Sociol.* 89:552–84

Hogan, D. P. 1978. The variable order of events in the life course. *Am. Sociol. Rev.* 43:573–86

Hogan, D. P. 1980. The transition to adulthood as a career contingency. *Am. Sociol. Rev.* 45:261–76

Huesmann, L. R., Eron, L. D., Lefkowitz, M. M. 1984. Stability of aggression over time and generations. *Dev. Psychol.* 20:1120–34

Jessor, R. 1983. The stability of change: psychosocial development from adolescence to young adulthood. In *Human Development: An Interactional Perspective*, ed. D. Magnusson. New York: Academic

Jessor, R., Donova, J., Costa, F. 1991. *Beyond Adolescence: Problem Behavior and Young Adult Development*. Cambridge: Cambridge Univ. Press.

Jessor, R., Jessor, S. L. 1977. *Problem Behavior and Psychosocial Development: A Longitudinal Study of Youth*. New York: Academic

Knight, B. J., Osborn, S. G., West, D. 1977. Early marriage and criminal tendency in males. *Br. J. Criminol.* 17:348–60

Lemert, E. 1951. *Sociol Pathology*. New York: McGraw-Hill

Loeber, R. 1982. The stability of antisocial child behavior: A review. *Child Dev.* 53:1431–46

Loeber, R., Stouthamer-Loeber, M. 1987. Prediction. In *Handbook of Juvenile Delinquency*, ed. H. C. Quay, pp. 325–82. New York: Wiley

Loeber, R., LeBlanc, M. 1990. Toward a developmental criminology. In *Crime and Justice*, ed. M. Tonry, N. Morris, 12:375–437. Chicago: Univ. Chicago Press

Long, J., Vaillant, G. H. 1984. Natural history of male psychological health, XI: Escape from the underclass. *Am. J. Psychol.* 141:341–46

Magnusson, D., Bergman, L. 1990. A pattern approach to the study of pathways from childhood to adulthood. See Robins & Rutter 1990, pp. 101–15

McCord, J. 1979. Some child-rearing antecedents of criminal behavior in adult men. *J. Pers. Soc. Psychol.* 37:1477–86

McCord, J. 1980. Patterns of deviance. In *Human Functioning in Longitudinal Perspective*, ed. S. B. Sells, R. Crandall, M. Roff, J. S. Strauss, W. Pollin, pp. 157–65. Baltimore: Williams & Wilkins

Moffitt, T. E. 1993. Adolescence-limited and life-course-persistent anti-social behavior: A developmental taxonomy. *Psychol. Rev.* 100: 674–701

Nagin, D., Paternoster, R. 1991. On the relationship of past and future participation in delinquency. *Criminology* 29:163–90

Olweus, D. 1979. Stability of aggressive reaction patterns in males: A review. *Psychol. Bull.* 86:852–75

Osborn, S. G. 1980. Moving home, leaving London, and delinquent trends. *Br. J. Criminol.* 20:54–61

Osborn, S. G., West, D. 1979. Marriage and delinquency: A postscript. *Br. J. Criminol.* 18:254–56

Osgood, D. W., Johnston, L. D., O'Malley, P. M., Bachman, J. G. 1988. The generality of deviance in late adolescence and early adulthood. *Am. Sociol. Rev.* 53:81–93

Rand, A. 1987. Transitional life events and desistance from delinquency and crime. See Wolfgang et al 1987, pp. 134–62

Rindfuss, R., Swicegood, C. G., Rosenfeld, R. 1987. Disorder in the life course: How common and does it matter? *Am. Sociol. Rev.* 52:785–801

Robins, L. 1966. *Deviant Children Grown Up.* Baltimore: Williams & Wilkins

Robins, L. 1978. Sturdy childhood predictors of adult antisocial behavior: Replications from longitudinal studies. *Psychol. Med.* 8:611–22

Robins, L., Rutter, M., eds. 1990. *Straight and Devious Pathways from Childhood to Adulthood.* Cambridge: Cambridge Univ. Press

Rogosa, D. 1988. Myths of longitudinal research. In *Methodological Issues in Aging Research,* ed. K. W. Schaie, R. T. Campbell, W. Meredith, S. C. Rawlings, pp. 171–209. New York: Springer

Rogosa, D., Brandt, D., Zimowski, M. 1982. A growth curve approach to the measurement of change. *Psychol. Bull.* 92:726–48

Rowe, D., Osgood, D. W. 1984. Heredity and sociological theories of delinquency: A reconsideration. *Am. Sociol. Rev.* 49:526–40

Rowe, A., Tittle, C. 1977. Life cycle changes and criminal propensity. *Sociol. Q.* 18:223–36

Rutter, M. 1988a. Longitudinal data in the study of causal processes: Some uses and some pitfalls. See Rutter 1988b, pp. 1–28

Rutter, M., ed. 1988b. *Studies of Psychosocial Risk: The Power of Longitudinal Data.* Cambridge: Cambridge Univ. Press

Rutter, M. 1989. Age as an ambiguous variable in developmental research: Some epidemiological considerations from developmental psychopathology. *Int. J. Behav. Dev.* 12:1–34

Rutter, M., Quinton, D., Hill, J. 1990. Adult outcomes of institution-reared children: Males and females compared. See Robins & Rutter 1990, pp. 135–57

Sampson, R. J., Laub, J. H. 1990. Crime and deviance over the life course: The salience of adult social bonds. *Am. Sociol. Rev.* 55:609–27

Shannon, L. 1988. *Criminal Career Continuity: Its Social Context.* New York: Human Sci.

Shover, N. 1985. *Aging Criminals.* Beverly Hills: Sage

Tonry, M. Ohlin, L. E., Farrington, D. P. 1991. *Human Development and Criminal Behavior: New Ways of Advancing Knowledge.* New York: Springer-Verlag

Vaillant, G. E. 1983. *The Natural History of Alcoholism.* Cambridge: Harvard Univ. Press

West, D. 1982. *Delinquency: Its Roots, Careers, and Prospects.* London: Heinemann

West, D., Farrington, D. 1977. *The Delinquent Way of Life.* London: Heinemann

Wheeler, S. 1961. Socialization in correctional communities. *Am. Sociol. Rev.* 26:697–712

White, J., Moffitt, T., Earls, F., Robins, L., Silva, P. 1990. How early can we tell?: Predictors of childhood conduct disorder and adolescent delinquency. *Criminology* 28:507–33

Wilson, J. Q., Herrnstein, R. 1985. *Crime and Human Nature.* New York: Simon & Schuster

Wolfgang, M., Figlio, R., Sellin, T. 1972. *Delinquency in a Birth Cohort.* Chicago: Univ. Chicago Press

Wolfgang, M., Thornberry, T., Figlio, R., eds. 1987. *From Boy to Man: From Delinquency to Crime.* Chicago: Univ. Chicago Press

SECTION II

Age, Crime, and Criminal Careers

S ince it was first observed by the Belgium statistician Adolphe Quetelet in 1831, no other fact about crime has been as widely accepted as the relationship between age and crime. The relationship, observed at the aggregate level, reveals an increase and peak in crime during the late-teenaged years followed by a steady decline during early adulthood. This relationship serves as the fundamental basis for the study of criminal careers and crime over the life course. Even though the majority of criminologists accept the observed relationship, like many facts in criminology, there is widespread dispute about the interpretation of the age-crime relationship.

One of the more important developments in the evolution of the life-course perspective has been research on criminal careers. This section begins with an introduction to age, crime, and criminal careers by Blumstein and his colleagues, who define a criminal career as the longitudinal sequence of crimes committed by an individual offender. Embedded within the criminal career concept are four components: (a) participation, (b) frequency, (c) duration of the criminal career, and (d) seriousness. Their paper also outlines a number of policy implications that underlie the criminal career perspective.

Fortunately, there exists some healthy disagreement among criminologists about the value of the criminal career perspective and its interpretation of the age-crime relationship, and the nature of offending behavior over the life course. In the second paper in this section, sociologists Michael Gottfredson and Travis Hirschi offer a serious challenge to mainstream thinking on criminal careers, age, and crime. In their comprehensive critique, Gottfredson and Hirschi challenge the criminal career perspective on its conceptual foundation, theoretical substance, methodological requirements, and ultimate policy prescriptions, concluding that the criminal career perspective is not adequately justified.

The papers in this section highlight some of the fundamental issues related to the nature of offending behavior. Having an appreciation of the current issues and debates surrounding age, crime, and criminal careers is crucial as one moves toward understanding criminal behavior over the life course.

SUGGESTED READINGS

Elliott, D. (1994). Serious violent offenders: Onset, developmental course, and termination. *Criminology, 32,* 1–22.

Farrington, D. (1986). Age and crime. In M. Tonry & N. Morris (Eds.), *Crime and justice: An annual review of research.* Chicago: University of Chicago Press.

Farrington, D. (1992). Explaining the beginning, progress, and ending of antisocial behavior from birth to adulthood. In J. McCord (Ed.), *Facts,*

frameworks, and forecasts: Advances in criminological theory (Vol. 3). New Brunswick, NJ: Transaction.

Hirschi, T., & Gottfredson, M. (1983). Age and the explanation of crime. *American Journal of Sociology, 89,* 552–584.

Wolfgang, M., Figlio, R., & Sellin, T. (1972). *Delinquency in a birth cohort.* Chicago: University of Chicago Press.

3

Introduction

Studying Criminal Careers

ALFRED BLUMSTEIN
JACQUELINE COHEN
JEFFREY ROTH
CHRISTY VISHER

THE CRIMINAL CAREERS CONCEPT

Although widely studied, crime is one of the most elusive subjects of social science research as well as a major public policy issue. It has been addressed by many scholars from a wide variety of disciplines; there has been extensive theorizing about its etiology; the public has consistently ranked crime as a serious problem; and there is intense public debate, even about facts, when considering alternative policies for dealing with crime. Yet, despite the importance of the issues and the amount of research, little definitive knowledge has been developed that could be applied to prevent crime or to develop efficient policies for reacting to crime. Over the past decade, however, some significant progress has been made, and much of that has focused on the "criminal career" paradigm.

A criminal career is the characterization of the longitudinal sequence of crimes committed by an individual offender. A previous National Research Council panel called for "research . . . directed at characterizing the patterns of individual criminal careers" (Blumstein, Cohen, & Nagin, 1978:78). This call was motivated in large part by the realization that crime is committed by individuals, even when they organize into groups, and that individuals are the focus of criminal justice decisions. Thus, a paradigm focusing attention on individuals might be most appropriate both for probing the causes of criminal behavior and for developing crime control policies intended to interrupt or modify criminal careers.

Much research on crime has been focused on aggregate crime rates, that is, crimes per capita in the general population. The criminal career approach partitions the aggregate rate into two primary components: participation, the distinction between those who commit crime and those who do not; and frequency, the rate of activity of active offenders. This partition is important

SOURCE: In A. Blumstein, J. Cohen, J. Roth, and C. Visher (Eds.). *Criminal Careers and Career Criminals*, pp. 12–30. Reprinted by permission of National Academy Press.

not only because the two components may be subject to very different influences, but also because different authorities have different levels of responsibility for control of the two components. In particular, education, social service, and mental health professionals all provide services that may reduce participation in crime, while controlling the rate of criminal activity is more central to the decisions of the criminal justice system. A decision on imprisonment, for example, often involves some concern for incapacitating a convicted offender, and so it is a matter of prime interest to estimate how many crimes in the community might be avoided by the removal of that offender.

In addition to the primary components of participation and frequency, two other dimensions that affect aggregate crime rates can be incorporated in the criminal career approach: duration, the length of an individual career (the time from first to last offense), and seriousness, which includes both the offenses committed and patterns of switching among offenses.

Separate consideration of participation, frequency, duration, and seriousness provides a finer resolution in the search for the factors associated with crime than do other common approaches. Traditional research on criminal behavior has often relied on aggregate arrest rates or recidivism statistics to develop or to test various causal models. These conventional measures of criminality, however, confound different aspects of individual offending patterns. For example, a drop in the aggregate crime rate may reflect a drop in the proportion of the population engaging in crime (level of participation), in the average number of crimes committed by active offenders in a given time (individual frequency), or in the average number of years over which offenders commit crimes (duration of activity). A causal factor could strongly affect one of these dimensions, but variation in the others might mask that relationship if the aggregate crime rate is used as the primary measure of crime. Thus, as in most research, when different factors affect different dimensions of a phenomenon of interest, it is extremely important to isolate those dimensions in order to assess the influence of any factor.

Different sets of "causes" may influence individuals' decisions to initiate criminal (or delinquent) activity, the frequency with which they commit crimes, the types of crimes committed, and their decisions to stop committing crimes. Attention to these separate dimensions of the criminal career can thus help to refine theories of criminal behavior, since some theoretical explanations may account for the initiation of deviant acts by teenagers, while very different theories may be more relevant to the termination of serious criminality by adults or to fluctuations in rates of offending during an active criminal career. Thus, basic knowledge about each component of individual criminal careers is fundamental for an understanding of how various factors and government policies may encourage or inhibit criminal activity.

For example, past research on the impact of unemployment on crime has resulted in inconsistent conclusions. However, the inconsistent results may be a consequence of the use of aggregate crime rates as the dependent variable. If the relationship between unemployment and criminal behavior were to be studied at the individual level, the effects might become more focused and consistent. One might hypothesize, for example, that variation in unemployment is not unlikely to have much influence on the initiation of criminal activity, which usually occurs in the teenage years, before most people have begun working, but that the opportunity for full-time employment leads to early termination of teenagers' criminal activity. Separation of the dimensions of individual careers might permit more precise tests of these hypotheses.

Criminal careers may vary substantially among offenders. At one extreme are offenders whose careers consist of only one offense. At the other extreme are "career criminals"—also variously characterized as dangerous, habitual, or chronic offenders—who commit serious offenses with high frequency over extended periods of time. Both of these extreme career types are of policy interest. Offenders with short careers who commit very few offenses are of interest for identifying external factors that foster early termination of careers and that can be affected by public policy. Such knowledge will be especially useful in the design of crime control policies, including prevention achieved through the imposition of sanctions for deterrent or rehabilitative purposes. Career criminals are of interest for formulating policies that can identify these offenders early in their careers and selectively target criminal justice resources at preventing their crimes, primarily through incarceration.

Individual-level data are fundamental to the analysis of criminal careers. An ideal approach for collecting data on the individual offender would involve getting a representative sample of offenders to maintain accurate logs of their daily criminal activity. In light of the obvious difficulties in mounting such an effort, two principal approaches have evolved for estimating the information that might be derived from those logs. One approach uses retrospective self-reports, typified by the work of Short and Nye (1958), West and Farrington (1977), Chaiken and Chaiken (1982a), and Elliott et al. (1983, 1985), which involves asking individuals to report on their offenses over a recent period. The other approach uses official records, typified by the work of Wolfgang, Figlio, and Sellin (1972), Blumstein and Cohen (1979), and Shannon (1982a, 1982b), in which arrests are viewed as a sample of the actual criminal activity that led to the arrests. Each of these approaches relies on different assumptions and introduces different distortions into the resulting descriptions of the underlying crime process.

In principle, offender self-reports could provide a complete picture of offending over time, but inaccuracies are introduced by respondents' selective nonresponse, intentional distortion, and inability to recall precise counts and sequences of previous crimes. In contrast, an offender's official arrest record provides counts and sequences of offenses, but only of those offenses recorded by police. The records therefore reflect only a sample of all the offense committed by an individual and may occasionally include notations of crimes that did not occur as charged.[1] As a sample of the underlying crime process, arrest

---

[1]In addition to the distortion that may result from differences between actual offenses and arrests, the issue of false arrests is an important concern when inferring crimes from arrests. It is well established that a majority of arrests fail to end in conviction even for

records are distorted by patterns in victims' willingness to report crimes to the police, by differential police attention to different crimes, and by police discretion in deciding which suspects to arrest, which arrests to record, and what charges to file. Arrest histories used in research may be incomplete because of failures to forward notations of all arrests or to include arrests recorded in jurisdictions other than the study site. Only recently has attention turned toward synthesis of criminal career data from both self-reports and official records.

Because of the limitations on the data from both sources, models are needed to convert the observed information into estimates of the principal dimensions of criminal careers. Such models have emerged only in the last decade, largely stimulated by the stochastic-process approach introduced by Avi-Itzhak and Shinnar (1973), which was followed several years later by empirical estimates of various career dimensions. Later, attention shifted to modeling the distributions of those dimensions and identifying their covariates (Chaiken & Chaiken, 1982a; Greenwood, 1982). This panel has contributed to that body by commissioning extensions of the modeling from the perspectives of economics (Flinn, Vol. II) and stochastic processes (Lehoczky, Vol. II).

CRIME CONTROL POLICIES

The criminal justice system's efforts to control crime take three forms: deterrence, rehabilitation, and incapacitation. Deterrence is the symbolic threat broadcast to actual and potential offenders by imposing punishment on identified offenders. Incapacitation is the removal of a convicted offender from the community, usually through imprisonment, to prevent the offenders from committing further crimes. Rehabilitation is the modification of an offender's criminal behavior. These efforts to control crime are carried out in conjunction with efforts to achieve other goals of the criminal justice system, such as imposing "deserved" punishment, enhancing public confidence in the justice system, and maintaining order in penal facilities.

Knowledge for Policy

Knowledge about criminal careers may be especially helpful in developing effective crime control policies. The appropriate response to crime will differ depending on whether the aggregate crime rate is the result of a small group of high-frequency offenders or a large group of offenders who commit

---

serious crimes. This differential raises questions about the validity of assuming that every arrest is properly associated with a crime and suggests using only those arrests that are followed by conviction. Two types of error are involved: using arrests as indicators of crimes probably involves some errors of commission because of false arrests; using only convictions is more likely to involve errors of omission. In adjudicating specific individuals, of course, the presumption of innocence makes the error or commission unacceptable. In assessing the relative validity of data for research purposes, however, there must be a relative weighing of these two types of error. Reports by criminal justice practitioners indicate that the errors of commission associated with using arrest records are far smaller than the errors of omission that would occur if only convictions were used.

Many of the ethical issues considered are matters of long-standing legal and philosophical debate. The resolution of some issues may rest on absolute principles, but more often it involves a balancing of competing ethical concerns. It is thus reasonable to anticipate that the principles governing the use of prediction-based classification rules as an aid to criminal justice decision makers will evolve, changing as public concerns about crime ebb and flow and as improved knowledge about individual criminal careers is developed.

DIMENSIONS OF CRIMINAL CAREERS

The panel's characterization of criminal careers partitions crime into four dimensions: one dimension describes the fraction of a population becoming offenders by virtue of participation in crime; three others describe active offenders in terms of the frequency, seriousness, and duration of their activity. The criminal career paradigm presumes that offending is not pervasive throughout a population, but is restricted to a subset of the population. This subset consists of active offenders—those who commit at least one crime during some observation period. It also presumes that the composition of active offenders varies over time as some criminal careers are initiated and others terminate.

Participation

The measurement of participation—the fraction of a population that is criminally active—depends on the scope of criminal acts considered and the length of observation periods.[2] Including minor infractions in the scope of crime types greatly increases the level of participation in offending in a population. Longer observation periods also increase participation measures, since more offenders who commit offenses only rarely will be included as will more offenders who are initiating or terminating their criminal activity. Conversely, restricting the criteria to focus only on serious offenses and using short observation periods will result in lower measures of current participation.

In any observation period, active offenders include both new offenders whose first offense occurs during the observation period and persisting offenders who began criminal activity in an earlier period and continue to be active during the observation period. Participation in any observation period thus depends on the number of individuals who become offenders and how long offenders remain active. The longer the duration of offending, the greater

---

[2]In the literature reviewed by the panel, the term "prevalence" is often used to refer to the current involvement of some portion of a sample in criminal activity, but occasionally to other measures of participation. The term "incidence" is usually used to refer to the per capita crime rate for the sample but occasionally to refer to individual frequency. In short, these terms have been used inconsistently by many researchers for decades. To avoid confusion, the panel adopted the vocabulary being introduced here. The relationship between the panel's framework and other individual and aggregate statistics on criminal behavior is discussed in the section, "Basic Definitions and Symbols."

the contribution of persisters to measured participation in successive observation periods.

Individual Frequency Rates, Seriousness, and Duration

Individual frequency rates—the number of crimes per year per active offender—vary substantially among offenders, with some having very high rates and others low rates of offending. For any individual, frequency rates may vary over time. Because they commit more crimes per unit of time, high-rate offenders contribute disproportionately to the total measured number of crimes.

Many different offense types may contribute to an individual's frequency rate. The scope of offending for individual offenders may vary from "specialists" (who engage predominantly in only one offense or a group of closely related offense types) to "generalists" (who engage in a wide variety of offense types). The degree of specialization may also vary across offense types, with some offense types committed predominantly by specialists and other types routinely committed by generalists. The mix of offense types committed by offenders may also vary over the course of their careers, with offenders becoming either more or less specialized, and with the mix of offense types escalating or de-escalating in seriousness.

The duration of criminal careers can also be expected to vary across individual offenders. It is likely that many criminal careers are very short, ending in the teenage years. However, some offenders continue to commit crimes into their 30s and even older ages. Thus, it is important to understand average *total* career length and the factors that distinguish offenders with long careers from offenders with short careers. But to understand the impact of decisions made about individual offenders, it is also extremely important to understand *residual* career length, the expected time remaining in an offender's criminal career at the time of the decision.

Basic Definitions and Symbols

To use these concepts to organize research results that have been developed in a variety of paradigms, the panel found it necessary to adopt consistent vocabulary and symbols for labeling the key dimensions that characterize individual criminal careers. This need arises from a confusion in the literature over specific terminology for individual and aggregate crime data. The confusion can be seen clearly, for example, in the variety of referents of the term "rate" in the literature: to a population (e.g., prevalence rate, the fraction of males ever participating in crime); to a time period (e.g., frequency rate, the individual's annual frequency of offending); or to both simultaneously (e.g., crime rate, the annual crime index per capita).[3]

---

[3]Crime itself is a heterogeneous phenomenon, and a variety of terminology has developed to distinguish more serious or less serious crimes. This report is primarily concerned with serious crimes, which are classified herein in several ways. *Personal* crimes

The symbols and definitions adopted by the panel are displayed in Table 3.1. Symbols in the second column describe the crime process, i.e., the actual offending process; symbols in the third column describe the arrest process from which much of the available information about the underlying crime process is derived.

We begin with the aggregate annual crime rate per capita (C) that is normally reported to the public in the press, and partition it into its component parts: one that focuses on the individual offender and his *individual offending frequency* measured in terms of crimes per year, λ, and another that describes the *current participation rate* of offenders in the population at any time (d). These three key variables are linked by the relationship $C = \lambda d$. Thus, for example, an aggregate crime rate of 1,000 crimes in a population based of 100,000 people could be a consequence of 10 criminals each committing an average of 100 crimes ($d = 10/100,000$, and $\lambda = 100$) or 100 criminals committing 10 crimes each ($d = 100/100,000$, and $\lambda = 10$). The two situations present different problems in the development of crime control strategies.

Much of the literature is not concerned with the current rate of participation in crime (d) but with the question of what fraction of a population has *ever* been involved in crime. This is simply the accumulation of new participants over time. We denote *cumulative participation* by the related symbol D.

Comparable symbols are defined for the arrest process, which is often the only source of information about individual criminal careers. The counterpart to the crime rate (C) is the number of *arrests* per capita per year, A. The average number of arrests experienced per year by active offenders is denoted by μ. The percent of a population that is arrested (or "busted") within some observation period is denoted by b. A relationship similar to that in the crime process exists for the arrest process, $A = \mu b$. Finally, as an analogue to the

---

encompass homicide, aggravated assault, and rape. Rape and homicide are relatively infrequent, and data are not usually reported separately by researchers for these crimes. The FBI includes these three crimes and robbery in their definition of *violent* crimes. *Safety* crimes include violent crimes and burglary. The five safety crimes plus larceny and auto theft are frequently referred to as *index* crimes, because they are included in the Part I crime index reported in the FBI's annual *Uniform Crime Reports.* In 1981, arson was added to the FBI's crime index; however, because reporting of arson was sporadic before that year, it is rarely included in the research reviewed here. *Property* crimes typically include burglary, larceny, and auto theft. In addition to the Part I index crimes, the FBI also uses the category of Part II crimes, which are recorded separately, are less often reported to police (e.g., white-collar crimes), are less serious (e.g., public order crimes), and include "victimless" crimes (e.g., prostitution, drug use). Some researchers also distinguish between a *felony* and a *misdemeanor:* the former is usually defined in statutes as any crime carrying a sentence length of at least 1 year. *Delinquency* has a less precise definition: it can refer to traditional youth crimes, such as truancy or underage drinking (sometimes called status offenses because they are only offenses as a result of the status, i.e., age, of the offender), or it can refer to any crime committed by someone under the age of majority.

Virtually all the research discussed in this report is on male offenders; hence, the pronoun "he" is used exclusively in referring to offenders.

Table 3.1 Glossary of Basic Symbols and Relationships

MEASURE	SYMBOL AND DEFINITION	
Measure Based on Crimes and Arrests	**Crime Process**	**Arrest Process**
Aggregate crime rate per capita per year	C Crimes per capita per year	A Arrests per capita per year
Individual frequency per active offender	λ Crimes per year per active offender	μ Arrests per year per active offender
Current participation rate	d Percent of a population committing a crime within a year ("doing")	b Percent of a population arrested for crimes within a year ("busted")
Cumulative participation rate	D Percent of a population ever committing a crime	B Percent of a population ever arrested
Aggregate crime rate per capita: frequency per active offender times participation rate	$C = \lambda d$	$A = \mu b$
Other Measures		
Arrest probability	q = Probability of arrest following a crime ($q = \mu/\lambda$)	
Career length	T = Total criminal career length	
Residual career length	T_R = Average time remaining in a criminal career	
Career dropout rate	δ = Fraction of a criminal population whose careers terminate during an observation period	

cumulative participation rate in crime, we denote the fraction of a population that is *ever* arrested as B.[4]

The arrest process can be viewed as a sampling from the crime process, since not all crimes result in arrest. This linkage is reflected in the "sampling probability" or the probability that a crime will result in an arrest, denoted by q. The two key individual rates, μ and λ, are thus linked through q by the relationship $\mu = \lambda q$. Thus, for example, if an offender commits 8 crimes per year and there is a 10 percent chance that commission of a crime will lead to an arrest, then the average arrest rate, μ should be 8(0.1) or 0.8 arrests per year.

The final principal construct for which we use symbols is the *total* criminal career length, T, denoting the number of years over which an offender is criminally active. In many cases, we are more interested in the *residual* career length, the number of *future* years a currently active offender is expected to remain active, and we denote this length by T_R. The fraction of careers that terminate during an observation period is denoted by the career dropout rate, δ.

Obviously, estimates of the criminal career dimensions represented by these symbols will vary by crime type, across different population groups, and

---

[4]Many studies use an alternative official-record indicator of an event, such as referral to juvenile court or conviction. For notational simplicity, we symbolize fractions involving all these events by B and b, but recognize in discussion the implications of these more stringent thresholds for empirical results.

in different settings. In the text of the report, we occasionally distinguish these different variations of the basic criminal career dimensions. The glossary presented in Table 3.1 should therefore be helpful as a continuing reference in reading that material.

Basic Model of a Criminal Career

The basic criminal career paradigm provides a framework for organizing knowledge about the dimensions that describe individual criminal behavior. It permits specifications or relationships among the dimensions and computation of statistics that describe offending in an observed sample, such as a cohort of individuals followed over time, a cross-section of active offenders arrested during some time interval, or matched control/experimental groups being studied to assess the impact of some intervention.

Figure 3.1 presents a highly simplified framework that introduces the essential concepts of the criminal career. The top of the figure represents a sequence of events during the criminal career of an active offender. On the line, the symbol $\times$ denotes the times at which the offender committed crimes. Symbols of crimes for which the offender was arrested are circled, and the crimes for which the arrest led to conviction are enclosed in a square. The shaded area indicates a period when the offender was incarcerated following conviction. In theory, all incidents marked $\times$ could be reported by the offender in a self-report survey, while only the circled ones could appear in an official arrest record.

A person initiates criminal activity at some time. That first offense may involve a conscious personal choice, it may follow from the development of a new set of associations developed, or it may be an inadvertent consequence of other changes in the individual's life. Once the offender has begun his criminal involvement, it continues for some period of time, perhaps increasing or decreasing in frequency. Finally, the person terminates his criminal career, possibly because of death, but more typically at a relatively young age, after which his probability of offending within any observation period is small enough to be ignored.

The minimum representation, which clearly omits many of the complexities of a real career, is represented in the lower portion of Figure 3.1. The offender is assumed to begin criminal activity at some "age of onset," a_O, but his official record does not reflect onset until some later time, at the point of his first arrest. Once begun, the offender continues to commit crimes at a constant rate λ during any time that he is not incarcerated. The career ends when the last crime is committed, represented at age a_T in Figure 3.1.

The representation in Figure 3.1 invokes three primary elements of information: the frequency or mean individual crime rate, λ, the age at career initiation, and the duration of the criminal career, T. Each of these three dimensions of a career varies across offenders. This variation may be influenced by personal events associated with the individual or by broader forces such as sanction levels or other community characteristics.

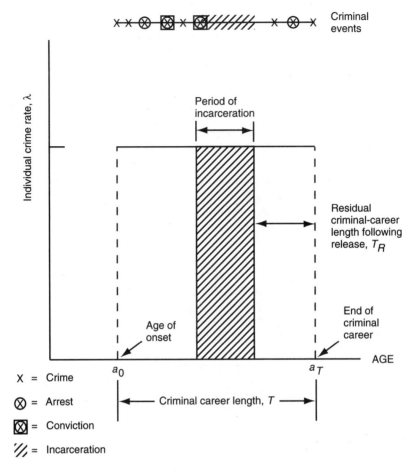

FIGURE 3.1 An individual criminal career

Extensions of the Basic Model

This simple representation can be extended to more richly describe a criminal career. Possibilities include a "start-up" time during which an offender's frequency increases, a decrease in frequency toward the end of a career, and sporadic spurts or intermittent recesses from criminal activity. If the intervals between spurts are much shorter than a typical sentence, the intermittent pattern may be ignored and the average λ used as a consideration in setting sentencing policy. But if the intervals of inactivity are long, then separate estimates are needed for high- and low-rate periods and for the duration of these periods, to adequately estimate average λ. In addition, spurts in activity make it difficult to obtain information from offenders for use in estimating average annual rates. Distinctions among different offense types can also be made, permitting attention to single offenses (e.g., "robbery careers") or to patterns of switching among offense types during a career. In this context, it is important to know whether offenders are more likely to be "specialists" (who engage in only one or a small group of offenses) or "generalists" (who switch more widely among a range of offenses). Last, extensions of the basic model can address whether offending patterns typically "escalate" in the seriousness of successive events so that crimes later in the career are more serious, or whether they peak in seriousness in mid-career and then begin to decline in seriousness as a career nears its end.

USING THE CRIMINAL CAREER PARADIGM

Interpreting Aggregate Crime Rates

The criminal career paradigm adopted here represents a departure from analyses that have focused on aggregate measures, such as incidence rates of crimes per capita or arrests per capita. Applying to active offenders and nonoffenders alike in a population, these aggregate measures confound the combined contribution of the extent of participation and the frequency of offending by active offenders. Despite this confounding of different aspects of individual offending, variations in aggregate measures have served as the basis for much of the broadly accepted current knowledge on the causes and correlates of crime.

Perhaps the most widely accepted view of crime is that it varies substantially with age. While varying in absolute magnitude, aggregate population arrest rates display a very consistent pattern—increasing rapidly during the juvenile years to reach peak rates in the late teens and then steadily declining.[5] Figure 3.2 illustrates this pattern for the FBI index offenses of robbery, aggravated assault, and burglary in 1983. Analyses of recidivism rates for identified offenders have also found a decline in criminal involvement for older offenders.[6] The declines in offending observed in aggregate data and recidivism measures have been characterized as "maturing out of crime" and have been attributed to physiological and social changes with age that lead to gradual reductions in criminal involvement.

These analyses, however, do not tell the full story. The distinctive age patterns in aggregate measures may be due either to changes in participation or in individual frequency rates for active offenders. In the former case, the peak rates of criminal activity would result from growing participation in crime during the late teen years, followed by declining participation as increasing number of offenders end their criminal careers. In the latter case, peak rates would arise from variations in the intensity of offending by a fairly fixed group of active offenders, with individuals' frequency rates increasing during the juvenile years and then gradually declining with age.

---

[5]Historically, arrest rates peaked in an offender's early twenties. This pattern was observed as early as 1831 in France (Quetelet, 1984); recent reviews of this research can be found in Greenberg (1983), Hirschi and Gottfredson (1983), and Farrington (1986).

[6]See, for example, Glueck and Glueck (1937, 1940), Sellin (1958), and more recently, studies of differential success on parole release (e.g., Hoffman and Beck, 1980; Rhodes et al., 1982; Bureau of Justice Statistics, 1984c).

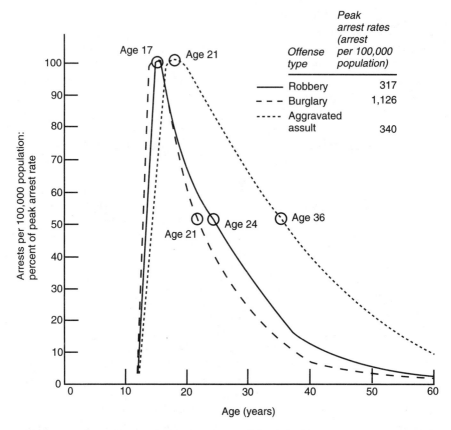

FIGURE 3.2 1983 U.S. age-specific arrest rates (arrests per 100,000 populations of each age). The curve for each offense type is displayed as a percentage of the peak arrest rate. The curves show the age at which the peak occurs (at 100 percent) and the age at which the rate falls to 50 percent of the peak rate.

Source: Federal Bureau of Investigation (1984).

Distinguishing between these alternative processes has both theoretical significance for understanding the causes of crime, as well as operational implications for efforts to control crime. From the theoretical perspective, the participation and frequency alternatives have implications for whether causes should be sought in broad social processes affecting the general population and people's movement into and out of criminal careers or in more isolated processes affecting only active offenders and their activity patterns. From a policy perspective, distinguishing between these alternatives has implications for the relative effectiveness of efforts to reduce peak levels of offending in the late teens by preventing participation by new offenders or by targeting intervention more narrowly at already active offenders.

Similar concerns about disentangling the relative contributions of participation, frequency, and duration emerge when considering other offender attributes. The sex of offenders is potentially an important factor in characterizing individual offending. Very large differences between males and females are observed both in aggregate arrest rates (see Table 3.2) and in recidivism rates (Bureau of Justice Statistics, 1984d), with substantially higher rates for males. Aggregate arrest rates also show large differences in levels of criminal activity between whites and blacks. As shown in Table 3.2, the differences between races increase as one focuses on more serious offense types, and have decreased in recent years. However, large differences between races are generally *not* found when recidivism rates for black and white offenders are compared (Wolfgang, Figlio, & Sellin, 1972:288–289; Blumstein & Graddy, 1982:283–284; Bureau of Justice Statistics, 1984d, Table 10). The differences in aggregate measures by sex and race reflect the combined contributions of differences in levels of participation in crime and differences in frequency for active offenders—distinct phenomena with very different policy implications.

Demographic Correlates of Criminal Careers

Demographic variables have received considerable attention, primarily because they are widely available in data on the general population, are easily observed by crime victims and police, and are routinely recorded for identification purposes in data from administrative and operational agencies. Data on dimensions of criminal careers are therefore widely available for different demographic subgroups defined in terms of age, sex, and race. The strong empirical associations observed between the demographic variables and aggregate arrest rates (see Table 3.2 and Figure 3.2, above) have generated substantial debate about the causes of subpopulation differences. But much ambiguity surrounds the underlying theoretical meaning of differences in criminal behavior between males and females (see Pollack, 1950; Adler, 1975; Nagel & Hagan, 1984), among racial and ethnic groups (e.g., Moynihan, 1965; Berger & Simon, 1974), and most recently, across age (Greenberg, 1983; Hirschi & Gottfredson, 1984; Greenberg, 1985; Wilson & Herrnstein, 1985; Farrington, 1986).

While demographic differences account for large portions of the variability in aggregate measures of criminal involvement, these differentials reflect relationships with other variables that are not yet well understood. For example, over the years, explanations offered for the differences between males and females have variously been biological differences, differences in moral training, differences in socialization experiences, and fewer criminal opportunities for girls because they are more closely supervised. These changes over time in interpretation of demographic differentials reflect the changing social contexts in which this research has been carried out.

Recently, Peterson and Hagan (1984) argued that criminal justice and research on differences between racial and ethnic groups should be viewed in an historical context. In the first half of this century, American research on

Table 3.2 U.S. Sex- and Race-Specific Arrest Rates in 1970 and 1980

Offense Type	ARRESTS PER **1,000** POPULATION				RATIOS[a]	
	MALES		**FEMALES**		**MALE/FEMALE**	
Sex-Specific Arrest Rates	1970	1980	1970	1980	1970	1980
All (except traffic)	76	81	12	14	6.3	5.6
All Index[b]	14	17	3	4	5.2	4.6
Property[c]	11	14	2	3	4.6	4.0
Violent[d]	2	3	0.2	0.3	8.0	8.3
Robbery	1	1	0.1	0.1	16.2	13.6
	WHITES		**BLACKS**		**BLACK/WHITE**	
Race-Specific Arrest Rates	1970	1980	1970	1980	1970	1980
All (except traffic)	35	40	107	97	3.1	2.4
All Index	6	8	28	29	4.7	3.7
Property	5	7	20	21	4.0	3.2
Violent	0.6	1	4	5	7.3	4.6
Robbery	0.2	0.3	3	3	15.4	10.3

Note: Rates are estimated from the number of reported arrests in 1980 (Federal Bureau of Investigation, 1981) and 1980 population figures (Bureau of the Census, 1983: Table 33). Similar data are available for adults and juveniles separately. Arrest rates for 1970 are estimated from the number of arrests reported in 1970 (Federal Bureau of Investigation, 1971) and 1970 population figures (Bureau of the Census, 1983: Table 33). To adjust for agencies not reporting to the FBI, reported arrests are increased by the ratio of total population available from the Bureau of the Census to the population covered by reporting agencies. This assumes that the arrest rates and population distribution in nonreporting agencies are similar to those available for reporting agencies.

[a]These ratios were computed before the arrest rates were rounded.

[b]Index rates include arrests for murder, rape, robbery, aggravated assault, burglary, larceny, and motor vehicle theft.

[c]Property rates include arrests for burglary, larceny, and motor vehicle theft.

[d]Violent rates include arrests for murder, rape, and aggravated assault.

criminal behavior focused on the criminality of newly arrived ethnic groups, the Irish and Italian immigrants in large urban areas (e.g., Glueck & Glueck, 1940). Researchers associated high crime rates among urban ethnic groups with a vast array of social problems, including low-paying jobs, poor housing, and weak ties to the "dominant" culture. Slowly the emphasis in racial/ethnic studies of criminal behavior has shifted to comparisons of white and black Americans. This shift in attention probably reflects the changing demographic composition in large cities from a variety of ethnic minorities to blacks as the dominant minority and the most recent arrivals to large urban areas. Even more recently, other racial/ethnic groups—Hispanics and Southeast Asians— have begun to receive special attention (see Moore et al., 1978; Zatz, 1984; LaFree, 1985).

The panel did not attempt to resolve the theoretical debates concerning age, sex, and racial/ethnic differences in criminal behavior. Empirical relationships are reported because so much of the research results are presented in these terms, and because the differences are often large in bivariate comparisons, robust in multivariate analyses, and stable across a variety of geographical and temporal settings and data collection methods. However, by allowing for different causal structures for the initiation, persistence, and termination of offending, the partitioning of the aggregate differentials into separate career dimensions should facilitate better theoretical interpretation. As suggested above, one finding of research invoking the criminal career paradigm has been that the demographic differentials arise more from differences in criminal participation patterns, rather than in the frequency or duration of individual offending.

Incapacitation, Rehabilitation, and Deterrence

Analyses that partition the effects of sanction among participation, frequency, and duration may provide valuable insights for improving the effectiveness of alternative crime control strategies. To date, for example, evaluations of deterrent effects have relied almost exclusively on aggregate crime rates, and evaluations of rehabilitative interventions have relied primarily on recidivism rates. To the extent that participation, duration, and frequency are differentially affected by deterrence, rehabilitation, or incapacitation policies, important relationships may be obscured in aggregate measures. Analyses of the separate effects may provide valuable insights for improving the crime control effectiveness of deterrence and rehabilitation policies. Crime control effectiveness may be improved by targeting some strategies at reducing participation, very different ones at encouraging career termination among active offenders, and still others at reducing frequency among active offenders.

Incapacitation, which is usually achieved by incarcerating active offenders, is frequently presented in terms of the criminal career paradigm. In Figure 3.3, the shaded area indicating crimes prevented during the period of incarceration represents the "incapacitative effect." Crime control effects through incapacitation increase with the magnitude of individual frequency, with the length of incarceration, and with the expected duration of the criminal career. More specifically, higher frequency means more crimes averted for each unit of time incarcerated. And longer career duration means less likelihood of wasting incarceration on offenders who would have ended their careers during the time they were incarcerated and would therefore not be committing any additional crimes whether incarcerated or not.

The incapacitative effect actually achieved will depend on the effectiveness of the criminal justice system in identifying and incarcerating offenders, especially those with the highest rates of offending. The incapacitative effect is reduced if criminals are not arrested, if arrested criminals are not convicted, if convicted criminals are not incarcerated, if sentences are short, or if parole is early. The incapacitative effect is further reduced if the crimes of an incarcerated offender are replaced by crimes by other offenders. This might occur, for

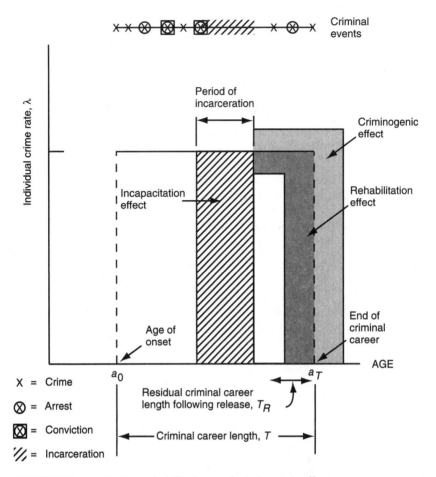

FIGURE 3.3 Incapacitation, rehabilitation, and criminogenic effects in an individual criminal career

example, if the offender is part of an organized illegal economic activity, like drug sales or burglaries organized by a fence; in this event, a replacement might simply be recruited from the available "labor market" to continue the crimes that would otherwise be committed by the incarcerated offender. If the offender is part of a crime-committing group, the remaining members of the group might continue their crimes, with or without recruiting a replacement. Group offending and its implications for crime control are addressed by Reiss (Volume II).

The criminal career construct discussed in this section is most directly related to incapacitation, with its fundamental objective of interrupting a criminal career, but it also relates directly to the other two modes of crime control used by the criminal justice system, rehabilitation and deterrence. In most evaluations of rehabilitation programs, effectiveness is measured in terms of the recidivism rate. Recidivism is usually measured as the fraction of a release group that is rearrested, usually within an observation period of 1 to 5 years.[7] If the offender depicted in Figure 3.3 received effective rehabilitative treatment in prison, its effect would be reflected as a change in his criminal career: as a reduction in his offending rate, as a shift to less serious crimes, or as a reduction in his career length. The crimes avoided by rehabilitation are depicted in Figure 3.3 by the dark gray area, "rehabilitation effect." These crimes are averted in addition to those averted through incapacitative effects during the period of imprisonment.

However, incarceration can also be counterproductive, criminogenic, if it leads to increases in postrelease criminality. This effect could be reflected by an increase in frequency or career length, depicted by the dotted area labeled "criminogenic effect," in Figure 3.3, or by an increase in the seriousness of crimes committed.[8] A criminogenic effect may result from an offender's enhanced identification as a "criminal," his learning new criminal techniques from fellow prisoners, or his strengthening ties to other offenders. The *net* rehabilitation effect is the rehabilitation effect less the criminogenic effect. No empirical comparison of these two effects has yet been carried out in the criminal career context. However, major reviews of evaluations of offender rehabilitation programs suggest that the net aggregate rehabilitation and criminogenic effect is small (Lipton, Martinson, & Wilks, 1975; Sechrest, White, & Brown, 1979).[9]

The third principal mode of crime control by the criminal justice system, in addition to incapacitation and rehabilitation, is deterrence. Deterrence is the crime-reduction effect achieved from the symbolic threat communicated to other offenders and to potential offenders by sanctions imposed on identified offenders.[10] The most common mode for examining the deterrent effect has

---

[7]Recidivism is often also measured by reconviction or recommitment to an institution. Indeed, there is considerable debate over the "true" value of recidivism, which is unwarranted since measurement at these different stages will provide different *numerical* values, but usually not different *relative* values when all measure the same process (see Blumstein & Larson, 1971). This discussion focuses on arrest, but it applies equally to any other recidivism event.

[8]A special case of this effect would be a postponement of the offender's criminal career, so that the residual career length after release assumes the same value it had when incarceration began. Thus, the delay in the career is equal to the period of incarceration, and the crimes avoided through incapacitation are exactly offset by the same number of crimes committed after the career would otherwise have ended. If this effect occurs, incarceration would delay crimes, but not reduce their number.

[9]Sechrest, White, and Brown (1979:34) caution that the poor quality of the evaluations, and the narrow range of options explored, militate against excessive pessimism concerning the potential of rehabilitation. But despite these qualifications, the failure of hundreds of evaluations to find demonstrable effects suggests that, given the current state of research methodology and correctional management, the net effect is fairly small.

[10]This effect is often characterized as "general deterrence" to distinguish it from "special deterrence," which refers to the effect of punishment on later behavior of the person punished. In this report special deterrence is considered an aspect of rehabilitation and the term deterrence refers to the broader crime-reduction effects achieved through general sanction policies.

been cross-sectional studies of jurisdictions with diverse sanction practices to examine the effect of aggregate crime rates of the sanction variation (controlling for other sources of variation in crime rate and in sanction policy). This research has yet to provide good estimates of the magnitude of deterrent effects (see Blumstein, Cohen, & Nagin, 1978). To determine the extent to which the deterrent effects of sanctions work by inhibiting career initiation, decreasing individual offending frequency, or encouraging career termination, it would be desirable for deterrence research to focus more specifically on the effect of community sanction levels on participation, and on the careers of active offenders.

SCOPE OF THE PANEL'S REPORT

The above discussion has presented the basic structural concepts involved in the criminal career paradigm. Aside from its intrinsic value, knowledge about the dimensions of criminal careers, their distribution in the population, and the factors that affect them, is important for a variety of policy uses:

- identifying variables associated with the most serious offenders (in terms of their criminal careers) so that such information may be used by decision makers, within legal and ethical constraints, to anticipate future criminal activity by an offender about whom they must make a processing decision;

- identifying variables that are widely but erroneously viewed as predictors of offenders' future criminal activity;

- improving identification of high-risk offenders and designing programs likely to be effective for them;

- better assessment of the magnitude of incapacitative effects under current or proposed imprisonment policies, possibly leading to more efficient use of limited prison space; and

- planning research programs that will build on existing knowledge and provide more effective policy directions over the next decade.

In its work, the panel focused primarily, though not exclusively, on criminal careers that involve robbery, burglary, and aggravated assault, including incidents leading to the victim's death. This decision was motivated by the scarcity of research on careers that involve only other offense types, by the priority given to those crimes by policy makers, and by the fear of those crimes expressed by the public (see, for example, Research and Forecasts, Inc., 1980). The following crime types were excluded from the panel's primary focus: arson, "white-collar" crime (e.g., embezzlement, securities fraud, mail fraud), and organized crime, for which neither extensive prior empirical research nor the requisite data exist; "victimless" crimes (e.g., prostitution, gambling, and drug use or possession); minor sex offenses and other deviant behaviors, for which offenders are commonly diverted from criminal justice to mental health or community treatment agencies; minor property offenses; and status offenses (acts that are illegal only when committed by juveniles). Although these types of offenses were not of primary interest, the panel did review studies that related them to the major crime types considered by the panel. For example, the panel was particularly interested in the relationship of minor delinquent acts to later adult careers involving robbery, burglary, and aggravated assault.

The panel also focused primarily, though not exclusively, on research that involved individual-level data on criminal careers of large samples representing clearly defined populations. Examples include analyses of arrest histories of an urban birth cohort, self-reports of offending by high school students, self-reports of incarcerated offenders, and arrest histories of criminals who are active during some observation period. Overall, the research reviewed by the panel represents most of the literature that is relevant to the study of individual criminal careers.

Several categories of research literature that study criminal behavior using paradigms other than the criminal career as defined in this report were not systematically included. Biographical and autobiographical case studies of individual offenders are excluded because the subjects are not generally representative of specific offender populations. Most ecological studies (jurisdiction-level analyses) generally relate aggregate crime measures to community or jurisdictional characteristics and do not include information about dimensions of individual criminal careers. Most recidivism studies lack sufficient detail on the number and timing of postrelease arrests that would be necessary for estimating annual offending frequencies and termination rates; hence, many research reports and program evaluations that used recidivism as the only measure of criminal behavior were not reviewed. Finally the research reviewed is primarily based on U.S. samples; a few studies of British and Danish populations are also included. The panel limited its review almost exclusively to studies published in English.

While much of the panel's work—as with all research—is concerned with the eventual development of causal theory, the panel did not pursue any particular theoretical tradition. This approach reflects the panel's recognition that synthesizing the available statistical descriptions of criminal careers will contribute to many theoretical approaches. However, development and refinement of causal theory about criminal careers should evolve from much more intensive investigation of the various dimensions of criminal careers than the literature now contains. Ideally, this investigation should proceed with a mixture of ethnographic studies to generate detailed hypotheses, longitudinal studies to explore temporal sequences, and field experiments to rigorously test hypotheses.

In considering the effect of influences possibly associated with reducing crime, the criminal career approach—with its focus on individual offenders—naturally suggests various influences that operate at the individual level to prevent initiation of a career, reduce the frequency of offending, interrupt the career, or encourage termination of a career. Individual-level influences on careers (e.g., maturation, family influences) and planned interventions grounded in knowledge about those influences (e.g., substance abuse treatment, incapacitation through incarceration) were reviewed by the panel. However, they are not the only ways in which individual careers are influenced. Individual criminal careers are also influenced in broader ways, such as through planned community-level interventions and uncontrolled events in the community (e.g., a factory shutdown). These other influences may operate through the social, economic, political, or environmental structure of the community in which individuals grow up or live, the social networks with which they become involved, or the deterrence effects generated by local sanctioning practices. Over time, all of these may change and therefore alter the nature of criminal careers. Therefore, their relationships to careers should be objects of future research. But because so little research is currently available that links these community-level effects to individual criminal careers, the panel did not address these broader relationships.

4

The True Value of Lambda Would Appear to be Zero

An Essay on Career Criminals, Criminal Careers, Selective Incapacitation, Cohort Studies, and Related Topics*

MICHAEL GOTTFREDSON

TRAVIS HIRSCHI

ABSTRACT The idea of selective incapacitation and the distinction between prevalence and incidence (participation and lambda) justify the search for a group of offenders whose criminality does not decline with age and who may be identified solely on the basis of legally relevant variables. This paper questions such research, arguing that the decline in age with crime characterizes even the most active offenders, and that the distinction between incidence and prevalence does not deserve the theoretical, research, or policy attention it has been claimed to merit (Farrington, 1985, Blumstein & Graddy, 1981–1982). In doing so, it relies on research results widely accepted in criminology. Thus, the current focus of criminological research on the "career criminal," on selective incapacitation, and on longitudinal research remains unjustified.

On March 26, 1982, 14 leading members of the criminological community in the United States met in Washington, D.C., to discuss the future of criminal justice research in this country. The priority area for future research listed first by this panel was "criminal careers." The idea of the career criminal has become so ingrained in American criminological thinking that the panel apparently saw no inconsistency between its substantive emphasis on criminal careers and its procedural view that "no worthwhile research program can be centrally planned" (Wilson, 1982). Four years later, the criminal career notion so dominates discussion of criminal justice policy and so

SOURCE: *Criminology,* Vol. 24, No. 2, pp. 213–234.

*This research was supported by grant SES8500244 from the National Science Foundation.

controls expenditure of federal research funds that it may now be said that criminal justice research in this country is indeed centrally planned.

Nearly every federal agency concerned with research on crime, delinquency, or criminal justice assumes the existence of the career criminal and consequently limits research outside this tradition—if only on the grounds that such research is less likely to deliver results of policy significance.[1] The academic community also tends to adopt career criminal terminology: the language of criminology is now saturated with the vocabulary of this perspective—with terms like *lambda, prevalence* and *incidence, onset* and *desistance, chronicity* and *selective incapacitation*. Being derived from policy concerns, career criminal terminology sounds immediately policy-relevant to those in charge of the nation's research agencies, and the circle is closed. Academics supply the terms that justify the funds provided them. Although not unique to criminology, it is clear that such closed systems survive turnover in those political appointees who direct the expenditure of public funds (whatever their politics). Of course they do more than survive. The large sums spent on pursuit of these terms convince many that the terms have value (which they by now do). On and on, round and round it goes.

If such systems are to be questioned, the questioning must come from the academic community. As of now, this is not being done. Those who make policy about criminal justice research are being advised by leading scholars to continue to concentrate their attention and resources on the career criminal.[2] This paper seeks to introduce some small degree of tension into this otherwise complacent system. It criticizes the career criminal and derivative concepts, evaluates the research on which they are based, and examines the policy (selective incapacitation) stemming from them.

THE CAREER CRIMINAL

The idea of the career criminal goes back to before the turn of the century, when many Western nations formed special committees to advise government on methods for dealing with the habitual offender (Carbonell & Megargee, nd). Since then, it has been a staple of criminal justice research and policy,

---

[1]According to James K. Stewart, Director of the National Institute of Justice, "Few issues facing criminal justice are more urgent than safeguarding the public from those who make a career of crime" (U.S. Department of Justice, 1983). According to Alfred S. Regnery, Administrator, Office of Juvenile Justice and Delinquency Prevention, "The main objective of our intervention strategies should be to incapacitate the small proportion of chronic, violent offenders" (Tracy, Wolfgang, & Figlio, 1985). In its announcement of research programs for fiscal 1986, the National Institute of Justice (U.S. Department of Justice, 1985) lists four areas relevant to crime causation: "crime control theory and policy," "offender classification and prediction of criminal behavior," "violent criminal behavior," and "drugs, alcohol, and crime." In all of these areas, the concepts critiqued in this paper can be fairly said to dominate the description of the agency's interests.

[2]One more example: the Attorney General's Task Force on Violent Crime (1981) told the Attorney General that as one of his first priorities he "should direct the National Institute of Justice and other branches of the Department of Justice to conduct research and development on federal and state career criminal programs. . . . "

particularly among those concerned with the control of crime. Current enthusiasm for the idea is not, however, the cumulative result of improvements in knowledge resulting from a hundred years of research. Rather, it can be traced to rediscovery of the chronic offender by Wolfgang, Figlio, and Sellin (1972). Walker (1985: 39) illustrates the reaction of the criminal justice community to this discovery: "Their landmark study *Delinquency in a Birth Cohort* is the single most important piece of criminal justice research in the last 25 years and has become a major influence on crime control thinking." The major finding of this study of about 10,000 young men living in Philadelphia is said to be that 627 of them account for the bulk of the crime in the entire group. According to Walker, "since Wolfgang first identified them, those 627 juveniles have inspired the freshest and most important thinking in criminal justice. They are the career criminals." Today, Wolfgang's career criminals appear under a number of aliases in almost all federally funded theory and research on crime. They are habitual offenders, chronic offenders, high rate offenders, or even offenders involved in "a sustained pattern of illegal acts."

Despite persistent interest in career criminals dating back 100 years, little improvement in the definition of them can be observed. According to Gladstone, the chair of an 1895 British committee, the habitual criminal is characterized by "the wilful persistence in the deliberately acquired habit of crime" (Morris, 1951:34). Some 50 years later, Morris (1951:6) provided three elements to define the habitual criminal: "(a) criminal qualities inherent or latent in the mental constitution; (b) settled practice in crime; (c) public danger." Petersilia, author of important research on career criminals for the Rand Corporation, writes (1980, Abstract) "a criminal career may consist of a single, undiscovered, venial lapse or a high level of sustained involvement in serious crime." Finally, even the United States Government provides a definition. According to the U.S. Department of Justice (1983), the career criminal is "a person having a past record of multiple arrests or convictions for serious crimes, or an unusually large number of arrests or convictions for crimes of varying degrees of seriousness."

If the career criminal (or his criminal career) can be identified by a state of mind, by the quality of the acts he commits, by the number of acts he commits, or even by a single, private, excusable lapse, the fact remains that the term is meant to serve a purpose. It is meant to distinguish some kinds of criminals from others. (These others are also variously labelled. They are nonchronic offenders, occasional offenders, sporadic offenders, or nonserious offenders.) If career criminals can be identified, there must be at least two types of criminals. And if there are two, there may be more than two. The concept of career criminals is thus conducive to efforts to classify offenders into distinct groups and, eventually, to efforts to seek unique causes and policy prescriptions for each type. These residual types and the theoretical and practical problems they presuppose are nowadays usually forgotten the moment they are created (for good reason), and as a consequence the idea of the career criminal does not in itself suggest complexity or difficulty. On the contrary, it suggests simple, clear-thinking policy directed at the heart of the crime problem. Whatever else it has come to mean, the idea of a career criminal suggests that some people pursue crime over an extended period of time, that the intention to pursue such activities may be determined in advance of their pursuit, and that the acts intended can be prevented by timely intervention by the state.

The theoretical and practical appeal of this idea is obvious. Sociologists who see crime as an alternate route to material success, economists who see crime as a form of employment, and psychologists and sociologists who see crime as a consequence of intense training in criminal values and techniques are likely to be comfortable with the notion of a career criminal. Their theories, after all, actually seek to explain such offenders. To the policy-oriented, the idea of a career criminal suggests the possibility of doing something to or for a small segment of the criminal population with notable reductions in crime rates. One currently popular policy option suggested by the career criminal notion is a sentencing strategy that seeks to imprison the career offender.

SELECTIVE INCAPACITATION

Selective incapacitation envisions identification of a small group of high-rate offenders early in their criminal careers in order to isolate them in such a way that they cannot pursue their criminal inclinations. Modern criminological research has held out the hope that such a dream may be realized, repeatedly telling us that the number of offenders responsible for the bulk of crime is remarkably small. In fact, the most frequently repeated finding of crime research is the Wolfgang disproportionality (about 6% commit more than half the crime). Wolfgang has not been alone in his pursuit of such disproportionality. Indeed, one might reasonably conclude that a competition exists among criminological researchers to maximize it. Thus, for example, Mednick (Mednick & Christiansen, 1977:1) reports that in a cohort he studied, "only 1% of the male population. . . accounts for *more than half of the offenses committed by the entire cohort*" (emphasis in original). Wilson and Herrnstein (1985:144) report that chronic offenders account for "as many as 75 percent of offenses" and also for "a disproportionately serious brand of crime." In fact, Cohen (1984) provides 13 additional estimates culled from recent research of the overinvolvement in crime of the active few.

Whatever the precise number of such inveterate criminals, they are sufficiently rare to be extremely attractive targets for crime control policy, suggesting as they do that with minimum effort and cost, maximum reduction in the crime rate may be achieved.

For such a dream to be realized, two conditions must obtain: First, selective incapacitation cannot simply duplicate existing criminal justice practices (which, after all, clearly involve highly selective processes). Second, those selected for incapacitation under proposed policies must be legally and socially eligible for such treatment.

As currently organized, the criminal justice system bases the decision to incapacitate offenders on the nature of their current offense and on the extent of their prior criminal record. Because the offender's prior record carries so much weight in the decision to incarcerate, those receiving prison sentences tend to be older than the average offender. For this reason, selective incapacitation envisions finding offender characteristics other than current offense and prior record predictive of subsequent criminal activity that can be legitimately employed in incarceration decisions. At the same time, selective incapacitation researchers recognize that utility and legitimacy are unlikely to come in a single package, that social predictors of crime provide a poor excuse for differential legal treatment. As a necessary consequence, researchers seek to base the incapacitation decision on characteristics of the criminal record not now considered by the criminal justice system. To do this, they must locate career criminals in the records of the criminal justice system. Such a search in the service of selective incapacitation has several ironies: it leads to an attempt to discover the very being whose discovery launched the search to begin with; it leads to an attempt to identify an obviously serious, dangerous offender whose character has gone unrecognized by criminal justice officials.

This point bears repeating until it is clear. Discovery of the career criminal by criminologists stimulated the idea of selective incapacitation. To implement the idea of selective incapacitation, one need only identify career criminals. Unfortunately, the career criminals who suggested the idea in the first place cannot be found when it comes time to implement the policy. Where did they go? What happened to them? It turns out that the particular career criminals identified in criminological research are no longer active and their replacements cannot be identified until they too are on the verge of "retirement." The 20-20 hindsight of career criminal research turns out to have been misleading. When asked to identify career criminals in advance of their criminal careers, the research community requests additional funding.

Still, the idea of imprisoning career criminals seems perfectly plausible. However, the idea has little merit. In fact, research has shown that the idea that "criminals" have "careers" is wrong. If crime represents a career, then it follows that it must have a beginning and an end, a determinable length, and a certain tendency or direction (for example, increasing skill, increasing seriousness, or increasing profitability). It follows further that those embarked on a criminal career may tend to specialize in certain crimes or to advance from one crime to another in predictable ways. These ideas survive as long as it takes to determine that the average burglar is about 16 and that he "advances" to robbery a few years later because burglary requires too much planning (for example, being at a particular place at a particular time). If there are lingering doubts about the veracity of the career criminal idea, the research literature should put them to rest. Consider the findings of Petersilia (1980): "the propensity to plan does not increase with age; it appears unlikely that the observed relation between declining arrests and age results from more skillful crimes by more seasoned criminals; the tendency to work alone becomes more pronounced as the career progresses; those who worked [at legitimate jobs] during their teens or early twenties . . .

had more police contacts and higher seriousness scores than those who were unemployed; few 'robbers' specialize in robbery."

There is, then, virtually no evidence of offense specialization anywhere in the life cycle of ordinary offenders (rape and assault are intermixed with crimes for pecuniary profit); most offenses do not require any particular skill (doors are simply smashed open), knowledge (little training is required to snatch a purse), or even expectation of great gain ("hand over all your big bills," the career criminal says to the cabbie); there is no evidence of escalation of any sort as the offender moves from adolescence to adulthood; and the crimes that occur most frequently are the crimes most frequently committed by "career" criminals.

One way to save the career criminal in the face of the overwhelming evidence that his career starts at the bottom and proceeds nowhere is to suggest that somewhere there is a set of offenders whose careers are not described by these tendencies, a set of offenders who continue to commit large numbers of offenses over an extended period of time. This subset of offenders must, by definition, also deviate from the general tendency of crime to decline with age.

AGE AND CRIME

Incapacitation researchers realize that, in general, the commission of crime declines with age and that in order for incapacitation to achieve maximum effectiveness it must occur during the time that the incapacitated offender would be committing criminal acts at a high rate. The decline in crime with age is therefore a direct threat to incapacitation policy. It makes little sense to attempt to prevent crime by locking up people who would not be committing crimes were they free. The decline in crime with age also suggests that the optimal point of intervention for purposes of incapacitation is just prior to the age at which crime peaks—that is, 13 or 14. This too is a direct threat to incapacitation policy since it suggests lengthy incarceration of children in the interest of crime prevention.

There is a potential solution to these unfortunate problems: if the true career criminal starts late and maintains a high level of criminal activity during his adulthood, the impediment to incapacitation policy presented by the general decline in crime with age is removed. Awareness of this solution has led recent incapacitation research to focus attention on adults. Strange to tell, it is now claimed that research has revealed existence of such offenders: high rate, chronic, persistent, habitual adult offenders.

The authors have spent some time investigating the relation between age and crime (Hirschi & Gottfredson, 1983). This investigation led to the conclusion that the propensity to commit criminal acts reaches a peak in the middle to late teens and then declines rapidly throughout life (see, for example, Figure 4.1, which shows Uniform Crime Report arrest rates for 1983, by age). Further, this distribution is characteristic of the age–crime relation regardless of sex, race, country, time, or offense. Indeed, the persistence of this relation across time and culture is phenomenal. As long as records have been kept, in all societies in which such records are available, it appears that crime is an activity highly concentrated among the young. These conclusions are controversial only insofar as they apply to other times and cultures. Current aggregate American age distributions of crime are not in serious dispute (Greenberg, 1985).

As is apparent from Figure 4.1, if the career criminal described by current incapacitation research exists, he is thoroughly disguised in arrest statistics for the general population. These statistics do not reveal a tendency for crime to level off at a high rate for any segment of the population. The issue thus turns directly on an empirical question: Is the age effect present in all segments of the population, including those now labelled "chronic offenders"?

Early research suggested that persons identified as offenders early in life were less likely to offend as they got older. In 1940, Glueck and Glueck reported the results of a long-term follow-up of 1,000 delinquents. The Gluecks recorded the offenses committed by the delinquents from the time they were 11 to the time they were 30. Being a true longitudinal study in which the same individuals are followed over time (the preferred research design of modern incapacitation researchers (Farrington, 1985), the Gluecks' study allows one to examine the age distributions of specific offenses. Some of these distributions are shown in Table 4.1.

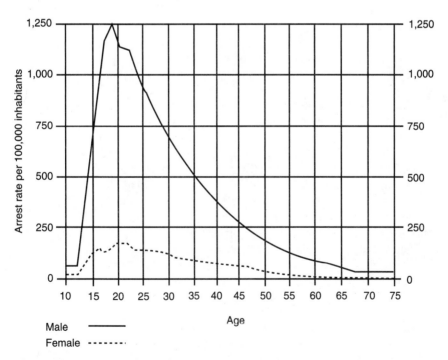

Male ———
Female ·······

FIGURE 4.1 Age-crime relationship

Source: U.S. Department of Justice, 1985b: 346

Table 4.1 Number of Arrests by Age and Type of Offense, Glueck Longitudinal Study of 1,000 Delinquents

Crime	Age 11–15	16–20	21–25	26–30
Property	829	1,272	613	390
Disorderly Conduct	286	580	755	483
Violence	33	115	183	147
Drunkenness	0	242	724	922
Family and Children	0	14	40	71
All Other Arrests	185	496	232	182
Total Arrests	1,333	2,719	2,547	2,195

SOURCE: Glueck and Glueck, 1940: 310.

Nothing in the Gluecks' longitudinal arrest data gives comfort to the career criminal notion. The age distribution of specific crimes in their data looks very much like the age distribution in the cross-sectional data of the Uniform Crime Reports shown earlier. Crime as a whole peaks in late adolescence because the disproportionately frequent property offenses peak then. Violent offenses peak in the early 20s. Such crime as drunkenness and family and child abuse appear to increase throughout the 20s. This too is no surprise. All available data, whatever the research design producing them, show these distributions. (It seems unlikely that those interested in incapacitation have in mind control of drunkenness and intrafamily violence.) It is therefore apparent that even in a sample selected for the delinquency of its members, crime declines with age.

Other research well known to criminologists strongly suggests the same conclusion. For example, research on the effectiveness of treatment for highly delinquent youth, research that has produced controversial findings with respect to the effectiveness of treatment, has always shown that even these youths "mature out" of crime (Empey & Erickson, 1972; Murray & Cox, 1979). The hypothesis that always competes with the hypothesis that the treatment has worked is the hypothesis that the observed decline in delinquency is a consequence of age. Maturational reform is so pervasively observed, even among serious delinquents (career criminals?) that it is the dominant explanation of change in criminal activity during the teen years.

Undaunted by such seemingly definitive research, researchers in the selective incapacitation tradition claim to have found a group whose crime rate fails to decline with age. The most influential work of this type is by Blumstein and Cohen (1979), whose study of offenders in Washington, D.C., is widely taken to show that crime does not decline with age among career criminals when the data are properly analyzed. According to Greenberg (1985), the Blumstein and Cohen study shows that "what seem to be age effects disappear when cohorts are followed over time," and Blumstein (1982) himself later summarizes his study as showing that "offenders who remain criminally active commit crimes at a fairly constant rate over age." Farrington (1985:33) is equally confident of these results:

> In a sample of adults arrested for serious crimes in Washington, D.C., [Blumstein and Cohen] found that the individual arrest rate decreased with age, from below 20 to above 30. However, they explained away this decrease on two grounds. First of all, there were cohort effects confounded with age, since arrest rates were higher among those born more recently. Secondly, the calculations did not take account of time incarcerated, which affected the older offenders more than the younger ones. When Blumstein and Cohen allowed for both of these effects in more sensitive analyses, they found that the arrest rate did not tend to decrease with age. They have consistently argued that the individual crime rate or incidence of offending is constant during a criminal career. What varies is onset and termination, not crime rate.

If Greenberg's and Farrington's (and Wilson and Herrnstein's (1985:138–139)) assessments of the Blumstein and Cohen research are correct, it seems fair to say that there is merit in pursuing the selective incapacitation research agenda. If, on the other hand, the data amassed by criminologists outside the incapacitation tradition are to be believed, it seems fair to say that the career criminal research agenda should be abandoned, along with the criminal justice policy it suggests.

The Blumstein and Cohen study leads to conclusions contrary to established facts in criminology and does not justify rejection of these facts. If this is correct, pursuit of an empirical basis for a policy of selective incapacitation of career offenders is a waste of scarce research resources and diverts public attention from crime control policies of potential merit. The discussion therefore turns directly to the Blumstein and Cohen study.

BLUMSTEIN AND COHEN, 1979

Given their policy problem, Blumstein and Cohen first confront the age distribution of crime as it has been revealed by official statistics as long as they have been collected. How, they ask, could crime rates appear to decline with age year after year if in fact the rate with which individuals engage in crime does not decrease as they grow older? The solution adopted is to suggest that what is observed as an age effect in each yearly depiction of the crime rate by age is in fact a rising crime rate effect. Persons born recently have higher rates of crime at all ages than do persons born earlier. Therefore, at any given point in time, the mix of cohorts yields the illusion of an age effect.

This explanation would be plausible if the world were invented in 1975. In order for it to be true, however, every new cohort since crime statistics were invented would have to be substantially more criminal than its predecessors.

Put another way, the Blumstein and Cohen hypothesis could be true if the crime rate had risen steadily throughout the lives of the oldest cohort in the comparison. Since the age distribution of crime has been invariant for at least 100 years, the Blumstein and Cohen hypothesis requires a steady increase in the rate of crime for about 170 years. One need not go back so far to prove them wrong. One need only show that the crime rate actually declined during portions of this period or that the age distribution of crime has survived the much-publicized current decline in the crime rate. Both are easily shown. Figure 4.2 shows the age distribution of male robbers as revealed by the Uniform Crime Reports for 1970, 1974, and 1983. The robbery rate in 1970 was low (very low by current standards). The robbery rate in 1974 was near its historic high, a rate not equaled as long as these statistics have been reported. The robbery rate in 1983 was down from the peak in the middle to late 1970s. As Figure 4.2 shows, apart from differences in levels of crime, the age distributions in these three periods are virtually indistinguishable from each other, contrary to the requirements of Blumstein and Cohen's logic.

It is still possible, however, to confuse offenders whose pattern of offending is consistent with an age effect with "career criminals" whose pattern of offending is inconsistent with an age effect. An age distribution of crime does not require that rates of crime by age be identical for all persons in the population. It does not require that crime rates for individuals actually decline during periods in which crime rates for the population as a whole are declining.

Consider statistics on the performance of professional baseball players (statistics that in many respects parallel crime statistics). A problem of considerable interest in such statistics is the length of the career of the superstar—that is,

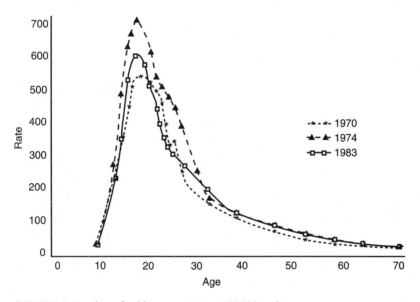

FIGURE 4.2 Number of robbery arrests per 100,000 males

until what age can superstars be expected to continue their excellence? One might conclude that age does not affect superstars to the same degree it affects ordinary players. After all, many superstars are still around and doing quite well at advanced ages (mid to late 30s). The data, however, show that (1) superstars have the same age curve as other ball players; and (2) at every age, superstars are better than other players at the same age (James, 1980). These facts leave an impression of unchanging performance over a restricted period of time because any player whose performance falls below the level acceptable for the major leagues is dropped from rosters regardless of prior record. The data also give the impression that the performance of superstars does not decline with age. But this is only because the performance of the superstar at advanced ages is well above that of ordinary young major league players. Mickey Mantle at 38 was better than Gene Michael at 28. Mickey Mantle at 38 was not, however, as good as Mickey Mantle at 28.

Applied to the crime rate, the baseball analogy suggests that crime may decline with age for several reasons: (1) some offenders so reduce the level of their criminal activity that they are no longer of interest to the criminal justice system; (2) some offenders continue a level of activity sufficient to be of interest to the criminal justice system, although this level is considerably below the level maintained during their peak years of activity; and (3) some offenders maintain a level of activity so high that they are removed from the game. In the criminal justice system as it now operates, superstars have the shortest rather than the longest careers.

Let us take these notions to an evaluation of the Blumstein and Cohen study: given their interest in discovering persistent offenders, Blumstein and Cohen's sample must be restricted to offenders somewhere between those who drop out because of insufficient activity and those who are forcefully removed because their level of activity is so high. Starting with the 5,338 offenders arrested for homicide, rape, robbery, aggravated assault, burglary, or auto theft in Washington, D.C., during 1973, Blumstein and Cohen proceed to the identification of offenders relevant to their concerns. Two additional criteria are applied to select their sample: (1) the offender must have turned 18 between 1963 and 1966, and (2) the offender's first reported adult arrest must have been at age 18, 19, or 20. Application of these criteria produced a sample of less than 200 offenders (Blumstein and Cohen do not report the exact number).

It is difficult to determine what population this sample represents. Presumably, it was selected to allow study of chronic offenders. It was widely represented as doing so (Wilson & Herrnstein, 1985:138). As indicated, such offenders are unlikely to be available to the sampling procedure employed by Blumstein and Cohen. Nonetheless, Blumstein and Cohen report good luck in finding a group of serious offenders among whom the rate of offending does not decline with age. "The results . . . strongly suggest that the previously observed effects of a decline in arrest rates with age . . . could well be artifacts." To understand the magnitude of this achievement, the reader should consult Figure 4.3, the age distribution of the full 1973 population of arrestees in Washington, D.C., as reported by Blumstein, Cohen, and Hsieh

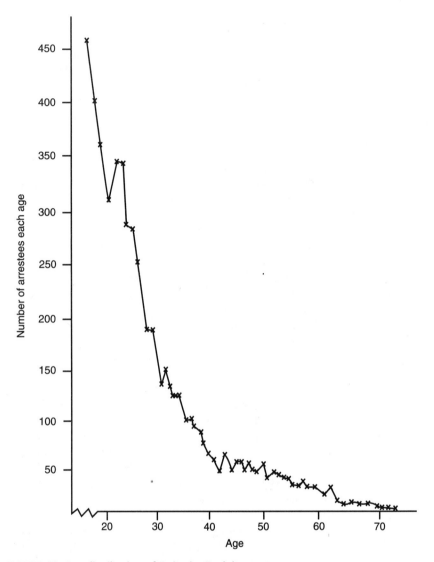

FIGURE 4.3 Age distribution of "criterion" adult arrestees in Washington, D.C. during 1973[a]

[a]"Criterion" arrestees include those adults arrested during 1973 for the index offenses of homicide, rape, robbery, aggravated assault, burglary, and auto theft (that is, arrestees for all index offenses other than larceny).

Source: Blumstein et al., 1982: 14.

(1982). How could a sample constructed from this population fail to reflect the overwhelming tendency of crime to decline with age in the parent population? To find the answer, one must come to grips with the implications of the Blumstein and Cohen sampling procedure. It turns out that the age effect apparent in Blumstein and Cohen's data is not an artifact. On the contrary, the conclusions of the Blumstein and Cohen study are themselves an artifact of their research procedures.

Recall that Blumstein and Cohen included offenders in their sample only if they had an arrest in 1973 and also had an arrest at age 18, 19, or 20, some time prior to 1973. Also recall that the question of interest is what the career criminal scientists have dubbed "lambda," the "average yearly individual arrest rate." (This figure, when precisely known, allows precise estimation of the savings in crime gained by a year of imprisonment.) In this case, lambda would be the average yearly arrest rate between 1966 and 1972 for persons between 21 and 27 arrested in 1973 and at least once subsequent to 1965. It is, for the "active individual criminals" identified by Blumstein and Cohen, .27, about one arrest every four years.

So, Blumstein and Cohen identify offenders arrested at two points in time, and they calculate the extent of their activity in the interim. This is identical to identifying ballplayers employed by the major leagues at two points in time and asking whether they were involved in professional baseball in the interim. It is neither very surprising nor very useful to learn that persons selected on the basis of predetermined characteristics actually possess those characteristics. Unfortunately, the utility of incapacitation depends on the ability to lock people up before they commit the offense defining them as persistent, and it is much more difficult to predict the occurrence of offenses than it is to count them after they have been committed. But for the moment, what is of interest is the significance of the Blumstein and Cohen data for their conclusion that crime does not decline with age among active offenders.

Consider the chances that an offender will be included with his cohort in the Blumstein and Cohen study: For the offender who turned 18, 19, or 20 in 1963 and was arrested in that year, it would be necessary that he be arrested again ten years later in order to be included. Ten years is, in arrest terms, a very long time. Only high-rate offenders would be expected to achieve this feat. However, recall the requirement that to be included in the sample the offender must have been arrested in 1973. What kind of long-term offender would still be on the street after such a lengthy period? Three kinds come to mind. The first is the undoubtedly mythical offender whose intelligence and sophistication make him a worthy adversary for the crime fighters of American fiction and public policy. Skilled in avoiding detection and presumably unlikely to be involved in robbery, aggravated assault, or narcotics, this sophisticated career criminal is by definition beyond the reach of meaningful selective incapacitation strategies. The second is a strangely sporadic or low-rate occasional offender whose arrests are sufficiently dispersed over time to reduce the likelihood of imprisonment (again, a curious although apparently frequent target of incapacitation researchers and "repeat offender" projects). The third is a high-rate offender who may have served a good deal of time in prison during the period in question but who happens to be free in 1973—that is, an offender already largely incapacitated under existing policy. Blumstein and Cohen do not attempt to count or describe their offenders in these terms, preferring to treat them as equally plausible targets of rational crime control policy.

Such lack of attention to the composition of the sample may have stemmed from the statistical difficulties involved in breaking an already small sample into subgroups. But such decomposition is required if one is to judge the policy significance of this research. It will be recalled that the life blood of selective incapacitation is the minute fraction of the offender population said to be responsible for the bulk (50% to 75%?) of criminal activity. Presumably Blumstein and Cohen have isolated the population of interest. But have they?

The group does appear to be small, representing less than 4% of those arrested in 1973. The group does not appear to be unusually active or chronic, however, at least in comparison to other adult offenders in the population from which Blumstein and Cohen drew their sample. In fact, a calculation shows that their 4% of offenders accounts for 4% of the arrests (hardly a group of "high-frequency, serious offenders" (Wilson & Herrnstein, 1985:138). In other words, a Washington arrestee selected at random would be as "active" or "chronic" as the arrestees so closely scrutinized by Blumstein and Cohen.

Farrington (1985) and Greenberg (1985) say that Blumstein and Cohen have uncovered a group of offenders whose criminal activity does not decline with age, thus providing potential targets for incapacitation policies and a justification for continuing research on the career criminal. They argue that the apparent decline in crime with age disappears when Blumstein and Cohen applies controls for cohort. Farrington (1985) argues further that part of the apparent age effect in the Blumstein and Cohen study was accounted for by differences in time incarcerated.

Neither of these points about the Blumstein and Cohen analysis is correct. Close examination of the Blumstein-Cohen data reveal that controls for cohort or time served were unnecessary because the Blumstein and Cohen sample was selected in such a manner that there was no correlation between age and crime from the beginning. Given the initial zero relation, control for cohort is hard to justify on statistical grounds (and there is certainly no substantive reason for such a control—any random variable would show the same result). Given the obvious connection between time served and frequency of criminal activity, the lack of a time-served effect gives additional reason for concern about the adequacy of the sample (and the effectiveness of an incapacitation policy). In any event, it is misleading to control for irrelevant variables and then suggest that such controls account for observed results. By doing so, Blumstein and Cohen imply that they know why age is related to crime—that it is an artifact of cross-sectional data and current incarceration practices—when in fact their research says nothing about this question and is incapable of saying anything about it. Making more of an issue that might seem by now settled, the discussion turns to a distinction much publicized in the career criminal literature, the distinction between incidence and prevalence.

CAREER CRIMINALS
OR CRIMINAL CAREERS?

If crime declines with age because low-rate, amateur, or occasional offenders offend only during the teen years and then drop out, while high-rate, professional, or chronic offenders start early and stay late, then it may be true (as many incapacitation researchers argue) that the greatest effect of imprisonment would be between ages 30 and 40 rather than at the peak age of offenses. Farrington (1985, Abstract) states this possibility as established fact: "Age-crime curves for individuals do not resemble the aggregate curve, since incidence does not change consistently between onset and termination." Farrington thus asserts what Blumstein and Cohen attempted to show, that differences in age-specific crime rates stem from changes in the number of active offenders rather than from changes in the frequency of offending among offenders. As has been seen, Blumstein and Cohen's methodology is not capable of supporting this assertion, especially in the face of good evidence to the contrary. What other evidence bears on Farrington's assertion?

Some evidence is provided by the longitudinal study of London youth by Farrington and his colleagues (Farrington, 1983). Portions of the data, along with the calculations of the authors of this paper, are reproduced as Table 4.2. The reader will note that the number of persons convicted of crimes is highest at age 17, that the number of convictions is highest at age 17, and that both persons convicted and convictions decline from this point. The similarity between offender and offense counts suggests that they are connected by a multiplier that remains reasonably constant throughout the 15 years the cohort is followed. This multiplier is one type of incidence rate for the sample, what some scholars refer to as "lambda." This incidence rate uses the number of offenders during a given time period as the denominator. (A more useful incidence rate uses the number of individuals in the population (offenders plus nonoffenders) as the denominator. The numerator in both cases is the number of offenses during the period.) Simple arithmetic reveals that the average annual lambda in the Farrington data is 1.294 (the total number of convictions divided by the total number of different persons convicted each year). Inspection of annual lambdas leads directly to the conclusion that lambda is invariant over the 15-year period of the study.[3] Because lambda is a constant over the period of the study, several things follow: (1) lambda, as one measure of the incidence of crime, does not vary by age; persons committing crimes at age 28 on the average commit as many crimes as those who commit crimes at age 10; (2) lambda can be calculated in the absence of expensive, time-consuming longitudinal research; and (3) lambda, as a measure of the

---

[3]An additional five years of follow-up data are available in draft form (Farrington, Gallagher, Morley, Ledger, & West, 1985). These new data, as predicted, would not alter the argument presented here. For example, in adding the five additional years of data, the average lambda changes from 1.294 to 1.288.

Table 4.2 Convictions at Each Age

Age	No. of First Convictions	No. of Different Persons Convicted	No. of Convictions	No. of Recidivists Convicted	Lambda
10	6	6	7	0	1.17
11	6	8	10	2	1.25
12	8	12	14	4	1.17
13	15	21	27	6	1.29
14	19	34	44	15	1.29
15	17	33	43	16	1.30
16	13	32	47	19	1.47
17	19	47	63	28	1.34
18	8	41	50	33	1.22
19	8	38	47	30	1.24
20	9	29	41	20	1.41
21	2	18	20	16	1.11
22	3	25	35	22	1.40
23	2	11	11	9	1.00
Total	136	367	475		$\overline{X} = 1.294$

SOURCE: Modified from Farrington (1983). Columns 4 and 5 were calculated by the authors of this paper.

incidence of crime, is, as defined, without theoretical or policy significance.[4] (Blumstein and Graddy (1981–1982) show that lambda is similarly insignificant with respect to race differences in offending—that is, that although race differences in prevalence are large, white offenders are as likely to recidivate as black offenders. This of course does not mean that black-white differences on the usual measure of incidence are without interest.)

---

[4]In the criminal careers literature, lambda is defined as the rate of offending by "active" offenders. The question is, given that one is a criminal, how many criminal acts does one commit during a specified period of time? This definition of "incidence" has implications not typically acknowledged by users of the term. It implies, for example, that the important questions for theory and policy have to do with how offenders vary among themselves, rather than with how offenders differ from nonoffenders. The vacuity of this kind of thinking about crime cannot be overestimated. No other area of scientific inquiry would accept the logic of this approach. What, this approach would ask, is the impact of interest rate increases on saving among those with savings accounts? (Rather than, what is the impact of interest rate increases on saving in general?) What, it would ask, distinguishes blacks who have had at least one heart attack from whites who have had at least one heart attack? (Rather than, what are the causes of heart attacks—and do they differ between blacks and whites?) The heart attack rate may be decomposed into at least two elements. For any given time period, there will be the proportion of people in a group who have had heart attacks (prevalence), there will be the number of heart attacks suffered by members of the group (incidence), and there will be the number of heart attacks suffered by those who had at least one heart attack during the period. The last named statistic (called lambda) connects the first two. It appears to have no other possible significance.

Having dispensed with lambda, the discussion can return to the career criminal. Taking into account age at first conviction in the Farrington data (column 1), we calculate that the number of "career criminals" (those with prior convictions) is highest at age 18, where 33 of the 41 persons convicted had been convicted previously. Apparently, the age distribution of career criminality is identical to the age distribution of noncareer criminality in Farrington's as in the Gluecks' data, and the assertion by Farrington is contrary to his own evidence. There is more contrary evidence.

When high-rate imprisoned offenders are asked for retrospective accounts of their criminal behavior, they report engaging in fewer crimes as they grow older.[5] For example, researchers for the Rand Corporation surveying a small group of California inmates found that "the overall amount of crime during [the reference period] declines linearly as a function of the respondent's age" (Peterson, Braiker, & Polich, 1980:49–50). Confronted once again by an age distribution contrary to the career criminal notion, incapacitation researchers invent a new strategy: "[The Rand researchers] using self-reported crime note that total crime rates for individuals tend to decrease with age of the offender. This decrease with age, however, is apparently associated with a decline in the number of different crime types committed by older offenders. Controlling for crime type [yet another lambda], older offenders report committing crimes at about the same rate as younger offenders" (Blumstein et al., 1982:8). In other words, Blumstein et al. tell us that offenders indeed commit fewer homicides, rapes, robberies, aggravated assaults, burglaries, and auto thefts as they age. He also tells us, however, that old rapists commit as many rapes as young rapists, that old robbers commit as many robberies as young robbers, that old burglars . . . etc. All of which means only that if one commits many crimes one is likely to commit many different crimes (criminal offenders, recall, do not specialize) and that if one commits few offenses one cannot commit many different kinds of offenses. This shows that older criminals do indeed slow down, a finding that comes as no surprise and a finding contrary to, rather than supportive of, a policy of selective incapacitation.

---

[5]Another property of lambda is that it depends heavily on the method of crime measurement. With self-report measures, lambda will vary in magnitude and meaning depending on the cutting point between offenders and nonoffenders. With self-report measures, one can ask: what is lambda for those committing more than 100 offenses during the specified reference period, or what is lambda for those committing at least one offense every day? Although precise numerical answers to these questions are possible, it is not clear what purpose they would serve.

Lambdas computed from official data are of course constrained in ways self-report (or victimization) lambdas are not. If, for example, felony conviction is the official criterion, annual lambdas will have a restricted upper limit, for reasons that are apparently of little interest to criminal career researchers. At the same time, if one uses an official criterion, the classification-counting rules are so limiting that counts of official transactions cannot meaningfully represent "the number of offenses committed by active offenders."

CONCLUSIONS

The heavy emphasis on the career criminal has paid little in the way of practical dividends and has limited thinking about crime to the repetition of pretentious slogans. Federal research policy has been captured by the career criminal notion. The favorite research design consistent with this idea requires following large numbers of people over long periods of time. In other words, the favorite design requires large outlays of funds concentrated on a small number of research institutions. This research policy therefore presupposes considerable confidence in the validity of the ideas being pursued, and considerable lack of confidence in alternative perspectives.

The evidence is clear that the career criminal idea is not sufficiently substantial to command more than a small portion of the time and effort of the criminal justice practitioner or academic community. Is there a policy-relevant alternative to the career criminal notion? Since the Enlightenment, many reasonable people have argued that the state exists in part to prevent crime. In a liberal society, the state prevents crime at least as much through the use of legal penalties as through the imprisonment or rehabilitation of criminals (Van den Haag, 1982). The theories of crime implicit in this strategy tend to reject the notion of a career criminal, not because they reject the idea that the criminal propensity is lodged in a small segment of the population, but because they accept the idea that the criminal propensity is lodged in the great bulk of the population. Whether advanced by economists (the rational choice theory) or by sociologists (social control theory), these explanations of crime share the view that crime occurs naturally in the absence of restraint. Crime, then, is merely natural, unskilled, unrestrained activity, activity carried on without regard to ordinary social or long-range consequences. The person committing criminal acts is thus a person relatively free of concern for the consequences of his acts, a person free to follow the impulse of the moment.

In this view (Hirschi & Gottfredson, 1986), one defining feature of the offender is a short-term orientation, a tendency to pursue immediate pleasure whatever its implications for the future. Another feature of the offender is what Short and Strodtbeck (1965) call social disability, a tendency to experience difficulty in managing the ordinary tasks of life. Such an offender is incapable of pursuing a career in the usual meaning of the term. When he is captured late in his "career" (whether by ordinary enforcement practices or by special repeat offender or career criminal units), it will tend to be for mundane public-order offenses more suggestive of failure than success, more suggestive of self-incapacitation than the need for public intervention. Nothing reviewed in this paper suggests discovery of any fact about crime or criminals contrary to this alternative perspective. Until such facts are discovered, the citizen would be well advised to continue to bolt the door despite the incapacitation of the wicked few.

REFERENCES

Attorney General's Task Force on Violent Crime
   1981   Final Report. Washington, D.C.: U.S. Department of Justice.

Blumstein, Alfred and Jacqueline Cohen
   1979   Estimation of individual crime rates from arrest records. Journal of Criminal
           Law and Criminology 70: 561–585.

Blumstein, Alfred, Jacqueline Cohen, and Paul Hsieh
   1982   The Duration of Adult Criminal Careers. Final Report to the National Insti-
           tute of Justice. Pittsburgh: Carnegie-Mellon University.

Blumstein, Alfred and Elizabeth Graddy
   1981–   Prevalence and recidivism in index arrests: A feedback model. Law and
   1982   Society Review 16: 265–290.

Carbonell, Joyce and Edwin I. Megargee
   nd   Early Identification of Future Career Criminals. Tallahassee: Florida State
           University.

Cohen, Jacqueline
   1984   Incapacitation. University of Illinois Law Review 2: 253.

Empey, LaMar T. and Maynard L. Erickson
   1972   The Provo Experiment. Lexington, MA: Heath

Farrington, David
   1983   Age and Crime. Unpublished. Cambridge: Cambridge University.

Farrington, David, Bernard Gallagher, Lynda Morley, Raymond St. Ledger, and
   Donald J. West
   1985   Cambridge Study in Delinquent Development: Long Term Follow-Up, First
           Annual Report to the Home Office. Cambridge: Cambridge University.

Federal Bureau of Investigation
   1984   Age Specific Arrest Rates. Washington, D.C.: U.S. Department of Justice.

Glueck, Sheldon and Eleanor Glueck
   1940   Juvenile Delinquents Grown Up. New York: Commonwealth Fund.

Greenberg, David
   1985   Age, crime, and social explanation. American Journal of Sociology 91: 1–21.

Hirschi, Travis and Michael Gottfredson
   1983   Age and the explanation of crime. American Journal of Sociology 89:
           552–584.
   1986   The distinction between crime and criminality. In Timothy Hartnagel and
           Robert Silverman (eds.), Critique and Explanation: Essays in Honor of
           Gwynne Nettler. New Jersey: Transaction.

James, Bill
   1980   The Baseball Abstract. New York: Ballantine.

Mednick, Sarnoff and Karl O. Christiansen
   1977   Biosocial Bases of Criminal Behavior. New York: Gardner.

Morris, Norval
   1951   The Habitual Criminal. Cambridge: Harvard University Press.

Murray, Charles and Louis Cox
   1979   Beyond Probation: Juvenile Corrections and the Chronic Delinquent. Beverly
           Hills: Sage.

Petersilia, Joan
  1980   Career criminal research. In Norval Morris and Michael Tonry (eds.), Crime
          and Justice: An Annual Review of Research, Vol. 2. Chicago: University of
          Chicago Press.

Peterson, Mark A., Harriet B. Braiker, and Suzanne M. Polich
  1980   Doing Crime: A Survey of California Prison Inmates. Santa Monica, CA:
          Rand.

Short, James and Fred Strodtbeck
  1965   Group Process and Gang Delinquency. Chicago: University of Chicago Press.

Tracy, Paul E., Marvin E. Wolfgang. and Robert M. Figlio
  1985   Delinquency in Two Birth Cohorts. Washington, D.C.: U.S. Department of
          Justice.

U.S. Department of Justice
  1983   Incapacitating Criminals: Recent Research Findings. Research in Brief. Wash-
          ington. D.C.: National Institute of Justice.
  1985a   Sponsored Research Programs, Fiscal Year 1986. Washington, D.C.: National
          Institute of Justice.
  1985b   Crime in the United States. 1983. Washington, D.C.: U.S. Government Print-
          ing Office.

Van den Haag, Ernest
  1982   Could successful rehabilitation reduce the crime rate? Journal of Criminal Law
          and Criminology 73: 1022–1035.

Walker, Samuel
  1985   Sense and Nonsense about Crime. Monterey: Brooks/Cole.

Wilson, James Q.
  1982   Memorandum to Deputy Attorney General Edward C. Schmults, May 24.

Wilson, James Q. and Richard Herrnstein
  1985   Crime and Human Nature. New York: Simon and Schuster.

Wolfgang, Marvin, Robert Figlio, and Thorsten Sellin
  1972   Delinquency in a Birth Cohort. Chicago: University of Chicago Press.

SECTION III

Life-Course Theories of Criminal Behavior

Life-course theories of criminal behavior have emerged in recent years from a variety of social science disciplines. Although these theories differ to varying degrees, they all recognize how influences can dynamically shape offending behavior over the life course. Many of these theories recognize that events and circumstances can materially alter criminal behavior over time. Moreover, some life-course theories of criminal behavior pay particular attention to whether turning points or events (e.g., marriage, job, childbirth, etc.) alter offending pathways. Life-course theories systematically examine the multitude of causal influences that shape offending behavior over time.

This section presents two contemporary life-course theories. The first selection, by psychologist Terrie Moffitt, represents a theory that identifies two distinct groups of offenders with unique features and explains their offending behavior. The two typologies, termed adolescent-limited offenders and life-course-persistent offenders, have distinct age-crime curves that magnify particular aspects of their antisocial behavior. The adolescent-limited typology captures both the upsurge of delinquency during adolescence as well as the remarkable downswing soon thereafter as adulthood approaches. According to Moffitt, the causal forces leading to adolescent-limited offending include an expanding maturity gap that magnifies the difference between adolescents' biological and social maturity. Many adolescents become frustrated by their inability to have adult privileges. While experiencing status frustration, some adolescents become susceptible to the negative influences of delinquent peers. Through a process of social mimicry and observational learning, adolescent-limited offenders engage in delinquency.

Moffitt's life-course-persistent typology recognizes that a small number of individuals are at risk for early delinquent participation, as well as serious and chronic offending. According to her theory, life-course persisters exhibit anti-social tendencies in early childhood that become amplified in certain familial and structural contexts, including poor neighborhoods and families with ineffective parental management. The combination of initial antisocial tendencies (e.g., difficult temperament, neuropsychological risks, etc.), and structural and familial deficits contribute to the formulation of an antisocial personality. Life-course persisters have limited academic success, and due to their antisocial interactional styles, are often marginalized in the elementary school environment. As a result of these accumulating risks, life-course-persistent offenders are at risk for early involvement in delinquency, drug use, and other antisocial behaviors.

The other theory discussed in this section is by criminologists Robert Sampson and John Laub. Building on the social control theory of Travis Hirschi, Sampson and Laub argue that despite the strong relationships between early childhood antisocial behavior, delinquency, and adult criminality, there are also important events and conditions that alter and redirect criminal pathways. Their theory of informal social control comprises three separate themes. First, they recognize that structural factors impact the development of social bonds. They argue, for example, that structural conditions such as poverty diminish the quality of parenting and other family processes, and together with weak ties to school, increase delinquency. Second, they argue that there is much stability in antisocial behavior across the lifespan. The combination of social conditions and labeling processes can lead to cumulative disadvantage and continuity in crime. Sampson and Laub also recognize that one of the strongest predictors of future crime is past participation. They observe that adult deviance relates strongly to previous deviant activity in adolescence and early childhood. Third, Sampson and Laub observe that the development of informal social capital in adulthood can alter criminal trajectories toward conformity. They argue that developing both strong social ties to a spouse (i.e., having a strong marriage) and employment commitment and stability can lead to an investment in conformity even among individuals who were seriously antisocial in adolescence and young adulthood.

The papers in this section illustrate some life-course theories of criminal behavior. These theories differ to varying degrees. For example, some life-course theories offer general explanations of criminal behavior, while others suggest that there are specific types of offending that require unique explanations. Both of the theories discussed, however, describe how certain influences shape offending behavior through developmental processes over the life course.

SUGGESTED READINGS

Agnew, R. (1997). Stability and change in crime over the life course: A strain theory explanation. In T. Thornberry (Ed.). *Developmental theories of crime and delinquency: Advances in criminological theory* (Vol. 7). New Brunswick, NJ: Transaction.

Catalano, R. F., & Hawkins, J. D. (1996). The social development model: A theory of antisocial behavior. In J. D. Hawkins (Ed.). *Delinquency and crime: Current theories.* New York: Cambridge University Press.

Hagan, J. (1997). Crime and capitalization: Toward a developmental theory of street crime in America. In T. Thornberry (Ed.). *Developmental theories of crime and delinquency: Advances in criminological theory* (Vol. 7). New Brunswick, NJ: Transaction.

Patterson, G., & Yoerger, K. (1993). Developmental models for delinquent behavior. In S. Hodgins (Ed.), *Mental disorder and crime.* Newbury Park, CA: Sage.

Thornberry, T. (1987). Toward an interactional theory of delinquency. *Criminology, 25,* 863–891.

5

Adolescence-Limited and Life-Course-Persistent Antisocial Behavior

A Developmental Taxonomy*

TERRIE E. MOFFITT

ABSTRACT   A dual taxonomy is presented to reconcile 2 incongruous facts about antisocial behavior: (a) It shows impressive continuity over age, but (b) its prevalence changes dramatically over age, increasing almost 10-fold temporarily during adolescence. This article suggests that delinquency conceals 2 distinct categories of individuals, each with a unique natural history and etiology: A small group engages in antisocial behavior of 1 sort or another at every life stage, whereas a larger group is antisocial only during adolescence. According to the theory of *life-course-persistent* antisocial behavior, children's neuropsychological problems interact cumulatively with their criminogenic environments across development, culminating in a pathological personality. According to the theory of *adolescence-limited* antisocial behavior, a contemporary maturity gap encourages teens to mimic antisocial behavior in ways that are normative and adjustive.

There are marked individual differences in the stability of antisocial behavior. Many people behave antisocially, but their antisocial behavior is temporary and situational. In contrast, the antisocial behavior of some people is very stable and persistent. Temporary, situational antisocial behavior is quite common in the population, especially among adolescents. Persistent,

SOURCE: *Psychological Review*, Vol. 100, No. 4, pp. 674–701. © 1993 by the American Psychological Association. Reprinted by permission.

*Work on this article was supported by the Violence and Traumatic Stress Branch of the National Institute of Mental Health (Grants MH43746, MH45070, and MH45548) and by the Program on Human Development and Antisocial Behavior, a joint project of the MacArthur Foundation and the National Institute of Justice. During writing, I was hosted by the Institute for Personality Assessment and Research of the University of California at Berkeley.

Without the persistent help of Avshalom Caspi, this article would not have been done. Other colleagues also helped to hone the ideas: Thomas Achenbach, Robert Cairns, Felton Earls, David Farrington, Bill Henry, Ben Lahey, Richard Linster, Rolf Loeber, stable antisocial behavior is found among a relatively small number of males whose behavior problems are also quite extreme. The central tenet of this article is that temporary versus persistent antisocial persons constitute two qualitatively distinct types of persons. In particular, I suggest that juvenile delinquency conceals two qualitatively distinct categories of individuals, each in need of its own distinct theoretical explanation.

Of course, systems for classifying types of antisocial persons have been introduced before (e.g., American Psychiatric Association, 1987; Chaiken & Chaiken, 1984; Hare, Hart, & Harpur, 1991; Jesness & Haapanen, 1982; Lahey et al., 1990; Megargee, 1976; Moffitt, 1990a; Quay, 1966; Warren, 1969). However, none of these classifications has acquired the ascendency necessary to guide mainstream criminology and psychopathology research. Indeed, "general" theories of crime (e.g., Gottfredson & Hirschi, 1990), comparisons of delinquent versus nondelinquent groups (e.g., Feehan, Stanton, McGee, Silva & Moffitt, 1990), and arraying samples of subjects along antisocial dimensions (e.g., Fergusson, Horwood, & Lloyd, 1991) remain the status quo.

Previous antisocial classification schemes may have failed to capture the imaginations of social scientists because, although they provided more or less accurate behavioral descriptions of antisocial subtypes, they offered relatively little in the way of etiological or predictive validity (Morey, 1991). A classification becomes a taxonomy if it engenders assertions about origins and outcomes by weaving a nomological net of relationships between the taxa and their correlates (Meehl & Golden, 1982). A taxon carries a network of meaning over and above a behavioral description; it includes implications for etiology, course, prognosis, treatment, and relations with other taxa. Previous classifications of antisocial behavior have not been extended into theories, and "it is theory that provides the glue that holds a classification together and gives it both its scientific and its clinical relevance" (Milton, 1991, p. 257; Quine, 1977). In this article, I elaborate on the distinction between temporary and persistent antisocial behavior and offer a pair of new developmental theories of criminal behavior that are based on this distinction. The theories are accompanied by refutable predictions.

If correct, this simple typology can serve a powerful organizing function, with important implications for theory and research on the causes of crime. For delinquents whose criminal activity is confined to the adolescent years, the causal factors may be proximal, specific to the period of adolescent development, and theory must account for the *dis*continuity in their lives. In contrast, for persons whose adolescent delinquency is merely one infliction in a continuous lifelong antisocial course, a theory of antisocial behavior must locate its causal factors early in their childhoods and must explain the continuity in their troubled lives.

Gerald Patterson, Steven Raudenbusch, Albert Reiss, Jr., Lee Robins, Robert Sampson, Richard Tremblay, Christy Visher, and Jennifer White. Ericka Overgard prepared the figures and edited the article.

Correspondence concerning this article should be addressed to Terrie E. Moffitt, Department of Psychology, University of Wisconsin at Madison, Madison, Wisconsin 53706-1611.

The dual taxonomy (and its two theories) that I propose in this article is best introduced with reference to the mysterious relationship between age and antisocial behavior. This relationship is at once the most robust and least understood empirical observation in the field of criminology.

AGE AND ANTISOCIAL BEHAVIOR

When official rates of crime are plotted against age, the rates for both prevalence and incidence of offending appear highest during adolescence; they peak sharply at about age 17 and drop precipitously in young adulthood. The majority of criminal offenders are teenagers; by the early 20s, the number of active offenders decreases by over 50%, and by age 28, almost 85% of former delinquents desist from offending (Blumstein & Cohen, 1987; Farrington, 1986). With slight variations, this general relationship between age and crime obtains among males and females, for most types of crimes, during recent historical periods and in numerous Western nations (Hirschi & Gottfredson, 1983). A prototype of the empirical curve of criminal offenses over age is shown in Figure 5.1.

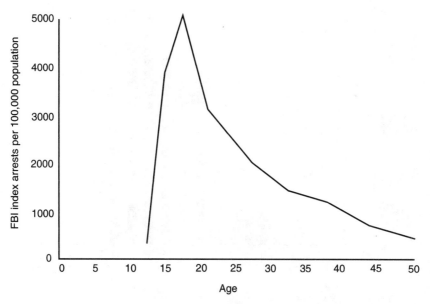

FIGURE 5.1 Age-specific arrest rates for United States Federal Bureau of Investigation's (FBI) index offenses in 1980. Index offenses include homicide, forcible rape, robbery, aggravated assault, burglary, larceny, and auto theft.

Source: From "Criminal Career Research: Its Value for Criminology" by A. Blumstein, J. Cohen, and D. P. Farrington, 1988, *Criminology, 26,* p. 11. Copyright 1988 by the American Society of Criminology.

Until recently, research on age and crime has relied on official data, primarily arrest and conviction records. As a result, the left-hand side of the age–crime curve has been censored. Indeed, in many empirical comparisons between early-onset and late-onset antisocial behavior, *early* has been artifactually defined as mid-adolescence on the basis of first police arrest or court conviction (cf. Farrington, Loeber, Elliott, et al., 1990; Tolan, 1987). However, research on childhood conduct disorder has now documented that antisocial behavior begins long before the age when it is first encoded in police data banks. Indeed, it is now known that the steep decline in antisocial behavior between ages 17 and 30 is mirrored by a steep incline in antisocial behavior between ages 7 and 17 (Loeber, Stouthamer-Loeber, Van Kammen, & Farrington, 1989; Wolfgang, Figlio, & Sellin, 1972). This extension to the age–crime curve is plotted in Figure 5.2. Furthermore, we may venture across disciplinary boundaries to add developmental psychologists' reports of

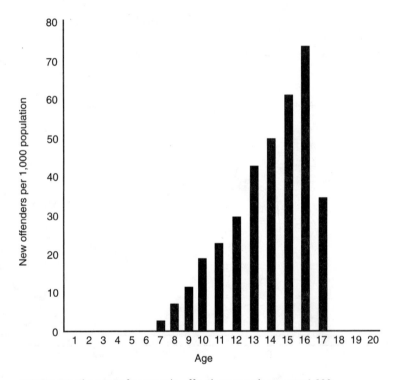

FIGURE 5.2 The rate of new male offenders at each age per 1,000 male population. Onset of offending was defined as the age at which a child was first taken into custody and designated delinquent by the police. Rates are based on a cohort of 9,945 boys born in 1945 in Philadelphia, Pennsylvania.

Source: From *Delinquency In a Birth Cohort* (p. 132) by M. E. Wolfgang, R. M. Figlio, and T. Sellin, 1972, Chicago: The University of Chicago Press. Copyright 1972 by The University of Chicago. Adapted by permission.

childhood aggression (Pepler & Rubin, 1991) and mental health researchers' reports of conduct disorder (Kazdin, 1987) to criminologists' studies of self-reported delinquency and official crime. So doing, it became obvious that manifestations of antisocial behavior emerge very early in the life course and remain present thereafter.

With the advent of alternate measurement strategies, most notably self-reports of deviant behavior, researchers have learned that arrest statistics merely reflect the tip of the deviance iceberg (Hood & Sparks, 1970; Klein, 1989). Actual rates of illegal behavior soar so high during adolescence that participation in delinquency appears to be a normal part of teen life (Elliott, Ageton, Huizinga, Knowles, & Canter, 1983). With the liberty of some artistic license, the curved line plotted in Figure 5.3 may be taken to represent what is currently known about the prevalence of antisocial behaviors over the life course.

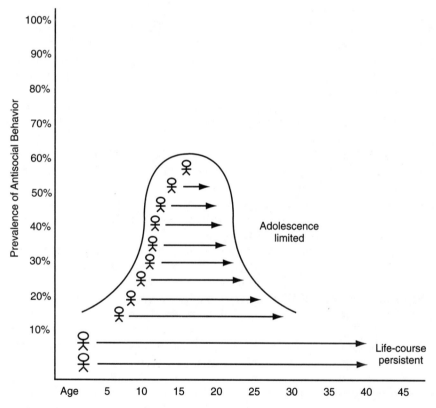

FIGURE 5.3 Hypothetical illustration of the changing prevalence of participation in antisocial behavior across the life course. (The solid line represents the known curve of crime over age. The arrows represent the duration of participation in antisocial behavior by individuals.)

Although there is widespread agreement about the curve of crime over age, there are few convincing explanations for the shape of the curve. Until recently, scholars still disagreed about whether the adolescent peak represented a change in prevalence or a change in incidence. Does adolescence bring an increment in the number of people who are willing to offend or does the small and constant number of offenders simply generate more criminal acts while they are adolescent? Empirical evaluations now suggest that the former explanation is correct. In his English study of offense rates over age, Farrington (1983) showed that the adolescent peak reflects a temporary increase in the number of people involved in antisocial behavior, not a temporary acceleration in the offense rates of individuals. This finding has been replicated in American samples (Wolfgang, Thornberry, & Figlio, 1987). The small human figures under the curve of Figure 5.3 portray these changes in prevalence.

But whence the increase in the prevalence of offenders? One possibility is that some phenomenon unique to adolescent development causes throngs of new adolescent offenders to temporarily join the few stable antisocial individuals in their delinquent ways. Figure 5.3 depicts the typological thesis to be argued here. A small group of persons is shown engaging in antisocial behavior of one sort or another at every stage of life. I have labeled these persons *life-course-persistent* to reflect the continuous course of their antisocial behavior. A larger group of persons fills out the age–crime curve with crime careers of shorter duration. I have labeled these persons *adolescence-limited* to reflect their more temporary involvement in antisocial behavior. Thus, timing and duration of the course of antisocial involvement are the defining features in the natural histories of the two proposed types of offenders.

Two oft-cited rules of thumb asserted by Robins (1978) seems to simultaneously assert and deny the life-course stability of antisocial behavior: "Adult antisocial behavior virtually *requires* childhood antisocial behavior [yet] most antisocial youths do *not* become antisocial adults" (p. 611). In fact, research has shown that antisocial behavior is remarkably stable across time and circumstances for some persons but decidedly unstable for most other people.

The stability of antisocial behavior is closely linked to its extremity. The extreme frequency of crime committed by a very few males is impressive; it has been repeatedly shown that the most persistent 5% or 6% of offenders are responsible for about 50% of known crimes (see Farrington, Ohlin, & Wilson, 1986, for a review). In their study of 10,000 men, Wolfgang et al. (1972) found that 6% of offenders accounted for more than half of the crimes committed by the sample; relative to other offenders, these high-rate offenders began their criminal careers earlier and continued them for more years. The relationship between stability and extremity is found in samples of children as well. In his analysis of a sample of third-grade boys, Patterson (1982) found that the most aggressive 5% of the boys constituted the most persistent group as well; 39% of them ranked above the 95th percentile on aggression 10 years later, and 100% of them were still above the median. Similarly, Loeber (1982) has reviewed research showing that stability of youngsters' antisocial behavior across time is linked with stability across situations and that both forms of stability are characteristic of a relatively small group of persons with extremely antisocial behavior.

Thus, in defiance of regression to the mean, a group of extremely antisocial persons remain extreme on measures taken at later ages and in different situations. Among other persons, however, temporary and situational manifestations of antisocial behavior (even to severe levels) may be quite common.

This point is vividly illustrated in a longitudinal investigation of a representative cohort of 1,037 New Zealand children born in 1972–1973. In this sample, I compared the base rates of persistent and temporary antisocial behavior problems (Moffitt, 1991). I identified a group of boys whose antisocial behavior was rated above average at each of seven biennial assessments (ages 3, 5, 7, 9, 11, 13, and 15). The boys were also rated as very antisocial by three different reporting agents (parents, teachers, and self). Five percent of the boys in the sample met these selection criteria. As a group, their mean antisocial ratings were more than a standard deviation above the norm for boys at every age. In contrast, fully two thirds of the remaining boys were rated above average on antisocial checklists as well but at only one or two ages or by only one reporter, illustrating that stability cannot be inferred from cross-sectional measures of extremity (Henry, Moffitt, Robins, Earls, & Silva, 1993). A disproportionate amount of the measured stability in the New Zealand sample could be attributed to the 5% of boys whose antisocial behavior was both extreme and consistent. For example, when these few boys were excluded from calculations, the 8-year stability coefficient for teacher ratings was reduced from .28 ($R^2 =$ .078) to .16 ($R^2 = .025$), indicating that 5% of the sample accounted for 68% of the sample's stability. (If antisocial behavior had been a stable characteristic throughout the sample, with most boys retaining their relative standing in the group across time, then excluding the top 5% of the sample should not have affected the stability coefficient.) In summary, there appear to be noteworthy individual differences in the stability of antisocial behavior.

I have alluded to the small number of persons in the general population whose antisocial behavior is life-course-persistent. In fact, epidemiological research has shown that there is remarkable uniformity in the prevalence rates of different manifestations of severe antisocial behavior: Regardless of their age, under 10% of males warrant an "official" antisocial designation. For example, about 5% of preschool boys are considered by their parents or caretakers to be "very difficult to manage" (McGee, Partridge, Williams, & Silva, 1991). The prevalence of conduct disorder among elementary-school-aged boys has been found to be between 4% and 9% in several countries (Costello, 1989; Rutter, Tizard, & Whitmore, 1970). About 6% of boys are first arrested by police as preteens (Moffitt & Silva, 1988c; Wolfgang et al., 1972); such early arrest is important because it is the best predictor of long-term recidivistic offending. The rate of conviction for a violent offense in young adult males is between 3% and 6% (Moffitt, Mednick, & Gabrielli, 1989), and about 4% of male adolescents self-report sustained careers of serious violence (three or more violent offenses per year for 5 years; Elliott, Huizinga, & Morse, 1986). Finally, the prevalence of men with antisocial personality disorder is estimated at about 4% to 5% (Davison & Neale, 1990; Robins, 1985).

It is possible, of course, that the persons who constitute these epidemiological statistics at different ages are all different individuals. However, the longitudinal data suggest otherwise: It is more likely that the remarkable constancy of prevalence rates reflects the reoccurrence of the same life-course-persistent individuals in different antisocial categories at different ages. Robins (1966, 1978) has shown that there are virtually no subjects with adult antisocial personality disorder who did not also have conduct disorder as children. White, Moffitt, Earls, Robins, and Silva (1990) found notable continuity from disobedient and aggressive behavior at age 3 to later childhood conduct disorder and thence to arrest by police in the early teen years. Loeber (1982) reviewed research that pinpoints a first arrest between ages 7 and 11 as particularly important for predicting long-term adult offending. Hare and McPherson (1984) have reported that a conviction for violence in the early 20s is characteristic of almost all men who become diagnosed with antisocial (psychopathic) personality disorder.

There are still gaps in the epidemiological database; each of the earlier cited studies connected only two or three points in the life course. Nonetheless, the consistency is impressive: A substantial body of longitudinal research consistently points to a very small group of males who display high rates of antisocial behavior across time and in diverse situations. The professional nomenclature may change, but the faces remain the same as they drift through successive systems aimed at curbing their deviance: schools, juvenile-justice programs, psychiatric treatment centers, and prisons. The topography of their behavior may change with changing opportunities, but the underlying disposition persists throughout the life course.

Whereas a few males evidence antisocial behavior that emerges in toddlerhood and is persistent thereafter, the majority of boys who become antisocial first do so during adolescence (Elliott, Knowles, & Canter, 1981). This tidal wave of adolescent onset has been studied in the aforementioned representative sample of New Zealand boys (Moffitt, 1991). Between ages 11 and 15, about one third of the sample joined the delinquent life-styles of the 5% of boys who had shown stable and pervasive antisocial behavior since preschool. As a group, these adolescent newcomers to antisocial ways had not formerly exceeded the normative levels of antisocial behavior for boys at ages 3, 5, 7, 9, or 11. Despite their lack of prior experience, by age 15, the newcomers equaled their preschool-onset antisocial peers in the variety of laws they had broken, the frequency with which they broke them, and the number of times they appeared in juvenile court (Moffitt, 1991). On the basis of such commonly used indexes of adolescent delinquency, the two delinquent groups were indistinguishable. Thus, if the sample was viewed only as an adolescent cross section, researchers would lose sight of the two delinquent groups' very different developmental histories, seeing only delinquents and nondelinquents.

Indeed, researchers and practitioners cannot yet effectively assign individual delinquent adolescents to meaningful subtypes on the basis of cross-sectional "snapshots" of their antisocial behavior during adolescence (Loeber & LeBlanc,

1990; Moffitt, 1990a). Again, the New Zealand sample provides an example: At age 15, both the childhood-persistent and adolescent-onset groups had members who scored more than 5 standard deviations above the mean on self-report delinquency, and by age 19 both groups had some members with more than 50 convictions for crimes in the New Zealand courts. Elliott and Huizinga (1984) reported similarly poor classification in a representative sample of American teens. They attempted to discriminate, at the time of first arrest, individual future career offenders from adolescence-limited offenders. Discrimination could not be improved beyond chance by entering the kinds of information typically available to officials: type of current offense, age, sex, race, class, involvement with delinquent peers, and attitudes toward deviance. Addition of measures of the extremity of self-reported delinquency and emotional problems improved prediction only 7% beyond chance. Earlier, I noted that the stability of antisocial behavior implies its extremity but that extremity does not imply stability; measures of the frequency or seriousness of adolescent offending will not discriminate very well between life-course-persistent and adolescence-limited delinquents. On the basis of their study and others, Elliott and Huizinga concluded that there is "no effective means for discriminating between the serious career offenders and nonserious offenders" (p. 98). A notable feature of the taxonomy introduced in this article is that knowledge of a subject's preadolescent behavior is *required* for making the differential diagnosis between the life-course-persistent and adolescence-limited types of antisocial teenager. Longitudinal designs are needed to collect the lifetime repeated measures that are needed to distinguish individual differences in the developmental course of antisocial behavior.[1]

I have argued in this section that juvenile delinquency conceals two categories of people. A very large group participates in antisocial behavior during adolescence. A much smaller group, who continues serious antisocial behavior throughout adulthood, is the same group whose antisocial behavior was stable across the years from early childhood. The categories remain hypothetical types, because no longitudinal study has yet repeatedly measured antisocial behavior in a representative sample of the same individuals from preschool to midlife. I describe in the next sections the two hypothetical types of antisocial youth: life-course-persistent and adolescence-limited. I argue that the two

---

[1]It may be countered that research has distinguished delinquent subtypes that are based on cross-sectional information. For example, the delinquent behaviors of the life-course-persistent type may be distinguished by relatively more overt aggression, whereas the adolescence-limited type may show relatively more covert offending under peer influence. I agree. Factor-analytic studies have revealed an aggressive "undersocialized" factor and a "socialized" peer-oriented factor (Quay, 1964a, 1964b, 1966), and meta-analytic studies have revealed "overt" and "covert" offense patterns (Loeber & Schmaling, 1985). However, such scale pairs are highly and positively correlated in adolescent samples, in which the evidence for offense versatility outweighs evidence for offense specialization (Klein, 1984; Robins, 1978). Cross-sectional classification has not proven effective at the level of the individual. My assertion that developmental history is needed for confident classification is buttressed by the repeated finding that age of onset of antisocial behavior problems is the single best predictor of adult criminal outcomes (Farrington, Loeber, Elliott, et al., 1990).

groups differ in etiology, developmental course, prognosis, and, importantly, classification of their behavior as either pathological or normative. The goal of this article is to proffer a description of the two types in the form of a set of testable predictions.

LIFE-COURSE-PERSISTENT ANTISOCIAL BEHAVIOR

My account of the life-course-persistent antisocial type follows this plan: In the first section, *Continuity of Antisocial Behavior Defined,* I provide a definition and description of persistent antisocial behavior. In the second section, *Beginnings: Neuropsychological Risk for Difficult Temperament and Behavioral Problems,* I present the hypothesis that persistent antisocial behavior has its origins in an interaction between children's neuropsychological vulnerabilities and criminogenic environments. In the third section, *Maintenance and Elaboration Over the Life Course: Cumulative Continuity, Contemporary Continuity, and Narrowing Options for Change,* I introduce the cumulative and contemporary processes that maintain antisocial behavior across time and that expand antisocial behavior into a pervasive adult life-style. In the fourth section, I summarize the theory's perspective on continuity, and in the fifth section, I make a case that life-course-persistent antisocial behavior is a form of psychopathology.

Continuity of Antisocial Behavior Defined

As implied by the label, continuity is the hallmark of the small group of life-course-persistent antisocial persons. Across the life course, these individuals exhibit changing manifestations of antisocial behavior: biting and hitting at age 4, shoplifting and truancy at age 10, selling drugs and stealing cars at age 16, robbery and rape at age 22, and fraud and child abuse at age 30; the underlying disposition remains the same, but its expression changes form as new social opportunities arise at different points in development. This pattern of continuity across age is matched also by cross-situational consistency: Life-course-persistent antisocial persons lie at home, steal from shops, cheat at school, fight in bars, and embezzle at work (Farrington, 1991; Loeber, 1982; Loeber & Baicker-McKee, 1989; Robins, 1966, 1978; White et al., 1990).

The concept of behavioral coherence, or *heterotypic continuity,* is invoked here to extend observations of continuity beyond the mere persistence of a single behavior to encompass a variety of antisocial expressions that emerge as development affords new opportunities. Heterotypic continuity refers to continuity of an inferred trait or attribute that is presumed to underlie diverse phenotypic behaviors (Kagan, 1969). As Kagan and Moss (1962) suggested, a specific behavior in childhood might not be predictive of phenotypically similar behavior later in adulthood, but it may still be associated with behaviors that are *conceptually* consistent with the earlier behavior.

Examples of heterotypic continuities have been reported by Ryder (1967), who found that childhood aggression, physical adventurousness, and nonconformity were related to adult sexual behavior. Another example of coherence is provided in a 22-year follow-up study of men and women who had been rated as aggressive by their peers in late childhood (Huesmann, Eron, Lefkowitz, & Walder, 1984). As adults, the men were likely to commit serious criminal acts, abuse their spouses, and drive while intoxicated, whereas the women were likely to punish their offspring severely. Another example of personality coherence is the finding that the developmental antecedents of erratic work histories may be found in phenotypically dissimilar attributes of difficult temperament in childhood (Caspi, Elder, & Bem, 1987). In addition, in their hallmark study, West and Farrington (1977) observed that stealing, alcohol abuse, sexual promiscuity, reckless driving, and violence were linked across the life course. The prognosis for the life-course-persistent person is bleak: Drug and alcohol addiction; unsatisfactory employment; unpaid debts; homelessness; drunk driving; violent assault; multiple and unstable relationships; spouse battery; abandoned, neglected, or abused children; and psychiatric illness have all been reported at very high rates for offenders who persist past the age of 25 (Farrington & West, 1990; Robins, 1966; Sampson & Laub, 1990). Thus, this theory of life-course-persistent antisocial behavior predicts continuity across the entire life course but allows that the underlying disposition will change its manifestation when age and social circumstances alter opportunities.

Although reports of the continuity of antisocial styles from childhood to young adulthood abound, the outcomes of antisocial individuals during midlife have seldom been examined. The pattern of official crime over age (Figure 5.1) implies that criminal offending all but disappears by midlife,[2] but there is no reason to expect that life-course-persistents miraculously assume prosocial tendencies after an antisocial tenure of several decades. Indeed, criminal psychopaths decrease their number of arrestable offenses at about age 40, but the constellation of antisocial personality traits described by Cleckley (1976) persists in male samples at least until age 69 (Harper & Hare, 1991). As I argue in the third section of this article (*Maintenance*), an analysis of the cumulative developmental forces underlying the continuity of aggression from childhood to adulthood will predict continuity on into midlife as well. Beyond young adulthood, the antisocial disposition of life-course-persistents may be expressed in a form that is simply not yet well measured by epidemiological surveys of official crime: One such possibility is neglect and abuse of family

---

[2]The conclusion that crime ceases in midlife may be premature; it is based on cross-sectional age comparisons of arrest and conviction rates. There are at least four reasons to doubt the conclusions that have been based on this method. First, official records underestimate the amount of true crime. Second, there may be justice-system biases toward underarrest and prosecution of older persons. Third, death and imprisonment may selectively remove persistent offenders from official crime statistics. Fourth, cross-cohort comparisons may mistake generational effects for age effects (Rowe & Tittle, 1977). Thus, until longitudinal researchers collect self-reports of crime in the same individuals from adolescence to old age, the midlife disappearance of crime will remain an empirical question.

members. Consistent with this hypothesis, Farrington and West (1990) found that half of the persistent offenders in the Cambridge longitudinal study self-reported having hit their spouses when they were interviewed at age 32. Fagan and Wexler (1987) reviewed studies showing that spouse battery is often preceded by a history of violence against strangers. Also, crime statistics show that, whereas property crimes peak in the teen years and drop thereafter, family violence offenses show a steady increase with age (Gottfredson & Hirschi, 1986). Research is needed that follows offenders into late adulthood while measuring multiple indicators of an antisocial life-style.

Beginnings: Neuropsychological Risk for Difficult Temperament and Behavioral Problems

If some individuals' antisocial behavior is stable from pre-school to adulthood as the data imply, then investigators are compelled to look for its roots early in life, in factors that are present before or soon after birth. It is possible that the etiological chain begins with some factor capable of producing individual differences in the neuropsychological functions of the infant nervous system. Factors that influence infant neural development are myriad, and many of them have been empirically linked to antisocial outcomes.

One possible source of neuropsychological variation that is linked to problem behavior is disruption in the ontogenesis of the fetal brain. Minor physical anomalies, which are thought to be observable markers for hidden anomalies in neural development, have been found at elevated rates among violent offenders and subjects with antisocial personality traits (Fogel, Mednick, & Michelson, 1985; E. Kandel, Brennan, & Mednick, 1989; Paulhus & Martin, 1986). Neural development may be disrupted by maternal drug abuse, poor prenatal nutrition, or pre- or postnatal exposure to toxic agents (Needleman & Beringer, 1981; Rodning, Beckwith, & Howard, 1989; Stewart, 1983). Even brain insult suffered because of complications during delivery has been empirically linked to later violence and antisocial behavior in carefully designed longitudinal studies (E. Kandel & Mednick, 1991; Szatmari, Reitsma-Street, & Offord, 1986). In addition, some individual differences in neuropsychological health are heritable in origin (Borecki & Ashton, 1984; Martin, Jardine, & Eaves, 1984; Plomin, Nitz, & Rowe, 1990; Tambs, Sundet, & Magnus, 1984; Vandenberg, 1969). Just as parents and children share facial resemblances, they share some structural and functional similarities within their nervous systems. After birth, neural development may be disrupted by neonatal deprivation of nutrition, stimulation, and even affection (Cravioto & Arrieta, 1983; Kraemer, 1988; Meany, Aitken, van Berkel, Bhatnagar, & Sapolsky, 1988). Some studies have pointed to child abuse and neglect as possible sources of brain injury in the histories of delinquents with neuropsychological impairment (Lewis, Shanok, Pincus, & Glaser, 1979; Milner & McCanne, 1991; Tarter, Hegedus, Winsten, & Alterman, 1984).

There is good evidence that children who ultimately become persistently antisocial do suffer from deficits in neuropsychological abilities. I have elsewhere reviewed the available empirical and theoretical literatures; the link between neuropsychological impairment and antisocial outcomes is one of the most robust effects in the study of antisocial behavior (Moffitt, 1990b; Moffitt & Henry, 1991; see also Hirschi & Hindelang, 1977). Two sorts of neuropsychological deficits are empirically associated with antisocial behavior: verbal and "executive" functions. The verbal deficits of antisocial children are pervasive, affecting receptive listening and reading, problem solving, expressive speech, and writing, and memory. In addition, executive deficits produce what is sometimes referred to as a comportmental learning disability (Price, Daffner, Stowe, & Mesulam, 1990), including symptoms such as inattention and impulsivity. These cognitive deficits and antisocial behavior share variance that is independent of social class, race, test motivation, and academic attainment (Moffitt, 1990b; Lynam, Moffitt, & Stouthamer-Loeber, 1993). In addition, the relation is not an artifact of slow-witted delinquents' greater susceptibility to detection by police; undetected delinquents have weak cognitive skills too (Moffitt & Silva, 1988a).

The evidence is strong that neuropsychological deficits are linked to the kind of antisocial behavior that begins in childhood and is sustained for lengthy periods. In a series of articles (Moffitt, 1990a; Moffitt & Henry, 1989; Moffitt & Silva, 1988b), I have shown that poor verbal and executive functions are associated with antisocial behavior, if it is extreme and persistent. In these studies, adolescent New Zealand boys who exhibited symptoms of both conduct disorder and attention-deficit disorder with hyperactivity (ADDH) scored very poorly on neuropsychological tests of verbal and executive functions and had histories of extreme antisocial behavior that persisted from age 3 to age 15. Apparently, their neuropsychological deficits were as long standing as their antisocial behavior; at ages 3 and 5 these boys has scored more than a standard deviation below the age norm for boys on the Bayley and McCarthy tests of motor coordination and on the Stanford-Binet test of cognitive performance. Contrast groups of boys with single diagnoses of either conduct disorder of ADDH did not have neuropsychological deficits or cognitive-motor delays, but neither were their behavior problems stable over time.

In a study designed to improve on measurement of executive functions (White, Moffitt, Caspi, Jeglum, Needles, & Stouthamer-Loeber, 1994), we gathered data on self-control and impulsivity for 430 Pittsburgh youths. Twelve measures were taken from multiple sources (mother, teacher, self, and observer) by using multiple methods (rating scales, performance tests, computer games, Q sorts, and videotaped observations). A linear composite of the impulsivity measures was strongly related to the 3-year longevity of antisocial behavior, even after controlling for IQ, race, and social class. Boys who were very delinquent from ages 10 to 13 scored significantly higher on impulsivity than both their nondelinquent and temporarily delinquent age-mates. Taken together, the New Zealand and Pittsburgh longitudinal studies suggest that neuropsychological dysfunctions that manifest themselves as poor scores on tests of language and self-control—and as the inattentive, overactive, and impulsive symptoms of ADDH—are linked with the early childhood emergence of aggressive antisocial behavior and with its subsequent persistence.

Neuropsychological Variation and the "Difficult" Infant Before describing how neuropsychological variation might constitute risk for antisocial behavior, it is useful to define what is meant here by neuropsychological. By combining *neuro* with *psychological,* I refer broadly to the extent to which anatomical structures and psychological processes within the nervous system influence psychological characteristics such as temperament, behavioral development, cognitive abilities, or all three. For example, individual variation in brain function may engender differences between children in activity level, emotional reactivity, or self-regulation (temperament); speech, motor coordination, or impulse control (behavioral development); and attention, language, learning, memory, or reasoning (cognitive abilities).

Children with neurological difficulties severe enough to constitute autism, severe physical handicap, or profound mental retardation are usually identified and specially treated by parents and professionals. However, other infants have subclinical levels of problems that affect the difficulty of rearing them, variously referred to as difficult temperament, language or motor delays, or mild cognitive deficits. Compromised neuropsychological functions are associated with a variety of consequences for infants' cognitive and motor development as well as for their personality development (Rothbart & Derryberry, 1981). Toddlers with subtle neuropsychological deficits may be clumsy and awkward, overactive, inattentive, irritable, impulsive, hard to keep on schedule, delayed in reaching developmental milestones, poor at verbal comprehension, deficient at expressing themselves, or slow at learning new things (Rutter, 1977, 1983; Thomas & Chess, 1977; Wender, 1971).

Hertzig (1983) has described an empirical test of the proposed relationship between neurological damage and difficult behavior in infancy. She studied a sample of 66 low-birth-weight infants from intact middle-class families. Symptoms of brain dysfunction detected during neurological examinations were significantly related to an index of difficult temperament taken at ages 1, 2, and 3 (Thomas & Chess, 1977; the index comprised rhythmicity, adaptability, approach–withdrawal, intensity, and mood). The parents of the children with neurological impairment and difficult temperament more often sought help from child psychiatrists as their children grew up, and the most frequent presenting complaints were immaturity, overactivity, temper tantrums, poor attention, and poor school performance. Each of these childhood problems has been linked by research to later antisocial outcomes (cf. Moffitt, 1990a, 1990b). Importantly, the impairments of the children with neural damage were not massive; their mean IQ score was 96 (only 4 points below the population mean). Hertzig's study showed that even subtle neurological deficits can influence an infant's temperament and behavior, the difficulty of rearing the infant, and behavioral problems in later childhood.

Child–Environment Covariation in Nature: A Source of Interactional Continuity Up to this point, I have emphasized in this article the characteristics of the developing child as if environments were held constant. Unfortunately, children with cognitive and temperamental disadvantages are not generally born into supportive environments, nor do they even get a fair chance of being randomly assigned to good or bad environments. Unlike the aforementioned infants in Hertzig's (1983) study of temperament and neuro-logical symptoms, most low-birth-weight infants are not born into intact, middle-class families. Vulnerable infants are disproportionately found in environments that will not be ameliorative because many sources of neural mal-development co-occur with family disadvantage or deviance.

Indeed, because some characteristics of parents and children tend to be correlated, parents of children who are at risk for antisocial behavior often in-advertently provide their children with criminogenic environments (Sameroff & Chandler, 1975). The intergenerational transmission of severe antisocial behavior has been carefully documented in a study of three generations (Huesmann et al., 1984). In that study of 600 subjects, the stability of individ-uals' aggressive behavior from age 8 to age 30 was exceeded by the stability of aggression across the generations: from grandparent to parent to child. Thus, with regard to risk for antisocial behavior, nature does not follow a 2 × 2 design with equal cell sizes.

Parents and children resemble each other on temperament and personality. Thus, parents of children who are difficult to manage often lack the necessary psychological and physical resources to cope constructively with a difficult child (Scarr & McCartney, 1983; Snyder & Patterson, 1987). For example, temperamental traits such as activity level and irritability are known to be partly heritable (Plomin, Chipuer, & Loehlin, 1990). This suggests that chil-dren whose hyperactivity and angry outbursts might be curbed by firm disci-pline will tend to have parents who are inconsistent disciplinarians; the parents tend to be impatient and irritable too. The converse is also true: Empirical evi-dence has been found for a relationship between variations in parents' warmth and infants' easiness (Plomin, Chipuer, & Loehlin, 1990).

Parents and children also resemble each other on cognitive ability. The known heritability of measured intelligence (Plomin, 1990; Loehlin, 1989) implies that children who are most in need of remedial cognitive stimulation will have parents who may be least able to provide it. Moreover, parents' cognitive abilities set limits on their own educational and occupational attainment (Barrett & Depinet, 1991). As one consequence, families whose members have below-average cognitive capacities will often be least able financially to obtain profes-sional interventions or optimal remedial schooling for their at-risk children.

Even the social and structural aspects of the environment may be stacked against children who enter the world at risk. Plomin and Bergeman (1990) have shown that there are genetic components to measures that are commonly used by developmental psychologists to assess socialization environments. For exam-ple, the Home Observation for Measurement of the Environment scale, the Moos Family Environment scales, and the Holmes and Rahe scales of stressful life events all revealed the influence of heritable factors when they were exam-ined with behavior genetic research designs (Plomin & Bergeman, 1990). Vulnerable children are often subject to adverse homes and neighborhoods because their parents are vulnerable to problems too (cf. Lahey et al., 1990).

Importantly, although examples from behavior genetics research have been cited in the previous three paragraphs, the perverse compounding of children's vulnerabilities with their families' imperfections does not require that the child's neuropsychological risk arose from any genetic disposition. In fact, for my purposes, it is immaterial whether parent–child similarities arise from shared genes or shared homes. A home environment wherein prenatal care is haphazard, drugs are used during pregnancy, and infants' nutritional needs are neglected is a setting where sources of children's neuropsychological dysfunction that are clearly environmental coexist with a criminogenic social environment.

Problem Child–Problem Parent Interactions and the Emergence of Antisocial Behaviors I believe that the juxtaposition of a vulnerable and difficult infant with an adverse rearing context initiates risk for the life-course-persistent pattern of antisocial behavior. The ensuing process is a transactional one in which the challenge of coping with a difficult child evokes a chain of failed parent–child encounters (Sameroff & Chandler, 1975). The assertion that children exert important effects on their social environments is useful in understanding this hypothetical process (Bell & Chapman, 1986). It is now widely acknowledged that personality and behavior are shaped in large measure by interactions between the person and the environment (cf. Buss, 1987; Plomin, DeFries, & Loehlin, 1977; Scarr & McCartney, 1983). One form of interaction may play a particularly important role both in promoting an antisocial style and in maintaining its continuity across the life course: *Evocative* interaction occurs when a child's behavior evokes distinctive responses from others (Caspi et al., 1987).

Children with neuropsychological problems evoke a challenge to even the most resourceful, loving, and patient families. For example, Tinsley and Parke (1983) have reviewed literature showing that low-birth-weight, premature infants negatively influence the behavior of their caretakers; they arrive before parents are prepared, their crying patterns are rated as more disturbing and irritating, and parents report that they are less satisfying to feed, less pleasant to hold, and more demanding to care for than healthy babies. Many parents of preterm infants hold unrealistic expectations about their children's attainment of developmental milestones, and these may contribute to late dysfunctional parent–child relationships (Tinsley & Parke, 1983). More disturbing, an infant's neurological health status has been shown to be related to risk for maltreatment and neglect (Friedrich & Boriskin, 1976; Frodi et al., 1978; Hunter, Kilstrom, Kraybill, & Loda, 1978; Milowe & Lowrie, 1964; Sandgrund, Gaines, & Green, 1974).

Numerous studies have shown that a toddler's problem behaviors may affect the parents' disciplinary strategies as well as subsequent interactions with adults and peers (Bell & Chapman, 1986; Chess & Thomas, 1987). For example, children characterized by a difficult temperament in infancy are more likely to resist their mothers' efforts to control them in early childhood (Lee & Bates, 1985). Similarly, mothers of difficult boys experience more problems in their efforts to socialize their children. Maccoby and Jacklin (1983) showed that over time these mothers reduce their efforts to actively guide and direct their children's behavior and become increasingly less involved in the teaching process. In a study of unrelated mothers and children, K. E. Anderson, Lytton, and Romney (1986) observed conduct-disordered and nonproblem boys interacting with mothers of conduct-disordered and nonproblem sons in unrelated pairs. The conduct-disordered boys evoked more negative reactions from both types of mothers than did normal boys, but the two types of mothers did not differ from each other in their negative reactions. It may well be that early behavioral difficulties contribute to the development of persistent antisocial behavior by evoking responses that exacerbate the child's tendencies (Goldsmith, Bradshaw, & Rieser-Danner, 1986; Lytton, 1990). "The child acts; the environment reacts; and the child reacts back in mutually interlocking evocative interaction" (Caspi et al., 1987, p. 308).

Such a sequence of interactions would be most likely to produce lasting antisocial behavior problems if caretaker reactions were more likely to exacerbate then to ameliorate children's problem behavior. To my knowledge, students of child effects have not yet tested for interactions between child behavior and parental deviance or poor parenting, perhaps because very disadvantaged families are seldom studies with such designs. Nonetheless, some data suggest that children's predispositions toward antisocial behavior may be exacerbated under deviant rearing conditions. In the New Zealand longitudinal study, there was a significant interaction effect between children's neuropsychological deficit and family adversity on one type of delinquent act: aggressive confrontation with a victim or adversary. Among the 536 boys in the sample, the 75 boys who had both low neuropsychological test scores and adverse home environments earned a mean aggression score more than four times greater than that of boys with either neuropsychological problems or adverse homes (Moffitt, 1990b). The index of family adversity included parental characteristics such as poor mental health and low intelligence as well as socioeconomic status. Behavior-genetic adoption studies of antisocial behavior often report a similar pattern of findings, wherein the highest rates of criminal outcomes are found for adoptees whose foster parents, as well as their biological parents, were deviant (e.g., Mednick, Gabrielli, & Hutchings, 1984). Thus, children's predispositions may evoke exacerbating responses from the environment and may also render them more vulnerable to criminogenic environments.

If the child who "steps off on the wrong foot" remains on an ill-starred path, subsequent stepping-stone experiences may culminate in life-course-persistent antisocial behavior. For life-course-persistent antisocial individuals, deviant behavior patterns later in life may thus reflect early individual differences that are perpetuated or exacerbated by interactions with the social environment: first at home, and later at school. Quay (1987) summarized this as "this youth is likely to be at odds with everyone in the environment, and most particularly with those who must interact with him on a daily basis to raise, educate, or otherwise control him. . . . This pattern is the most troublesome to society, seems least amenable to change, and has the most pessimistic prognosis for adult adjustment" (p. 121).

However, inauspicious beginnings do not complete the story. In the New Zealand study, for example, a combination of preschool measures of antisocial behavior and cognitive ability was able to predict 70% of the cases of conduct disorder at age 11 but at the cost of a high false-positive rate (White et al., 1990). The next section explores the specific interactional processes that nourish and augment the life-course-persistent antisocial style beyond childhood.

Maintenance and Elaboration Over the Life Course: Cumulative Continuity, Contemporary Continuity, and Narrowing Options for Change

In the previous section, the concept of evocative person–environment interaction was called on to describe how children's difficult behaviors might affect encounters with their parents. Two additional types of interaction may help to explain how the life-course-persistent individual's problem behavior, once initiated, might promote its own continuity and pervasiveness. *Reactive* interaction occurs when different youngsters exposed to the same environment experience it, interpret it, and react to it in accordance with their particular style. For example, in interpersonal situations where cues are ambiguous, aggressive children are likely to mistakenly attribute harmful intent to others and then act accordingly (Dodge & Frame, 1982). *Proactive* interaction occurs when people select or create environments that support their styles. For example, antisocial individuals appear to be likely to affiliate selectively with antisocial others, even when selecting a mate. Some evidence points to nonrandom mating along personality traits related to antisocial behavior (Buss, 1984), and there are significant spouse correlations on conviction for crimes (e.g., Baker, Mack, Moffitt, & Mednick, 1989).

The three types of person–environment interactions can produce two kinds of consequences in the life course: *cumulative consequences* and *contemporary consequences* (Caspi & Bem, 1990). Early individual differences may set in motion a downhill snowball of cumulative continuities. In addition, individual differences may themselves persist from infancy to adulthood, continuing to influence adolescent and adult behavior in a proximal contemporary fashion. Contemporary continuity arises if the life-course-persistent person continues to carry into adulthood the same underlying constellation of traits that got him into trouble as a child, such as high activity level, irritability, poor self-control, and low cognitive ability.

The roles of cumulative and contemporary continuities in antisocial behavior have been explored by Caspi, Bem, and Elder (1989; Caspi et al., 1987), using data from the longitudinal Berkeley Guidance Study. They identified men who had a history of temper tantrums during late childhood (when tantrums are not developmentally normative). Then they traced the continuities and consequences of this personality style across the subsequent 30 years of the subjects' lives and into multiple diverse life domains: education, employment, and marriage. A major finding was that hot-tempered boys who came from middle-class homes suffered a progressive deterioration of socioeconomic status as they moved through the life course. By age 40, their occupational status was indistinguishable from that of men born into the working class. A majority of them held jobs of lower occupational status than those held by their fathers at a comparable age. Did these men fail occupationally because their earlier ill-temperedness started them down a particular path (cumulative consequences) or because their current ill-temperedness handicapped them in the world of work (contemporary consequences)?

Cumulative consequences were implied by the effect of childhood temper on occupational status at midlife: Tantrums predicted lower educational attainment, and educational attainment, in turn, predicted lower occupational status. Contemporary consequences were implied by the strong direct link between ill-temperedness and occupational stability. Men with childhood tantrums continued to be hot-tempered in adulthood, where it got them into trouble in the world of work. They had more erratic work lives, changing jobs more frequently and experiencing more unemployment between ages 18 and 40. Ill-temperedness also had a contemporary effect on marital stability. Almost half (46%) of the men with histories of childhood tantrums had divorced by age 40 compared with only 22% of other men.

Elsewhere, I describe in detail some of the patterns of interaction between persons and their social environments that may promote antisocial continuity across time and across life domains (Caspi & Moffitt, 1995). Two sources of continuity deserve emphasis here because they narrow the options for change. These processes are (a) failing to learn conventional prosocial alternatives to antisocial behavior and (b) becoming ensnared in a deviant life-style by crime's consequences. These concepts have special implications for the questions of why life-course-persistent individuals fail to desist from delinquency as young adults and why they are so impervious to intervention.

A Restricted Behavioral Repertoire This theory of life-course-persistent antisocial behavior asserts that the causal sequence begins very early and the formative years are dominated by chains of cumulative and contemporary continuity. As a consequence, little opportunity is afforded for the life-course-persistent antisocial individual to learn a behavioral repertoire of prosocial alternatives. Thus, one overlooked and pernicious source of continuity in antisocial behavior is simply a lack of recourse to any other options. In keeping with this prediction, Vitaro, Gagnon, and Tremblay (1990) have shown that aggressive children whose behavioral repertoires consist almost solely of antisocial behaviors are less likely to change over years than are aggressive children whose repertoires comprise some prosocial behaviors as well.

Life-course-persistent persons miss out on opportunities to acquire and practice prosocial alternatives at each stage of development. Children with poor self-control and aggressive behavior are often rejected by peers and adults (Coie, Belding, & Underwood, 1988; Dodge, Coie, & Brakke, 1982; Vitaro et al, 1990). In turn, children who have learned to expect rejection are likely in later settings to withdraw or strike out preemptively, precluding opportunities to affiliate with prosocial peers (Dodge & Newman, 1981; Dodge & Frame, 1982; LaFrenier & Sroufe, 1985; Nasby, Hayden, & DePaulo, 1980). Such children are robbed of chances to practice conventional social skills. Alternatively, consider this sequence of narrowing options: Behavior problems at school and failure to attain basic math and reading skills place a limit on the variety of job skills that can be acquired and thereby cut off options to pursue legitimate employment as an alternative to the underground economy (Farrington, Gallagher, Morley, Ledger, & West, 1986; Maughan, Gray, & Rutter, 1985; Moffitt, 1990a). Simply put, if social and academic skills are not mastered in childhood, it is very difficult to later recover lost opportunities.

Becoming Ensnared by Consequences of Antisocial Behavior Personal characteristics such as poor self-control, impulsivity, and inability to delay gratification increase the risk that antisocial youngsters will make irrevocable decisions that close the door of opportunity. Teenaged parenthood, addiction to drugs of alcohol, school dropout, disabling or disfiguring injuries, patchy work histories, and time spent incarcerated are *snares* that diminish the probabilities of later success by eliminating opportunities for breaking the chain of cumulative continuity (Cairns & Cairns, 1991; J. Q. Wilson & Herrnstein, 1985). Similarly, labels accrued early in life can foreclose later opportunities; an early arrest record or a "bad" reputation may rule out lucrative jobs, higher education, or an advantageous marriage (Farrington, 1977; Klein, 1986; West, 1982). In short, the behavior of life-course-persistent antisocial persons is increasingly maintained and supported by narrowing options for conventional behavior.

Interventions with life-course-persistent persons have met with dismal results (Lipton, Martinson, & Wilks, 1975; Palmer, 1984; Sechrest, White, & Brown, 1979). This is not surprising, considering that most interventions are begun relatively late in the chain of cumulative continuity. The forces of continuity are formidable foes (Caspi & Moffitt, 1993). After a protracted deficient learning history, and after options for change have been eliminated, efforts to suppress antisocial behavior will not automatically bring prosocial behavior to the surface in its place. Now-classic research on learning shows conclusively that efforts to extinguish undesirable behavior will fail unless alternative behaviors are available that will attract reinforcement (Azrin & Holz, 1966). My analysis of increasingly restricted behavioral options suggests the hypothesis that opportunities for change will often be actively transformed by life-course-persistents into opportunities for continuity: Residential treatment programs provide a chance to learn from criminal peers, a new job furnishes the chance to steal, and new romance provides a partner for abuse. This analysis of life-course-persistent antisocial behavior anticipates disappointing outcomes when such antisocial persons are thrust into new situations that purportedly offer the chance "to turn over a new leaf."

The Reason for Persistence:
Traits, Environments, and Developmental Processes

According to some accounts of behavioral continuity, an ever-present underlying trait generates antisocial outcomes at every point in the life span (e.g., Gottfredson & Hirschi, 1990). By other accounts, antisocial behavior is sustained by environmental barriers to change (e.g., Bandura, 1979, pp. 217–224). In this theory of life-course-persistent antisocial behavior, neither traits nor environments account for continuity.

True, the theory begins with a trait: variation between individuals in neuropsychological health. The trait is truly underlying in that it seldom comes to anyone's attention unless an infant is challenged by formal examinations; it is manifested behaviorally as variability in infant temperament, developmental milestones, and cognitive abilities.

Next, the theory brings environments into play. Parents and other people respond to children's difficult temperaments and developmental deficits. In nurturing environments, toddlers' problems are often corrected. However, in disadvantaged homes, schools, and neighborhoods, the responses are more likely to exacerbate than amend. Under such detrimental circumstances, difficult behavior is gradually elaborated into conduct problems and a dearth of prosocial skills. Thus, over the years, an antisocial personality is slowly and insidiously constructed. Likewise, deficits in language and reasoning are incrementally elaborated into academic failure and a dearth of job skills. Over time, accumulating consequences of the youngster's personality problems and academic problems prune away the options for change.

This theory of life-course-persistent antisocial behavior emphasizes the constant process of reciprocal interaction between personal traits and environmental reactions to them. The original attribute is thus elaborated on during development, to become a syndrome that remains conceptually consistent, but that gains new behavioral components (Caspi & Bem, 1990). Through that process, relatively subtle childhood variations in neuropsychological health can be transformed into an antisocial style that pervades all domains of adolescent and adult behavior. It is this infiltration of the antisocial disposition into the multiple domains of a life that diminishes the likelihood of change.

When in the life course does the potential for change dwindle to nil? How many person–environment interactions must accumulate before the life-course-persistent pattern becomes set? I have argued that a person–environment interaction process is needed to predict emerging antisocial behavior, but after some age will the "person" main effect predict adult outcomes alone? An answer to these questions is critical for prevention efforts. The well-documented resistance of antisocial personality disorder to treatments of all kinds seems to suggest that the life-course-persistent style is fixed sometime before age 18 (Suedfeld & Landon, 1978). Studies of crime careers reveal that it is very unusual for males to first initiate crime after adolescence, suggesting that if an adult is going to be antisocial, the pattern must be established by late adolescence (Elliott, Huizinga, & Menard, 1989).[3] At the same time, efforts to

---

[3]Between 9% and 22% of males not arrested as juveniles are arrested as adults, suggesting that adult-onset offenders constitute between 5% and 15% of all males (for a review see Farrington, Ohlin, & Wilson, 1986). However, estimates that are based on such official data are too high because most offenders engage in crime for some time before they are first arrested. Longitudinal studies of self-report delinquency show that only 1% to 4% of males commit their first criminal offense after age 17 (Elliott, Huizinga, & Menard, 1989). Adult-onset crime is not only very unusual, but it tends to be low rate, nonviolent (Blumstein & Cohen, 1987), and generally not accompanied by the many complications that attend a persistent and pervasive antisocial life-style (Farrington, Loeber, Elliott, et al., 1990).

predict antisocial outcomes from childhood conduct problems yield many errors (e.g., White et al., 1990). These errors seem to suggest that antisocial styles become set sometime after childhood.

Unfortunately, the extant longitudinal database does not provide a sound basis for conclusions. Typically, childhood behavior problems are assessed at only one time point from a single source, thereby lumping the many children who are temporarily or situationally aggressive with the few children who are on a persistent and pervasive trajectory. Outcomes are also typically assessed at a single point, often during late adolescence when temporary delinquents and future persisters are lumped together. According to my theory, such predictive designs should yield large numbers of false positives and false negatives. Analyses should ask, when between preschool and late adolescence can *stable–pervasive* antisocial behavior problems best predict antisocial outcomes among adults?

Life-Course-Persistent
Antisocial Behavior as Psychopathology

The life-course-persistent antisocial syndrome, as described here, has many characteristics that, taken together, suggest psychopathology. For example, the syndrome is statistically unusual; much research converges to suggest that it is characteristic of about 5% of males (Robins, 1985). Its rarity is thus consistent with a simple statistical definition of abnormality.

The theoretical syndrome is also characterized by tenacious stability across time and in diverse circumstances. This high-probability response style is relied on even in situations where it is clearly inappropriate or disadvantageous (Caspi & Moffitt, 1995), especially if these are a very limited repertoire of alternative conventional behaviors (Tremblay, 1991). Life-course-persistent antisocial behavior is thus maladaptive in the sense that it fails to change in response to changing circumstances.

The syndrome of life-course-persistent antisocial behavior described here has a biological basis in subtle dysfunctions of the nervous system (Moffitt, 1990b). (I reiterate my assertion that biological origins are in no way deterministic. Rather, individual variations in nervous system health provide raw material for subsequent person–environment interactions.)

The syndrome is associated with other mental disorders. There is good evidence that such "comorbidity" is associated with long-term continuity. An impressive body of research documents an overlap between persistent forms of antisocial behavior and other conditions of childhood such as learning disabilities and hyperactivity (cf. Moffitt, 1990a). Three studies (Elliott, Huizinga, & Menard, 1989; Farrington, Loeber, & Van Kammen, 1990; Moffitt, 1990a) have now shown that the presence of multiple behavioral disorders predicts persistence of illegal behavior over the course of years. This proliferation of mental disorders is common among life-course persistent antisocial persons. For example, in the Epidemiological Catchment Area (ECA) study of mental disorders among 19,000 adults, over 90% of the cases with antisocial personality disorder had at least one additional psychiatric diagnosis. (Evidence of onset before adulthood is required for the diagnosis of antisocial personality disorder, confirming persistence in the ECA cases.) The comorbid conditions that disproportionately affected antisocial adults were mania, schizophrenia, drug and alcohol abuse, depression, and anxiety disorders (Robins & Regier, 1991).

Of course, no one or two of these parameters is enough to warrant the classification of life-course-persistent antisocial behavior as psychopathology. Nonetheless, when taken together they form a more persuasive argument that persons whose antisocial behavior is stable and pervasive over the life course may constitute a category that is distinct from persons whose antisocial behavior is short term and situational.

ADOLESCENCE-LIMITED
ANTISOCIAL BEHAVIOR

My account of the adolescence-limited antisocial type will follow this plan: In the first section, *Discontinuity: The Most Common Course of Antisocial Behavior,* I provide a definition and description of this ubiquitous form of antisocial behavior. In the second section, *Beginnings: Motivation, Mimicry and Reinforcement,* I present three etiological hypotheses. Adolescence-limited antisocial behavior is motivated by the gap between biological maturity and social maturity, it is learned from antisocial models who are easily mimicked, and it is sustained according to the reinforcement principles of learning theory. In the third section, I answer the question, *Why doesn't every teenager become delinquent?* In the fourth section *Desistence From Crime: Adolescence-Limiteds Are Responsive to Shifting Reinforcement Contingencies,* I explain how temporary delinquents come to be exempted from the processes of continuity. In the fifth section, *Adolescence-Limited Delinquency and Secular Change,* I locate adolescence-limited delinquency in its recent historical context. In the sixth section, I make a case that the antisocial behavior of adolescence-limited delinquents is best regarded as adaptive social behavior.

Discontinuity: The Most Common Course
of Antisocial Behavior

As implied by the proffered label, discontinuity is the hallmark of teenaged delinquents who have no notable history of antisocial behavior in childhood and little future for such behavior in adulthood. However, the brief tenure of their delinquency should not obscure their prevalence in the population or the gravity of their crimes. In contrast with the rare life-course-persistent type, adolescence-limited delinquency is ubiquitous. Several studies have shown that about one third of males are arrested during their lifetime for a serious criminal offense, whereas fully four fifths of males have police contact for some minor infringement (Farrington, Ohlin, & Wilson, 1986). Most of these police contacts are made during the adolescent years. Indeed numerous rigorous self-report studies have now documented that it is statistically aberrant to refrain from crime during adolescence (Elliott et al., 1983; Hirschi, 1969; Moffitt & Silva, 1988c).

Compared with the life-course-persistent type, adolescence-limited delinquents show relatively little continuity in their antisocial behavior. Across age, change in delinquent involvement is often abrupt, especially during the periods of onset and desistence. For example, in my aforementioned longitudinal study of a representative sample of boys, 12% of the youngsters were classified as new delinquents at age 13; they had no prior history of antisocial behavior from age 5 to age 11. Between age 11 and age 13, they changed from below the sample average to 1.5 standard deviations above average on self-reported delinquency (Moffitt, 1990a). By age 15, another 20% of this sample of boys had joined the newcomers to delinquency despite having no prior history of antisocial behavior (Moffitt, 1991). Barely into mid-adolescence, the prevalence rate of markedly antisocial boys had swollen from 5% at age 11 to 32% at age 15. When interviewed at age 18, only 7% of the boys denied all delinquent activities. By their mid-20s, at least three fourths of these new offenders are expected to cease all offending (Farrington, 1986).

Adolescence-limited delinquents may also have sporadic, crime-free periods in the midst of their brief crime "careers." Also, in contrast with the life-course-persistent type, they lack consistency in their antisocial behavior across situations. For example, they may shoplift in stores and use drugs with friends but continue to obey the rules at school. Because of the chimeric nature of their delinquency, different reporters (such as self, parent, and teacher) are less likely to agree about their behavior problems when asked to complete rating scales or clinical interviews (Loeber, Green, Lahey, & Stouthamer-Loeber, 1990; Loeber & Schmaling, 1985).

These observations about temporal *in*stability and cross-situational *in*consistency are more than merely descriptive. They have implications for a theory of the etiology of adolescence-limited delinquency. Indeed, the flexibility of most delinquents' behavior suggests that their engagement in deviant life-styles may be under the control of reinforcement and punishment contingencies.

Unlike their life-course-persistent peers, whose behavior was described as inflexible and refractory to changing circumstances, adolescence-limited delinquents are likely to engage in antisocial behavior in situations where such responses seem profitable to them, but they are also able to abandon antisocial behavior when prosocial styles are more rewarding. They maintain control over their antisocial responses and use antisocial behavior only in situations where it may serve an instrumental function. Thus, principles of learning theory will be important for this theory of the cause of adolescence-limited delinquency.

A theory of adolescence-limited delinquency must account for several empirical observations: modal onset in early adolescence, recovery by young adulthood, widespread prevalence, and lack of continuity. Why do youngsters with no history of behavior problems in childhood suddenly become antisocial in adolescence? Why do they develop antisocial problems rather than other difficulties? Why is delinquency so common among teens? How are they able to spontaneously recover from an antisocial life-style within a few short years?

Just as the childhood onset of life-course-persistent persons compelled me to look for causal factors early in their lives, the coincidence of puberty with the rise in the prevalence of delinquent behavior compels me to look for clues in adolescent development. Critical features of this developmental period are variability in biological age, the increasing importance of peer relationships, and the budding of teenagers' self-conscious values, attitudes, and aspirations. These developmental tasks form the building blocks for a theory of adolescence-limited delinquency.

Beginnings: Motivation, Mimicry, and Reinforcement

Who do adolescence-limited delinquents begin delinquency? The answer advanced here is that their delinquency is "social mimicry" of the antisocial style of life-course-persistent youths. The concept of social mimicry is borrowed from ethology. Social mimicry occurs when two animal species share a single niche and one of the species has cornered the market on a resource that is needed to promote fitness (Moynihan, 1968). In such circumstances, the "mimic" species adopts the social behavior of the more successful species to obtain access to the valuable resource. For example, cowbird chicks, who are left by their mothers to be reared in the nests of unsuspecting parent birds, learn to behave like the parent birds' own true chicks and thus stimulate the parents to drop food their way. Social mimicry may also allow some species to safely pass among a more successful group and thus share access to desired resources. For example, some monkey species have learned to mimic bird calls. One such species of monkeys, rufous-naped tamarins, is able to share the delights of ripe fruit after a tree has been located by tyrant flycatchers, whose superior avian capacities in flight and distance vision better equip them to discover bearing trees. Similarly, zebras are sensitive to the social signals of impalas and gazelles and thus benefit from the latter species' superior sensitivity to approaching predators (E. O. Wilson, 1975).

If social mimicry is to explain why adolescence-limited delinquents begin to mimic the antisocial behavior of their life-course-persistent peers, then, logically, delinquency must be a social behavior that allows access to some desirable resource. I suggest that the resource is mature status, with its consequent power and privilege.

Before modernization, biological maturity came at a later age, social adult status arrived at an early age, and rites of passage more clearly delineated the point at which youths assumed new roles and responsibilities. In the past century, improved nutrition and health care have decreased the age of biological maturity at the rate of three tenths of a year per decade (Tanner, 1978; Wyshak & Frisch, 1982). Simultaneously, modernization of work has delayed the age of labor-force participation to ever later points in development (Empey, 1978; Horan & Hargis, 1991; Panel on Youth of the President's Science Advisory Committee, 1974). Thus, secular changes in health and work have lengthened the duration of adolescence. The ensuing gap leaves modern teenagers in a

5- to 10-year role vacuum (Erikson, 1960). They are biologically capable and compelled to be sexual beings, yet they are asked to delay most of the positive aspects of adult life (see Buchanan, Eccles, & Becker, 1992, for a review or studies of the compelling influence of pubertal hormones on teens' behavior and personality). In most American states, teens are not allowed to work or get a driver's license before age 16, marry or vote before age 18, or buy alcohol before age 21, and they are admonished to delay having children and establishing their own private dwellings until their education is completed at age 22, sometimes more than 20 years after they attain sexual maturity. They remain financially and socially dependent on their families of origin and are allowed few decisions of any real import. Yet they want desperately to establish intimate bonds with the opposite sex, to accrue material belongings, to make their own decisions, and to be regarded as consequential by adults (Csikszentmihalyi & Larson, 1984). Contemporary adolescents are thus trapped in a *maturity gap*, chronological hostages of a time warp between biological age and social age.

This emergent phenomenology begins to color the world for most teens in the first years of adolescence. Steinberg has shown that, between ages 10 and 15, a dramatic shift in youngsters' self-perceptions of autonomy and self-reliance takes place. Moreover, the timing of the shift of individuals is connected with their pubertal maturation (Steinberg, 1987; Steinberg & Silverberg, 1986; Udry, 1988). At the time of biological maturity, salient pubertal changes make the remoteness of ascribed social maturity painfully apparent to teens. This new awareness coincides with their promotion into a high school society that is numerically dominated by old youth. Thus, just as teens begin to feel the discomfort of the maturity gap, they enter a social reference group that has endured the gap for 3 to 4 years and has already perfected some delinquent ways of coping with it. Indeed, several researchers have noted that this life-course transition into high school society may place teens at risk for antisocial behavior. In particular, exposure to peer models, when coupled with puberty, is an important determinant of adolescence-onset cases of delinquency (Caspi, Lynam, Moffitt, & Silva, 1993; Magnusson, 1988; Simmons & Blyth, 1987).

Life-course persistent youngsters are the vanguard of this transition. Healthy adolescents are capable of noticing that the few life-course-persistent youths in their midst do not seem to suffer much from the maturity gap. (At a prevalence rate of about 5%, one or two such experienced delinquents in every classroom might be expected.) Already adept at deviance, life-course-persistent youths are able to obtain possessions by theft or vice that are otherwise inaccessible to teens who have no independent incomes (e.g., cars, clothes, drugs, or entry into adults-only leisure settings). Life-course-persistent boys are more sexually experienced and have already initiated relationships with the opposite sex.[4]

---

[4]Several longitudinal studies have shown that a history of antisocial behavior predicts early sexual experience for males relative to their age peers (Elliott & Morse, 1987; Jessor, Costa, Jessor, & Donovan, 1983; Weiher, Huizinga, Lizotte, & Van Kammen, 1991). Specifically, almost all of the sexual experience of an early adolescent cohort is concentrated among the most seriously delinquents 5% of its boys (Elliott & Morse, 1987).

Life-course-persistent boys appear relatively free of their families of origin; they seem to go their own way, making their own rules. As evidence that they make their own decisions, they take risks and do dangerous things that parents could not possibly endorse. As evidence that they have social consequence in the adult world, they have personal attorneys, social workers, and probation officers; they operate small businesses in the underground economy; and they have fathered children (Weiher, Huizinga, Lizotte, & Van Kammen, 1991). Viewed from within contemporary adolescent culture, the antisocial precocity of life-course-persistent youths becomes a coveted social asset (cf. Finnegan, 1990a, 1990b; Jessor & Jessor, 1977; Silbereisen & Noack, 1988). Like the aforementioned bird calls that were mimicked by hungry tamarin monkeys, antisocial behavior becomes a valuable technique that is demonstrated by life-course-persistents and imitated carefully by adolescence-limiteds. The effect of peer delinquency on the onset of delinquency is among the most robust facts in criminology research (Elliott & Menard, 1996; Jessor & Jessor, 1977; Reiss, 1986; Sarnecki, 1986). However, is there evidence consistent with a social mimicry interpretation? I describe the evidence in the next section.

Social Mimicry and the Relationships Between Life-Course-Persistent and Adolescence-Limited Delinquents One hypothesized by-product of the maturity gap is a shift during early adolescence by persistent antisocial youth from peripheral to more influential positions in the peer social structure. This shift should occur as aspects of the antisocial style become more interesting to other teens. In terms of its epidemiology, delinquent participation shifts from being primarily an individual psychopathology in childhood to a normative group social behavior during adolescence and then back to psychopathology in adulthood. Consider that the behavior problems of the few pioneering antisocial children in an age cohort must develop on an individual basis; such early childhood pioneers lack the influence of delinquent peers (excepting family members). However, near adolescence, a few boys join the life-course-persistent ones, then a few more, until a critical mass is reached when almost all adolescents are involved in some delinquency with age peers. Elliott and Menard (1996) have analyzed change in peer group membership from age 11 to age 24 in a national probability sample. Their data show a gradual population drift from membership in nondelinquent peer groups to membership in delinquent peer groups up to age 17; the trend reverses thereafter. For example, 78% of 11-year-olds reported no or minimal delinquency among their friends. In contrast, 66% of 17-year-olds reported substantial delinquency on the part of the friends in their group.

The word *friends* in the previous sentence seems to imply a personal relationship between life-course-persistents and adolescence-limiteds that is implausible. Much evidence suggests that, before adolescence, life-course-persistent antisocial children are ignored and rejected by other children because of their unpredictable, aggressive behavior (Coie et al., 1988; Dodge et al., 1982). After adolescence has passed, life-course-persistent adults are often described as lacking the capacity for loyalty or friendship (Cleckley, 1976;

Robins, 1958). At first, these observations may seem contrary to my assertion that life-course-persistents assume social influence over youths who admire and emulate their style during adolescence. However, it is important to recall that social mimicry required no exchange of affection between the successful birds and their monkey mimics. In this theory, adolescents who wish to prove their maturity need only notice that the style of life-course-persistents resembles adulthood more than it resembles childhood. Then they need only observe antisocial behavior closely enough and long enough to imitate it successfully. What is contended is that adolescence-limited youths should regard life-course-persistent youths as models, and life-course-persistent teens should regard themselves as magnets for other teens. Neither perception need involve reciprocal liking between individuals.

A modeling role would imply that measures of exposure to delinquent peers (e.g., knowledge of their delinquency behavior or time spent in proximity to them) should be better predictors of self-delinquency then measures of relationship quality (e.g., shared attitudes or attachment to delinquent peers). Few studies have parsed peer-delinquency effects into separate components, but two findings consistent with this prediction have been reported from the National Youth Survey, a representative sample of more than 1,500 teens. Agnew (1991) examined relationship characteristics in interaction with levels of peer delinquency. He argued that attachment to peers should encourage deviance if peers are delinquent but discourage it if they are not. Agnew's results showed that such interaction terms were good predictors. However, the results also showed that time spent with delinquent peers was a stronger unique predictor of self-delinquency than the interaction between peer attachment and peer crime. Warr and Stafford (1991) found that the knowledge of friends' delinquent behavior was 2.5 to 5 times more important for self-delinquency than friends' attitudes about delinquency. (This pattern has been replicated in another sample by Nagin & Paternoster, 1991.) Moreover, the effect of peer delinquency was direct; it was not mediated by influencing the respondents' attitudes to be more like those of deviant peers. These findings are not consistent with the notion that teens take up delinquency after pro-delinquency attitudes are transferred in the context of intimate social relations. Rather, Warr and Stafford concluded that the data on peer effects are best interpreted in terms of imitation or vicarious reinforcement.

A magnet role would imply that children who were rejected and ignored by others should experience newfound "popularity" as teens, relative to their former rejected status. That is, life-course-persistent youth should encounter more contacts with peers during adolescence when other adolescents draw near so as to imitate their life-style. Some research is consistent with this interpretation. For example, in a study of 450 students in middle school, aggressive youths who were rejected by their peers reported that they did not feel lonely, whereas submissive rejected youths did feel lonely (Parkhurst & Asher, 1992). Similarly, aggressive seventh-graders in the Carolina Longitudinal Study were rated as popular as often as nonaggressive youths by both teachers and themselves and were as likely as other youths to be nuclear members of peer groups

(Cairns, Cairns, Neckerman, Gest, & Gariépy, 1988). In their review of peer-relationship studies, Coie, Dodge, and Kupersmidt (1990) noted that the relationship between overt aggression and peer rejection is weaker or absent in adolescent samples compared with child samples. Findings such as these suggest that aggressive teens experience regular contacts with peers, however short-lived. Similarly, in the Oregon Youth Study, rejection by peers at age 10 was prognostic of greater involvement with delinquent peers 2 years later (Dishion, Patterson, Stoolmiller, & Skiller, 1991). Although the Oregon researchers interpreted their results as suggesting that aggressive children seek delinquent friends, their data are equally consistent with my interpretation that aggressive youths begin to serve as a magnet for novice delinquents during early adolescence. Definitive sociometric research must follow up aggressive–rejected children to test whether they develop networks in adolescence that include late-onset delinquents of the adolescence-limited type.

Researchers from the Carolina Longitudinal Study have carefully documented that boys with an aggressive history do participate in peer networks in adolescence but that the networks are not very stable (Cairns et al., 1988). Consistent with a social mimicry hypothesis, delinquent groups have frequent membership turnover. In addition, the interchanges between network members are characterized by much reciprocal antisocial behavior (Cairns et al., 1988). Reiss and Farrington (1991) have shown that the most experienced high-rate young offenders tend to recruit different co-offenders for each offense.

Life-course-persistents serve as core members of revolving networks, by virtue of being role models or trainers for new recruits (Reiss, 1986). They exploit peers as drug customers, as fences, as lookouts, or as sexual partners. Such interactions among life-course-persistent and adolescence-limited delinquents may represent a symbiosis of mutual exploitation. Alternatively, life-course-persistent offenders need not even be aware of all of the adolescence-limited youngsters who imitate their style. Unlike adolescence-limited offenders, who appear to need peer support for crime, life-course-persistent offenders are willing to offend alone (Knight & West, 1975). The point is that the phenomena of "delinquent peer networks" and "co-offending" during the adolescent period do not necessarily connote supportive friendships that are based on intimacy, trust, and loyalty, as is sometimes assumed. Social mimicry of delinquency can take place if experienced offenders actively educate new recruits. However, it can also take place if motivated learners merely observe antisocial models from afar.

Reinforcement of Delinquency by its "Negative" Consequences For teens who become adolescence-limited delinquents, antisocial behavior is an effective means of knifing-off childhood apron strings and of proving that they can act independently to conquer new challenges (Erikson, 1960). Hypothetical reinforcers for delinquency include damaging the quality of intimacy and communication with parents, provoking responses from adults in positions of authority, finding ways to look older (such as by smoking cigarettes, being tattooed, playing the big spender with ill-gotten gains), and tempting fate (risking pregnancy, driving while intoxicated, or shoplifting under the noses of clerks). None of these putative reinforcers may seem very pleasurable to the middle-aged academic, but each of the aforementioned consequences is a precious resource to the teenager and can serve to reinforce delinquency. Block and Niederhoffer (1958) have offered an anthropological perspective: "It is almost as if the contemporary young person, in the absence of puberty rituals and ordeals, is moved to exclaim: If you don't care to test us, then we will test ourselves!" (p. 28).

I suggest that every curfew violated, car stolen, drug taken, and baby conceived is a statement of personal independence and thus a reinforcer for delinquent involvement. Ethnographic interviews with delinquents reveal that proving maturity and autonomy are strong personal motives for offending (e.g., Goldstein, 1990). Such hypothetical reinforcing properties have not been systematically tested for most types of delinquent acts. However, epidemiological studies have confirmed that adolescent initiation of tobacco, alcohol, and drug abuse are reinforced because they symbolize independence and maturity to youth (D. Kandel, 1980; Mausner & Platt, 1971).

In summary, in this narrative account of the etiology of adolescent-onset delinquency I have emphasized three conditions: motivation, mimicry, and reinforcement. I have suggested that a secular change in the duration of adolescence has generated an age-dependent motivational state. In addition, life-course-persistent antisocial models must be available so that their delinquent behaviors can be imitated. Finally, adolescents' fledgling attempts to mimic antisocial styles will continue if they are socially reinforced by the "negative consequences" of crime.

Why Doesn't Every Teenager Become Delinquent?

The proffered theory of adolescence-limited delinquency regards this sort of delinquency as an adaptive response to contextual circumstances. As a consequence, the theory seems to predict that every teen will engage in delinquency. Data from epidemiological studies using the self-report method suggest that almost all adolescents do commit some illegal acts (Elliott et al., 1983). In addition, even studies using official records of arrest by police find surprisingly high prevalence rates (for a review see Farrington, Ohlin, & Wilson, 1986). Nevertheless, some youths commit less delinquency than others, and a small minority abstains completely. Unfortunately, almost no research sheds light on the characteristics of teens who abstain from antisocial behavior altogether. Speculations are thus ill-informed by empirical observations. However, some predictions may be derived from the present theory of adolescence-limited delinquency. The predictions center on two theoretical prerequisites for adolescent-onset delinquency: the motivating maturity gap and antisocial role models. Some youths may skip the maturity gap because of late puberty or early initiation into adult roles. Others may find few opportunities for mimicking life-course-persistent delinquent models.

Some youths who refrain from antisocial behavior may, for some reason, not sense the maturity gap and therefore lack the hypothesized motivation for experimenting with crime. Perhaps such teens experience very late puberty so that the gap between biological and social adulthood is not signaled to them early in adolescence. For example, Caspi and Moffitt (1991) have shown that girls who do not menstruate by age 15 tend not to become involved in delinquency; in fact they evidence fewer than normal behavior problems as teens. Perhaps other abstainers belong to cultural or religious subgroups in which adolescents are given legitimate access to adult privileges and accountability. In his vivid ethnographic account of "old heads" and teenaged boys in a poor black neighborhood, Anderson (1990) described how mature community leaders drew certain boys into their own work and social lives, deliberately and publicly initiating the boys into manhood (and preventing delinquent involvement).

Some nondelinquent teens may lack structural opportunities for modeling antisocial peers. Adolescent crime rates are generally lower in rural areas than in inner-city areas (Skogan, 1979, 1990). Teens in urban areas are surrounded by a greater density of age peers (and have readier unsupervised access to them through public transportation and meeting venues such as parks and shopping malls) than are teens in relatively isolated rural areas. For instance, Sampson and Groves (1989) determined that the strongest community-level correlate of local rates of robbery and violence was the presence of "unsupervised groups of teenagers hanging out and making a nuisance" (p. 789). In that study, more traditional community correlates of crime, such as socioeconomic status, residential mobility, and ethnicity, were mediated by the teenaged social scene. School structures may also constrain or facilitate access to life-course-persistent models. Caspi et al. (1993) found that early puberty was associated with delinquency in girls but only if they had access to boys through attending coed high schools. Girls who were enrolled in girls' schools did not engage in delinquency. In that study, the difference in delinquent involvement between coed and single-sex school settings could not be explained by any personal or family characteristics that may have influenced how the girls came to be enrolled in their schools; access to delinquent role models was clearly the best explanation for the girls' behavior problems.

Youths may also be excluded from opportunities to mimic antisocial peers because of some personal characteristics that make them unattractive to other teens or that leave them reluctant to seek entry to newly popular delinquent groups. Shedler and Block (1990) found such an effect on the use of illegal drugs. They compared the personality styles of three adolescent groups: teens who abstained from trying any drug, teens who experimented with drugs, and teens who were frequent heavy drug users. Adolescents who experimented were the best adjusted teens in the sample. As expected, frequent users were troubled teens, who were alienated and antisocial. However, the abstainers were also problem teens: They were "relatively tense, overcontrolled, emotionally constricted, . . . somewhat socially isolated and lacking in interpersonal skills" (p. 618). This personality style was not a consequence of failing to try drugs. Rather, it was an enduring personality configuration. At age 7, these abstainers had been prospectively described by raters as "overcontrolled, timid, fearful and morose . . . , they were not warm and responsive, not curious and open to new experience, not active, not vital, and not cheerful" (pp. 619–620). Similarly, Farrington and West (1990) reported that boys from criminogenic circumstances who did not become delinquent seemed nervous and withdrawn and had few or no friends. These provocative findings remind us that deviance is defined in relationship to its normative context. During adolescence, when delinquent behavior becomes the norm, nondelinquents warrant our scientific scrutiny.

In summary, this theory of adolescence-limited delinquency suggests that adolescents who commit no antisocial behavior at all have either (a) delayed puberty, (b) access to roles that are respected by adults, (c) environments that limit opportunities for learning about delinquency, (d) personal characteristics that exclude them from antisocial peer networks, or (e) all four. Research is needed to determine whether or not abstaining from delinquency is necessarily a sign of good adolescent adjustment.

Desistence From Crime: Adolescence-Limiteds Are
Responsive to Shifting Reinforcement Contingencies

By definition, adolescence-limited delinquents generally do not maintain their delinquent behavior into adulthood. The account of life-course-persistent persons I made earlier in this article required an analysis of maintenance factors. In contrast, this account of adolescence-limited delinquents demands an analysis of desistence: Why do adolescence-limited delinquents desist from delinquency? This theory's answer: Healthy youths respond adaptively to changing contingencies. If motivational and learning mechanisms initiate and maintain their delinquency, then, likewise changing contingencies can extinguish it.

Preoccupied with explaining the origins of crime, most theories of delinquency have neglected to address the massive shift in the prevalence of criminal involvement between adolescence and adulthood. Gove (1985) reviewed six of the most influential theories of deviance: labeling theory, conflict theory, differential association theory, control theory, anomie theory, and functional theory. He concluded, "All of these theoretical perspectives either explicitly or implicitly suggest that deviant behavior is an amplifying process that leads to further and more serious deviance" (p. 118). A general application of an amplifying process to all delinquency is inconsistent with the empirical observation that desistence from crime is the normative pattern.

Waning Motivation and Shifting Contingencies In contrast with amplifying theories, the present maturity-gap theory does anticipate desistence. With the inevitable progression of chronological age, more legitimate and tangible adult roles become available to teens. Adolescence-limited delinquents gradually experience a loss of motivation for delinquency as they exit the maturity gap. Moreover, when aging delinquents attain some of the privileges they coveted as teens, the consequences of illegal behavior shift from rewarding to punishing, *in their perception.* An adult arrest record will limit their job opportunities, drug abuse keeps them from getting to work on time, drunk driving is costly, and bar fights lead to accusations of unfit parenthood. Adolescence-limited delinquents have something to lose by persisting in their antisocial behavior beyond the teen years.

There is some evidence that many young adult offenders weigh the relative rewards from illegal and conventional activities when they contemplate future offending. In a study of three samples, the effect of age on criminal participation was mediated by young men's expectations about whether illegal earnings would exceed earnings from a straight job (Piliavin, Thornton, Gartner, & Matsueda, 1986). Important for this theory, research shows that "commitment costs" are among the factors weighed by young adults when they decide to discontinue offending. In the criminological subfield of perceptual deterrence research, commitment costs are defined as a person's judgment that past accomplishments will be jeopardized or that future goals will be foreclosed (Williams & Hawkins, 1986). Criminal behavior incurs commitment costs if it risks informal sanctions (disapproval by family, community, or employer) as well as formal sanctions (arrest or conviction penalty). Given that very few delinquent acts culminate in formal sanctions, perceptual deterrence theories consider informal sanctions as keys to deterrence. Paternoster and colleagues have tested the proposed effects of commitment costs and informal sanctions in a follow-up study of 300 young adults. They found that criminal offending 1 year later was best predicted by prospective indexes of commitment costs ($r = -.23$) and informal sanctions ($r = -.40$). Those variables outdid gender, perceived risk of arrest, grade point average, and peer attachment (Paternoster, Saltzman, Waldo, & Chiricos, 1983).[5]

Options for Change Consistent with this motivational analysis, the antisocial behavior of many delinquent teens has been found to decline after they leave high school (Elliott & Voss, 1974), join the army (Elder, 1986; Mattick, 1960), marry a prosocial spouse (Sampson & Laub, 1990), move away from the old neighborhood (West, 1982), or get a full-time job (Sampson & Laub, 1990). As these citations show, links between the assumption of adult roles and criminal desistance have been observed before. The issue left unaddressed by theory is why are some delinquents able to desist when others are not? What

---

[5]Deterrence effects on crime are controversial. However, most past studies of deterrence have few implications for my theory of desistence among adolescence-limited delinquents for several reasons: (a) Some compare aggregate-level crime rates across places or periods that differ on severity of formal penalties. Such designs ignore the influence of individuals' perceptions about the certainty of sanctions. (b) Some use cross-sectional correlations between past offending and current perceptions of sanction certainty. Such designs evaluate the effects of experience on perceptions, not the effect of perceptions on future offending. They show only that experienced criminals know that the risk of arrest is inconsequential. (c) Most focus on the severity and certainty of formal legal sanctions, ignoring informal sanctions from the broader social context. People have concerns about nonlegal problem consequences of illicit behaviors, whether they expect to get caught or not (Nagin & Paternoster, 1991). (d) Most fail to study general samples during the age when the desistence process peaks, instead studying high school students or midlife prison inmates. Only the study by Paternoster et al. (1983) has compared prospective measures of individual perceptions of formal and informal sanctions on the later offending behavior of young adult subjects.

enables adolescence-limited delinquents to make these (often abrupt) transitions away from crime? Why do adolescence-limited delinquents come to realize that they have something to lose, whereas life-course-persistent delinquents remain undeterred? Here, two positions are advanced: unlike their life-course-persistent counterparts, adolescence-limited delinquents are relatively exempt from the forces of (a) cumulative and (b) contemporary continuity.

First, without a lifelong history of antisocial behavior, the forces of cumulative continuity have had fewer years in which to gather the momentum of a downhill snowball. Before taking up delinquency, adolescence-limited offenders had ample years to develop an accomplished repertoire of prosocial behaviors and basic academic skills. These social skills and academic achievements make them eligible for postsecondary education, good marriage, and desirable jobs.

The availability of alternatives to crime may explain why some adolescence-limited delinquents desist later than others. (As shown in Figure 5.1, the desistence portion of the age–crime curve slopes more gradually than the abrupt criminal initiation portion.) Although the forces of cumulative continuity build up less momentum over the course of their relatively short crime careers, many adolescence-limited youths will fall prey to many of the same snares that maintain continuity among life-course-persistent persons. Those whose teen forays into delinquency inadvertently attracted damaging consequences may have more difficulty desisting. A drug habit, an incarceration, interrupted education, or a teen pregnancy are snares that require extra effort and time from which to escape. Thus, this theory predicts that variability in age at desistence from crime should be accounted for by the cumulative number and type of ensnaring life events that entangle persons in a deviant life-style.

Second, in stark contrast with the earlier account of life-course-persistent offenders, personality disorder and cognitive deficits play no part in the delinquency of adolescence-limited offenders. As a result, they are exempt from the sources of contemporary continuity that plague their life-course-persistent counterparts. In general, these young adults have adequate social skills, they have a record of average or better academic achievement, their mental health is sturdy, they still possess the capacity to forge close attachment relationships, and they retain the good intelligence they had when they entered adolescence. One study of girls who grew up in institutional care has illustrated that individual differences influence which adolescents are able to attain prosocial outcomes in young adulthood (Quinton & Rutter, 1988). In that study, some girls reared in institutions were able to escape adversity for advantage through marriage to a supportive husband, but a constellation of individual psychological attributes determined which girls were able to marry well.

At the crossroads of young adulthood, adolescence-limited and life-course-persistent delinquents go different ways. This happens because the developmental histories and personal traits of adolescence-limiteds allow them the option of exploring new life pathways. The histories and traits of life-course-persistents have foreclosed their options, entrenching them in the antisocial path. To test this hypothesis, research must examine conditional effects of individual histories on opportunities for desistence from crime.

Adolescence-Limited Delinquency and Secular Change

I have suggested that adolescence-limited delinquency is a byproduct of modernization, an adolescent adaption to a maturity gap engendered by the opposing social forces of improved health and a smaller, better educated work force. If this theory is correct, then secular changes should have rendered the age–crime curve relatively steeper with increasing modernization. The theory predicts that, in contemporary preindustrial nations and in earlier historical periods, the age–crime curve should have a flatter kurtosis; in other words, it will lack the characteristic sharp peak between the ages of 15–18.

Empirical data support this prediction. Greenberg (1985) compared crime statistics from the mid-1800s to 1980s in the United States, France, Norway, and Holland. He also made cross-cultural comparisons between India and Uganda and more industrialized nations. The results show that the steepness of the age–crime curve is indeed greatest during recent times and among modern nations. Farrington (1986) compared the relationship between age and crime for English males using British Home Office statistics from 1938, 1961, and 1983. His results, reproduced in Figure 5.4, show that the rate of offending by adolescents increased considerably over this historical period.

Diverse factors may be influential in accounting for the changing nature of the age–crime curve (J. Q. Wilson, 1983). However, I suggest that many of these factors are the very features of modernization and modernity invoked in this theory of adolescence-limited delinquency. The earlier age of puberty and the extension of the period of childhood are generally overlooked as by-products of modernization, but they have important implications for the experience of youths. The years between 1938 and 1983, covered in the study by Farrington (1986), also witnessed an incremental displacement of sons by their mothers as the family's secondary breadwinners (Modell, Furstenberg, & Hershberg, 1976). The shift of work away from farms, trades, and small family businesses to factories and service industries has stopped adolescents from sharing the daily lives of older relatives. As Anderson (1990) has observed, fewer and fewer "old heads" are initiating young proteges into the adult world. Teens are less well-integrated with adults than ever before. What has emerged is an age-bounded ghetto (Schwendinger & Schwendinger, 1985) from within which it seems advantageous to mimic deviant behavior.

Important for this theory, additional data suggest that secular changes may have influenced the age pattern of some crimes but not all. A comparison of the age–crime curve for data from the Federal Bureau of Investigation's *Uniform Crime Reports* for 1940, 1960, and 1980 showed that the adolescent peakedness of the curves for most crimes increased in a linear fashion over the 40-year period (Steffensmeier, Allan, Harer, & Streifel, 1989). However, the authors noted that

> the shift toward more peaked distributions is greater for some types of offenses than for others. The shifts are comparatively small for the person crimes and for those property offenses primarily involving older offenders (e.g., fraud and forgery), while the shifts are moderate to substantial for

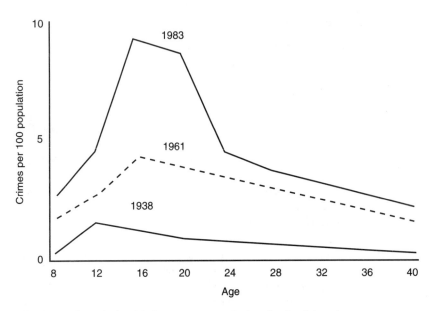

FIGURE 5.4 The relationship between age and crime for English males. The graphs show the rate of findings of guilt and cautions per 100 population for indictable offenses in the years 1938, 1961, and 1983, as reported by the British Home Office.

Source: From "Age and Crime" by D. P. Farrington, 1986, *Crime and Justice: An Annual Review of Research, 7,* p. 192. Copyright 1986 by The University of Chicago. Adapted by permission.

the youth-oriented, low-yield property offenses (e.g., robbery and burglary), public order offenses, and the substance-abuse offenses. (p. 823)

Steffensmeier's finding of different curves for different offenses is consistent with the distinction I have made between two hypothetical types of offenders. On the one hand, life-course-persistent offenders (with mild neuropsychological impairment, poor self-control, pathological interpersonal relationships, weak connections to other people, and a lifelong antisocial personality configuration) should account for violence against persons as well as for crimes committed in late life. On the other hand, adolescence-limited offenders should account primarily for crimes that serve to meet adolescents' lust for acknowledgment and privilege: theft, vandalism, public order, and substance abuse.

Adolescence-Limited Antisocial Behavior
Is Not Pathological Behavior

In an earlier section, it was contended that life-course-persistent antisocial behavior represented an especially pernicious and tenacious form of psychopathology. My view of adolescence-limited delinquency is strikingly different: Its prevalence is so great that it is normative rather than abnormal. It is flexible and adaptable rather than rigid and stable; most delinquent careers are of relatively short duration because the consequences of crime, although rein-forcing for youths caught inside the maturity gap, become punishing to youths as soon as they age out of it. Instead of a biological basis in the nervous system, the origins of adolescence-limited delinquency lie in youngsters' best efforts to cope with the widening gap between biological and social maturity. Moreover, neither this theory nor the empirical evidence suggests that there are links between mental disorders and short-term adolescent delinquency.

According to this theory of adolescence-limited delinquency, the behav-ior of youths who make the transition to delinquent groups near adolescence is readily understood as a group social phenomenon, it does not represent individual-level deviance. Quay (1987) concurred:

> A second pattern . . . involves behavior of a less overtly aggressive and inter-personally alienated nature. In fact, good peer relations in the context of delinquency are at the core of this pattern. . . . There is little, if any, reason to ascribe psychopathology to youths manifesting this pattern; it may well represent an adjustive response to environmental circumstances. (p. 131)

It is my stance that individual characteristics will not predict adolescence-lim-ited offending; it is a product of an interaction between age and historical period. True, past studies have reported low to moderate correlations between adolescent delinquency and individual difference variables (such as IQ). However, none of these studies excluded life-course-persistent subjects before analysis. Thus, it remains unclear whether the obtained correlations represent linear monotonic relationships between variables or "outlier" effects of the extreme scores of life-course-persistent subjects. For example, in the New Zealand sample, the often-reported 8 point IQ difference (Hirschi & Hindelang, 1977) between delinquents and nondelinquents obtains, but it is the pooled result of a 1-point mean deficit for adolescence-onset delinquents and a 17-point mean deficit for childhood-onset delinquents. The same pattern obtained for measures of reading achieve-ment and impulsivity (Moffitt, 1990a; White et al., 1994).

The Evidence and the Alternatives

In this theory of adolescence-limited delinquency, I have made several novel propositions. I have suggested that adolescence-onset delinquency constitutes social mimicry of a pathological type of antisocial child. I have suggested that the motivation for such mimicry follows from a maturity gap between biolog-ical adulthood and ascribed adulthood. I have suggested that delinquent mimicry is reinforced by its own consequences while a youth is inside the maturity gap. I have suggested that those consequences lose their rewarding properties after youths age out of the gap, extinguishing delinquency. All three of the components of this theory are needed to support my assertion that adolescence-limited delinquency is not psychopathology. Because of the newness of this set of hypotheses, there is yet no literature of studies specifi-cally designed to test them. Nonetheless, it was possible to glean from the existing literature empirical evidence in support of most aspects of the theory.

There is some evidence for the mimicry component. A drift into delinquent peer relationships does match the timing of the maturity gap. As predicted, most teens appear to engage in delinquency because they are simply aware of delinquent peer behavior, not because they share attitudes of close friendships with delinquents. Conversely, the most experienced early-onset delinquents do interact with other adolescents, albeit briefly and with their trademark antisocial style.

There is some evidence for the motivational component. The maturity gap has widened during this century, and, as predicted by the theory, the change has coincided with a differential increase in teen crime. After puberty, youngsters' thoughts do turn increasingly to proving their own adultness, and, as predicted by the theory, the particular types of crimes that increased among adolescents this century are ones that satisfy wishes for adult privileges.

There is less evidence for the reinforcement component. Research suggests that youngsters take up drug and alcohol use because it makes them feel independent, but studies of the symbolic reward values of other delinquent acts have not yet been reported. There is better evidence that the informal consequences of crime become deterrents after young adults exit the maturity gap. As predicted, young adults' desistence from crime is influenced by their expectancies of informal sanctions from family, employer, and community.

To date, almost no studies have discriminated childhood-onset persistent delinquents from adolescence-onset delinquents and then examined the specific correlates of delinquency in the latter group. Because the available literature mixes the two types of delinquents, it is difficult to evaluate the predictions from this theory against extant findings. However, in evaluating the empirical foundation for this theory of adolescence-limited delinquency, it is helpful to contrast the theory with its most favored predecessors: control theories and social learning theories.

Control theories of delinquency point to weak social controls, such as lax supervision by adults or weak bonds to parents, as the causes of burgeoning delinquency (e.g., Hirschi, 1969). The database for control theories is a cross-sectional correlation between measures of delinquency and supervision in adolescent samples. Research has yet to demonstrate that parenting practices change before teen's interest in problem behavior begins.[6] More critical, control theories do not explain why antisocial behavior per se is the outcome of weakened social control systems. Why do unsupervised teens not mow lawns for the elderly? Why don't weakly attached youths gather in groups to do more algebra homework? In answer, social control theories rely on the philosophical assumption that all humans are inherently antisocial; crime must thus emerge

---

[6]Indeed, some research indicates that changes in parental behavior may be a *child effect*. Steinberg (1981, 1987) has shown that pubertal maturation precedes emotional distance and less authoritarian parenting. There is much evidence for the activational effects of pubertal hormones on problem behavior and on escalation of parent–child conflict (Buchanan, Eccles, & Becker, 1992). In the Oregon Youth Study, parental monitoring and discipline fell to insignificance as predictors of delinquent outcome when the child's prior antisocial behavior was entered first (Dishion, Patterson, Stoolmiller, & Skinner, 1990).

spontaneously, by default, whenever social controls are weakened. A taxonomic theory cannot afford the luxury of this philosophical premise about the universal mainsprings of human behavior. I offer instead an answer that links individual motivation for crime to its ecological context: Algebra homework does not make a statement about independence; it does not assert that a youth is entitled to be taken seriously. Crime does. How do pubescent teens come to know about antisocial behavior and its effects? I have suggested that they vicariously observe the life-styles of the life-course-persistent youths in their midst. Control theories assert that, in the absence of any such models, innocents would invent delinquency.

Calling on learning theory to explain juvenile delinquency, as I have done in this section, is not unique. Social learning theories have suggested that delinquency follows the learning of attitudes conducive to crime (e.g., Sutherland & Cressey, 1978). However, social learning theories of delinquency have not asked, why do so many people learn the attitudes at the same life stage? Why do they learn them so rapidly? What suddenly motivates that learning? What reinforces it? Who are the "teachers"? Why are deviant attitudes unlearned so readily a few years later? Social leaning theories describe aspects of the process by which an individual acquires delinquent skills. However, without a motivational component, social learning theories do not address the inescapable epidemiological facts about adolescent delinquency. This developmental analysis of adolescence-limited delinquency invokes the maturity gap as an explanation for the motivation and timing of adolescence-limited delinquency. The concept of social mimicry is borrowed to explain why healthy adolescents adopt the style of youths who have been antisocial since early childhood. Thus, this narrative attempts to answer some questions begged by earlier theories.

COMPARING THESE TWO THEORIES
WITH OTHERS

Students of antisocial behavior have been blessed with a number of thoughtful theories. As a group, the theories have tended to be "general" theories of crime; each extends its causal explanation to all offenders.

General theories that summon sociological processes to explain crime and delinquency have provided valuable insights about the proximal mechanisms that promote juvenile delinquency (e.g., Becker, 1968; Cloward & Ohlin, 1960; Hagan, 1987; Hirschi, 1969; Lemert, 1967; Shaw & McKay, 1942; Sutherland & Cressey, 1978). However, sociologists have trained their lenses on the adolescent age period, when the peak prevalence of criminal involvement occurs, and when antisocial behavior is most easily studied with survey methods (Hagan, Gillis, & Simpson, 1985; Sampson & Laub, 1992). Historically, reliance on legal definitions of antisocial behavior and record sources of data kept delinquency researchers focused on the adolescent onset of illegal behavior. Consequently, many delinquency theories have failed to address the stability of antisocial behavior that begins *before* adolescence, during early childhood. In addition, most sociological theories invoke amplifying causal mechanisms that seem to ignore the empirical facts about the enormous amount of desistence from crime that happens soon *after* adolescence (Gove, 1985). Causal factors such as low social class, unemployment, cultural approval for violence, and deviant labels do not seem to remit contemporaneously with that undeniable downward shift in the prevalence of offenders during early adulthood.

General theories that invoke causal variables from personality psychology or biology have taught researchers much about how individual differences predispose toward crime (e.g., Bowlby, 1988; Buikhuisen, 1987; Cloninger, 1987; Eysenck, 1977; Gorenstein & Newman, 1980; Mednick, 1977). However, these theories, too, fail to provide a satisfying account. Because such theorists have trained their lenses on early childhood and adulthood (often to the neglect of adolescence), they have failed to anticipate the enormous surge in the prevalence of antisocial involvement that occurs *during* adolescence. Such theories typically rely on the stability of individual differences in traits such as impulsivity, neuroticism, autonomic nervous system reactivity, or low intelligence. Psychological theories cannot explain the onset and desistence of adolescent delinquency without positing compelling reasons for a sudden and dramatic population shift in criminogenic traits followed by return to baseline a few years later.

Despite the imperfect fit of many existing theories to the epidemiological facts, data in partial support of each theory abound. The resulting stalemate has engendered among students of crime a gentlemen's agreement to disagree. The dual taxonomy described in this article argues that this compromise may be needless. The competing theories may all be correct, but the processes they describe may fit better for different types of delinquents or may operate at different developmental stages in the natural history of antisocial behavior. Among the many mechanisms touted by this developmental taxonomy, few are brand new. What is new is the way in which many different theories of delinquency have been integrated under a taxonomic umbrella.

Indeed, this developmental taxonomy may serve to reconcile disagreements, controversies, and the misunderstandings in research on antisocial behavior. For example, the developmental taxonomy may account for effects that appear, disappear, and reappear as a function of the age of research subjects. Behavior-genetic studies have shown that childhood aggression and adult crime are heritable, whereas juvenile delinquency is much less so (DiLalla & Gottesman, 1989; Edelbrock, Rende, Plomin, & Thompson, 1995). Other correlates show also strong relationships to antisocial behavior when it is measured in children and adults but only weak relationships to antisocial behavior measured during adolescence. Such age-related fluctuations in effect size have been noticed for the associations among antisocial behavior and social class (Elliott & Huizinga, 1983), gender (Smith & Visher, 1980), and reading problems (B. Maughan, personal communication, October 1990; Murray, 1976).

These disappearing effects yield (unnecessary) controversy; they may be an inadvertent consequence of mixing apples with oranges when using adolescents as research samples. I have here proposed that the ratio of life-course-persistents to their social mimics will differ as a function of the age of the research sample. Samples of antisocial children and adults should contain relatively more life-course-persistent subjects, but in samples of delinquent teens, adolescence-limited subjects will far outnumber their persistent peers. Consequently, effect sizes for the correlates of persistent antisocial behavior should be attenuated in adolescent samples, and developmental interpretations of cross-sectional data will be confounded. Note one implication: Juvenile delinquents may not be the best group to study if researchers wish to detect the correlates of persistent crime or antisocial psychopathology.

STRATEGIES FOR RESEARCH

Epidemiological Predictions

According to the theory, natural histories of antisocial behavior should be found at predictable prevalence rates in samples followed from childhood until adolescence. Less than 10% of males should show extreme antisocial behavior that begins during early childhood and is thereafter sustained at a high level across time and across circumstances, throughout childhood and adolescence. A much larger number of males, a majority, should show similar levels of antisocial behavior during the adolescent age period but should fail to meet research criteria for a childhood history of stable and pervasive problem behavior. Teenaged males who abstain from any and all delinquency should be relatively rare. False-positive subjects, who meet criteria for a stable and pervasive antisocial childhood history and yet recover (eschew delinquency) after puberty, should be extremely rare.

A specific research design is needed to evaluate whether these epidemiological parameters will be borne out. Samples should be representative to tap the population range of natural histories. The same individuals should be studied longitudinally to describe the trajectories of individuals as opposed to population shifts. Reports of antisocial behavior should be gathered from multiple sources to tap pervasiveness across circumstances. Antisocial behavior should be assessed repeatedly from childhood through adolescence to capture stability and change across time. Measures of antisocial behavior should be sensitive to developmental heterogeneity to tap individual differences while allowing for the emergence of new forms of antisocial behavior (e.g., automobile theft) or for the forsaking of old forms (e.g., tantrums).

If appropriate research designs fail to yield the predicted individual natural histories (or growth curves), at or near the predicted base rates, then the theory is wrong. However, if subjects are found who match the natural histories of this taxonomy, then the following hypotheses may be tested about differential predictors and outcomes.

Predictions About Differential Correlates of Life-Course-Persistent and Adolescence-Limited Antisocial Behavior

According to the theory, the life-course-persistent type has its origins in neuropsychological problems that assume measurable influence when difficult children interact with criminogenic home environments. Beginning in childhood, discipline problems and academic failures accumulate increasing momentum, cutting off opportunities to practice prosocial behavior. As time passes, recovery is precluded by maladaptive individual dispositions and narrowing life options, and delinquents are channeled into antisocial adult lifestyles. Thus, the strongest prospective predictors of persistent antisocial behavior are anticipated to be measures of individual and family characteristics. These measures include health, gender, temperament, cognitive abilities, school achievement, personality traits, mental disorders (e.g., hyperactivity), family attachment bonds, child-rearing practices, parent and sibling deviance, and socioeconomic status, *but not age.*

According to the description of adolescence-limited delinquency, youths with little risk from personal or environmental disadvantage encounter motivation for crime for the first time when they enter adolescence. For them, an emerging appreciation of desirable adult privileges is met with an awareness that those privileges are yet forbidden. After observing their antisocial peers' effective solution to the modern dilemma of the maturity gap, youths mimic that delinquent solution. Perversely, the consequences of delinquency reinforce and sustain their efforts, but only until aging into adulthood brings a subjective shift in the valence of the consequences of crime. Then such offenders readily desist from crime, substituting the prosocial skills they practiced before they entered adolescence. This narrative suggests a direct contrast with the predictions made for persistent antisocial behavior. Individual differences should play little or no role in the prediction of short-term adolescent offending careers. Instead, the strongest prospective predictors of short-term offending should be knowledge of peer delinquency, attitudes toward adulthood and autonomy, cultural and history context, *and age.*

If life-course-persistent and adolescence-limited delinquents, defined on the basis of their natural histories, do not show the predicted differential patterns of correlates, then the theory is wrong.

Predictions About Types of Offenses

According to the theory, the two types will engage in different patterns of offending. Adolescence-limited offenders should engage primarily in crimes that symbolize adult privilege or that demonstrate autonomy from parental control; vandalism, public order offenses, substance abuse, "status" crimes such as running away, and theft. Life-course-persistent offenders should spawn a wider variety of offenses, including types of crimes that are often committed by lone offenders. Thus, in addition to the aforementioned crime types, they should commit more of the victim-oriented offenses, such as violence and fraud.

If groups of life-course-persistent and adolescence-limited delinquents, defined on the basis of their natural histories, do not show the predicted differential patterns of antisocial behaviors, then the theory is wrong.

Predictions About Desistence From Crime

According to this theory, transition events in the life course are *not* unconditional determinants of desistence from crime. Indeed, events such as marriage, employment, or military service can provide opportunities for desistence, but such events can also provide opportunities for continuity. According to this theory, individuals' reactions to life-transition events will vary predictably, depending on their personal antisocial histories. Adolescence-limited delinquents can profit from opportunities for desistence, because they retain the option of successfully resuming a conventional life-style. Life-course-persistent delinquents may make transitions into marriage or work, but their injurious childhoods make it less likely that they can leave their past selves behind; they should select jobs and spouses that support their antisocial style, and they should express antisocial behavior at home and at work.

If life-course-persistent and adolescence-limited delinquents, defined on the basis of their natural histories, do not show the predicted differential responses to young-adulthood transitions, then the theory is wrong.

Predictions About Teenagers
Who Abstain From Delinquency

I have proposed that adolescence-limited delinquency does not constitute pathology. Rather, it is social activity that is normative as well as understandable from the perspective of contemporary teens. If this assertion is true, the existence of people (however few) who abstain from all delinquency during their adolescent years requires explanation. Earlier, I suggested that adolescents who commit no antisocial behavior have either (a) pathological characteristics that exclude them from peer networks, (b) structural barriers that prevent them from learning about delinquency, or (c) no experience of the maturity gap (because of late puberty or early access to adult roles).

If adolescence-limited delinquents and abstainers, defined on the basis of their natural histories, do not differ in their predicted ways, then that part of the theory is wrong.

Predictions About the Longitudinal Stability
of Antisocial Behavior

I have proposed that most adults who behave in an antisocial fashion are the same individuals who began antisocial behavior in early childhood. During the peak participation period of adolescence, those persistent individuals will be masked by the "noise" of their more numerous mimics. Following from this observation, estimates of the individual stability of antisocial behavior are expected to violate the *longitudinal law*, which states that relationships between variables become weaker as the time interval between them grow longer (Clarke & Clarke, 1984). One study has found evidence that the longitudinal law is violated in this way when antisocial behavior is studied in the same individuals over time. Stattin and Magnusson (1984) reported that adult crime was predicted more strongly by behavior at age 10 then by behavior between ages 15 and 17. This prediction awaits additional corroboration.

CONCLUSIONS

The bulk of research, including the longitudinal research, on antisocial behavior continues to be performed on adolescent subjects. This is unfortunate. If the taxonomy introduced here has merit, then studying offenders at the peak participation age offers the least favorable prospects for understanding the sort of antisocial subjects who will develop an adult career of crime and violence. Researchers will learn more about the etiology of severe, persistent antisocial behavior if they single out childhood-onset persistent cases for study and if they begin their studies during infancy, or even prenatally, and follow the same individuals to adulthood. In the past, cross-sectional comparisons that lumped all delinquents together may have resulted in attenuated effect sizes. This probably obscured some potential causal factors from view and produced underestimates of the importance of others. Indeed, it is likely that most of the research findings cited in this article were attenuated. If the theory is correct, then the empirical footing for it could have been clearer if the distinction between persistent and temporary delinquents had been made in past research. In our past efforts to uncover the causes of persistent predatory crime, we have been studying many of the right variables but in the wrong subjects and at the wrong point in the life course.

Also unfortunate is that almost none of the contemporary theories of delinquency do a good job explaining delinquency that begins in adolescence and ends soon after. Our failure as a field to recognize the heterogeneity of adolescent delinquency may have caused us to overlook important theoretical variables, such as biological age, or structural factors in schools and neighborhoods that determine access to antisocial models. Research is needed that analyzes the roles of biological age and attitudes about maturity in the onset of teenaged delinquency. Delinquency theories are woefully ill-informed about the phenomenology of modern teenagers from their own perspective. I fear that we cannot understand adolescence-limited delinquency without first understanding adolescents.

REFERENCES

Agnew, R. (1991). The interactive effect of peer variables on delinquency. *Criminology, 29,* 47–72.

American Psychiatric Association. (1987). *Diagnostic and statistical manual of mental disorders* (3rd ed., rev.). Washington, DC: Author.

Anderson, E. (1990). *Streetwise.* Chicago: University of Chicago Press.

Anderson, K. E., Lytton, H., & Romney, D. M. (1986). Mothers' interactions with normal and conduct-disordered boys: Who affects whom? *Developmental Psychology, 22,* 604–609.

Arzin, N.H., & Holz, W. C. (1966). Punishment. In W. K. Honig (Ed.), *Operant behavior: Areas of research and application* (pp. 390–477). New York: Appleton-Century-Crofts.

Baker, L. A., Mack, W., Moffitt, T. E., & Mednick, S. A. (1989). Etiology of sex differences in criminal convictions in a Danish adoption cohort. *Behavior Genetics, 19,* 355–370.

Bandura, A. (1979). The social learning perspective: Mechanisms of aggression. In H. Toch (Ed.), *Psychology of crime and criminal justice* (pp. 193–236). Prospect Heights, IL: Waveland Press.

Barrett, G. V., & Depinet, R. L. (1991). A reconsideration of testing for competence rather than for intelligence. *American Psychologist, 46,* 1012–1024.

Becker, G. S. (1968). Crime and punishment: An economic approach. *Journal of Political Economy, 76,* 169–217.

Bell, R. Q., & Chapman, M. (1986). Child effects in studies using experimental or brief longitudinal approaches to socialization. *Developmental Psychology, 22,* 595–603.

Bloch, H. A., & Niederhoffer, A. (1958). *The gang: A study in adolescent behavior.* New York: Philosophical Library.

Blumstein, A., & Cohen, J. (1987). Characterizing criminal careers. *Science, 237,* 985–991.

Blumstein, A., Cohen, J., & Farrington, D. P. (1988). Criminal career research: Its value for criminology. *Criminology, 26,* 1–35.

Borecki, I. B., & Ashton, G. C. (1984). Evidence for a major gene influencing performance on a vocabulary test. *Behavior Genetics, 14,* 63–80.

Bowlby, J. (1988). Developmental psychiatry comes of age. *American Journal of Psychiatry, 145,* 1–10.

Buchanan, C. M., Eccles, J. S., & Becker, J. B. (1992). Are adolescents the victims of ranging hormones: Evidence for activational effects of hormones on moods and behavior at adolescence. *Psychological Bulletin, 111,* 62–107.

Buikhuisen, W. (1987). Cerebral dysfunctions and persistent juvenile delinquency. In S. A. Mednick, T. E. Moffitt, & S. A. Stack (Eds.), *The causes of crime: New biological approaches* (pp. 168–184). Cambridge, England: Cambridge University Press.

Buss, D. M. (1984). Toward a psychology of person–environment correspondence: The role of spouse selection. *Journal of Personality and Social Psychology, 47,* 361–377.

Buss, D. M. (1987). Selection, evocation, and manipulation. *Journal of Personality and Social Psychology, 53,* 1214–1221.

Cairns, R. B., & Cairns, B. D. (1991). *Adolescence in our time: Lifelines and risks.* Unpublished manuscript.

Cairns, R. B., Cairns, B. D., Neckerman, H. J., Gest, S. D., & Gariépy, J.-L. (1988). Social networks and aggressive behavior: Peer support or peer rejection? *Developmental Psychology, 24,* 815–823.

Caspi, A., & Bem, D. J. (1990). Personality continuity and change across the life course. In L. Pervin (Ed.), *Handbook of personality theory and research* (pp. 549–575). New York: Guilford Press.

Caspi, A., Bem, D. J., & Elder, G. H., Jr. (1989). Continuities and consequences of interactional styles across the life course. *Journal of Personality, 57,* 375–406.

Caspi, A., Elder, G. H., & Bem, D. J. (1987). Moving against the world: Life-course patterns of explosive children. *Developmental Psychology, 23,* 308–313.

Caspi, A., Lynam, D., Moffitt, T. E., & Silva, P. A. (1993). Unraveling girls' delinquency: Biological, dispositional, and contextual contributions to adolescent misbehavior. *Developmental Psychology, 29,* 19–30.

Caspi, A., & Moffitt, T. E. (1991). Individual differences are accentuated during period of social change: The sample case of girls at puberty. *Journal of Personality and Social Psychology, 61,* 157–168.

Caspi, A., & Moffitt, T. E. (1993). Continuity amidst change: A paradoxical theory of personality coherence. *Psychological Inquiry, 4,* 247–271.

Caspi, A., & Moffitt, T. E. (1995). The continuity of maladaptive behavior: From description to understanding in the study of antisocial behavior. In D. Cicchetti & D. Cohen (Eds.), *Manual of developmental psychopathology.* New York: Wiley.

Chaiken, M. R., & Chaiken, J. M. (1984). Offender types and public policy. *Crime and Delinquency, 30,* 195–226.

Chess, S., & Thomas, A. (1987). *Origins and evolution of behavior disorders: From infancy to early adult life.* Cambridge, MA: Harvard University Press.

Clarke, A. D. B., & Clarke, A. A. M. (1984). Constancy and change in the growth of human characteristics. *Journal of Child Psychology and Psychiatry, 25,* 191–210.

Cleckley, H. (1976). *The mask of sanity* (5th ed.). St. Louis, MO: Mosby.

Cloninger, C. R. (1987). A systematic method for clinical description and classification of personality variants. *Archives of General Psychiatry, 44,* 573–588.

Cloward, R. A., & Ohlin, L. E. (1960). *Delinquency and opportunity.* New York: Free Press of Glencoe.

Coie, J. D., Belding, M., & Underwood, M. (1988). Aggression and peer rejection in childhood. In B. Lahey & A. Kazdin (Eds.), *Advances in clinical child psychology* (Vol. 2, pp. 125–158). New York: Plenum Press.

Coie, J. D., Dodge, K., & Kupersmidt, J. (1990). Peer group behavior and social status. In S. R. Asher & J. D. Coie (Eds.), *Peer rejection in childhood* (pp. 17–59). Cambridge, England: Cambridge University Press.

Costello, E. J. (1989). Developments in child psychiatric epidemiology. *Journal of the American Academy of Child and Adolescent Psychiatry, 28,* 836–841.

Cravioto, J., & Arrieta, R. (1983). Malnutrition in childhood. In M. Rutter (Ed.), *Developmental neuropsychiatry* (pp. 32–51). New York: Guilford Press.

Csikszentmihalyi, M., & Larson, R. (1984). *Being adolescent: Conflict and growth in the teenage years.* New York: Basic Books.

Davison, G. C., & Neale, J. M. (1990). *Abnormal psychology* (5th ed.). New York: Wiley.

DiLalla, L. F., & Gottesman, I. I. (1989). Heterogeneity of causes for delinquency and criminality: Lifespan perspectives. *Development and Psychopathology, 1,* 339–349.

Dishion, T. J., Patterson, G. R., Stoolmiller, M., & Skinner, M. L. (1990). *An ecological analysis of boys' drift to antisocial peers: From middle childhood to early adolescence.* Unpublished manuscript, Oregon Social Learning Center, Eugene.

Dishion, T. J., Patterson, G. R., Stoolmiller, M., & Skinner, M. L. (1991). Family, school, and behavioral antecedents to early adolescent involvement with antisocial peers. *Developmental Psychology, 27,* 172–180.

Dodge, K. A., Coie, J. D., & Brakke, N. P. (1982). Behavior patterns of socially rejected and neglected preadolescents: The roles of social approach and aggression. *Journal of Abnormal Child Psychology, 10,* 389–410.

Dodge, K. A., & Frame, C. L. (1982). Social cognitive biases and deficits in aggressive boys. *Child Development, 53,* 629–635.

Dodge, K. A., & Newman, J. P. (1981). Biased decision-making processes in aggressive boys. *Journal of Abnormal Psychology, 90,* 375–379.

Edelbrock, C., Rende, R., Plomin, R., & Thompson, L. A. (1995). Genetic and environmental effects on competence and problem behavior in childhood and early adolescence. *Journal of Child Psychology and Psychiatry, 36,* 775–785.

Elder, G. H., Jr. (1986). Military times and turning points in men's lives. *Development Psychology, 22,* 233–245.

Elliott, D. S., Ageton, S. S., Huizinga, D., Knowles, B. A., & Canter, R. J. (1983). *The prevalence and incidence of delinquent behavior: 1976–1980* (The National Youth Survey Report No. 26). Boulder, CO: Behavioral Research Institute.

Elliott, D. S., & Huizinga, D. (1983). Social class and delinquent behavior in a national youth panel: 1976–1980. *Criminology, 21,* 149–177.

Elliott, D. S., & Huizinga, D. (1984, April). *The relationship between delinquent behavior and ADM problems.* Paper presented at the AD-ADMA/OJJDP State-of-the-Art Research Conference on Juvenile Offenders with Serious Drug, Alcohol, and Mental Health Problems, Rockville, MD.

Elliott, D. S., Huizinga, D., & Menard, S. (1989). *Multiple problem youth: Delinquency, substance use, and mental health problems.* New York: Springer-Verlag.

Elliott, D. S., Huizinga, D., & Morse, B. (1986). Self-reported violent offending: A descriptive analysis of juvenile violent offenders and their offending careers. *Journal of Interpersonal Violence, 1,* 472–514.

Elliott, D. S., Knowles, B., & Canter, R. (1981). *The epidemiology of delinquent behavior and drug use among American adolescents: 1976–1980* (The National Youth Survey Project Report No. 14).

Boulder, CO: Behavioral Research Institute.

Elliott, D., & Menard, S. (1996). Delinquent friends and delinquent behavior: Temporal and developmental patterns. In D. Hawkins (Ed.), *Some current theories of deviance and crime.* New York: Springer-Verlag.

Elliott, D. S., & Morse, B. J. (1987). Drug use, delinquency, and sexual activity. In C. Jones & E. McAnarney (Eds.), *Drug abuse and adolescent sexual activity pregnancy, and parenthood* (pp. 32–60). Washington, DC: U.S. Government Printing Office.

Elliott, D. S., & Voss, H. L. (1974). *Delinquency and dropout.* Lexington, MA: Heath.

Empey, L. T. (1978). *American Delinquency.* Homewood, IL: Dorsey Press.

Erikson, E. H. (1960). Youth and the life cycle. *Children Today, 7,* 187–194.

Eysenck, H. J. (1977). *Crime and personality.* London: Routledge.

Fagan, J., & Wexler, S. (1987). Crime at home and in the streets: The relationship between family and stranger violence. *Violence and Victims, 2,* 5–23.

Farrington, D. P. (1977). The effects of public labelling. *British Journal of Criminology, 27,* 112–125.

Farrington, D. P. (1983). Offending from 10 to 25 years of age. In K. Van Dusen & S. A. Mednick (Eds.), *Prospective studies of crime and delinquency* (pp. 17–38). Boston: Kluwer-Nijhoff.

Farrington, D. P. (1986). Age and crime. In M. Tonry & N. Morris (Eds.), *Crime and Justice: An Annual Review of Research* (Vol. 7, pp. 189–250). Chicago: University of Chicago Press.

Farrington, D. P. (1989). Early predictors of adolescent aggression and adult violence. *Violence and Victims, 4,* 79–100.

Farrington, D. P. (1991). Antisocial personality from childhood to adulthood. *The Psychologist, 4,* 389–394.

Farrington, D. P., Gallagher, B., Morley, L., Ledger, R. J., & West, D. J. (1986).

Unemployment, school leaving and crime. *British Journal of Criminology, 26,* 335–356.

Farrington, D. P., Loeber, R., Elliott, D. S., Hawkins, D. J., Kandel, D. B., Klein, M. W., McCord, J., Rowe, D., & Tremblay, R. (1990). Advancing knowledge about the onset of delinquency and crime. In B. Lahey & A. Kazdin (Eds.), *Advances in clinical child psychology* (Vol. 13, pp. 283–342). New York: Plenum Press.

Farrington, D. P., Loeber, R., & Van Kammen, W. B. (1990). Long-term criminal outcomes of hyperactivity-impulsivity-attention deficit and conduct problems in childhood. In L. N. Robins & M. R. Rutter (Eds.), *Straight and devious pathways from childhood to adulthood* (pp. 62–81). Cambridge, England: Cambridge University Press.

Farrington, D., Ohlin, L., & Wilson, J. Q. (1986). *Understanding and controlling crime.* New York: Springer-Verlag.

Farrington, D. P., & West, D.J. (1990). The Cambridge study of delinquent development: A long-term follow-up of 411 London males. In H. J. Kerner & G. Kaiser (Eds.), *Kriminalitat* (pp. 117–138). New York: Springer-Verlag.

Feehan, M., Stanton, W., McGee, R., Silva, P. A., & Moffitt, T. E. (1990). Is there an association between lateral preference and delinquent behavior? *Journal of Abnormal Psychology, 99,* 198–201.

Fergusson, D. M., Horwood, L. J., & Lloyd, M. (1991). A latent class model of child offending. *Criminal Behavior and Mental Health, 1,* 90–106.

Finnegan, W. (1990a, September). Out there, I. *The New Yorker.* p. 51–86.

Finnegan, W. (1990b, November). Out there, II. *The New Yorker.* pp. 60–90.

Fogel, C. A., Mednick, S. A., & Michelson, N. (1985). Minor physical anomalies and hyperactivity. *Acta Psychiatrica Scandinavica, 72,* 551–556.

Friedrich, W. N., & Boriskin, J. A. (1976). The role of the child in abuse. *American Journal of Orthopsychiatry, 46,* 580–590.

Frodi, A. M., Lamb, M. E., Leavitt, L. E., Donovan, W. L., Neff, C., & Sherry, D. (1978). Fathers' and mothers' responses to the faces and cries of normal and premature infants. *Developmental Psychology, 14,* 490–498.

Goldsmith, H. H., Bradshaw, D. L., & Rieser-Daner, L. A. (1986). Temperament as a potential developmental influence on attachment. In J. V. Lerner & R. M. Lerner (Eds.), *Temperament and social interaction during infancy and childhood* (pp. 5–34). San Francisco: Jossey-Bass.

Goldstein, A. P. (1990). *Delinquents on delinquency.* Champaign, IL: Research Press.

Gorenstein, E. E., & Newman, J. P. (1980). Disinhibitory psychopathology: A new perspective and a model for research. *Psychological Review, 87,* 301–315.

Gottfredson, M., & Hirschi, T. (1986). The value of lambda would appear to be zero: An essay on career criminals, criminal careers, selective incapacitation, cohort studies, and related topics. *Criminology, 24,* 213–234.

Gottfredson, M., & Hirschi, T. (1990). *A general theory of crime.* Stanford, CA: Stanford University Press.

Gove, W. R. (1985). The effect of age and gender on deviant behavior: A biopsychosocial perspective. In A. Rossi (Ed.), *Gender and the life course* (pp. 115–144). Chicago: Aldine.

Greenberg, D. F. (1985). Age, crime, and social explanation. *American Journal of Sociology, 91,* 1–21.

Hagan, J. (1987). Class in the household: A power-control theory of gender and delinquency. *American Journal of Sociology, 92,* 788–816.

Hagan, J., Gillis, A. R., & Simpson, J. (1985). The class structure of gender and delinquency: Toward a power-control theory of common delinquent behavior. *American Journal of Sociology, 90,* 1151–1179.

Hare, R. D., Hart, S. D., & Harpur, T. J. (1991). Psychopathy and the *DSM–IV* criteria for antisocial personality disorder. *Journal of Abnormal Psychology, 100,* 391–398.

Hare, R. D., & McPherson, L. M. (1984). Violent and aggressive behavior by criminal psychopaths. *International Journal of Law and Psychiatry, 7,* 35–50.

Harpur, T. J., & Hare, R. D. (1991). *The assessment of psychopathy as a function of age.* Unpublished manuscript, University of British Columbia, Vancouver, British Columbia, Canada.

Henry, B., Moffitt, T. E. Robins, L. N., Earls, F., & Silva, P. A. (1993). Early family predictors of child and adolescent antisocial behavior: Who are the mothers of delinquents? *Criminal Behavior and Mental Health, 3,* 97–118.

Hertzig, M. (1983). Temperament and neurological status. In M. Rutter (Ed.), *Developmental neuropsychiatry* (pp. 164–180). New York: Guilford Press.

Hirschi, T. (1969). *Causes of delinquency.* Berkeley, CA: University of California Press.

Hirschi, T., & Gottfredson, M. (1983). Age and the explanation of crime. *American Journal of Sociology, 89,* 552–584.

Hirschi, T., & Hindelang, M. J. (1977). Intelligence and delinquency: A revisionist review. *American Sociological Review, 42,* 571–587.

Hood, R., & Sparks, R. (1970). *Key issues in criminology.* New York: McGraw-Hill.

Horan, P. M., & Hargis, P. G. (1991). Children's work and schooling in the late nineteenth-century family economy. *American Sociological Review, 56,* 583–596.

Huesmann, L. R., Eron, L. D., Lefkowitz, M. M., & Walder, L. O. (1984). Stability of aggression over time and generations. *Developmental Psychology, 20,* 1120–1134.

Hunter, R. S., Kilstrom, N., Kraybill, E. N., & Loda, F. (1978). Antecedents of child abuse and neglect in premature infants: A prospective study in a new born intensive care unit. *Pediatrics, 61,* 629–635.

Jesness, C. F., & Haapanen, R. A. (1982). *Early identification of chronic offender.* Sacramento, CA: Department of Youth Authority.

Jessor, R., Costa, F., Jessor, L., & Donovan, J. E. (1983). Times of first intercourse: A prospective study. *Journal of Personality and Social Psychology, 44,* 608–626.

Jessor, R., & Jessor, S. L. (1977). *Problem behavior and psychosocial development: A longitudinal study of youth.* San Diego, CA: Academic Press.

Kagan, J. (1969). The three faces of continuity in human development. In D. A. Goslin (Ed.), *Handbook of socialization theory and research* (pp. 983–1002). Chicago: Rand McNally.

Kagan, J., & Moss, H. A. (1962). *Birth to maturity.* New York: Wiley.

Kandel, D. (1980). Drug and drinking behavior among youth. *Annual Review of Sociology, 6,* 235–285.

Kandel, E., Brennan, P. A., & Mednick, S. A. (1989). Minor physical anomalies and parental modeling of aggression predict to violent offending. *Acta Psychiatrica Scandanavica, 78,* 1–5.

Kandel, E., & Mednick, S. A. (1991). Perinatal complications predict violent offending. *Criminology, 29,* 519–530.

Kazdin, A. E. (1987), *Conduct disorders in childhood and adolescence.* Newbury Park, CA: Sage.

Klein, M. W. (1984). Offense specialization and versatility among juveniles: A review of the evidence. *British Journal of Criminology, 24,* 185–194.

Klein, M. W. (1986). Labelling theory and delinquency policy. *Criminal Justice and Behavior, 13,* 47–79.

Klein, M. (1989). Watch out for that last variable. In S. Mednick, T. Moffitt, & S. A. Stack (Eds.), *The cause of crime: New biological approaches* (pp. 25–41). Cambridge, England: Cambridge University Press.

Knight, B. J., & West, D. J. (1975), Temporary and continuing delinquency.

British Journal of Criminology, 15, 43–50.

Kraemer, G. W. (1988). Speculations on the developmental neurobiology of protest and despair. In P. Simon, P. Soubrie, & D. Widlocher (Eds.), *Inquiry into schizophrenia and depression: Animal models of psychiatric disorders* (pp. 101–147). Basel, Switzerland: Karger.

LaFrenier, P., & Sroufe, L. A. (1985). Profiles of peer competence in the preschool: Interrelations between measures, influence of social ecology, and relation to attachment history. *Developmental Psychology, 21,* 56–69.

Lahey, B. B., Frick, P. J., Loeber, R., Tannenbaum, B. A., Van Horn, Y., & Christ, M. A. G. (1990). *Oppositional and conduct disorder: I. A meta-analytic review.* Unpublished manuscript.

Lee, C. L., & Bates, J. E. (1985). Mother-child interaction at age two years and perceived difficult temperament. *Child Development, 56,* 1314–1323.

Lemert, E. M. (1967). *Human deviance, social problems, and social control.* Englewood Cliffs, NJ: Prentice Hall.

Lewis, D. O., Shanok, S. S., Picus, J. H., & Glaser, G. H. (1979). Violent juvenile delinquents: Psychiatric, neurological, psychological and abuse factors. *Journal of the American Academy of Child Psychiatry, 2,* 307–319.

Lipton, D., Martinson, R., & Wilks, J. (1975). *The effectiveness of correctional treatment: A survey of treatment evaluation studies.* New York: Praeger.

Loeber, R. (1982). The stability of antisocial and delinquent child behavior: A review. *Child Development, 53,* 1431–1446.

Loeber, R., & Baicker-McKee, C. (1989). *The changing manifestations of disruptive/antisocial behavior from childhood to early adulthood: Evolution of tautology?* Unpublished manuscript, Western Psychiatric Institute, University of Pittsburgh, Pittsburgh, PA.

Loeber, R., Green, S., Lahey, B., Stouthamer-Loeber, M. (1990). Optimal informants on childhood disrup-

tive behaviors. *Development and Psychopathology, 1,* 317–337.

Loeber, R., & LeBlanc, M. (1990). Toward a developmental criminology. In M. Tonry & N. Morris (Eds.), *Crime and justice* (Vol. 12, pp. 375–473). Chicago: University of Chicago Press.

Loeber, R., & Schmaling, K. B. (1985). Empirical evidence for overt and covert patterns of antisocial conduct problems: A meta analysis. *Journal of Abnormal Child Psychology, 13,* 337–353.

Loeber, R., Stouthamer-Loeber, M., Van Kammen, W., & Farrington, D. P. (1989). Development of a new measure of self-reported antisocial behavior for young children: Prevalence and reliability. In M. Klein (Ed.), *Cross-national research in self-reported crime and delinquency* (pp. 203–226). Boston: Kluwer-Nijhoff.

Loehlin, J. C. (1989). Partitioning environmental and genetic contributions to behavioral development. *American Psychologist, 44,* 1285–1292.

Lynam, D., Moffitt, T., & Stouthamer-Loeber, M. (1993). Explaining the relation between IQ and delinquency: Class, race, test motivation, school failure, or self-control? *Journal of Abnormal Psychology, 102,* 187–196.

Lytton, H. (1990). Child and parent effects in boys' conduct disorder: A reinterpretation. *Developmental Psychology, 26,* 683–697.

Maccoby, E. E., & Jacklin, C. N. (1983). The "person" characteristics of children and the family as environment. In D. Magnusson & V. L. Allen (Eds.), *Human development: An interactional perspective* (pp. 75–92). San Diego, CA: Academic Press.

Magnusson, D. (1988). *Individual development from an interactional perspective: A longitudinal study.* Hillsdale, NJ: Erlbaum.

Martin, N. G., Jardine, R., & Eaves, L. J. (1984). Is there only one set of genes for different abilities? *Behavior Genetics, 14,* 355–370.

Mattick, H. W. (1960). Parolees in the army during World War II. *Federal Probation, 24,* 49–55.

Maughan, B., Gray, G., & Rutter, M. (1985). Reading retardation and antisocial behavior: A follow-up into employment. *Journal of Child Psychiatry and Psychology, 26,* 741–758.

Mausner, B., & Platt, E. S. (1971). *Smoking: A behavioral analysis.* Elmsford, NY: Pergamon Press.

McGee, R., Partridge, F., Williams, S. M., & Silva, P. A. (1991). A twelve-year follow up of preschool hyperactive children. *Journal of the American Academy of Child and Adolescent Psychiatry, 30,* 224–232.

Meany, M. J., Aitken, D. H., van Berkel, C., Bhatnagar, S., & Sapolsky, R. M. (1988). Effect of neonatal handling on age-related impairments associated with the hippocampus. *Science, 239,* 766–768.

Mednick, S. A. (1977). A bio-social theory of the learning of law-abiding behavior. In S. A. Mednick & K. O. Christiansen (Eds.). *Biosocial bases of criminal behavior* (pp. 1–8). New York: Gardner Press.

Mednick, S. A., Gabrielli, W. F., & Hutchings, B. (1984). Genetic influences in criminal behavior: Some evidence from an adoption cohort. *Science, 224,* 891–893.

Meehl, P. E., & Golden, R. R. (1982). Taxometric methods. In P. C. Kendall & J. N. Butcher (Eds.), *Handbook of research methods in clinical psychology* (pp. 127–181). New York: Wiley.

Megargee, E. (1976). The prediction of dangerous behavior. *Criminal Justice and Behavior, 3,* 3–21.

Millon, T. (1991). Classification in psychopathology: Rationale, alternatives, and standards. *Journal of Abnormal Psychology, 100,* 245–261.

Milner, J. S., & McCanne, T. R. (1991). Neuropsychological correlates of physical child abuse. In J. S. Milner (Ed.), *Neuropsychology of aggression* (pp. 131–145). Norwell, MA: Kluwer Academic.

Milowe, I. D., & Lowrie, R. S. (1964). The child's role in the battered child syndrome. *Journal of Pediatrics, 65,* 1079–1081.

Modell, J., Furstenberg, F. F., & Hershberg, T. (1976). Social change and transitions to adulthood in historical perspective. *Journal of Family History, 12,* 7–32.

Moffitt, T. E. (1990a). Juvenile delinquency and attention-deficit disorder: Development trajectories from age 3 to 15. *Child Development, 61,* 893–910.

Moffitt, T. E. (1990b). The neuropsychology of delinquency: A critical review of theory and research. In N. Morris & M. Tonry (Eds.), *Crime and justice* (Vol. 12, pp. 99–169). Chicago: University of Chicago Press.

Moffitt, T. E. (1991, September). *Juvenile delinquency: Seed of a career in violent crime, just sowing wild oats—or both?* Paper presented at the Science and Public Policy Seminars of the Federation of Behavioral, Psychological, and Cognitive Sciences, Washington, DC.

Moffitt, T. E., & Henry, B. (1989). Neuropsychological assessment of executive functions in self-reported delinquents. *Development and Psychopathology, 1,* 105–118.

Moffitt, T. E., & Henry B. (1991). Neuropsychological studies of juvenile delinquency and violence: A review. In J. Milner (Ed.), *The neuropsychology of aggression* (pp. 67–91). Norwell, MA: Kluwer Academic.

Moffitt, T. E., Mednick, S. A., & Gabrielli, W. F. (1989). Predicting criminal violence: Descriptive data and predispositional factors. In D. Brizer & M. Crowner (Eds.), *Current approaches to the prediction of violence* (pp. 13–34). Washington, DC: American Psychiatric Association.

Moffitt, T. E., & Silva, P. A. (1988a). IQ and delinquency: A direct test of the differential detection hypothesis. *Journal of Abnormal Psychology, 97,* 330–333.

Moffitt, T. E., & Silva, P. A. (1988b). Neuropsychological deficit and self-reported delinquency in an unselected birth cohort. *Journal of the American Academy of Child and Adolescent Psychiatry, 27,* 233–240.

Moffitt, T. E., & Silva, P. A. (1988c). Self-reported delinquency: Results from an instrument for New Zealand. *Australian and New Zealand Journal of Criminology, 21,* 227–240.

Morey, L. C. (1991). Classification of mental disorder as a collection of hypothetical constructs. *Journal of Abnormal Psychology, 100,* 289–293.

Moynihan, M. (1968). Social mimicry: Character convergence versus character displacement. *Evolution, 22,* 315–331.

Murray, C. A. (1976). *The line between learning disabilities and juvenile delinquency.* Washington, DC: U.S. Department of Justice.

Nagin, D., & Paternoster, R. (1991). The preventive effects of the perceived risk of arrest: Testing an expanded conception of deterrence. *Criminology: 29,* 561–588.

Nasby, W., Hayden, B., & DePaulo, B. M. (1980). Attributional bias among aggressive boys to interpret unambiguous social stimuli as displays of hostility. *Journal of Abnormal Psychology, 89,* 459–468.

Needleman, H. L., & Beringer, D. C. (1981). The epidemiology of low-level lead exposure in childhood. *Journal of Child Psychiatry, 20,* 496–512.

Palmer, T. (1984). Treatment and the role of classification: A review of basics. *Crime and Delinquency, 30,* 245–267.

Panel on Youth of the President's Science Advisory Committee. (1974). *Transition to adulthood.* Chicago: University of Chicago Press.

Parkhurst, J. T., & Asher, S. R. (1992). Peer rejection in middle school: Subgroup differences in behavior, loneliness, and interpersonal concerns. *Developmental Psychology, 28,* 231–241.

Paternoster, R., Saltzman, L. E., Waldo, G. P., & Chiricos, T. G. (1983). Perceived risk and social control: Do sanctions really deter? *Law & Society Review, 17,* 457–479.

Patterson, G. R. (1982). *Coercive family process.* Eugene, OR: Castalia.

Paulhus, D. L., & Martin, C. L. (1986). Predicting adult temperament from minor physical anomalies. *Journal of Personality and Social Psychology, 50,* 1235–1239.

Pepler, D., & Rubin, K. (Eds.). (1991). *The development and treatment of childhood aggression.* Hillsdale, NJ: Erlbaum.

Piliavin, I., Thornton, C., Gartner, R., & Matsueda, R. (1986). Crime, deterrence, and rational choice. *American Sociological Review, 51,* 101–119.

Plomin, R. (1990). The role of inheritance in behavior. *Science, 248,* 183–188.

Plomin, R., & Bergeman, C. S. (1990). The nature of nurture: Genetic influence on "environmental" measures. *Behavioral and Brain Sciences, 14,* 373–386.

Plomin, R., Chipuer, H. M., & Loehlin, J. C. (1990). Behavioral genetics and personality. In L. A. Pervin (Ed.), *Handbook of personality theory and research* (pp. 225–243). New York: Guilford Press.

Plomin, R., DeFries, J. C., & Loehlin, J. C. (1977). Genotype-environment interaction and correlation in the analysis of human behavior. *Psychological Bulletin, 88,* 245–258.

Plomin, R., Nitz, K., & Rowe, D. C. (1990). Behavioral genetics and aggressive behavior in childhood. In M. Lewis & S. M. Miller (Eds.), *Handbook of developmental psychopathology* (pp. 119–133). New York: Plenum Press.

Price, B. H., Daffner, K. R., Stowe, R. M., & Mesulam, M. M. (1990). The comportmental learning disabilities of early frontal lobe damage. *Brain, 113,* 1383–1393.

Quay, H. C. (1964a). Dimensions of personality in delinquent boys as inferred from the factor analysis of case history data. *Child Development, 35,* 479–484.

Quay, H. C. (1964b). Personality dimensions in delinquent males as inferred from the factor analysis of behavior ratings. *Journal of Research in Crime and Delinquency, 1,* 33–37.

Quay, H. C. (1966). Personality patterns in preadolescent delinquent boys. *Educational and Psychological Measurements, 16,* 99–110.

Quay, H. C. (1987). Patterns of delinquent behavior. In H. C. Quay (Ed.), *Handbook of juvenile delinquency* (pp. 118–138). New York: Wiley.

Quine, W. V. O. (1977). Natural kinds. In S. P. Schwartz (Ed.), *Naming, necessity and natural kinds* (pp. 155–175). Ithaca, NY: Cornell University Press.

Quinton, D., & Rutter, M. (1988). *Parenting breakdown: The making and breaking of intergenerational links.* Aldershot, England: Avebury.

Reiss, A. J., Jr. (1986). Co-offender influences on criminal careers. In A. Blumstein, J. Cohen, J. A. Roth, & C. Visher (Eds.), *Criminal careers and career criminals* (pp. 121–160). Washington, DC: National Academy Press.

Reiss, A. J., Jr.., & Farrington, D. P. (1991). Advancing knowledge about co-offending: Results from a prospective longitudinal survey of London males. *Journal of Criminal Law and Criminology, 82,* 360–395.

Robins, L. N. (1966). *Deviant children grown up.* Baltimore, MD: Williams & Wilkins.

Robins, L. N. (1978). Sturdy, childhood predictors of adult antisocial behavior: Replications from longitudinal studies. *Psychological Medicine, 8,* 611–622.

Robins, L. N. (1985). Epidemiology of antisocial personality. In J. O. Cavenar (Ed.)., *Psychiatry* (Vol. 3, pp. 1–14). Philadelphia: Lippincott.

Robins, L. N., & Regier, D. A. (1991). *Psychiatric disorders in America.* New York: Free Press.

Rodning, C., Beckwith, L., & Howard, J. (1989). Characteristics of attachment organization and play organization in prenatally drug-exposed toddlers. *Development and Psychopathology, 1,* 277–289.

Rothbart, M. K., & Derryberry, D. (1981). Development of individual differences in temperament. In M. E. Lamb & A. L. Brown (Eds.), *Advances in developmental psychology* (Vol. 1, pp. 37–66). Hillsdale, NJ: Erlbaum.

Rowe, A. R., & Tittle, C. R. (1977). Life cycle changes and criminal propensity. *The Sociological Quarterly, 18,* 223–236.

Rutter, M. (1977). Brain damage syndromes in childhood: Concepts and findings. *Journal of Child Psychology and Psychiatry, 18,* 1–22.

Rutter, M. (Ed.). (1983). *Developmental neuropsychiatry.* New York: Guilford Press.

Rutter, M., Tizard, J., & Whitmore, K. (1970). *Education, health and behaviour.* London: Longman.

Ryder, R. G. (1967). Birth to maturity revisited: A canonical analysis. *Journal of Personality and Social Psychology, 1,* 168–172.

Sameroff, A., & Chandler, M. (1975). Reproductive risk and the continuum of caretaking casualty. In F. Horowitz, M. Hetherington, S. Scarr-Salapatek, & G. Siegel (Eds.), *Review of child development research* (Vol. 4, pp. 187–244). Chicago: University of Chicago Press.

Sampson, R. J., & Groves, W. B. (1989). Community structure and crime: Testing social disorganization theory. *American Journal of Sociology, 94,* 774–802.

Sampson, R. J., & Laub, J. H. (1990). Crime and deviance over the life course: The salience of adult social bonds. *American Sociological Review, 55,* 609–627.

Sampson, R. J., & Laub, J. H. (1992). Crime and deviance in the life course. *Annual Review of Sociology, 18,* 63–84.

Sandgrund, A. K., Gaines, R., & Green, A. (1974). Child abuse and mental retardation: A problem of cause and effect. *American Journal of Mental Deficiency, 79,* 327–330.

Sarnecki, J. (1986). *Delinquent networks.* Stockholm: National Council for Crime Prevention.

Scarr, S., & McCartney, K. (1983). How people make their own environments: A theory of genotype → environment effects. *Child Development, 54,* 424–435.

Schwendinger, H., & Schwendinger, J. S. (1985). *Adolescent subcultures and delinquency.* New York: Praeger.

Sechrest, L., White, S.O., & Brown, E. D. (Eds.). (1979). *The rehabilitation of criminal offenders: Problems and prospects.* Washington, DC: National Academy of Sciences.

Shaw, C. R., & McKay, H. D. (1942). *Juvenile delinquency and urban areas.* Chicago: University of Chicago Press.

Shedler, J., & Block, J. (1990). Adolescent drug use and psychological health. *American Psychologist, 45,* 612–630.

Silbereisen, R. K., & Noack, P. (1988). On the constructive role of problem behavior in adolescence. In N. Bolger, A. Caspi, G. Downey, & M. Moorehouse (Eds.), *Person in context: Developmental processes* (pp. 152–180). Cambridge, England: Cambridge University Press.

Simmons, R. G., & Blyth, D. A. (1987). *Moving into adolescence: The impact of pubertal change and school context.* New York: Aldine de Gruyter.

Skogan, W. G. (1979). Crime in contemporary America. In H. D. Graham & T. R. Gurr (Eds.), *Violence in America: Historical and comparative perspectives* (pp. 375–391). Beverly Hills, CA: Sage.

Skogan, W. G. (1990). *Disorder and decline.* New York: Free Press.

Smith, D. A., & Visher, C. A. (1980). Sex and involvement in deviance/crime: A quantitative review of the empirical literature. *American Sociological Review, 45,* 691–701.

Snyder, J., & Patterson, G. (1987). Family interaction and delinquent behavior. In H. Quay (Ed.), *Handbook of juvenile delinquency* (pp. 216–243), New York: Wiley.

Stattin, H., & Magnusson, D. (1984). *The roles of early aggressive behavior for the frequency, the seriousness, and the types of later criminal offenses* (report). Stockholm: University of Stockholm, Department of Psychology.

Steffensmeier, D. J., Allan, E. A., Harer, M. D., & Streifel, C. (1989). Age and the distribution of crime. *American Journal of Sociology, 94,* 803–831.

Steinberg, L. (1981). Transformations in family relations at puberty. *Developmental Psychology, 17,* 833–840.

Steinberg, L. (1987). Impact of puberty on family relations: Effects of pubertal status and pubertal timing. *Developmental Psychology, 23,* 451–460.

Steinberg, L., & Silverberg, S. B. (1986). The vicissitudes of autonomy in early adolescence. *Child Development, 57,* 841–851.

Stewart, A. (1983). Severe perinatal hazards. In M. Rutter (Ed.), *Developmental neuropsychiatry* (pp. 15–31). New York: Guilford Press.

Suedfeld, P., & Landon, P. B. (1978). Approaches to treatment. In R. Hare & D. Schalling (Eds.), *Psychopathic behaviour* (pp. 347–376). New York: Wiley.

Sutherland, E., & Cressey, D. R. (1978). *Criminology.* Philadelphia: Lippincott.

Szatmari, P., Reitsma-Street, M., & Offord, D. (1986). Pregnancy and birth complications in antisocial adolescents and their siblings. *Canadian Journal of Psychiatry, 31,* 513–516.

Tambs, K., Sundet, J. M., & Magnus, P. (1984). Heritability analysis of the WAIS subtests: A study of twins. *Intelligence, 8,* 283–293.

Tanner, J. M. (1978). *Fetus into man.* Cambridge, MA: Harvard University Press.

Tarter, R. E., Hegedus, A. M., Winsten, N. E., & Alterman, A. L. (1984). Neuropsychological, personality and familial characteristics of physically abused delinquents. *Journal of the American Academy of Child Psychiatry, 23,* 668–674.

Thomas, A., & Chess, S. (1977). *Temperament and development.* New York: Brunner/Mazel.

Tinsley, B. R., & Parke, R. D. (1983). The person–environment relationship: Lessons from families with preterm infants. In D. Magnusson & V. L. Allen (Eds.), *Human development: An interactional perspective* (pp. 93–110). San Diego, CA: Academic Press.

Tolan, P. H. (1987). Implications of age on onset for delinquency risk. *Journal of Abnormal Child Psychology, 15,* 47–65.

Tremblay, R. E. (1991). Aggression, pro-social behavior, and gender: Three magic words, but no magic wand. In D. Pepler & K. Rubin (Eds.), *The development and treatment of childhood aggression* (pp. 71–77). Hillsdale, NJ: Erlbaum.

Udry, J. R. (1988). Biological predispositions and social control in adolescent sexual behavior. *American Sociological Review, 53,* 709–722.

Vandenberg, S. C. (1969). A twin study of spatial ability. *Multivariate Behavioral Research, 4,* 273–294.

Vitaro, F., Gagnon, C., & Tremblay, R. E. (1990). Predicting stable peer rejection from kindergarten to grade one. *Journal of Clinical Child Psychology, 19,* 257–264.

Warr, M. & Stafford, M. (1991). The influence of delinquent peers: What they think or what they do? *Criminology, 29,* 851–866.

Warren, M. Q. (1969) The case for differential treatment of delinquents. *Annals of the American Academy of Political Science, 381,* 47–59.

Weiher, A., Huizinga, D., Lizotte, A. J., & Van Kammen, W. B. (1991). The relationship between sexual activity, pregnancy, delinquency, and drug abuse. In D. Huizinga, R. Loeber, & T. Thornberry (Eds.), *Urban delinquency and substance abuse: A technical report* (chapter 6). Washington DC: Office of Juvenile Justice and Delinquency Prevention.

Wender, P. H. (1971). *Minimal brain dysfunction in children.* New York: Wiley.

West, D. J. (1982). *Delinquency.* Cambridge, MA: Harvard University Press.

West, D. J., & Farrington, D. P. (1977). *The delinquent way of life.* New York: Crane Russak.

White, J., Moffitt, T. E., Caspi, A., Jeglum, D., Needles, D., & Stouthamer-Loeber, M. (1994). Measuring impulsivity and examining its relationship to delinquency. *Journal of Abnormal Psychology, 103,* 192–205.

White, J., Moffitt, T. E., Earls, F., Robins, L. N., & Silva, P. A. (1990). How early can we tell? Preschool predictors of boys' conduct disorder and delinquency. *Criminology, 28,* 507–533.

Williams, K. R., & Hawkins, R. (1986). Perceptual research on general deterrence: A review. *Law & Society Review, 20,* 545–572.

Wilson, E. O. (1975). *Sociobiology.* Cambridge, MA: Harvard University Press.

Wilson, J. Q. (1983). Crime and American culture. *The Public Interest, 70,* 22–48.

Wilson, J. Q., & Herrnstein, R. J. (1985). *Crime and human nature.* New York: Simon & Schuster.

Wolfgang, M. E., Figlio, R. M., & Sellin, T. (1972). *Delinquency in a birth cohort.* Chicago: University of Chicago Press.

Wolfgang, M. E., Thornberry, T. P., & Figlio, R. M. (1987). *From boy to man, from delinquency to crime.* Chicago: University of Chicago Press.

Wyshak, G., & Fritsch, R. E. (1982). Evidence for a secular trend in age of menarche. *New England Journal of Medicine, 306,* 1033–1035.

6

A Life-Course Theory of Cumulative Disadvantage and the Stability of Delinquency*

ROBERT J. SAMPSON

JOHN H. LAUB

Although often lumped together, longitudinal and developmental approaches to crime are not the same. Longitudinal research invokes a methodological stance—collecting and analyzing data on persons (or macrosocial units) over time. Ironically, however, one of the objections to existing longitudinal research has been that it often looks like, or produces results equivalent to, cross-sectional research (Gottfredson & Hirschi, 1987). Critics of longitudinal research have a valid point—many studies simply investigate between-individual relationships using a static, invariant conception of human development. For example, showing an "effect" of social class at time one on crime at time two requires a longitudinal design, but substantively such an effect says nothing about within-individual change, dynamic or sequential processes, or whether in fact "time" really matters. Hence longitudinal studies often borrow the tools of cross-sectional analysis but do not inform about how individuals progress through the life course. Perhaps most important, until recently longitudinal research has labored under the trinity of dominant criminological theories—strain, control, and cultural deviance—all of which are inherently static in their original conceptualization. It is little wonder that the mismatch of static theory with longitudinal data has produced unsatisfactory results.

By contrast, developmental approaches are inextricably tied to dynamic concerns and the unfolding of biological, psychological, and social processes through time. Rutter and Rutter (1993) propose an admittedly "fuzzy" but nonetheless useful definition of development as "systematic, organized, intra-individual change that is clearly associated with generally expectable age-related progressions and which is carried forward in some way that has

SOURCE: In T. P. Thornberry (Ed.). *Developmental theories of crime and delinquency: Advances in criminological theory,* pp. 133–161. Reprinted by permission of Transaction Books.

*We thank Terry Thornberry for helpful comments on a previous draft. This paper stems from an ongoing project using the archives of Sheldon and Eleanor Glueck, and draws in part from our recent book *Crime in the Making: Pathways and Turning Points Through Life.* Financial support from the Russell Sage Foundation (grant #998.958) is gratefully acknowledged.

implications for a person's pattern or level of functioning at some later time" (1993:64). Development is thus focused on systematic change, especially how behaviors set in motion dynamic processes that alter future outcomes.

With respect to crime, Loeber and LeBlanc (1990:451) argue that "developmental criminology" recognizes both continuity and within-individual changes over time, focusing on "life transitions and developmental covariates . . . which may mediate the developmental course of offending." This strategy has also been referred to as a "stepping stone approach" where factors are time ordered by age and assessed with respect to outcome variables (see Farrington, 1986). A similar orientation can be found in interactional theory (Thornberry, 1987), which embraces a developmental approach and asserts that causal influences are reciprocal over the life course.

In this paper, we take seriously the conceptions of time and systematic change implied by a developmental approach. We do so with reference to a particularly vexing problem that has led to much debate in criminology—continuity (or stability) in criminal behavior. As reviewed below, there is evidence that antisocial and criminal behaviors are relatively stable over long periods of the life course. Yet while most criminologists can agree on the basic facts, the implications of this stability are contentious. Namely, the fact of stability can be interpreted from both a developmental and a time-invariant, static perspective. Our purpose is to lay out these competing viewpoints on the issue from the perspective of our recent theoretical framework on age-graded informal social control (Sampson & Laub, 1993). We specifically propose that sources of continuity stem in large part from developmental processes that we term "cumulative disadvantage" (Sampson & Laub, 1993; Laub & Sampson, 1993). The idea of cumulative disadvantage draws on a dynamic conceptualization of social control over the life course, integrated with the one theoretical perspective in criminology that is inherently developmental in nature—labeling theory.

EVIDENTIARY BACKDROP

The facts appear straightforward. For some time now research has shown that individual differences in antisocial behavior are relatively stable over time. For example, Olweus's (1979) review of sixteen studies on aggressive behavior revealed "substantial" stability—the correlation between early aggressive behavior and later criminality averaged .68 (1979:854–55). Loeber (1982) completed a similar review of the extant literature in many disciplines and concluded that a "consensus" has been reached in favor of the stability hypothesis: "children who initially display high rates of antisocial behavior are more likely to persist in this behavior than children who initially show lower rates of antisocial behavior" (1982:1433). In addition to earlier classic studies (e.g., Glueck & Glueck, 1930, 1968; Robins, 1966), more recent works documenting stability in delinquent behavior across time include West and Farrington (1977), Bachman et al. (1978), and Wolfgang et al. (1987).

The linkage between childhood delinquency and adult outcomes is also found across domains that go well beyond the legal concept of crime (e.g., excessive drinking, traffic violations, marital conflict or abuse, and harsh discipline of children). Huesmann et al. (1984) report that aggression in childhood was related not just to adult crime but marital conflict, drunk driving, moving violations, and severe punishment of offspring. Other studies reporting a coalescence of delinquent and "deviant" acts over time include Glueck and Glueck (1968), Robins (1966), and West and Farrington (1977). As Caspi and Moffitt (1993: 2) note, continuities in antisocial behavior have also been replicated in nations other than the United States (e.g., Canada, England, Finland, New Zealand, and Sweden) and with multiple methods of assessment (e.g., official records, teacher ratings, parent reports, peer nominations). Taken as a whole, these different studies across time, space, and method yield an impressive generalization that is rare in the social sciences.

To be sure, behavioral stability in criminal conduct is not perfect or inevitable. As we have reviewed elsewhere, there are considerable discontinuities in crime throughout life that must be explained (Sampson & Laub, 1992). For example, while studies do show that antisocial behavior in children is one of the best predictors of antisocial behavior in adults, "most antisocial children do not become antisocial as adults" (Gove, 1985:123; see also Robins, 1978). Similarly, Cline (1980:669–670) concludes that there is far more heterogeneity in criminal behavior than previous work has suggested, and that many juvenile offenders do not become career offenders. For these reasons we view intra-individual change and "turning points" as integral to developmental theories of criminal behavior (Laub & Sampson, 1993). Nonetheless, we restrict our attention in this article to an explanation of the stability of delinquency from a developmental framework.

THE DEVELOPMENTAL STATUS OF CRIMINOLOGICAL THEORY

How might criminological theory explain behavioral stability? The simple answer is that the question has been largely ignored by criminologists despite the long-standing evidence. Especially from a sociological framework, criminologists have not paid much attention to the developmental implications of early antisocial behavior and its stability through time and circumstance (Sampson & Laub, 1992). This is not surprising, however, since traditional criminological theory is decidedly nondevelopmental in nature. Take, for example, the three dominant perspectives on crime—control, strain, and cultural deviance. Each of these perspectives seeks to explain why some individuals engage in crime and not others—a between-individual mode of inquiry.[1] Thus each tends to assign causal priority to the *level* of competing variables (e.g., degree of attachment to parents vs. delinquent definitions) among individuals, which are then tested for relative effects with cross-sectional designs (see Thornberry, 1987 for a similar discussion).

When the evidence on stability has been seriously considered by criminologists, static explanations also predominate (for an overview see Sampson & Laub, 1993). These generally involve the interpretation of stability as arising from a "latent trait" that is time invariant (e.g., extroversion, low IQ). But if a trait is time-invariant, do we need to follow persons longitudinally? Gottfredson and Hirschi (1990:237) answer this very question in the negative and criticize developmental criminology for neglecting its own evidence on the stability of personal characteristics. Specifically, Gottfredson and Hirschi (1990) interpret stability from the viewpoint of a personality trait—low self-control—that causes crime at all ages. In other words, Gottfredson and Hirschi's theory posits a trait of low self- control that differs among individuals but remains constant over time within a given person. Since within-individual change is excluded from the theory by definition, they view behavioral change as "illusory" or "alleged" (Hirschi & Gottfredson, 1993:51).[2]

The implications for a developmental strategy are profound. As Nagin and Farrington (1992:501) trace them: "Once relevant time-stable individual differences are established, subsequent individual experiences and circumstances will have no enduring impact on criminal (or noncriminal) trajectories." The time-invariant or static viewpoint argues therefore that stability in crime over the life course is generated by population *heterogeneity* in an underlying criminal propensity that is established early in life and remains stable over time (see also Wilson & Herrnstein, 1985). Precisely because individual differences in the propensity to commit crime emerge early and are stable, childhood and adult crime will be positively correlated. It then follows that the correlation between past and future delinquency is not causal but spurious because of population heterogeneity. The hypothesized sources of early propensity cover a number of factors, but in addition to self-control leading candidates in the criminological literature include temperament, IQ, and hyperactivity (Wilson & Herrnstein, 1985).

A time-invariant or static interpretation is perhaps understandable when considered along with the larger intellectual history of developmental research. Following what Dannefer (1984) terms the "ontogenetic" model, the dominant view of human development has been one of "maturational unfolding" irrespective of context. That is, the environment is seen as the stage on which life patterns are played out—one that has no real bearing on the structure of development.[3] Hence developmental approaches almost always look to the early childhood years as the shaper of all that follows. In an incisive essay, the psychologist Jerome Kagan (1980:44) argues that this strategy represents a "faith in connectedness" where notions of stability comport with larger ideas on the universe as a rational order undisturbed by arbitrariness, contingency, and situation. He suggests that the assumption of stability of structures goes back to "the Greek notion that immutable entities lay behind the diversity and cyclicity in nature's rich display" (1980:45). Kagan even asserts that a wide-spread faith in connectedness by Western scholars has led developmentalists to be "permissive regarding the validity of supporting facts, and eager for any evidence that maintains the belief" (1980:44). Like the existentialists who vigorously challenged the notion of continuity of experience, emphasizing instead the freedom of choice to abrogate one's past, Kagan (1980:53) views the hypothesis of a static, unbroken trail from childhood to adulthood as fundamentally flawed and rooted in philosophical belief rather than scientific fact.

Whatever the epistemological underpinnings, the dominant criminological theories of the last three decades—strain, control, and cultural deviance—have also been treated as largely static in their predictions. This is not to say that they are devoid of developmental *implications* (see especially Thornberry, 1987; Loeber & Le Blanc, 1990), only that the leading theoretical trio is rooted in "between-individual" rather than temporal thinking. Yet as we shall now see, there is one theoretical tradition, currently in eclipse, that was formed with developmental processes in mind.[4]

LABELING THEORY RECONSIDERED

As Loeber and La Blanc (1990:421) have argued, labeling theory is the only criminological theory that is truly developmental in nature because of its explicit emphasis on processes over time. Although labeling theorists have addressed a number of diverse issues, of particular relevance for developmental theories of criminal behavior is the attention drawn to the potentially negative consequences of being labeled for understanding subsequent behavior. For example, Lemert (1951) maintained that societal reactions to primary deviance may create problems of adjustment that foster additional deviance or what he termed "secondary deviance."

In general, labeling theorists have conceptualized this process as the "stigmatizing" and "segregating" effects of social control efforts (Paternoster and Iovanni 1989:375). As Lemert has explained: Primary deviance is assumed to arise in a wide variety of social, cultural, and psychological contexts, and at best has only marginal implications for the psychic structure of the individual; it does not lead to symbolic reorganization at the level of self-regarding attitudes and social roles. Secondary deviation is deviant behavior, or social roles based upon it, which becomes means of defense, attack, or adaptation to overt and covert problems created by the societal reaction to primary deviation. In effect, the original "causes" of the deviation recede and give way to the central importance of the disapproving, degradational, and isolating reactions of society (Lemert 1972:48).

Labeling may thus lead to an alteration of one's identity, exclusion from "normal routines" or "conventional opportunities," and increased contact with and support from deviant subgroups. All three, in turn, may lead to further deviance. Contrary to past characterizations of labeling theory, Paternoster and Iovanni emphasize the contingent nature of these developmental processes (1989:375–381; see also Tittle, 1975). Similar to historical sociologists' concerns with contingency and "path dependency" (Aminzade, 1992), they stress that "we should not expect labeling effects to be invariant across societal subgroups" (1989:381). Paternoster and Iovanni also note that the "stigmatizing and exclusionary effects" of labeling "act as intervening variables in the escalation to secondary deviance" (1989:384).

The role of the criminal justice system in the labeling process is especially important. Garfinkel (1956) describes this process as a "status degradation ceremony." From a developmental perspective, formal degradation ceremonies like those surrounding felony trials are most salient with respect to later behavioral outcomes. For example, successful degradation ceremonies that lead to felony convictions may increase the probability of negative job outcomes in later life. As Becker argues, the designation of "deviant" or "criminal" often becomes a "master status" whereby "the deviant identification becomes the controlling one" (1963:33–34). The concept of a deviant career thus suggests a stable pattern of deviant behavior that is sustained by the labeling process (Becker, 1963:24–39). In a similar vein, Schur (1971) refers to this process as *role engulfment*.

In a recent review of the empirical research on labeling theory, Paternoster and Iovanni (1989) argue that the "secondary deviance hypothesis" has not been adequately tested. In large part this is because the complexities of labeling theory have not been fully explicated in extant research. In particular, Paternoster and Iovanni (1989:384) contend that "by failing to consider the requisite intervening effects, the bulk of these studies do not constitute a valid test of labeling theory." From a developmental perspective, it is also notable that the follow-up periods in most tests of labeling have been quite short and rarely include the developmental transition from adolescence to adulthood (but see Farrington et al., 1978). For example, a common scenario has been to test the effects of police contacts or court referrals on future delinquency *within* the juvenile career (see e.g., Thomas & Bishop, 1984; Smith & Paternoster, 1990).

Recent research by Link (1982; 1987; Link et al., 1989; 1987) on mental health may provide guidance for criminologists interested in alternative conceptualizations of labeling theory compared to those found in criminology (see also Paternoster & Iovanni, 1989). Link developed a "modified labeling theory," which like Paternoster and Iovanni, moves beyond simplistic statements about the direct effects of labeling and provides a specification of the intervening mechanisms and developmental process. Building on Scheff's (1966) labeling theory, Link argues that official labeling and subsequent stigmatization generate negative consequences regarding social networks, jobs, and self-esteem in the lives of mental patients (see Link et al., 1989).

The first step in this model is a focus on beliefs about devaluation and discrimination. The key idea is that individuals (patients and nonpatients) internalize societal conceptions and beliefs about mental illness. The result is that "patients' expectations of rejection are an outcome of socialization and the cultural context rather than a pathological state associated with their psychiatric condition" (Link et al., 1989:403). The second step is official labeling through contact with treatment providers. This step is important because the label applied at the individual level personalizes societal beliefs about devaluation and discrimination towards patients. The third step in Link's model focuses on the patients' responses to their stigmatizing status, including secrecy and withdrawal. The fourth step emphasizes the consequences of the stigma process on patients' lives. Although potentially beneficial, secrecy and withdrawal may also have negative consequences for individual patients by limiting life chances. This effect is consistent with the idea of secondary deviation as developed by Lemert (1951). The fifth and final step in the process is vulnerability to future disorder. As a result of earlier processes, patients may suffer from poor self-esteem, diminished network ties, and experience unemployment (or underemployment) as a result of their own and others' reaction to their label. These deficits increase the risk of further disorder in the future.

Link and his colleagues have demonstrated empirical support for this modified conception of labeling processes (see Link, 1982; 1987; Link et al., 1989; 1987). Most important for our purposes is the finding that labeling has negative consequences in the lives of psychiatric patients regarding work status, income, friendships, family relations, and mate selection. Link's program of research steers attention away from static and "deterministic" aspects of labeling and focuses instead on the more subtle—and clearly indirect—consequences of labeling for later behavior. This emphasis is consistent with a developmental, stepping-stone perspective. In fact, Link (1982:203, n.2) notes that labeling effects are produced "incrementally," and should be thought of as "a series of reinforcing conditions." While it may be the case (as critics of labeling theory have long contended) that the labeling of deviance is initially the result of actual differences in behavior (see e.g., Gove, 1980), this fact is not inconsistent with the notion that such labeling may causally influence the later direction of developmental trajectories over the life course.

Despite its obvious affinity to a life course, developmental framework, labeling theory has rarely been viewed from this perspective. For the most part, research on labeling has consisted of cross-sectional studies or panel studies entailing modest follow-up periods *within* rather than *across* developmental phases. With their focus on deviant identity and "psychic change," labeling analysts have also undertheorized the role of social structural constraints. As described more below, structural effects of labeling may emerge through social allocation mechanisms that have nothing to do with a redefinition of the self or other social-psychological processes that operate within the individual. In particular, the structural consequences of labeling during adolescence (e.g., long-term incarceration as a juvenile) on later adult outcomes have not been fully incorporated into extant labeling theory. Although we suspect much more is at work in the form of ideological resistance, these lacunas have no doubt contributed to the received wisdom that labeling theory is "discredited." We think otherwise, and thus turn to an integration of the dynamic aspects of labeling theory with social control theory, and then apply this perspective to findings of stability produced by criminological research. As a backdrop, we first provide a brief overview of the social control portion of our theory.

EXTENDING AN AGE-GRADED THEORY OF INFORMAL SOCIAL CONTROL

The central idea of social control theory—that crime and deviance are more likely when an individual's bond to society is weak or broken—is an organizing principle in our theory of social bonding over the life course (Sampson & Laub, 1993). The life course has been defined as "pathways through the age differentiated life span" (Elder, 1985:17), in particular the "sequence of culturally defined age-graded roles and social transitions that are enacted over time" (Caspi et al., 1990:15). Two central concepts underlie the analysis of life course dynamics. A *trajectory* is a pathway or line of development over the life span such as worklife, parenthood, and criminal behavior. Trajectories refer to long-term patterns of behavior and are marked by a sequence of transitions. *Transitions* are marked by life events (e.g., first job or first marriage) that are embedded in trajectories and evolve over shorter time spans (see also Elder, 1985:31–32).

Following Elder (1985), we differentiate the life course of individuals on the basis of age and argue that the important institutions of both formal and informal social control vary across the life span. However, we emphasize the role of age-graded informal social control as reflected in the structure of interpersonal bonds linking members of society to one another and to wider social institutions (e.g., work, family, school). Unlike formal sanctions that originate in purposeful efforts to control crime, informal social controls "emerge as by-products of role relationships established for other purposes and are components of role reciprocities" (Kornhauser, 1978:24).

Although traditional control theory (e.g., Hirschi, 1969) is static, we believe its integration with the life course framework may be used to understand the dynamics of both continuity and change in behavior over time. In particular, a major thesis of our work is that social bonds in adolescence (e.g., to family, peers, and school) and adulthood (e.g., attachment to the labor force, cohesive marriage) explain criminal behavior regardless of prior differences in criminal propensity—that age-graded changes in social bonds explain changes in crime. We also contend that early (and distal) precursors to adult crime (e.g., conduct disorder, low self-control) are mediated in developmental pathways by key age-graded institutions of informal and formal social control, especially in the transition to adulthood (e.g., via employment, military service, marriage, official sanctions).

In uniting continuity and change within the context of a sociological understanding of crime through life, a major concept in our framework is the dynamic process whereby the interlocking nature of trajectories and transitions generate *turning points* or a change in life course (Elder, 1985:32). Adaptation to life events is crucial because the same event or transition followed by different adaptations can lead to different trajectories (Elder, 1985:35). That is, despite the connection between childhood events and experiences in adulthood, turning points can modify life trajectories—they can "redirect paths." For some individuals, turning points are abrupt—radical "turnarounds" or changes in life history that separate the past from the future (Elder et al., 1991:215).

For most individuals, however, we conceptualize turning points as "part of a process over time and not as a dramatic lasting change that takes place at any one time" (Pickles & Rutter, 1991:134; Rutter, 1989; Clausen, 1993). The process-oriented nature of turning points leads to a focus on incremental change and age-related progressions and events, which carry forward or set in motion dynamic processes that shape future outcomes (Rutter & Rutter, 1993:64). In our theoretical model, turnings points may be positive or negative because they represent "times of decision or opportunity when life trajectories may be directed on to more adaptive or maladaptive paths" (Rutter & Rutter, 1993:244). As Rutter and Rutter recognize, "Life-span transitions have a crucial role in the processes involved, strengthening emerging patterns of behavior or providing a means by which life trajectories may change pattern" (1993:109; see also Maughan & Champion, 1990:310). This variability results because life transitions do not have the same impact on everyone. For instance, getting married may be beneficial or deleterious depending on "*when* a person marries, *whom* a person marries, the *quality* of the relationship formed and whether or not *changes* in social group and life patterns are involved" (Rutter & Rutter, 1993:356, emphasis in the original). Although not usually thought of as such, some turning points are thus negative, serving to exacerbate early trajectories of antisocial conduct.

CUMULATIVE DISADVANTAGE

We believe that a developmental conceptualization of labeling theory, integrated with the age-graded theory of informal social control previously outlined, provides an alternative way of thinking about trait-based interpretations of behavioral stability. Consider first an often neglected fact about stability. As reviewed by Rutter and Rutter (1993:77–79), psychological traits usually thought of as having the greatest biological basis—e.g., activity level and temperament—in fact show relatively low stability from childhood to adulthood. By contrast, even though aggression is arguably less likely than these studied traits to result from biological differences, it shows the *highest* stability.

Why should this be so? A clue is that aggression is a social behavior that, by definition, involves interpersonal interaction. Moreover, aggression and conduct disorder often generate immediate and harsh responses by varying segments of society compared to most personality traits. As we shall elaborate, aggression tends to foster physical counterattacks, teacher and peer rejection, punitive discipline, parental hostility, and harsh criminal justice sanctions. The common feature to all these responses is retaliation and attempts at control and domination.

Logically, then, the fact that much delinquency starts early in the life course implies that retaliatory efforts to suppress it also begin early. These repressive efforts accrete incrementally over time to produce developmental effects. Specifically, we argue that antisocial children replicate their antisocial behavior in a variety of social realms in part because of the differing reactions that antisocial behavior brings forth (Caspi, 1987). Maladaptive behaviors are "found in interactional styles that are sustained both by the progressive accumulation of their own consequences (cumulative continuity) and by evoking maintaining responses from others during reciprocal social interaction (interactional continuity)" (Caspi et al., 1987:313, emphasis added). The combination of interactional and cumulative continuity over time is thus inherently a social process.

Invoking a state dependence argument (see Nagin & Paternoster, 1991), our theory incorporates the causal role of prior delinquency in facilitating adult crime through a process of "cumulative disadvantage." The state dependence component implies that committing a crime has a genuine behavioral influence on the probability of committing future crimes. In other words, crime itself—whether directly or indirectly—causally modifies the future probability of engaging in crime (Nagin & Paternoster, 1991:166). Although this role is potentially direct, we emphasize a developmental model where delinquent behavior has a systematic attenuating effect on the social and institutional bonds linking adults to society (e.g., labor force attachment, marital cohesion). For example, delinquency may spark failure in school, incarceration, and weak bonds to the labor market, in turn increasing later adult crime (Tittle, 1988:80). Serious sanctions in particular lead to the "knifing off" (Moffitt, 1993) of future opportunities such that labeled offenders have fewer options for a conventional life.

The cumulative continuity of disadvantage is thus not only a result of stable individual differences in criminal propensity, but a dynamic process whereby childhood antisocial behavior and adolescent delinquency foster adult crime through the severance of adult social bonds. From this view, similar to what Thornberry (1987) has termed interactional theory, weak social bonding serves as a mediating and hence causal sequential link in a chain of adversity between childhood delinquency and adult criminal behavior. We further believe that this process of cumulative disadvantage is linked to four key institutions of social control—family, school, peers, and state sanctions.

Family

The importance of family management and socialization practices (e.g., monitoring and supervision, consistent punishment, and the formation of close social bonds among parents and children) for explaining crime and delinquency has been well established (see e.g., Loeber & Stouthamer-Loeber, 1986:29). When considering the role of families and crime, however, criminologists generally view childrearing in a static framework that flows from parent *to* child. This static view ignores the fact that parenting styles are also an adaptation to children in a process of reciprocal interaction. An example of interactional continuity in the family is when the child with temper tantrums provokes angry and hostile reactions in parents, which in turn feeds back to trigger further antisocial behavior by the child. In support of this idea, there is evidence that styles of parenting are very sensitive to these troublesome behaviors on the part of children.

Lytton (1990) has written an excellent overview of this complex body of research, which he subsumes under the theoretical umbrella of "control systems theory." This theory argues that parent and child display reciprocal adaptation to each other's behavior level, leading to what Lytton calls "child effects" on parents. One reason for these child effects is that reinforcement does not work in the usual way for conduct disordered children. As Lytton (1990:688) notes, conduct disordered children "may be underresponsive to social reinforcement and punishment." Hence normal routines of parental childrearing become subject to disruption based on early antisocial behavior—i.e., children themselves differentially engender parenting styles likely to further exacerbate antisocial behavior.

The behavior that prompts parental frustration is not merely aggressiveness or delinquency, however. Lytton (1990:690) reviews evidence showing a connection between a child being rated "difficult" in preschool (e.g., whining, restlessness, strong-willed resistance) and the child's delinquency as an adolescent—a relation that holds independent of the quality of parents' childrearing practices. For example, Olweus (1980) showed that mothers of boys who displayed a strong-will and hot temper in infancy later became more permissive of aggression, which in turn led to greater aggressiveness in middle childhood. Moreover, there is experimental evidence that when children's inattentive and noncompliant behavior is improved by administering stimulant drugs, their mothers become less controlling and mother-child interaction patterns are nearly normalized (Lytton, 1990:688). All of this suggests that parenting, at least in part, is a reaction to children's temperament, especially difficult ones.

Although rarely studied directly, it seems likely that delinquent behavior and other deliberate violations of parental authority spark retaliation in the form of harsh physical punishment and, in some cases, parental abuse. In turn, child abuse and violent punishment have been linked to later violent offending on the part of victims (Widom, 1989). To the extent that children's appraisals of themselves are powerfully influenced by negative parental labeling (Matsueda, 1992), the consequences of violent interactional styles, parent-child conflict, and violent punishment for later life are potentially quite large.

In any case, our point is that interactional continuity begins in the family. This is not a simultaneous relationship at one point in time so much as a reinforcing cycle that builds over time to further increase the probability of antisocial behavior (see also Thornberry, 1987:869). In Nagin and Paternoster's (1991) terminology, this process captures the state dependence effect of prior delinquency on future crime.

School and Peers

Many years ago, the Gluecks observed that poor school attachment may be a consequence of misbehavior more than a cause (1964:23). Teachers may be particularly sensitive to unruly and difficult children, leading to rejection of the child or at least a strained teacher-student relationship. This rejection undermines the attachment of the child to the school, and ultimately, the child's performance in the school. More recent evidence on the reciprocal relationship between delinquency and school attachment has been uncovered in research by Liska and Reed (1985), Olweus (1983), and Thornberry et al. (1991).

Similar processes have been revealed for peer interactions. For instance, children who are aggressive are more likely to be rejected by their peers compared with less aggressive children (see Cairns & Cairns, 1992; Coie et al., 1991; Dodge, 1983; Patterson et al., 1989). This process creates a vicious cycle of negative interactions and is consistent with Caspi's (1987) idea of interactional continuity. Dishion and his colleagues (1991) have also found that poor family practices, peer rejection, and academic failure at age ten increased the likelihood of involvement with antisocial peers at age twelve. In this sense, peer rejection and the deviant peer group contribute to the maintenance of antisocial behavior through mid-adolescence (see also Thornberry et al., 1994). Although further discussion is beyond the scope of this article, the existing evidence thus suggests that the reciprocal interactional dynamics of teacher and peer rejection contribute to the continuity of aggression and other forms of delinquent behavior.

Criminal Justice and Institutional Reaction

Cumulative disadvantage is generated most explicitly by the negative structural consequences of criminal offending and official sanctions for life chances. The theory specifically suggests a "snowball" effect—that adolescent delinquency and its negative consequences (e.g., arrest, official labeling, incarceration) increasingly "mortgage" one's future, especially later life chances molded by schooling and employment. For example, it has long been the case that many jobs formally preclude the hiring of ex-prisoners (Glaser, 1969:233–238). Experimental studies have also shown that employers are reluctant to consider ex-offenders as potential employees (Boshier & Johnson, 1974; Dale, 1976; Finn & Fontaine, 1985).

The stigma associated with arrest and conviction extends to membership in trade unions, "bonding" applications, and licensing restrictions (see Davidenas, 1983). For example, many trade unions deny membership to ex-offenders (Dale, 1976:324), while the standard commercial blanket bond contains a provision that nullifies coverage if employers have knowingly hired any person with a criminal record (Dale, 1976: 326). The result is that ex-offenders are barred from employment where bonding is required (e.g., security guards, hotel workers). Of course, these are precisely the sort of low-skilled jobs that are compatible with the educational and work-history profiles of most offenders.

The licensing of government-regulated private occupations yields even more structural constraints on the reintegration of ex-offenders. As an example, in only four states can an ex-offender work as a barber without interference by the state licensing agency because of criminal conduct (Dale, 1976:330). Although there is considerable state-by-state variation, licensing boards bar ex-offenders from literally hundreds of other occupations, including apprentice electrician, billiards operator, and plumber (Singer, 1983:246 and Dale, 1976). Again, these seem to be primary "escape routes" from a disadvantaged past were it not for the criminal record.

Arrest, conviction, and imprisonment are clearly stigmatizing, and those so tarnished face structural impediments to establishing strong social ties to conventional lines of adult activity—regardless of their behavioral predispositions (see also Schwartz & Skolnick, 1964; Thornberry & Christenson, 1984; Burton et al., 1987). Drawing on the thesis of cumulative disadvantage, there is thus support for hypothesizing that incarceration has negative effects on job stability and employment in adulthood (see especially Bondeson, 1989; Freeman, 1991). The logic of this theoretical perspective in turn points to a possible *indirect* role of delinquency and official sanctioning in generating future crime.

Although long-term assessments are rare, there is some developmental evidence that bears on this thesis. As part of a larger project, we have analyzed the natural histories originally gathered by Glueck and Glueck (1950, 1968) of 500 delinquents and 500 control subjects matched on age, IQ, ethnicity, and neighborhood deprivation (see Sampson & Laub, 1993 for details). To test the cumulative disadvantage thesis, we examined the role of job stability at ages seventeen—twenty-five and twenty-five–thirty-two as an intervening link between incarceration and adult crime. In doing so we controlled for theoretically relevant factors in the etiology of job stability. As Gottfredson and Hirschi (1990) argue, those individuals with low self-control and tendencies toward crime are also the same individuals likely to have unstable histories in employment and other conventional lines of activity. Accordingly, we controlled for official arrest frequency, unofficial delinquency, and sample attrition risk. Moreover, previous research (e.g., Robins, 1966; Vaillant, 1983) in conjunction with our own qualitative analysis revealed the important role of drinking in understanding patterns of job stability—heavy or abusive drinkers tend to either drift from job to job or be fired from their jobs at a rate much higher than nondrinkers. Excessive drinking that began in adolescence (age nineteen or younger) was thus also controlled. Finally, we used empirical methods that took into account persistent unobserved heterogeneity in criminal behavior (Nagin & Paternoster, 1991).

Using this multimethod, multimeasure approach, we found that length of juvenile incarceration had the largest overall effect on later job stability—regardless of prior crime, excessive adolescent drinking, and exclusion risk. Even though all the delinquent boys were incarcerated at some point, those incarcerated for a longer period of time had trouble securing stable jobs as they entered young adulthood compared to delinquents with a shorter incarceration history. Since unofficial propensity to deviance, sample selection bias, drinking, unobserved heterogeneity, and prior criminal history were controlled (the latter influencing the length of confinement), it seems unlikely that the result is spurious.

Our analyses also underscored the deleterious role that incarceration may play in developmental trajectories of employment in later periods of adulthood (ages twenty-five–thirty-two). Length of incarceration in both adolescence *and* young adulthood had significant negative effects on job stability at ages twenty-five–thirty-two (Sampson & Laub, 1993:167–168). These results are noteworthy not only because confounding "propensity" factors were taken into account (e.g., crime and drinking), but also for the long-term negative consequences of juvenile incarceration independent of adult incarceration (Laub & Sampson, 1994). Apparently, the structural disadvantages accorded institutionalized adolescents are so great (e.g., through dropping out of high school, record of confinement known to employers) that their influence lingers throughout adult development. We tested the idea of cumulative effects by also examining the duration of incarceration from adolescence (< seventeen) through the transition to young adulthood (ages seventeen–twenty-five). As the total time served in juvenile and adult correctional facilities increased, later job stability decreased (controlling for prior record and unofficial deviance).

Although limited, the data thus suggest that looking only at the direct effects of official sanctions is misleading. Length of incarceration—whether as a juvenile or adult—has little direct bearing on later criminal activity when job stability is controlled. This does not imply unimportance, however, for there is evidence that the effect of confinement may be indirect and operative in a developmental, cumulative process that reproduces itself over time (see also Hagan & Palloni, 1990). Consistent with the theoretical idea of cumulative continuity and state (duration) dependence (Nagin & Paternoster, 1991; Featherman & Lerner, 1985), incarceration appears to cut off opportunities and prospects for stable employment later in life. This "knifing off" has important developmental implications—job stability and also marital attachment in adulthood are significantly related to changes in adult crime (Sampson & Laub, 1993, ch. 7). Namely, the stronger the adult ties to work and family, the less crime and deviance among both delinquents and controls. Therefore, even if the direct effect of incarceration is zero or possibly even negative (i.e., a deterrent), its indirect effect may well be criminogenic (positive) as structural labeling theorists have long argued.

Other Evidence

Although infrequently studied over significant periods of human development, there is additional evidence of cumulative continuity arising from state sanctions and the attenuation of social bonds to employment. Based on the Cambridge Study in Youth Development, Farrington (1977) found that convictions increased the probability of future offending. Using the same longitudinal data, research by Nagin and Waldfogel (1992) supports the cumulative continuity thesis in showing a destabilizing effect of convictions on the labor market prospects of London boys. More recently, and again using the

Cambridge data, Hagan (1993) has shown that delinquency increases the probability of future unemployment, regardless of prior differences in criminal propensity. Thornberry and Christenson (1984) have similarly shown a lagged positive effect of criminal involvement on future adult unemployment, controlling for prior propensities to unemployment.

In perhaps the most impressive set of findings, Richard Freeman has analyzed the National Longitudinal Survey of Youth (NLSY) to estimate effects of jail time, probation, conviction, and arrests (charges) on whether individuals were employed (and for how many weeks) for each year from 1980 to 1988. Control variables included sociodemographic characteristics (e.g., education, region, age) and self-reported use of drugs and alcohol. Net of these factors, Freeman's results showed that serious involvement with the criminal justice system had large long-term effects on employment. Specifically, men in jail as of 1980 had lower employment in all succeeding years than other men with comparable characteristics (Freeman 1991:11). Similar results obtained for the number of weeks worked in the years previous to the interview follow-up. Interestingly, there was no effect of conviction but very large effects for jail time. As Freeman concludes: "The relation between incarceration and employment is "causal" rather than the result of fixed unobserved personal characteristics that are correlated with crime and employment: proportionately fewer youths who had been incarcerated worked years afterward than did nonincarcerated youths with similar initial employment experiences" (1991:1).

Freeman also investigated these relationships using the Boston Youth Survey of out-of-school young men conducted during the height of the Boston labor market boom in the 1980s. To adjust for individual differences, Freeman's analyses controlled for age, race, education, grades in school, living arrangements, public housing, marital status. religious attendance, household size, alcohol use, and gang membership. Similar to the NLSY findings, his results showed that criminal offending and sanction experiences—especially jail time—severely restricted future opportunities in the labor market. In fact, Freeman's multivariate analyses "confirm that having been in jail is the single most important deterrent to employment" (1991:13). This result held up when unobserved heterogeneity in individual differences in employment proclivities were controlled.

Freeman's consistent research findings from very different samples underscore the fact that we do not necessarily need to assume that personal "identities" change as a result of labeling and state sanctions. Rather, we take a more rational choice approach that focuses on endogenous decisions about the utility of labor market participation and adherence to conventional norms (see also Cook, 1975). In other words, once severe sanctions like incarceration have been imposed, labor market decisions take on new meaning—especially when weighed against the opportunities provided by the innovation and expansion of drug economies in recent years (Freeman 1991:22). From this view, labels work cumulatively through the structural transformation of one's stake in conformity to conventional society.

STRUCTURAL LOCATION AND CONTINUITY

To this point we have examined how involvement in delinquent behavior and criminal sanctioning during the transition from adolescence to young adulthood constrains subsequent development. Although this is certainly a developmental issue, Jessor et al. (1991:252) argue "that there might well be very different outcomes of the same attribute, depending on the stage of the life course, the time in history, the particular cultural and social context, and the relevant aspects of the larger social setting." In their recent longitudinal study, Jessor and his colleagues (1991) found that despite continuity in problem behavior from adolescence to young adulthood, there was little evidence of "spillover" effects into other areas of adult life (e.g., work, education, family, friendships, and mental health). For this sample, delinquency does not appear to be a major handicap with respect to adult outcomes. However, the participants of Jessor et al.'s study (1991:268) consisted largely of middle-class youth drawn from a "normal" sample.

Along similar lines, Hagan's (1991) research suggests that the deleterious effect of adolescent deviance on adult stratification outcomes is greatest among lower class boys, especially as mediated by police contacts. Middle-class boys who escaped the negative consequences of official labeling did not suffer impairment in adult occupational outcomes as a result of their adolescent delinquency. Avoiding the snares of arrest and institutionalization thus provided opportunities for prosocial attachments among middle-class youth to take firm hold in adulthood.

Recent experimental research on domestic violence provides even more compelling evidence of the interaction of structural location and sanctions. Randomized experiments in Milwaukee, Miami, Colorado Springs, and Omaha all revealed that arrest reduced repeat violence among the employed but *increased* it among the unemployed (Sherman, 1992; 1993:10). In other words, sanctioning tends to aggravate crime when administered in populations with low "stakes in conformity." Much like Braithwaite's (1989) theory of re-integrative shaming, Sherman (1993) argues that stigmatizing punishment among the disaffected works only to increase "defiant" recidivism. In particular, he posits that criminal justice sanctions provoke future defiance of the law when offenders have weak social bonds to both sanctioning agents and the wider community.

These studies suggest that the concepts of knifing off and cumulative continuity are most salient in explaining the structurally constrained life chances of the disadvantaged urban poor. In other words, cumulative disadvantage, state-dependence, and location in the class structure appear to interact. Among those in advantaged positions that provide continuity in social resources over time, both nondelinquents and delinquents alike are presumably not just more motivated, but better able structurally to establish binding ties to conventional lines of adult activity (Laub & Sampson, 1993:307). If nothing else, incumbency in prosocial middle-class roles provides advantages in maintaining the status quo and counteracting negative life events (e.g., being fired). Legal deterrents work better here, reducing future offending as classical theory suggests they should (Sherman, 1992).

Among the disadvantaged, things seem to work differently. Deficits and disadvantages pile up faster, and this has continuing negative consequences for later development in the form of "environmental traps" (Maughan & Champion, 1990:308). Perhaps most problematic, the process of cumulative disadvantage restricts future options in conventional domains that provide opportunities for social "interdependence" (e.g., stable employment) while simultaneously encouraging options within subcultures that "reject the rejectors" (Braithwaite, 1989:102). Maughan and Champion (1990:308) argue that this process takes on the characteristics of a "conveyor belt" that is extremely difficult to manage or jump off—especially for the disadvantaged. Thus one cannot ignore the effects of larger social contexts (social structure and living conditions) on development (Rutter & Rutter, 1993:34–37).

IMPLICATIONS

Our synthesis of cumulative disadvantage and state dependence recasts in a structural and developmental framework the original contentions of labeling theory that official reactions to primary deviance (e.g., arrest) may create problems of adjustment (e.g., unemployment) that foster additional crime in the form of secondary deviance (e.g., Lemert, 1951; Becker, 1963). Similar to Becker's concept of a deviant career sustained by the labeling process, Hagan and Palloni (1990) suggest that continuity in delinquent behavior may result from a structural imputation process that begins early in childhood (see also Tittle, 1988:78–81; Laub & Sampson, 1993). Indeed, the stability of behavior may reflect more the stability of social *response* than the time-invariance of an individual trait. As we have argued, aggression is a social behavior embedded in ongoing social interactions with salient others.

Taking a similar position, Dannefer (1987:216) argues that most developmental research is too quick to attribute continuity to time-stable traits and social-psychological processes rather than "structured mechanisms of social allocation producing similar differentiating tendencies in successive cohorts." The channeling of prior differences and the tendency toward cumulation of both advantage and disadvantage is so general that it has been referred to as the "Matthew effect"—"To him who hath shall be given; from him who hath not shall be taken away that which he hath" (see Dannefer, 1987:216). The Matthew effect underscores what Smith (1968) has called "vicious and benign circles" of development. Or as John Clausen puts it—"early advantages become cumulative advantages; early behaviors that are self-defeating lead to cumulative disadvantages" (1993:521).

Patterson (1993) has offered the most telling metaphor for understanding the developmental risks of cumulative disadvantage—the "chimera." Patterson and his colleagues (1989) have examined the developmental course of antisocial behavior and delinquency across a developmental trajectory involving family, school, and peers. Their model consists of a series of action-reaction sequences across the developmental stages of early childhood, middle childhood, and late childhood and adolescence. Patterson argues that antisocial behavior leads to a "cascade" of secondary problems (e.g., school failure, peer rejection, depressed mood, and involvement with deviant peers) and he is quite explicit that "for problems produced at later stages, antisocial behavior is only an indirect determinant" (Patterson & Yoerger, 1993:145).

Appropriately, then, Patterson (1993) refers to the antisocial trait as a "chimera"—a hybrid where qualitative shifts in problem behavior (e.g., academic failure, peer rejection, etc.) as well as new forms of antisocial behavior (e.g., substance abuse) are "grafted" onto a core antisocial trait. From our perspective, the grafting process, the "piling up" of disadvantage, and the resultant chimera of a persistent criminal career is likely to interact with race and structural location (Hagan, 1991; Jessor et al., 1991; Thornberry, 1987). Namely, there is increasing evidence that the probability of adolescent risks becoming transmuted into adverse adult circumstances is greatest among those in disadvantaged racial and economic positions.

On a final note, we stress that our theorizing of cumulative continuity and the causal role of salient life experiences in adulthood does not negate the potential importance of self-selection and individual differences. By distinguishing self-selection from cumulative continuity we incorporate the independent effects of both early delinquency (or individual propensity) and the dimensions of adult social bonding on adult crime. This distinction is consistent with recent research on homophily in social choices across the life course. As Kandel et al. (1990:221) state: "although individual choices are made, in part, as a function of the individual's prior attributes, values, and personality characteristics, involvement in the new relationship has further effects and influences on that individual." Similarly, Rutter et al. (1990) and Quinton et al. (1993) found homophily in the choice of marital partners but also a substantial effect of marital cohesion and stable family life that held after taking planning of marriage partners into account. We found a similar phenomenon in our reanalyses of the Gluecks' data (see Sampson & Laub, 1993; Laub & Sampson, 1993).

An important roadblock to integrating trait-based models with life-course theory is thus conceptual and turns on what we believe is an incorrect interpretation of homophily. To assume that individual differences influence the choices one makes in life (which they certainly do), does not mean that social mechanisms emerging from those choices can then have no causal significance.[5] Choices generate constraints *and* opportunities that themselves have effects not solely attributable to individuals. As situational theorists have long pointed out, the same person—with the same attributes and traits—acts very different in different situations. For these reasons, the integration of rational choice, situational, and social control theories with a life-course perspective that respects yet is not reducible to individual differences seems a promising avenue of future advances in criminological theory (see also Nagin & Paternoster, 1993).

NOTES

1. Even if we grant the argument that strain and cultural deviance theories are macro-level in nature (e.g., Bernard, 1987), most applications still pose static questions (e.g., whether between-societal differences in crime rates are associated with variations in income inequality).

2. It is with no small irony that stability can only be established with longitudinal data, yet its existence had led to static explanations.

3. Life-span developmental psychology does incorporate historical change, although developmental processes are still usually treated as invariant within cohorts (Danneter, 1984:105).

4. One might also argue that social learning theory is developmental in nature,

since it deals with processes that unfold over time. Still, the causal variables emphasized in social learning theory to date (e.g., deviant peers) tend to be static just like those in strain, control, and cultural deviance. Perhaps this is not surprising given the theoretical compatibility of social learning and cultural deviance theories (see Kornhauser, 1978). In any event, the developmental cast of social learning theory, although beyond the scope of this paper, deserves consideration in future theoretical work.

5. We should also note that even homophily, though usually attributed to self selection, is profoundly shaped by structural constraints beyond the pale of individual choice (see generally Blau, 1977).

REFERENCES

Aminzade, Ronald. 1992. "Historical Sociology and Time." *Sociological Methods and Research* 20: 456–80.

Bachman, Jerald, Patrick O'Malley, and Jerome Johnston. 1978. *Youth in Transition, Volume VI: Adolescence to Adulthood—Change and Stability in the Lives of Young Men.* Ann Arbor, MI: University of Michigan Press.

Becker, Howard. 1963. *Outsiders: Studies in the Sociology of Deviance.* New York: Free Press.

Bernard, Thomas. 1987. "Testing Structural Strain Theories." *Journal of Research in Crime and Delinquency* 24: 262–80.

Blau, Peter. 1977. *Inequality and Heterogeneity.* New York: Free Press.

Bondeson, Ulla V. 1989. *Prisoners in Prison Societies.* New Brunswick, NJ: Transaction Publishers.

Boshier, Roger, and Derek Johnson. 1974. "Does Conviction Affect Employment Opportunities?" *British Journal of Criminology* 14: 264–68.

Braithwaite, John. 1989. *Crime, Shame, and Reintegration.* Cambridge: Cambridge University Press.

Burton, Velmer, Francis Cullen, and Lawrence Travis. 1987. "The Collateral Consequences of a Felony Conviction: A National Study of State Statutes." *Federal Probation* 51: 52–60.

Cairns. Robert B., and Beverly Cairns. 1992. "The Sociogenesis of Aggressive and Antisocial Behavior." In *Facts, Frameworks, and Forecasts: Advances in Criminological Theory,* vol. 3, ed. Joan McCord, 157–91. New Brunswick, NJ: Transaction Publishers.

Caspi, Avshalom. 1987. "Personality in the Life Course." *Journal of Personality and Social Psychology* 53: 1203–13.

Caspi, Avshalom, and Terrie E. Moffitt. 1995. "The Continuity of Maladaptive Behavior: From Description to Understanding in the Study of Antisocial Behavior." In *Manual of Developmental Psychopathology,* ed. Dante Cicchetti and Donald Cohen, 472–511. New York: Wiley.

Caspi, Avshalom, Glen H. Elder, Jr., and Ellen S. Herbener. 1990. "Childhood Personality and the Prediction of Life-Course Patterns." In *Straight and Devious Pathways from Childhood to Adulthood,* ed. Lee Robins and Michael Rutter, 13–35. Cambridge: Cambridge University Press.

Caspi, Avshalom, Glen H. Elder, Jr., and Daryl J. Bem. 1987. "Moving Against the World: Life-Course Patterns of Explosive Children." *Developmental Psychology* 23: 308–13.

Coie, J. D., M. Underwood. and J. E. Lochman. 1991. "Programmatic Intervention with Aggressive Children in the School Setting." In *The Development and Treatment of Childhood Aggression,* ed. D. J. Pepler and K. H. Robin, 389–410. Hillsdale, NJ: Erlbaum.

Clausen, John. 1993. *American Lives: Looking Back at the Children of the Great Depression.* New York: Free Press.

Cline, Hugh F. 1980. "Criminal Behavior over the Life Span." In *Constancy and Change in Human Development,* ed. Orville G. Brim Jr. and Jerome Kagan, 641–74. Cambridge: Harvard University Press.

Cook, Philip J. 1975. "The Correctional Carrot: Better Jobs for Parolees." *Policy Analysis* 1:11–54.

Dale, Mitchell. 1976. "Barriers to the Rehabilitation of Ex-Offenders." *Crime and Delinquency* 22: 322–37.

Dannefer, Dale. 1984. "Adult Development and Social Theory: A Paradigmatic Reappraisal." *American Sociological Review* 49: 100–16.

———. 1987. "Aging as Intracohort Differentiation: Accentuation, the Matthew Effect, and the Life Course." *Sociological Forum* 2: 211–36.

Davidenas, J. 1983. "The Professional License: An Ex-Offender's Illusion." *Criminal Justice Journal* 7: 61–69.

Dishion, Thomas J., Gerald R. Patterson, M. Stoolmiller, and M. L. Skinner. 1991. "Family, School, and Behavioral Antecedents to Early Adolescent Involvement with Antisocial Peers." *Developmental Psychology* 27: 172–80.

Dodge, Kenneth A. 1983. "Behavioral Antecedents of Peer Social Status." *Child Development* 54: 1386–99.

Elder, Glen H., Jr. 1985. "Perspectives on the Life Course." In *Life Course Dynamics,* ed. Glen H. Elder Jr., 23–49. Ithaca: Cornell University Press.

Elder, Glen H. Jr., Cynthia Gimbel, and Rachel Ivie. 1991. "Turning Points in Life: The Case of Military Service and War." *Military Psychology* 3: 215–31.

Farrington, David P. 1977. "The Effects of Public Labeling." *British Journal of Criminology* 17: 112–25.

———. 1986. "Stepping Stones to Adult Criminal Careers." In *Development of Antisocial and Prosocial Behavior,* ed. Dan Olweus, Jack Block, and Marian Radke-Yarrow, 359–84. New York: Academic Press.

Farrington, David P., S. G. Osborn, Donald West. 1978. "The Persistence of Labelling Effects." *British Journal of Criminology* 18: 277–84.

Featherman, David, and Richard Lerner. 1985. "Ontogenesis and Sociogenesis: Problematics for Theory and Research about Development and Socialization Across the Lifespan." *American Sociological Review* 50: 659–76.

Finn, R. H., and P. A. Fontaine. 1985. "The Association between Selected Characteristics and Perceived Employability of Offenders." *Criminal Justice and Behavior* 12: 353–65.

Freeman, Richard. 1991. "Crime and the Employment of Disadvantaged Youth." Cambridge: Harvard University, National Bureau of Economic Research.

Garfinkel, Harold. 1956. "Conditions of Successful Degradation Ceremonies." *American Journal of Sociology* 61: 420–24.

Glaser, Daniel. 1969. *The Effectiveness of a Prison and Parole System.* Abridged edition. Indianapolis: Bobbs-Merrill Co.

Glueck, Sheldon, and Eleanor Glueck. 1930. *500 Criminal Careers.* New York: A.A. Knopf.

————. 1950. *Unraveling Juvenile Delinquency.* New York: Commonwealth Fund.

————. 1964. *Ventures in Criminology.* Cambridge: Harvard University Press.

————. 1968. *Delinquents and Nondelinquents in Perspective.* Cambridge: Harvard University Press.

Gottfredson, Michael, and Travis Hirschi. 1987. "The Methodological Adequacy of Longitudinal Research on Crime." *Criminology* 25: 581–614.

Gottfredson Michael, and Travis Hirschi. 1990. *A General Theory of Crime.* Stanford: Stanford University Press.

Gove, Walter R. 1980. *The Labeling of Deviance: Evaluation of a Perspective.* 2d ed. Beverly Hills, CA: Sage.

————. 1985. "The Effect of Age and Gender on Deviant Behavior: A Biopsychosocial Perspective." In *Gender and the Life Course,* ed. Alice S. Rossi, 115–44. New York: Aldine.

Hagan, John. 1991. "Destiny and Drift: Subcultural Preferences, Status Attainments, and the Risks and Rewards of Youth." *American Sociological Review* 56: 567–82.

————. 1993. "The Social Embeddedness of Crime and Unemployment." *Criminology* 31: 465–91.

Hagan, John, and Alberto Palloni. 1990. "The Social Reproduction of a Criminal Class in Working-Class London, Circa 1950–1980." *American Journal of Sociology* 96: 265–99.

Hirschi, Travis. 1969. *Causes of Delinquency.* Berkeley: University of California Press.

Hirschi, Travis, and Michael Gottfredson. 1993. "Commentary: Testing the General Theory of Crime." *Journal of Research in Crime and Delinquency* 30: 47–54.

Huesmann, L. Rowell, Leonard D. Eron, Monroe M. Lefkowitz, and Leopold O. Walder. 1984. "Stability of Aggression over Time and Generations." *Developmental Psychology* 20: 1120–34.

Jessor, Richard, John E. Donovan, and Frances M. Costa. 1991. *Beyond Adolescence: Problem Behavior and Young Adult Development.* Cambridge: Cambridge University Press.

Kagan, Jerome. 1980. "Perspectives on Continuity." In *Constancy and Change in Human Development,* ed. Orville G. Brim Jr. and Jerome Kagan, 26–74. Cambridge: Harvard University Press.

Kandel, Denise, Mark Davies, and Nazli Baydar. 1990. "The Creation of Interpersonal Contexts: Homophily in Dyadic Relationships in Adolescence and Young Adulthood." In *Straight and Devious Pathways from Childhood to Adulthood,* ed. Lee Robins and Michael Rutter, 221–41. New York: Cambridge University Press.

Kornhauser, Ruth. 1978. *Social Sources of Delinquency.* Chicago: University of Chicago Press.

Laub, John H., and Robert J. Sampson. 1993. "Turning Points in the Life Course: Why Change Matters to the Study of Crime." *Criminology* 31: 301–25.

————. 1994. "The Long-Term Effect of Punitive Discipline." In *Coercion and Punishment in Long-Term Perspectives,* ed. Joan McCord, 247–258. Cambridge: Cambridge University Press.

Lemert, Edwin. 1951. *Social Pathology.* New York; McGraw-Hill.

————. 1972. *Human Deviance, Social Problems, and Social Control.* 2d ed. Englewood Cliffs, NJ: Prentice Hall.

Link, Bruce. 1982. "Mental Patient Status, Work, and Income: An Examination of the Effects of a Psychiatric Label." *American Sociological Review* 47: 202–15.

————. 1987. "Understanding Labeling Effects in the Area of Mental Disorders: An Assessment of the Effects of Expectations of Rejection." *American Sociological Review* 52: 96–112.

Link, Bruce, Francis Cullen, James Frank, and John F. Wozniak. 1987. "The Social Rejection of Former Mental Patients: Understanding Why Labels Matter." *American Journal of Sociology* 92: 1461–1500.

Link, Bruce, Francis Cullen, Elmer Struening, Patrick Shrout, and Bruce

Dohrenwend. 1989. "A Modified Labeling Approach to Mental Disorders: An Empirical Assessment." *American Sociological Review* 54: 400–423.

Liska, Allen, and Mark Reed. 1985. "Ties to Conventional Institutions and Delinquency: Estimating Reciprocal Effects." *American Sociological Review* 50: 547–60.

Loeber, Rolf. 1982. "The Stability of Antisocial Child Behavior: A Review." *Child Development* 53: 1431–46.

Loeber, Rolf, and Magda Stouthamer-Loeber. 1986. "Family Factors as Correlates and Predictors of Juvenile Conduct Problems and Delinquency." In *Crime and Justice,* vol. 7, ed. Michael Tonry and Norval Morris, 29–149. Chicago: University of Chicago Press.

Loeber, Rolf, and Marc Le Blanc. 1990. "Toward a Developmental Criminology." In *Crime and Justice,* volume 12, ed. Michael Tonry and Norval Morris, 375–437. Chicago: University of Chicago Press.

Lytton, Hugh. 1990. "Child and Parent Effects in Boys' Conduct Disorder: A Reinterpretation." *Developmental Psychology* 26: 683–97.

Matsueda, Ross. 1992. "Reflected Appraisals, Parental Labeling, and Delinquency: Specifying a Symbolic Interactionist Theory." *American Journal of Sociology* 97: 1577–1611.

Maughan, Barbara, and Lorna Champion. 1990. "Risk and Protective Factors in the Transition to Young Adulthood." In *Successful Aging,* ed. Paul Baltes and M. Baltes, 296–331. Cambridge: Cambridge University Press.

Moffitt, Terrie E. 1993. "Life-course Persistent and Adolescence Limited Antisocial Behavior: A Developmental Taxonomy." *Psychological Review* 100: 674.

Nagin, Daniel, and Raymond Paternoster. 1991. "On the Relationship of Past and Future Participation in Delinquency." *Criminology* 29: 163–90.

———. 1993. "Enduring Individual Differences and Rational Choice Theories of Crime." *Law and Society Review* 27: 201–30.

Nagin, Daniel and David P. Farrington. 1992. "The Stability of Criminal Potential From Childhood to Adulthood." *Criminology* 30: 235–60.

Nagin, Daniel, and Joel Waldfogel. 1992. 'The Effects of Criminality and Conviction on the Labour Market Status of Young British Offenders." Unpublished manuscript. Pittsburgh: Carnegie Mellon University.

Olweus, Dan. 1979. "Stability of Aggressive Reaction Patterns in Males: A Review." *Bulletin* 86: 852–75.

———. 1980. "Familial and Temperamental Determinants of Aggressive Behavior in Adolescent Boys." *Developmental Psychology* 16: 644–60.

———. 1983. "Low School Achievement and Aggressive Behavior in Adolescent Boys." In *Human Development: An Interactional Perspective,* ed. David Magnusson and Vernon L. Allen, 353–65. New York: Academic.

Paternoster, Raymond, and Leeann Iovanni. 1989. "The Labeling Perspective and Delinquency: An Elaboration of the Theory and an Assessment of the Evidence." *Justice Quarterly* 6: 359–94.

Patterson, Gerald R. 1993. "Orderly Change in a Stable World: The Antisocial Trait as a Chimera." *Journal of Consulting and Clinical Psychology* 61: 911–19.

Patterson, Gerald R., and Karen Yoerger. 1993. "Developmental Models for Delinquent Behavior." In *Mental Disorder and Crime,* ed. Sheilagh Hodgins, 140–72. Newbury Park, CA: Sage.

Patterson, Gerald R., Barbara D. DeBaryshe, and Elizabeth Ramsey. 1989. "A Developmental Perspective on Antisocial Behavior." *American Psychologist* 44: 329–35.

Pickles, Andrew, and Michael Rutter. 1991. "Statistical and Conceptual Models of 'Turning Points' in Developmental Processes." In *Problems and Methods in Longitudinal Research: Stability and Change,* ed. David Magnusson,

Lars Bergman, Georg Rudinger, and Bertil Torestad, 133–65. New York: Cambridge University Press.

Quinton, David, Andrew Pickles, and Barbara Maughan, and Michael Rutter. 1993. "Partners, Peers, and Pathways: Assortative Pairing and Continuities in Conduct Disorder." *Development and Psychopathology* 5: 763–83.

Robins, Lee N. 1966. *Deviant Children Grown Up.* Baltimore: Williams and Wilkins.

———. 1978. "Sturdy Childhood Predictors of Adult Antisocial Behavior: Replications from Longitudinal Studies." *Psychological Medicine* 8: 611–22.

Rutter, Michael. 1989. "Pathways from Childhood to Adult Life." *Journal of Child Psychology and Psychiatry* 30: 25–31.

Rutter, Michael, D. Quinton, and J. Hill. 1990. "Adult Outcomes of Institution-reared Children: Males and Females Compared." In *Straight and Devious Pathways from Childhood to Adulthood,* ed. Lee Robins and Michael Rutter, 135–57. New York: Cambridge University Press.

Rutter, Michael, and Marjorie Rutter. 1993. *Developing Minds: Challenge and Continuity Across the Life Span.* New York: Basic Books.

Sampson, Robert J., and John H. Laub. 1992. "Crime and Deviance in the Life Course." *Annual Review of Sociology* 18: 63–84.

———. 1993. *Crime in the Making: Pathways and Turning Points Through Life.* Cambridge: Harvard University Press.

Scheff, Thomas H. 1966. *Becoming Mentally Ill.* Chicago: Aldine.

Schur, Edwin M. 1971. *Labeling Deviant Behavior.* New York: Harper and Row.

Schwartz, Richard, and Jerome Skolnick. 1964. "Two Studies of Legal Stigma." In *The Other Side: Perspectives on Deviance,* ed. Howard Becker, 103–117. New York: Free Press.

Sherman, Lawrence. 1992. *Policing Domestic Violence.* New York: Free Press.

———. 1993. "Defiance, Deterrence, and Irrelevance: A Theory of the Criminal Sanction." *Journal of Research in Crime and Delinquency* 30: 445–73.

Singer, Richard. 1983. "Conviction: Civil Disabilities." In *Encyclopedia of Crime and Justice,* ed. Sanford Kadish, 243–48. New York: Free Press.

Smith, Brewster. 1968. "Competence and Socialization." In *Socialization and Society,* ed. John Clausen, 270–320. Boston: Little Brown.

Smith, Douglas, and Raymond Paternoster. 1990. "Formal Processing and Future Delinquency: Deviance Amplification as Selection Artifact." *Law and Society Review* 24: 1109–31.

Thomas, Charles, and Donna Bishop. 1984. "The Effect of Formal and Informal Sanctions on Delinquency: A Longitudinal Comparison of Labeling and Deterrence Theories." *Journal of Criminal Law and Criminology* 75: 1222–45.

Thornberry, Terence P. 1987. "Toward an Interactional Theory of Delinquency." *Criminology* 25: 863–91.

Thornberry, Terence P., and R.L. Christenson. 1984. "Unemployment and Criminal Involvement: An Investigation of Reciprocal Causal Structures." *American Sociological Review* 49: 398–411.

Thornberry, Terence P., Alan J. Lizotte, Marvin D. Krohn, Margaret Farnworth, and Sung Joon Jang. 1991. "Testing Interactional Theory: An Examination of Reciprocal Causal Relationships among Family, School, and Delinquency." *Journal of Criminal Law and Criminology* 82: 3–35.

———. 1994. "Delinquent Peers, Beliefs, and Delinquent Behavior: A Longitudinal Test of Interactional Theory." *Criminology* 32: 47–84.

Tittle, Charles. 1975. "Deterrents or Labeling?" *Social Forces* 53: 399–410.

———. 1988. "Two Empirical Regularities (maybe) in Search of an Explanation: Commentary on the Age-Crime Debate." *Criminology* 26: 75–86.

Vaillant, George E. 1983. *The Natural History of Alcoholism*. Cambridge: Harvard University Press.

West, Donald J., and David P. Farrington. 1977. *The Delinquent Way of Life*. London: Heinemann.

Widom, Cathy S. 1989. "The Cycle of Violence." *Science* 244: 160–66.

Wilson, James Q., and Richard Herrnstein. 1985. *Crime and Human Nature*. New York: Simon and Schuster.

Wolfgang, Marvin E., Terence P. Thornberry, and Robert Figlio. 1987. *From Boy to Man: From Delinquency to Crime*. Chicago: University of Chicago Press.

SECTION IV

Empirical Tests
of Life-Course Theories

Despite the recency of life-course theories of crime causation, a number of empirical tests have emerged in recent years examining many of the key aspects of these theories. This section presents empirical tests of the life-course theories discussed in the previous section. These selections illustrate many of the current methods used to examine life-course theories of crime.

Terrie Moffitt's recent developmental theory of offending behavior presented in Section III identifies two discrete groups of offenders: adolescent-limited and life-course persisters. The first article in this section by Daniel Nagin and his colleagues uses data from the Cambridge Study in Delinquent Development to examine characteristics associated with specific types of offenders. Their analyses reveals some overlap and some important differences between discrete offender groups consistent with Moffitt's theory. For example, the authors find the employment histories of low-risk offenders, such as those in the adolescent-limited group, to be similar to nonoffenders and substantially better than chronic, life-course persistent offenders. Nagin and his colleagues, however, also find that adolescent-limited offenders continue to drink heavily and use drugs, participate in fights, and engage in other minor forms of deviance through adulthood.

The second study by sociologist Julie Horney and her colleagues examines how local life circumstances and events shape short-term changes in criminal offending patterns. This study has direct implications for Sampson and Laub's age-graded theory of offending. Horney and her colleagues administered life event history calendars to a sample of male felons in Nebraska to identify specific criminal incidents as well as changes in salient life events, such as employment and marriage. Using hierarchical linear modeling techniques, their results reveal that individual offending patterns are associated with changes in local life circumstances. Specifically, they find that attending school or living with a wife reduces offending in the short-term, but using drugs or living with a girlfriend actually increases offending. Results of the study by Horney and her colleagues are largely consistent with Sampson and Laub's age-graded theory of informal social control.

The papers in this section present readers with an appreciation of empirical research on current life-course theories of offending behavior. Empirical research does not occur in a vacuum. Rather, any one study must be placed into the wider body of empirical research that informs any particular theory. These studies, however, reflect recent and rigorous empirical tests of life-course theories and should expose readers to empirical examinations of life-course theories.

SUGGESTED READINGS

Kratzer, L., & Hodgins, S. (1999). A typology of offenders: A test of Moffitt's theory among males and females from childhood to age 30. *Criminal Behaviour and Mental Health, 9*, 57–73.

Moffitt, T., Caspi, A., Dickson, N., Silva, P., & Stanton, W. (1996). Childhood-onset versus adolescent-onset antisocial conduct problems in males: Natural histories from ages 3 to 18 years. *Development and Psychopathology, 8*, 399–424.

Simons, R., Wu, C.-I., Conger, R., & Lorenz, F. (1994). Two routes to delinquency: Differences between early and late starters in the impact of parenting and deviant peers. *Criminology, 32,* 247–275.

Thornberry, T., Lizotte, A., Krohn, M., & Jang, S. (1989). Delinquent peers, beliefs, and delinquent behavior: A longitudinal test of interactional theory. *Criminology, 32,* 47–83.

Tibbetts, S. G., & Piquero, A. R. (1999). The influence of gender, low birth weight, and disadvantaged environment in predicting early onset of offending: A test of Moffitt's interactional hypothesis. *Criminology, 37*(4), 843–877.

7

Life-Course Trajectories of Different Types of Offenders*

DANIEL S. NAGIN
DAVID P. FARRINGTON
TERRIE E. MOFFITT

ABSTRACT The point of departure for this paper is Nagin and Land (1993), who identified four distinctive offending trajectories in a sample of 403 British males—a group without any convictions, "adolescence-limiteds," "high-level chronics," and "low-level chronics." We build upon that study with a detailed analysis of the distinguishing individual characteristics, behaviors, and social circumstances from ages 10 through 32 of these four groups. The most salient findings concern the adolescence-limiteds. By age 32 the work records of the adolescence-limiteds were indistinguishable from the never-convicted and substantially better than those of the chronic offenders. The adolescence-limiteds also seem to have established better relationships with their spouses than the chronics. The seeming reformation of the adolescence-limiteds, however, was less than complete. They continued to drink heavily and use drugs, get into fights, and commit criminal acts (according to self-reports).

The aim of life-course and developmental theories of crime and deviance (Farrington, 1986b; Hawkins et al., 1986: Huizinga et al., 1991; Loeber & LeBlanc, 1990; Moffitt, 1993; Sampson & Laub, 1991, 1993) is to document and explain the evolution of crime and deviance from childhood through adulthood. To varying degrees these theories emphasize some combination of the following arguments: The progression or trajectory of offending across ages will differ among individuals; the determinants of antisocial behavior are age graded and vary over the life course: antisocial behaviors themselves are sequenced; and time-stable individual differences have an enduring impact on antisocial behavior.

SOURCE: *Criminology,* Vol. 33, No. 1, pp. 111–139.

*This work was supported by the National Science Foundation under grants SES—9023109 and SES—9210437. We thank John Laub and anonymous referees for comments and suggestions for elaboration.

The point of departure for this paper is Nagin and Land (1993), who identified four distinctive offending trajectories in a sample of 403 British males who were tracked from ages 8 to 32. A group who had never been convicted were labeled "nonconvicted." A group who ceased their offending (as measured by conviction) by their early twenties were labeled "adolescence-limiteds," after Moffitt (1993). Also identified were two chronic offender groups: "high-level chronics," who offended at a high level through much of the observation period, and "low-level chronics," who offended at a low level throughout the observation period.

This paper advances the life-course and developmental literature in two ways. First, it builds upon Nagin and Land with a detailed analysis of the distinguishing individual characteristics, behaviors, and social circumstances from ages 10 through 32 of the above four groups. Here the objective is to elaborate upon life-course and developmental theory. Of specific interest are the theories of Moffitt (1993) and Sampson and Laub (1991, 1993). Both theories predict the sorts of distinctive trajectories identified in Nagin and Land, but each offers a fundamentally different explanation for the desistance of the adolescence-limiteds and the continued offending of the chronics. The second aim is methodological—to demonstrate a new approach to identifying characteristics of population groups with distinctive offending trajectories, which is based on nested chi-squared tests.[1]

The most salient findings reported here concern the adolescence-limiteds. By age 32 the work records of the adolescence-limiteds were indistinguishable from the never-convicted and substantially better than those of the high- and low-level chronics. The adolescence-limiteds also seem to have established better relationships with their spouses than the chronics. The seeming reformation of the adolescence-limiteds, however, was less than complete. They continued to drink heavily, use drugs, and get into fights. While their official criminal records ceased many years before, they were still committing criminal acts, such as stealing from their employer, according to their self-reports.

NAGIN AND LAND STUDY

Among the best-documented facts about crime is the age-crime curve. On average, rates of offending rise rather rapidly during early adolescence, reach a peak in the late teenaged years, and then begin a gradual but steady decline thereafter (Farrington, 1986; Hirschi & Gottfredson, 1983). To be sure, this trajectory does not hold for all types of crime (Farrington, 1986a; Wilson &

---

[1]The Nagin and Land study also included an analysis of the distinguishing characteristics of the four groupings described above. This study goes beyond that analysis in several important ways. It examines a far richer set of potentially distinguishing characteristics. Among these are measurements made at age 32, none of which was included in Nagin and Land. Also, the method used to search for distinguishing characteristics is an advance over Nagin and Land. (See also note 11.)

Herrnstein, 1985), but it is the typical pattern. Nagin and Land examined whether this aggregate-level pattern held at the level of the individual.[2] Specifically, Nagin and Land examined whether there were distinctive age-crime trajectories within the population. As described above, four such distinctive trajectories were found: the never-convicted (NCs), the adolescence-limiteds (ALs), the high-level chronics (HLCs), and the low-level chronics (LLCs).

Table 7.1 reports the average rate of conviction by age for the three groups with at least one conviction, the HLCs, LLCs, and ALs. Observe that the trajectory of offending differs dramatically across groups. The HLC age-conviction curve follows the contour of the typical age-crime curve based on aggregate data—a rather steep rise to a peak at about age 18 and a gradual decline thereafter (Farrington, 1986a; Hirschi & Gottfredson, 1983). The rising portion of the AL curve follows this conventional contour, but upon reaching a peak at about age 16 the rate begins a precipitous decline; by age 22 the rate is zero, where it remains for the rest of the observation period. The LLC curve is also distinctive. While there is a clear rise through early adolescence, it remains relatively stable after age 18. By age 20 the LLCs are more active than the ALs and by age 30 the rates of the HLCs and the LLCs have nearly converged. These results imply that explanations of the age-crime curve at the level of the individual cannot be the same as explanations of average population tendencies.

The model used in the Nagin and Land analysis to identify heterogeneity in offending trajectories was specified to explore a number of issues in the "criminal career debate" (Blumstein et al., 1988a, 1988b; Gottfredson & Hirschi, 1986, 1987, 1988). One component of the model was included to test for discrete jumps from periods of offending inactivity to activity (onset) and from periods of activity to inactivity (desistance). Another component of the model was designed to examine various questions concerning offending patterns during periods of activity. It is this component of the model that is relevant here because it was used to identify the distinctive trajectories described above. The discussion that follows is intended as a nontechnical summary of how this method "works."

The model assumes that during periods of activity individuals commit crimes according to a Poisson process, $P(N_{it}; \lambda_{it})$, where N_{it} is the actual number of crimes committed by individual i in period t and λ_{it} is the expected rate of crime commission for that individual in that period. λ_{it} can be thought of as a parameter capturing the underlying propensity to offend, which in general will not correspond to the actual number of offenses due to the intervention of chance events (e.g., availability of offending opportunities or being ill for part of the period).

Nagin and Land estimated the following relationship of λ_{it} to potential covariates:

---

[2]In the Nagin and Land analysis the unit of observation was the individual. We therefore refer to the age-crime relationship thus derived as an individual rather than aggregate relationship.

Table 7.1 Average Biannual Rate of Conviction (×10) by Age and Offender Type

Age	OFFENDER TYPE High-Level Chronic	Adolescence-Limited	Low-Level Chronic
10–11	2.1	.8	0.0
12–13	5.0	2.4	.5
14–15	9.0	5.5	1.7
16–17	14.6	5.7	1.7
18–19	16.5	4.9	1.8
20–21	11.5	1.0	3.1
22–23	7.5	0.0	3.6
24–25	5.6	0.0	2.6
26–27	3.8	0.0	3.3
28–29	5.2	0.0	2.4
30–31	3.5	0.0	2.6
N	52	51	42

$$ln\ (\lambda_{it}) = \gamma_0 + \delta\ X_i + \beta_1\ Age_{it}\ \beta_2\ Age^2_{it},$$

where X_i is a vector of time-stable characteristics of individual i, Age_{it} is individual i's age in t, and Age^2_{it} is age squared in t.[3] $Ln(\lambda_{it})$ is specified as a quadratic function of age to test whether at the level of the individual, λ follows the single-peaked function characterizing age-crime curves based on aggregate data. A single-peaked age-λ curve is implied if $\beta_1 > 0$ and $\beta_2 < 0$. Another possibility is that at the level of the individual, λ is invariant with age. Such a relationship, which is predicted by Blumstein and Cohen (1979), is implied by $\beta_1 = \beta_2 = 0$.

Nagin and Paternoster (1991) and Nagin and Farrington (1992a, 1992b) have pointed out the importance of controlling for unmeasured time-stable individual differences in the analysis of longitudinal data. As specified in Equation 1, the model assumes that λ_{it} is *completely* determined by *measured* time-stable characteristics of the individual and by age. Results reported in Nagin and Farrington (1992a, 1992b) demonstrate that this assumption is seriously flawed. Those analyses reveal that patterns of offending over time are influenced to a very substantial degree by unmeasured characteristics of individuals or their environment.

The basic innovation of Nagin and Land was to allow for such heterogeneity but without making a specific assumption about its distribution in the population (e.g., normal, gamma, log-normal).[4] This was done by adapting a

---

[3]A log-linear relationship between λ_{it} and potential covariates is assumed to ensure that a basic assumption of the Poisson distribution, $\lambda > 0$, is fulfilled in model estimation.

[4]If unobserved heterogeneity is ignored, the parameters of Equation 1 could be estimated by a standard Poisson regression.

semiparametric maximum likelihood estimation procedure, similar to that proposed by Heckman and Singer (1984), that approximates any unspecified continuous distribution of unobserved heterogeneity with a linear combination of discrete distributions. Intuitively, the estimation procedure accomplishes this task as follows. Suppose unbeknownst to us there were two distinct groups in the population: youth offenders, constituting 50% of the population, who up to age 18 have a λ of five and who after age 18 have a λ of one; and adult offenders, constituting the other 50% of the population, whose offending trajectory is the reverse of that of the youth offenders— through age 18 their λ equals one and after age 18 their λ increases to five. If one had longitudinal data on the recorded offenses of a sample of individuals from this population, one would observe two distinct groups: a clustering of about 50% of the sample, who generally have many offenses prior to age 18 and relatively few offenses after age 18, and another 50% clustering with just the reverse pattern.

Suppose these data were analyzed under the assumption that the age-λ trajectory is identical across all individuals. The estimated value of λ would be a "compromise" estimate of about three for all ages, from which one would mistakenly conclude that in this population the rate of offending is invariant with age. If the data were analyzed using the approach employed in Nagin and Land, which specifies the likelihood function as a composite of several distributions (i.e., a mixing distribution), no such mathematical "compromise" would be necessary. The parameters of one component of the mixing distribution would effectively be used to accommodate (i.e., match) the youth offender data, whose offending declines with age, and another component of the mixing distribution would be available to accommodate the adult offender data, whose offending increases with age. Exploiting this approach, which is sensitive to developmental heterogeneity, Nagin and Land detected the four offending trajectories to be described further in this article.

DATA

The Nagin and Land analysis and this extension to it uses a panel data set assembled by David Farrington and Donald West. The panel is a prospective longitudinal survey of 411 males from a working-class area of London. Data collection began in 1961–62, when most of the boys were about age 8. Criminal involvement is measured by convictions for criminal offenses and is available for all individuals in the sample through age 32, with the exception of eight individuals who died prior to this age.[5]

The Nagin and Land and present analyses are based on the data for the 403 individuals for whom there was a complete conviction history between the

---

[5]The conviction counts do not include convictions for traffic offenses or for offenses deemed to be of minor seriousness (e.g., drunkenness or simple assault).

10th and the 32nd birthdays. Of these, 36% had at least one conviction. For those who were convicted, the average number of convictions over the observation period was 4.4.

To the extent possible, all of the sample were interviewed at approximate two-year intervals until they were age 18 and then again at age 32.[6] Parents, teachers, and friends were also interviewed. Based on these contacts an impressive variety of measurements were made. Through childhood and adolescence, data are available on psychological characteristics, such as IQ, risk-taking behavior, and neuroticism; on socialization variables, such as parental supervision and attachment; and on family background variables, such as criminality of parents and siblings, income, separation from parents, and family size. Beginning in late adolescence, data were also collected on drug and alcohol use, sexual activity, family formation patterns, and employment status. For a complete discussion of the data set, see Farrington and West (1990).

This analysis attempts to make maximum use of the rich variety of measurements available in this data set. Representative variables from the following categories were contrasted across the four offender categories:

1. *Delinquent, Criminal, and Imprudent Behaviors,* which includes self-reported crime and delinquency, early or promiscuous sexual behavior, illicit drug use, and alcohol abuse.

2. *Intelligence and Attainment,* which includes IQ and success in school and in the labor market.

3. *Hyperactivity, Impulsivity, and Attention Deficit (HIA),* which comprises reports by teachers, parents, and the individual himself of restlessness, impulsive and daring behavior, and an inability to concentrate.

4. *Relationship with Family and Friends,* which measures the strength and quality of the attachments to others, as a child and an adult.

5. *Antisocial Family and Parenting Factors,* which comprises measurements taken during early adolescence of parental child-rearing practice and of the antisocial behavior of parents and siblings.

6. *Socioeconomic Deprivation,* which measures economic and physical deprivation experienced by the individual during early adolescence.

IDENTIFYING DISTINGUISHING CHARACTERISTICS OF OFFENDER GROUPS

Our method for identifying distinguishing characteristics of offenders is a two-stage procedure. In the first stage individuals in the estimation sample are assigned to one of the four offender categories. Such an assignment process was necessary, for example, to compile the summary statistics in Table 7.1. In the

---

[6]Subsamples were also interviewed at ages 21 and 25, but these data were not used in this study.

second stage distinctive group characteristics are identified with a model-search procedure designed to identify the most parsimonious model for explaining the data.

It is not possible to determine definitively an individual's offender-group membership.[7] Individuals can, however, be sorted among the offender categories based on the probability of their belonging to the various groups. Specifically, based on the model coefficient estimates, the probability of observing each individual's longitudinal pattern of offending is computed conditional on his being, respectively, an HLC, LLC, AL, or NC. The individual is assigned to the group with the highest *ex post* probability of having generated the individual's observed pattern of offending. This probability equals $P(y_i/j, x_i)\gamma_j$, where j (= HLC, LLC . . .) is an index of group membership, y_i is a vector comprising a count of individual i's convictions in each period t, and γ_j is the estimated proportion of the population in each group. These proportions are among the model parameter estimates.

Based on this procedure, an individual with a cluster of offenses in adolescence but none thereafter, in all likelihood, will be assigned to the AL category. Alternatively, an individual whose history of recorded offenses begins in his late teens and continues on through his twenties is likely to be categorized as a LLC, whereas an individual who offends at a comparatively high rate throughout the observation period will likely be assigned to the HLC group. Finally, this "maximum probability" procedure always assigns individuals with no convictions to the NC category.

As a first step toward identifying characteristics and behaviors that distinguish among the HLCs, LLCs, ALs, and NCs, all variables measuring such characteristics/behaviors were recoded into a binary format. Specifically, the transformed variable was coded as 1 if the individual scored "high" on the potential risk factor (e.g., low IQ, criminal parent) or antisocial behavior (e.g., heavy drinking, using drugs) and 0 if the individual scored low. The definition of "high" was operationalized by prevalence (e.g., used drugs) or by the individual scoring in the highest/lowest quartile of the measurement scale (e.g., persons in the lowest quartile of the IQ distribution were coded as having a low IQ).

Variables were measured dichotomously for two reasons. First, the methodology described below for identifying distinguishing group characteristics would be extremely awkward to implement if the full range of categorical responses present in the raw data were maintained. Second, dichotomous coding serves the interests of comparability and is in accordance with a "risk factor" approach. Moreover, since most variables were originally measured in a small number of categories and because fine distinctions between categories

---

[7]The offender groupings are defined by a vector of age-indexed λ's. Because the model assumes that the underlying process of actual offending has a stochastic component as defined by the Poisson distribution, the actual number of offenses committed by an individual at a specified age from a given group will in general not be the same as the underlying group average rate.

could not be made very accurately, dichotomizing does not involve a great loss of information (Farrington & Hawkins, 1991).

By dichotomizing the variables of interest, the data can be summarized in the form of two-dimensional contingency tables wherein one dimension is offender type and the other is the level of the risk factor or behavior (e.g., lives in a crowded house (y/n), unstable job record (y/n)). As shown in Figure 7.1, the entries in the table are determined by the proportion of each group that is high on the risk factor/behavior, where π_h, π_l, π_a, and π_n, are, respectively, that proportion for the HLCs, LLCs, ALs, and NCs.

The objective of identifying distinctive group characteristics is statistically equivalent to determining whether subsets of the groups have the same or different π's. Some of the possibilities are summarized in Figure 7.2. The null and general models capture the two extremes: In the null model, all the π's are the same, which implies that all the offender groups are equivalent on the variable. In the general model, all the π's are different, which implies that each group is distinctive with regard to the variable.

As indicated in Figure 7.2, the null model is a one-parameter model and the general model is a four-parameter model. In between these two extremes there are a number of two- and three-parameter models that are of theoretical interest. Consider first the two-parameter models. One is called the criminal model, in which $\pi_h = \pi_a = \pi_l > \pi_n$. In the criminal model all criminal groups possess the characteristic to an equal degree regardless of whether they are active at the time of the measurement (i.e., the ALs might be the same as the HLCs and LLCs on some variable measured at age 32, long after the ALs have desisted as measured by conviction).

Within the class of two-parameter models some other interesting possibilities include the high/low-level chronic model ($\pi_h = \pi_l > \pi_a = \pi_n$) and the high-level chronic/adolescence-limited model ($\pi_h = \pi_a > \pi_l > \pi_n$). The former model implies that on some characteristics the HLCs and LLCs are equivalent, but distinctive from the ALs and NCs, who in turn are indistinguishable on that characteristic. This model implies that chronic offenders, as measured by conviction, are distinctive from desisters and nonoffenders. In contrast the HLC/AL model is expected to apply if distinctive characteristics temporally vary in conjunction with periods of high offending activity. Recall from Table 7.1 that the HLCs and ALs have markedly higher rates of conviction than LLCs (and NCs) up to age 19. Also listed among the two-parameter models are the HLC, LLC, and AL models. Each of these is a model in which the group after which the model is named is

OFFENDER GROUPING				
		HLC	AL	LLC	NC
Risk factor/	Present	π_h	π_a	π_l	π_n
behavior	Absent	$1 - \pi h$	$1 - \pi a$	$1 - \pi l$	$1 - \pi n$

FIGURE 7.1 Two-dimensional contingency table: Offender grouping by behavior

Null—one-parameter model
($\pi_h = \pi_l = \pi_a > \pi_n$)

Two-parameter models

High-level chronic and adolescence-limited
($\pi_h = \pi_a > \pi_l > \pi_n$)

High/low-level chronic
($\pi_h = \pi_l > \pi_a > \pi_h$)

Criminal
($\pi_h = \pi_l = \pi_a > \pi_n$)

High-level chronic
($\pi_h > = \pi_l = \pi_a > \pi_n$)

Low-level chronic
($\pi_l > \pi_h = \pi_a = \pi_n$)

Adolescence-limited
($\pi_a > \pi_h = \pi_l > \pi_n$)

Criminal/high-level chronic—three-parameter model
($\pi_h > \pi_l = \pi_a > \pi_n$)

General—four-parameter model
($\pi_h \neq \pi_a \neq \pi_l \neq \pi_n$)

FIGURE 7.2 Nested model types

disproportionately high on the characteristic compared with all other groups, who are in turn indistinguishable on the characteristic (e.g., $\pi_a > \pi_h = \pi_l = \pi_n$). Such models are of special interest because they imply that some risk factor/behavior uniquely distinguishes some group.[8]

Figure 7.2 lists only one of the many possible three-parameter models, the criminal/high-level chronic model ($\pi_h > \pi_l = \pi_a > \pi_n$). In this model all the criminal groups are high on the characteristic compared with the NCs, but the HLCs are particularly high. In the domain of three-parameter models, other interesting possibilities exist but they are not listed because the analyses did not find such possibilities to be the "preferred" model.

The basic testing strategy for identifying the "preferred" model involves a systematic search for the model that best explains the data with the fewest parameters. This was done as follows: The explanatory power of the most parsimonious model, the one-paramater null model, is first compared with the least parsimonious, four-parameter general model. This test was performed using the likelihood ratio statistic (G^2 statistic) to calibrate the change in explanatory power. This statistic, which equals twice the absolute value of the difference in the log likelihoods of the competing models, is distributed as chi-squared with degrees of freedom equal to the difference in the number of parameters of the two models. Thus, in the contrast between the general and null models, the degrees of freedom of the chi-squared test statistic is three (= 4 minus 1).

The loss of explanatory power of the null model compared with the general model was deemed significant if the *p*-value of the test statistic was less than .1. If the loss was not significant for $\alpha = .1$, model testing was stopped and the null model was designated the "best fitting" model.[9]

This test procedure is equivalent to using the chi-squared test of independence to test whether group membership is independent of the specified behavior/risk characteristic. Independence implies that there are no cross-group differences in the proportion, π_j, who have the specified behavior/characteristic. Lack of independence implies that there is cross-group variation in such proportions, and thus testing moved on to explore the explanatory power of the various two-parameter models.

---

[8]Other possible two-parameter models include the LLC/AL model ($\pi_l = \pi_a > \pi_h = \pi_n$) and models in which the inequality is reversed (e.g., $\pi_a < \pi_l = \pi_h = \pi_n$). These models are not included in Figure 7.2 because they are theoretically improbable and indeed did not arise as the "preferred" model for describing any specific characteristic.

[9]The choice of a *p*-value delimiting significant versus nonsignificant loss of explanatory power is in the end a matter of judgment. For several reasons we chose a *p*-value of .1, which is large by conventional standards. First, this analysis is inherently exploratory in nature. Thus, it is not clear which model should be given the special standing of the "null" hypothesis. Indeed, for some variables what we call the "null" model is a theoretically interesting possibility that in conventional testing would be given the status of the "alternative" hypothesis. To be sure we implicitly gave the model with the least number of parameters the status of the "null hypothesis" by our selection of a .1 *p*-value cutoff versus, for example, a .5 cutoff. Still, in the spirit of exploratory analysis we did not want to set too stringent a standard for concluding that there may be differences across groups. Also, another reason for use of the more "lenient" .1 significance cutoff was concern about statistical power in light of the relatively small sizes of the criminal groups.

In testing the two-parameter models, loss of explanatory power was again gauged relative to the general, four-parameter model using a .1 p-value to define a significant loss of explanatory power. Typically, at most only one of the two-parameter models met the $p = .1$ threshold of no significant loss of explanatory power (i.e., had a p-value greater than .1). In this case that model was designated the best-fitting model. When two or more of the two-parameter models meet the $p = .1$ criterion, classical statistical theory provides no firm theoretical basis for model selection because the competing two-parameter models are not nested (i.e., one model is not a special case of the other).[10] In this case the two-parameter model with the largest p-value (i.e., smallest decline in explanatory power relative to the general model) was designated as the best-fitting model. If none of the two-parameter models exceeded the $p = .1$ threshold, testing moved on to examine various possible three-parameter models using the same rules as applied to the two-parameter models.[11]

RESULTS

Table 7.2 compares offending patterns of all groups, including NCs, based on self-reports of offending as well as conviction rate. The self-report summary statistics for theft and burglary are mean rates over the measurement period.[12] The general delinquency statistic (which includes burglary, vehicle theft, theft from a vehicle, shoplifting, vandalism, violence, and drug use) measures the mean prevalence of these behaviors in each group. Thus, it is a measure of the "variety" of delinquent behaviors that are engaged in. An individual is regarded as engaging in the specified behavior if he reports one or more acts of that behavior. For the age 14 self-reports, the measurement period is up to and including age 14. For the age 18 and 32 measurements, the self-reports are, respectively, for the past three and five years.

Table 7.2 reveals that at all ages the three criminal groups had higher self-reported offending rates than the NCs. As reported in Table 7.3, these

---

[10]By contrast, all the other models in Figure 7.2 are nested within the general model so that use of the likelihood ratio statistic to test for a significant loss of explanatory power relative to the general model is statistically appropriate.

[11]As previously noted, Nagin and Land also did an analysis of distinguishing characteristics of the HLCs, ALs, LLCs, and NCs. That analysis was based on series of paired t-tests exhaustively comparing the groups (e.g., t-tests of the HLCs vs. ALs, HLCs vs. LLCs, ALs vs. NCs, etc.). This procedure is inferior to that used here because our chi-squared testing procedure jointly tests for cross-group differences. Also, the testing approach used here systematically explores best-fitting model options.

[12]A common feature of data on self-reported criminality is that it is highly skewed; a few individuals report a very large number of offenses. Sample means are very sensitive to values of such outlying data points, particularly in small data sets such as this. In computing the means reported in Table 7.2, we recoded all self-reports greater than 30 events to equal 30. This procedure, we believe, was generally successful in reasonably summarizing the "central tendency" of the data. One exception is the comparatively high mean theft rate for the ALs at age 30, which is attributable to a single individual.

Table 7.2 Multiple Measures of Crime and Delinquency by Age

	High-Level Chronic	Adolescence-Limited	Low-Level Chronic	Never Convicted
Age 14				
Conviction Rate (×10)	5.00	2.35	.48	.00
General Delinquency	2.88	2.26	2.38	1.37
Burglary	2.88	1.94	1.36	.12
Theft	.73	.69	.50	.06
Age 18				
Conviction Rate (×10)	14.62	5.69	1.90	.00
General Delinquency	3.10	2.50	1.95	.93
Burglary	3.31	.77	.68	.01
Theft	5.29	1.19	.66	.10
Age 32				
Conviction Rate (×10)	3.46	0.00	2.62	0.00
General Delinquency	1.45	1.00	1.15	.42
Burglary	.14	.04	.24	.00
Theft	.12	.76	.17	.00

differences were, with one exception, always statistically significant (i.e., the null model never applied).[13] This finding is noteworthy because none of the ALs had been convicted since age 22, yet at age 32 their offending behavior, as measured by self-reported general deviance and theft, was indistinguishable from that of the HLCs and LLCs. We return to this finding below.

The summary offending statistics in Table 7.2 also generally support the distinctiveness of the HLCs. At ages 14 and 18 the conviction rate of the HLCs was well above the rates of all other groups; the same pattern of pronounced difference is present in the self-reported rate of burglary and also of theft but at age 18 only. Interestingly, for the more broad-based general delinquency measure, the mean rate of the HLCs at ages 14 and 18 is only modestly larger than the companion rates for the ALs and HLCs.

Consider next Table 7.3, which reports the best-fitting model for "delinquent, criminal, and imprudent behaviors." The first column of this table lists the model types that were selected at least once as the "best-fitting" model for this category of variables. Thus, for example, the null model, where $\pi_h = \pi_l = \pi_a = \pi_n$ was selected as the best-fitting model for heavy gambling, a variable measured at age 32. The implication is that at age 32 there was no significant difference across groups, including the NCs, in the proportion who were heavy gamblers. Similarly, the model-search procedure revealed that at age 32 there was no difference in the proportion of HLCs and LLCs who acknowledged committing at

---

[13]The one exception is for burglary at age 32, for which, as discussed below, the high/low-level chronic model best fits the data.

Table 7.3 Delinquent, Criminal, and Imprudent Behaviors

Model Type	Age 10	Age 14	Age 18	Age 32
Null				
High-Level Chronic		Self-Reported Theft		Heavy Gambler Tax Evasion Self-Reported Burglar Antisocial
High/Low-Level Chronic				
High-Level Chronic/ Adolescence-Limited		Smokes Regularly Had Sex	Self-Reported General Delinquency Self-Reported Theft Frequently in Group Fights Fights at Soccer Matches High Self-Reported Violence Has Used Marijuana and Other Drugs	
Criminal	Primary School Truancy Troublesome	Self-Reported General Delinquency Self-Reported Burglary Fights Outside Home Steals Outside Home	Unprotected Sex Multiple Sex Partners Drives While Drunk Heavy Drinker Fights After Drinking Heavy Gambler	Self-Reported General Delinquency Self-Reported Theft Drives While Drunk Fights Outside Home Heavy Smoker Used Drugs in Past 5 Years
Criminal/High-Level Chronic		Frequently Truant Frequently Lies	Self-Reported Burglar	Used Marijuana in Past 5 Years Heavy Drinker

least one burglary and that this proportion was in turn higher than the propor-tion for ALs and NCs, who in turn themselves were not significantly different. As a consequence, the high/low-level chronic model ($\pi_h = \pi_l > \pi_a = \pi_n$) is listed as the best-fitting model for the variable "self-reported burglar" at age 32. The same pattern was also found for "antisocial" at age 32, and therefore this variable is also associated with the high/low-level chronic model.

There are a number of noteworthy patterns in this table. First, at ages 14 and 18, when the ALs and HLCs are at their peak offending rates, the groups were also collectively more likely than the LLCs and NCs to engage in vio-lence, use drugs, smoke regularly, and have sex, as evidenced by our finding that the high-level chronic/adolescence-limited model is the best-fitting model for these variables at these ages. In contrast, at age 10, the three crimi-nal groups were similar in their antisocial behavior, as measured by trouble-someness and truancy. This is evidenced by the criminal model ($\pi_h = \pi_l = \pi_a > \pi_n$) being the best-fitting model for these age-b variables. Second, by age 32 all three offending groups were more likely than the NCs to be fighting, using drugs, and abusing alcohol, as evidenced by the finding that the criminal model is again the best-fitting model.

These results suggest that "reformation" of the ALs based on their post-teen conviction rates is more apparent than real. However, inspection of Table 7.4, which reports the best-fitting model for "intelligence and attainment" mea-surements, suggests that this conclusion is an oversimplification. At age 18, when the HLCs, LLCs, and ALs are in the midst of their peak period of offend-ing, their performance in the legal labor market compared to the NCs is poor. The three criminal groups are significantly more likely to hold unskilled jobs, be unemployed, and score high on an overall index of employment instability.[14] By age 32, the employment patterns of the ALs have changed dramatically. On all criteria of labor market success they are indistinguishable from the NCs. In con-trast, the HLCs and LLCs continue to be disproportionately employed in inse-cure, low-paying jobs. Thus, it is no coincidence that at age 32 the HLCs and LLCs are also disproportionately of low socioeconomic status, live in homes that are in poor condition, and are "social failures" (on a composite nine-point scale; see Farrington, 1989) compared with ALs and NCs.

Table 7.5 reports best-fitting models for "relationships with family and friends." Through age 18 there are no notable differences across groups. By age 32 interesting differences have emerged. While all groups are equally likely to have a wife or cohabitee, the criminal groups are more likely than NCs to have been divorced or separated and to have a child living elsewhere. In this respect the ALs are indistinguishable from the HLCs and LLCs.

The high family-dissolution rates of the ALs compared with the NCs may, however, be measuring family breakups that occurred years earlier. This

---

[14]These differences are further corroborated by observations of West and Farrington (1977), who report that at age 18 convicted youth were far more likely to be employed in insecure, "dead-end" jobs, such as day laborers, rather than in jobs offering the prospect of job security and advancement, such as an apprenticeship.

Table 7.4 Intelligence and Attainment

Model Type	Age 10	Age 14	Age 18	Age 32
Null				
High/Low-Level Chronic	Low Junior School Attainment Low Secondary School Tracking Low Verbal IQ		Low-Take Home Pay Difficulty Reading	Low Take-Home Pay Frequent Unemployment Unstable Job Record Social Failure Low SES Poor Home Conditions
Criminal	Low Nonverbal IQ	Low Verbal IQ Low Nonverbal IQ Left School Early	Has Unskilled Job	
Criminal/High-Level Chronic			Unstable Job Record High Unemployment	

Table 7.5 Relationship with Family and Friends

Model Type	Age 10	Age 14	Age 18	Age 32
Null	Peers Rate Unpopular	Teacher Rate Unpopular	Married, Separated, or Cohabitating	No Wife/Cohabitee Argues Frequently with Wife/Cohabitee
High-Level Chronic			Poor Relationship with Parents	
High/Low-Level Chronic				Hits Wife/Cohabitee Doesn't Get Along with Wife/Cohabitee
Criminal		Delinquent Acquaintances		Divorced or Separated Had Child Living Elsewhere

interpretation is supported by more contemporaneous measurements of the quality of attachments to family; the HLCs and LLCs, but not the ALs, appear to continue to have difficulty in establishing enduring and constructive attachments. Specifically, the HLCs and LLCs disproportionately report that they hit their wife/cohabitee and that they do not get along with her.[15]

Tables 7.6, 7.7, and 7.8 report findings for "*HIA*," "antisocial family and parenting factors," and "socioeconomic deprivation," respectively. The results confirm a host of factors distinguishing criminals from NCs that have been previously documented in this and other data sets. One or more of the criminal groups were more likely than NCs to be impulsive, lack concentration, have criminal parents or siblings, have grown up in economically deprived households, and have had parents who were criminal, disharmonious, or poor at childrearing. These characteristics do not, however, distinguish very well among the criminal groups. While there is some indication that the HLCs were especially lacking in their ability to concentrate and that they had disproportionately grown up in a deprived home setting, evidence is scant of cross-group differences among criminal groups in "HIA," "antisocial family and parenting factors," and "socioeconomic deprivation."[16]

To sum up, our most striking findings concern the ALs. In some domains of life activities their behavior follows a trajectory that parallels that of their criminal behavior as measured by conviction. At age 18 the ALs, like the HLCs and LLCs, scored high on all measures of job instability. By age 32 the labor market performance of the ALs was indistinguishable from the NCs and markedly better than the HLCs and LLCs, who unlike the ALs, continued to be active offenders, as measured by their conviction rate. Our analyses also suggest that by age 32 the ALs have had greater success than the HLCs and LLCs in developing strong (positive) attachment with their spouse.

In other domains of activity, however, the label adolescence-limited belies the reality of the group's typical behavior. At age 32 the ALs continued to engage in property crime, in particular, theft (as opposed to burglary). Further analyses suggest that a principal victim of the stealing of ALs is their employer; at age 32, 43% of the ALs admitted to stealing from their employer in the past five years, whereas only 18% of the NCs reported such behavior.

Also, based on their self-reported behavior, the ALs continued disproportionately to use illicit drugs, drink heavily, and get into fights. This pattern of

---

[15]We do not have data on the timing of the divorces and separations. To the extent that the divorces and separations of the ALs occurred at ages more proximate to their peak years of offending, the personal and social circumstances that gave rise to such family breakups may have changed in major ways by age 32.

[16]As previously noted, the Nagin and Land analysis of distinguishing characteristics was more limited than that reported here. For those variables that overlap, the results are largely identical. The only noteworthy divergence in findings is that in Nagin and Land LLCs were found to be disproportionately low in IQ compared with the ALs and HLCs. Our model-testing procedure did not show this difference to be significant. Nagin and Land also found that compared with the HLCs and LLCs the ALs were more popular and less prone to poor junior school performance. This same pattern was again found in this analysis, but it was not significant with the testing procedure used here.

Table 7.6 Hyperactivity, Impulsivity, and Attention Deficit

Model Type	Age 10	Age 14	Age 18	Age 32
High-Level Chronic	Lacks Concentration and Restless			
High-Level Chronic/ Adolescence-Limited		Daring		
Criminal	Daring Psychomotor Impulsivity		High Self-Reported Impulsivity	High Self-Reported Impulsivity
Criminal/High-Level Chronic		Lacks Concentration		

Table 7.7 Antisocial Family and Parenting Factors (≤ 14 years old)

Model Type	Age 10	Age 14
Null	Authoritarian Parents Not Praised by Parents	
High-Level Chronic	Delinquent Older Sibling Low Parental Interest in Education	
High/Low-Level Chronic	Harsh or Erratic Child-Discipline	Poor Parental Rearing Marital Disharmony
Criminal	Criminal Parent Marital Disharmony Poor Supervision Poor Parental Child-Rearing	

Table 7.8 Socioeconomic Deprivation (≤ 14 years old)

Model Type	Age 10	Age 14
Null	Low SES Poor Housing	
High-Level Chronic	Low Family Income	
Criminal	Crowded Housing Boy Physically Neglected	Crowded Housing

behavior not only points to the distinctiveness of the ALs but also is puzzling. Prior research has repeatedly documented that illicit drug and alcohol abuse are associated with job failure and dysfunctional family relationships (see Jessor et al., 1991; Robins, 1966; Sampson & Laub, 1993), yet our results seemingly suggest no such relationship for the ALs.

To probe this anomaly further, we examined the relationship between illicit drug use and job instability separately for each group. The results of this analysis are reported in Table 7.9 in the form of a series of contingency tables relating illicit drug use to job instability for each group at ages 18 and 32.[17] Also reported are the chi-squared tests of independence. For these 2 × 2 tables the degrees of freedom is one.

Inspection of Table 7.9 reveals several distinctive patterns. First, there is no relationship between drug use and job instability for the HLCs and LLCs at age 18 or 32; for these two groups job instability is high regardless of drug use status. For example, at age 32, 47.6% of the HLCs using illicit drugs had unstable job records. For those who were not using illicit drugs, a nearly identical

---

[17]Job instability is a composite measure based on number of jobs held over a specified period, average number of weeks unemployed over the past year, longest time on any job, and number of times fired.

Table 7.9 Drug Use and Job Instability by Group

	AGE 18			**AGE 32**	
	High-Level Chronics				
	High Job Instability			**High Job Instability**	
	Y	N		Y	N
Illicit Drug Use Y	54.8%	45.2%	**Illicit Drug Use**	47.6%	52.4%
Illicit Drug Use N	50.0	50.0		52.2	47.8
	chi sq. = .11			chi. sq. = .09	
	Adolescence-Limiteds				
	High Job Instability			**High Job Instability**	
	Y	N		Y	N
Illicit Drug Use Y	61.9%	38.1%	**Illicit Drug Use**	38.5%	61.5%
Illicit Drug Use N	18.5	81.5		8.3	91.7
	chi sq. = 9.49*			chi. sq. = 6.35*	
	Low-Level Chronics				
	High Job Instability			**High Job Instability**	
	Y	N		Y	N
Illicit Drug Use Y	30.0%	70.0%	**Illicit Drug Use**	55.6%	44.4%
Illicit Drug Use N	30.0	70.0		31.3	68.8
	chi sq. = 0.00			chi. sq. = 1.79	
	Never-Convicted				
	High Job Instability			**High Job Instability**	
	Y	N		Y	N
Illicit Drug Use Y	22.4%	77.6%	**Illicit Drug Use**	31.0%	69.0%
Illicit Drug Use N	11.4	88.6		17.6	82.4
	chi sq. = 4.42*			chi. sq. = 2.95	

Note: Table entries are row percentages.

*Significant at 5%.

percentage had unstable job records—52.2%. Second, unlike for the chronics, for the ALs (and NCs) there is a pronounced relationship between drug use and job instability at both ages. Combined, these two results imply that it is the chronics, not the ALs, who deviate from the conventional wisdom that drug use increases the risk of poor labor market performance. It appears that the drug use and job instability of the HLCs and LLCs reflect a lifetime inability to conform with conventional norms of behavior.

A third salient pattern is that at age 32 the ALs who do not use drugs have markedly lower levels of job instability than the NCs—8.3% for the ALs versus 17.6% for the NCs. While we can offer no explanation for this difference, it does reconcile the seeming inconsistency that the ALs have a higher rate of illicit drug use than the NCs but the same rate of job instability.[18]

How do we interpret the findings? The ALs appear to be engaged in what might be characterized as circumscribed deviance. At age 32 they seem to be careful to avoid committing crimes with a high risk of conviction, which might jeopardize their stable work careers, or to engage in behaviors, like spousal assault, that might harm their familial relationships. Instead, they seem to restrict their deviance to behaviors less likely to result in official sanction or disrupt intimate attachments.[19]

The behavior of the ALs, thus, exhibits both continuity and change. This dualism in their behavior is striking. Whereas in some domains the deflection of their behavioral trajectory away from antisocial and self-destructive behaviors is so complete that they are indistinguishable from the NCs, in other domains there is no apparent change in the behavioral trajectory that characterized the generalized deviance of their youth, at least in comparison with the chronic offender groups.

DISCUSSION

Our findings document important differences in the life-course trajectories of the four groups identified in Nagin and Land. The two chronic offender groups, the adolescence-limiteds, and the never-convicted not only have distinctive life-course trajectories as measured by their age-graded conviction rate, they also manifest important cross-group differences in other domains of behavior. We interpret this evidence as generally confirming the usefulness of the offender typology identified in Nagin and Land.

Our results, we believe, are particularly relevant to the theories of Moffitt (1993) and Sampson and Laub (1993). Moffitt advances a theory predicting some of the differences in offending trajectory found in Nagin and Land. She argues that a small proportion of the population constitutes what she calls life-course persistent deviants. This group comprises individuals in whom cumulative interactions between family adversity and neuropsychological deficits predispose them to chronic deviance throughout their

---

[18]We also conducted a parallel set of analyses relating heavy drinking with job instability. While for the overall sample there is a significant positive association between these two variables, for the subsamples defined by the four groupings the association is generally not significant. The pattern of results, however, generally conforms to those for drug use and job instability.

[19]Our finding that the ALs commonly continue to steal from their employers is potentially but not necessarily at odds with this explanation of the ALs behavior. The likelihood of being caught for stealing at work is generally very low.

lives. Such deficits, she argues, result from such factors as maternal drug abuse, poor prenatal nutrition, or pre- or post-natal exposure to toxic agents (e.g., lead) or from heritable variation and are manifested early in life in such behaviors as attention deficit disorder, impulsivity, hyperactivity, and learning disorders. Her theory also includes a second, much larger population group—adolescence-limited offenders. Those in this group, like the life-course persistent deviants, are heavily involved in crime and delinquency during their youth. She argues that the onset of delinquent behavior among the adolescence-limiteds results from their mimicking the antisocial life-style of the life-course persistent youth. However, unlike offending by the life-course persistents, offending within the adolescence-limited subpopulation declines precipitously after about age 18.[20]

The Sampson and Laub theory does not specifically invoke terms such as life-course persistent and adolescence-limited, but it does effectively predict the existence of such groups. Drawing from the life-course perspective developed by Elder (1975, 1985, 1992), Dannefer (1984), and others, and from social control theory, Sampson and Laub attempt to account for the desistance from deviance of most delinquent youth in the context of a theory that takes into account the enormous body of evidence showing the continuity of individual antisocial behavior. In a nutshell, Sampson and Laub argue that enduring attachments to work and family have a comparably powerful influence as stable individual differences on the unfolding of deviant behaviors through the life course. Thus, they argue that even individuals who were severely delinquent in their youth will desist from such antisocial behavior as adults if they have the good fortune to encounter the "right" mate or employer.

The finding that at age 18 the ALs were indistinguishable from the HLCs in terms of attachments to work and family but by age 32 were indistinguishable from the NCs in this regard is a key prediction of both theories but for very different reasons. In the context of the Sampson and Laub theory, this finding is consistent with the hypothesized socializing influence of strong social bonds. The ALs theoretically desisted because they developed such bonds, and the HLCs (and LLCs) did not desist because they failed to develop such bonds. In the Moffitt theory the ALs develop strong attachments to work and family for the same reason they desist from delinquency: Youthful delinquency followed by adult bonding to work and family constitute a sequence of normal developmental stages (for males). Her life-course persistents are the exceptions who, because of their neurological deficits combined with adverse family circumstances in early childhood, are unable to conform to legal norms or to establish social bonds.

Aspects of the design of the Farrington and West data set did not allow us to conduct a definitive empirical test that could decide in favor of one causal process over the other. According to Moffitt's causal account, neuropsychological deficits prevent desistance. To test this, prospective childhood indicators of neuropsychological deficit such as attention problems, impulsivity, low IQ, and

---

[20]Her theory does not anticipate the low-level chronics identified in Nagin and Land.

reading failure should characterize chronics relative to adolescence-limiteds. But our findings for such measures at ages 10, 14, and 18 were equivocal (see Tables 7.4 and 7.6). Moffitt's predictions address developmental patterns of antisocial behavior per se, which are better measured by self-reports and informant reports. Our court conviction data, however, do not operationalize antisocial behavior closely enough for a strong test of her taxonomic theory.

According to Sampson and Laub's causal account, social bonds cause desistance. To test this, prospective young-adulthood indicators of strong bonds to work or spouse should characterize adolescence-limiteds relative to chronics. But our findings at age 32 were 12 years past the turning point of desistance (age 20), and our findings at age 18 were equivocal (see Tables 7.4 and 7.5). Measures of bonds more proximal to the turning point are needed to demonstrate temporal precedence of bonds; our data waves were not timed closely enough for a strong test of social control theory.

CONCLUSIONS

Two sets of findings from this study stand out: (1) the discrepancy between the results obtained from official data and self-report data and (2) the continued involvement of the ALs in drugs, alcohol, and violence outside the home. We comment on these in turn.

Our analyses of conviction records led us to conclude that a group of research subjects had desisted from crime participation near age 20, whereas analyses of the subjects' self-reports implied that they were still participating, as much as 12 years later. This incompatibility of results is reminiscent of a much earlier controversy about the measurement of offender participation: Incompatibility between results of official versus self-report studies of juvenile delinquency was a pivotal methodological issue for criminologists in the 1970s. Hindelang et al. (1979) argued that the discrepancy was illusory because juvenile self-reports probably tap a more trivial domain of offending than do official data. It is not clear that the discrepancy in our study can be dispensed with as easily. The self-reports of our subjects at age 32 tapped nontrivial offenses: drunk driving, fighting outside the home, drug use, burglary, and theft. To be sure some convictions for certain of these offenses, such as drunk driving and brawling, are not included in the conviction counts. Thus, the discrepancy between self-report versus official-record findings may in part be a measurement artifact. This observation cannot, however, fully resolve the discrepancy because the convictions for theft and burglary are included in the conviction data.

Our study thus raises a new methodological issue—a discrepancy between official records and the self-reports of *adults* who reported *non-trivial* crimes. Resolution of this issue will be important for future research because almost all published findings about criminal careers to date rely on official data. Contemporary longitudinal self-report studies are now beginning to follow their samples into adulthood; these studies will soon provide a data base for self-report studies of criminal careers. Our findings may be a harbinger of a methodological controversy to come on the horizon.

Consider next the finding of the continued drug and alcohol abuse and ongoing violent behavior of the ALs. To our knowledge this result is not anticipated by any life-course or developmental theory, including the Moffitt and Sampson/Laub theories. If this result is replicated in other data sets, extant theory will necessarily have to be expanded to account for it.

We offer here the outline of one possible explanation based on social control theory. Social control theory focuses on the crime-inhibiting effects of external control mechanisms—bonds to work, family, and the community. Individuals are deterred from deviant behavior by the threat that their accumulated investment in such bonds will be lost if their involvement in deviance is discovered. The effectiveness of these control mechanisms depends on at least two factors: (1) the degree of condemnation of the behavior by relevant parties in the individual's community and (2) the risk of detection for engaging in the behavior either through official labeling (e.g., conviction) or through nonformal social mechanisms (e.g., word of mouth).

Viewed from the perspective of these underlying assumptions of control theory, the behavior of the ALs is less perplexing. They seem to be restricting their deviance to forms of behavior that are least likely to jeopardize their jobs and marriages. Specifically, they seem to avoid committing crimes with a comparatively high risk of conviction (e.g., burglary) or that might harm familial relationships (e.g., spousal assault). Instead they seem to restrict their deviance to behaviors less likely to result in official sanction or to disrupt intimate attachments, such as theft, heavy drinking, and barroom brawling.

This explanation for the behavior of the ALs is also relevant to the prior discussion of the methodological implications of our findings. If ALs adopted a strategy of engaging selectively in offenses with low risk of detection by police, future research on criminal careers will have to incorporate the construct of detection risk, in just the way that studies of juvenile delinquency were obligated by Hindelang et al. (1979) to incorporate considerations of offense seriousness.

Our interpretation of the behaviors of the ALs, however, begs a number of theoretical and empirical issues.[21] Among these are: What accounts for the continued desire of the ALs to engage in such imprudent and dangerous behaviors as illicit drug use, heavy drinking, and fighting? Is this desire a reflection of the same individual characteristics or social circumstances that prompted such behaviors in their youth? If the desistance of the ALs from certain sorts of deviant behaviors can be explained by instrumental considerations, why do not these considerations affect the behavior of the HLCs and LLCs? Further research and theory development are needed to answer these and related questions.

---

[21]We also stress that we offer here only one possible explanation based on social control theory. Other theories can also plausibly explain the continued deviance of the ALs. A reviewer uttered a subcultural explanation: It may be the case that stealing from "the boss," heavy drinking, and barroom brawling are not considered to be "real" crimes in the working-class subculture in which the ALs live.

REFERENCES

Blumstein, Alfred and Jacqueline Cohen
  1979   Estimation of individual crime rates from arrest records. Journal of Criminal Law and Criminology 70:561–585.

Blumstein, Alfred, Jacqueline Cohen, and David P. Farrington
  1988a   Criminal career research: Its value for criminology. Criminology 26:1–35.
  1988b   Longitudinal and criminal career research: Further clarifications. Criminology 26:57–74.

Dannefer, Dale
  1984   Adult development and social theory: A paradigmatic reappraisal. American Sociological Review 49:100–116.

Elder, Glen
  1975   Age differentation and the life course. In Alex Inkeles (ed.), Annual Review of Sociology. Palo Alto, Calif.: Annual Reviews.
  1985   Perspectives on the life course. In Glen Elder (ed.), Life Course Dynamics. Ithaca, N.Y.: Cornell University Press.
  1992   The life course. In Edgar F. Borgatta and Marie L. Borgatta (eds.), The Encyclopedia of Sociology. New York: Macmillan.

Farrington, David P.
  1986a   Age and crime. In Michael Tonry and Norval Morris (eds.), Crime and Justice: An Annual Review of Research. Vol. 7. Chicago: University of Chicago Press.
  1986b   Stepping stones to adult criminal careers. In Dan Olweus, Jack Block, and Marian R. Yarrow (eds.), Development of Antisocial and Prosocial Behavior. New York: Academic Press.
  1989   Self-reported and official offending from adolescence to adulthood. In Malcolm W. Klein (ed.), Cross-National Research in Self-Reported Crime and Delinquency. Dordrecht, Netherlands: Kluwer.

Farrington, David P. and J. David Hawkins
  1991   Predicting participation, early onset, and later persistence in officially recorded offending. Criminal Behaviour and Mental Health 1:1–33.

Farrington, David P. and Donald J. West
  1990   The Cambridge study in delinquent development: A prospective longitudinal survey of 411 males. In Hans–Jurgen Kerner and Gunter Kaiser (eds.), Criminality: Personality, Behavior and Life History. New York: Springer-Verlag.

Gottfredson, Michael and Travis Hirschi
  1986   The true value of lambda would appear to be zero: An essay on career criminals, criminal careers, selective incapacitation, cohort studies, and related topics. Criminology 24:213–234.
  1987   The methodological adequacy of longitudinal research on crime. Criminology 24:581–614.
  1988   Science, public policy, and the career paradigm. Criminology 26:37–56.

Hawkins, J. David, D.M. Lisher, R.F. Catalano, and M.O. Howard
  1986   Childhood predictors of adolescent substance abuse: Toward an empirically grounded theory. Journal of Children in Contemporary Society 8:11–48.

Heckman, James and Burton Singer
  1984   A method for minimizing the impact of distributional assumptions in econometric models for duration data. Econometrica 52:271–320.

Hindelang. Michael J., Travis Hirschi, and Joseph G. Weis
  1979   Correlates of delinquency: The illusion of discrepancy between self-report and official measures. American Sociological Review 44:975–1014.

Hirschi, Travis and Michael Gottfredson
  1983   Age and the explanation of crime. American Journal of Sociology 89:552–584.

Huizinga, David, Finn–Aage Esbensen, and Anne Wylie Weiher
  1991   Are there multiple paths to delinquency? Journal of Criminal Law and Criminology 82:83–118.

Jessor, Richard, John E. Donovan, and Francis M. Costa
  1991   Beyond Adolescence: Problem Behavior and Young Adult Development. New York: Cambridge University Press.

Laub, John H. and Robert J. Sampson
  1993   Turning points in the life course: Why change matters to the study of crime. Criminology 31:301–326.

Loeber, Rolf and Marc LeBlanc
  1990   Toward a developmental criminology. In Michael Tonry and Norval Morris (eds.), Crime and Justice: An Annual Review of Research. Vol. 12. Chicago: University of Chicago Press.

Moffitt, Terrie E.
  1993   Adolescence-limited and life-course persistent antisocial behavior: A developmental taxonomy. Psychological Review 100:674–701.

Nagin, Daniel S. and David P. Farrington
  1992a   The onset and persistence of offending. Criminology 30:501–523.
  1992b   The stability of criminal potential from childhood to adulthood. Criminology 30:235–260.

Nagin, Daniel S. and Kenneth C. Land
  1993   Age, criminal careers, and population heterogeneity: Specification and estimation of a nonparametric, mixed Poisson model. Criminology 31:327–362.

Nagin. Daniel S. and Raymond Paternoster
  1991   On the relationship of past to future delinquency. Criminology 29:163–189.

Robins, Lee N.
  1966   Deviant Children Grown Up. Baltimore: Williams and Wilkins.

Sampson, Robert J. and John H. Laub
  1991   Crime and deviance over the life course: The salience of adult social bonds. American Sociological Review 55:608–627.
  1993   Crime in the Making: Pathways and Turning Points through the Life Course. Cambridge, Mass.: Harvard University Press.

West, Donald J. and David P. Farrington
  1977   The Delinquent Way of Life. London: Heinemann.

Wilson, James Q. and Richard Herrnstein
  1985   Crime and Human Nature. New York: Simon & Schuster.

8

Criminal Careers in the Short-Term

Intra-Individual Variability in Crime and Its Relation to Local Life Circumstances*

JULIE HORNEY

D. WAYNE OSGOOD

INEKE HAEN MARSHALL

ABSTRACT   We analyze month-to-month variations in offending and life circumstances of convicted felons to understand change in criminal behavior. We extend previous applications of social control theory by considering whether local life circumstances that strengthen or weaken social bonds influence offending over relatively short periods of time. We seek to determine whether formal and informal mechanisms of social control affect the likelihood of committing nine major felonies. We employ a hierarchical linear model that provides a within-individual analysis as we explore factors that determine the pattern of offending. The results suggest that meaningful short-term change in involvement in crime is strongly related to variation in local life circumstances.

SOURCE: *American Sociological Review,* Vol. 60, pp. 655–673. Reprinted by permission of the American Sociological Assn.

*Direct all correspondence to Julie Horney, Department of Criminal Justice, Annex 37, University of Nebraska at Omaha, Omaha, NE 68182 (Internet: jhorney@fa-cpacs. unomaha.edu). This research was supported by grant # 89-IJ-CX-0030 from the National Institute of Justice, Office of Justice Programs. U.S. Department of Justice. Points of view or opinions in this document are those of the authors and do not necessarily represent the official position or policies of the U.S. Department of Justice. The authors thank the administration and staff of the Diagnostic and Evaluation Unit of the Nebraska Department of Corrections for facilitating the interviews; the respondents who participated in interviews; Allison Brown-Corzine, Mickey Coffey, Kelly Green, Tara Ingram, Lisa Lannin, Kit Lemon, Carol Marshall, and Mike Mead for their valuable research assistance: Stephen Raudenbush for providing statistical software and valuable advice: and three anonymous *ASR* reviewers for offering helpful suggestions. An earlier version of this paper was presented to the American Society of Criminology in November 1993. [Reviewers acknowledged by the authors include Daniel S. Nagin.—*ED.*]

ssues of continuity and change have recently come to the fore in criminology. Two influential theoretical statements have focused on the continuity in criminal behavior and challenged the importance of social factors during adulthood (Wilson & Herrnstein, 1985; Gottfredson & Hirschi, 1990). Both theories assume that a basic propensity to commit crime is *established early in life and persists throughout the life course.* This propensity is the key to understanding criminal behavior. This view implies that life events after childhood are of little, if any, explanatory importance. Thus, events such as changes in position in the social structure or assumption of new roles that increase social integration would have no bearing on adult crime.

Sampson and Laub (1993) took a very different perspective in their life-span approach to the study of crime. While they acknowledged that measures of illegal behavior are highly correlated over time, they argued that such continuity does not preclude large and systematic changes for many individuals. Their empirical research, which tracked individuals across large segments of the life-span, documented substantial changes in offending. They explain these patterns of change in terms of variation in social control.

The purpose of the present study is to fill an important gap in our knowledge about change in criminal behavior during adulthood. Rather than examine extended time periods, we conduct a fine-grained analysis of month-to-month change in criminal behavior over three years for a sample of serious offenders. Thus, we forego the broad sweep of trajectories over the life-span in favor of a more detailed mapping of the correspondence between offending and current circumstances.

SOCIOLOGICAL THEORY
AND CRIME BY ADULTS

Although the sociological tradition is compatible with the study of changes in offending during adulthood, most work on this topic stems from other traditions, such as developmental perspectives (Moffitt, 1993; Patterson & Yoerger, 1993) and the criminal careers perspective (Blumstein, Cohen, Roth, & Visher, 1986). The limited role of sociology in this area is perhaps understandable in that prominent sociological theories primarily concern juvenile delinquency rather than adult crime. For instance, Shaw and McKay's (1942) classic theory of social disorganization portrayed delinquency as arising from adults' inability to supervise their children's activities, and there is no obvious generalization to crime by adults.

Other sociological theories are more pertinent to adult offending, either because they entail types of socialization that have long-term implications or because they specify general social processes that are not limited to a particular age. An example of the first type of theory is Cohen's (1955) strain theory, which explains delinquency as stemming from socialization that leaves lower-class adolescents unprepared to compete by middle-class standards.

Differential association theory (Sutherland & Cressey, 1955) and its social learning variations (Akers, 1985; Elliott, Huizinga, & Ageton, 1985) exemplify the second type of theory—they predict that changing from a conventional peer or reference group to a deviant one leads to crime, regardless of age. It is not simply associations that create change, but rather the learning or influence that follows from such associations, which takes time. These two types of theory imply that change in criminal behavior is nonexistent or very gradual. Thus, these theories do not predict the month-to-month correspondence between offending and social factors that we investigate in the present study.

Two other veins of sociological theory imply more immediate effects of changing life circumstances during adulthood. Social control theory, as described in Hirschi's early work, proposes that social bonds prevent crime and deviance (Hirschi, 1969). Because crime results directly from the absence of bonds rather than from some mediating process, social control theory predicts relatively rapid changes in criminal behavior in response to changing life circumstances. Immediate effects also follow from rational choice or opportunity theories, such as routine activities theory (Cohen & Felson, 1979). This approach emphasizes the role of social conditions in creating situations conducive to crime. When applied to individual offending, routine activities theory predicts that adults' involvement in crime will increase or decrease as their roles and relationships change their "daily round" of activities so as to present more or fewer opportunities for offending.

LONGITUDINAL DESIGNS
AND THE ANALYSIS OF CHANGE

A reliance on cross-sectional designs has limited the ability of criminologists to study change. Cross-sectional designs preclude separating the effects of extrinsic variables from the effects of enduring individual differences. For example, the finding that men in stable marriages commit fewer crimes than those not involved in such relationships can be interpreted either as evidence of the social control function of marriage or as evidence that offending and failure to develop a stable marriage are both indicators of a single underlying trait, such as self-control. Thus, Farrington (1988, 1992) and others have argued that longitudinal research designs are needed to appropriately address questions relating to change in criminal behavior.

Even when longitudinal data have been collected, analyses have rarely assessed within-individual change, such as determining whether individuals commit more crimes when unemployed than when employed. Most longitudinal data currently available for studying criminal behavior were obtained infrequently, thus making the analysis of within-individual change difficult, if not impossible. With widely spaced waves of data collection and correspondingly few alternations of conditions, there must be greater dependence on aggregation in order to have enough variability to study. Nagin and Farrington (1992a, 1992b) demonstrated how relationships detected through the cross-sectional analysis of longitudinal data can be spurious and suggested the use of statistical methods that control for "persistent unobserved heterogeneity" (i.e., stable individual differences in rates of offending).

Gottfredson and Hirschi (1990) argued that longitudinal designs intended to study changes in offending offer no real advantage and waste resources because there is *little reason to believe that ordinary events are important determinants of offending.* In fact, they contended "that crime-relevant characteristics of people cause all of these events" (p. 237). Testing this contention requires analyses of within-individual change.

CONCEPTIONS OF CHANGE
IN CRIMINAL BEHAVIOR

One of the most comprehensive longitudinal data sets in criminological research was collected by Glueck and Glueck (1950). Challenging the notion that ordinary events do not matter, Sampson and Laub (1990, 1993; Laub & Sampson, 1993) re-analyzed the Gluecks' data using more sophisticated techniques and evaluated the findings in light of current theory. In their "socio-genic" theoretical model, they proposed that regardless of an individual's delinquent or antisocial background, criminal behavior would still be influenced in adulthood by institutions of informal social control, such as family or work. Thus, from a social control approach, Sampson and Laub (1990) suggested that "childhood pathways to crime and deviance can be significantly modified over the life course by adult social bonds" (p. 611).

The Gluecks' data came from interviews at ages 14, 25, and 32 with delinquent and nondelinquent boys matched on a number of social variables. Sampson and Laub (1990, 1993) constructed an overall measure of crime frequency and considered its relation to three key independent variables: job stability, commitment (a combined measure of the respondent's work, education, and economic ambitions), and attachment to spouse. They controlled for criminal "propensity" by performing separate analyses for the delinquent and nondelinquent samples and by studying relationships within a given age range while controlling for delinquency at earlier ages. Although they found clear evidence of stability of offending over time, job stability and marital attachment emerged as significant predictors of adult crime and deviance, even after childhood delinquency and crime in young adulthood were controlled. Accordingly, Sampson and Laub (1990) concluded that "both continuity and change are evident, and that trajectories of crime and deviance are systematically modified by social bonds to adult institutions of informal social control" (p. 625).

Laub and Sampson (1993) discussed the nature of change and provided illustrations of three kinds of change. What Caspi and Moffitt (1993) refer to as "systematic" or "deep" change is depicted by a high-rate offender who ceases offending completely, whereas what Laub and Sampson called "modified" change is exemplified when a high-rate offender starts offending at a lower rate. A third kind of change is illustrated by an offender switching from burglary to robbery. Although Laub and Sampson were most interested in the first two kinds of change, all fit within their conceptualization of change. Appropriate to their life-course perspective and their focus on the alteration of life trajectories, they implicitly conceptualize change as an enduring modification of behavior patterns.

Laub and Sampson's (1993) perspective also led them to look to the role of institutions, such as employment and marriage, to understand how social bonds structure the process of change. Transitions into such institutions are traditionally considered to be unidirectional (i.e., these transitions represent stages of development or permanent changes in state). A young man joins the work force or marries and starts a family, and his social investment in these institutions accumulates from that point on. Nevertheless, adult lives are not always so orderly, especially the lives of serious criminal offenders. Not only do role transitions often fail to follow an orderly progression (Rindfuss, Swicegood, & Rosenfeld, 1987), but reversals of transitions may be common, as when employment is terminated or a marriage is dissolved. In their qualitative analysis of the life-history records of men from the Gluecks' study, Laub and Sampson (1993) described how some men experienced declines in job stability when the labor market changed and how others, who had married and initially got along well with their spouses, had marriages unravel ("there were separations, followed by reconciliations, followed by further separations" [p. 317]). When these scenarios were played out, "crime and deviance became more pronounced over time due to the severing of social ties to work and family" (p. 317).

Sampson and Laub (1990, 1993) have made a major contribution to criminology by showing that a focus on stability or continuity of offending is insufficient for understanding adult criminal behavior. By showing how adult social bonds can alter life trajectories, they demonstrated that change matters. The long-term view of change Sampson and Laub provided can be seen only when looking back on a relatively long segment of an individual's life course. It is also the only picture of change that can emerge when our view of the life course is constructed from infrequent measurements. We believe it may also be productive to consider a short-term view of change and ask whether levels of criminal activity shift in response to alterations in "local life circumstances." We introduce the term "local life circumstances" to emphasize conditions in an individual's life that can fluctuate relatively frequently. Because these life circumstances may be constantly shifting, any resulting changes in criminal behavior may be transient rather than enduring. The same circumstances that lead one person to an altered life trajectory because the circumstances endure (a stable marriage, for example), may produce only transient change in another individual if the circumstances are fleeting (a marriage that lasts only a few months or years).

LOCAL LIFE CIRCUMSTANCES AND SHORT-TERM VARIATION IN CRIMINAL CAREERS

Within the criminal careers paradigm (Blumstein et al., 1986), the study of change has emphasized the determinants of career initiation or termination; persistence in offending has generally been viewed simply as the converse of desistence. Research on persisting careers has focused almost exclusively on the frequency of committing crimes (incidence) and has generally assumed that offending occurs at a constant rate.

There have been few attempts to look at within-individual variability in offending over relatively short periods of time. Horney and Marshall (1991) found that incarcerated offenders described considerable month-to-month variability in levels of offending, and that activity patterns varied by type of crime. Nagin and Land (1993) found that models of offending that incorporate an intermittency parameter that allowed for periods of activity and inactivity performed better than models without such a parameter. Thus, they established that there is genuine within-individual change over time in offending. They observed, however, that "notwithstanding its contribution to the model fit, the concept of intermittency is problematic because a promising theoretical explanation for why it should occur has yet to be offered" (p. 357).

We believe one plausible explanation for intermittency is that the same kind of social control variables that Sampson and Laub (1990, 1993) found to alter trajectories of criminal offending are also responsible for short-term variation in criminal behavior. In other words, whether an individual offends at a particular time depends on whether he or she is employed, married, or going to school at that time. Although a persistent underlying trait like self-control can influence both an individual's overall level of offending and his or her overall stability of marriage and employment, that shared influence does not mean that a relationship between offending and the life circumstance is necessarily spurious. It is still possible that involvement in those social institutions influences the likelihood of offending *during the time of involvement.* The high crime rate of the most persistent offender, rather than indicating a total lack of investment in social institutions, may instead reflect alternating periods of criminal activity and inactivity. A coherent causal pattern would be indicated if the relatively infrequent and brief periods of inactivity correspond to sporadic episodes of social bonding.

Some theorists have dealt with the role of more localized life circumstances in determining criminal offending. Farrington (1992), for example, asserted that

> . . . short-term, situationally-induced motivating factors that are conducive to offending include boredom, frustration, alcohol consumption, getting fired from a job, or quarreling with a wife or girlfriend. Slightly longer-lasting life circumstances or events may also be important, such as unemployment, drug addiction, and shortage of money. (p. 278)

Unfortunately, empirical evidence of relationships between such factors and offending is scarce.

Farrington, Gallagher, Morley, St. Ledger, and West (1986) analyzed data from the Cambridge Youth Study, which was collected in two-year waves, and found that boys in their sample had higher crime rates during periods of unemployment than they did during periods of employment. Unfortunately, their analysis was hampered by the fact that only 95 of the 399 youths had committed offenses, and only 11 had at least one offense when unemployed and one offense when employed. The authors appropriately noted a self-selection problem—that the youths who were unemployed could differ in many ways from those who were employed, and the higher crime rate during unemployment could occur because both variables were related to some other causal factor. They attempted to control for this possibility by restricting the analysis to youths who had been unemployed and had committed officially recorded crimes, but this resulted in very small numbers of youths. When, in their "most important test of the effect of unemployment" (p. 345) they also required minimum periods of unemployment, the resulting analysis was based on only 36 youths. The authors suggested that to determine whether individual offending varies with conditions like employment, larger samples and samples of persons with relatively high offending rates must be studied.

THE CURRENT STUDY

In the current study, we explore the role of local life circumstances as determinants of change in criminal behavior. Our data were obtained through a retrospective survey in which more than 600 serious offenders provided a month-by-month account of criminal offenses and local life circumstances. Our analysis extends Sampson and Laub's (1993) application of social control theory to criminal career trajectories by considering whether local life circumstances that strengthen or weaken social bonds influence offending over relatively short periods of time. We focus on informal mechanisms of social control and ask if the likelihood of offending is affected by going to school, being employed, living with a wife or girlfriend, drinking heavily, or using drugs. We also consider the impact of formal social control mechanisms by asking whether individuals are less likely to offend when they are on probation or parole. We employ hierarchical linear modeling to obtain a within-individual analysis of factors that determine the patterning of offending.

METHODOLOGY

The data presented here are based on interviews conducted with 658 newly convicted male offenders sentenced to the Nebraska Department of Correctional Services during a nine-month period in 1989–1990. A few inmates incarcerated during that time could not be interviewed for various logistical reasons; 94 percent of those invited to participate completed interviews. This sample was 57.3 percent White and had a mean age of 28.1 years. Although this sample is not representative of the general population, it is suited to addressing the impact on criminal behaviors of changes in local life circumstances. The short-term variability we wish to study is far greater in this sample than it is in most others, owing to the prison respondents' high rates of offending and the considerable instability of their lives in terms of marriage, employment, and so forth.

Because we sampled incarcerated offenders, our sample is not representative of the general population of offenders. We must assume we have over-sampled men who commit more crimes, those who commit crimes for which it is easier to be caught and convicted, and those who are less able to avoid detection.

Survey Instrument

We used a modified version of a survey instrument used in the RAND Corporation's Second Inmate Survey (Chaiken & Chaiken, 1982). The 48-page instrument generally required a 45- to 90-minute interview. In the critical section of the interview, two calendars—an "event calendar," and a "crime calendar"—were used to establish the reference period and to record detailed information. Respondents were asked to consider a reference period based on the date of the arrest that led to the current incarceration. The reference period included the months up to and including the month of arrest for the calendar year of arrest and the two calendar years preceding the year of arrest. The measurement periods thus varied across respondents from 25 months to 36 months. All months outside the reference period as well as any months during which the respondent had been locked up were crossed out on the calendars. The remaining months were considered "street months."

The event calendar was then used to record various life circumstances. The respondent was asked to identify those street months during which he had been on probation, on parole, going to school, working, living with a wife, living with a girlfriend, drinking heavily, or using drugs (other than prescription drugs or marijuana). The interviewer placed a check beside the appropriate items for those months. The crime calendar was created in the same manner to determine the months during which the respondent committed any burglaries, personal robberies, business robberies, assaults, thefts, auto thefts, frauds, forgeries, or drug deals.

Research indicating that personal memories are organized as "autobiographical sequences" (Bradburn, Rips, & Shevell, 1987) suggests that the use of life-history calendars helps to facilitate recall. Evidence of the reliability of retrospective data collected through life-history calendars is available from studies that have gathered the retrospective data within a longitudinal research design. Freedman, Thornton, Camburn, Alwin, and Young-DeMarco (1988) found that 91 percent of respondents gave identical answers about 1980 school attendance (whether attending school in a particular month) in 1980 interviews and 1985 interviews, while 83 percent gave identical responses about employment.

In a similar study, Caspi and Amell (1994) used a life-history calendar to obtain retrospective data about monthly life events that had been concurrently reported three years earlier. They compared reports of whether the respondent was living with parents, cohabiting with a partner, the primary caregiver for a child, attending school, involved in job training, employed, and searching for employment or receiving unemployment benefits. Over 90 percent of the reports matched with regard to status for the month of the first interview.

Statistical Model

Hierarchical linear modeling (HLM), a generalization of multiple regression for nested or repeated-measures data, was developed by Bryk and Raudenbush (1992) and other statisticians. Raudenbush (1993) presented a binomial version of the model that is suited to a research design like ours, which includes many waves of dichotomous data for each subject. We will first describe the HLM model for continuous data. Then we will turn to the distinctive features of the binomial version.

HLM is one of several methods developed in recent years for analyzing data containing multiple observations for each individual. These methods provide a general format for analyses that allow effects to vary randomly across cases (Goldstein, 1987; Mason, Wong, & Entwistle, 1983), and they follow from earlier statistical developments extending random-coefficient models (Hsiao, 1986, chap. 6, esp. pp. 151–53). These models can also be viewed as extensions or generalizations of analysis of variance for repeated measures designs (Bryk & Raudenbush, 1992, chap. 2) and as elaborations of models for "pooled time-series and cross-sections" found in econometrics (Sayrs, 1989). We have chosen Bryk and Raudenbush's HLM because it is flexible and is described well in available publications. Also, a computer program for implementing the version of the method for continuous data is commercially available (Bryk, Raudenbush, & Congdon, 1993), and a version of HLM for dichotomous data has been developed.

Within-person Model HLM separates within-person and between-persons models, as in repeated-measures analysis of variance. These models are distinct, but closely linked, linear models. In an HLM analysis, the within-person model must be considered first because it determines the meaning of the between-persons model. Equation 1 presents the basic elements of the within-person models used in our analysis:

$$Y_{ij} = \beta_{0,i} + \beta_{1,i} T_{ij} + \beta_{2,i} X_{ij} + r_{ij} \tag{1}$$

where i is the index for persons, j is the index for occasions, T is an interval measure of time (months in our study), and X is an explanatory variable that varies over time for at least some of the respondents. In our application the explanatory variable is a local life circumstance like employment or marriage.

Notice that the parameters, β, can take different values for different individuals because they carry the subscript i. $\beta_{0,i}$ is the individual's intercept, which will be the fitted value of the dependent variable, crime, when both T and X equal 0; $\beta_{1,i}$ is the amount this person's level of crime (Y) changes per unit of time; and r_{ij} corresponds to the unexplained variance for this specific observation on Y. Against the backdrop of the time trend for each individual, the outcome also varies as a function of the local life circumstance, and $\beta_{2,i}$ reflects the magnitude of this relationship.

Between-persons Model   In most applications, including ours, the primary results of interest are the parameters of the between-persons model. In HLM, the individual-level parameters from the within-person model serve as dependent variables for the between-persons model, leading to a separate equation for each parameter:

$$\beta_{0,i} = \gamma_{0,0} + u_{0,i} ; \qquad\qquad (2)$$

$$\beta_{1,i} = \gamma_{1,0} + u_{1,i} ; \qquad\qquad (3)$$

$$\beta_{2,i} = \gamma_{2,0}. \qquad\qquad (4)$$

In the general HLM model, these between-persons equations may include additional explanatory variables for characteristics that do not change over the period of study (e.g., race and sex), but this feature play's a minor role in the present study because our theoretical interests involve change in local life circumstances.[1] In the present study, the between-persons models are simple because each model involves a single parameter, γ (with one exception discussed below). In this case, the γ parameters reflect the average level of the corresponding within-person parameters, which in turn indicate individual-level intercepts, time trends, and effects of the local life circumstance.

Error Terms   In equations 2 and 3, the person-specific error terms, $u_{0,i}$ and $u_{1,i}$, mean that the between-persons model treats $\beta_{0,i}$ and $\beta_{1,i}$ as random effects (i.e., as having meaningful variance across individuals). The error term in equation 2, $u_{0,i}$, allows for random variation in the form of individual differences in the average level of offending, which typically is the principal source of correlated error when applying ordinary least squares regression to panel data. This term appears in the variance-components models found in the pooled time-series literature (Sayrs, 1989) and is equivalent to the persistent heterogeneity that is a central feature of Nagin and Farrington's work (1992a, 1992b).

Equation 3 shows how HLM generalizes this principle to other elements of the within-person model, making this a "random coefficients" model. In this case, the error term, $u_{1,i}$, reflects unexplained variability in linear time trends. Thus, including this error term allows the linear time trends to vary across individuals. This term helps correct for a second type of problem of independence because it allows for gradual change over time, which is a major source of serially correlated error. Equation 4 does not contain an error term because

---

[1]Elaborating this aspect of the models, to assess whether the impact of local life circumstances varies across groups, would be an appropriate direction for future research.

there is no a priori reason to assume that the effects of local life circumstances vary across individuals.

We can form an overview of the between-persons model by substituting equations 2, 3, and 4 into equation 1:

$$Y_{ij} = (\gamma_{0,0} + \gamma_{1,0}T_{ij} + \gamma_{2,0}X_{ij})$$

[Effects on Y]

$$+ (u_{0,i} + u_{1,i}T_{ij} + r_{ij}). \tag{5}$$

[Composite error term]

This arrangement makes apparent the composite error term, which resolves the problems of independence that arise with multiple measures of Y for each respondent. Similar composite error terms are characteristic of repeated-measures analysis of variance and variance components models for pooled time-series.

Within-person Change The estimate of the impact of the local life circumstance X that is captured by $\gamma_{2,0}$ in equation 4 represents the combined effects of differences between individuals in their average circumstances and within-person change over time in this circumstance (Bryk & Raudenbush, 1992:117–23). This is inappropriate because our substantive interest is in change. An estimate that is restricted to within-person change can be obtained by two modifications to the preceding equations. First, the values for X in equation 1 are transformed to deviations from each individual's mean calculated across the entire period of observations:

$$X^{\star}_{ij} = X_{ij} - \overline{X}_{i.}.$$

Second, the individual means, $\overline{X}_{i.}$, are included as an explanatory variable in the equation for overall individual differences (equation 2):

$$\beta_{0,i} = \gamma_{0,0} + \gamma_{0,1}\overline{X}_{i.} + u_{0,i}.$$

Under this formulation, $\gamma_{0,1}$ reflects the effects of between-persons differences in average local life circumstances, while $\gamma_{2,0}$ (from equation 4) satisfies our need for an estimator that reflects the effects of within-person change.[2]

Model Estimates An HLM analysis yields estimates of the between-persons parameters, their standard errors, and their statistical significance. The results also include estimates of the magnitude and reliability of the variance components of random effects. HLM uses the covariances among the errors of the βs to

[2]Fixed-effects estimators for panel data also restrict the analysis to within-individual change. Both the fixed-effects approach and our approach limit the analysis to deviations from individual means on X. In fixed-effect models the same transformation is applied to Y, whereas we accomplish the same result with random effects by including the individual mean of X as a predictor. The fixed-effects approach is difficult to apply to discrete outcomes when there are more than a few waves of data (Greene, 1990:656–88), but our model gives us one of its principal advantages.

derive generalized least squares estimates of the γs. In this fashion, HLM capitalizes on any interdependence among the within-person components to increase the efficiency of the estimates and to gauge their standard errors. Bryk and Raudenbush (1992) presented the statistical theory underlying HLM in an extended treatment that is not highly technical. The method relies on iterative estimates of the true variance and the error variance of the $\beta_{k,i}$, which are derived through a Bayesian weighting of information from the within-person and between-persons portions of the analysis. HLM also capitalizes on the EM algorithm, developed by Dempster et al., (1977), to make use of data from all respondents, including respondents with insufficient data for separate estimation of the within-person parameters. As with most methods for analyzing continuous dependent variables, HLM assumes that errors for particular observations, $r_{i,j}$, are normally distributed. Furthermore, treatment of the within-person parameters as random effects requires specification of their error distributions, and these error terms, $u_{1,i}$, are also assumed to be normally distributed.

The HLM model does not require that each person provide data on any particular set of occasions, which means that the method is suitable for irregular data sets, unlike many other approaches to analyzing panel data. This flexibility arises because the parameters of interest, the between-persons parameters, γ, are defined in relation to the within-person parameters, β. Thus, the analysis does not hinge on having a particular set of observation times for Y, but rather on the available observations of Y providing enough information to estimate the individual-level βs. HLM gauges the precision of these person-specific estimates from information such as the number of data points and the variances of Y, T, and X for the respondent.

Binomial HLM   The statistical model for the binomial version of HLM closely follows the format of the basic HLM model (Raudenbush, 1993). The within-person model becomes a logistic regression:

$$\log_n [odds\ (Y_{ij} = 1)] = \beta_{0,i} + \beta_{1,i}T_{ij} + \beta_{2,i}X_{ij}. \tag{6}$$

Thus, the fitted values from the within-person model no longer refer directly to levels of Y. Instead this is a linear model of the logit, which is the natural logarithm of the odds that the dichotomous Y variable will take on the value 1, (i.e., an offense occurred this month) rather than the alternative value of 0 (i.e., no offense this month). Also, the within-person model no longer includes an error term because the logistic model is inherently probabilistic. This use of the logistic regression model brings to HLM a standard approach for correcting the problems that would result from applying ordinary least squares regression to a dichotomy.

Equations 2, 3, and 4 still define an appropriate between-persons model, despite the change to the logistic within-person model.[3] Of course, these equations now reflect average values of βs that are logistic coefficients rather than ordinary regression coefficients. No change in the between-persons model is necessary, however, because the within-person coefficients (which serve as the dependent variables) are continuous and have meaningful intervals. The generalized least squares derivation of the estimates of the between-persons parameters remains applicable, although the weighting of the variance components changes according to the precision of logistic regression estimates. Because the logistic regression model is nonlinear in relation to the observed values of Y, the estimation requires an iterative reweighting of the within-person data.

Our Full Model Our analysis extends the simple model presented above in two respects. First, the analyses include seven local life circumstances rather than the single X in the example. All life circumstances are dichotomies (coded 1 if the feature is present and 0 if not) extracted from the event calendars in the same fashion as the measures of offending. The specific life circumstances are supervision by the justice system (probation or parole), attending school, working, living with a wife, living with a girlfriend, heavy alcohol use, and use of illicit drugs other than marijuana.

We also extended the simple model by including a more elaborate control for individual time trends. Because the analysis includes up to 36 waves of data for each respondent, it would be unreasonable to assume that individual time trends are so consistent as to be linear. Instead, the basic model allows a greater flexibility in the time trend through a third-order polynomial function of time. The within-person intercept and all three powers of time were specified as random effects. As a result, changes over time in offending are attributed to substantive variables only if offending closely tracks that variable over time. More gradual or diffuse changes are instead attributed to the individual time trend.

The final element of the model is a dummy variable indicating the month of the arrest leading to the current incarceration.[4] This variable corrects the offense rate for this specific month, which is artificially high due to our sample

---

[3]The coefficients for the between-persons model represent conditional relationships in that the analysis controls for individual relationships in that the analysis controls for individual differences in overall rates of offending. Because the binomial model is nonlinear in relation to probabilities, these conditional within-individual relationships tend to be stronger than the marginal relationship to the explanatory variables to the average rates of offending for the entire population (Zeger, Liang, & Albert, 1988). We report only conditional relationships because our focus is on change within individuals over time.

[4]The time variables were transformed to reduce the correlations among the components and improve the efficiency of the estimation of the model. These transformations have no impact on the substantive results of the model, but they must be taken into account in order to reproduce the average time curves. The last wave of data collection was given a value of 0 on the components of the polynomial of time, making the dummy code for the last month orthogonal to the other time components. To give the linear component a mean of 0 across persons, a value of 0 was assigned to 15.4 months before the final month. The squared term for month was this value multiplied by itself and divided by 10 (to reduce its range and place its coefficient in a more useful range). We subtracted 8 from the result, to give it a mean of 0. Finally, the cubed power of time was formed as the product of the linear and square terms, divided by 10.

selection criteria. Fifty-three percent of the sample reported one or more offenses for this month versus 32 percent for all other months.[5] Because this variable refers to a single month, it was defined as a fixed effect.

RESULTS

The analysis was limited to respondents who contributed information on the full set of variables for at least 10 "street months." Though HLM does not require any minimum number, respondents with fewer months of data would contribute little to the analysis. Only 41 of the 658 respondents failed to meet this criterion; the remaining 617 respondents provided data for an average of 28.36 months.

The analysis was conducted separately for each of four measures of offending. The first measure, "any crime," was coded 1 for months in which a respondent reported committing at least one of the nine felonies. The other measures of offending referred to specific crimes: property crime (burglary, personal robbery, business robbery, theft, auto theft, forgery, and fraud), assault, and drug crime (dealing). Table 8.1 reports descriptive information on the measures used in the analysis.

Because our analysis focuses on within-person change, our ability to detect the impact of local life circumstances is largely dependent on the number of respondents who experience change on those variables. Column 2 of Table 8.1 reports that proportion of respondents who had at least one transition during the period of study for each of the local life circumstances (e.g., from student to nonstudent or nonstudent to student, as opposed to always a student or never a student). Fully 85 percent of the sample experienced at least one transition over this interval of no more than three years, and over one-half experienced two or more transitions.

Summary Statistics for Change in Offending

Table 8.2 presents some simple summary statistics about the changes in offending following changes in local life circumstances. These statistics reflect periods that begin with a change in a local life circumstance (e.g., starting school) and end with either a change in offending (for our "any crime" measure), a subsequent change in that local life circumstance (e.g., stopping school), or the end of the period of observation. The odds of starting crime is computed for periods preceded by a month for which no crime was reported; it is the ratio of the number of instances in which a subsequent crime was reported divided by the number of instances in which no offense was reported throughout the period.

---

[5]The rate still falls well below 100 percent because: (1) arrest could occur more than a month after the actual offense; (2) a small proportion of respondents were incarcerated for offenses not included in the measure (e.g., drunk driving); and (3) some respondents claimed not to have committed the offense for which they were incarcerated, although they admitted to other offenses.

Table 8.1 Descriptive Statistics for Variables Used in the Analyses: Male Offenders in Nebraska, 1989–1990

Variable	Proportion of Months	Proportion of Sample with Change in Status
Measures of Offending		
Any Crime	.33	
Property Crime	.11	
Assault	.06	
Drug Crime	.23	
Explanatory Variables		
Probation or Parole	.11	.25
School	.11	.25
Work	.65	.58
Live with Wife	.19	.12
Live with Girlfriend	.29	.30
Heavy Drinking	.28	.19
Illegal Drug Use	.24	.22

Note: N = 617 individuals; 17,500 street months.

The odds of stopping crime is the comparable ratio for periods preceded by a month in which an offense occurred. The odds ratios and log odds in Table 8.2 indicate that changes in offending depend on changes in local life circumstances. Thus, for men on probation or on parole, the odds ratio of .42 for starting crime (.69 divided by 1.63) indicates that the odds of starting to offend are over twice as high after probation or parole stops as after the supervision starts. The odds ratio of .74 for stopping crime (.49 divided by .66) indicates that the odds of stopping crime are greater after probation or parole stops than after the supervision starts.

The results presented in Table 8.2 suggest that changes in offending systematically follow changes in local life circumstances. Typically, the odds of a change in offending roughly double (or are halved) following a change in a local life circumstance, such as marriage, employment, or drug use. Furthermore, the two directions of change in the explanatory variables typically have comparable relationships with criminal behavior, as is assumed in the HLM analysis. For instance, moving in with one's wife doubles the odds of stopping offending (compared to moving away), and moving away from one's wife doubles the odds of starting to offend (compared to moving in). The largest discrepancy is for living with a girlfriend. The odds of stopping offending were considerably lower after moving away from a girlfriend, but starting to offend was unrelated to this variable. The presence of a single discrepancy of this limited magnitude is not surprising from such a simple and ad hoc summary of the data.

Table 8.2 Odds of Changes in Offending Following Changes in Local Life Circumstances: Male Offenders in Nebraska, 1989–1990

Life Circumstance	Odds of Crime Starting	Odds of Crime Stopping
Probation or Parole		
Starts	.69	.66
Stops	1.63	.49
Odds Ratio	.42	.74
Log Odds	−.86	−.30
School		
Starts	.33	.36
Stops	.76	.25
Odds Ratio	.43	.70
Log Odds	−.84	−.35
Work		
Starts	.33	.36
Stops	.76	.25
Odds Ratio	.43	.70
Log Odds	−.84	−.35
Live with Wife		
Starts	.62	.75
Stops	1.20	.42
Odds Ratio	.52	.56
Log Odds	−.66	−.59
Live with Girlfriend		
Starts	1.02	.25
Stops	1.11	.66
Odds Ratio	.92	2.64
Log Odds	−.09	.97
Heavy Drinking		
Starts	.51	.42
Stops	.25	1.12
Odds Ratio	2.09	2.67
Log Odds	.74	.98
Illegal Drug Use		
Starts	.59	.20
Stops	.27	.37
Odds Ratio	2.16	1.86
Log Odds	.77	.62

Note: Odds ratios greater than 1 and positive log odds indicate greater odds of starting crime after the local life circumstance starts and greater odds of stopping crime after the local life circumstance stops.

Variance Components

The HLM analyses provide greater statistical control and allow us to gauge the precision of our results. Table 8.3 shows results for the variance components of the model. Estimates of variance components are provided for unconditional models, which include the time trends but not the explanatory variables, and conditional models, which include all variables. Preliminary analyses indicated that the higher-order elements of the polynomial time trend were not justified for some of the measures of offending. For all measures, there was substantial variation in average level of offending, as reflected by the size and reliability of the variance components for the within-person intercepts. This replicates Nagin and Farrington's (1992a, 1992b) finding that there are substantial individual differences in propensities to offend, and extends that finding to a prison population with a much higher overall rate of offending.

Effects of Local Life Circumstances

Table 8.4 reports the estimates of the within-person effects of local life circumstances from the binomial HLM analyses. The table includes the logistic coefficients, γ (as in $\gamma_{2,0}$ in equation 4), their standard errors, and the odds ratios corresponding to the coefficients. (Coefficients for the time trends and

Table 8.3 Variance Components for Random Effects in Binomial Hierarchical Linear Models: Male Offenders in Nebraska, 1989–1990

Type of Crime and Model Term	UNCONDITIONAL MODEL			CONDITIONAL MODEL		
	Reliability	Variance	χ^2	Reliability	Variance	χ^2
Any Crime'						
Intercept	.81	11.298	4,398.2*	.76	8.750	4,498.3*
Month	.42	.026	1,202.9*	.40	.025	1,157.0*
$(Month)^2$	.26	.011	763.0*	.24	.011	715.0*
$(Month)^3$	.16	.007	465.3	.14	.006	432.1
Property Crime						
Intercept	.66	7.061	4,781.6*	.62	6.161	3,957.4*
Month	.22	.008	628.9	.21	.008	623.2
$(Month)^2$	.16	.007	513.3	.16	.007	507.8
Assault						
Intercept	.56	4.799	3,922.4*	.53	4.617	3,509.6*
Month	.17	.007	429.6	.17	.007	427.3
Drug Crime						
Intercept	.72	14.324	5,445.0*	.66	12.701	5,015.8*
Month	.32	.020	1,035.8*	.30	.022	932.2*
$(Month)^2$	.21	.013	624.7	.18	.012	523.7

*$p < .05$ (two-tailed tests)

Note: All terms had 616 degrees of freedom, except the intercepts in the conditional models, which had 609.

Table 8.4 Logistic Coefficients (γ) and Odds Ratios from Binomial Hierarchical Linear Models of Monthly Offending in Relation to Change in Life Circumstances: Male Offenders in Nebraska, 1989–1990

Life Circumstance	ANY CRIME γ	Odds Ratio	PROPERTY CRIME γ	Odds Ratio	ASSAULT γ	Odds Ratio	DRUG CRIME γ	Odds Ratio
Probation or Parole	-.21 (.20)	.81	-.27 (.20)	.76	.06 (.22)	1.06	.08 (.28)	1.08
School	-.73* (.18)	.48	-.25 (.20)	.78	-.17 (.23)	.84	-.94* (.24)	.39
Work	.13 (.11)	1.14	.25* (.12)	1.28	-.28 (.16)	.76	.11 (.15)	1.11
Live with Wife	-.52 (.29)	.59	-.19 (.31)	.82	-.84* (.38)	.43	-.48 (.39)	.62
Live with Girlfriend	.50* (.17)	1.64	.25 (.18)	1.28	-.06 (.23)	.94	.49* (.21)	1.63
Heavy Drinking	.39 (.21)	1.48	.63* (.23)	1.88	.31 (.29)	1.36	.53 (.29)	1.71
Illegal Drug Use	1.81* (.19)	6.10	.43* (.20)	1.54	.73* (.27)	2.07	2.75* (.25)	15.70

*$p < .05$ (two-tailed tests)

Note: Numbers in parentheses are standard errors.

between-persons differences in the local life circumstances, which are not of substantive interest for this analysis, are available on request from the authors.)

Use of illegal drugs was related to all four measures of offending. Use of drugs had an especially strong association with involvement in drug dealing—the logistic coefficient of 2.75 corresponds to a 15-fold increase in the odds of drug crime during months of drug use. Although the relationship of illegal drug use to property crimes and assaults is less extreme, it is still substantial. During months of drug use, the odds of committing a property crime increased by 54 percent, and odds of committing an assault increased by over 100 percent. Combining these for the summary index, illegal drug use increased the odds of committing any crime by sixfold.

Our findings on the impact of drug use are consistent with studies of heroin addicts that have compared periods of addiction with periods of nonaddiction. Ball, Shaffer, and Nurco (1983) and Anglin and Speckart (1986) found substantially higher self-reported crime-commission rates during periods of addiction. Our results indicate that drug use apparently has the same kind of deleterious effects, even when a criterion less stringent than addiction is used (i.e., monthly use) and when drugs other than heroin are considered (i.e., illegal drugs other than marijuana; very few of our respondents used heroin).

Heavy drinking was positively related to the four measures of offending, significantly so for property offenses. Indeed, heavy drinking was more strongly related to commission of property crimes than was illicit drug use. Although not statistically significant, coefficients relating heavy drinking to commission of any crime and to commission of a drug crime are sizable as well. Their relatively large standard errors result from the limited number of individuals who had changes in their heavy drinking status (see Table 8.1).

Table 8.4 shows that living with a wife is associated with lower levels of offending, but living with a girlfriend is associated with higher levels. Living with a girlfriend significantly raised the odds of offending by over 64 percent for commission of any crime and for commission of a drug crime. The relationship of living with a wife to these measures of offending was of equal magnitude, but was not statistically significant (again because of the small number of individuals with change on this variable). There was a statistically significant decrease of 57 percent in the odds of committing an assault when living with a wife.

These results are in accord with Sampson and Laub's (1993) finding that marital attachment was one of the strongest predictors of adult criminality, even after childhood delinquency and early adult criminality were controlled. Their composite measure of marital attachment was based on interview data and included the respondent's assessment of the general marital relationship, his attitude toward marital responsibility, and, for the final wave of data, a measure of family cohesiveness. Although we do not have measures of marital attachment, we do have the comparison of living with a wife and living with a girlfriend. If we assume that formalizing a relationship through marriage indicates attachment, then the lesser attachment may explain why living with a girlfriend does not lower the odds of offending. We have no explanation for the unexpected increase in the odds of offending associated with living with a girlfriend.

Changing life circumstances in the domains of work and school also contributed to the odds of offending in any given month. Attending school had uniformly beneficial consequences, significantly reducing the odds of involvement in any crime by 52 percent and the odds of involvement in drug crimes by 61 percent. Working was only weakly related to all of the measures of offending. Surprisingly, the odds of committing a property crime increased by 28 percent in the months when men worked. Though this was statistically significant, it is exceeded by an opposite, but not significant, coefficient for commission of assault. Because changes in work status were common, these coefficients have the smallest standard errors.

We viewed employment as an important aspect of social bonding that should reduce the likelihood of offending. Our crude measure (respondents simply reported whether they worked during a given month) may be responsible for the weak results on lowered odds of offending. We measured none of the aspects of attachment to a job that Sampson and Laub (1993) considered; our measure did not even distinguish part-time from full-time employment, or temporary from permanent work. The surprising increase in the odds for commission of a property crime may reflect the increased opportunities for theft and perhaps also for forgery or fraud that are available in the workplace. The only aspect of local life circumstances that was not related to any of the indices of offending was justice supervision in the form of probation or parole.

Reduced Models We also estimated two reduced models using subsets of the seven local life circumstances. One model excludes the substance use variables of heavy drinking and illegal drug use. This reduced model is useful for two purposes. First, it is informative about potential indirect effects that might be mediated by the impact of substance use. Attending school, being employed, and living with a wife could reduce crime indirectly by reducing substance use. Comparing this reduced model to the full model gives little evidence of this. Relationships that were significant in the full model typically changed little when we did not control for substance use. There was one notable change, however: Living with a wife became significantly and negatively related to the general measure of crime ($\gamma = -.61$, s.e. $= .29$), which adds consistency to the previous pattern of results. Nevertheless, it does not appear that controlling for substance use obscured important effects.

This reduced model is also of interest because the causal role of the substance use variables is subject to an alternative interpretation. Heavy alcohol use and illegal drug use are deviant or conventionally disapproved behaviors, as are our measures of crime. Thus, rather than influencing crime, these behaviors may be alternative manifestations of the same factors that lead to crime (Osgood, Johnston, O'Malley, & Bachman, 1988:81–83). That would imply that their relationship is spurious rather than causal, an issue that the present analysis cannot resolve. The reduced model is useful in this regard because it provides estimates of the effects of the other local life circumstances, unbiased by any potential spurious relationship between crime and substance use.

The second reduced model concerns probation or parole, the only local life circumstance that was not related to any of the indices of offending in the full models. These results may arise because the impact of probation or parole is indirect, being mediated by intermediate effects of supervision, such as reducing illegal drug use and promoting employment. The second reduced model addresses this possibility by excluding all measures of local life circumstances other than justice supervision, thereby ruling out any indirect effects. Even in this model, there are no significant effects of justice supervision on offending.

Though three of the four coefficients indicate lower rates of offending during justice supervision, the relationships are weak, reflecting a 26 percent reduction in odds of offending at most. Clearly, justice supervision did not produce substantial reductions in crime among these serious offenders. These results are consistent with previous findings in the perceptual deterrence literature that the threat of formal sanctions is much less effective in altering behavior than are informal processes of social control (Paternoster & Iovanni, 1986; Paternoster, Saltzman, Waldo, & Chiricos, 1983).

DISCUSSION

Our results provide clear evidence of meaningful short-term change in involvement in crime, and this change is strongly related to variation in local life circumstances. Our use of a hierarchical linear model allowed us to rule out criminal propensity as a confounding variable by controlling for individual differences in the overall probability of offending. Thus, our results cannot be explained by the possibility that drug use, unstable marriage, and criminal offending are all indicators of an underlying stable trait—a lack of self-control, for example. Rather, we found that, regardless of overall level of offending, these men were more likely to commit crimes when using illegal drugs and conversely were less likely to commit crimes when living with a wife.

Figure 8.1 illustrates the implications of the estimates in Table 8.4. This figure shows that, even in the presence of substantial individual differences in the propensity to offend, varying local life circumstances produce dramatic changes in rates of offending. Probabilities of committing a crime by three hypothetical individuals who offend at average, low, and high rates (corresponding to monthly probabilities of .33, .06, and .80 when all X variables are at their means) are portrayed. They begin this period living with wives and not using drugs or using alcohol heavily. The horizontal axis indicates changes that occur from one month to the next, and the lines plot the corresponding changes in rates of offending. For comparison, a fourth line indicates the overall time trend when local life circumstances are held constant. Although changes in life circumstances have greater effects for the average- and high-rate offenders, offense rates for all three hypothetical individuals vary markedly with changes in living arrangements, school attendance, and substance use.

We believe that measuring offending activity in fairly short units of time is important for understanding the relationship between life events and criminal behavior. As Freedman et al. (1988) noted, "the traditional panel study provides only multiple snapshots of individual lives" (p. 39). When one- or two-year intervals are used, the correspondence between events in time may be missed, especially in the unstable lives of serious offenders. To detect change over brief time spans, it is also important to use self-reports of criminal activity. Although official records may be good indicators of the overall level of criminal activity, measures of arrests or convictions have base rates

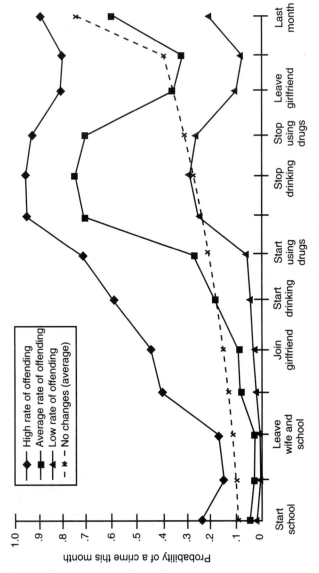

FIGURE 8.1 The effect of changing life circumstances on the probability of committing a crime: three hypothetical individuals

that are too low to allow meaningful estimation of the relationship of offending to local life circumstances.

We used life-event calendars to collect retrospective data in one-month units. Although studies on the reliability of such techniques (Freedman et al., 1988; Caspi & Amell, 1994) have been encouraging, Freedman et al. (1988) reported that "one important issue in obtaining retrospective data appears to be the degree of volatility of the activity patterns, since respondents find it more difficult to recall widely fluctuating event patterns" (p. 66). Because we studied a population with considerable volatility in their activity patterns, it would be extremely beneficial to replicate this study with a longitudinal design that allows the prospective collection of data at short intervals.

The measurement of offending and life circumstances at frequent intervals over a relatively short period of time provides a different perspective on change than that provided by Sampson and Laub (1990, 1993; Laub & Sampson, 1993). Whereas their long-term perspective showed that life events could modify criminal career trajectories, our short-term perspective has shown that local life circumstances can change criminal careers by modifying the likelihood of offending *at particular times.*

Because we looked at only a tiny portion of the life course, we cannot say whether the changes we observed represent alterations in life trajectories for some individuals, nor can we assess the degree of continuity in these respondents' criminal careers. We are encouraged, however, that the underlying processes involved in producing short-term change may be the same processes that produce "deep" change, or the alteration in a life trajectory. Living with a wife reduces the short-term likelihood of committing crime; a stable marriage and attachment to a spouse may lead to the long-term cessation of offending.

We have made no attempt to explain the processes underlying change. As we noted in our introduction, social control and rational choice (or opportunity) theories provide the most relevant sociological perspectives. Sampson and Laub (1993) emphasized the role of "*informal* social controls that emerge from the role reciprocities and structure of interpersonal bonds linking members of society to one another and to wider social institutions such as work, family, and school" (p. 18) and contended that "adult social ties are important insofar as they create interdependent systems of obligation and restraint that impose significant costs for translating criminal propensities into action" (p. 141). Their focus on the quality or strength of these social ties goes beyond what we could assess with our simple indicators. Their results suggest that we might have found stronger relationships between offending and local life circumstances if we had been able to appreciate more fully the level of investment those circumstances represented for individuals.

Rational choice or routine activity perspectives may also provide useful frameworks for thinking about the role of local life circumstances. When individuals are married and living with their spouses, their perceptions of the consequences of crime may change, either because they view themselves as having more to lose, or because a sense of shame is enhanced when the reactions of a significant other person are considered. When individuals are using drugs, on the other hand, they may become even more present-oriented, judge the utility of committing a crime to be greater, and give lesser consideration to sanctions and shame. Involvement in marriage and family, school, and work may also be important because of the role these institutions play in structuring daily activities. Time devoted to activities related to those institutions is time unavailable for "hanging out" on the streets or in bars and may therefore reduce an individual's exposure to situations conducive to involvement in criminal behavior.

Reconciling Continuity and Change

We cannot assume that the local life circumstances we studied were randomly distributed among offenders. Probably, they were to some extent determined by time-stable characteristics of the individuals. Our results in no way negate findings of long-term continuity—individuals do differ in their long-term criminal propensities and in their abilities to maintain stable schooling, employment, and marriages.

We believe that these tendencies interact with each other in complex ways and that contrasting continuity with change is a false dichotomy. As Rowe and Osgood (1984) noted, long-term correlates of offending, even genetic factors, do not rule out important social influences on crime because social processes may be essential links in the chain of causes that produce those relationships. For example, Booth and Osgood (1993) found that the positive relationship of testosterone levels to adult offending was mediated by current social integration. Thus, although continuity over the life course supports the importance of early influences, it has no direct bearing on the contribution of social factors during adulthood.

One view of the interplay between continuity and change can be found in the recent work of Nagin and Paternoster (1993), who showed how theories of criminal opportunity and rational choice can be linked to theories that focus on enduring individual differences in propensities. Using scenarios presented to college undergraduates, they found that a measure of self-control was directly related to decisions to commit offenses and indirectly related to intentions to offend through self-control's influence on judgments about total sanctions, the perceived utility of committing the offense, and shame. Yet even after differences in self-control were accounted for, decisions to offend were still influenced by the attractiveness of the target, the ease of committing the crime, and perceptions of the costs and benefits of committing the crime. As Nagin and Paternoster (1993) noted, "a belief that variation in offending is reflective of variations in criminal propensity or poor self-control does not preclude the possibility that would-be offenders are sensitive to the attractions and deterrents of crime" (p. 490).

Gottfredson and Hirschi (1990), while arguing for the central role of a time-stable criminal propensity, acknowledged a role for immediate circumstances in determining when and where crimes are committed. They have reconciled the seeming contradiction by distinguishing between self-control—"relatively stable differences across individuals in the propensity to commit criminal (or equivalent) acts" (p. 137)—and the criminal acts themselves—"short-term, circumscribed events that presuppose a peculiar set of necessary conditions (e.g., activity, opportunity, adversaries, victims, goods)" (p. 137). Yet Gottfredson and Hirschi (1990) denied a role for life circumstances beyond the immediate situation, such as those we have studied, by arguing that these ordinary events are caused by the individual's crime-relevant characteristics and thus are only spuriously connected to crime.

We have shown that less immediate local life circumstances are also important. These circumstances may provide an essential intermediate level of analysis that can be linked both to enduring individual differences rooted in early childhood experience and to the immediate circumstances in which criminal acts occur. Our results closely parallel those of Nagin and Paternoster (1993). They showed that, although individuals with low self-control discounted the costs of crime relative to individuals with high self-control, they were not insensitive to costs. We have shown that, although individuals with a high propensity to offend maintain few social bonds to society relative to individuals with a low propensity, they are not insensitive to those bonds. Persons with a high propensity for crime may be unlikely to graduate from school, unlikely to maintain meaningful employment, and unlikely to stay in stable, committed marriages. Even so, they may *sometimes* go to school, *sometimes* work, and *sometimes* live with a wife, and *at those times* they are less likely to commit crimes. Likewise the high-propensity individuals may be more likely than others to be involved with drugs and heavy alcohol use, but *sometimes* they do not use these substances, and *when they do not,* they are less likely to commit crimes.

We believe our findings also provide a link to the long-term change described by Sampson and Laub (1993). The combined effects of several crime-inhibiting local life circumstances may lead to the accumulation of enough social capital to motivate an individual to work at maintaining the social bonds. The maintenance of the bonds may, in turn, provide additional social capital and further reduce offending. If such a process continues to spiral, it could produce the kind of incremental change that results in a major alteration of a life trajectory. Just as lives are built one day at a time, over-arching life-span trajectories can only evolve from responses to daily social realities. Inevitably, short-term and long-term analyses of change must converge. Achieving this convergence would lend considerable support to our theories, and the effort will provide a richer appreciation of the task of explaining how individual lives evolve.

In sum, our findings strongly support the conclusion that continuity and change are not opposites, but rather are two faces of intertwined causal processes. Our results forcefully demonstrate that social events during adulthood are related to crime. Contrary to the image presented by some theorists of crime, life after puberty does matter. Yet changes in offending during adulthood do not negate the importance of enduring individual differences in criminal propensity or of related constructs like self-control. Instead, our results suggest that differences among individuals combine with their shifting social environments to produce current levels of criminal activity.

REFERENCES

Akers, Ronald. 1985. *Deviant Behavior: A Social Learning Approach.* Belmont, CA: Wadsworth.

Anglin, M. Douglas and George Speckart. 1986. "Narcotics Use, Property Crime, and Dealing: Structural Dynamics Across the Addiction Career." *Journal of Quantitative Criminology* 2:355–75.

Ball, John, John Shaffer, and David Nurco. 1983. "The Day-to-Day Criminality of Heroin Addicts in Baltimore; A Study in the Continuity of Offense Rates." *Drug and Alcohol Dependence* 12:119–42.

Blumstein, Alfred, Jacqueline Cohen, Jeffrey A. Roth, and Christy Visher, eds. 1986. *Criminal Careers and "Career Criminals."* 2 vols. Washington, DC: National Academy Press.

Booth, Alan and D. Wayne Osgood. 1993. "The Influence of Testosterone on Deviance in Adulthood: Assessing and Explaining the Relationship." *Criminology* 31:93–117.

Bradburn, Norman M., Lance J. Rips, and Steven K. Shevell. 1987. "Answering Autobiographical Questions: The Impact of Memory and Inference on Surveys." *Science* 236:157–61.

Bryk, Anthony S. and Stephen W. Raudenbush. 1992. *Hierarchical Linear Models: Applications and Data Analysis Methods.* Newbury Park, CA: Sage.

Bryk, Anthony, Stephen W. Raudenbush, and Richard Congdon. 1993. *HLM Version 3.* Chicago, IL: Scientific Software International.

Caspi, Avshalom and James Amell. 1994. "The Reliability of Life History Calendar Data" (DPPP Technical Report 94–101). University of Wisconsin, Madison. WI.

Caspi, Avshalom and Terrie Moffitt. 1993. "Continuity Amidst Change: A Paradoxical Theory of Personality Coherence." *Psychological Inquiry* 4:247–71.

Chaiken, Jan M. and Marcia Chaiken. 1982. *Varieties of Criminal Behavior.* Santa Monica, CA: Rand Corporation.

Cohen, Albert. 1955. *Delinquent Boys.* New York: Free Press.

Cohen, Lawrence E. and Marcus Felson. 1979. "Social Change and Crime Rate Trends: A Routine Activity Approach." *American Sociological Review* 44:588–608.

Dempster, A. P., N. M. Laird, and D. B. Rubin. 1977. "Maximum Likelihood from Incomplete Data Via the EM Algorithm." *Journal of the Royal Statistical Society, Series B* 39:1–8.

Elliot, Delbert, David Huizinga, and Suzanne Ageton. 1985. *Explaining Delinquency and Drug Use.* Beverly Hills, CA: Sage.

Farrington, David P. 1988. "Studying Changes Within Individuals: The Causes of Offending." Pp. 158–83 in *Studies of Psychosocial Risk: The Power of Longitudinal Data,* edited by M. Rutter. New York: Cambridge University Press.

———. 1992. "Explaining the Beginning, Progress, and Ending of Antisocial Behavior from Birth to Adulthood," Pp. 253–86 in *Facts, Frameworks, and Forecasts,* edited by J. McCord. New Brunswick, NJ: Transaction.

Farrington, David P., Bernard Gallagher, Lynda Morley, Raymond J. St. Ledger, and Donald J. West. 1986. "Unemployment, School Leaving, and Crime." *British Journal of Criminology* 26:335–56.

Freedman, Deborah, Arland Thornton, Donald Camburn, Duane Alwin, and Linda Young-DeMarco. 1988. "The Life History Calendar: A Technique for Collecting Retrospective Data." *Sociological Methodology* 18:37–68.

Glueck, Sheldon and Eleanor Glueck. 1950. *Unraveling Juvenile Delinquency.* New York: Commonwealth Fund.

Goldstein, Harvey. 1987. *Multilevel Models in Educational and Social Research.* London, England: Oxford University Press.

Gottfredson, Michael and Travis Hirschi. 1990. *A General Theory of Crime.* Stanford, CA: Stanford University Press.

Greene, William H. 1990. *Econometric Analysis.* New York: Macmillan.

Hirschi, Travis. 1969. *Causes of Delinquency.* Berkeley, CA: University of California Press.

Horney Julie and Ineke Haen Marshall. 1991. "Measuring Lambda through Self-Reports." *Criminology* 29:471–95.

Hsiao, Cheng. 1986. *Analysis of Panel Data.* Cambridge, England: Cambridge University Press.

Laub, John H. and Robert J. Sampson. 1993. "Turning Points in the Life Course: Why Change Matters to the Study of Crime." *Criminology* 31:301–25.

Mason, William M., George M. Wong, and Barbara Entwistle. 1983. "Contextual Analysis through the Multilevel Linear Model." *Sociological Methodology* 13:72–103.

Moffitt, Terrie E. 1993. "Adolescence-Limited and Life-Course-Persistent Antisocial Behavior: A Developmental Taxonomy." *Psychological Review* 100:674–701.

Nagin, Daniel S. and David P. Farrington. 1992a. "The Stability of Criminal Potential from Childhood to Adulthood." *Criminology* 30:236–60.

———. 1992b. "The Onset and Persistence of Offending." *Criminology* 30:525–45.

Nagin, Daniel S. and Kenneth C. Land. 1993. "Age, Criminal Careers, and Population Heterogeneity: Specification and Estimation of a Nonparametric, Mixed Poisson Model." *Criminology* 31:327–62.

Nagin, Daniel S., and Raymond Paternoster. 1993. "Enduring Individual Differences and Rational Choice Theories of Crime." *Law and Society Review* 27:467–96.

Osgood, D. Wayne, Lloyd D. Johnston, Patrick M. O'Malley, and Jerald G. Bachman. 1988. "The Generality of Deviance in Late Adolescence and Early Adulthood." *American Sociological Review* 53:81–93.

Paternoster, Raymond and LeeAnn Iovanni. 1986. "The Deterrent Effect of Perceived Severity: A Reexamination." *Social Forces* 64: 751–77.

Paternoster, Raymond, Linda Saltzman, Gordon Waldo, and Theodore Chiricos. 1983. "Perceived Risk and Social Control: Do Sanctions Really Deter?" *Law and Society Review* 17:457–79.

Patterson, Gerald R., and K. Yoerger. 1993. "Developmental Models for Delinquent Behavior." Pp. 140–72 in *Crime and Mental Disorder,* edited by S. Hodgins. Newbury Park, CA: Sage.

Raudenbush, Stephen W. 1993. "Posterior Model Estimation for Hierarchical Generalized Linear Models with Applications to Dichotomous and Count Data." College of Education, Michigan State University, East Lansing, MI. Unpublished manuscript.

Rindfuss, Ronald R., C. Gray Swicegood, and Rachel A. Rosenfeld. 1987. "Disorder in the Life Course: How Common and Does It Matter?" *American Sociological Review* 52:785–801.

Rowe, David C. and D. Wayne Osgood. 1984. "Heredity and Sociological Theories of Delinquency: A Reconsideration." *American Sociological Review* 49:526–40.

Sampson, Robert J. and John H. Laub. 1990. "Crime and Deviance over the Life Course: The Salience of Adult Social Bonds." *American Sociological Review* 55:609–27.

———. 1993. *Crime in the Making: Pathways and Turning Points through Life.* Cambridge, MA.: Harvard University Press.

Sayrs, Lois W. 1989. "Pooled Time Series Analysis" (Sage University Paper series on Quantitative Applications in the Social Sciences, 07–070). Newbury Park, CA: Sage.

Shaw, Clifford R. and Henry D. McKay. 1942. *Juvenile Delinquency and Urban Areas*. Chicago, IL: University of Chicago Press.

Sutherland, Edwin H. and Donald R. Cressey. 1955. *Principles of Criminology*. 5th ed. Philadelphia, PA: J. B. Lippincott.

Wilson, James Q. and Richard Herrnstein. 1985. *Crime and Human Nature*. New York: Simon and Schuster.

Zeger, S. L., K-Y. Liang, and P. S. Albert. 1988. "Models for Longitudinal Data: A Generalized Estimating Equation Approach." *Biometrics* 44:1049–60.

SECTION V

Developmental Versus Static Theories

Current Debates

The articles in Section V focus on debates in the area of developmental and static theories of crime. In recent years, the field of criminology has witnessed a debate that strikes at the core of the discipline. According to one group of scholars, theories that take into consideration an individual's development over the life course; the transitions and trajectories that mark involvement in criminal offending; and the reasons for initiation, progression, and cessation of criminal offending are the best approaches for studying and understanding criminal behavior over time. Other scholars, however, argue that developmental models of offending are more complex than is necessary, and generally provide little added explanatory power above and beyond what has been revealed from cross-sectional approaches.

In their comprehensive article, sociologists Travis Hirschi and Michael Gottfredson point out that both longitudinal and cross-sectional research produces equivalent findings about the correlates of delinquency. According to these scholars, since the causes of crime at one age identify the causes of crime at other ages, developmental theories and research are unnecessary. Hirschi and Gottfredson argue that when individuals change their course of offending, it is not due to institutional or environmental influences. According to their viewpoint, decisions precede actions such that individuals select themselves (i.e., self-selection) into more prosocial institutions (such as a good marriage) that coexist with changes in criminal behavior.

In reply to Hirschi and Gottfredson, criminologists Robert Sampson and John Laub make the case for a life-course approach to the study of criminal behavior over time. Unlike the static approach advocated by Hirschi and Gottfredson, Sampson and Laub embrace a dynamic perspective that allows for both stability and change in offending throughout the life-course. Built on their age-graded theory of informal social control, this approach focuses on the structure of interpersonal bonds linking members of society to one another and to wider social institutions such as work, family, and school. Sampson and Laub further argue that some of these informal social controls can alter individuals' criminal conduct. Therefore, in their view, behavioral change is not a product of self-selection, but rather a product of the salient influences that flow from the development of meaningful ties to occupational and marital institutions.

The papers included in this section illustrate some of the central debates between developmental and static theories of criminal behavior. The implications arising from the debates have much to offer with regard to how researchers study crime over the life-course.

SUGGESTED READINGS

Bartusch, D., Lynam, D., Moffitt, T., & Silva, P. (1997). Is age important? Testing a general versus a developmental theory of antisocial behavior. *Criminology, 35,* 13–48.

Huizinga, D., Esbensen, F., & Weiher, A. (1991). Are there multiple paths to delinquency. *Journal of Criminal Law and Criminology, 82*(1), 83–118.

Loeber, R., Wei, E., Stouthamer-Loeber, M., Huizinga, D., & Thornberry, T. P. (1999). Behavioral antecedents to serious and violent offending: Joint analyses from the Denver Youth Survey,

Pittsburgh Youth Study, and the Rochester Youth Development Study. *Studies on Crime and Crime Prevention, 8*(2), 245–263.

Paternoster, R. & Brame, R. (1997). Multiple routes to delinquency: A test of developmental and general theories of crime. *Criminology, 35*(1), 49–84.

Simons, R., Johnson, C., Conger, R., & Elder, G., Jr. (1998). A test of latent trait versus life-course perspectives on the stability of adolescent antisocial behavior. *Criminology, 36*(2), 217–243.

9

Control Theory and
the Life-Course Perspective

TRAVIS HIRSCHI

MICHAEL R. GOTTFREDSON

ABSTRACT Recent discussions of the merits of longitudinal and cross-sectional research conclude that the two methods produce equivalent findings about the correlates of delinquency. If this conclusion is correct (and we believe that it is), attention in the field should shift to the substantive findings of research and their interpretation or explanation. Theories or perspectives in the field should be required to attempt to account for these common findings, and may be judged by their ability to do so and by their further contributions to research design.

I n 1983, we advanced the hypothesis that the age distribution of crime is invariant across social and cultural conditions. From this hypothesis, others seemed to us to follow. For example, if the age distribution is invariant:

- it cannot be accounted for by any variable or combination of variables currently available to criminology.

- the conceptual apparatus that has grown up around the age effect is almost certainly redundant or misleading.

- identification of the causes of crime at one age may suffice to identify them at other ages as well—if so, cohort or longitudinal studies of crime are unnecessary (Hirschi & Gottfredson, 1983).

Editors and referees were at some pains to convince us before the article was published that we should acknowledge what they called the "life-course perspective" on the age issue, but we were insufficiently conversant with the perspective to do so. There was an additional reason for our hesitancy. To the extent we understood the life-course perspective, it seemed diametrically opposed to our conclusions, and therefore could not be accepted without abandoning them.

In the age-crime "debate" that followed, the attention of critics focused mainly on our invariance thesis (Greenberg, 1985; Farrington, 1986;

SOURCE: *Studies on Crime and Crime Prevention*, Vol. 4, No. 2, 131–142. Reprinted by permission of Scandinavian University Press.

Steffensmeier et al., 1989; Tittle, 1988), and its implications for criminal career or longitudinal research (Blumstein et al., 1988). The life-course perspective was occasionally raised as an alternative approach to the age question (Hagan & Palloni, 1988), but we again ignored it as we developed the theoretical and policy implications of an invariant age-crime relation in a series of works culminating in *A General Theory of Crime* (Gottfredson & Hirschi, 1990).

In the course of our work, we reached the conclusion that several facts about crime had been well-established. We continue to argue the basic validity of these facts and their consistency with control theory (Hirschi & Gottfredson, 1994), and continue to consider them central to theorizing in the field. As is well known, debates about facts are often thinly disguised debates about theory. Is the disagreement between control theory and the life-course perspective a disagreement about facts or theory? The answer to this question should have much to say about social policy and future research directions in criminology.

Interestingly enough, the same considerations apply to methodological disputes. While typically phrased as factual or logical in nature, they too often conceal theoretical differences among proponents of various designs. Judging from the nature of the debate between advocates of longitudinal and cross-sectional designs, it may be fair to say that it has more to do with the theories underlying these designs than with the strengths and weaknesses of the designs themselves. Thus, those whose theories of crime are consistent with a life-course perspective have defended longitudinal research, while those advocating control theory have been satisfied with cross-sectional designs.

Apart from general or platitudinous assertions about causal ordering, which interestingly enough are almost always divorced from concrete predictions, there has been little or no direct discussion of the scientific or logical merits of the designs at issue. Rather what has been stated clearly is that some perspectives or theories require longitudinal data for their exposition and validation. These perspectives, it turns out, simply include the longitudinal design as part of their axiomatic system. Included in these perspectives are the career criminal, life-course, developmental, and interactionist models. Together these models have attracted a large number of adherents, and spawned a large amount of research—so much so that it may not be inappropriate to suggest that a new discipline has emerged.[1]

The control model also views research design issues from the point of view of theory, and from the requirements of the facts it considers established. This perspective assumes that people choose situations, or select experiences, that they act and are acted upon, all of which makes assignment of cause and effect

---

[1]In our view the body of literature centering on life-course studies has all of the features of the positivistic disciplines discussed in Hirschi and Gottfredson (1990): centering first on identification of a problem to be addressed by the scientific method; apparently open to the facts whatever they may happen to be; ultimately driven by basic behavioral assumptions and adherence to particular methodologies.

ambiguous and potentially misleading. In our version, it also assumes that crime declines with age. For these reasons, longitudinal data may be excessively complicated and difficult to interpret.

If this characterization of the disagreement is correct, discussion of the determinants of delinquency is best preceded by frank admission that theory or explanation rather than research design is at the heart of the matter. If so, we should ask which of the perspectives is more consistent with established facts, and which offers the more useful and provocative predictions for criminology and public policy.

Fortunately for the field, criminologists tend to agree about the correlates of juvenile delinquency. As a matter of fact, two proponents of the longitudinal/developmental school have put the matter to a test in the empirical literature. LeBlanc (1989) and Loeber and LeBlanc (1989) examined our assertion that the basic findings about crime and delinquency produced by cross-sectional and longitudinal designs are the same. Their conclusion could not be more straightforward:

> If we leave this methodological question aside and address the knowledge-building question, all these reviews point to a common conclusion. Longitudinal surveys have confirmed cross-sectional surveys when it comes to findings concerning the correlates of crime. This is a major argument of the Gottfredson and Hirschi (1987) critique. And we find this argument impossible to reject because the reviews of Farrington et al. (1986) and Blumstein et al. (1986) do not propose new facts on correlates that were produced by longitudinal surveys (LeBlanc, 1989:383).

If LeBlanc's and Loeber and LeBlanc's characterization of the field is correct (see also Tittle & Ward, 1993), a description of "agreed upon" correlates of delinquency should provide an important starting point for resolution of the theoretical issues just described. In addition to agreement about basic correlates, we would add that there is general agreement in the field about the nature of delinquency—about how it should be measured, about its stability, and its relation to other problem behaviors.

Correlates of Delinquency   The reviews referred to by Loeber and LeBlanc were both undertaken by panels of scholars, one on behalf of the National Academy of Sciences, and the other on behalf of the MacArthur Foundation. Both groups may fairly be characterized as favoring career or developmental models for the study of crime and delinquency. Both confirm the now familiar *major* correlates of delinquency as including age, gender, race or ethnicity, intelligence, school performance, and peer and family relations (see also Rutter & Giller, 1984; Wilson & Herrnstein, 1985; Gottfredson & Hirschi, 1990; Farrington, 1992). We use the term "major" advisedly. Study after study documents that these variables account for the great bulk of the variation in delinquency that we are now able to explain. Indeed, it is probably not an overstatement to say that any study not finding these correlates is prima facie suspect. Agreement of this magnitude is fundamentally important to a scientific field. It allows it to put aside basic issues of fact and turn to new findings of potential significance for theory and policy.

Are these facts relevant to the disagreement between the life-course and control theory points of view? It seems to us that they are, that there should be tension between a theory that sees correlates as "age-graded" and a conclusion that the major correlates of crime do not depend on age. For that matter, emphasis on change, if it is to be theoretically meaningful, must suggest that the configuration of crime-causal variables shifts significantly over time or over the life-course. In this sense, the life-course perspective is not dependent on a set of agreed upon correlates of crime. As a result, it is not a theory in the classical sense, but a post hoc descriptive scheme focused on discrete events or series of events that may or may not occur in the lives of individuals.

Versatility It is now widely understood that the basic versatility of offenders extends within and bèyond the realm of delinquency. Indeed, it appears that the best available operational measure of the propensity to offend is a count of the number of distinct problem behaviors engaged in by a youth (that is, a variety scale) (Hindelang, Hirschi, & Weis, 1981; Robins & Ratcliff, 1978). There is a general tendency to engage in a wide variety of offenses, including legal and illegal drug use, and to manifest behavioral problems in school and occupational settings, to have difficulty making and retaining friends and to be involved in a variety of accidents (for reviews, see Junger, 1994; Britt, 1994; Sorensen, 1994; Strand & Garr, 1994). As a result of this finding of generality, theories focusing on specific causes for specific behaviors would not seem to be indicated, a conclusion shared by the control and life-course perspectives.

Having said this, however, it must be noted that the life-course interpretation of versatility differs markedly from our own. The life-course view is that specific events (sometimes referred to as "turning points") cause or prevent specific forms of crime. To make these events causal, the life-course perspective is forced to exclude them from the realm of deviant behavior or crime. From the perspective of control theory, the same events are within the realm of deviance and thus predictable from the concept of self-control. Alleged causal connections from one perspective between unemployment and property crime or between marriage failure and drinking are from the other perspective merely illustrations of the versatility of offenders and the enduring consequences of low self-control.

Stability A second area of agreement in the field as a whole concerns the stability of individual differences in the propensity to engage in delinquent and deviant acts from childhood to adulthood. Farrington (1992:258) has recently summarized the research on this issue: "There is clearly continuity over time in antisocial tendency. In other words, the antisocial child tends to become the antisocial teenager and the antisocial adult. . . . The relative orderings of any cohort of people on antisocial tendency is significantly consistent over time."[2] This finding, deducible from an invariant age effect, is largely responsible for the character of current control theory formulations.

In the disagreement between control theory and the life-course perspective, the stability question often surfaces as a distinction between person and variable stability, but the evidence suggests that this distinction cannot be critical to the disagreement between these two perspectives. The stability finding is based on correlation coefficients in which measures of some attribute are taken for individuals at different points in time. These correlations reflect the relative rank ordering of individuals on the attribute at different points in time. They do not presuppose, as is occasionally suggested (Sampson & Laub, 1992), that the level of the attribute for each individual is identical at every point in time. Indeed, when it comes to crime, this is decidedly not the case. The effect of age on crime, especially as it applies to particular crimes, is nowhere in dispute. Thus, references to control theory that suggest that it ignores that concept of change in crime over the life-course simply misrepresent this theoretical tradition (Hirschi & Gottfredson, 1983).[3]

A third area of general agreement concerns the *age* effect on crime. Not coincidentally, *interpretation* of the age effect is the source of considerable disagreement between the life-course and control perspectives. The nature of the general agreement in the field can be easily summarized. There is a strong and robust association between antisocial behaviors and age, with antisocial behaviors tending strongly to peak in late adolescence and to decline precipitously and continuously throughout life. Our view, for which we find considerable support in the empirical literature (e.g., Farrington, 1986; Britt, 1992; Nagin & Land, 1993; Wilson & Daly, 1993), is that age has a direct effect on problematic behavior, that there are no substantively important deviations from the general age distribution that can be traced to characteristics of persons, historical or cohort effects. Although some variability is found for some offenses and in some data sets, this variability is quite small compared with the robust nature of the general age effect, and is perhaps best thought of as reflecting misconceptualization of the dependent variable.

A constant effect of age on crime (or any other behavior) is anathema to the life-course tradition. This tradition is in fact based on assumptions explicitly contrary to a ubiquitous age-crime relation. Matilda White Riley has summarized the life-course perspective as a set of working principles (WP), most of which deny the possibility of a large or important direct effect of age on crime:

---

[2]Farrington goes on to say: "However, the behavioral manifestations of this tendency change over time, and it is important to document and explain these changing manifestations." From the life-course point of view, this is indeed what is problematic. From the control theory point of view, the important point is to understand the nature of the tendency from the character of its behavioral consequences—that is, why these behaviors should be characterized as manifestations of a *particular* underlying phenomenon. Of course, from a control perspective, the ability to say that a type of behavior *manifests* some underlying tendency yields the argument to control theory.

[3]It is ironic that we are criticized by some for arguing that change is universal and by others for presenting a theory that denies the possibility of change.

WP-1. Aging is not a unitary or exclusively biological process; it is multifaceted, composed of interdependent biological, psychological and social processes.

WP-2. Within each age stratum, individuals engage actively in a complex of roles (e.g., at work, in the family, in the community) that can continually influence the way they grow older, their capacities, motivations, and attitudes, and the other people with whom they interact; these roles set limits to, but also provide opportunity for, individual initiative and enterprise.

WP-5. The life-course patterns of individuals are affected by the character of the cohort to which they belong and by those social, cultural, and environmental changes to which their cohort is exposed in moving through each of the successive age strata (Riley, 1986:157–58).

Put the other way around, our age and crime argument violates almost all of the working principles of the life-course perspective. Where the life-course perspective says aging is not a unitary or biological process, we say that with respect to crime it is useful to see aging in precisely this way. Where the life-course perspective says the effects of age are a function of the role complex in which people are engaged, we argue that age effects on crime are invariant across roles (demographic or institutional factors). Where the life-course perspective says that the effects of age vary from cohort to cohort, we argue that age effects are invariant over time and place.

Perhaps not surprisingly, our argument about age effects on crime may be said to embody almost all of the "fallacies" identified by the life-course perspective. We based our conclusion originally on what Riley calls the life-course fallacy (basing conclusions about the effects of age on cross-sectional data); we explicitly embraced what she calls the cohort-centrism and age-reification fallacies. Indeed, her wording of these particular fallacies is virtually identical to our conclusions about age effects!

Nevertheless, whatever the disagreements about how age should be treated and interpreted, the form and extent of the relation between age and problem behaviors is not in serious dispute (for a recent summary of the statistics in this area as they apply to serious criminal offenders, see Gottfredson & Gottfredson (1992)). Thus the basic issue even here is theoretical, and one that should be decided on the basis of readily available data.

With respect specifically to crime, the life-course perspective is required to assume that important variations in age distributions are concealed by aggregate data, that good jobs hasten the decline in post-adolescence and that prisons delay it. Once again, these are issues addressed by substantial bodies of research that in our view clearly favor the control theory perspective. Prisons, jobs and marriages may appear to affect desistence under uncontrolled conditions, even when extensive statistical adjustments are made for previous misconduct, but they turn out to have little or no effect when experimental controls or rigorous controls for causal order are applied.

Interestingly enough, if the focus is on the determinants of *delinquency*, the distinction between the life-course and control perspectives is moot. Within the period where behavior has traditionally been defined as "delinquent," the relation between age and delinquency is not problematic. Delinquency simply increases with age, and this relation has not been shown to interact with, or be a spurious consequence of, other variables (Tittle & Ward, 1993). The empirical dispute about age thus focuses on the period of life subsequent to adolescence, when rates of crime and delinquency are declining. The significance of the decline in crime with age is difficult to overestimate. For one thing, it suggests that most of the variability in delinquency and crime is produced early in life, a fact of enormous consequence for theory and policy. For another, it suggests that the problem of crime is largely the problem of delinquency. Because the peak age of crime comes so early in the life-course, the vast majority of the acts of concern to criminologists are committed by young people. As a result, the current fascination with factors affecting post-adolescent crime trajectories is hard to justify on theoretical or policy grounds (especially when we know the decline will occur in any event).

Apparent Institutional Effects Surprisingly, another area of potential agreement in the delinquency literature is in the finding that people involved with prosocial institutions have relatively low delinquency rates, whereas those involved with antisocial institutions—for example, gangs, prisons, delinquent spouses—have relatively high delinquency rates. More significantly, such people are likely to have lower or higher rates than would be predicted from their prior records of delinquency, suggesting that the institutional experience has either a protective or corrosive effect on the subsequent behavior of the individual. A recent example of this thinking is provided by Laub and Sampson, who report from the Gluecks' data that, holding constant prior tendency, incarceration and job instability increase the chances of subsequent misconduct, while a stable job and a good marriage decreases these chances. Laub and Sampson argue that such findings cannot be understood as a consequence of self-selection to the "treatment," but illustrate instead automatic consequences of the establishment of social relations (1993:308, quoting Coleman, 1990:300). In fact, longitudinal and cross-sectional data also do not disagree on this point.

Findings identical to those of Laub and Sampson are easily uncovered in cross-sectional data. For example, the cross-sectional Richmond Youth Survey (see Hirschi, 1969, for details of data collection and definition of variables) reveals similar institutional "effects" for many variables. Holding constant prior delinquency by restricting attention to the delinquent group, we find "good" effects for "good" institutions or social relations and "bad" effects for "bad" institutions or social relations. Thus, among white male delinquents (as measured by police records), recent *non-delinquency* (as measured by self-reports) is four times more likely among those in good schools (schools where almost all teachers reportedly care about their students) than among those in bad schools; three times more likely among delinquent boys with good friends as measured by arrests than among delinquent boys with bad friends by the same measure; five times more likely among delinquent boys with good friends as measured by their reports of teacher's ratings than among delinquent boys with bad friends by the same measure. At the same time, non-delinquency is four times more likely among delinquent boys who have never been excluded from school than among delinquent boys who have been suspended.

According to life-course logic, such "turning points" in adolescent life have remarkable power to reduce or exacerbate delinquent tendencies. If these effects are real, there is no need to wait for the adult-years to see change in the life-trajectories of delinquents.

From our perspective, these apparent effects and identical findings reported in the life-course literature are a consequence of self-selection and statistical regression. Put in theoretical terms, they are a straightforward consequence of failure to take into consideration the decision-making capacities of the individuals making up our samples. In our view, it is illegitimate to wish away the capacities of individuals to seek and find environments compatible with their wishes and desires. Laub and Sampson argue that entrance into an institution represents an increase in social capital such that concern for self-selection is unreasonable. Their position appears reasonable when applied to those who seek to increase their social capital by establishing interpersonal relations or social bonds and thereby restricting their own behavior, especially deviant behavior. In fact, however, this process would merely account for the apparently good effects of good institutions. (The decision to change was made prior to involvement with the "change-producing" institutions.) The narratives reported by Sampson and Laub (1993) suggest as much. Former offenders say they "decided" to settle down, get a job or get married before they actually did so. Control theory, unlike life-course theory, accepts the notion that decisions precede actions.

Applying the idea of social capital to those choosing not to enter such institutions will illustrate its limitations. Would those resisting marriage, schooling, employment and the like benefit equally (i.e., increase their social capital) were they to be assigned to these institutions? Control theory says no, assuming that people uninterested in the restrictions of social institutions (unmotivated to change) are less likely to enter them and less likely to be affected by them. Put another way, people are not empty vessels into which self-restraint may be poured. The idea that unrestrained individuals passively acquire restrictions from accidental exposure is contrary to control theory's vision of man as an active decision-maker and is also, in our view, contrary to the facts.

EXPLAINING DELINQUENCY

When we first attempted to understand the correlates of delinquency from a theoretical point of view, we decided that versatility was the primary or central issue, that our first task was to understand the source of versatility, to find what seemingly diverse behaviors have in common that accounts for their tendency to appear together in the behavioral repertoires of individuals. High levels of versatility or variety seemed to us (and others as well, e.g., Jessor & Jessor,

1977; Robins, 1966; Hirschi, 1969) to be established fact. It seemed obvious, too, that identification of the common element in delinquent behaviors must precede theoretical explanation. After all, without such identification, we would not know what it was we were trying to explain.

The control theory solution to this problem distinguishes it most clearly from alterative theories, including the life-course perspective. In our version, control theory asserts that delinquent acts are a subset of acts that produce immediate benefit at the risk of long term cost, and that such acts tend to be engaged in by those relatively unlikely to consider the long term implications of their current behavior. With this solution to the versatility problem, control theory reduces the causal significance of life-course events, and indeed tends to see such events as themselves consequences of the mechanism that explains versatility.

There are other potential solutions to the versatility problem. One is strictly empirical, identifying through the pattern of correlations in the data a "latent trait" that accounts for the tendency of "items" to correlate, a factor that can then be used in subsequent empirical analyses of treatment effects or life-course events. One problem with the latent trait approach is that it fails to identify the boundaries of the trait on theoretical grounds and therefore has no means to distinguish it from measures of treatments and life-course events. In the general social science literature, this is equivalent to failure to specify in advance predictor and treatment variables, a problem we regard as all too common in the life-course literature.

A second solution in psychology is to identify a personality trait or syndrome that accounts for the various "types" of behavior that are found together. Common examples include aggressiveness, impulsivity, and psychopathy. Two problems were suggested to us in reviewing these constructs (Gottfredson & Hirschi, 1993). The first might be called the problem of under-inclusion. For example, aggression does well with homicide and rape but seems to have difficulty with drug use, truancy and accidents. The second is the problem of over-inclusion, by which people are compelled or driven to the acts explained by the trait that explains them. It seems to us that almost all personality explanations of versatility have this problem. We do not see from the data how such a deterministic stance can be justified. Because the life-course perspective gains much of its appeal from its similar rejection of such determinism, it is misleading and unfair for life-course adherents to depict control theory as deterministic (e.g., Sampson & Laub, 1993). In fact, the data suggest to us that it is easy to over-explain behaviors that come and go over the life-course, that even among the most active offenses are rare events. Elements of chance and choice must certainly be involved in them (Matza, 1964).

A third solution to the problem of versatility might be called the parallel causation model. Various acts appear together in the same individual because they are caused by the same set of hereditary and environmental conditions. For example, kids from broken homes who associate with gangs will tend to use drugs and engage in theft. Although this approach makes more sense when it recognizes versatility than when it predicts specialization (which it tends to do), it remains conceptually limited.

A fourth solution argues that one of the behaviors in the set causes the others. Drug use causes theft, truancy, and gang affiliation; drinking causes job instability, accidents, and homicide; problem behaviors in the classroom cause juvenile delinquency. This solution denies conceptual equivalence among the behaviors in question, and along with the third solution tends to be favored by the life-course perspective because it denies that something in the individual or in the acts themselves accounts for their tendency to go together.

We took two approaches to versatility. In the first we asked what the acts or behaviors had in common. In the second we asked what characteristic of individuals might be consistent with this property of deviant acts. The first question led us away from traditional definitions that rely on political or disciplinary terms to describe the behaviors of interest. Thus, we did not ask what delinquent or criminal acts have in common, nor did we seek the underlying theme in deviant behavior, aggression or attention deficit disorder. Rather, we tried to remind ourselves that versatility clearly extends beyond the borders of such concepts.[4] In the end, we concluded that the acts that tend to be found together in the behavior of offenders share a common feature: they carry for the individual involved in them the risk of long term negative consequences. Upon inspection, these acts have other common, if less defining, features. They require little effort, skill or planning; their execution and benefits are obvious to anyone in the situation; they require no particular tutelage or training.

This characterization, coupled with good evidence of stability of individual differences in involvement in such acts, suggested a property of individuals as the source and explanation of differential involvement or diversity. We labelled this property self-control. We were cognizant of the long history of this concept in psychology, and of the similarity and differences in our use of this term and its use by others. It does not denigrate previous work to argue that our meaning of the term is in some respects different, having been derived from a particular conception of a set of deviant, criminal and reckless acts. Rather, it seems to us fair to say that some of the concern with previous uses of the term should focus on the differences between our concept and previous ideas as well as the similarities between our work and what is after all a strong research tradition in psychology (Mischel, 1983; Block et al., 1988).[5]

Is it logical to assume that the concept of self-control can account for the other correlates of delinquency? It seemed to us that the answer is yes and no.

---

[4]It is hard to avoid leaving the impression that we are interested only, or mainly, in a subset of those acts that typically go together. Thus the title of our book, *A General Theory of Crime,* suggests that we are mainly concerned with acts that violate the criminal law, and those examining our argument frequently remark on our definitions of crime as pertaining to acts of force and fraud. Other scholars comment *after* reading our work that we seem more concerned with deviant behavior than with crime. The fact of the matter is that there is as yet no vocabulary that allow us to capture the wide range of phenomena of interest with a single term.

[5]If we appear over-sensitive on this issue, perhaps we should point out that a measure based on interpretation of Rorschach responses initially labeled "self-control" by the Gluecks has recently been used in a comparison of the life-course and self-control perspectives (Laub & Sampson, 1993: 305–6).

Although we argue that self-control is a general cause of crime, we do not argue that it is the sole cause of crime. Indeed, our analysis of delinquent and criminal acts argues that "lack of restraint" is only one of several conditions necessary, and collectively sufficient, for such acts to occur. These other conditions are usually considered "opportunity" factors. They are responsible for a good deal of the variation in the delinquent and deviant acts over time and space and over the life-course. (They account for within-individual variability, as well as the absolute frequency of the acts in question).

On the other hand, self-control accounts for a good portion of the major, agreed-upon determinants of delinquency. As we have tried to show, self-control acconts for family factors, since many of these processes are implicated in the production of self-control in the child. It accounts for school-behavioral factors, because these too are to some large degree products of low self-control. It accounts for peer factors, seeing them as a product of self-selection and institutional sorting processes. It accounts for the failure of efforts to treat delinquents or to deter them by the threat of punishment. It predicts the *apparent* success of involvement in conventional institutions and relationships.

Together, the concepts of opportunity and self-control provide a system for organizing the determinants of delinquency, and for approaching many of the traditional problems of the field (Hirschi & Gottfredson, 1994).

RESEARCH DIRECTIONS

Given the broad popularity of the life-course perspective, and its apparent compatibility with a variety of theoretical orientations, it is reasonable to assume that it will continue to influence the study of crime and delinquency. Given its specific ties to *social-control* theory (Sampson & Laub, 1993), it seems likely that its compatibility with self-control theory will continue to be explored (see Nagin & Paternoster, 1994). As these efforts proceed, it seems to us important to keep in mind general, agreed-upon facts about crime. These facts may help assess that applicability to crime of a scheme developed in other areas to explain other phenomena. The life-course perspective may help us understand why World War II is the defining moment in the lives of those who experienced it; it may account for the salience of the undergraduate experience in the lives of upper middle class males. But its application to crime may be as inappropriate as the highly popular economic view that crime is a rational *occupational* choice. We have argued elsewhere that wholesale application of disciplinary perspectives has greatly impeded progress in the understanding of crime and delinquency. Earlier we suggested that the life-course perspective shares many features of established disciplines, not the least of which is the idea that the concerns of the discipline outweigh those of the phenomenon to be explained. The persistent tendency of the life-course perspective to be at odds with the field on interpretation of major facts, and its tendency to dismiss traditional methodological concerns in favor of explanations consistent with its own presuppositions, suggests the need for caution.

REFERENCES

Block, J., Block, J. H. & Keys, S. (1988). Longitudinally foretelling drug usage in adolescence: Early childhood personality and environmental predictors. *Child Development* 59: 336–55.

Blumstein, A., Cohen, J., & Farrington, D. P. (1988). Criminal career research: Its value for criminology. *Criminology* 26:1–35.

Blumstein, A., Cohen, J., Roth, J. & Visher, C. (1986). *Criminal careers and "career criminals."* Washington, D.C.: National Academy Press.

Britt, C. (1992). Constancy and change in the U.S. age distribution of crime: A test of the invariance hypothesis. *Journal of Quantitative Criminology* 8:175–87.

Britt, C. (1994). Versatility. In: Hirschi, T., & Gottfredson, M., eds. *The Generality of Deviance,* New Brunswick, NJ: Transaction Publishers.

Coleman, J. S. (1990). *Foundations of social theory.* Cambridge, Mass: Harvard University Press.

Farrington, D. (1986). Age and crime. In: Tonry, M. & Morris, N., eds. *Crime and justice: An annual review of research.* Chicago: University of Chicago Press.

Farrington, D. (1992). Explaining the beginning, progress, and ending of antisocial behavior from birth to adulthood. In: McCord, J., ed. *Facts, frameworks, and forecasts,* vol. 3 in *Advances in criminological theory.* New Brunswick, NJ: Transaction Publishers.

Farrington, D., Ohlin, L. & Wilson, J. Q. (1986). *Understanding and controlling crime.* New York: Springer-Verlag.

Greenberg, D. F. (1985). Age, crime, and social explanation. *American Journal of Sociology* 91:1–21.

Gottfredson, S. D. & Gottfredson, D. (1992). *Incapacitation strategies and the career criminal.* Sacramento: California Department of Justice Monograph no. 8.

Gottfredson, M. R. & Hirschi, T. (1990). *A general theory of crime.* Stanford, CA: Stanford University Press.

Gottfredson, M. & Hirschi, T. (1993). A control theory interpretation of psychological research on aggression. In: Felson, R.R. & Tedeschi, J.T., eds. *Aggression and violence: social interactionist perspectives.* Washington, D.C.: American Psychological Association.

Hagan, J. & Palloni, A. (1988). Crimes as social events in the life course. *Criminology* 26:87–100.

Hindelang, M., Hirschi, T., & Weis, J. (1981). *Measuring delinquency.* Beverly Hills, CA: Sage.

Hirschi, T. (1969). *Causes of delinquency.* Berkeley: University of California Press.

Hirschi, T. & Gottfredson, M. (1983). Age and the explanation of crime. *American Journal of Sociology* 89: 552–84.

Hirschi, T. & Gottfredson, M. (1990). Substantive positivism and the idea of crime. *Rationality and Society* 2:412–28.

Hirschi, T. & Gottfredson, M. (1994). *The generality of deviance.* New Brunswick, NJ: Transaction Publishers.

Jessor, R. & Jessor, S. (1977). *Problem behavior and psychosocial development: A longitudinal study of youth.* New York: Academic Press.

Junger, M. (1994). Accidents. In: Hirschi, T. & Gottfredson, M., eds. *The generality of deviance.* New Brunswick, NJ: Transaction Publishers.

Kempf, K. L. (1993). The empirical status of Hirschi's control theory. In: Adler, F. & Laufer, W. eds. *New directions in criminological theory.* New Brunswick, NJ: Transaction Publishers.

Laub, J. H. & Sampson, R. J. (1993). Turning points in the life course: Why change matters to the study of crime. *Criminology* 31:302–25.

LeBlanc, M. (1989). Designing a self-report instrument for the study of the development of offending from childhood to adulthood: Issues and problems. In: Klein, M. V., ed. *Cross-National Research in Self-Reported Crime and Delinquency.* NATO ASI Series. vol. 50. Boston: Kluwer Academic Publishers.

Loeber, R. & LeBlanc, M. (1990). Toward a developmental criminology. In: Tonry, M. & Morris, N. eds. *Crime and justice: An annual review,* vol. 11. Chicago: University of Chicago Press.

Matza, D. (1964). *Delinquency and drift.* New York: Wiley.

Michel, W. (1983). Delay of gratification as process and as person variable in development. In: Magnusson, D. & Allen, V. eds. *Human development: An interaction perspective,* New York: Academic Press.

Nagin, D. S. & Land, K. C. (1993). Age, criminal careers, and population heterogeneity: Specification and estimation of a nonparametric, mixed Poisson model. *Criminology* 31: 327–62.

Nagin, D. S. & Paternoster, R. (1994). Personal capital and social control: The deterrence implications of a theory of individual differences in criminal offending. *Criminology* 32:581–606.

Riley, M. W. (1986). Overview and highlights of a sociological perspective. In: Sorenson, A. B., Weinert, F. & Sherrod, L. R., eds. *Human development and the life course.* Hillsdale, NJ: Erlbaum.

Robins, L. (1966). *Deviant children grown up.* Baltimore: Williams and Wilkins.

Robins, L. & Ratcliff, K. (1978). Risk factors in the continuation of childhood antisocial behavior in adulthood. *International Journal of Mental Health* 7:96–116. In: Farrington, D. P., ed. *Psychological Explanations of Crime.*

Aldershot, Eng.: Dartmouth Publishing Company (1994).

Rutter, M. & Giller, H. (1984). *Juvenile delinquency: Trends and perspectives.* New York: Guilford.

Sampson, R. J. & Laub, J. H. (1990). Crime and deviance over the life-course. The salience of adult social bonds. *American Sociological Review* 55:609–27.

Sampson, R. J. & Laub, J. H. (1993). *Crime in the making.* Cambridge, MA: Harvard University Press.

Sorensen, D. (1994). Motor vehicle accidents. In: Hirschi, T. & Gottfredson, M., eds. *The Generality of Deviance.* New Brunswick, NJ: Transaction Publishers.

Steffensmeier, D. J., Andersen, A. E., Harer, M. D. & Streifel, C. (1989). Age and the distribution of crime. *American Journal of Sociology* 94:803–831.

Strand, G. & Garr, M. (1994). Driving under the influence. In: Hirschi, T. & Gottfredson, M., eds. *The Generality of Deviance,* New Brunswick, NJ: Transaction Publishers.

Tittle, C. (1988). Two empirical regularities (maybe) in search of an explanation: Commentary on the age/crime debate. *Criminology* 26:75–85.

Tittle, C. R. & Ward, D. A. (1993). The interaction of age with the correlates and causes of crime. *Journal of Quantitative Criminology* 9:3–53.

Wilson, J. Q. & Herrnstein, R. (1985). *Crime and Human Nature.* New York: Simon and Schuster.

Wilson, M. & Daly, M. (1993). A Lifespan Perspective on Homicidal Violence: The Young Male Syndrome. In: Block, C. R. & Block, R. L., eds. *Questions and Answers in Lethal and Non-lethal Violence 1993,* eds. FBI Academy, Quantico, VA.

10

Understanding Variability in
Lives Through Time
Contributions of
Life-Course Criminology

ROBERT J. SAMPSON
JOHN H. LAUB

ABSTRACT   This paper examines the distinguishing features of a life-course perspective on crime. Integrated with an age-graded theory of informal social control, we argue that the nuts and bolts of life-course inquiry—especially aging (social and biological), stability and change, human agency, cohort, and historical period—yield powerful insights directly related to the substantive phenomenon of crime. We also identify points of both agreement and disagreement with Hirschi and Gottfredson's static perspective on crime, attempting to reconcile, or, where necessary, clarify differences in theoretical outlook. Our main goal is to highlight the implications of static and dynamic perspectives on the life course for future research in criminology.

I n our recent book, *Crime in the Making: Pathways and Turning Points Through Life* (Sampson & Laub, 1993), we explicated and tested an age-graded theory of informal social control and crime over the life course. Although drawing on diverse theoretical positions in sociology and developmental psychology, two seminal works in criminology influenced much of our thinking—*Causes of Delinquency* (Hirschi, 1969) and *A General Theory of Crime* (Gottfredson & Hirschi, 1990). In particular, our theory draws heavily on Hirschi's classic study of *social* control, and further suggests the conditions under which Gottfredson and Hirschi's theory of *self* control can be integrated with a life-course perspective to better understand variations in crime both between individuals and within individuals over time.

In *Control Theory and the Life Course Perspective* (1995), Hirschi and Gottfredson criticize both the fundamental premises of life-course research and the specific theory advanced in our book. Because our embrace of their work

SOURCE: *Studies on Crime and Crime Prevention*, Vol. 4, No. 2, pp. 143–158. Reprinted by permission of Scandinavian University Press.

was partial and at times frankly critical, alas we are not surprised that their assessment of the life-course perspective is likewise critical. But their present critique is scholarly, challenging, and generative of a healthy debate that we believe has important implications for future criminological research. Indeed, complete consensus in a field of scholarly inquiry is boring, and usually indicates a lack of theoretical excitement. Fortunately, criminology has always been a leader in sponsoring sharp theoretical debates, and we are pleased to continue that tradition.

Our goal in this paper, then, is to reflect on the implication of the life-course perspective for criminology against the backdrop of Hirschi and Gottfredson's critique. Because most of their criticisms are by now familiar to criminologists and no new data are presented, we see little need to rehash old debates. For example, we are fairly sure that the "criminal career" debate has grown tiresome for all parties concerned. Our strategy is thus to highlight thematic issues in a way that sheds new light on the distinguishing features of the life-course perspective. We also hope to identify points of both agreement and disagreement with Hirschi and Gottfredson in an attempt to reconcile, or, where necessary, clarify remaining differences in theoretical outlook. Readers can then judge for themselves which perspective asks the most interesting questions, is most compatible with the extant data, and provides a more compelling vision for future research in the field of criminology. For the benefit of readers new to the life-course literature, and to correct apparent misunderstandings in Hirschi and Gottfredson (1995), we begin with a brief review of the life-course perspective and our theoretical framework (Sampson & Laub, 1992, 1993; Laub & Sampson, 1993).

THE LIFE-COURSE PERSPECTIVE
AND SOCIAL INQUIRY

The life course may be conceptualized as trajectories and transitions through the age-differentiated life span (Elder, 1975, 1985), in particular the "sequence of culturally defined age-graded roles and social transitions that are enacted over time" (Caspi et al., 1990:15). A *trajectory* is a pathway or line of development over the life span in such areas as work, marriage, parenthood, or criminal behavior. Trajectories often refer to long-term patterns and sequences of behavior. *Transitions* are marked by specific life events (e.g., first job or onset of crime) and are embedded in trajectories and evolve over shorter time spans— "changes in state that are more or less abrupt" (Elder, 1985:31–32). Some transitions are age-graded and some are not; hence, what is often assumed to be important is the normative timing and sequencing of change in roles, statuses, or other socially defined positions along some consensual dimension. As a result, life-course analyses often focus on the consequences of the duration of time (spells) between a change in state and the ordering of major life events for later social development.

The interlocking nature of trajectories and transitions may generate "turning points" or change in the life course (Elder, 1985:32). Adaptation to life events is crucial because the same event or transition followed by different adaptations can alter the ongoing course of trajectories (Elder, 1985:35). In other words, while the long-term view embodied by the life-course focus on trajectories implies a connection between childhood events and experiences in adulthood (continuity), the simultaneously shorter-term view implies that transitions or turning points can modify (change) the course of life trajectories—they can "redirect paths." Social institutions and triggering life events that are hypothesized to modify trajectories include school, work, military induction, imprisonment, and marriage.

In addition to the study of stability *and* change in lives through time, the life-course framework encompasses other major themes: 1) a concern with the changing social meanings of age, not of biological age, 2) human agency in choice making, 3) intergenerational transmission of social patterns (the notion of "linked" or interdependent lives), and 4) the role of macro-level events (e.g., Great Depression, World War II) and structural location (e.g., ecological context) in shaping individual life histories.

In short, the major objective of the life-course perspective is to link social history and social structure to the unfolding of human lives. Life-course inquiry directs special attention to the dynamics of aging, cohort effects, historical context (period), and the social influence of age-graded transitions. To address these substantive phenomena, individual lives are studied through time, ideally but not necessarily with a prospective longitudinal design. By raising theoretical questions and providing a framework that guides research in terms of problem identification and formulation, variable selection and rationale, and strategies of design and analysis, the life-course perspective approximates to a research paradigm.

AN AGE-GRADED THEORY
OF INFORMAL SOCIAL CONTROL

The central idea of social control theory—that crime and deviance are more likely when an individual's bond to society is weak or broken—is an organizing principle in our theory of social bonding over the life course. Following Elder (1975), we differentiate the life course of individuals on the basis of age and argue that the important institutions of both formal and informal social control vary across the life span. However, we emphasize the role of age-graded *informal* social control as reflected in the structure of interpersonal bonds linking members of society to one another and to wider social institutions (e.g., work, family, school). Unlike formal sanctions which originate in purposeful efforts to control crime, informal social controls "emerge as by-products of role relationships established for other purposes and are components of role reciprocities" (Kornhauser, 1978:24).

Rejecting an "ontogenetic" or invariant conception of human development, our theoretical framework follows a "sociogenic" developmental strategy in studying the life course (Sampson & Laub, 1993, chap. 1). Developmental approaches to life course generally focus on the sequences of biological, psychological, and social processes through time, especially how behaviors set in motion dynamic processes that may alter future outcomes. Applied to crime, the life-course perspective recognizes both continuity and within-individual changes over time, focusing on "life transitions and developmental covariates . . . which may mediate the developmental course of offending" (Loeber & LeBlanc, 1990:451). The specific analytical approach we take views social development as best represented by a network of causal factors in which dependent variables become independent variables over time (Loeber & LeBlanc, 1990:433). This strategy has also been referred to as a "stepping stone approach" where factors are time ordered by age and assessed with respect to outcome variables (see Farrington, 1986). Interactional theory (Thornberry, 1987; Thornberry et al., 1994) embraces a similar developmental approach by arguing that causal influences are reciprocal over time.

The first theoretical building block in *Crime in the Making* focuses on the mediating role of social bonds to family and school in explaining child and adolescent delinquency (Sampson & Laub, 1993, chapters 4–5). The second building block theorizes about continuities in antisocial behavior from childhood throughout adulthood across a variety of domains (e.g., temper tantrums, crime, alcohol abuse, domestic violence). As elaborated below, we specifically posit both a state-dependence and population heterogeneity interpretation of the connection between child and adult outcomes.

A third and major thesis of our work is that salient life events and social bonds in adulthood—especially *attachment to the labor force and cohesive marriage* – explain variations in criminal behavior independent of prior differences in criminal propensity. In order words, we contend that trajectories of crimes are subject to modification by key institutions of social control in the transition to adulthood (e.g., employment, military service, and marriage). In contrast to many life-course models, we emphasize the quality or strength of social ties in these transitions more than their timing. For example, the occurrence of marriage *per se* may not increase social control, but close emotional ties and mutual investment increase the social bond between individuals and, all other things being equal, should lead to a reduction in criminal behavior. Employment by itself also does not necessarily increase social control. It is employment coupled with job stability, commitment to work, and mutual ties binding workers and employers that should increase social control and lead to a reduction in crime.

Having outlined the bare bones of a life-course perspective along with our age-graded theory of informal social control and crime, we now turn to sources of both agreement and disagreement with Hirschi and Gottfredson.

DEMONSTRATING STABILITY
REQUIRES LONGITUDINAL DATA

Ironically, the crux of Hirschi and Gottfredson's (HG) theory rests on the stability of individual differences in self-control and crime—the demonstration of which requires longitudinal data. "The stability finding is based on correlation coefficients in which measures of some attribute are taken for individuals *at different points in time*" (1995:134, emphasis added). Researchers cited approvingly as demonstrating stability in self control and/or crime (e.g., Jack Block, David Farrington, Lee Robins) are also premier advocates of a developmental or life-course perspective. Without the findings produced by longitudinal research, HG's theory thus has no empirical foundation.[1]

Obviously aware of this conundrum (1990:230–232), they are forced to argue that we need no more (longitudinal) research on stability because it has already been shown (by longitudinal research). Taken literally, that is, HG are calling upon criminologists to abandon empirical efforts to falsify their own theory. A more plausible interpretation, however, is that Gottfredson and Hirschi (1986) pushed the logic of their theory to the extreme so as to force a confrontation with the then hegemonic position of the "criminal career" model (Blumstein et al., 1986). Fair enough, but it now seems time to put the "criminal career" weaponry behind us and move on to a more rigorous assessment of stability and change in crime over the life course. As an independent observer has recently commented: "Gottfredson and Hirschi have provided us with the strongest incentive in years to try large-scale protracted prospective longitudinal studies" (Janson, 1994:420).

EXPLAINING STABILITY: THE POPULATION
HETEROGENEITY (STATIC) VIEW

Of course, correlations of stability by themselves tell us nothing about causal process. So to explain stability Gottfredson and Hirschi (1990) propose an individual-level attribute—low self-control—that causes crime at all ages. In other words, Gottfredson and Hirschi's theory posits that self-control differs between individuals but remains constant over time within a given person. This time-invariant or static viewpoint thus argues that stability in crime over the life course is generated by population *heterogeneity* in an underlying

---

[1]In some cases longitudinal data may be gathered cross-sectionally, as exemplified by the use of the retrospective life-history calendar to reconstruct life histories (for an excellent example of this strategy see Horney et al., 1995). But this does not change the fact that the phenomena of stability and change, and the ultimate data and analysis used to assess them, are dynamic in nature. Recognizing this strategy of data collection also seems to take some of the sting out of Gottfredson and Hirschi's (1990, chap. 11) charge that longitudinal research is always expensive and time consuming.

criminal tendency that is established early in life and then remains stable over time. Because individual differences in the propensity to commit crime are stable by adolescence, juvenile and adult crime will be positively but spuriously correlated (due to heterogeneity).

Before entertaining a competing conception of stability over the juvenile and adult years, we would point out a potential contradiction in Gottfredson and Hirschi's theory concerning childhood. This clearly argues that self-control must be taught, that this process is dependent on child rearing, and that it becomes set at about age eight (1990, chap. 5). If this be true, then self-control *changes* over the life-course of children from age zero to about eight. And by defining crime as acts that involve force taken in the pursuit of self interest, one has to conclude that such behavior is rampant among children. Several things follow: "crime" increases from infancy to about age eight and then declines before rising again later in adolescence: intra-individual variability in self-control depends on age; thereby self-control and the causes of "crime" follow an age-graded pattern. So it might be said that HG propose a dynamic theory of child rearing to age eight and from thereafter a static theory. That is, their time-stable heterogeneity thesis actually refers to middle childhood onward. (A time-stable thesis from birth is possible, and has been so invoked by behavioral genetic theorists).

STATE DEPENDENCE
AND CUMULATIVE CONTINUITY

Population heterogeneity is not the only hypothesis to account for the link between delinquency and crime over time. *State dependence* points to the causal role of prior delinquency in facilitating future crime (Nagin & Paternoster, 1991). Although this role is potentially direct and may involve reinforcement on reduced inhibition, we emphasize a developmental model where antisocial behavior has a systematic attenuating effect on the social and institutional bonds linking adults to society (e.g., labor force attachment, marital cohesion). The idea of *cumulative continuity* suggests that delinquency incrementally mortgages the future by generating negative consequences for life chances, especially among stigmatized and institutionalized youth. For example, juvenile incarceration may spark failure in school, unemployment, and weak community bonds, leading in turn to increasing adult crime. In this way, delinquency may lead to the "knifing off" of future opportunities and options for a conventional life. The cumulative continuity of disadvantage is thus not only a result of stable individual differences in criminal propensity, but a *dynamic* process whereby childhood antisocial behavior and adolescent delinquency intensify adult crime through the severance of adult social bonds. On this view, weak social bonding serves as a mediating and hence causal sequential link in a "chain of adversity" between childhood delinquency and adult criminal behavior.

From a research design perspective, the predictions of a "pure" heterogeneity hypothesis may be distinguished from state dependence theory. As

Nagin and Farrington (1992:501) note: "Once relevant time-stable individual differences are established, subsequent individual experiences and circumstances will have no enduring impact on criminal (or noncriminal) trajectories." That is, correlations among adult behaviors (e.g., job instability and crime) are completely spurious and will disappear once controls are introduced for prior individual-level differences in propensity or low self-control (see Gottfredson & Hirschi, 1990:154–168).

Although prior research clearly suggests a link between childhood and adult deviance, the data do not support a pure heterogeneity hypothesis. To evaluate this claim we analyzed the natural histories of two groups of boys who differed dramatically in childhood antisocial behavior and delinquency that followed into adulthood. These life histories were originally gathered by the Gluecks from 500 delinquents and 500 control subjects matched on age, IQ, ethnicity, and neighborhood deprivation. An extensive body of data (e.g., official records, observations, personal interviews with subjects, parents, spouses, neighbors, and employers) was collected on these individuals in childhood, adolescence, young adulthood, and adulthood. Our analyses of these data revealed independent effects of marital attachment and job stability on adult crime. These results were consistent for a wide variety of outcome measures, control variables (e.g., childhood antisocial behavior; IQ, personality attributes), and analytical techniques—including methods that estimate persistent unobserved heterogeneity in criminal propensity (see Sampson & Laub, 1993, chap. 7–8). The research findings of Nagin and Paternoster (1991) also militate against a simple heterogeneity thesis.

Perhaps more interesting, our research also supported the cumulative continuity or *indirect* causation hypothesis. Specifically, adult social ties to work and family were influenced by prior delinquency and official sanctions. Incarceration as a juvenile and as a young adult was negatively related to later job stability, which in turn was negatively related to continued involvement in crime over the life course. Although we found little direct effect of incarceration on subsequent criminality, the indirect "criminogenic" effects through job stability appeared substantively important. Recent research also supports the cumulative continuity thesis by showing detrimental effects of delinquent behavior (Hagan, 1993) and incarceration (Freeman, 1991) on the labor market prospects of young males.

In short, we believe that Hirschi and Gottfredson are too quick to attribute continuity only to time-stable individual traits, thereby neglecting "structured mechanisms of social allocations" (Dannefer, 1987). The channeling of prior differences and the tendency toward cumulation of both advantage and disadvantage is so general that is has been referred to as the "Matthew effect"—"To him who hath shall be given; from him who hath not shall be taken away that which he hath" (Dannefer, 1987:216). Patterson (1993) has offered perhaps the most telling metaphor for understanding the developmental risks of cumulative disadvantage—the "chimera." Examining the course of antisocial behavior, Patterson's model consists of a series of action-reaction sequences across the developmental stages of early childhood, middle childhood, late childhood, and adolescence. He argues that antisocial behavior leads to a "cascade" of secondary problems (e.g., school failure, peer rejection, depressed mood, and involvement with deviant peers) and he is quite explicit that "for problems produced at later stages, antisocial behavior is only an indirect determinant" (Patterson & Yoerger, 1993:145). Appropriately, then, Patterson (1993) refers to the antisocial trait as a "chimera"—a hybrid where qualitative shifts in problem behavior (e.g., academic failure, peer rejection), as well as new forms of antisocial behavior (e.g., substance abuse) are "grafted" onto a core antisocial trait.

Choice and selection

It is important to stress that our theorizing of cumulative continuity and the causal role of salient life experiences in adulthood does not negate HG's emphasis on self-selection and individual differences. By distinguishing self-selection from cumulative continuity we incorporate the independent effects of *both* individual propensity and the dimensions of adult social bonding on adult crime. This distinction is consistent with recent research on homophily in social choices across the life course. As Kandel et al. (1990:221) observe: "although individual choice are made, in part, as a function of the individual's prior attributes, values, and personality characteristics, involvement in the new relationship has further effects and influences on that individual." Similarly, Rutter et al. (1990) and Quinton et al. (1993) found homophily in the choice of marital partners but also a substantial effect of marital cohesion and stable family life that held after the planning of marriage partners was taken into account. We found a similar phenomenon in our re-analyses of the Gluecks' data (Laub & Sampson, 1993).

A major block to integrating selection based models with life-course criminology is thus conception and turns on what we believe is an incorrect interpretation of homophily. For example, HG (1995:138) claim that we view people as "empty vessels" and "passive". Nowhere in our writing, in the account just noted, or in the life-course perspective more generally, does such a notion arise. To assume that individual differences influence the choices one makes in life (which they certainly do), does not mean that social mechanisms emerging from those choices can then have no causal significance.[2] Choices generate constraints *and* opportunities that themselves have effects not solely attributable to individuals. As Horney et al. (1995) observe:

> Persons with a high propensity for crime may be unlikely to graduate from school, unlikely to maintain meaningful employment, and unlikely to stay in stable, committed marriages. Even so, they may *sometimes* go to school, *sometimes* work and *sometimes* live with a wife, and *at those times* they are less likely to commit crimes. Likewise the high-propensity individuals may be involved with drugs and heavy alcohol use, but *sometimes* they do not use these substances and *when they do not* they are less likely to commit crimes.

---

[2] As noted in Laub and Sampson (1993), even homophily, though usually attributed to self-selection, is profoundly shaped by structural constraints.

The peer-delinquency correlate is another example of the dual influence of selection and causation—we may choose our friends but they still influence our behavior (see especially Thornberry et al., 1994). As situational theorists have long pointed out, the same person—with the same attributes and traits—often acts very differently in different situations.

We think it is resolved, therefore, that heterogeneity and state dependence need not be mutually exclusive phenomena—both operate over the life-course of individuals. Put more concretely and integrating the theory of Gottfredson and Hirschi as at one point they seem to allow (1990:87–88, 115), stable levels of self-control combine with time-varying social factors (including but limited to social controls) to explain criminal offending across the life-course. From this view, drug or alcohol intoxication, job instability, and other "local life circumstances" (Horney et al., 1995) attain causal significance. Hence if Gottfredson and Hirschi's theory relaxes the rigid assumption of an "invariant" direct effect of self-control on adult behavior, many new research opportunities emerge. The integration of rational choice, situational, and social control theories with a life-course perspective that respects yet is not reducible to individual differences in self-control seems an especially promising avenue of future advances in criminological theory (see Nagin & Paternoster, 1993).

CHANGE MATTERS TOO

Whether generated by self-selection or cumulative disadvantage, a focus on stability is nonetheless insufficient for understanding crime over the life course. Stability correlations, corrected for measurement error, average about .6 to .7—leaving roughly 50% of the variance to change (see also Janson, 1994). Relatedly, the prediction literature in criminology has long been plagued with high hopes yet weak results—false positives and false negatives are rife. More generally, lives are often unpredictable and dynamic; *exogenous* changes are ever present. Many changes in life result from chance or random events in individual lives (Laub & Sampson, 1993), while other changes in life direction stem from macro-level "exogenous shocks" largely beyond the pale of individual choice (e.g., war, depression, natural disasters, revolutions, plant closings, industrial restructuring).

We shall not repeat our findings on how changes in the adult life course influence changes in crime because that was a central and lengthy component of *Crime in the Making* (see also Laub & Sampson, 1993). Suffice to say that our theory and analysis suggest that turning points in the adult life-course—especially regarding employment, the military, and marriage—predict changes in crime. In other words, there is much intra-individual variability in the adult life-course that, by definition, is not reducible to levels of self-control that remain constant within individuals.

Other research has also begun to demonstrate the independent explanatory power of adult life-course changes on adult deviance, self-selection notwithstanding (e.g., Rutter et al., 1990; Farrington & West, 1995). In probably the most sophisticated micro-level research to date, Horney et al. (1995) show the life-course effects of within-individual changes in drug use, schooling, and marriage on changes in criminal offending, independent of propensity. Overall, extant research contradicts the argument put forth by self-control theory that changes in life events can have *no* explanatory power.

Versatility and the "opportunity" clause

It is important to note that the logic of versatility works against the claim that "opportunity" explains all within-individual variability in crime not accounted for by low self-control (1995:140). Consider that HG rely heavily on empirical evidence showing versatility in crime—offenders tend not to specialize. The logical implication is that opportunities are ubiquitous for an undifferentiated or non-specialized propensity—*some* crime is always possible for those low in self-control. To use but one example, it cannot reasonably be claimed that periods of quiescence or intermittency in a high-rate offender's career are due to lack of "opportunity." (The exception would seem to be incarceration or complete disability, factors we explicitly controlled in our empirical analysis). To be sure, inner-city ghetto youth might not be able to commit insider trading, and rich suburbanites might not have access to drug trafficking networks in their neighborhoods. But if there is no specialization in propensity as HG claim (1990:91–97), every day, every one, has the opportunity to commit some crime or break some law. If so inclined, we can all: steal from a store; hit a neighbor, friend, or spouse; break the window or a car; or whatever. Using ubiquitous "opportunity factors" as a catch-all to explain away variations in crime not attributed to self control thus reduces the plausibility and testability of their theory.

EXPLAINING THE CORRELATES

In another apparent source of disagreement Hirschi and Gottfredson pit the life-course perspective against the "agreed-upon" correlates of delinquency, implying that longitudinal research is unnecessary because it produces the same correlates as cross-sectional research.[3] We are surprised that HG see consensus in the field on correlates of delinquency such as social class, race, and IQ. Arguments about all three correlates continue to abound.

Even assuming consensus on the list of correlates, however, there is little if any consensus in the field of criminology over *why* or *how* these correlates come about. Indeed, HG seem to agree that the fact of a correlation is merely the beginning of matters—more interesting are the explanatory mechanisms. For example, going back to *Causes of Delinquency* (1969), Hirschi has been embroiled in disputes over why peer delinquency is such a strong correlate of

---

[3]It would seem that, by this logic, we do not need more cross-sectional research either because it too keeps producing the same correlates.

delinquency. He asserts the importance of self-selection and "flocking together," while others point to social learning and peer influence. Obviously, the development of new knowledge in criminology will involve explicating the processes and intervening mechanisms that explain correlates such as delinquent peers. This research effort will involve both cross-sectional and longitudinal designs—the choice of which should depend on the theory involved. HG should be free to test cross-sectional hypotheses without recourse to longitudinal data—and likewise dynamic theories (e.g., Thornberry, 1987) should not be required to embrace static research designs. In this sense we agree with HG insofar as we understand their position.

Where we do disagree concerns their claim (p. 133) that our age-graded theory rests upon correlates at odds with known research. Readers of our book will discover that in childhood our theory focuses on family process (e.g., discipline, monitoring, attachment), in adolescence our attention expands to schools, peer groups, and the juvenile justice system, while in the transition to young adulthood we focus on the institutions of employment, marriage, prison, and the military. These are age-graded institutions in a legal as well as developmental sense—being drafted by the army is not relevant to a 10 year old, nor is marriage or employment. And we doubt that, say, parental supervision is a good candidate for understanding crime in middle age.

Because it is nowhere in dispute that individuals face shifting sources of social control as they age, the only way Hirschi and Gottfredson's critique makes logical sense is to assert that all explanatory variables, at all ages, are simple *outcomes* (manifestations) of one prior variable—low self-control. Again they make just such an argument, claiming, for example, that unemployment–crime and divorce–crime connections are "merely illustrations of the versatility of offenders and the enduring consequences of low self-control" (p. 9). In other words, HG are forced by the logic of self-control theory to conceptualize all instance of unemployment and divorce as forms of "offending" or "criminality."[4] And though ambiguous in their writings, if *social* controls are rendered completely endogenous by self-control theory (including, for example, parental attachment and supervision), Hirschi's theory and empirical findings in *Causes of Delinquency* must also be rejected.

Of course, this returns us once again to the selection-causation debate for which we have already stated our position. We would add here only that nowhere did we say that all correlates need to be (or are) age-graded, nor that life-course research designs are always necessary. Rather, we posited a theory that directs attention to age-graded processes of informal social control over the life course, and thereby a longitudinal design. As long as we do not foist our choice of theory upon others, we do not see how HG can disagree with our methodological stance: "There must be an intimate connection between the conceptualization of a problem and the design of research focused on that problem" (Gottfredson & Hirschi, 1990:252).

---

[4]If they do allow "exogenous" (i.e., non self-control) variations in these constructs across time, then our change arguments takes hold.

ON AGE, CRIME, AND VARIABILITY IN LIVES

In criticizing the life-course perspective, Hirschi and Gottfredson continue to rely on their well-known thesis of age-crime invariance. Downplaying secular change in particular, they state that ". . . there are no substantively important deviations from the general age distribution that can be traced to characteristics of persons, historical, or cohort effects" (1995:135). As noted before, much has been written on this issue and we do not wish to cover all known territory. We thus restrict our attention to key points that bear on research design and testing the age-crime thesis.

First, from a life-course perspective the aggregate age-invariance thesis is difficult, if not impossible, to falsify because invariance is defined to include variance. In other words, departures from the age-invariance pattern are treated as "insubstantial," and in fact HG allow variance in the parameters of the age-crime curve (such as mean and variance). But unless there is a stated threshold or agreed-upon calibration of variation, there can be no resolution. For example, what are we to make of findings such as those of Greenberg (1994), who shows that the age of peak involvement in homicide declined from age 24 in 1952 to age 18 in 1987? He concluded that "If this is not evidence for dramatic historical variability, it is hard to imagine what would be" (p. 370). From the static perspective these variations are just noise, while from the life-course perspective it is precisely these sorts of historical shifts that are interesting and must be explained. Specifying and accounting for age-crime parameter variance (e.g., mean, kurtosis) under conditions of "mathematical form" (shape) invariance has been suggested as one way to break the stalemate (see Britt, 1994:378).

Second, the explicit prediction of Hirschi and Gottfredson's theory is that age-crime trajectories are invariant across individuals. This prediction has been directly tested in a series of recent analyses by Nagin and colleagues (see e.g., Nagin & Land, 1993). Their results show differential trajectories of offending through time that do not match the aggregate age-crime curve and that cannot be interpreted from the perspective of a time-stable trait alone (Nagin, Farrington, & Moffitt, 1995; see also Harada, 1994).

Third, within historical periods there is also much more heterogeneity (lack of invariance?) in the aggregate age by crime-type relationship than HG seem willing to acknowledge. For example, Hirschi and Gottfredson claim that:

> Because the peak age of crime comes so early in the life course, the vast majority of the acts of concern to criminologists are those committed by young people. As a result, the current fascination with factors affecting post-adolescent crime trajectories is hard to justify on theoretical or policy grounds (1995:136).

Yet the fact is that the majority of arrestees are adults, a matter of deep policy concern reflected in rising U.S. imprisonment rates. 1990 data from the *Uniform Crime Reports* (UCR) reveal that adults age 21 or older represented 69 percent of those arrested for violent 69 percent of those arrested for violent crime, 53 percent of those arrested for property crime, and 70 percent of those arrested for total crime. UCR data from 1988 shows that the mean age of arrestees was 28 for violent crime and 25 for property crime. Self-reported offending data and victims' reports of the ages of offenders also demonstrate that adults are heavily involved in criminal behavior, especially domestic violence. Empirically, then, we do not see how post-adolescent crime is a problem that can be trivialized.

Other forms of deviance such as gambling, savings and loan fraud, ghost payrolling, police corruption, alcoholism, and alimony default show an even greater divergence from the aggregate age-crime pattern.[5] Moreover, in contrast to ordinary crimes, age curves for lucrative criminality not only peak much later but tend not to decline rapidly with age (Steffensmeier et al., 1989:827). Interestingly, these patterns shed another light on HG's argument—if "crime" declines with age and self-control remains stable, then other forms of non-crime "deviance" must take up the slack (Gottfredson & Hirschi, 1990:91–94). But this is another way of saying there is an age-graded pattern of deviance (heterotypic continuity) across the life-course.

Finally, the invariance thesis does not leave room for variations in the social, historical, and cultural context of aging itself. As Modell (1989) shows, the cultural cues for appropriate developmental transitions throughout an individual's life course have dramatically shifted over this century. Birth, puberty, and death are biological facts, but social definitions of age status, normative divisions of the life-course, and age norms as expressed in timetables for lines of action are socially constructed. Consistent with this idea, Harada (1994) finds that the criminal behavior of school-age youths in Japan is more related to "social" age (measured as school year) than "biological" age. Moreover, the life-course timing of biological events clearly matters, as shown in the link between age at menarche and female delinquency (Caspi et al., 1993).

Against the backdrop of a general age-crime curve, and consistent with the working principles of a life-course perspective, the data thus conflict with the strict age-invariance thesis that: 1) all antisocial behaviors peak in late adolescence, 2) there are no substantive individual, cohort, historical, or cultural differences in this relationship, and 3) all anti-social behaviors decline precipitously and continuously throughout life.

THINKING ABOUT EXPERIMENTS

Hirschi and Gottfredson suggest that a life-course perspective is undermined by experimental research and treatment literature showing little or no effect of "institutions" on crime (see also Gottfredson & Hirschi, 1990:236–239). We

---

[5]Although beyond the scope of this paper, a related concern is HG's restricted definition of "crime" limited to acts of force or fraud committed *in the pursuit of self-interest* (1990:15). Crimes not obviously regulated by self-interest, such as collective violence, terrorism, hate violence, ethnic cleansing, civil warfare, suicide bombings, and so on, are bracketed by their theory as irrelevant to the age-crime debate. Although difficult to accurately measure, we find these offenses quite interesting theoretically and are not convinced that they follow an invariant age-crime curve.

agree that such research is relevant to the debate, but observe that few, if any, research efforts have randomly allocated jobs (especially residential-based job training) or marriages.[6] Also, the effectiveness of rehabilitative interventions in reducing criminal behavior is not as dismal as common wisdom ("nothing works") allows (Andrews et al., 1990).

We wonder as well why Hirschi and Gottfredson did not turn the experimental spotlight on the thesis that increasing self-control—which according to their theory can be taught—reduces crime. Extending the logic of a selection critique, will not conduct disordered children with low self-control disrupt efforts at family management (Lytton, 1990), hence producing "spurious" family effects? In this sense children contaminate or select the "treatment"—in fact, by running away from home, children may be said to "choose" their parental dosage. And since "such treatment must come from adults" (Gottfredson & Hirschi, 1990:269), why would we expect low self-control adults (the ones with poor child-rearing skills) to *change*? That is, how does one induce a low self-control parent to care about their child if change in adulthood is not possible?

All told, we find the experimental literature on treatment to be neutral with respect to both life-course *and* self-control theory. Gottfredson and Hirschi (1990:269) would apparently agree: "In our view, treatment need not be derived from or consistent with a theory of crime causation . . . It is, therefore, an illegitimate criticism of positivistic theories and the crime-causal research they generate to say that they have spawned or somehow supported ineffective treatment efforts."

CONCLUSION

The field of criminology in indebted to Hirschi and Gottfredson for redirecting our attention to the importance of early child rearing. The resulting concept of self-control is also clearly important, and will continue to guide empirical research. But, since it seems equally clear that self-control is only one factor among many, we are puzzled about why they insist that low self-control is the cause of crime for all individuals, at all ages, at all times, and in all places. Lest there by any confusion on the sweeping nature of their claim: "low self-control is a unitary phenomenon that absorbs its causes such that it becomes, for all intents and purposes, *the* individual-level cause of crime" (Gottfredson & Hirschi, 1990:232, emphasis in original). Pushing further the logic of the

---

[6]One analogy has been the random allocation of financial aid in the Transitional Aid Research Project (TARP), which yielded controversial and complex results that provide ammunition to both sides. The only research design of which we are aware that assigned *residential-based* job training to ex-felons is the Job Corps program where economically disadvantaged, high-rate youthful offenders were removed from their neighborhoods and provided 7-month job training. Compared with the control group, there was a significant reduction in future recidivism (Mallar et al., 1982). Even here, however, the results are not definitive and selection bias remains a concern.

claim that crime propensity is a "property of individuals" (1995:21), that "only crime can predict crime" (1990:233), and hence that meaningful individual (and macrosocial?) change is not possible, Hirschi and Gottfredson (1995) seems to conclude that criminology has nothing to learn from other disciplines, and certainly from no theory other than self-control theory.

To be sure, this isolationist view and rejection of the life-course perspective, along with sociological theories in general, is consistent with Hirschi's (1979) earlier position against theoretical integration. Arguing for theoretical parsimony and consistency, they would no doubt say we have integrated theoretical assumptions and ideas that are fundamentally contradictory—especially the co-existence of stability and change. But this critique is itself based on epistemological assumptions about the ordered and predictable ways in which lives unfold (Kagan, 1980).[7] In other words, it is questionable whether the notion of consistency is one that should be applied to understanding the human experience. Individuals confront ambiguity, change, and contradictions throughout their lives; indeed, constructing a coherent personal narrative on sometimes disorderly lives is one of the dominant struggles that life-course research has uncovered (Cohler, 1982).

In conclusion, then, we hope to have shown that the nuts and bolts of life-course inquiry—aging (social and biological), narrative (see also Abbott, 1992), stability, change, human agency, cohort, and historical period—yield powerful insights directly related to the substantive phenomenon of crime. We hope as well that we have demonstrated that our theory of informal social control is not owned by a particular research design. We view controls as varying within and between individuals, through historical time, and across place—consequently, control theory may be tested at the individual level (both cross-sectionally and longitudinally), historically, and at the macrosocial level, again both cross-sectionally and longitudinally. We thus believe the life-course perspective presents an exciting and challenging research agenda for criminology, and that the empirical evidence will continue to underscore the utility of a dynamic understanding of crime over the life course. But only time, of course, will tell.

REFERENCES

Abbott, A. (1992). From causes to events: Notes on narrative positivism. *Sociological Methods and Research* 20:428–455.

Andrews, D., Zinger, I., Hoge R., Bonta, J., Gendreau, P. & Cullen, F. (1990). Does correctional treatment work? A clinically relevant and psychologically informed meta-analysis. *Criminology* 28:369–404.

Blumstein, A., Cohen, J., Roth, J. A. & Visher, C. A., eds. (1986). *Criminal careers and "career criminals"*. Washington, D.C.: National Academy Press.

---

[7]For example, Jerome Kagan argues that notions of stability comport with larger ideas on the universe as a rational order undisturbed by arbitrariness, contingency, and situation. He suggests that this "faith in connectedness" has led developmental psychologists to be permissive regarding the validity of facts supporting the hypothesis of a static, unbroken trail from childhood to adulthood (1980:44).

Britt, C. L. (1994). Model specification and interpretation: A reply to Greenberg. *Journal of Quantitative Criminology* 10:375–379.

Caspi, A., Lynam, D., Moffitt, T. & Silva, P. (1993). Unraveling girls' delinquency: Biological, dispositional, and contextual contributions to adolescent misbehavior. *Developmental Psychology* 29:19–30.

Caspi, A., Elder, G. H. Jr. & Herbener, E.S. (1990). Childhood personality and the prediction of life-course patterns. In: Robins, L. & Rutter, M., eds. *Straight and Devious Pathways from Childhood to Adulthood*. Cambridge: Cambridge University Press.

Cohler, B. (1982). Personal narrative and the life course. Life-Span Development and Behavior, Vol. 4. New York: Academic.

Dannefer, D. (1987). Aging as intracohort differentiation: Accentuation, the Matthew effect, and the life course. *Sociological Forum* 2:211–236.

Elder, G.H., Jr. (1975). Age differentiation and the life course. *Annual Review of Sociology* 1:165–190.

Elder, G.H., Jr. (1985). Perspectives on the life course. In: Elder, G.H., Jr. *Life Course Dynamics*. Ithaca: Cornell University Press.

Farrington, D. P. (1986). Stepping stones to adult criminal careers. In: Olweus, D., Block, J. & Radke-Yarrow, M., eds. *Development of Antisocial and Prosocial Behavior*, New York: Academic Press.

Farrington, D. P. & West, D. J. (1995). The effects of marriage, separation, and children on offending by adult males. In: Smith Blau, Z. & Hagan, J., eds. *Current Perspectives on Aging and the Life Cycle*. Volume 4: *Delinquency and Disrepute in the Life Course: Contextual and Dynamic Analyses*. CT: JAI Press.

Freeman, R. (1991). Crime and the employment of disadvantaged youth. Cambridge: National Bureau of Economic Research Working Paper 3875.

Gottfredson, M. & Hirschi, T. (1986). The true value of lambda would appear to be zero: An essay on career criminals, criminal careers, selective incapacitation, cohort studies, and related topics. *Criminology* 24: 213–234.

Gottfredson, M. & Hirschi. T. (1990). *A General Theory of Crime*. Stanford: Stanford University Press.

Greenberg, D. F. (1994). The historical variability of the age-crime relationship. *Journal of Quantitative Criminology* 10:361–373.

Hagan, J. (1993). The social embeddedness of crime and unemployment. *Criminology* 31:465–491.

Harada, Y. (1994). A longitudinal analysis of juvenile arrest histories of the 1970 birth cohort in Japan. In: Weitekamp, E. & Kerner, H.-J., eds. *Cross-national longitudinal research on human development and criminal behavior*. Dordrecht/Boston/London: Kluwer.

Hirschi, T. (1969). *Causes of delinquency*. Berkeley: University of California Press.

Hirschi, T. (1979). Separate and unequal is better. *Journal of Research in Crime and Delinquency*. 16:34–38.

Hirschi, T. & Gottfredson, M. (1995). Control theory and the life course perspective. *Studies on Crime and Crime Prevention*, 4:131–143.

Horney, J. D., Osgood, W. & Marshall, I. (1995). Criminal careers in the short term: Intra-individual variability in crime and its relation to local life circumstances. *American Sociological Review* 60: 655–673.

Janson, C.-G. (1994). A case for a longitudinal study. In: Weitekamp, E. & Kerner, H.-J., eds. *Cross-National Longitudinal Research on Human Development and Criminal Behavior*. Dordrecht/Boston/London: Kluwer.

Kagan, J. (1980). Perspectives on continuity. In: Brim Jr., O.G. & Kagan, J., eds. *Constancy and Change in Human Development*. Cambridge: Harvard University Press.

Kandel, D., Davies, M. & Baydar, N. (1990). The creation of interpersonal contexts: Homophily in dyadic relationships in adolescence and young adulthood. In: Robins, L. & Rutter,

M., eds. *Straight and Devious Pathways from Childhood to Adulthood*. New York: Cambridge University Press.

Kornhauser, R. (1978). *Social sources of delinquency*. Chicago: University of Chicago Press.

Laub, J. H. & Sampson, R. J. (1993). Turning points in the life course: Why change matters to the study of crime. *Criminology* 31:301–325.

Loeber, R. & LeBlanc, M. (1990). Toward a developmental criminology. In: Tonry, M. & Morris, N., eds. *Crime and Justice* (Volume 12). Chicago: University of Chicago Press.

Lytton, H. (1990). Child and parent effects in boys' conduct disorder: A reinterpretation. *Developmental Psychology* 26: 683–697.

Mallar, C., Kerachsky, S., Thornton, C. & Long, D. (1982). Evaluation of the economic impact of the job corps program. Third follow-up report. Princeton, N.J.: Mathematica Policy Research, Inc.

Modell, J. (1989). *Into one's own: From youth to adulthood in the United States, 1920–1975*. Berkeley: University of California.

Nagin, D. & Paternoster, R. (1991). On the relationship of past and future participation in delinquency. *Criminology* 29: 163–190.

Nagin, D. & Paternoster, R. (1993). Enduring individual differences and rational choice theories of crime. *Law and Society Review* 27:467–496.

Nagin, D. & Farrington, D. (1992). The onset and persistence of offending. *Criminology* 30:501–523.

Nagin, D. & Land, K. (1993). Age, criminal careers, and population heterogeneity: Specification and estimation of a nonparametric, mixed poisson model. *Criminology* 31:327–362.

Nagin, D., Farrington, D. & Moffitt, T. (1995). Life-course trajectories of different types of offenders. *Criminology* 33: 111–140.

Patterson, G. R. (1993). Orderly change in a stable world: The antisocial trait as a chimera. *Journal of Consulting and Clinical Psychology* 61:911–919.

Patterson, G. R. & Yoerger, K. (1993). Developmental models for delinquent behavior. In: Hodgins, S., ed. *Mental Disorder and Crime*. Newbury Park, CA: Sage.

Quinton, D., Pickles, A., Maughan, B. & Rutter, M. (1993). Partners, peers, and pathways: Assortative pairing and continuities in conduct disorder. *Development and Psychopathology* 5:763–783.

Rutter, M., Quinton, D. & Hill, J. (1990). Adult outcomes of institution-reared children: Males and females compared. In: Robins, L. & Rutter, M., eds. *Straight and Devious Pathways from Childhood to Adulthood*. New York: Cambridge University Press.

Sampson, R. J. & Laub, J. H. (1992). Crime and deviance in the life course. *Annual Review of Sociology* 18:63–84.

Sampson, R. J. & Laub, J. H. (1993). *Crime in the making: Pathways and turning points through life*. Cambridge: Harvard University Press.

Steffensmeier, D., Allan, E., Harer, M. & Sreifel, C. (1989). Age and the distribution of crime. *American Journal of Sociology* 94:803–831.

Thornberry, T. P. (1987). Toward an interaction theory of delinquency. *Criminology* 25:863–891.

Thornberry, T.P., Lizotte, A., Krohn, M., Farnworth, M. & Sung Joon Jang. (1994). Delinquent peers, beliefs, and delinquent behavior: A longitudinal text of interactional theory. *Criminology* 32:47–84.

Understanding Persistence in Criminal Behavior

O ne of the more recognized findings in criminological research is that offending behavior is highly stable over time and across situations. In fact, prior offending participation is perhaps the strongest predictor of future offending behavior. The two articles included in this section illustrate varying approaches toward examining offending stability.

One of the most important studies on offending stability was conducted by Huesmann and his colleagues in 1984. Using data from over 600 persons in New York State spanning a 22-year period, the study revealed a number of interesting findings. First, the more aggressive 8-year-olds at the beginning of the study were found to be the more aggressive 30-year-olds at the end of the study. Second, early aggressiveness was predictive of antisocial behavior in the future, including spouse abuse, traffic violations, and physical aggression. Third, the stability of aggression across generations was higher than within individual stability across ages. Huesmann and his colleagues argued that aggression is a persistent trait that is highly stable across time and situations that can be influenced by situational variables.

Of more recent interest in criminology is the issue of understanding whether offending stability reflects a state dependent (SD) or persistent heterogeneity (PH) process. Although it is clear that there is a strong correlation between past offending and offending in the future, criminologists assert that the interpretation of the relationship is currently unclear. One view holds that persistent individual level differences (i.e., heterogeneity) in criminal propensity actually render the positive association between past and future offending spurious, because the tendency to offend remains stable or fixed over time. A competing view argues that past offending behavior is causally linked with future crime. In other words, previous offending experiences further increase, for reasons such as social learning, labeling, and so on, the likelihood of criminal activity in the future.

Applying these dual interpretations of offending stability (PH vs. SD), the second paper by Paternoster and his colleagues extends this issue to assess stability in offending for discrete groups of offenders. Their study examines whether persistent heterogeneity and state-dependent interpretations hold for high and low criminal-propensity offenders. Using data from males that were released from training schools in North Carolina, the results reveal that (1) both heterogeneity and state-dependent effects impact offending stability, and (2) these effects are largely, but not exclusively, invariant across high and low criminal propensity groups. The study by Paternoster and his colleagues is consistent with theories that allow for both persistent heterogeneity and state dependent effects in criminal careers, and that do not make distinctions between discrete offending groups.

Offending stability represents an important issue in criminology. The papers included in this section illustrate both the complexity in empirically examining the positive association between past and future offending as well as in identifying the most defensible interpretation of the relationship. The empirical research to date suggests that both state-dependent and persistent heterogeneity interpretations may be necessary for a more complete understanding of criminal behavior over the life course.

SUGGESTED READINGS

Dean, C. W., Brame, R., & Piquero, A. R. (1996). Criminal propensity, discrete offender groups, and persistence in crime. *Criminology, 34,* 547–574.

Nagin, D., & Paternoster, R. (1991). On the relationship between past and future offending. *Criminology, 29,* 163–190.

Nagin, D., & Farrington, D. (1992). The stability of criminal potential from childhood to adulthood. *Criminology, 30,* 235–260.

Olweus, D. (1979). Stability of aggressive reaction patterns in males: A review. *Psychological Bulletin, 86,* 852–875.

Robins, L. (1978). Sturdy predictors of adult antisocial behavior: Replications from longitudinal studies. *Psychological Medicine, 8,* 611–622.

11

Stability of Aggression
Over Time and Generations*

L. ROWELL HUESMANN
LEONARD D. ERON
MONROE M. LEFKOWITZ
LEOPOLD O. WALDER

ABSTRACT   In a study spanning 22 years, data were collected on the aggressiveness of over 600 subjects, their parents, and their children. Subjects who were the more aggressive 8-year-olds at the beginning of the study were discovered to be the more aggressive 30-year-olds at the end of the study. The stability of aggressive behavior was shown to be very similar to the stability of intellectual competence, especially for males. Early aggressiveness was predictive of later serious antisocial behavior, including criminal behavior, spouse abuse, traffic violations, and self-reported physical aggression. Furthermore, the stability of aggression across generations within a family when measured at comparable ages was even higher than the within individual stability across ages. It is concluded that, whatever its causes, aggression can be viewed as a persistent trait that may be influenced by situational variables but possesses substantial cross-situational constancy.

I nterpersonal aggression is a problem whose dimensions in terms of cost to life and property are obviously staggering. Decades of research into the root causes of aggression have yielded numerous models purporting to explain the ontogeny of different aspects of aggressive behavior. Yet, there is little sign that the responses of either the criminal justice or psychological establishments based on these theories have had much impact. It now seems clear that a major reason for such failures is that aggression is a relatively stable, self-perpetuating

SOURCE: *Developmental Psychology,* Vol. 20, No. 6, pp. 1120–1134. © 1984 by the American Psychological Assn. Reprinted by permission.

*This study was supported in part by Grant MH-34410 to Leonard D. Eron from the National Institute of Mental Health. Portions of this article were presented at the meetings of the Society for Research on Child Development in Detroit, Michigan, in April 1983. The first two authors contributed equally to the article, with Eron primarily responsible for initiating the study and providing the theoretical framework and Huesmann primarily responsible for directing the collection and analysis of the data.

Eric Dubow, Richard Romanoff, Rafi Seli, and Patty Warnick-Yarmel assisted in collection and analysis of the data.

behavior that is not readily amenable to change by the time it usually comes to the attention of society.

Aggression as a characteristic way of solving social problems usually emerges early in life. Genetic, physiological, and other constitutional factors undoubtedly play a role in many cases, but the presence of the "appropriate learning conditions" is probably more important in most cases (Eron, Walder, & Lefkowitz, 1971; Lefkowitz, Eron, Walder, & Huesmann, 1977). The "appropriate learning conditions" seem to be those in which the child has many opportunities to observe aggression, in which the child is reinforced for his or her own aggression, and in which the child is the object of aggression. Nevertheless, in such situations only some children become seriously aggressive. Yet by themselves, simple observational learning and reinforcement models do not seem to be adequate explanations. An extensive array of environmental, familial, and child characteristics have been shown to be weakly predictive of which child will be more aggressive; yet, none could be called a sufficient or necessary condition for antisocial aggression. Severe antisocial, aggressive behavior seems to occur only when there is a convergence of a number of these factors during a child's development (Eron, 1982).

Despite the considerable evidence that severe, antisocial aggression is greatly affected by the environmental and learning conditions to which the child is exposed, there is accumulating evidence that each individual develops a characteristic level of aggressiveness, which remains relatively stable across situations. The current study extends the investigation of this stability across decades and generations. However, the stability of aggressive behavior over shorter time periods has already been documented by Olweus (1979). In his review of 16 separate studies with lags ranging from 6 months to 21 years, Olweus has demonstrated the stability of aggressive behavior in males. The disattenuated stability coefficients ranged from .98 for Olweus' (1977) own study of eighty-five 13-year-olds in Sweden over a 1-year lag to .36 for Kagan and Moss's (1962) study of thirty-six 5-year-olds, who were followed for 18 years. Unfortunately, only one investigation with a lag of 5 years or more involved a substantial sample size—Eron, Huesmann, Lefkowitz, and Walders's (1972) study of 211 boys and 216 girls over a 10-year lag. Olweus (1978) found that stability coefficients generally decreased linearly with lag. However, his data also reveal that for the same length lag, stabilities are greater for older boys than younger boys. Thus, the decrease in stability with time is almost certainly nonlinear and approaches asymptote for longer lags.

In his 1979 review, Olweus reported little stability data for girls. However, limited data do exist. In their longitudinal study of children from age 8 to 19, Eron et al. (1972) found that the stability of aggression for girls was slightly higher than for boys. However, Olweus (1981) located five other longitudinal studies involving girls, and among these the stability of aggression for the girls was consistently lower than for comparable samples of boys. Nevertheless, aggression in girls has been reasonably stable in all of these investigations.

Two very recent reports have added to the evidence suggesting that aggression is a stable trait. Roff and Wirt (1984) followed a sample of over 500 low-peer-status boys and over 500 low-peer-status girls through archival record sources into young adulthood. They found that primary school measures of aggression were significantly related to later delinquency and criminal behavior for males but not for females. However, Moskowitz and Schwartzman (1983) followed a sample of 377 aggressive or aggressive and withdrawn children for 3 years and found substantial stabilities for both boys and girls.

Although these existing studies seem to establish fairly clearly that aggressiveness is not a transient behavior for most children, they can be criticized on a number of grounds. In many of the studies, for example, Kagan and Moss (1962), the sample size was quite small, and the longitudinal correlations may therefore be inaccurate estimations of the population correlations. In several studies, for example, Roff and Wirt (1984), only a subsample of children who were initially at the extremes of the distribution were retested. Such a restriction in the range of the sample may yield stability coefficients that underestimate the population coefficients. Although Olweus (1979) eliminated from his review studies in which the primary measure of aggression at both times was self-report, communalities in other measurement procedures over time may have contributed to the apparent stability. Finally, although aggression has been measured in a variety of ways in the existing studies, only a few researchers have examined the extent to which their measures of childhood aggression relate to adult criminality and antisocial behavior in males and females.

The current study has overcome most of these problems. In it a substantial sample of males and females were examined at three times over the course of 22 years on multiple measures of aggression, including antisocial and criminal behavior. The stability of an hypothesized latent trait of aggression was then tested with linear structural models that allow the different measures of aggression to be integrated.

METHOD

Subjects

The subjects originally comprised the entire population of youngsters enrolled in the third grade in a semi-rural county in New York State (Columbia County). This included approximately 870 youngsters whose modal age at the time was 8 years. These youngsters were tested in their classrooms with a variety of procedures. We also interviewed personally approximately 75% of their mothers and fathers. Ten years later, we reinterviewed 427 of the original subjects (211 boys, 216 girls; modal age, 19). A small subsample was also interviewed at modal age 13, but these data reflect too limited and biased a sample to be considered in this article. However, the stability data from both the 10-year lag and the two 5-year lags have been reported elsewhere (Eron et al., 1972; Lefkowitz, Eron, Walder, & Huesmann, 1972; Olweus, 1979).

In 1981 we again tracked down as many of the original subjects as possible. Their modal age was now 30. We were able to locate and interview 295 of the original subjects in person and another 114 by mail and telephone for a total of 409 (198 males, 211 females). We were also successful in obtaining interviews with the spouses of 165 of the interviewed subjects and with 82 of the subjects' own children who at the time were approximately the same age as the subjects when first seen in 1960. Children under 5 were not interviewed, and only one child (the oldest) from each family was interviewed. Nevertheless, the 82 children interviewed represent over half of those reinterviewed subjects who had children. Thus, there are substantial samples of data on aggression about and from three generations within the subject's family: the subject and the subject's spouse, the subject's parents, and the subject's child.

In addition to the interview, we obtained data from the New York State Divisions of Criminal Justice Services and Motor Vehicles about the subjects who were interviewed and any other subjects who were in the original sample but whom we did not see for follow-up interviews. We obtained at least some data from these archives on 542 of our original subjects. Coupled with the interview data, this gave us some 1981 follow-up data on 632 of our original subjects (358 males, 274 females). Of these, 366 had also been interviewed after the 10-year lag in 1970.

Early Measures

Beginning from a definition of aggression as "an act whose goal response is injury to an organism or organism surrogate" (Dollard, Doob, Miller, Mower, & Sears, 1939, p. 11), Eron and his colleagues developed in the 50s a technique for measuring a child's aggressiveness in everyday life (Eron et al., 1971; Walder, Abelson, Eron, Banta, & Laulicht, 1971).

This technique, the peer-nomination index of aggression, was used as the primary measure of child aggression in 1960. With this procedure, each child's aggression score is derived from the responses of a sample of his or her peers— usually classmates. The procedure is to have all children in the sample name as many other children in the sample as they wish who behave in a certain way, for example, "Who pushes or shoves children?" The aggression score is the percentage of times a child is nominated on 10 aggression items out of the potential number of times he or she could have been nominated. The scale was established only after an extensive developmental period and possesses exceptional psychometric properties. In a recent sample of 748 children, the scale's internal consistency (coefficient alpha) was found to be .96 and its 1-month test–retest reliability was .91 (Huesmann, Lagerspetz, & Eron, 1984). Its criterion validity has been established by numerous studies relating children's peer nomination scores to their scores on other measures of aggression (Eron et al., 1971). Its construct validity has been established by its ability to predict the gender, age, and other differences that most theories of aggression predict (Eron et al., 1971; Lefkowitz, Eron, Walder, & Huesmann, 1977; Huesmann et al., 1984).

Over the course of 25 years, the peer-nomination measure has been used in at least 10 countries in over 50 different studies with consistent success (e.g., Feshbach & Singer, 1971; Olweus, 1979; Pitkannen-Pulkkinen, 1979; Sand et al., 1975).

Another variable recorded during the first wave that reflects primarily the subject's parents' aggression was the severity of punishment the parents reported they would use in response to specific misdeeds by the subject. The misdeeds were the same as those used in the peer-nomination questions. In addition to the aggression measures, we obtained an IQ score for each child during the first wave with the California Test of Mental Maturity (Sullivan, Clark, & Tiegs, 1957). The stability of intellectual competence over time will be reported for our sample to provide an anchor for the interpretation of the stability of aggression. Because IQ and aggression are usually negatively correlated, the effects of IQ also were partialed out from the stability coefficients for aggression.

Later Measures

Indications of the subjects' aggression 22 years later at age 30 were derived from self-ratings, ratings of the subject by the spouse, and citations of offenses by the New York State Divisions of Criminal Justice and Traffic. Self-ratings included the sum of Minnesota Multiphasic Personality Inventory (MMPI) scales *F*, 4 and 9, which previous research (Huesmann, Lefkowitz, & Eron, 1978) has indicated is a reliable and valid measure of overt aggression, and the subject's self-report of committing physical aggression against others. Ratings by the spouse of the subject's aggression included behavior directed toward him or her by the subject. The items came from the Straus Home Violence Questionnaire (Straus, Giles, & Steinmetz, 1979). The Criminal Justice scores were the total number of convictions in New York State in the previous 10 years and ratings of the seriousness of the corresponding offenses. The latter is a system used by the New York State Criminal Justice Division in which each type of offense is assigned a specific seriousness score (Rossi, Bose, & Berk, 1974). Two other measures of aggressiveness obtained from state records were each subject's total number of moving traffic violations and number of convictions for driving while intoxicated. For subjects who had children we also obtained ratings of how severely they would punish their children for specific misdeeds. This measure was the same one used with their own parents 22 years earlier. For the 82 children whom we were able to interview individually, we also obtained self-ratings of aggression on the same 10 items used in the peer-nomination questionnaire, as well as self-ratings of the extent to which they engaged in aggressive fantasy. Finally, all interviewed subjects and children were given the Wide Range Achievement Test (WRAT; Jastak & Jastak, 1978) to measure their intellectual competence.

On the subsample of 366 subjects who had been interviewed in 1970, three primary measures of aggression were obtained. These measures were peer-nominated aggression, the sum of MMPI scales *F*, 4 and 9, and their self-ratings of physical aggression. These measures have been described in other publications (e.g., Lefkowitz et al., 1977).

Procedure

The procedures used in the first and second waves of the study (1960, age 8; 1970, age 19) have been reported in detail elsewhere (Eron et al., 1971; Lefkowitz et al., 1977). Therefore, we will describe here only the procedures used during the last data collection in 1981.

Subjects were contacted by mail and telephone. Addresses were obtained from local directories, a network of informants, newspaper stories, and newspaper advertisements. Subjects were paid $40.00 for an interview lasting 1 to 2 hr. The interview was administered in our field office on a microcomputer. The questions were displayed on a TV-type monitor and answered by the respondent typing into the computer keyboard. With this procedure, the subjects' responses were immediately punched into the computer and stored on floppy disks, which were then read by more powerful computers. This was an efficient, time-saving, relatively error-free procedure. Respondents learned the procedure quickly, enjoyed the novelty, and were reassured of the confidentiality of their responses. It is very likely that using the computerized interview added to the validity of information obtained.

At the close of the interview, the subject was asked for permission to contact the spouse for an interview, and if the subject had a child age 6 to 12, permission was sought to interview that child, or the oldest such child, if there were more than one. Spouses were also paid $40.00 per interview and children were paid $20.00. Subjects who were unable to come to the field office for interviews were interviewed by telephone and asked to fill out a mail questionnaire. They were paid $40.00 if the interview was sent back within 2 weeks. Certain of the measures that required personal interaction, the WRAT for example, were eliminated for the postal and telephone sample. However, for those measures that could be obtained through the mail, the results were merged with those obtained in the regular procedure. Spouses and children were not interviewed by mail.

RESULTS

The effect of attrition over 22 years on the composition of the sample was evaluated by examining the mean 1960 peer-nominated aggression scores for subjects who were interviewed either personally or by mail with those who were not interviewed at all in 1981. Male subjects who were *not* interviewed in 1981 had a significantly higher mean aggression score in 1960 than male subjects who were interviewed (17.3 versus 12.9), $F(1, 294) = 6.6$, $p < .01$. However, there was no difference between the personal and postal interview groups. As for the female subjects, there were no significant differences in 1960 aggression score among any of the groups, whether interviewed by mail or in person. Male subjects, of course, had significantly higher aggression scores than females in each group.

Longitudinal Correlations
of Aggression Within Individuals

Correlations between the early and later measures of aggression are shown in Table 11.1. It is apparent that over 22 years there is good predictability from early aggression to later aggression, especially in the case of males. Also in this table are the correlations between the early IQ measure, the California Test of Mental Maturity, and the Spelling, Reading, and Arithmetic scores of the WRAT 22 years later. It is apparent that the stability of aggression holds up across method, informant, and situation as well as time. Especially impressive is the correlation between aggression at age 8 and later encounters with the law, as indicated by driving and criminal offenses.

The correlations in Table 11.1 must be taken as lower bounds for the true stability of aggression (Block, 1963). There are at least four identifiable factors that would lead to an underestimation of the population true score correlations. First, of course, is the limited reliability of some of the measures. Although the peer-nominations and the standardized tests (MMPI and WRAT) have reasonably high reliabilities (.85 to .95), the data gathered from archival records have unknown reliabilities, and some of the other rating scales have only moderate reliabilities. Thus, the observed correlations will be attenuated from the true score correlations. Second, because a disproportionate number of the original subjects who were not interviewed were high-aggressive males, the range of aggression scores in the male sample has been truncated. This restriction in range would also be expected to bias the sample correlations below the population correlations. Third, the distributions of scores on several of the rating scale measures of aggression are highly positively skewed with standard deviations exceeding the mean. For example, for boys for the 1960 peer-nominated measure of aggression, skewness was 2.4 and for 1980 self-ratings of physical aggression skewness was 3.9. As a result, the correlation coefficient is theoretically limited to have a maximum of less than 1, and the correlation as a measure of stability underweights the concentration of scores at the low end of the scale and overweights extreme scores.

One can at least partially correct for the bias due to the skewed distributions by appropriate transformations of raw scores, for example, log, logit, or square root. In Table 11.1 the correlations that changed more than a few points following such transformations are indicated in parenthesis. In the remainder of this article all correlations will be based on scores that have been transformed to reduce their skewness. The last, but perhaps most important, reason why the correlations underestimate the stability of aggression is that the measures of aggression at ages 8 and 30 are not identical. Each may be measuring a slightly different aspect of aggressive behavior, and the correlations only measure the stability of the aspects common to the measures.

Table 11.1   Correlations of Peer-Nominated Aggression and IQ at Age 8 with Aggression and Intellectual Competence at Age 30

Age 30 Measures	Males			Females		
	N	Age 8 Aggression r	Age 8 IQ r	N	Age 8 Aggression r	Age 8 IQ r
Aggression						
MMPI Scales F+ 4 + 9	190	.30****	-.19***	209	.16** (.20***)	—
Spouse Abuse	88	.27***	—	74	—	—
Punishment of Child by Subject	63	.24*	—	96	.24**	-.21***
Criminal Justice Convictions	335	.24****	-.15***	207	— (.10)	—
Seriousness of Criminal Acts	332	.21****	-.14***	207	— (.15**)	—
Moving Traffic Violations	322	.21****	-.10*	201	—	—
Driving While Intoxicated	322	.29***** (.24*****)	—	201	—	—
Self-Rating of Physical Aggression	193	.25***** (.29*****)	—	209	—	—
Intellectual Competence						
WRAT Spelling	136	-.30*****	.54*****	158	-.35*****	.44*****
Reading	136	-.20**	.56*****	158	-.37*****	.47*****
Arithmetic	136	-.20**	.55*****	158	-.35***** (-.43*****)	.42*****

Note: The correlations shown in parentheses are those that changed .04 or more when skew-correcting transformations were applied. MMPI = Minnesota Multiphasic Personality Inventory; WRAT = Wide Range Achievement Test. Correlations under .10 are not shown. Significance tests are two-tailed.

* p < .10. ** p < .05. *** p < .01. **** p < .001.

Adult Behaviors for High- and Low-Aggressive Children

A more representative demonstration of the stability of aggression that is less sensitive to these biases can be obtained by comparing groups of high- and low-aggressive 8-year-olds on their later behaviors. These relations are shown graphically in Figures 11.1 to 11.4. The boys and girls were divided separately into high-, medium-, and low-aggressive groups according to whether they fell in the upper quartile, lower quartile or middle 50% for their gender on peer-nominated aggression at age 8. Then the groups' mean scores on aggressive behaviors at age 30 were compared. As these graphs show, the high group

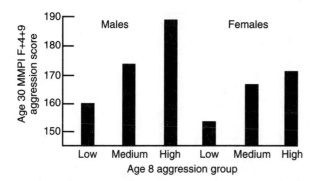

FIGURE 11.1 Mean aggression score on Minnesota Multiphasic Personality Inventory Scales F + 4 + 9 at age 30 according to a subject's peer-nominated aggression score at age 8. The group differences are significant for females, $F(2, 155) = 5.17$, $p < .007$, and for males, $F(2, 132) = 9.60$, $p < .0001$.

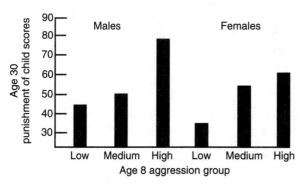

FIGURE 11.2 Mean score on punishment of child at age 30 according to a subject's peer-nominated aggression score at age 8. The group differences are marginally significant for females, $F(2, 93) = 2.33$, $p < .10$, and for males, $F(2, 60) = 2.94$, $p < .06$.

of aggressive eight-year-old males scored significantly higher 22 years later on the MMPI aggression measure, on the punishment of their children, on criminal convictions, on seriousness of criminal offenses, on moving traffic violations, and on drunk driving. They also scored higher on aggression toward their spouses although the difference was not significant due to the small number of highly aggressive male subjects whose spouses could be interviewed (N = 14). The females classified in the high-aggression group at age 8 also scored significantly higher on the MMPI aggression scale, on punishment, and on criminality 22 years later, although the differences were less significant than for males. Unlike the males, moreover, the high-aggressive females did not differ from the other females in number of traffic violations by age 30.

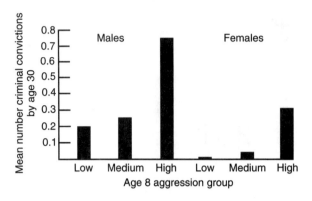

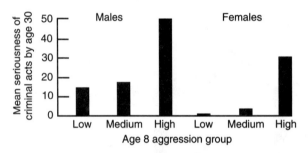

FIGURE 11.3 Mean criminal justice convictions and mean seriousness of crimes up to age 30 according to a subject's peer-nominated aggression score at age 8. The group differences are significant for males, $F(2, 319) = 4.87$, $p < .01$ and $F(2, 319) = 4.13$, $p < .02$.

Child Aggression and Adult Criminality

Perhaps the most impressive aspects of both the longitudinal correlations and the bar graphs is the relation between peer-nominated aggressive behavior at age 8 and adult criminality. The children who are nominated as more aggressive by their third-grade classmates on the average commit more serious crimes as adults. In Table 11.2 the exact conviction rate is shown for each group of males and females. These data convincingly indicate that the peer nominations are measuring more than transient "boisterousness and incivility" (Cook, Kendzierski, & Thomas, 1983). These peer-nominations measure a characteristic aggressiveness in many children that evidences itself in severe antisocial behavior as a young adult.

Aggression, Intellectual Functioning, and Child Rearing

As has been demonstrated previously (Lefkowitz et al., 1977), aggression is significantly related to IQ; so it is fair to ask how much of the stability of aggression results from its correlation with intelligence. In this particular sample, IQ and aggression at age 8 were moderately correlated negatively (–.27, $p < .001$

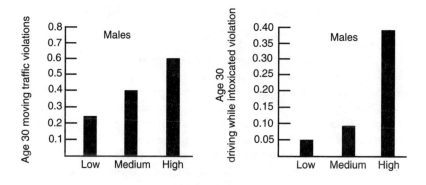

Age 8 aggression group

FIGURE 11.4 Mean traffic violations for male subjects up to age 30 according to their peer-nominated aggression score at age 8. The group differences are highly significant, $F(2, 319) = 4.23$, $p < .015$, for moving violations and $F(2, 319) = 10.4$, $p < .0001$ for intoxication.

Table 11.2 Proportion of Subjects Convicted for a Crime in New York State Before Age 30 According to Gender and Peer-Nominated Aggression at Age 8

Sex	Age 8 Peer-Nominated Aggression		
	Low	**Medium**	**High**
Males	9/90 (10%)	25/163 (15%)	19/82 (23%)
Females	0/49 (0.0%)	2/110 (1.8%)	3/48 (6.3%)

for boys and $-.32$, $p < .001$ for girls). The relative contribution of the stability of IQ to the stability of aggression was evaluated by partial correlation analysis. These partial correlations of aggression over time with age 8 IQ partialed out are almost identical to the raw correlations. Thus, although IQ and aggression are related at age 8, the relation of early aggression to later aggression is independent of the relation between IQ and aggression. Whatever effect IQ has on aggression, it has already taken place before age 8 because subsequent change in aggression is no longer affected by IQ to any appreciable extent.

The overall predictability of adult aggression was evaluated with multiple regression equations using early aggression, birth factors, socioeconomic factors, intellectual factors and child–rearing styles as predictors. Multiple correlations of .37 to .45 were obtained indicating that 15% to 20% of the variance in adult aggression is predictable over 22 years from these measures. As expected, by far the most significant regression coefficient belonged to early aggression for both boys and girls.

Path Analyses for Stability of Aggression
Within Individuals

In Table 11.3, the skew-corrected correlations are shown for the rating scale measures over all three waves of measurement. If one compares the correlations from age 8 to 19 on those waves' common measures (peer nominations) with the correlations from age 19 to age 30 on those waves common measures (MMPI F + 4 + 9 and Self-Rated Physical Aggression), one must conclude that stability seems to increase with age. In addition, aggression seems to be more stable for males than for females. However, as mentioned above, even the skew-corrected correlations probably underestimate the stability of aggression because the aggression measures are not perfectly reliable and because different measures of aggression were used in the different waves. One way to surmount this problem is by estimating coefficients of a structural model involving a latent variable representing the "trait" of aggression. A reasonable model for estimating stability is shown in Figure 11.5. The latent variables are denoted by round nodes and the manifest variables by square nodes. The blank latent variables represent all determinants of the manifest variables other than aggression and random error. For the model in Figure 11.5, the error variance of each manifest variable was specified a priori on the basis of previous reliability analyses. In addition, the degree to which a manifest variable measured the latent trait of aggression over time was assumed to be invariant. This yielded a model with 13 parameters and 21 equations having 8 degrees of freedom. The model was identified, although equality constraints had to be relaxed slightly to achieve standardized parameters.

The parameters of the model were estimated with the LISREL program (Joreskog & Sorbom, 1978). From the chi-square statistic one can see that the model fits the data well with the parameter values shown. The 11-year stability coefficients for the latent trait of aggression are .634 and .727, respectively. To obtain the 22-year coefficient, we multiply these and obtain .461. In Figures 11.6 and 11.7, separate stability analyses are provided for males and females under the same model. Their 22-year stability coefficients are .50 and .34, respectively. Taken together, these stability analyses provide compelling evidence that aggressive behavior remains remarkably stable after a child is 8 years old. It appears substantially more stable for boys than for girls, but this depends upon the manifestation of aggression one chooses to analyze. For both genders stability increases with age.

Correlations of Aggression Across Generations

So far we have only discussed the stability of aggressive behavior within an individual's own lifespan. However, as indicated above, data were collected in this study not only on the aggressiveness of the subject but also on the aggressiveness of the subjects' parents and the subjects' children. Because the sample of subjects for whom all such data are available is only 82 children, the data cannot be analyzed separately by subject's gender. In Table 11.4 the skew-corrected correlations between the major measures of parental, subject, and child aggression are shown. Parent–child communalities are revealed both by

Table 11.3 Intercorrelations of Skew-Corrected Scores on Rating Scale Measures of Aggression

MALES

Measure	Age 8 Peer Agg	Age 19 Peer Agg	Age 19 MMPI F+4+9	Age 19 Phys Agg	Age 30 MMPI F+4+9	Age 30 Phys Agg	Age 30 Spouse Abuse
Age 8 Aggression							
Peer Aggression							
Age 19 Aggression							
Peer Aggression	.44****						
MMPI F+4+9	.28****	.40****					
Physical Aggression	.13*	.42****	.28****				
Age 30 Aggression							
MMPI F+4+9	.32****	.35****	.55****	.23***			
Physical Aggression	.29****	.41****	.22***	.27****	.33****		
Spouse Abuse	.25**	.25**	—	.16	.19*	.46****	
Punishment Child	.26**	.40**	.24	—	.22	.18	—

FEMALES

Measure	Age 8 Peer Agg	Age 19 Peer Agg	Age 19 MMPI F+4+9	Age 19 Phys Agg	Age 30 MMPI F+4+9	Age 30 Phys Agg	Age 30 Spouse Abuse
Age 8 Aggression							
Peer Aggression							
Age 19 Aggression							
Peer Aggression	.36****						
MMPI F+4+9	.13*	.34****					
Physical Aggression	.19***	.13*	.20***				
Age 30 Aggression							
MMPI F+4+9	.20***	.22***	.45****	.11			
Physical Aggression	—	.14*	.28****	.18**	.45****		
Spouse Abuse	—	—	.30**	—	.34***	.34***	
Punishment Child	.27***	—	—	.37***	.13	.24**	—

Note: A logit transformation was used with the peer-nominations, which are proportions, and a log transformation on the self-ratings. Correlations under .10 are not shown. Significance tests are two-tailed.
* $p < .10$. ** $p < .05$. *** $p < .01$. **** $p < .001$.

the parent–subject correlations and by the subject–child correlations. However, because the measure of the subject's parents' aggression was only indirect (via their punishment of their children), more emphasis should be placed on the subject–child correlations. It is clear from these data that aggressive parents have more aggressive children. Aggression appears to be not only a stable characteristic within individuals but one that is transmitted across generations. One might wonder whether such cross-generational consistency could be explained by consistencies across generations in social class and intelligence.

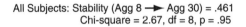

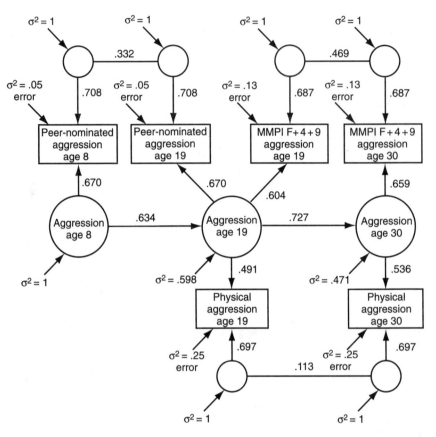

FIGURE 11.5 A structural model showing the stability of an hypothesized latent trait of aggression within all subjects over 22 years.

However, the correlations in Table 11.4 do not change substantially when the parents' social class and the child's IQ at age 8 are partialed out.

Path Analysis of Stability
of Aggression Across Generations

In Figure 11.8 a structural model for cross-generational stability is presented. A slightly different approach was adopted for the cross-generational structural model. Because reciprocal parent–child influences are certainly feasible, the model does not include hypothesized causal directions. The stability coefficients represent simple correlations between the hypothesized latent variables. For this analysis, the within-subject stability and the measurement parameters relating

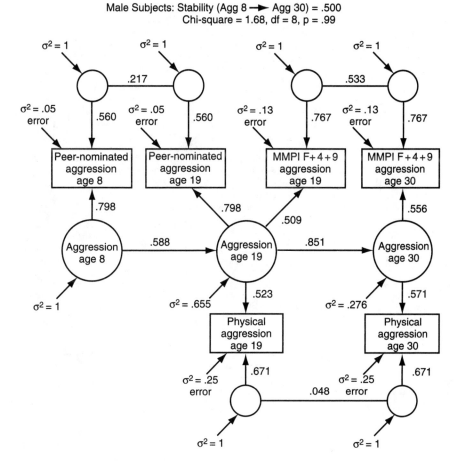

FIGURE 11.6 A structural model showing the stability of an hypothesized latent trait of aggression within male subjects over 22 years.

the latent variables to the manifest were fixed at the values derived in Figure 11.5. Therefore, the model has 11 free parameters for 28 equations relating the manifest variables. The derived parameter values fit the data extremely well, yielding a chi-square of 17.4 with 17 degrees of freedom. All of the stability parameters are significantly different from zero.

Remarkably, the results indicate that stability across generations is not of a different order than stability within the subject's own lifespan up to 22 years. Actually the subject's aggression relates even higher to the child's aggression 22 years later than to the subject's own aggression over that period. Grandparents' (subject's parents') aggression (as measured by punishment of the subject in 1960) also relates highly to the subject's aggression 22 years later and relates moderately to the grandchild's aggression. However, because

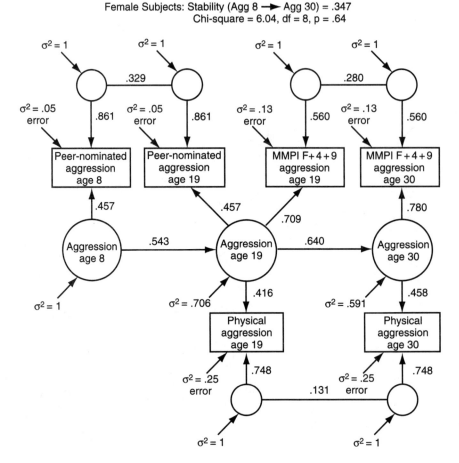

FIGURE 11.7 A structural model showing the stability of an hypothesized latent trait of aggression within female subjects over 22 years.

only one measure of the grandparents' aggression was obtained (punishment style) and because this was a relatively poor measure of aggression (.436 weight in model), the coefficients from the grandparents' aggression may be overestimates.

The derived coefficients in Figure 11.8 suggest that age is an important situational variable influencing the stability of aggressive behavior across generations. A child's aggression relates strongest to his or her parents' aggression when the parents were about the same age. Thus, the highest stability was found between a subject's aggression at age 8 and the subject's child's aggression 22 years later when that child was also about 8 years old. The contemporaneous aggression of the parent does not appear to be as important in determining a child's aggressiveness as was the parent's own aggressiveness as a

Table 11.4 Correlations of Skew-Corrected Measures of Aggression Across Generations

Measure	Parent's Aggression (When Subject Age 8) Punishment of Subject	Subject's Aggression				
		Age 8 Peer-Nominated	Age 19 Peer-Nominated	Age 19 MMPI F+4+9	Age 30 MMPI F+4+9	Age 30 Punishment of Child
Parents' Aggression (when subject age 8)	1.00	.25***	—	.13**	.14***	.25***
Child's Aggression (when subject age 30)						
Self-Rating	—	.31***	—	—	.26**	.31***
Aggressive Fantasy	.17	.40****	.13	—	.27***	.34***

Note. A logit transformation was used with the peer-nominations, which are proportions, and a log transforms with the subject's self-ratings. MMPI = Minnesota Multiphasic Personality Inventory. Correlations under .10 are not shown. Significance tests are two-tailed.

** $p < .05$. *** $p < .01$. **** $p < .001$.

child. This is particularly notable because the aggressiveness of the other parent (the subject's spouse) was not figured into the relation. Of course, the aggression of the spouse does correlate quite significantly with the subject's aggression as an adult (.20 to .30 depending on the measure); so the stability to some extent may be a function of both parents' aggressiveness. Finally, the higher stability for same-age aggression undoubtedly reflects the fact that the appropriateness of specific aggressive behaviors is age related.

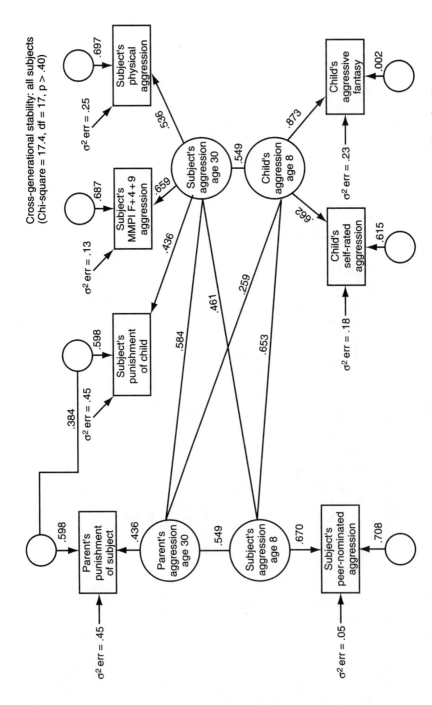

FIGURE 11.8 A correlational model showing the stability of a latent trait of aggression across three generations within a family.

DISCUSSION

Severe antisocial aggressive behavior seems to occur most often when there is a convergence of predisposing and precipitating factors (Eron, 1982). However, once a characteristic style of aggressive responding develops, it seems to persist. On the basis of the current data on more than 600 subjects who were followed from age 8 to 30, we have estimated the stability of aggression over 22 years to be about .50 for boys and .35 for girls. These estimates are consistent with previous findings for shorter periods when one corrects for differing measurement techniques (Olweus, 1979). Moreover, we have shown that the early aggressiveness displayed in school has a reasonable chance of turning into severe antisocial aggressiveness in a young adult. Such aggressiveness may manifest itself in criminal behavior, physical aggression, and child abuse in both genders, and in spouse abuse and driving behaviors for males. We also demonstrated that aggressiveness is transmitted across generations within families.

If aggression were mostly situationally determined, one would certainly not expect stability coefficients of the magnitude we have reported. At the same time, the stability described in this article is a stability of individual differences and of relative position in a population, not a stability of absolute level. Characteristic forms and amounts of aggression change dramatically with age (Eron, Huesmann, Brice, Fischer, & Mermelstein, 1983) and situation. Some situations are much more likely to elicit aggressive behaviors than others. What remains reasonably constant is the aggressiveness of an individual relative to the population. The child who is at the top of the distribution for 8-year-olds is likely to be near the top of the distribution for 30-year-olds two decades later.

It is apparent that many individuals are characterized by a propensity to respond in an aggressive manner to a variety of interpersonal situations. This propensity or disposition becomes apparent early on in their development and continues to characterize their behavior as they grow into adulthood. The development of aggressive behavior, at least in this large sample of subjects, is testimony more to constancy than change in human development (Brim & Kagan, 1980). Where lie the roots of this consistency? How does the aggressive disposition take hold and persist across varied environmental conditions?

Although this article was not directed at elaborating the causes of aggression, one cannot discuss the stability of aggression without some attention to the issues. The data reported here, showing predictability of aggression across three generations as well as from childhood to adulthood within a single life span, cannot discriminate between genetic, constitutional, and/or environmental explanations. Unfortunately, this particular research program was not originally designed to investigate genetic and constitutional precursors (Eron, Laulicht, Walder, Farber, & Spiegel, 1961), and the opportunity to collect data relevant to a biological hypothesis was lost during the first wave of the study. In the second and third waves, an attempt was made to collect some such measures. For example, during the second wave, current height and weight of the subjects were recorded, but no relation was found to current or previous aggression for either males or females. At that time we also collected birth record information for all those subjects born in New York State. A significant relation was found for boys between birth weight and peer-nominated aggression at age 8, with birth weights in the middle range related to the highest aggression (Lefkowitz et al., 1977). Although there was no relation between birth weight and aggression at age 19, there were positive relations between current weight and aggression for females at age 30. Another indicator that early physiological development may affect later aggression was the finding that mother's age at time of birth was significantly related to boy's aggression at age 19. Those male subjects whose mothers were over 35 at the time of their boy's birth were most aggressive as measured both by self-ratings and peer nominations (Lefkowitz et al., 1977). Although neurological damage during birth that might lead to heightened aggressive behavior is more frequent among children born to older mothers, there are equally plausible psychological explanations for the heightened aggression of such offspring. Finally, in the last wave of the study, we also collected blood samples from our male subjects in order to determine level of testosterone and to relate those results to level of aggression. For the 60 male subjects who complied with the request, there was no significant relation between testosterone level and aggression.

Although much of these data are suggestive of a role for constitutional, physiological, or genetic factors in stability, all of the data also can be incorporated into an environmental or learning explanation. Reports of our previous findings (e.g., Eron et al., 1972; Lefkowitz et al., 1977) have stressed the importance of the learning conditions for aggression in a child's development. Our current results are not inconsistent with such a view. Aggressive dispositions can be learned. Youngsters are often directly reinforced for acting aggressively by increased attention as well as by the material and psychological rewards that are often the consequents of such behavior. Examples of aggressive behavior are abundantly available in the media as well as at home, at school, and in the neighborhood. The learning of aggressive attitudes is facilitated when respected and glorified figures, for example, professional athletes, movie stars, and political figures, engage in various kinds of aggressive behavior for which they reap many rewards. It is easy for a youngster to justify aggressive solutions to problems by referring to norms for such behavior promulgated by the media and others (Huesmann et al., 1984). Aggression can be learned early in life (Eron et al., 1983) and may be learned very well, generalizing to many situations. Aggressive individuals actively seek out and create situations in which they can often be observed (Bowers, 1973; Olweus, 1978), and due to their past conditioning histories, they may be exquisitely sensitive to aggressive cues in the environment (Berkowitz, 1978). Thus, though the individual's environment and learning conditions may change radically, aggression can persist.

Quite probably the impressive stability of aggressive behavior across time and generations is a product both of the continuity of constitutional factors and the continuity of environmental factors. Certainly constitutional characteristics including genetic factors (Lagerspetz & Lagerspetz, 1974; Christiansen, 1977), hormonal factors (Kreuz & Rose, 1972; Rada, Kellner, & Winslow, 1976), and neurological trauma (Mark & Ervin, 1970) play some role in aggressive behavior. Just as certainly, a person's environment and learning history strongly influence his or her aggressive tendencies (Bandura, 1973; Berkowitz, 1962; Eron et al., 1971; Huesmann et al., 1984). The relative importance of these factors is arguable. What is not arguable is that aggressive behavior, however engendered, once established, remains remarkably stable across time, situation, and even generations within a family.

REFERENCES

Bandura, A. (1973). *Aggression: A social learning analysis.* Englewood Cliffs, NJ: Prentice Hall.

Berkowitz, L. (1962). *Aggression: A social psychological analysis.* New York: McGraw-Hill.

Berkowitz, L. (1978). External determinants of impulsive aggression. In W. W. Hartsup & J. de Wit (Eds.), *Origins of aggression* (pp. 147–165). The Hague: Mouton.

Block, J. (1963). The equivalence of measures and the corrections for attenuation. *Psychological Bulletin, 60,* 152–156.

Bowers, K. S. (1973). Situationalism in psychology: An analysis and critique. *Psychological Review 80,* 307–336.

Brim, O. Jr., & Kagan, J. (Eds.) (1980). *Constancy and change in human development.* Cambridge, MA: Hammond University Press.

Christiansen, K. O. (1977). A review of studies of criminality among twins. In S. A. Mednick & K. O. Christiansen (Eds.), *Biosocial basis of criminal behavior,* New York: Gardner.

Cook, T. D., Kendzierski, D. A., & Thomas, S. V. (1983). The implicit assumptions of television research: An analysis of the NIMH report on Television and Behavior. *Public Opinion Quarterly, 47,* 161–201.

Dollard, J., Doob, L. W., Miller, N. E., Mower. O. H., & Sears, R. R. (1939). *Frustration and aggression.* New Haven: Yale University Press.

Eron, L. D. (1982). Parent child interaction, television violence and aggres-

sion of children. *American Psychologist, 27,* 197–211.

Eron, L. D., Huesmann, L. R., Brice, P., Fischer, P., & Mermelstein, R. (1983). Age trends in the development of aggression, sex typing and related television habits. *Developmental Psychology 19,* 71–77.

Eron, L. D., Huesmann, L. R., Lefkowitz, M. M., & Walder, L. O. (1972). Does television violence cause aggression? *American Psychologist, 27,* 253–263.

Eron, L. D., Laulicht, J. H., Walder, L. O., Farber, I. E., & Spiegel, J. P. (1961). Application of role and learning theories to the study of the development of aggression in children. *Psychological Reports, 9,* 291–334. (monograph supplement 2-V9).

Eron, L. D., Walder, L. O., & Lefkowitz, M. M. (1971). *Learning of aggression in children.* Boston: Little, Brown.

Feshbach, S., & Singer, R. D. (1971). *Television and aggression: An experimental field study.* San Francisco: Jossey-Bass.

Huesmann, L. R., Lagerspetz, K., & Eron. L. D. (1984). Intervening variables in the television violence-aggression relation: Evidence from two countries. *Developmental Psychology, 20,* 746–775.

Huesmann, L. R., Lefkowitz, M. M., & Eron, L. D. (1978). Sum of MMPI Scales F, 4 and 9 as a measure of aggression. *Journal of Consulting and Clinical Psychology, 46,* 1071–1078.

Jastak, J. F., & Jastak, S. (1978). *Wide Range Achievement Test. Manual of Instructions. Revised Edition.* Wilmington, DE: Jastak Associates.

Joreskog. K. G., & Sorbom, D. *LISREL IV Manual.* (1978). Chicago: National Educational Resources.

Kagan, J., & Moss, H. A. (1962). *Birth to maturity: A study in psychological development.* New York: Wiley.

Kreuz, L. F., & Rose, R. M. (1972). Assessment of aggressive behaviors and plasma testosterone in a young criminal population. *Psychosomatic Medicine, 34,* 321–332.

Lagerspetz, K., & Lagerspetz, K. Y. H. (1974). Genetic determination of aggressive behavior. In I. H. F. von Abeelen (Ed.), *Behavioral genetics* (pp. 321–346). Holland: North Holland Publishing.

Lefkowitz, M. M., Eron, L. D., Walder, L. O., & Huesmann, L. R. (1972). Television violence and child aggression: A follow-up study. In G. A. Comstock & E. A. Rubinstein (Eds.), *Television and social behavior* (Vol. 3. pp. 35–135). Washington, DC: U.S. Government Printing Office.

Lefkowitz, M. M., Eron, L. D., Walder, L. O., & Huesmann, L. R. (1977). *Growing up to be violent: A longitudinal study of the development of aggression.* New York: Pergamon.

Mark, V., & Ervin, F. (1970). *Violence and the brain.* New York: Harper & Row.

Moskowitz, D. S., & Schwartzman, A. E. (1983, April). *Stability and change in aggression and withdrawal in middle childhood and adolescence.* Paper presented as the Society for Research on Child Development, Detroit.

Olweus, D. (1977). Aggression and peer acceptance in adolescent boys: two short-term longitudinal studies of ratings. *Child Development, 48,* 1301–1313.

Olweus, D. (1978). *Aggression in the schools: Bullies and whipping boys.* Washington, DC: Hemisphere.

Olweus, D. (1979). The stability of aggressive reaction patterns in human males:

a review. *Psychological Bulletin, 85,* 852–875.

Olweus, D. (1981). Continuity in aggressive and withdrawn, inhibited behaviour patterns. *Psychiatry and Social Science,* I, 141–159.

Pitkannen-Pulkkinen, L. (1979). Self-control as a prerequisite for constructive behavior. In S. Feshbach & A. Fraczek (Eds.), *Aggression and behavior change* (pp. 250–270). New York: Praeger.

Rada, R. T., Kellner, R., & Winslow, W. W. (1976). Plasma testosterone and aggressive behavior. *Psychosomatics, 17,* 138–142.

Roff, J. D., & Wirt, R. D. (1984). Childhood aggression and social adjustment as antecedents of delinquency. *Journal of Abnormal Child Psychology, 12,* 111–126.

Rossi, P., Bose, C., & Berk, R. (1974). The seriousness of crime, normative structure and individual differences. *American Sociological Review, 39,* 224–237.

Sand, E. A., Emery-Hauzeur, C., Buki, H., Chauvin-Faures, C., Sand-Ghilain, J., & Smets, P. (1975). *L'Échec Scolarie Précole Variables Associes-Prédiction.* Bruxelles: Ministere de L'Éducation Nationale.

Straus, M. A., Giles. R. J., & Steinmetz, S. K. (1979). *Behind closed doors: Violence in the American family.* New York: Doubleday/Anchor.

Sullivan, E. T., Clark, W. W., & Tiegs, E. W. (1957). *California Short Form Test of Mental Maturity.* Los Angeles: California Test Bureau.

Walder, L., Abelson, R., Eron, L. D., Banta, T. J., & Laulicht, J. H. (1961). Development of a peer-rating measure of aggression. *Psychological Reports, 9,* 497–556, (monograph supplement 4–19).

12

Generality, Continuity, and Change in Offending

RAYMOND PATERNOSTER
CHARLES W. DEAN
ALEX PIQUERO
PAUL MAZEROLLE
ROBERT BRAME

ABSTRACT   A number of criminological theories make either implicit or explicit predictions about the empirical relationship between prior and future offending behavior. Some argue that time-stable characteristics such as criminal propensity should account for any positive correlation between past and future criminal behavior for all individuals. Others contend that the positive association between offending behavior at different points in time are partly causal and partly spurious. Still others anticipate that different patterns will emerge for different groups (distinguished by their criminal propensity) of individuals. Using a longitudinal data set comprised of 848 training school releasees, we test various hypotheses emanating from these different theoretical perspectives. The results indicate that (1) both stability and change have causal implications for one's offending behavior and (2) with but one exception, these effects do not vary between high and low criminal propensity groups.

INTRODUCTION

I t has been noted that theoretical controversies in criminology rarely involve disputes about facts; instead they often involve disputes about the *interpretation* of facts (Hirschi & Gottfredson, 1995). One of the most consistent and resilient facts in criminology is the positive correlation between past and future criminal behavior. While there is no dispute about the existence of this fact, there is a great deal of disagreement about what it means. The purpose of this paper is to review briefly some of the prominent explanations for the relationship between past and future crime. These different explanations, though sharing some common ground, differ in ways that have critical implications for the development of theory and public policy. We then attempt to organize these

SOURCE: *Journal of Quantitative Criminology,* Vol. 13, No. 3, pp. 231–266. Reprinted by permission of Plenum Publishing Corporation.

explanations by creating a framework of theory types. While we do not wish to oversimplify the content of these theories, we do think that our proposed framework highlights some important issues and suggests that theory development and testing is at an important crossroad. In devising this vocabulary, we contend that some theories are far less parsimonious than others. The primary research question addressed in this paper is whether the additional complexity of some theories is worth their added weight. We try to answer this question by testing some hypotheses deduced from these more complex theories.

EXPLAINING THE RELATIONSHIP
BETWEEN PRIOR AND FUTURE OFFENDING

Nagin and his colleagues (Nagin & Paternoster, 1991; Nagin and Farrington, 1992a, 1992b) have suggested two processes that could account for the strong positive correlation between past and future offending. One process implicates differences between individuals in their latent tendency to commit crime (e.g., criminal propensity, impulsivity, and present orientation). These differences are established early in life and are time stable. Whether these individual differences in criminal propensity or criminal potential are due to constitutional factors and personality traits (Wilson & Herrnstein, 1985) or differences in upbringing (Gottfredson & Hirschi, 1990), the common ground among these theories is their view that "bad apples" are created by forces that operate early in life. These "bad apples" begin offending early in life, exhibit great versatility in offending, and are more likely to offend throughout life, resulting in a positive correlation between sundry types of past and future problem behavior. Since the process generating the relationship is due to persistent differences between individuals along an underlying dimension of criminal propensity, this view can be conveniently labeled the "population heterogeneity" position (Hsiao, 1986, pp. 172–180; Nagin & Paternoster, 1991). According to this view, repeated offending among crime-prone individuals is simply a series of continuing realizations of a relatively stable underlying crime producing process. In causal terms, the positive correlation between past and future offending is spurious insofar as variation in both variables is the outcome of a common cause. For those who accept a population heterogeneity explanation, adequate controls for stable criminal propensity should cause the association between prior and future behavior to vanish.

Theories of population heterogeneity do not rule out the possibility that "change" may occur (e.g., previous offenders may find a good job and/or partner, and subsequently desist from crime).[1] What they do rule out, however,

---

[1]Some population heterogeneity theories are compatible with the notion that there may be some *absolute* change in criminal propensity and associated characteristics over time but preclude the possibility of *relative* change (i.e., changes in relative standing within the population in the likelihood of committing crime) (Gottfredson & Hirschi, 1990). Other population heterogeneity theories seem to be more hostile to the idea of absolute change as well as relative change (Wilson & Herrnstein, 1985).

is a *causal relationship* between life changes and transitions away from offending behavior. Any observed relationship between life events and desistance from crime is attributed solely to self-selection. That is, once time-stable differences in criminal potential are held constant, the effects of life events of all sorts (including prior episodes of offending behavior) should have no effect on subsequent offending. According to this view, "bad apples" simply do not secure meaningful, stable jobs or emotionally warm and rewarding social relationships. Not quite so bad "bad apples," however, may a priori decide to secure jobs, find meaningful relationships, and cease offending. In other words, the moderate "bad apples" sort themselves into somewhat better situations than their extreme "bad apple" counterparts. Consequently, in a pure population heterogeneity explanation, the very intention of the moderate "bad apples" to make positive changes constitutes evidence that they are not really the worst of the "bad apples," that the "reform" is merely apparent, and that the underlying process is one of self-selection, rather than one of cause and effect (Hirschi & Gottfredson, 1995).

A second explanation for the observed correlation between past and future offending argues that there is a genuine causal link between past and future criminal behavior. This link, commonly referred to as the *state-dependent* effect, suggests that the commission of criminal acts reduces inhibitions and/or strengthens motivations to commit crime. There are any number of specific mechanisms that can account for this state dependent effect. For example, the commission of crimes with impunity may weaken persons' perceptions of the certainty of punishment, weaken their bond to conventional others or their commitments to conventional roles, strengthen their affiliation with deviant others leading to increased social reinforcement for crime and more criminal opportunities, or result in labeling and one's exclusion from the normal routines of life. Clearly, state dependent effects are compatible with numerous extant criminological theories. The common ground they share is the expectation that the commission of criminal acts has a causal effect on the commission of subsequent criminal behaviors. Contrary to heterogeneity explanations, life events (e.g., marriage, job, changes in friendship groups, and involvement in criminal behavior) can have a genuine causal effect on future behavior. In other words, committing criminal acts can make things worse for offenders if they desire a more conventional life; moreover, changes in the life situations of those who have offended in the past may subsequently lead to long-term (Sampson & Laub, 1993) or short-term (Horney et al., 1995) redemption.

It can be appreciated that heterogeneity and state-dependent theories offer very different understandings of the processes that result in a positive correlation between past and future criminality. In their pure form, heterogeneity theories (like those of Gottfredson and Hirschi and of Wilson and Herrnstein) can be construed as static processes (Nagin & Farrington, 1992a) because they disallow any genuine causal effect of prior behavior on future behavior. They also discount the possibility that experiences or major life events can alter one's destined pattern of offending after the die is cast.[2] State-dependent theories, in contrast, are dynamic in that they both allow for a causal effect of prior on future behavior and are compatible with the idea that changes in life circumstances can affect one's proclivity to offend.

Thus far, we have drawn a clear distinction between static population heterogeneity theories, on the one hand, and dynamic state dependent theories, on the other. There is now in the literature an ongoing debate as to whether or not the added complexity of a dynamic theory is superior to the simpler static model (Gottfredson & Hirschi, 1990; Sampson & Laub, 1993, 1995; Laub & Sampson, 1993; Hirschi & Gottfredson, 1995). As we argue below, however, there is more than one dimension of complexity to consider in current debates over criminological theory.

Though differing in the causal importance attached to prior criminal behavior and the theoretical importance of change, the kinds of heterogeneity and state-dependent theories we have alluded to above share a common theme—they essentially argue that there is a common explanation of crime that applies to all members of the population. As such, they share the characteristic of being general theories of crime. For example, Gottfredson and Hirschi (1990) clearly argue that all crime and analogous acts can be attributed to variations in self-control and available opportunities. Similarly, Wilson and Herrnstein (1985) suggest that what they call serious predatory crime can be linked to a time-stable cluster of characteristics including impulsivity, poor conditionability, and a weak conscience. In addition to these obviously general theories, many theories of crime that are dynamic also posit one or a few causes of crime. For Agnew (1992) it is strain, for Akers (1985) it is differential reinforcement, for Lemert (1951, 1972) it is negative labeling, for Thornberry (1987) it is the dynamic interplay of peers and informal social controls, and for Tittle (1995) it is a balance between control exercised and control experienced.

An interesting example of how theoretical generality can unite those who disagree about the salience of dynamic influences on offending can be found in the dialogue of Gottfredson and Hirschi (1990) and Sampson and Laub (1993). Indeed, their points of agreement are as revealing as their points of contention.

---

[2]It should be noted in Gottfredson and Hirschi's theory, low self-control is the product of failed early childhood socialization practices. Until the end of early childhood, then, interventions that improve those socialization practices should be effective at modifying one's level of self-control. This "window of opportunity" closes around age 8, however, and relative standing on self-control within any given age cohort after that time is predicted to be resistant to intervention. Thus, their theory is dynamic up to about age 8 and is static thereafter.

Gottfredson and Hirschi also claim that self-control does not explain all variation in offending; even those with low self-control need opportunities to commit crimes. In the limiting case of a complete absence of opportunity, they would argue that offending is physically impossible. We make two observations about this: (1) the opportunity to commit some kind of crime is certainly ubiquitous, particularly when one considers that offenders are often versatile creatures (Blumstein et al., 1986:5); and (2) some criminal behaviors may open up new opportunities for crime while closing off those for noncrime, and some noncriminal behaviors may open up opportunities for a conventional life while closing off those for a criminal life. The latter observation, that past crime has important causal consequences for involvement in crime in the future, is of central interest to us in this paper.

To Sampson and Laub (1993), crime can be understood as the product of informal social controls. To be sure, the specific sources of informal control (e.g., family, school, marriage, and employment) change over time. The source of informal control, however, is less important than the overall quantity and quality of control to which one is subject. In short, crime is inhibited when persons are bonded to conventional institutions. Gottfredson and Hirschi's theory, on the other hand, looks to internal controls (what they call self-control) to explain the process that restrains individuals from becoming involved in crime.

A key point of contention between the theory of Gottfredson and Hirschi and that of Sampson and Laub is whether controls on behavior, whatever their source, are subject to variation within individuals over time. Gottfredson and Hirschi argue that within-individual variation (beyond age 8) is not problematic, whereas Sampson and Laub contend that it is central to understanding why some people persist in a life of problem behaviors (including crime) while others turn their lives around. Despite their different perspectives on the importance of static and dynamic processes, however, Sampson and Laub and Gottfredson and Hirschi apparently agree that a *single* theory is sufficient to explain variation in offending behavior throughout the population. Indeed, what the static theories of Gottfredson and Hirschi and Wilson and Herrnstein have in common with the dynamic theories of Agnew, Thornberry, Akers, Tittle, and Sampson and Laub is that all offenders follow a single pathway to crime. Thus, it is possible to articulate either static or dynamic theories of crime that are general in scope—that is, the causes of offending are presumed to be the same for all persons.

It is perhaps fruitful to view theoretical generality as a type of null hypothesis (Osgood & Rowe, 1994), which asserts that only one theoretical model is needed to account for variation in offending behavior. In deference to the principle of parsimony, we should want to relax the constraint of a single theory only if the additional complexity of a "multiple pathways" theory significantly increases our understanding of the etiology of crime.

Recent work in developmental theory relaxes the assumption of generality and, in so doing, adds further complexity to the theoretical picture. Contemporary developmental theory emerged partly in response to empirical findings from the criminal career literature that suggested the existence of distinct types of offenders such as early starters, late starters, persisters, desisters, occasionals, and chronics (Blumstein et al., 1986, 1988; Barnett et al., 1985, 1989, 1992). In essence, the criminal career literature led to a burgeoning taxonomy of offender types. This work did not extend beyond the classification stage, however, as criminal career researchers were better at identifying offender types than explaining them. Contemporary developmental theories entered this hiatus by rejecting the assumption of general causality and assuming that different offense patterns may need to be understood as resulting from unique causal processes (Osgood & Rowe, 1994). Rather than positing a general causal process that applies to all offenders to varying degrees, developmental theorists hypothesized that offenders differ in kind rather than only in degree (Loeber & LeBlanc, 1990). In this view, a unique causal process is required to explain the behavior of different kinds of offenders. In other words, different offenders have very distinctive sequelae.

In addition to the identification of different offender types, empirical work in the criminal career tradition also noted the simultaneous existence of continuity and change in offending. While it appeared that many offenders consistently committed crimes over long periods of time, others' involvement was more intermittent, beginning later and ending earlier. In addition to explaining behavioral continuity, then, the task taken on by developmental theorists was to explain variations in offending over the life course. The intermittent and seemingly nonrandom patterns of much criminal offending led contemporary developmental theorists to question the static position taken by some general theories of crime. Almost by definition, the developmental view grants a prominent role to changes in life circumstances as well as the experience, rewards, and consequences of prior actions in the explanation of persistent offending. Thus, in focusing attention on how changes in life circumstances affect changes in offending, developmental perspectives are friendly to the idea that changing life circumstances can have causal implications for future involvement in crime. They are also friendly to the idea that involvement in crime in the past can have a causal impact on whether one continues to offend in the future. In short, a prominent theme of contemporary developmental theories can be found in their focus on dynamic rather than static causes of crime.

In reconciling both continuity and change in criminal offending, some prominent examples of developmental theory have adopted both a dynamic and static perspective to theory by applying each process to different offender types. For example, Moffitt and her colleagues (1993, 1994, 1996) and Patterson and his colleagues (1989, 1993) reject the assumption that there is a general theory of crime and argue for the existence of two distinct offender groups. One of these offender groups is characterized primarily by continuity in offending, the other by change. Moffitt refers to these two groups as life-course persistent and adolescent-limited offenders while Patterson refers to them as early- and late-starters.

Though differing in subtle ways, Moffitt and Patterson offer very comparable explanations for the behavior of persons who begin offending early in life and persist in their problem behaviors over the life course. Both presume that the one who begins offending early and continues offending is characterized by early behavior problems, parent–child conflict, and poor socialization. These poorly socialized children eventually fail in their family life, their school work, and their relationships with others. They "miss out on opportunities to acquire and practice prosocial alternatives at each stage of development" (Moffitt, 1993, p. 683). Essentially, some children are never effectively socialized, never learn to control or channel their antisocial behavior, and act impulsively and aggressively as children, adolescents, and adults.

It is clear from their discussion of etiology that Moffitt's life-course persistent and Patterson's early starting offenders follow a pathway to offending that resembles in many ways the pathway to low self-control developed by Gottfredson and Hirschi (1990). The early-starters and life-course persistent offenders are "bad apples" who exhibit significant deficits in early childhood socialization and rarely get back on track. This explanation for life-course continuity, like the one offered by Gottfredson and Hirschi (1990), allows for some dynamic variation during early childhood which gives way to a largely static process by the beginning of adolescence. Assuming such an explanation is correct, any correlation between dynamic variables and continued offending within this group is likely to be spurious since both will be the result of ineffective socialization.[3]

---

[3]Our position, that Patterson's explanation for the early-starting offender is a static one, may be controversial. This is because when they have described their theory, Patterson and his colleagues have hinted that the early starting offender may at some point be profoundly and causally affected by other deviant peers. That is, even though they possess a high propensity for and considerable experience with antisocial behavior, early-starters are said to *require* other deviant peers to become delinquent. This was the reading of the theory adopted by Simons *et al.* (1994) in their empirical test of the Patterson model. Essentially, this position asserts that the early-starting route to delinquency is a dynamic one because delinquent peers play an important causal role in transforming a "bad child" into a delinquent. Although a detailed discussion of this issue is beyond the scope of the present paper, we would like to provide some rationale for our position. In a nutshell, for several reasons we are very skeptical of any strong causal effect for delinquent peers in the Patterson early-starter group.

First, we take Patterson *et al.* at their word when they propose that their theory is a typological one. In numerous publications they emphasize the fact that they are positing two different routes to delinquency, i.e., that there are "two very different developmental paths leading to juvenile delinquency . . . they differ both in terms of the determinants that bring them about and in terms of the long-term outcomes of following one path or the other" (Patterson & Yoerger, 1993, p. 166). The "two very different" routes to delinquency is seriously compromised if peers play an important causal role for both the early- and the late-starting offender. Patterson and colleagues are adamant that the primary causal factor in accounting for the late-starting offender is the influence of delinquent peers. Their typological distinction is clear if it is maintained that the primary causal actor for the early-starter is inadequate socialization. Ultimately, we think that their distinction becomes blurred and seriously compromised if they attribute significant causal import to delinquent peers within both the early- and the late-starting group. In this case, the distinction between the early- and the late-starters seems merely to be a matter of degree and not kind.

Second, the precise causal role played by delinquent peers within the early-starting group is not clearly specified, and when sketched out, it remains unconvincing. It should be remembered that those in the early-starting group are the product of ineffective parental socialization. More important, they already exhibit a diverse repertoire of antisocial behavior —they are destructive, aggressive, and confrontational with both other children and adults. They appear to show little regard for either the feelings or the possessions of others. In sum, they appear to us to be both fully capable and experienced in committing antisocial acts. Why do they need other antisocial peers to do things they are both skilled and experienced in doing? Patterson and colleagues seem to answer this question by stating that peers are needed to *amplify* the early starter's antisocial tendency. It is not clear what amplify means in their theory, but we assume it means that peers are needed to broaden the targets for the early-starters antisocial acts. If all peers do is to broaden the supply of targets, is the only important role they play that of providing opportunities to commit delinquent acts? This position is neither very dynamic nor at odds with the position adopted by Gottfredson and Hirschi (1990), who note that delinquent peers may be important in providing youths with low self-control a steady state of criminal opportunities.

Finally, in describing the role played by delinquent peers among the early-starting group, Patterson and colleagues have suggested that the apparent correlation with

Both Moffitt and Patterson adopt a more dynamic position when explaining adolescent-limited or late-starting offending. The stances of Moffitt and Patterson on the explanation of offending that is limited to the adolescent phase of the life course, however, continue to be quite similar to each other. To both, individuals who begin offending in adolescence will generally not continue to offend beyond. Within this group, however, whatever offending does occur will depend largely on life circumstances such as conflict with or divorce between parents, parental unemployment, assertions of adolescent independence, and most importantly, falling into the wrong crowd. Thus, the primary causes of offending among those who do not fit into the life-course persistent or early-start group are salient life circumstances. Logically, changes in those circumstances can causally affect the risk of involvement in offending.[4] For individuals in the adolescence-limited and late-starting groups, prior criminal acts may causally affect current and future offending by further alienating parents and conventional peers and diminishing conventional alternatives to crime. Similarly, changes in life circumstances may lead to crime desistance as partners are secured and careers or vocational training initiated. Contrary to the early-starter/life-course persistent offender, then, the behavior of the late-starter/adolescence-limited offender is predicted to be driven by a much more dynamic, state-dependent process.

It would appear from this brief discussion that current criminological theory is in disarray, even when it is directed at the single problem of accounting for the relationship between prior and current offending. We now offer an organizing theme that classifies theory along two dimensions, whether it is static or dynamic and whether it is general or developmental. Figure 12.1 illustrates our fourfold classification scheme.

Static general theories of crime presume that there is a general cause of crime for all offenders and that, once the causal process has played out, change is unlikely. This is what characterizes a pure population heterogeneity theory. Examples include Wilson and Herrnstein (1985) and Gottfredson and Hirschi (1990). A dynamic/general theory is slightly more complex. It maintains the assumption of general causality, but rejects the assumption that changes in life circumstances cannot materially affect one's offending. An example of

---

delinquent peers may be noncausal. That is, they at times suggest that their empirical finding of a positive correlation between delinquent peers and the delinquency of the early starter may be due to a selection phenomenon—i.e.. that "birds of a feather flock together." Patterson and Yoerger (1993, pp. 147, 149) have noted, for example, that ". . . problem children tend to be selected as friends by isolated or rejected children" and that the early-starter is free to shop for social groups that match their own proclivities." If antisocial children "shop around" for other antisocial children with whom to commit delinquent offenses, how is it that they play an important causal role in the continuation or amplification of offending?

[4]According to Moffitt (1993), some dynamic factors such as destructive reactions by others to negative behavior can begin a chain reaction that culminates in a transition from adolescence-limited offending to life course-persistent offending.

	General	**Developmental**
Static	Wilson & Herrnstein (1985) Gottfredson & Hirschi (1990)	Moffitt (life course persistent) Patterson (early starter)
Dynamic	Sampson and Laub (1993) Agnew (1992) Tittle (1995)	Moffitt (adolescent limited) Patterson (late starter)

FIGURE 12.1 Classification scheme of criminological theory.

dynamic, general theory is Sampson and Laub's (1993) theory of age-graded informal social control.

A developmental theory relaxes both assumptions. It assumes that causality is not general and that different causal processes explain different offender types. The causal process involved, however, may be either static, as when it adopts the position that crime throughout the life course is due to persistent individual differences in criminal propensity produced by ineffective socialization, or dynamic, as when it adopts the position that prior crime and changes in life circumstances may causally affect current and future crime. As can be discerned, dynamic/developmental theory is far less parsimonious and more complex than dynamic/general theory, and the latter is less parsimonious than static/general theory. The question motivating this research is whether the additional complexity of some theories is necessary.

OVERVIEW OF PRIOR RESEARCH

Prior research in this area suggests that some complexity above and beyond that anticipated by general static models may be required. For example, Nagin and Paternoster (1991) found that both persistent individual differences in criminal propensity and prior offending behavior exerted significant effects on self-reported offending (theft) patterns in a convenience sample of South Carolina high school students. This finding was replicated within sampling error (using a broader set of delinquent behaviors as outcomes) by a recent analysis of the National Youth Survey self-report data by Paternoster and Brame (1997). In their analysis of the Glueck's long-term follow-up of Boston males, Sampson and Laub (1993) concluded that both stable individual differences and past offending patterns were important in the explanation of future offending behavior.

Nagin and Farrington (1992a) also discovered important heterogeneity effects in the Cambridge Study in Delinquent Development data comprised of a 22 year follow-up of inner-city London males. Their analysis did not, however, find the strong state-dependent effects that were evident in the Nagin and Paternoster, Paternoster and Brame, and Sampson and Laub studies. Consequently, they concluded that persistent individual differences were the predominant cause of variation in future offending behavior. Nevertheless, a close review of their empirical results suggests that state-dependent influences, though greatly reduced after the introduction of controls for persistent unobserved heterogeneity, were still evident.[5]

In sum, a variety of studies using different outcomes, different samples, different control variables, and different model specifications seems to yield similar conclusions in at least one respect—changes in prior offending behavior appears to have important implications for one's future offending behavior that cannot be explained solely by a process of self-selection.

The extant literature also reports results that bear on the question of whether general theories are sufficient or whether typological models are more realistic. Patterson (1993), for example, predicted that parental discipline and monitoring practices would be associated with antisocial behavior by the fourth grade of school and that changes in antisocial behavior after that time would be associated with changing levels of unsupervised street time and involvement with deviant peers. Using data from his ongoing Oregon Youth Survey, Patterson (1993, pp. 914–915) estimated the parameters of this model and found that it reproduced the covariance matrix of the study variables within sampling error.

Simons et al. (1994) examined panel data on 177 midwestern boys from small towns in the midwestern United States. Based on the work of Patterson and his colleagues, they predicted that the process driving arrest outcomes would differ across samples stratified by age at first arrest. Their analysis uncovered evidence consistent with this prediction. Specifically, among those arrested by approximately age 14, they found that parental monitoring and disciplinary practices predicted "a coercive, noncompliant orientation" in interactions with other people. Within this "early-onset group," those possessing this oppositional/defiant orientation were found to be more likely to succumb to involvement with deviant peers and, in turn, experience more frequent future involvement with the criminal justice system (Simons et al., 1994, p. 260).

Among those arrested later on (after age 14), however, Simons and his colleagues (1994, p. 262) found that effective parental monitoring and disciplinary practices were associated with lower levels of involvement with deviant peers and, in turn, lower frequencies of future contact with the criminal justice system. Unlike the early-onset group, oppositional/defiant orientation exerted

---

[5]Another study using the Cambridge data conducted by Nagin and Land (1993) also estimated a state-dependent effect. However, the state-dependent effect was apparently estimated within the framework of a probit model where observed, but not unobserved, heterogeneity was controlled. Review of the tables of Nagin and Land (1993) indicates that the probit coefficient for prior convictions is very similar to the probit coefficient for prior convictions without controls for persistent unobserved heterogeneity reported by Nagin and Farrington (1992a). A recent reanalysis of the Cambridge data by Land and Nagin (1996), however, reports a strong effect for "any prior convictions" on contemporary conviction frequency with a model that incorporates a nonparametric specification of unobserved heterogeneity. Taken together, the various analyses of the Cambridge data appear to suggest that both stable individual differences and prior offending behavior have important implications for future offending behavior.

no effect on future criminal justice system involvement in the later-onset group. On the basis of this evidence, Simons and his colleagues concluded that distinct processes were responsible for the future offending behavior of those who began offending early and those who began offending after age 14.

Dean et al. (1996) assessed whether the correlates of post-age 16 offending persistence (defined as the time to first arrest after release from training school) varied significantly between groups of North Carolina training school releasees stratified by age at first adjudication. They found that child abuse victimization and number of juvenile adjudications exerted different effects between the early (onset occurred before 12 years of age) and the late (onset occurred at or after 12 years of age) groups. Nevertheless, they also discovered that these results were sensitive to the age cutoff points used to define the groups and that when other cutting points were used the differences vanished.

More recently, Paternoster and Brame (1997) used the National Youth Survey data to examine the effects of prior offending behavior and delinquent peer exposure on participation and frequency of contemporary offending. This study was limited because onset ages were not available in the data. Nevertheless, they did use the subsample of respondents who were age 11 or 12 at the first wave of the survey to create "antisocial propensity" groups based on both attitudinal and behavioral measures. They then compared the effects of delinquent peer exposure and prior offending behavior on the outcomes between high and low antisocial propensity groups. Their analysis revealed that the effects of both variables were comparable across the groups.

Nagin and his colleagues (Nagin & Land, 1993; Nagin et al., 1995) have taken a somewhat different approach to the study of whether different etiological processes explain offending behavior. Using data from the Cambridge Study in Delinquent Development and a model that probabilistically assigned individuals to distinct offending "trajectories," they inductively identified four different longitudinal offending patterns. One group, the "high-rate chronics," exhibited relatively high conviction frequencies over a sustained period of time. A second group, the "adolescence-limiteds," were convicted during adolescence but tended to cease offending as they moved into adulthood. Nagin and his colleagues concluded that these two groups bore strong resemblance to the life course-persistent and adolescence-limited offenders described by Moffitt (1993). A third group that offended at low rates beginning in late adolescence and persisting into adulthood, not "anticipated" by Moffitt and Patterson, was also discovered. The fourth group was comprised of individuals in the Cambridge study who were not convicted at all.

A key aspect of the analyses reported by Nagin and Land (1993, 1996) as well as Nagin et al. (1995) was an assessment of whether individuals in the various groups differed from each other on behavioral measures that did not include offending. A number of results from this assessment seem noteworthy. First, at ages 14 and 18, the adolescence-limited and high-rate chronic groups reported greater drug use, smoking, and sexual promiscuity than their low-level chronic and never convicted counterparts.

At age 32, the three groups of individuals who had been convicted at least once exhibited greater levels of fighting as well as greater levels of drug and alcohol use than the never convicted group. Interestingly, by age 32, the adolescent-limited and never-convicted groups were much more successful in the labor market than the chronic low- and high-rate groups. The adolescent-limited and never-convicted groups also appeared to have higher-quality attachment to their families by age 32 than the chronic offending group.[6] One anomalous result was that adolescent-limited offenders did not always desist completely. Within this group, nontrivial levels of theft and embezzlement were still evident well into adulthood.

Nagin et al. (1995) observed, in summary, that drug use, alcohol use, theft, and rowdy behavior (e.g., fighting) appear to comprise a pattern of "circumscribed deviance" for the adolescent-limited group, while more malignant forms of deviance were in evidence for the chronic offending groups. The adolescent-limited group, thus, exhibits some deviance but generally it is the kind of deviance that is "less likely to result in official sanction or disrupt intimate attachments" (Nagin et al., 1995, p. 132). Alternatively, say Nagin and his colleagues (1995, p. 136), such activities may not be regarded as serious infractions within the "working class subculture in which the AL's live."

Moffitt and her colleagues (1996) recently assessed the antisocial conduct problems of a retrospective 1972–1973 birth cohort of 457 Dunedin, New Zealand, males from age 3 to age 18. Five groups of individuals were cobbled together based on a number of measures of conduct problems within the longitudinal data: (1) individuals who engaged in extreme antisocial behavior during both childhood and adolescence (about 7% of the sample), (2) individuals who engaged in extreme antisocial behavior as adolescents but not as children (about 24% of the sample), (3) individuals who engaged in extreme childhood antisocial behavior but abstained from such behavior during adolescence (about 6% of the sample), (4) individuals who refrained from extreme antisocial behavior throughout the entire follow-up period (about 6% of the sample), and (5) a "normal" group that included 58% of the birth cohort and did not meet the criteria for inclusion in any of the other groups. Comparison of the early- and late-onset groups revealed that they differed in their tendencies to drop out of school, strength of attachments to their families, and personality profiles.

In sum, the various studies we have examined provide mixed signals on the propriety of studying different developmental pathways to offending behavior. While some analyses suggest that distinct causal processes may be responsible for the continued offending behavior of early- and late-onset groups, others indicate that there may be a great deal of similarity as well. Still other studies speak to the question of whether groups defined on the basis of the offending

---

[6]In considering these findings of "attachment quality," Nagin et al. (1995) noted that the adolescent-limited group might still have been quite susceptible to divorce and family breakup in the years most approximate to their peak period of offending. They suggest this in the wake of their finding that divorce patterns by age 32 did not vary among the three groups of offenders.

behavior they exhibit are comparable on a number of characteristics that do not include offending. These studies generally suggest that offending groups resembling those described by Moffitt and Patterson may indeed differ from each other in interesting ways. Nevertheless, they do not resolve the question of whether these differences are of causal significance and whether a theory that anticipates differences in degree rather than differences in kind can account for them as well.

HYPOTHESES

In this paper, we derive some hypotheses that constitute a test of some of the implications of developmental and general theory. Because of the centrality of the issue, each of the hypotheses concerns the possible causal impact of prior on current criminal offending. Starting from the premise that, other things equal, the most parsimonious theory is the preferred one, we ask whether (1) prior behavior has a causal effect on future behavior once time-stable differences in criminal propensity have been controlled and (2) whether there are unique causal pathways to offending in that prior behavior has a causal impact on the behavior of one type of offender but not another.

From the general perspective of Gottfredson and Hirschi (1990, pp. 154–168) and Wilson and Herrnstein (1985), we derive the following prediction:

H_1: The relationship between prior and future offending behavior will be positive, but after controlling for persistent individual differences, this positive relationship will vanish.

This hypothesis is derived from a pure or "strong" version of heterogeneity theory, as it predicts that all continuity in offending is due to time-stable individual differences in criminal propensity. As argued by Nagin and Paternoster (1991) and Nagin and Farrington (1992a), many other theories, such as differential association, social control, and strain theory, would make a different prediction:

H_2: The relationship between prior and future offending behavior will be positive and will continue to be positive even after persistent individual differences have been controlled.

Confirmation of this second hypothesis would constitute evidence that "change matters" (Laub & Sampson, 1993). In other words, changes in life circumstances may have causal significance for offending that cannot be ignored. We view the second hypothesis as a mixed model, or a "weak" form of the previous heterogeneity hypothesis, since it allows for both population heterogeneity and significant causal change. Finally, the typological theories recently advanced by Moffitt (1993) and Patterson et al. (1989) would make yet another prediction:

H_3: For those with high criminal propensity, the causal effect of prior behavior on future behavior should be trivial while, for those with low criminal propensity, the effect should be substantial.

Confirmation of this third hypothesis would constitute evidence that continuity and change in offending may be subject to different causal processes for different types of individuals. Persistence in offending may be due to time-stable differences in criminal propensity among a small group of "hardcore" offenders (the "bad apples"), while the intermittent offending of a larger pool of offenders may be due to state-dependent processes of change and adaptation to change. We characterize this as a "category-dependent" hypothesis since population heterogeneity is predicted to dominate in one group (those who onset early), while state-dependent processes dominate in the other group (those who onset later).[7]

METHODS

Data

The data for this study were comprised of 838 releasees from North Carolina Division of Youth Services training schools during the 1988–1989 calendar years. All subjects were between 16 and 18 years of age at the time of their release (average age = 16.210 years), and the analysis includes over 98% of the individuals in this age range who were released in 1988–1989 (a small number of cases were deleted due to missing data on one or more covariates). Individuals who were younger than 16 at the time of their release were not included in the analysis because subsequent arrest information was not uniformly available for these youngsters until they reached age 16. A search of arrest records for these subjects was conducted in November 1994 and the current analysis includes information on yearly arrest counts between the date of release and the search date.

A number of background variables were collected from the official Division case files on each of the 838 individuals. Table 12.1 presents descriptive statistics for all of the variables included in the analysis. The majority of the subjects were male and nonwhite. The average age of first adjudication was slightly greater than 14 years and the mean number of prior adjudications was about 2.2, although there was considerable variation about the mean for both of these variables. The average length of confinement in the juvenile training school was just under 11 months (but the sample median was eight months).

Table 12.1 also shows that about 20% of the sample had experienced at least one incident of child abuse that had been reported to authorities. More commonly, nearly 40% of the sample had been diagnosed with some type of learning disability and about 40% of the sample lived in a household that received some form of government assistance (e.g., welfare payments, food stamps, etc.). The vast majority of youngsters in the release cohort did not live in a two-parent household and slightly over one-third had parents and/or siblings who possessed a criminal record. A small minority of releasees had

---

[7]We thank one of the reviewers of this article for suggesting these descriptive characterizations of our hypotheses.

Table 12.1 Descriptive Statistics

Variable	Mean	SD	Range
Demographic Characteristics (N = 838)			
Sex (0 = Female/1 = Male)	0.882	0.323	0 to 1
Race (0 = White/1 = Nonwhite)	0.549	0.498	0 to 1
Prior Offending Behavior (N = 838)			
Age at First Adjudication	14.307	1.537	7 to 17
Number of Prior Adjudications	2.189	1.650	0 to 8
Time Incarcerated (Months)	10.845	7.772	0 to 52
Indicator Variables (0 = No/1 = Yes) (N = 838)			
Reported Child Abuse	0.195	0.396	0 to 1
Learning Disability Designation	0.394	0.489	0 to 1
Family Receives Government Assistance	0.383	0.486	0 to 1
Not Living in a Two-Parent Household	0.829	0.376	0 to 1
Criminal History Among Other Family	0.365	0.482	0 to 1
Mental Deficit and Assaultive Behavior	0.080	0.271	0 to 1
Time-Varying Variables (N = 4529)			
Time Index	3.235	1.588	1 to 6
Arrested in Previous Year (0 = No/1= Yes)	0.236	0.425	0 to 1
Count of Arrests in Current Year	0.465	0.963	0 to 11

been diagnosed with a severe disorder that consists of both mental or intellectual deficiencies and serious episodes of assaultive behavior. Children classified into this category are referred to as "Willie M" cases and receive intensive treatment or services in areas where particular needs are identified (details are discussed by Weisz et al., 1990). These data were used to create a multiwave panel that varied from 4 to 6 years in length. Thus, some individuals were followed for as few as 4 full years ($n = 47$), others were followed for 5 years ($n = 405$), while still others were followed for 6 full years ($n = 386$).

A key component of the tests performed in this analysis is the definition of high and low criminal propensity groups. Unfortunately, there is no single widely accepted definition of criminal propensity (Simons et al., 1994, p. 267; Moffitt, 1994, pp. 28–29; Patterson et al., 1989, p. 331, 1992, pp. 335–341; Patterson, 1993, pp. 913–914; Nagin et al., 1995, p. 112; Nagin and Farrington, 1992b, pp. 504–506). Nevertheless, Nagin and Farrington (1992b) argue that "[i]t is well documented that early onset of delinquent behavior is predictive of more persistent future offending" (p. 503; see also Farrington et al., 1990, pp. 290–293; Patterson et al., 1992, pp. 339–340; Moffitt, 1993, p. 694; Sampson & Laub, 1995, pp. 149–150; Horney et al., 1995, p. 671). Thus, while criminal propensity itself may be difficult to define there seems to be considerable agreement that an early onset of offending behavior is an indicator of relatively high propensity to engage in crime and delinquency. For example, according to Gottfredson and Hirschi (1990), those who initiate offending early in life exhibit comparatively low levels of self-control (i.e., high criminal propensity) throughout the life course (see also

Gottfredson & Hirschi, 1986, p. 223, 1988, pp. 39–40). Similar themes are expressed in the work of other theorists as well (see, e.g., Moffitt, 1993, p. 694, 1994, p. 46; Loeber & LeBlanc, 1990, pp. 394–395).

In short, onset age appears to be a useful index for criminal propensity. While it is not yet clear whether onset age is itself causally important, all seem agreed that early onset of criminal behavior is not a harbinger of good things to come.[8] As such, those with early onset ages are generally viewed as being at highest risk for long-term chronic offending patterns, while those with later onset ages are generally viewed as being at somewhat lower risk for these malignant outcomes. For theorists such as Gottfredson and Hirschi and Sampson and Laub, factors that predict future problem behavior in early- and late-onset groups are hypothesized to be the same—those who onset late just possess them to a lesser degree. For taxonomic theorists such as Moffitt and Patterson, however, the factors that lead to offending are actually thought to be very different between the two groups. The question for our research is whether the difference between these groups is one of degree or kind.

Finally, the data facilitate calculation of the number of arrest events that occurred during each full year of the follow-up period (see Table 12.1). They also provide a reasonable base of information upon which to address the questions discussed above. First, the analysis attempts to identify the effect of prior arrests on future arrests under the restrictive assumption that a single process generated the data for all 838 individuals. Then, using varying onset ages as cutting points, this equal-effects constraint is relaxed to test the hypothesis that prior arrests exert similar effects on subsequent arrests regardless of one's membership in an early- or late-onset group.

Analysis Methods

The dependent variable is a count of arrest events within each year of the panel. Thus, a statistical model that takes the discrete features of the dependent variable and the lack of independence of multiple observations on the same individual into account is required. As Land (1992) argues, it is conventional to assume that data such as these are generated by a Poisson process with discrete density

$$\text{pr}(n_{it}) = e^{-\lambda_{it}}\lambda_{it}^{y_{it}}/y_{it}!, \qquad y_{it} = 0, 1, \ldots \tag{1}$$

where λ is the Poisson parameter and is allowed to depend on vectors of time-stable and time-varying covariates, by the equality

$$\lambda_{it} = \exp(x'_i\theta + t\gamma + z_{it}\eta) \tag{2}$$

where

$$z_{it} = \begin{cases} 1, & \text{if individual } i \text{ was arrested in previous year} \\ 0, & \text{otherwise} \end{cases}$$

---

[8]In sum, while it may seem that the age at which one onsets offending is a mere calendrical event, it proxies for latent criminal propensity.

t is a time index which ranges from 1 to 6 and indexes one's temporal position within the follow-up period, and x_i is a vector of covariates that do not change over time (i.e., sex, race, etc.).

In the special case where λ adequately captures both the mean and the variance of the outcome variable y_{it}, then the parameters of Eq. (2) can be estimated by maximum-likelihood methods for Poisson regression. In regression analyses of crime count outcomes (including the current analysis), however, the mean-variance equality is often violated by substantial over dispersion in the data (see Table 12.1). A common remedy for this problem is to augment Eq. (2) to include a random disturbance term,

$$\lambda_{it} = \exp(x'_i\theta + t\gamma + z_{it}\eta + \varepsilon_{it}) \tag{3}$$

under the assumption that $\exp(\varepsilon)$ is distributed as $\Gamma(1, \alpha)$ where the parameters $\theta, \gamma, \eta,$ and α are estimated from the data by maximum-likelihood methods (see, e.g., Land et al., 1996, p. 396; Hausman et al., 1984, p. 922). The probability of the number of events for individual i at time t to enter the likelihood is

$$p(n_{it}) = \int_0^\infty p(n_{it}|\lambda_{it})\, f\,(\lambda_{it})\; d\lambda_{it}$$

$$= \left(\frac{\Gamma(n_{it} + v)}{n_{it}!\;\Gamma(v)}\right)\left(\frac{v}{v + \lambda_{it}}\right)^v\left(\frac{\lambda_{it}}{v + \lambda_{it}}\right)^{n_{it}} \tag{4}$$

where $\Gamma(\bullet)$ is the gamma function, which is easily evaluated using most statistical computing packages and $v = 1/\alpha$ (see, e.g., SAS Institute, 1990, p. 551).[9] This specification provides a baseline to which more complex models that take the lack of independence among within-subject observations into account may be compared.

To confront the lack of independence in the data due to multiple observations per individual, a random-effects specification of Eq. (3) is employed. The specification for this problem is similar to that of Eq. (3) except that we now enter a different probability into the likelihood. Following Hausman *et al.* (1984, p. 927), we assume that the ratio $v/(1 + v)$ is distributed as a beta random variable, $B(a, b)$, with parameters a and b estimated from the data. The probability to enter the likelihood is then given by

$$p(n_{i1}, \ldots, n_{iT}) = \left(\frac{\Gamma(a + b)\Gamma(a + \Sigma\lambda_{it})\Gamma(b + \Sigma n_{it})}{\Gamma(a)\Gamma(b)\Gamma(a + b + \Sigma\lambda_{it} + \Sigma n_{it})}\right)$$

$$\times\left(\prod_{t=1}^T \frac{\Gamma(\lambda_{it} + n_{it})}{\Gamma(\lambda_{it})\Gamma(n_{it} + 1)}\right) \tag{5}$$

Maximizing the likelihood based on the probability in Eq. (5) facilitates the control of persistent unmeasured covariates of λ. A number of covariates, as discussed above, are also included in the specification to control for observable

---

[9]We note that this specification is equivalent to the NEGBIN II model discussed by Cameron and Trivedi (1986).

persistent individual differences that affect λ. The likelihood function and computational details for estimating the parameters of the negative binomial model and the random-effects negative binomial model are discussed by Greene (1995, pp. 570–571).[10]

RESULTS

The core problem to be addressed by this analysis is twofold. First, we wish to consider whether the effect of prior arrests on future arrests is spurious. This is equivalent to testing whether the parameter estimate of η in Eq. (3) is different from zero after controlling for both persistent observed and unobserved differences between individuals. The analysis was also designed to assess whether the maximum-likelihood estimate of η differs between those who were first adjudicated at an early age and those who were first adjudicated later on.

We begin by considering whether the effect of prior arrests on subsequent arrests varies between models that make very different assumptions: (1) there are no persistent unobserved differences between individuals that relate to arrest frequency, and (2) such differences are present and must be taken into account in order to assess properly the process that generates the data. Table 12.2 presents Models 1 and 2, which are estimated with controls for the full set of covariates (with the exception of age at first adjudication) described in Table 12.1.[11] Figure 12.2 graphically displays the corresponding confidence intervals for the structural effects reported in Table 12.2 for Model 1 and Model 2. From these figures one can easily see the full range of the expected effect for each estimated parameter.

Model 1 is a negative binomial regression analysis based on the assumption that the specification includes no important omitted time stable covariates [i.e., estimated according to Eq. (3) above]. Model 2 relaxes this assumption at the cost of one parameter estimate (i.e., one degree of freedom). A test of whether the log-likelihoods of Models 1 and 2 are different is, therefore, a test of the plausibility of the exhaustive specification assumption (i.e., that there is no persistent unobserved heterogeneity). Twice the difference between these

---

[10]Although useful for our purposes, this specification makes assumptions about the process generating persistent heterogeneity. Incorrect specification of this process affects the efficiency of the estimator resulting in deflated standard errors and, therefore, inflated t ratios. Land and Nagin have developed a semiparametric estimator that makes no assumptions about the distribution of persistent unobserved heterogeneity in the population (Nagin & Land, 1993; Land et al., 1996; Land & Nagin, 1996). Unfortunately, the software to estimate their semiparametric mixed Poisson model is not widely available. To assess whether our model provides a reasonable approximation to the observed frequencies, we generated the theoretical relative frequency distribution from Eq. (5) based on a specification that included only indicator variables for the time index. In support of the specification we have chosen, we found considerable congruence between the observed frequencies and those expected from evaluating Eq. (5). We report the results of this investigation in the Appendix.

[11]Age at first adjudication was not included as a covariate in this analysis because its values were used as the basis for dividing the sample into low and high criminal propensity groups.

Table 12.2 Full Sample Negative Binomial Regression Models Estimated Under Assumptions of Zero Persistent Unobserved Heterogeneity (Model 1) and Nontrivial Persistent Unobserved Heterogeneity (Model 2)

Variable	MODEL 1. NO CONTROL FOR PERSISTENT UNOBSERVED HETEROGENEITY ($N = 838$)			MODEL 2. PERSISTENT UNOBSERVED HETEROGENEITY CONTROLLED ($N = 838$)		
	Parameter Estimate	SE	|t| Ratio	Parameter Estimate	SE	|t| Ratio
Constant	−1.738	0.138	12.58	−1.199	0.211	5.67
Number of Juvenile Adjudications	0.036	0.018	1.93	0.034	0.023	1.52
Race = Nonwhite	0.304	0.064	4.71	0.421	0.075	5.64
Sex = Male	0.787	0.100	7.86	0.962	0.129	7.44
Reported Child Abuse	0.159	0.075	2.12	0.141	0.090	1.57
Learning Disability	0.024	0.064	0.37	0.073	0.075	0.97
Mental Deficit/Assaultive Behavior	−0.019	0.121	0.16	0.090	0.131	0.68
No Two-Parent Household	0.230	0.083	2.75	0.248	0.099	2.49
Family Criminal History	0.244	0.061	4.03	0.231	0.073	3.16
Government Assistance	−0.030	0.064	0.47	−0.044	0.076	0.57
Time Incarcerated	0.003	0.004	0.76	−0.002	0.005	0.39
Time Index (γ)	−0.183	0.019	9.75	−0.165	0.019	8.82
Arrested in Previous Year (η)	0.631	0.071	8.82	0.228	0.074	3.09
α	1.713	0.116	14.75			
a				6.714	1.040	6.47
b				2.884	0.544	5.30
Log-Likelihood	−3942.64			−3886.14		
Number of Parameter Estimates	14			15		

log–likelihood values is distributed as a chi-square random variable with one degree of freedom, and in this case, the test statistic is statistically significant [$\chi^2_{(1)} = 113.0$, $P < 0.05$]. On the basis of this result, the hypothesis of no persistent unobserved heterogeneity seems to be inconsistent with the data.

The next item of interest in Table 12.2 is the variable effect of η under the assumption of no time-stable individual differences (Model 1) and after that assumption has been relaxed (Model 2). The η term, it will be remembered, measures the effect of prior arrests on future arrests. Under Hypothesis 1, we would expect this to be zero once measured and unmeasured sources of persistent heterogeneity have been controlled. In particular, the quantity $\delta = \eta_{M1} - \eta_{M2}$ is of interest and an examination of Table 12.2 indicates that δ is sizable and of substantive importance ($\delta = 0.631 - 0.228 = 0.402$). The imposition of statistical controls for persistent unobserved heterogeneity leads to a

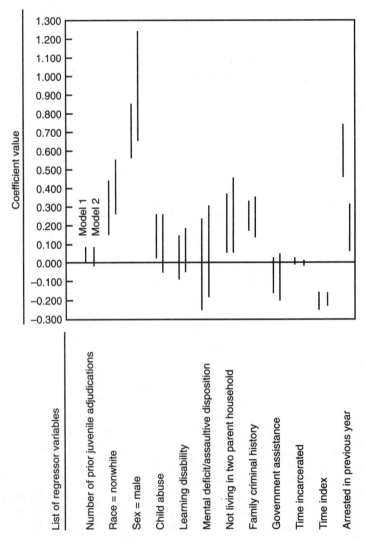

FIGURE 12.2 Ninety-five percent confidence intervals for parameter estimates associated with Models 1 and 2. The 95% intervals are computed under the assumption that repeated random sampling from the target population would yield a sampling distribution for each regression coefficient. This sampling distribution is assumed to be approximately normal. For each coefficient the 95% interval is bounded by the 2.5th percentile and the 97.5th percentile of that sampling distribution.

dramatic deterioration in the estimate of the effect of prior arrests on future arrests [i.e., $\delta/\eta_{MI}) \times 100 = 63.9\%$ reduction in the value of η].[12] Nevertheless, consistent with Hypothesis 2, the estimate of η was positive and statistically significant under both specifications. The most reasonable conclusion on the basis of this evidence is that, *ceteris paribus,* prior arrests increase the frequency of future arrests. Moreover, these results run counter to the predictions of theories such as Gottfredson and Hirschi's (1990) and Wilson and Herrnstein's (1985), models that anticipate static causal processes. Our findings in this regard corroborate those of Land and Nagin (1996), who also reported evidence of persistent heterogeneity (continuity) and state dependence (change).

Table 12.3 provides some insight into the difference in the effect of prior behavior between Model 1 and Model 2. To construct this table, all variables except the indicator variable signifying whether one was arrested in the previous year were constrained to their mean values; we then multiplied the mean variable vector by the estimated regression coefficients with the prior behavior variable set to 0.0 and 1.0, respectively. To secure the probabilities associated with Model 1, we evaluated Eq. (4), and to secure the probabilities associated with Model 2. we evaluated Eq. (5). As might be expected from the results in Table 12.2, the effect of being arrested in the previous period is attenuated as one moves from Model 1 to Model 2.

Although the models presented in Table 12.2 provide evidence in favor of dynamic rather than static theoretical perspectives, they do not confront the possibility accommodated by developmental theorists that there are qualitatively different groups whose behaviors are generated by distinct causal processes. In particular, these theories predict that the continued offending behavior of those with extremely high levels of criminal propensity will be caused by a different set of factors than those associated with low-criminal propensity individuals. Among the most prominent of these factors is the effect of prior behavior on future behavior.

To test the state dependence/persistent heterogeneity implications of the Moffitt and Patterson developmental theories, we divided the sample into two groups: those who were first adjudicated at an early age and those who were first adjudicated later on. While the literature does not offer specific guidance about the exact cutoff point that should be used to define the low and high propensity groups, the age cutoffs herein are consistent with what has been used by others (Simons et al., 1994, p. 267; LeBlanc & Frechette, 1989, p. 105; Loeber & LeBlanc, 1990, p. 395; Patterson et al., 1992, p. 336; Farrington et al., 1990, p. 325; Stattin & Magnusson, 1995, pp. 418–419, 423). Consequently,

---

[12]Ideally, we would conduct a formal test of the hypothesis that $\delta = 0$. The test statistic would be distributed as a standard normal variable z. Unfortunately, the existing theory for testing this hypothesis requires either (1) that one know the covariance between the coefficients whose difference is being tested or (2) that the covariance can be assumed to be zero. When the samples on which the coefficients are estimated are independent, the second assumption is reasonable. In this case, however, the models are estimated on the same sample, the coefficients used in the computation of δ are not independent, and we do not know their covariance.

Table 12.3 Expected Relative Frequency Distributions for Arrests During a 1-Year Period Showing Estimated Effect of Prior Behavior With and Without Controls for Persistent Unobserved Heterogeneity

Number of Arrests	MODEL 1. NO CONTROL FOR PERSISTENT UNOBSERVED HETEROGENEITY		MODEL 2. PERSISTENT UNOBSERVED HETEROGENEITY CONTROLLED	
	Arrest in Prior Period = 0	Arrest in Prior Period = 1	Arrest in Prior Period = 0	Arrest in Prior Period = 1
0	0.760	0.643	0.755	0.706
1	0.166	0.199	0.162	0.187
2	0.049	0.084	0.049	0.062
3	0.016	0.038	0.018	0.024
4	0.005	0.018	0.007	0.010
5+	0.004	0.018	0.009	0.011

Note. Expected relative frequency distributions were calculated by constraining all variables to their sample means (except the indicator variable for one or more arrests in the previous period) and evaluating the probability density for a negative binomial model and a random-effects negative binomial model.

models were estimated using four cutoff points: (1) age 11 and younger, (2) age 12 and younger compared to age 13 and older, (3) age 13 and younger compared to age 14 and older, and (4) age 14 and younger compared to age 15 and older.

Using the first age cutoff point, we divided the sample into two groups: those who were first adjudicated at or before age 11 and those who were adjudicated at or after age 12. The results of this estimation are presented in Table 12.4 as Models 3 and 4. Only 52 individuals could be classified as early starters using this scheme and the estimation routine failed to reach convergence using the full set of covariates. We were able to achieve convergence with a model that included the intercept, a time trend indicator, and a prior arrest indicator (as well as the random effects parameters). The log-likelihood for this specification on the entire sample was -3940.12 (with five parameter estimates) while the sum of the log-likelihood values in the separate group equations was -3936.88 (with 10 parameter estimates). Twice the difference between the summed log-likelihood of Models 3 and 4 and the constrained log-likelihood is distributed as a chi-square random variable with $10 - 5 = 5$ degrees of freedom. The test statistic provides no support for rejecting the null hypothesis that the population coefficients are the same for each of the groups $[\chi_5^2 = 6.48, P > 0.05]$.

In words, the dynamic effect of prior on future behavior is comparable between the low and the high criminal propensity groups. This result is counter to the predictions of the Moffitt and Patterson theories and Hypothesis 3, which anticipate that the effect of prior behavior will be contingent on established levels of criminal propensity. Consistent with the predictions of general theorists, the results point to invariance in the process leading to future offending behavior. As demonstrated below, this conclusion is robust to the choice of cutoff points.

Table 12.4 Negative Binomial Regression Models Comparing Those Adjudicated at or Before Age 11 (Model 3) and Those Adjudicated at or After Age 12 (Model 4)

Variable	Model 3 (N = 52)			Model 4 (N = 786)		
	Parameter Estimate	SE	ltl Ratio	Parameter Estimate	SE	ltl Ratio
Constant	0.939	0.603	1.56	0.464	0.122	3.79
Time Index (γ)	−0.239	0.076	3.12	−0.155	0.019	8.13
Arrested in Previous						
Year (η)	0.284	0.264	1.07	0.199	0.076	2.62
a	6.340	4.398	1.44	5.269	0.759	6.93
b	2.393	1.446	1.65	1.865	0.302	6.16
Log-Likelihood	−290.76			−3646.12		
Number of Parameter Estimates	5			5		

Despite this result, it might be argued that the likelihood difference test is inappropriate when interest centers on a difference between specific coefficients because the chi-square statistic must be very large to reject the null hypothesis when there are many degrees of freedom involved. To address this possibility, a direct test of the hypothesis that $\delta = 0$ (ignoring the possibility of other similarities and differences) was calculated using a large sample test statistic, z, which is distributed as a standard normal random variable.

$$z = |\delta| / [\sigma^2(\eta_{Mi}) + \sigma^2(\eta_{Mj})]^{1/2} \qquad (6)$$

where $i \neq j$ and, in the case at hand, $\delta = \eta_{M3} - \eta_{M4} = 0.085$. This result follows the convention of calculating the difference and the variance of the difference between two independent random normal variables (Clogg et al., 1995, pp. 1276–1277). In the case of the hypothesis that $\delta = \eta_{M3} - \eta_{M4} = 0$, the obtained test statistic is not statistically significant at conventional levels ($z = 0.31$, $P > 0.05$). As such, there is no basis in the current data for concluding that the effects of prior arrests vary between those who were first adjudicated at or before age 11 and those first adjudicated later on.

The results of this analysis using the second cutoff point (those age 12 or younger compared to those 13 or older) are presented in Table 12.5 as Models 5 and 6. These models were estimable with the full set of covariates. Two tests were conducted to assess the plausibility of the hypothesis that the effect of prior arrests on future arrests is the same between the early and late first adjudication groups (i.e., $\delta = \eta_{M5} - \eta_{M6} = 0$). The first assessment was a global test of the hypothesis that none of the differences between parameter estimates in Models 3 and 4 was greater than zero. To conduct this test, we sum the log-likelihood values of Models 5 and 6. This summed log-likelihood [$\log(L) = -3877.08$] is based on a total of 30 parameter estimates. Twice the difference between the summed log-likelihood of Models 5 and 6 and the constrained

**Table 12.5 Negative Binomial Regression Models Comparing
Those Adjudicated at or Before Age 12 (Model 5)
and Those Adjudicated at or After Age 13 (Model 6)**

	MODEL 5 (*N* = 101)			MODEL 6 (*N* = 737)		
Variable	Parameter Estimate	SE	Itl Ratio	Parameter Estimate	SE	Itl Ratio
Constant	0.509	0.836	0.61	−1.415	0.227	6.22
Number of Juvenile Adjudications	−0.022	0.066	0.33	0.039	0.026	1.51
Race = Nonwhite	0.377	0.229	1.65	0.428	0.078	5.45
Sex = Male	−0.033	0.544	0.06	1.057	0.137	7.68
Reported Child Abuse	0.568	0.256	2.22	0.057	0.102	0.56
Learning Disability	0.168	0.203	0.83	0.055	0.079	0.69
Mental Deficit/Assaultive Behavior	0.234	0.348	0.67	0.052	0.143	0.37
No Two-Parent Household	0.317	0.347	0.91	0.232	0.103	2.24
Family Criminal History	0.086	0.218	0.40	0.256	0.077	3.28
Government Assistance	−0.109	0.250	0.43	−0.010	0.081	0.13
Time Incarcerated	−0.006	0.014	0.44	0.000	0.005	0.09
Time Index (γ)	−0.229	0.060	3.80	−0.154	0.020	7.66
Arrested in Previous Year (η)	0.183	0.183	1.00	0.246	0.081	3.03
a	9.388	4.96	1.89	6.819	1.182	5.77
b	2.775	1.53	1.82	3.136	0.675	4.64
Log Likelihood	−514.66			−3362.42		
Number of Parameter Estimates	15			15		

log-likelihood of Model 2 is distributed as a chi-square random variable with $30 - 15 = 15$ degrees of freedom. The test statistic provides no support for rejecting the null hypothesis that the population coefficients are the same for each of the groups [$\chi^2_{(15)} = 18.12$, $P > 0.05$].

A direct test of the hypothesis that $\delta = \eta_{M5} - \eta_{M6} = 0$ indicates that the difference is not statistically significant at conventional levels ($z = 0.32$, $P > 0.05$). As such, there is no basis in the current data for concluding that the effects of η vary between those who were first adjudicated early and those first adjudicated later on.

We now turn to a third version of the test for differences between groups distinguished by age at first adjudication. In this third version, the cutoff point for the early first adjudication group was raised to include all individuals who were age 13 or younger at the time of their first adjudication. All individuals who were older than 13 at the time of their first adjudication were included in the late first adjudication group. The models for the early and late first adjudication groups, so defined, are presented in Table 12.6 as Models 7 and 8, respectively. The sum of the log-likelihood values for these two group-specific

Table 12.6 Negative Binomial Regression Models Comparing Those Adjudicated at or Before Age 13 (Model 7) and Those Adjudicated at or After Age 14 (Model 8)

Variable	Model 7 (N = 197)			Model 8 (N = 641)		
	Parameter Estimate	SE	|t| Ratio	Parameter Estimate	SE	|t| Ratio
Constant	−0.774	0.455	1.70	−1.217	0.262	4.65
Number of Juvenile Adjudications	0.029	0.042	0.68	0.016	0.031	0.53
Race = Nonwhite	0.295	0.145	2.04	0.465	0.092	5.04
Sex = Male	0.388	0.262	1.48	1.088	0.153	7.08
Reported Child Abuse	0.322	0.152	2.12	0.074	0.115	0.64
Learning Disability	0.067	0.135	0.49	0.065	0.089	0.72
Mental Deficit/Assaultive Behavior	0.219	0.242	0.91	−0.000	0.162	0.00
No Two-Parent Household	0.437	0.233	1.88	0.180	0.115	1.56
Family Criminal History	0.123	0.132	0.93	0.265	0.089	2.96
Government Assistance	−0.162	0.143	1.14	0.015	0.094	0.16
Time Incarcerated	−0.002	0.008	0.25	−0.003	0.008	0.38
Time Index (γ)	−0.187	0.042	4.48	−0.155	0.022	7.15
Arrested in Previous Year (η)	0.221	0.136	1.62	0.232	0.088	2.62
a	6.909	2.246	3.08	6.914	1.267	5.46
b	3.918	1.599	2.45	2.684	0.582	4.61
Log-likelihood	−1064.36			−2813.33		
Number of Parameter Estimates	15			15		

regressions was −3877.69 (based on 30 parameter estimates). A comparison of this summed log-likelihood value to the baseline value of Model 2 yields a nonsignificant test statistic [$\chi^2_{(15)} = 16.90$, $P > 0.05$]. Furthermore, a direct comparison of the estimated values of η between the early and the late adjudication group [using the z test in Eq. (5)] provides no support for the conclusion that $\delta = 0$ in the population ($z = 0.07$, $P > 0.05$).

Finally, we consider a fourth test for differences between groups distinguished by age at first adjudication. The early first adjudication group included all individuals who were age 14 or younger at the time of their first adjudication. All individuals who were 15 or older at the time of their first adjudication were included in the late first adjudication group. The models for the two groups are presented in Table 12.7 as Models 9 and 10. The sum of the log-likelihood values for these two equations was −3879.35 (based on 30 parameter estimates). A comparison of this summed log-likelihood value to the baseline value of Model 2 yields a nonsignificant test statistic [$\chi^2_{(15)} = 13.58$, $P > 0.05$]. Direct comparison of the estimated values of η between the early

Table 12.7 Negative Binomial Regression Models Comparing Those Adjudicated at or Before Age 14 (Model 9) and Those Adjudicated at or After Age 15 (Model 10)

Variable	MODEL 9 (N = 375)			MODEL 10 (N = 463)		
	Parameter Estimate	SE	ltl Ratio	Parameter Estimate	SE	ltl Ratio
Constant	−1.119	0.312	3.58	−1.263	0.311	4.05
Number of Juvenile Adjudications	0.028	0.031	0.89	0.013	0.044	0.29
Race = Nonwhite	0.416	0.108	3.83	0.429	0.108	3.98
Sex = Male	0.886	0.178	4.97	1.031	0.194	5.30
Reported Child Abuse	0.236	0.123	1.92	0.041	0.133	0.31
Learning Disability	−0.034	0.106	0.33	0.147	0.107	1.38
Mental Deficit/Assaultive Behavior	0.136	0.183	0.74	0.014	0.194	0.07
No Two-Parent Household	0.416	0.152	2.74	0.101	0.139	0.72
Family Criminal History	0.212	0.102	2.07	0.235	0.106	2.22
Government Assistance	−0.117	0.109	1.07	0.057	0.114	0.50
Time Incarcerated	−0.007	0.006	1.27	0.008	0.010	0.81
Time Index (γ)	−0.176	0.027	6.38	−0.154	0.026	5.83
Arrested in Previous Year (η)	0.159	0.103	1.54	0.294	0.109	2.69
a	6.980	1.618	4.31	6.749	1.455	4.64
b	3.307	0.943	3.51	2.689	0.711	3.78
Log-Likelihood	−1876.83			−2002.52		
Number of Parameter Estimates	15			15		

and the late adjudication group [using the z test in Eq. (5)] provides no support for the conclusion that $\delta = 0$ in the population ($z = 0.90$, $P > 0.05$).

Thus far, the results provide support for the idea that both stable individual differences and the effect of prior arrests (a state dependent effect) have implications for the yearly frequency of offending in these data. The results, thus far, do not support the idea that prior behavior exerts different effects between the early and late onset groups. In sum, the effect of prior arrests on future arrests appears to be positive, statistically significant, and of similar magnitude regardless of whether one was first adjudicated early or late.

One possible criticism of our analysis as presented thus far is that our theoretical interest centers on the invariance of the state-dependent effect, while our models have been estimated to allow for differences between the groups on all effects. In order to examine the robustness of our results to an alternative specification, we estimated models including an indicator variable for one's age at first adjudication (0 = late first adjudication; 1 = early first adjudication), an indicator variable for whether one was arrested in the previous year (0 = not arrested in the previous year; 1 = arrested in the previous year), a product of the age at first adjudication indicator and the prior arrest indicator, and all of the covariates included in the previous specifications. A test of the hypothesis of invariant state-dependent effects in this specification is given by a z test on the null hypothesis that the product term coefficient is equal to zero in the population.

Table 12.8 presents the results of this analysis using the age division schema employed in our previous tests. Models 11, 12, and 13 all suggest that the effect of the interaction between whether one was adjudicated early or late and arrest in the previous period is only trivially different from zero in the population. The estimates obtained from Model 14, however, lead us to a somewhat more qualified conclusion on this matter.

The estimated effect of prior arrests on future arrests in Model 14 does appear to depend on whether one was first adjudicated at or before age 14. Inspection of the coefficients reveals that the estimated value of η for those who were first adjudicated at or after age 15 was 0.339. The comparable effect among those who were first adjudicated at or before age 14, however, was 0.129. The z value associated with the product of the early first adjudication indicator and the prior arrest indicator is -1.80, which is statistically significant at the 95% confidence level (using a one-tailed test).

To investigate this result more closely, we eliminated the variables that were not statistically significant at the 95% confidence level from Model 14 and estimated the reduced version of the specification as Model 15.[13] The results of this specification led us to exactly the same conclusions as those obtained under Model 14. The effect of prior arrests was significantly weaker within the group of individuals who were first adjudicated at or before age 14 compared to those who were first adjudicated at a later age.

Summary of Results

Because we have covered much ground in this paper, we briefly summarize our results in this section. It should be recalled that there were two primary questions driving the analysis. First, we examined the relative utility of static and dynamic models of offending frequency. The decrease in the magnitude of prior arrest effects after persistent individual differences were controlled was substantial. This finding is testimony to the important role that continuity and stability play in the process driving offending careers (Gottfredson & Hirschi, 1990; Nagin & Paternoster, 1991; Nagin & Farrington, 1992). Consistent with Hypothesis 2 (and counter to Hypothesis 1—the "strong" heterogeneity hypothesis), the effect of prior arrest on future arrest was positive, statistically significant, and substantively important even after controlling for persistent individual differences. This result provides empirical support for the predictions of dynamic theorists such as Sampson and Laub (1993, 1995)

---

[13]A test of whether the log-likelihood of Model 15 differs significantly from the summed log-likelihood values of Models 9 and 10 yields $\chi^2_{(19)} = 15.62$. which is not statistically significant at a 95% confidence level.

Table 12.8 Investigation of Interactions Between First Adjudication Age and Prior Offending Behavior

Variables	Model 11 Parameter Estimate	Model 11 |t| Ratio	Model 12 Parameter Estimate	Model 12 |t| Ratio	Model 13 Parameter Estimate	Model 13 |t| Ratio	Model 14 Parameter Estimate	Model 14 |t| Ratio	Model 15 Parameter Estimate	Model 15 |t| Ratio
Constant	-1.183	5.57	-1.189	5.58	-1.177	5.50	-1.228	5.83	-1.173	6.09
Number of Juvenile Adjudications	0.030	1.30	0.030	1.24	0.022	0.89	0.025	1.02		
Race = Nonwhite	0.420	5.62	0.422	5.63	0.415	5.56	0.419	5.62	0.400	5.59
Sex = Male	0.959	7.39	0.956	7.37	0.944	7.29	0.956	7.39	0.974	7.73
Reported Child Abuse	0.138	1.45	0.141	1.49	0.141	1.54	0.139	1.54		
Learning Disability	0.067	0.88	0.071	0.94	0.067	0.90	0.066	0.89		
Mental Deficit/Assaultive Behavior	0.083	0.63	0.086	0.64	0.089	0.68	0.094	0.72		
No Two-Parent Household	0.246	2.47	0.248	2.48	0.244	2.45	0.247	2.48	0.245	2.52
Family Criminal History	0.230	3.13	0.231	3.14	0.226	3.09	0.229	3.14	0.239	3.31
Government Assistance	-0.046	0.60	-0.045	0.59	-0.040	0.53	-0.044	0.57		
Time Incarcerated	-0.002	0.46	-0.002	0.46	-0.003	0.69	-0.003	0.68		
Time Index (γ)	-0.165	8.82	-0.165	8.82	-0.165	8.85	-0.165	8.82	-0.165	8.85
Arrested in Previous Year (η)	0.228	3.01	0.241	3.08	0.276	3.34	0.339	3.57	0.331	3.49
First Adjudicated at Age										
≤11	0.116	0.71								
≤12			0.098	0.80						
≤13					0.172	1.71				
≤14							0.146	1.66	0.184	2.33
Arrested in Previous Year × Age at First Adjudication Group	-0.001	0.01	-0.088	0.55	-0.145	1.15	-0.210	1.80	-0.205	1.76
a	6.714	6.44	6.692	6.49	6.811	6.38	6.794	6.41	6.64	6.44
b	2.881	5.28	2.871	5.31	2.945	5.24	2.944	5.24	2.84	5.31
Log-Likelihood	-3885.81		-3885.84		-3884.66		-3884.16		-3887.16	
Number of Parameter Estimates	17		17		17		17		17	

and Loeber and LeBlanc (1990), which anticipate that transitions and change will also play important roles in the process driving offending careers. On balance, these results highlight the theoretical importance of studying *both* continuity and change. A mixed model (the "weak" heterogeneity hypothesis) that combines both heterogeneity and state dependence would seem to be consistent with the data.

Although the analysis provided strong support for the importance of dynamic models that adequately partition stability and change, the results of our assessment of Hypothesis 3 were somewhat more equivocal. The majority of our analyses failed to substantiate the more complex arguments offered by developmental theorists (the category-dependent hypothesis). We do note, however, that one of our specifications did suggest that state-dependent effects are less salient for those who were first adjudicated at or before age 14 compared to those who were first adjudicated at or after age 15. This result strikes us as being consistent with the predictions offered by developmental theorists, but the lack of robustness in this result to slight variations in the early/late onset sample division scheme leaves us with some question about whether the result is artifactual. Indeed, we can think of no good reason for believing a priori that this difference should occur yet not be apparent with any other age division schemes.[14]

In sum, our analysis questions the assumption of developmental theorists that prior behavior will exert different effects between high and low criminal propensity groups. The statistical models estimated herein revealed relatively robust and stable effects of prior arrests on future arrests regardless of onset age.

DISCUSSION AND CONCLUSIONS

At the inception of this paper, we suggested that criminological theories can usefully be organized within a two-dimensional framework. Some theories, such as those of Wilson and Herrnstein (1985) and Gottfredson and Hirschi (1990), can best be thought of as static/general theories. Pure static/general theories adopt the position that differences in crime for all offenders are due to time-stable differences in an underlying trait or characteristic that can be termed "criminal propensity." Once formed, criminal propensity is an enduring characteristic that affects the life events of individuals but is not, in turn, affected by those events. Other theories, such as Sampson and Laub's (1993) theory of age-graded informal controls, also apply to all individuals but relax the stability constraint that is a defining feature of Gottfredson and Hirschi's model. Still other theories add to this theoretical complexity by relaxing both the assumption of a general causal process and static causality. These developmental theories anticipate multiple

---

[14]We also estimated a model that examined the interaction using a cutoff that classified individuals into the early start group if they were first adjudicated at or before age 15. This analysis revealed no support for the hypothesis that prior arrests exerted different effects on future arrests between the early- and the late-onset groups.

pathways to offending. Within different developmental typologies, the process leading to offending may be either static or dynamic.

As can be discerned, the static/general theory is far more parsimonious than the dynamic and developmental models. Our purpose in this paper has been to determine if the added complexity of these dynamic and developmental theories is necessary. We have tested key hypotheses bearing on the validity of all of these approaches. One unequivocal conclusion from our analyses is that purely static or purely dynamic models of criminal offending do not appear to fit the facts. The evidence at hand clearly indicates that the relationship between past and future criminal offending cannot be attributed solely to persistent individual differences in criminal propensity nor solely to state-dependent processes of change and adaptation to change. We conclude, therefore, that continuity *and* change matter and that observed change cannot be attributed to a process of self-selection. Our findings, therefore, are more compatible with the theories of Sampson and Laub (1993; Laub & Sampson, 1993) and Nagin & Paternoster (1993, 1994), which recognize the theoretical importance of stability but do not trivialize the possibility that people can be profoundly affected by the changes in their lives.

Our reading of the evidence with respect to general vs. developmental models of offending lead us to believe that the complexity inherent in developmental models is probably not necessary, though we remain open on this important question. When separate models of criminal offending were estimated for those with low and high criminal propensity (as measured by age of onset), we found more similarities than differences. Most important, we found no evidence that state dependent effects were more pronounced within the group low in criminal propensity. This finding was robust with respect to the cutoff point for the onset age of offending. It was also relatively robust with respect to method. When product terms of age of onset by prior offending were included in pooled models, the interaction terms were, with one exception, insignificant. The exception was when the age of onset was 14 years old and younger and 15 years and older.[15] From our reading of developmental theory we have no reason for attributing particular significance to those who onset by age 14. In view of this latter finding, however, and the evidence in support of developmental theory from other research discussed earlier in this paper, the jury may still be out on the importance of unique pathways to criminal offending.

In sum, what is clear and noncontroversial is that evidence is mounting that a mixture of both continuity and change are required to account for long-term

---

[15]As to why an onset age of 14 would be so critical relative to other ages, we can offer only some conjecture at this point. It should be remembered that our data reflect the onset age of adjudication. It may well be that a first adjudication by age 14 follows a substantial amount of prior involvement in crime not captured by official statistics. Thus, adjudication by age 14 simply reflects the criminal justice system's response to established antisocial behavioral tendencies. Given our indicator of propensity, and the expectation that the causes of early adolescent delinquency may reflect antisocial tendencies, it is not surprising that the effect of prior arrest on future arrests is lower in this group of delinquents. In other words, adjudication catches up with latent criminal propensity by age 14.

patterns in criminal offending (Nagin & Farrington, 1992a, 1992b; Nagin & Land, 1993; Sampson & Laub, 1993; Horney et al., 1995; Farrington & West, 1995). We therefore dissent from the thoughtful positions of Gottfredson and Hirschi (1986) with respect to both the idea that change is causally unimportant and its methodological implication that longitudinal research is unnecessary. Indeed, the findings from this research, and other analyses leading to similar conclusions, could not have been derived from cross-sectional studies. We believe that findings like ours have important things to say for the refinement of criminological theory.

REFERENCES

Agnew, R. (1992). Foundation for a general strain theory of crime and delinquency. *Criminology* 30:47–87.

Akers, R. (1985). *Deviant Behavior.* Wadsworth, Belmont, CA.

Barnett, A., and Lofaso, A. J. (1985). Selective incapacitation and the Philadelphia cohort data. *J. Quant. Criminol.* 1:3–36.

Barnett, A., Blumstein, A., and Farrington, D. P. (1989). A prospective test of a criminal career model. *Criminology* 27:373–385.

Barnett, A.. Blumstein, A., Cohen, J., and Farrington, D. P. (1992). Not all criminal career models are equally valid. *Criminology* 30:133–140.

Blumstein, A., Cohen, J., Roth, J., and Visher, C. (1986). *Criminal Careers and "Career Criminals,"* National Academy Press, Washington, DC.

Blumstein. A., Cohen. J., and Farrington, D. P. (1988). Criminal career research; Its value for criminology. *Criminology* 26: 1–35.

Cameron, A. C., and Trivedi, P. K. (1986). Econometric models based on count data: Comparisons and applications of some estimators and tests. *J. Appl. Econometr.* 1:29–53.

Clogg, C. C., Petkova. E., and Haritou, A. (1995). Statistical methods for comparing regression coefficients between models. *Am. J. Sociol.* 100(5): 1261–1293.

Dean, C. W., Brame. R., and Piquero, A. R. (1996). Criminal propensities, discrete groups of offenders, and persistence in crime. *Criminology* 34: 547–574.

Farrington, D. P., and West, D. J. (1995). The effects of marriage, separation, and children on offending by adult males. In Blau, Z. S., and Hagan, J. (eds.), *Current Perspectives on Aging and the Life Cycle. Vol. 4: Delinquency and Disrepute in the Life Course: Contextual and Dynamic Analyses.* JAI Press, Greenwich, CT.

Farrington. D., Loeber, R., Elliott, D., Hawkins, J. D., Kandel, D., Klein. M., McCord. J., Rowe, D., and Tremblay, R. (1990). Advancing knowledge about the onset of delinquency and crime. In Lahey, B., and Kazdin, A. (eds.), *Advances in Clinical Child Psychology,* Plenum Press, New York.

In contrast, the stronger state-dependent effect for official delinquents whose first adjudication occurred at or after age 15 may coincide with time-specific criminogenic influences such as a pronounced influence of peers as one becomes free of parental control, critical period events (entering high school), biological transformations in the transition to puberty, and changes in social experiences (having sexual intercourse). In sum, the volatility of life during adolescence may accentuate the negative effects of an arrest on future behavior, generating a strong state-dependent effect for those who onset later.

Gottfredson, M., and Hirschi, T. (1986). The true value of lambda would appear to be zero: An essay on career criminals, criminal careers, selective incapacitation, cohort studies, and related topics. *Criminology* 24:213–234.

Gottfredson, M., and Hirschi, T. (1988). Science, public policy, and the career paradigm. *Criminology* 26:37–55.

Gottfredson, M., and Hirschi, T. (1990). *A General Theory of Crime,* Stanford University Press, Stanford, CA.

Greene, W. (1995). *LIMDEP Version 7.0 User's Manual,* Econometrics Software, Belport, NY.

Hausman, J., Hall, B. H., and Griliches, Z. (1984). Econometric models for count data with an application to the patents–R&D relationship. *Econometrica* 52(4):909–938.

Hirschi, T. (1969). *Causes of Delinquency,* University of California Press, Berkeley.

Hirschi, T., and Gottfredson, M. (1995). Control theory and the life-course perspective. *Stud. Crime Crime Prevent. Biann. Rev.* 4:131–142.

Horney, J., Osgood, D. W., and Marshall, I. (1995). Criminal careers in the short term: Intra-individual variability in crime and its relation to local life circumstances. *Am. Sociol. Rev.* 60:655–673.

Hsiao, C. (1986). *The Analysis of Panel Data,* Cambridge University Press, New York.

Land, K. C. (1992). Models of career criminals: Some suggestions for moving beyond the current debate. *Criminology* 30:149–155.

Land, K. C., and Nagin, D. S. (1996). Micro-models of criminal careers: A synthesis of the criminal careers and life course approaches via semiparametric mixed Poisson regression models, with empirical applications. *J. Quant. Criminol.* 12(1):163–191.

Land, K. C., McCall, P. L., and Nagin, P. S. (1996). A comparison of Poisson, negative binomial, and semiparametric mixed Poisson regression models, with empirical applications to criminal careers data. *Sociol. Methods Res.* 24:387–442.

Laub, J., and Sampson. R. (1993). Turning points in the life course: Why change matters to the study of crime. *Criminology* 31:301–326.

LeBlanc, M., and Frechette, M. (1989). *Male Criminal Activity from Childhood Through Youth,* Springer-Verlag, New York.

Lemert, E. (1951). *Social Pathology,* McGraw–Hill, New York.

Lemert, E. (1972). *Human Deviance, Social Problems, and Social Control,* Prentice–Hall, Englewood Cliffs, NJ.

Loeber, R., and LeBlanc, M. (1990). Toward a developmental criminology. In Tonry, M., and Morris, N. (eds.). *Crime and Justice: An Annual Review of Research, Vol. 12,* University of Chicago Press, Chicago, IL.

Moffitt, T. (1993). Adolescent-limited and life-course persistent antisocial behavior: A developmental taxonomy. *Psychol. Rev.* 100:674–701.

Moffitt. T. (1994). Natural histories of delinquency. In Weitekamp, E., and Hans-Jurgen. K. (eds.), *Cross-National Longitudinal Research on Human Development and Criminal Behavior,* Kluwer Academic, Dordreeht, The Netherlands.

Moffitt, T., Caspi. A., Dickson, D., Silva, P., and Stanton, W. (1996). Childhood-onset vs. adolescent-onset antisocial conduct problems in males: Natural history from ages 3 to 18 years. *Dev. Psychopathol.* 8:399–424.

Nagin, D. S., and Farrington, D. (1992a). The stability of criminal potential from childhood to adulthood. *Criminology* 30:235–260.

Nagin, D. S., and Farrington, D. (1992b). The onset and persistence of offending. *Criminology* 30:501–523.

Nagin, P., and Land, K. (1993). Age, criminal careers, and population heterogeneity: Specification and estimation of a nonparametric, mixed Poisson model. *Criminology* 31:327–362.

Nagin, D., and Paternoster, R. (1991). On the relationship of past and future participation in delinquency. *Criminology* 29:163–190.

Nagin, D., and Paternoster, R. (1993). Enduring individual differences and rational choice theories of crime. *Law Soc. Rev.* 27:467–496.

Nagin, D., and Paternoster, R. (1994). Personal capital and social control: The deterrence implications of a theory of individual differences in criminal offending. *Criminology* 32:581–606.

Nagin, D., Farrington, D., and Moffitt, T. (1995). Life-course trajectories of different types of offenders. *Criminology* 33:111–139.

Osgood, D. W., and Rowe, D. C. (1994). Bridging criminal careers, theory, and policy through latent variable models of individual offending. *Criminology* 32:517–554.

Paternoster, R., and Brame, R. (1997). Multiple routes to delinquency? A test of developmental and general theories of crime. *Criminology* 35:49–84.

Patterson, G. (1993). Orderly change in a stable world: The antisocial trait as a chimera. *J. Consult. Clin. Psychol.* 61:911–919.

Patterson, G., and Yoerger, K. (1993). Developmental models for delinquent behavior. In Hodgins, S. (ed.), *Mental Disorder and Crime,* Sage, Newbury Park, CA.

Patterson, G., DeBaryshe, B., and Ramsey, E. (1989). A developmental perspective on antisocial behavior. *Am. Psychol.* 44:329–335.

Patterson, G., Crosby, L., and Vuchinich, S. (1992). Predicting risk for early police arrest. *J. Quant. Criminol.* 8:335–355.

Sampson, R., and Laub, J. (1993). *Crime in the Making: Pathways and Turning Points Through Life.* Harvard University Press, Cambridge, MA.

Sampson, R., and Laub, J. (1995). Understanding variability in lives through time: Contributions of life-course criminology. *Stud. Crime Crime Prev. Biann. Rev.* 4:143–158.

SAS Institute (1990). *SAS Language,* SAS Institute, Cary, NC.

Simons, R., Wu, C-I., Conger, R., and Lorenz, F. (1994). Two routes to delinquency: Differences between early and late starters in the impact of parenting and deviant peers. *Criminology* 32:247–275.

Stattin, H., and Magnusson, D. (1995). Onset of official delinquency. Its co-occurrence in time with educational, behavioral, and interpersonal problems. *Br. J. Criminol.* 35:417–449.

Thornberry, T. (1987). Towards an interactional theory of delinquency. *Criminology* 25:863–891.

Tittle, C. R. (1995). *Control Balance: Toward a General Theory of Deviance.* Westview Press, Boulder, CO.

Weisz, J., Walter, B., Weiss, B., Fernandez, G., and Mikow, V. (1990). Arrests among emotionally disturbed violent and assaultive individuals following minimal vs. lengthy intervention through North Carolina's Willie M Program. *J. Consult. Clin. Psychol.* 58:72–78.

Wilson, J.. and Herrnstein. R. (1985). *Crime and Human Nature,* Simon and Schuster, New York.

APPENDIX

Comparison of Observed and Expected Arrest Proportions by Year of Follow-Up

Number of Arrests	YEAR 1 Observed Proportion	Expected Proportion	YEAR 2 Observed Proportion	Expected Proportion	YEAR 3 Observed Proportion	Expected Proportion
0	0.683	0.671	0.667	0.675	0.712	0.704
1	0.168	0.197	0.196	0.195	0.159	0.183
2	0.075	0.070	0.084	0.069	0.070	0.061
3	0.041	0.029	0.033	0.029	0.039	0.025
4	0.019	0.014	0.011	0.013	0.010	0.011
5	0.011	0.007	0.007	0.007	0.002	0.006
6	0.001	0.004	0.001	0.004	0.006	0.003
7	0.002	0.002	0.000	0.002	0.001	0.002
8			0.000	0.001		
9			0.001	0.001		
10						
11						
Total	838		838		838	
θ	0.445		0.428		0.298	

Number of Arrests	YEAR 4 Observed Proportion	Expected Proportion	YEAR 5 Observed Proportion	Expected Proportion	YEAR 6 Observed Proportion	Expected Proportion
0	0.746	0.744	0.812	0.812	0.782	0.786
1	0.158	0.164	0.126	0.128	0.158	0.143
2	0.062	0.051	0.043	0.034	0.028	0.041
3	0.018	0.019	0.009	0.012	0.016	0.015
4	0.006	0.008	0.008	0.005	0.008	0.006
5	0.007	0.004	0.003	0.002	0.003	0.003
6	0.001	0.002			0.003	0.001
7	0.001	0.001			0.000	0.001
8	0.001	0.001			0.000	0.001
9					0.000	0.000
10					0.000	0.000
11					0.003	0.000
Total	838		791		386	
θ	0.104		−0.277		−0.121	

Note: θ is the estimated value of an intercept term for each year of the follow-up period, and the beta parameters were estimated as $a = 4.8228$ and $b = 1.4791$. Test of whether observed and expected frequencies differ from each other: $\chi^2_{(44)} = 50.57$, $P > 0.05$.

SECTION VII

Examining Desistance from Criminal Behavior

D esistance from criminal behavior represents a relatively underexplored area within criminology. In this section of the book, two articles examine both the processes and distinct correlates of criminal desistance. These papers provide good illustrations of the diverse methodological approaches currently employed for examining criminal desistance.

Sociologists Neal Shover and Carol Thompson present an early attempt at studying the reasons why offenders refrain from criminal activity. Using data from the Rand Inmate Survey, the authors examine factors correlated with desistance from crime upon release from prison. Additionally, their study bears directly on whether age has direct or indirect effects on desistance. The findings by Shover and Thompson reveal that the odds of desistance increase with age and education, when expectations for criminal gains are low, and when expectations of possible confinement are high. According to these results, both age and prior experience with crime are salient in the desistance process.

In a more recent study, John Laub and his colleagues explore how marriage alters offending trajectories over time. Using data from the classic study of 500 delinquent men from Boston, the authors find that desistance from crime is facilitated by the development of quality marital bonds, and that this influence is gradual and cumulative over time. The analysis by Laub and his colleagues illustrates, in studying the desistance process, the importance of examining marital quality as opposed to simply the occurrence of a marriage.

Although criminal desistance still remains an underresearched area, new studies are emerging that examine whether predictors of desistance differ for male and female offenders or for different types of offenders. The two articles in this section illustrate current thinking on desistance as well as the complex research strategies employed to better understand the desistance process.

SUGGESTED FUTURE READINGS

Baskin, D., Sommers, I., & Fagan, J. (1994). Getting out of the life: Crime desistance by female street offenders. *Deviant Behavior* (15), 125–149.

Bushway, S., Piquero, A., Mazerolle, P., Broidy, L., & Cauffman, E. (2000). A developmental framework for empirical research on desistance. Manuscript under review.

Farrington, D. & Hawkins, J. D. (1991). Predicting participation, early onset and later persistence in officially recorded offending. *Criminal Behaviour and Mental Health, 1,* 1–33.

Farrington, D. P., & West, D. J. (1995). Effects of marriage, separation, and children on offending by adult males. In Z.S. Blau and J. Hagan (Eds.). *Current Perspectives on Aging and the Life Cycle* (Vol. 4). Greenwich, CT: JAI Press.

Uggen, C., & Kruttschnitt, C. (1998). Crime in the breaking: Gender differences in desistance. *Law and Society Review, 32,* 339–366.

13

Age, Differential Expectations, and Crime Desistance*

NEAL SHOVER

CAROL Y. THOMPSON

ABSTRACT   We specify an individual-level model linking crime desistance to estimates of legal risk, differential expectations, degree of past success at legitimate and criminal pursuits, and age. OLS and logistic regression procedures are used to estimate the model using longitudinal data on serious, previously imprisoned offenders. As predicted, age decreases estimates of the likely payoffs from crime and legitimate employment. Contrary to predictions, age is unrelated to the perceived legal risk of renewed criminal participation. Age, past success at avoiding confinement, expectations of success from crime, and level of education are significant predictors of crime desistance. Neither the perceived legal risk of crime nor expectations of success through straight pursuits significantly predict desistance. We suggest an interpretation for these anomalous findings.

The past decade has witnessed substantial renascent interest in the variable careers and criminal participation of street offenders (e.g., Blumstein et al., 1988; Petersilia, 1980). This movement has focused new attention on crime desistance, that is, the termination of criminal careers (e.g., Ohlin et al., 1988). No one disputes that the overwhelming majority of street offenders, including those whose criminal participation extends into adulthood, eventually desist from serious criminal activities. The positive relationship between age and desistance among adults is supported by official crime statistics, self-report studies, cohort follow-up investigations, and offender autobiographies (Farrington, 1986; Gartner & Piliavin, 1988; Shover, 1985).

SOURCE: *Criminology*, Vol. 30, No. 1, pp. 89–104.

*The data used in the paper were collected originally by the Rand Corporation and were made available by the Inter-University Consortium for Political and Social Research. Neither the collector of the original data nor the consortium bears any responsibility for the analysis or interpretations presented here. We are grateful to Michael Benson and anonymous reviewers for comments on an earlier draft.

Historically, the desistance phenomenon has been approached inferentially (Ohlin et al., 1988). The lion's share of research on the later stages of criminal careers has focused on recidivism or the *failure to desist* from renewed criminal participation. Because most studies of recidivism are motivated by interest in parole prediction or other policy questions, there are few theoretical explanations for desistance (e.g., Glaser, 1964, 1980). We draw primarily from ethnographic investigations to construct an individual-level model linking age, degree of past success at legitimate and criminal pursuits, expectations about the likely payoffs from criminal and noncriminal behavior, estimates of legal risk, and crime desistance. We then evaluate the model using longitudinal data from a sample of serious offenders. We note points of similarity between our findings and reports by other investigators who have employed similar samples and longitudinal data.

THE DESISTANCE PROCESS

Two logically complementary constructions of the theoretical link between age and crime desistance have been offered. The first genre of explanation posits a direct, positive relationship between the two. Many age-related biopsychosocial factors thought to be related to criminal participation presumably contribute to crime desistance as well (Gove, 1985). Walsh (1986:150) suggests, for example, that aging makes offenders "less audacious" and, therefore, less interested in crime and other high-risk pursuits. Perhaps the best known example of a direct-effects hypothesis stresses the importance of aging-produced *maturation* and its dampening effects on criminal proclivities (Glueck & Glueck, 1937). Although this hypothesis has been criticized on several grounds (e.g., Gartner & Piliavin, 1988), the possibility of other direct links between age and crime desistance cannot be ruled out (Wilson & Herrnstein, 1985). Shover (1985) suggests, for example, that aging improves offenders' ability and inclination to calculate more precisely and carefully the results of past and prospective criminal involvement and the result is an increased probability of desistance.

Grounded securely in findings from ethnographic investigations, a second type of explanation hypothesizes significant indirect links between age and desistance. Compatible with social learning theory (Akers, 1985), the fundamental assumptions underlying this construction are simple and straightforward: To the extent offenders meet with self-defined success from crime, they will be optimistic about the potential payoffs from continued criminal participation and will be unlikely to desist; to the extent they meet with failure from crime, they will be unlikely to expect a reversal of this pattern and will be more likely to desist.

Success at criminal pursuits strengthens commitment to criminal others and criminal lines of action and erodes the perceived formal risk of crime. Using the metric of thieves and hustlers, those who earn well from crime while serving little time in prison are successful (Shover, 1973). Despite whatever short-term monetary success they may enjoy, however, very few street offenders attain long-lasting financial success illegally. Their criminal financial gains are dissipated quickly on alcohol and other drugs, ostentatious consumption, and "good times."Their performance avoiding imprisonment is no better; aging and criminal experience do not improve significantly their odds of avoiding arrest, conviction, and confinement. For the overwhelming majority of street offenders, extended involvement in crime brings only penury, interspersed with modest, quickly depleted criminal gains and repeated imprisonment. This is the most important reason they eventually lose confidence in prospects for achieving success by committing street crimes (Walsh, 1980).

But these are not the only reasons crime becomes less attractive with increasing age. Shover (1983, 1985) contends that aging offenders gradually become aware of time–until–death as a finite, diminishing resource and that they become increasingly unwilling to risk wasting their remaining years in prison. Experience managing criminal pursuits eventually causes them also to grow "progressively weary" at the "hassle of everyday boundary maintenance and their feelings of being expatriated from conventional society" (Adler, 1985:132). Even the daily routines of managing criminal involvement become tiring and burdensome to aging offenders. Many lower their material aspirations and find increasing interest and satisfaction in emergent goals, such as contentment and peace of mind that are experienced as antithetical to criminal participation. Consequently, the allure of crime diminishes substantially as offenders get older. According to Maguire (1982:89),

> The impetus to think seriously about [desistance] seems to come in many cases from a gradual disenchantment with the criminal life in its totality: the inability to trust people; the frequent harassment by the police; the effects on wives and children when the offender is in prison; and [other hassles]. As people grow older such a process can become more painful and depressing and the optimistic outlook can give way to a feeling of being caught in a trap.

This growing disenchantment with the criminal life also causes offenders to lower their expectations for achieving success via criminal means.

What is true of the effects of criminal performance is also true of offenders' performance in legitimate roles and employment: The degree of success they have known in the past determines their estimates of the likely payoff from more of the same. Most street offenders have known little success in the legitimate work world, in part because it is difficult to reconcile sustained criminal involvement with the demands of a 40–hour workweek. Confinement further expropriates the young, energetic years and may leave offenders ill-prepared and demographically mismatched for many conventional occupations and career timetables. Prospects can be particularly bleak for those who have served multiple prison terms. Too late they see how repeated confinement severely constrains prospects for a successful and rewarding straight life. Their underclass background and blue-collar or menial employment experiences also cause many street offenders eventually to scale down their legitimate expectations. Coupled with growing disenchantment with the criminal life, alternative and noncriminal life-styles become increasingly apparent and attractive to street offenders as they get older. This does not mean, however, that the *expected* rewards of noncrime increase since aging offenders come to have a very accurate assessment of their legitimate prospects (Shover, 1985).

In sum, we suggest theoretically that increasing age and past performance in straight and criminal pursuits determine the offender's *differential expectations*. These are "factors that reliably influence the decision to engage or not to engage in criminal acts" (Hirschi, 1986:116). They include general, pan-situational constraints on decision making and situational components that are determined by one's momentary perceptions of needs, opportunities, and risks (Glaser, 1980). We hypothesize that age and minimal success at crime cause offenders eventually to reduce their expectations for achieving success by continued or renewed criminal participation. Although age may be unrelated to expectations for achieving success by straight pursuits, past success at legitimate employment does increase straight expectations.

Changes in the perceived formal risk of criminal participation also may contribute to desistance as street offenders get older (Glassner et al., 1983). Some investigators suggest that offenders grow increasingly preoccupied with and fearful of the legal risks of crime. Cusson and Pinsonneault (1986:76) assert that "it is clear that, with age, criminals raise their estimates of the certainty of punishment." Fear of reimprisonment was the "primary motive" of self-defined desisters in a sample of adult offenders (Meisenhelder, 1977:322). The same is reported by Cromwell et al. (1991:83), who state that "for most of the desisters we interviewed . . . the final decision to terminate a criminal lifestyle was primarily the result of their increasing fear of punishment." As these authors see it, age increases the perceived legal risk of criminal participation and that increases the odds of desistance. Shover cautions (1985:126) that the relationship between age and estimates of legal risk may not be direct but mediated by differential expectations; risk may increase only if criminal expectations are reduced or straight expectations are raised. Nevertheless, a direct and positive link between age and risk reflects the reports of most investigators who have explored desistance. It also reflects the results of research on samples drawn from the general population (e.g., Grasmick & Bursik, 1990; Grasmick & Milligan, 1976; Tittle, 1980).

Past research has shown that aging offenders who manage to establish a secure and rewarding social niche and to develop commitment to conventional lines of activity significantly improve their odds of desistance (Glaser, 1964; Irwin, 1970; Meisenhelder, 1977; Reitzes, 1955; Shover, 1985; West, 1978). Establishment of this stake in conformity "give[s] meaning to life and provide[s] an incentive for respecting the law" (Cusson & Pinsonneault, 1986:80). Recent analysis of longitudinal data collected by the Gluecks finds support again for the importance of these conventional social bonds (Sampson & Laub, 1990). Due to the lack of data on the number and strength of postrelease social bonds and legitimate activities, we were unable to test this part of the theory of desistance (Shover, 1985).[1]

---

[1]This contention is counter to the argument presented by Gottfredson and Hirschi (1990).

Figure 13.1 depicts the theoretical model we have elaborated. This ethnographically based explanation as yet "has not been confirmed by deductive analyses of hard data" (Gartner & Piliavin, 1988:300). The remainder of this paper rectifies this omission. We explore empirically the causal connections among age, offenders' criminal and straight expectations, perceived formal risks of criminal participation, and desistance from crime.

DATA

Data for the independent variables in Figure 13.1 were collected in 1978, when investigators from the Rand Corporation administered the Rand Inmate Survey (RIS) to 1,469 male inmates of 12 prisons in Texas, Michigan, and California (Peterson et al., 1982). On average the subjects were approximately 27 years of age and had two previous felony convictions. Approximately two-thirds of them were black, Hispanic, or another minority. Although the precise relationship of this sample to larger populations of theoretical and substantive interest is unknown, the sample does capture serious offenders, the object of considerable public and official concern.

In addition to questions about past criminal behavior, the RIS measured respondents' confinement history, earnings from legitimate employment during their most recent stay in the free community, earnings from crime during the same period, and estimates of the risks and rewards of future straight and criminal activities. The questionnaire was administered to groups of between

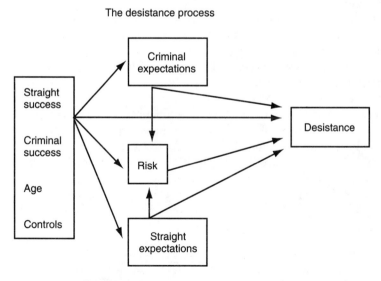

FIGURE 13.1 The desistance process

20 and 30 prisoners in classrooms, visiting rooms, or other available space inside the prisons. It was not anonymous.

In 1984, Rand investigators examined state "rap sheets" and correctional records for follow-up data on the post release criminal activities of the inmates who completed the RIS. Klein and Caggiano (1986:5) report that 184 of the original cohort either were deceased or still incarcerated in 1984. A comparison of the original RIS inmates with the remaining subjects indicated the two groups were similar in age, number of prior felony convictions, current conviction offense, and percent minority (1986:6). Of the 1,285 subjects who were available for follow-up, 1,023 were released at least 36 months before rap sheets were generated. Our analysis utilizes only the 948 inmates from this 36-months cohort who were 18 years of age or older at the time of the original RIS.

Rand investigators collected three categories of follow-up data: arrests, convictions, and incarcerations that occurred during the 36 months following release from prison. Because arrests are events that are closer to former prisoners' behavior than conviction or incarceration, we decided to use arrest data to construct a dichotomous measure of desistance: 0 = at least one arrest within 36 months of release and 1 = no arrests within 36 months of release. The longitudinal design produced by merging the RIS and follow-up data allows us to specify and examine properly relationships among key variables in the theory of desistance we have outlined.

The RIS questionnaire was lengthy and very detailed. Because 50% of the respondents had 11 years of education or less, it may have required knowledge and skills beyond those of many of the respondents. Field notes from researchers indicate that poor reading skills caused some respondents to code multiple responses to some items and that many were confused about some questions. We considered two strategies for handling missing data produced by these and other problems: imputation and available case analysis. Imputation procedures treat substituted values as real data in statistical analysis. The resulting tests of significance for filled in data are underestimated, particularly when errors are large (Little & Rubin, 1989). Although imputation is preferred when estimating the mean of a variable, it is generally regarded as inappropriate for estimating regression coefficients or probit and logit models (Dubin & Rivers, 1989; Little & Rubin, 1989; Hosmer & Lemeshow, 1989). Available case analysis, on the other hand, uses only cases without missing values. When the complete cases can be considered a random subsample of the original sample, subsequent analyses can be considered unbiased. If missing values are pervasive, however, statistical estimates may not be representative of the original sample (Little & Rubin, 1987). Both imputation and available case analysis require analytic compromises. Because ordinary least squares (OLS) and logistic regression techniques are used in this analysis, we decided in favor of using the unbiased statistical estimates provided by listwise deletion of cases with missing data.[2]

---

[2]The percentage of data missing for each variable is: marital status (0.6%), race (0.6%), education (0.5%), work (1.2%), criminal success (10.7%), straight success (5.3%), confinement

As a first step in exploring the links between age and desistance, we created measures of past success at straight and criminal pursuits, straight and criminal expectations, and the estimated legal risk of criminal participation. The variable straight success represents the offender's success at legitimate pursuits in the immediate pre-imprisonment period, and the variables criminal financial success and confinement avoidance measure the offender's past success at crime. Although Rand investigators did not collect data on the post-release employment and social circumstances of cohort members, data are available on their *preimprisonment* marital status. We included it as a control variable in the analysis. Race, level of education, and past legitimate employment (work) also were included as controls. The operationalization of all variables is described in the Appendix.

ANALYSIS AND RESULTS

Our primary analytic objective is to explore the viability and causal nature of the proposed relationships in Figure 13.1. Formal methods of statistical modeling, such as covariance analysis, require complete data and exactly specified a priori substantive and measurement theory. When these requirements are not met, models cannot be estimated reliably. Therefore, to achieve our primary goal, the major theoretical variables in the desistance process are explicated individually using regression analysis. The findings then may be used to refine the model and as a guide for future investigations.

We begin by determining the predictors of straight and criminal expectations. The OLS regression results in Table 13.1 reveal age to be the only significant predictor of straight expectations (Beta = −.100). As predicted, increasing age dampens optimism for achieving success via legitimate pursuits. Table 13.1 also included the regression results for criminal expectations. It shows that age (Beta = −.134), criminal financial success (Beta = .162), and confinement avoidance (Beta = .087) are significant predictors of criminal expectations. These statistical relationships are in the predicted directions, thus confirming the negative effect of age on expectations of criminal success. They also confirm that success at crime increases criminal expectations.

Table 13.1 also shows the predictors of risk. Risk increases as straight expectations increase (Beta = . 139), and it decreases as criminal expectations increase (Beta = −.089). Increases in risk are associated also with increasing education (Beta = .101) and with being white (Beta = .105). All of these relationships are in the predicted direction. Contrary to predictions, we did not find age to be a significant predictor of risk. The findings, however, are consistent with the suggestion by Maguire (1982) and Shover (1985) that the effect of aging on risk is mediated by differential expectations. It is also possible that

avoidance (4.2%), straight expectations (8.6%), criminal expectations (8.9%), risk (8.0%), age (0%) and desistance (0%).

Table 13.1 Standardized Estimates from OLS Regression for Straight Expectations, Criminal Expectations, and Risk

Independent Variable	DEPENDENT VARIABLE		
	Straight Expectations	Criminal Expectations	Risk
Criminal Expectations			−.089*
			(−.054)
Straight Expectations			.139***
			(.094)
Straight Success	.047	−.033	.045
	(.0003)	(−.0002)	(.0002)
Criminal Financial	−.052	.162***	−.018
Success	(−.0001)	(.0002)	(−.0000)
Confinement Avoidance	−.041	.087*	.002
	(−.164)	(.396)	(.006)
Marital Status	.034	−.045	−.047
	(.241)	(−.364)	(−.226)
Age	−.100*	−.134***	.041
	(−.041)	(−.062)	(.011)
Race	−.034	−.065	.105**
	(−.204)	(−.436)	(.417)
Education	.066	.050	.101**
	(.352)	(.298)	(.361)
Work	−.012	−.063	−.007
	(−.077)	(−.477)	(−.033)
R^2	.02	.08	.06
N	711	709	663

Note: Standardized regression coefficients shown with unstandardized coefficients in parentheses.
* $p < .05$
** $p < .01$
*** $p < .001$

this finding is an artifact of studying an already incarcerated cohort with little variation in risk levels.

The logistic regression findings in Table 13.2 indicate that age (b = .026), education (b = .388), criminal expectations (b = −.064), and confinement avoidance (b = −.295) significantly predict desistance. The odds of desistance increase with age and education, and they decrease as confinement avoidance and criminal expectations increase.[3]

---

[3]In a separate logistic regression analysis, we operationalized desistance as 0 = at least one criminal conviction in the 36 months following release from prison and 1 = no convictions. The results using this measure are substantially similar. The principal difference was the absence of a significant relationship between confinement avoidance and desistance. This suggests that past success at avoiding confinement may increase the resolve of prosecutors, probation investigators, and judges to see that defendants pay for their misdeeds by imprisonment thereby reducing to insignificance the advantage it affords offenders at the front end (arrest) stage of the criminal process.

Table 13.2 Logistic Regression Predicting Desistance

Independent Variable	b	Independent Variable	b
Work	.348	Straight Expectations	.018
	(.239)		(.029)
Education	.388*	Criminal Financial Success	–.00002
	(.155)		(.477)
Age	.026*	Confinement Avoidance	–.295*
	(.012)		(.121)
Marital Status	–.371	Straight Success	–.0001
	(.212)		(.0002)
Race	.001	Risk	–.079
	(.172)		(.043)
Criminal Expectations	–.064*	Intercept	–.014
	(.027)		(.779)

Note: Unstandardized regression coefficients shown with standard errors in parentheses.
–2 log likelihood = 839.798; df = 651; p = .0000; N = 663.
Correctly predicted 63.8%.
McFadden's R^2 = .04.
*2.0 times the standard error.

DISCUSSION AND CONCLUSIONS

Nearly all of the relationships reported here are in the predicted direction, and they lend support to the model of crime desistance developed from ethnographic research. Moreover, they are consistent generally with reports by other investigators. Using a longitudinal research design and a sample of serious offenders similar to those of this study, Piliavin et al. (1986:118) show that the effect of age on renewed criminal participation is mediated by offenders' belief that expected earnings from crime "are greater than or equal to expected earnings from a straight job." We find that the probability of desistance from criminal participation increases as expectations for achieving friends, money, autonomy, and happiness via crime decrease (criminal expectations b = – .064). Piliavin et al. (1986) further show that self-reported desistance is not affected by offenders' average monthly income from legitimate employment in the year preceding incarceration. Our findings are similar.

Failure to find a link between perceived legal risk and desistance is consistent with Piliavin et al. (1986) but contrary to our prediction. One possible explanation for this may lie in a distinction between distal measures of risk perception and risk perceptions occurring in the immediate context of decision-making about specific criminal opportunities. It is evident increasingly that measures of the latter are better predictors than more remote ones. Piliavin et al. (1986) show, for example, that risk perceptions fluctuate "substantially" over a nine-month period of time. Risk perceptions, they suggest, "may be conditioned by elements within the immediate situation confronting the individual . . . [such that] perceptions of the opportunity, returns, and support for crime within a given situation may influence . . . perceptions of risks and the extent to which those risks are discounted" (1986:115). Others have demonstrated the potential merit of a situational approach to risk estimates (e.g., Ekland–Olson et al., 1984; Rankin & Wells, 1983; Shover & Honaker, 1991).

Piliavin et al. (1986) failed to find a predicted positive relationship between straight expectations and crime desistance. So did we; straight expectations fail to make a difference in postrelease desistance. Although we can only speculate as to the reasons for this, we emphasize that our measures of differential expectations are distal measures. We cannot rule out the possibility that in the RIS sample straight expectations more proximate to subjects' actual criminal decision-making situations constrained their chances of desistance.

The fact that the RIS sample consists of prison inmates, many of them recidivists, means we cannot determine how much their behavior reflects innate differences in decision-making styles or experiential effects, that is, the effects of past success in committing crime and avoiding arrest (Gottfredson & Hirschi, 1990; Nagin & Paternoster, 1991). This may explain why we do not find a direct relationship between age and risk. The lack of comparative data on never-incarcerated offenders makes it impossible to examine the merits of these interpretations. More important, it could be argued that the criminal calculus and behavior of RIS subjects, precisely because they had demonstrated a willingness to commit serious crimes and had done so successfully in the past, limit the external validity of these findings. Generalizations beyond the study population must be made, therefore, with caution. Data and sample limitations notwithstanding, the findings support theoretical explanations that emphasize both direct and indirect links between age and desistance.

REFERENCES

Adler, Patricia
    1985   Wheeling and Dealing. New York: Columbia University Press.

Akers, Ronald L.
    1985   Deviant Behavior: A Social Learning Approach. 3d ed. Belmont, Calif.:
            Wadsworth.

Blumstein, Alfred, Jacqueline Cohen, and David P. Farrington
    1988   Criminal career research: Its value for criminology. Criminology 26:1–36.

Cromwell, Paul F., James N. Olson, and D'Aunn Wester Avary
    1991   Breaking and Entering: An Ethnographic Analysis of Burglary. Newbury Park,
            Calif.: Sage.

Cusson, Maurice and Pierre Pinsonneault
    1986   The decision to give up crime. In Derek B. Cornish and Ronald V. Clarke
            (eds.), The Reasoning Criminal. New York: Springer-Verlag.

Dubin, Jeffrey A. and Douglas Rivers
    1989   Selection bias in linear regression, logit and probit models. Sociological Meth-
            ods and Research 18:360–390.

Ekland–Olson, Sheldon, John Lieb, and Louis Zurcher
    1984   The paradoxical impact of criminal sanctions: Some microstructural findings.
            Law & Society Review 18:159–178.

Farrington, David P.
    1986   Age and crime. In Michael Tonry and Norval Morris (eds.), Crime and Justice: An Annual Review of Research. Vol. 7. Chicago: University of Chicago Press.

Gartner, Rosemary and Irving Piliavin
    1988   The aging offender and the aged offender. In P. B. Baltes, D. L. Featherman, and R. M. Lerner (eds.), Life-Span Development and Behavior. Vol. 9. Hillsdale, N.J.: Lawrence Erlbaum.

Glaser, Daniel
    1964   Effectiveness of a Prison and Parole System. Indianapolis, Ind.: Bobbs-Merrill.

    1980   The interplay of theory, issues, policy, and data. In Malcolm Klein and Katherine Tielmann (eds.), Handbook of Criminal Justice Evaluation. Beverly Hills, Calif.: Sage.

Glassner, Barry, Margaret Ksander, Bruce Berg, and Bruce D. Johnson
    1983   A note on the deterrent effect of juvenile vs. adult jurisdiction. Social Problems 31:219–221.

Glueck, Sheldon and Eleanor Glueck
    1937   Later Criminal Careers. New York: Commonwealth Fund.

Gottfredson, Michael R. and Travis Hirschi
    1990   A General Theory of Crime. Stanford, Calif.: Stanford University Press.

Gove, Walter R.
    1985   The effect of age and gender on deviant behavior: A biopsychosocial perspective. In Alice S. Rossi (ed.), Gender and the Life Course. New York: Aldine.

Grasmick, Harold G. and Robert J. Bursik, Jr.
    1990   Conscience, significant others, and rational choice: Extending the deterrence model. Law & Society Review 24:837–861.

Grasmick, Harold G. and Herman Milligan, Jr.
    1976   Deterrence theory approach to socioeconomic/demographic correlates of crime. Social Science Quarterly 57:608–617.

Hirschi, Travis
    1986   On the compatibility of rational choice and social control theories of crime. In Derek B. Cornish and Ronald V. Clarke (eds.), The Reasoning Criminal. New York: Springer-Verlag.

Hosmer, David and Stanley Lemeshow
    1989   Applied Logistic Regression. New York: John Wiley & Sons.

Irwin, John
    1970   The Felon. Englewood Cliffs, N.J.: Prentice-Hall.

Klein, Steven P. and Michael N. Caggiano
    1986   The Prevalence, Predictability, and Policy Implications of Recidivism. Santa Monica, Calif.: Rand.

Little, Roderick and Donald Rubin
    1987   Statistical Analysis with Missing Data. New York: John Wiley & Sons.

    1989   The analysis of social science data with missing values. Sociological Methods and Research 18:293–325.

Maguire, Mike, in collaboration with Trevor Bennett
    1982   Burglary in a Dwelling. London: Heinemann.

Meisenhelder, Thomas N.
    1977   An exploratory study of exiting from criminal careers. Criminology 15:319–334.

Nagin, Daniel S. and Raymond Paternoster
    1991   On the relationship of past to future participation in delinquency. Criminology 29:163–189.

Ohlin, Lloyd, Alfred Blumstein, Kenneth Adams, Douglas Anglin, Arnold Barnett, Robert Boruch, Peter Greenwood, Albert Reiss, and Lawrence Sherman
    1988   Final report of the desistance-persistence working Group Program on Human Development and Criminal Behavior. Castine Research Corporation, Maine. Photocopy.

Petersilia, Joan
    1980   Criminal career research: A review of recent evidence. In Norval Morris and Michael Tonry (eds.), Crime and Justice: An Annual Review of Research. Vol. 2. Chicago: University of Chicago Press.

Peterson, Mark, Jan Chaiken, Patricia Ebener, and Paul Honig
    1982   Survey of Prison and Jail Inmates: Background and Method. Santa Monica, Calif.: Rand.

Piliavin, Irving, Rosemary Gartner, Craig Thornton, and Ross Matsueda
    1986   Crime, deterrence, and rational choice. American Sociological Review 51:101–119.

Rankin, Joseph H. and L. Edward Wells
    1983   The social context of deterrence. Sociology and Social Research 67:18–39.

Reitzes, Dietrich C.
    1955   The effect of social environment upon former felons. Journal of Criminal Law, Criminology and Police Science 46:226–231.

Sampson, Robert J. and John H. Laub
    1990   Crime and deviance over the life course: The salience of adult social bonds. American Sociological Review 55:602–627.

Shover, Neal
    1973   The social organization of burglary. Social Problems 20:499–514.

    1983   The later stages of ordinary property offender careers. Social Problems 31:208–218.

    1985   Aging Criminals: Beverly Hills, Calif.: Sage.

Shover, Neal and David Honaker
    1991   The socially bounded decision making of persistent property offenders. Howard Journal of Criminal Justice 31: 276–294.

Tittle, Charles R.
    1980   Sanctions and Social Deviance: The Question of Deterrence. New York: Praeger.

Walsh, Dermot
    1980   Break-Ins: Burglary from Private Houses. London: Constable.

    1986   Heavy Business. London: Routledge & Kegan Paul.

West, W. Gordon
    1978   The short term careers of serious thieves. Canadian Journal of Criminology 20:169–190.

Wilson, James Q. and Richard J. Herrnstein
    1985   Crime and Human Nature. New York: Simon & Schuster.

APPENDIX

Operationalization of Variables

Age	Response to the question: How old were you on your last birthday?
Race	1 = white 0 = other
Work	0 = no jobs during last period of time in free community 1 = one or more jobs
Marital Status	0 = not married 1 = married
Education	0 = 6th grade or less 1 = 7th through 11th grade 2 = high school or more
Desistance	0 = at least one arrest within 36 months of release 1 = no arrests within 36 months of release
Criminal Financial Success	Self-reported average monthly income from crime during last period of time in the free community
Confinement Avoidance	Total number of adult felony convictions/total number of prison terms ever served (including the current term), plus one-half the total number of jail terms ever served
Straight Success	Self-reported average monthly income from legitimate employment during last period of time in the free community
Criminal Expectations	Summated index (alpha = .67) created from the matrix question, What are the chances each of these things would happen to you from doing crimes?: Having friends, Being my own man, Having a lot of money, and Being happy. Response options were 1 = no chance, 2 = low chance, 3 = even chance, 4 = high chance, 5 = certain.
Straight Expectations	Summated index (alpha = .67) created from the matrix question, What are the chances each of these things would happen to you if you did not do crimes?: Having friends, Being my own man, Having a lot of money, and Being happy. Response options were 1 = no chance, 2 = low chance, 3 = even chance, 4 = high chance, 5 = certain.
Risk	Summated index (alpha = .76) created from the matrix question, What are the chances each of these

things would happen to you from doing crimes?:
Getting arrested, and Going to prison for years.
Response options were 1 = no chance, 2 = low
chance, 3 = even chance, 4 = high chance,
5 = certain.

14

Trajectories of Change in Criminal Offending

Good Marriages and the Desistance Process*

JOHN H. LAUB

DANIEL S. NAGIN

ROBERT J. SAMPSON

ABSTRACT Building on Sampson and Laub (1993), we draw an analogy between changes in criminal offending spurred by the formation of social bonds and an investment process. This conceptualization suggests that because investment in social relationships is gradual and cumulative, resulting desistance will be gradual and cumulative. Using a dynamic statistical model developed by Nagin and Land (1993), we test our ideas about change using yearly longitudinal data from Glueck and Glueck's (1950, 1968) classic study of criminal careers. Our results show that desistance from crime is facilitated by the development of quality marital bonds, and that this influence is gradual and cumulative over time.

When and how do criminal offenders desist? Although the relationship between age and criminal behavior has animated much recent research in criminology, the questions of change in criminal offending and the attendant issue of measuring such change have received little attention. We emphasize the central role of social bonds in the movement away from criminal and antisocial behavior patterns. The emergence of social bonds can be likened to an investment process in that social bonds do not arise intact and full-grown but develop over time like a pension plan funded by regular installments. As the investment in social bonds grows, the incentive for avoiding crime increases because more is at stake. Thus, while seminal events can dramatically alter longstanding patterns of behavior, we expect that desistance from crime will be gradual and will accompany the accumulation of social bonds (Horney, Osgood, & Marshall, 1995:671).

SOURCE: *American Sociological Review,* Vol. 63, pp. 225–238. Reprinted by permission.

Sampson and Laub (1993) pose an age-graded theory of informal social control in which social bonding in the form of strong ties to work and family plays an important role in the movement away from crime for previously criminal youths. They find that individuals who desist from crime are significantly more likely to have entered into stable marriages and steady employment. Thus, Sampson and Laub contend, marriage and work act as "turning points" in the life course and are crucial in understanding the processes of change.

We emphasize that turning points are "triggering events" that are, in part, exogenous—that is, they are chance events. If these events were entirely the result of conscious calculations or enduring patterns of behavior, we could not argue for the independent role of social bonds in shaping behavior. It could be argued, for example, that the association between desistance and adult social bonds is instead attributable to a selection process (Gottfredson & Hirschi, 1990). A large body of research documents an association between enduring individual characteristics—low intelligence and impulsiveness, for example—and criminality. The distribution of these persistent individual differences, which we call persistent heterogeneity, is highly skewed right (Nagin & Paternoster, 1991). It may be that those who desist from crime as young adults are in the middle range of the skewed tail: They are sufficiently prone to crime, to be delinquent and unattached in their youth, but not so crime-prone to persist in their criminality and detachment in their adult years. Although we do not fully accept this rather deterministic view of human destiny (and its attendant optimism about the ability to predict adult outcomes from childhood patterns), our empirical analyses must address this argument.

Here we move beyond Sampson and Laub's prior work (1993; Laub & Sampson, 1993). First, we test their predictions using a dynamic statistical model drawn from Nagin and Land (1993; also see Land, McCall, & Nagin, 1996). Sampson and Laub's analyses to date have used mainly "static" tests, albeit with longitudinal data, in which behavior at one time is related to variables measured in prior periods. This strategy establishes causal order, but it does not capture the progression of change. Here we examine multiple periods of behavior that capture not only the cumulative impact of change but the time path by which change is achieved.

Second, we explicate the underlying process of social bonding over the life course. A change in criminal trajectory does not necessarily result from marriage and work alone. Rather, it is a response to an enduring attachment that emerges from entering into a marriage or a job. Here we build on Laub and Sampson (1993:310–11) and Nagin and Paternoster (1994:586–88) who liken the emergence of social bonds to an investment process. This theoretical viewpoint has implications for the underlying dynamics of the desistance process: Unlike the criminal careers paradigm, in which desistance is modeled as abrupt, we anticipate a gradual movement away from criminal offending.

Third, we show that individual characteristics and family circumstances measured in childhood that are known to predict delinquency and adult criminality have a limited capacity to predict desistance. This further supports our contention that adult social bonds are important in understanding changes in criminal trajectories.

DATA AND METHODS

We analyze the criminal histories of 500 delinquent boys who were followed into adulthood by Glueck and Glueck (1950, 1968). The Gluecks' prospective study of the formation and development of criminal careers was initiated in 1940 and also included a control group of 500 nondelinquent boys. As our interest is in desistance from crime, we exclude the Gluecks' nondelinquent sample from our study.

The data collection process took place over 25 years, from 1940 through 1965. After an initial interview at age 14 (on average), subjects were followed up at ages 25 and 32. The data were collected using a multimethod strategy that included interviews with the subjects and their families and with key informants such as social workers, school teachers, neighbors, employers, and criminal justice officials (Glueck & Glueck, 1950:41–53). Interview data were supplemented by field investigations that gathered information from the records of public and private agencies. These data verified and amplified the case materials collected during the interviews (Glueck & Glueck, 1950, 1968; Sampson & Laub, 1993).

Key Measures

The following measures covering childhood, adolescence, and adulthood were selected (Sampson & Laub, 1993:47–63; Sampson & Laub, 1994:530–31).

Individual Differences Measures of individual differences include verbal intelligence, personality traits, and childhood behaviors. *Verbal intelligence* was assessed using the Wechsler-Bellevue IQ test; scores were coded into eight categories ranging from 1 (120 and above) to 8 (59 and below). The mean verbal IQ score for the delinquent sample was 88.6 (Glueck & Glueck, 1950:356).

From psychiatric assessments we used four dichotomous variables that tap *personality traits:* extroverted ("uninhibited in regard to motor responses to stimuli"); adventurous ("desirous of change, excitement, or risk"); egocentric ("self-centered"); and aggressive ("inclined to impose one's will on others").

To capture *childhood behaviors* we used a dichotomous indicator based on teachers' and parents' reports that the subject engaged in violent and habitual temper tantrums while growing up. Another measure of childhood behavior (difficult child) indicated whether the subject was overly restless and irritable.

Family Differences Included here are *family poverty* (indicated by a combination of low income and reliance on public assistance), *family size* (number of children), and *parental criminality and alcohol abuse* (determined from official records and interview data). In addition, we used three measures of family process—*parental style of discipline, mother's supervision,* and *parent–child attachment.* Parenting style was measured by summing three variables describing the discipline and punishment practices of mothers and fathers to create a measure that combined mother's and father's discipline—*erratic/harsh discipline.*

Adolescent Behavior *Antisocial conduct in adolescence* was measured in two ways. One indicator is the *average annual frequency of arrests* up to age 17 while not incarcerated. A second measure is a composite "unofficial" scale (ranging from 1 to 26) of self-, parent-, and teacher-reports of delinquent behavior (e.g.. stealing, vandalism) and other misconduct (e.g., truancy, running away) not necessarily known to the police. In addition, we use self-reported *age of onset of misbehavior* to create a dichotomous variable (coded 1 if age of onset is earlier than age 8). Finally, *attachment to school* is a composite measure that combines the boy's attitude toward school and his academic ambition.

Adult Criminal Behavior Information on *criminal activity through age 32* was drawn from official criminal histories at the state and national levels.

Adult Social Bonds All of the social bond measures were taken from the age-32 interview. *Job stability* is measured by a standardized composite scale of employment status, stability of most recent employment, and work habits. *Attachment to spouse* is a standardized composite scale derived from interview data describing the general conjugal relationship during the follow-up period plus a measure of the cohesiveness of the family unit. (For details, see Sampson & Laub, 1993:143–45.)

In addition to *marital status at age 32,* we included a variable from the age 25 interview indicating whether a child was born within seven months of the date of marriage and the birth was not recorded as premature or if pregnancy at marriage is acknowledged by the couple. We label this variable *"shotgun" marriage.*

Measuring Adult Desistance

We anticipate that individuals who enter early into a marriage that subsequently evolves into a strong attachment, hereafter referred to as an "ex-post good marriage," will desist the soonest. Testing this dynamic prediction requires that we operationalize the concept of desistance. Our perspective emphasizes gradual change, that is, we do not expect criminal activity to drop abruptly to zero. Rather we expect a gradual decline toward zero or a very low rate of offending.

Consider two hypothetical offending trajectories. In both trajectories, the individual's rate of offending rises throughout adolescence, reaches a peak at about age 18, and declines thereafter. However, for one individual, the rate of decline is rapid, so that by age 25 his rate of offending is negligible. In contrast, the rate of decline for the second individual is more gradual, so that by age 32 his rate is substantially less than at age 18 but is still far from zero. By any reasonable conception of desistance, the former individual has desisted, but not the latter.

The analytical challenge is to devise a statistical procedure for identifying such distinctive offending trajectories. We use the semiparametric Poisson mixture model (SPMM) (Nagin & Land, 1993; also see Land et al., 1996).[1] The model assumes that, during periods of criminal activity, individuals commit crimes according to a Poisson process with rate λ_{it}, where parameter λ_{it} is the expected rate of crime commission for that individual in that period. A graph of individual i's λ_{it} over time specifies that individual's offending trajectory.

Nagin and Land (1993) approximate the limitless heterogeneity in possible offending trajectories with a finite number of distinctive groups that vary not only in terms of the *level* of offending but also in the *rate of change* in offending over time. To do this the offending trajectory for each group is assumed to be a quadratic function of age:

$$\ln(\lambda_{it}^j) = \beta_0^j + \beta_1^j \, Age_{it} + \beta_2^j \, Age_{it}^2, \tag{1}$$

where superscript j denotes group j, age_{it} is individual i's age in period t, and age_{it}^2 is i's age squared in period t.[2] Note that all of the parameters of the quadratic function are group-specific. This allows groups to have distinctive offending trajectories in terms of both level and pattern of change over time. The larger the group's constant term, β_0^j, the higher its "base" offending rate. The parameters β_1^j and β_2^j define the shape of the trajectory.[3]

An example illustrates how the estimation procedure extracts the group-specific trajectories and their proportional representation in the population. Suppose there are two distinct groups in the population: (1) youthful offenders who make up 50 percent of the population and who, up to age 18, have a λ of 5 and after age 18 have a λ of 1; and (2) adult offenders who make up the other 50 percent of the population, whose offending trajectory is the reverse of that of the youthful offenders—through age 18 their λ equals 1 and after age 18 their λ increases to 5.

Suppose these data are analyzed under the assumption that the age to λ trajectory was identical across all individuals. The estimated value of λ would be a "compromise" estimate—about 3 for all ages. From this value we would

---

[1] A detailed discussion of the likelihood function of the semiparametric mixed Poisson regression model and a comparison of its estimates with those from regular Poisson and negative binomial analyses can be found in Land et al. (1996).

[2] A log-linear relationship between λ_{it} and potential covariates is assumed to ensure that a basic assumption of the Poisson distribution, $\lambda > 0$, is fulfilled.

[3] The model also includes a second component called "intermittency," which allows for periods of inactivity within the criminal career. The intermittency component of the model specifies that with probability, π_{it}, individual i in period t will be inactive and thus will have no recorded offenses. Intermittency is modeled as a probit that is a quadratic function of age.

mistakenly conclude that in this population the rate of offending does not vary with age. If the data are analyzed using the SPMM, which specifies the likelihood function as a mixing distribution, this mathematical "compromise" would not be necessary. The parameters of one component of the mixing distribution would accommodate (i.e., match) the youth offending portion of the data in which offending declines with age, and another component of the mixing distribution would accommodate the adult offender data in which offending increases with age.

Controlling for Enduring Individual Differences

There is a strong bivariate association in the Gluecks' data between desistance and the formation of strong marital bonds. This association may reflect the preventive effect of marriage or it may be an artifact of a selection process. The criminally active who eventually desist may represent individuals with a low level of "criminal propensity." In the parlance of Gottfredson and Hirschi (1990), the desisters are individuals with comparatively more self-control, or in the Moffitt (1993) taxonomy, they are "adolescent-limited" offenders. According to either theory, desisters are more likely than nondesisters to form strong marital bonds, but not because desistance and strong marital bonds are causally related. Rather the association reflects enduring individual differences that are causes of both desistance and the formation of a strong marriage.

To control for such enduring individual differences we use SPMM's ability to identify which group trajectory best matches an individual's offending history. While an individual's offender-group membership cannot be determined definitively, individuals can be sorted among offender categories based on the probability of their belonging to the various groups. Based on the model coefficient estimates, the probability of observing each individual's longitudinal pattern of offending is computed conditional on his belonging to each group. The individual is then assigned to the group with the highest ex-post probability of having generated his observed pattern of offending. For each individual i, the probability of his belonging to group j is:

$$P(j|y_i, x_i) = \frac{P(j|y_i, x_i)\pi_j}{\Sigma_j P(j|y_i, x_i)\pi_j}, \tag{2}$$

where y_i is a vector representing a count of individual i's arrests in each period t and π_j is the estimated proportion of the population in each group j.

These group assignments control for enduring individual differences in two ways. They serve as control variables in regressions that analyze the link between the timing of entry into an ex-post good marriage and the timing of the decline in offending. They also identify subsamples of individuals with similar offending trajectories. Within these more homogeneous subsamples, which include groups that show the strongest evidence of desistance from crime by age 32, we test whether the desistance process was accelerated by early entry into a strong marriage.

RESULTS

Our analysis proceeds in two stages. In the first stage, we apply the SPMM to the delinquent sample of 480 youths in the Gluecks' data.[4] In the second stage of the analysis, we examine the relationship between the timing of marriage and desistance from criminal activity.

First-Stage Analysis

Exploratory analysis suggested that a four-group model best fit the data.[5] Figure 14.1 shows the four offending trajectories identified by the model. Although individuals in this sample were selected on the basis of their being active delinquents in their youth, by age 32 the distribution of their offending mirrors that of the general population—it is skewed right. Group 1 is a small but prominent group of high-rate chronic offenders. Based on the maximum probability rules described above, only 11 individuals were assigned to this group. Another 95 individuals were assigned to Group 2, which includes chronic offenders who offend at a more modest rate. Finally, Groups 3 and 4 constitute the largest share of the sample, 220 and 154 individuals, respectively. These individuals have either effectively desisted or are near desistance by age 32.

Figure 14.2 compares the actual and predicted offending trajectories for each group. The correspondence between actual and predicted is generally close for all four groups.

Group 1 includes individuals who remain high-rate offenders throughout the adult observation period. Their peak average offending rate of nearly 3 arrests per year occurs at age 25 and declines only to about 2 arrests per year by age 32. This group constitutes only a small percentage of the sample—2.8 percent based on the model's parameters. Group 2 also is comprised of individuals who can be characterized as chronic offenders. This group, which accounts for an estimated 25.7 percent of the sample, differs from Group 1 only in degree: Through the adult years the estimated average offending rate of Group 2 is about 60 percent of that of Group 1. Otherwise Group 2's offending trajectory mirrors that of Group 1, reaching a peak at about age 25 and slowly declining thereafter. But even at age 32, those in Group 2 average about .8 arrests per year.

Groups 3 and 4 are the largest groups making up an estimated 42.5 percent and 28.9 percent of the sample, respectively. While both groups have modestly high rates of offending through their teenage years, by age 32 the average arrest

---

[4]Unfortunately, the original records for 20 cases were lost in the process of archiving, leaving 480 cases available for our analysis. Previous analyses revealed nothing unusual about these 20 lost cases (Sampson & Laub, 1993).

[5]Although there is no definitive statistic for determining the optimal number of groups, the Bayesian Information Criterion (BIC) provides a good benchmark (D'Unger et al., 1998). By this criterion, the four-group model improves on a three-group model. As the five-group model was not estimable, we concluded that the four-group model was best. The parameter estimates of the model are available from the authors on request.

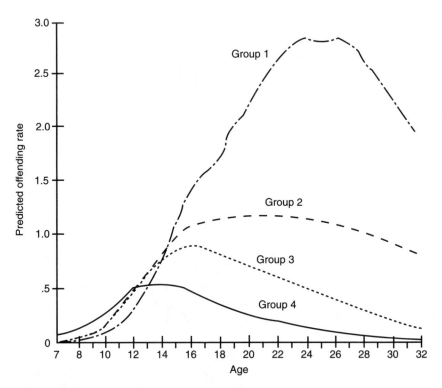

FIGURE 14.1 Predicted offending trajectories, by age

rates are small: For Group 4 it approaches 0 (.02 arrests per year). Figure 14.1 indicates that effectively this group had desisted from offending for nearly a decade. At age 32 the estimated offending rate of Group 3 is only .1 arrests per year, which implies an average time between arrests of about 10 years. The effective desistance of Group 3 members by age 32 appears to have occurred more gradually than that for Group 4 members, as throughout their twenties those in Group 3 have modestly high arrest rates.

Table 14.1 presents group means on a variety of individual characteristics, behaviors, and life-course outcomes. We combine Groups 1 and 2 because of the small numbers in Group 1. Consider first the "unofficial" delinquency measure under "Adolescent Behavior." Although Groups 1 and 2 had more adolescent delinquent activity than did members of Groups 3 and 4, the difference is modest—15.6 for Groups 1 and 2 versus 14.0 for Group 3 and 13.6 for Group 4.[6] Thus, *conditional upon having a juvenile record,* the intensity of

---

[6]Significance tests are based on a likelihood-ratio test of whether the group membership variables add significantly to the explained variation in the response variable. This test assumes that group assignments are made without error. They are not. However, group assignment probabilities, according to the maximum probability rule, are typically very high. When this is the case, inferences are scarcely affected by formal correction for assignment uncertainty (Roeder, Lynch, & Nagin, 1997).

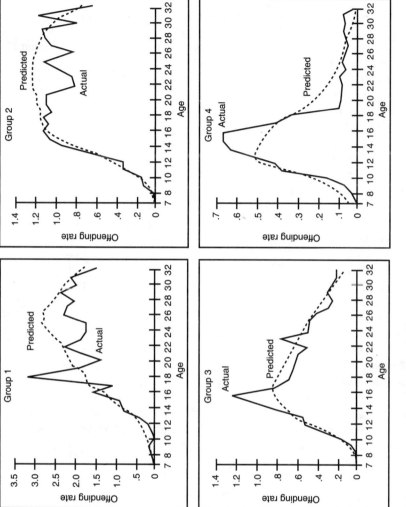

FIGURE 14.2 Actual and predicted offending rates by age, for groups

adolescent delinquency seems to be only moderately predictive of eventual desistance. This important point is often overlooked in discussions of desistance from crime in adulthood.

The variables measuring individual and family differences in childhood were selected because research on the Gluecks' data (Sampson & Laub, 1993) as well as on other data (Loeber & Stouthamer-Loeber, 1986; Nagin & Farrington, 1992; Nagin, Farrington, & Moffitt, 1995) has shown that these childhood factors predict juvenile delinquency and in some instances, predict adult criminality. Our concern, however, is with desistance.

Only family size distinguishes the groups—on average the desisters come from somewhat smaller families, 5.5 and 5.2 for Groups 3 and 4, respectively, versus 6.0 for Groups 1 and 2. None of the other variables measuring

**Table 14.1 Comparison of Group Means
for Selected Characteristics, by Group Membership**

Characteristic	Groups 1 and 2	Group 3	Group 4
Individual Differences in Childhood			
Verbal IQ	5.63	5.49	5.44
Percent Extroverted	67.0	53.1	55.8
Percent Adventurous*	66.0	52.7	50.6
Percent Egocentric	12.3	15.9	9.7
Percent Aggressive	14.2	15.9	15.6
Percent Tantrums	44.3	41.4	34.4
Percent Difficult	55.8	60.9	57.9
Family Differences in Childhood			
Poverty	.10	.08	.00
Family Size*	6.00	5.34	5.23
Parental Crime/Alcohol Abuse	2.06	1.94	2.04
Erratic Discipline	.13	−.15	−.08
Supervision	1.39	1.47	1.42
Attachment to Family	3.07	3.13	3.10
Adolescent Behavior			
Arrest Frequency*	.45	.45	.37
Unofficial Delinquency*	15.6	14.0	13.6
Percent Attached to School*	21.6	35.9	39.7
Percent Early Onset	15.4	14.1	9.6
Adult Social Bonds			
Percent Divorce/Separation by Age 32*	38.5	18.9	10.3
Percent "Shotgun" Marriage*	40.8	34.4	18.4
Percent Married by Age 32*	30.8	50.7	80.3
Quality of Marriage at Age 32*	− 2.01	−.47	.69
Job Stability at Age 32*	− 3.16	− 1.37	.50
Number of Cases	106	220	154

Note. *Differences are jointly significant at $p < .05$ level (see footnote 6).

family factors—poverty, parental criminality, and childrearing practices—distinguish the groups; only one of the individual characteristics—whether the boy was judged "adventurous"—differentiates the groups. The percentages of subjects who in childhood were extroverted, egocentric, aggressive, difficult, or prone to temper tantrums all fail to differentiate the Group 1 and 2 non-desisters from the two desister groups. We suspect that the limited capacity of these childhood factors to differentiate group membership stems from the relatively small differences across groups in the intensity of their adolescent delinquency. Put differently, while prior research has shown that childhood and family differences are "sturdy" predictors of antisocial behavior (Robins, 1978), the capacity of these differences to predict future desistance from such behavior seems to be limited. Nagin et al. (1995) also found that these variables had a limited capacity to predict desistance among active offenders in a more contemporary sample of 411 British males born in 1951–1954.

The variables measuring adult social bonds show that desister groups (Groups 3 and 4) are significantly and substantially less likely to be divorced or separated or to have been involved in "shotgun" marriages. They also have significantly higher scores on two indices of social bonds—the quality of the marriage bond at age 32 for those who are married and job stability for the period from age 25 to 32.

The pronounced association between membership in Group 3 or 4 and the strength of adult social bonds is consistent with our view of change over time; but it is also consistent with a selection process view. Table 14.2 illustrates the potential selection problem. Model 1 shows a regression of the marriage quality index at age 32 on our measure of "unofficial" delinquency. There is a pronounced negative association between the intensity of unofficial delinquency and this index of a good marriage—those with fewer delinquent acts as reported by various informants tend to have more successful marriages, a result consistent with the past-as-prologue-to-future argument that underlies the selection interpretation of the desistance-social bond association. However, once group membership controls are entered into the regression (Model 2), the association between the intensity of delinquency and the good marriage quality index is reduced to zero. This result is strong evidence that using group membership as a control effectively takes into account enduring individual differences.

Second-Stage Analysis

In the second stage of our analysis, we test two key predictions on gradual change: (1) Individuals who early on become involved in marriages that evolve into good marriages will desist from crime the soonest, and (2) as a result of

Table 14.2 Coefficients from Regressions of the Marriage Quality Index Scores on Unofficial Delinquency and Group Membership

Independent Variable	Model 1	Model 2
Unofficial Delinquency	−.055*	−.004
	(−2.08)	(−.17)
Groups 1 and 2 Membership	—	− 2.685**
		(−9.54)
Group 3 Membership	—	−1.154**
		(−5.04)
Constant	.362	.742*
	(.93)	(2.07)
R^2	.01	.34
Number of Cases	311	311

Note: Numbers in parentheses are *t*-ratios.
*p < .05   **p < .01 (two-tailed tests)

the growing investment in ex-post good marriages, the magnitude of the preventive effect of the marital bond will grow over time.

In the Poisson regression analyses that follow, the dependent variable is the number of arrests of individual i in period t, where periods are defined as two-year intervals beginning with age 17 and ending at age 32 (i.e., $i = 17$–18, 19–20, . . . , 31–32). Independent variables include dummy variables for age for each period, which control for changes in offending due to the effect of "age" (Hirschi & Gottfredson, 1983). To control for persistent heterogeneity, the model specification also includes the individual's juvenile arrest frequency rate *and* dummy variables indicating group membership.[7]

The key component of the specification for testing our hypotheses concerning the preventive effect of the marriage bond is a series of period dummy variables designed to capture the impact of the quality and timing of the marriage on the offending rate. To illustrate, for an individual who marries in the 23–24 age period, his dummy variable for "marriage period" equals 1 in the period of the marriage (age 23–24 in this example) and 0 in all other periods. The dummy variables "one period before marriage period" and "two periods before marriage period" are, respectively, set equal to 1 in the first and second periods prior to the marriage. Similarly, the dummy variables for one, two, and three periods after the marriage are set equal to 1 in the first, second, and third periods following marriage, respectively. The model also includes a companion set of dummy variables that in a similar manner distinguish the timing of ex-post good marriages, defined by having a marriage quality score at age 32 greater than the sample median.

Our model emphasizes that the preventive effect emanates from the quality of the marriage bond, not from the existence of marriage itself. Thus, we do not expect any systematic relationship between the timing of the marriage and the offense rate as captured by the coefficients for the marriage period dummy variables. In contrast, we anticipate that the coefficients for the good marriage period dummy variables will display a pattern suggesting an enduring and growing preventive effect. In other words, all of the good-marriage coefficients will be negative and their absolute magnitudes will increase from the onset of the good marriage forward. This prediction captures our argument that ex-post good marriages have a preventive effect dating from the initial period of the marriage onward, and that the preventive effect will grow with time. We make no predictions about the signs of the coefficients for the one and two periods before a good marriage, but if there is a preventive effect stemming from courtship, the coefficients will also be negative for the courtship period.

The results are reported in Table 14.3. Observe that the group membership coefficients are large and significant. All of the coefficients of the dummy variables in the model can be interpreted as the natural logarithm of the proportional difference from a reference group. For the group membership variables, the reference group is Group 4. Thus, in any given period, members of Groups 1 and 2 have mean arrest rates 14 times larger than their Group 4 counterparts.

---

[7]We also conducted the analyses including both juvenile arrest frequency and unofficial delinquency in the models. The results were virtually identical.

Table 14.3 Coefficients from Poisson Regressions of Arrest Rate on the Timing and Quality of Marriage

Independent Variable	Estimate	t-Ratio
Marriage Period – 2	.036	(.50)
Marriage Period – 1	–.072	(–1.00)
Marriage Period 0	–.212**	(–2.62)
Marriage Period + 1	–.029	(–.37)
Marriage Period + 2	.115	(1.43)
Marriage Period + 3	.378***	(4.81)
Good-Marriage Period – 2	–.024	(–.19)
Good-Marriage Period – 1	–.202	(–1.41)
Good-Marriage Period 0	.332**	(2.67)
Good-Marriage Period + 1	–.216	(–1.57)
Good-Marriage Period + 2	–.860***	(–4.76)
Good-Marriage Period + 3	–1.154***	(–5.87)
Groups 1 and 2	2.610***	(30.04)
Group 3	1.630***	(18.88)
Age at Marriage		
17 to 18	.667***	(8.78)
19 to 20	.448***	(5.58)
21 to 22	.481***	(5.79)
23 to 24	.475***	(5.87)
25 to 26	.355***	(4.29)
27 to 28	.213**	(2.53)
29 to 30	.139	(1.61)
Juvenile Arrest	.010	(.13)
Constant	–2.021***	(–19.18)
Number of Observations	2,799	

$*p < .05$ $**p < .01$ $***p < .001$ (two-tailed tests)

Similarly, the Group 3 arrest rate is estimated to be 5 times larger. Note, however, that the arrest rates for Group 4 members are very small by their mid-twenties so that these large multiples exaggerate the absolute difference in the offending rate, particularly in the case of Group 3. Not surprisingly, the coefficients of the dummy variables for age also imply a steady decline in the expected arrest rate from age 17 onward.

The coefficients for the marriage-timing dummy variables measure the preventive impact of marriage alone.[8] For these variables the reference group is "not married." The estimates suggest an initial preventive effect—the coefficient

---

[8]Because the model specifically distinguishes ex-post good marriages, the marriage-alone impact estimates can also be interpreted as measuring the impact of an ex-post "bad" marriage as evidenced by a marriage quality score below the sample median.

for the period of marriage is negative and significant, but for periods after the marriage the coefficients change sign and become positive, implying that marriage alone may even increase crime. Indeed, by three periods after marriage the increase is statistically significant. Likelihood-ratio tests show that the six marriage-timing variables add significantly to the explanatory power of the model ($\chi^2 = 35.2$, d.f. $= 6$).

We turn now to the results concerning the preventive effects of ex-post good marriages. The coefficients for one and two periods before a good marriage are both negative, suggesting a courtship effect, but neither is statistically significant. The results for the periods after a good marriage accord with our prediction but with one important exception. In all of the periods following an ex-post good marriage there is a significant preventive effect that increases over time. By construction, the coefficient estimates measure the preventive effect of a good marriage compared to marriage alone. Thus, the reference group is individuals who entered into marriages that were evaluated as "not-good" by the marriage quality index. The results imply that in the first period after marriage, persons who enter into an ex-post good marriage have an offending rate that is 19 percent less than a person who is one period into an ex-post "not-good" marriage. By the second period after marriage, this difference grows to 58 percent, and by the third period the difference is an even more substantial 68 percent. These estimates suggest that the influence on offending of a strong marital bond is large and that influence increases over time. The exception to the predicted pattern occurs in the initial period of the good marriage. The results show a positive and significant increase in the expected arrest rate of nearly 40 percent compared to entry into an ex-post "not-good" marriage.

Another natural reference category for calibrating the impact of a good marriage is no marriage. This impact can be obtained by summing the period-specific coefficients for marriage and good marriage (e.g., one period after marriage and one period after good marriage). Table 14.4 reports these results using the reference groups of "not married" and "not good marriage" alone. The results are not substantially sensitive to the choice of reference group. When "not married" is the reference group, there is no statistically significant initial period increase in crime and the post-marriage preventive effect grows over time. When "not good marriage" is the reference group there is an initial increase in crime, but by the first period after marriage there is a preventive effect that thereafter grows large. The insensitivity of the results to choice of reference group is another reflection of the finding that marriage alone seems to have no enduring preventive effect.

Table 14.5 reports regression results similar to those in Table 14.3, but for each group separately. Holding constant the degree of desistance by age 32 provides further protection from selection biases contaminating our test of the preventive effect of a good marriage. The results for Group 3 mirror the findings for the combined sample: There is evidence of a short-term preventive effect of marriage alone, but no enduring impact. Also, as in the combined sample, there is a growing preventive effect of a good marriage. While

**Table 14.4 Magnitude of the Good-Marriage Effect:
Percentage Difference from Reference Group, by Marriage Period**

	REFERENCE GROUP	
Period	Not Married	"Not-Good" Marriage
Good-Marriage Period – 2	1.2	2.4
Good-Marriage Period – 1	–24.0	–18.3
Initial Good-Marriage Period	12.7	39.4
Good-Marriage Period + 1	–21.7	–19.4
Good-Marriage Period + 2	–52.5	–57.7
Good-Marriage Period + 3	–53.8	–68.3

the estimated decline in arrests in the first period after a good-marriage is not statistically significant, the magnitude of the point estimate of the "good-marriage effect" is still substantial—a 21-percent decline compared to entry into an ex-post not-good marriage. The effects for two and three periods after a good marriage are statistically significant and resemble the estimated preventive effects for the full sample, 50-percent and 64-percent declines, respectively. The coefficient of the initial good-marriage period remains positive and substantial in magnitude, a 75-percent increase.

The results for Group 4 are qualitatively similar, but the good-marriage effect is significant only in the second period after the good marriage. The weaker results are likely attributable to the rapid decline in arrest rates that all members of this group experience beginning in their late teenage years. Because this decline occurs prior to the age that most married, it is difficult to measure the impact of marriage on offending for Group 4.

Finally, the combined Groups 1 and 2 consist of individuals who even at age 32 continued to have moderate-to-high arrest rates. Still, by age 32 their rates of offending have declined by about 30 percent to 40 percent from their peaks at age 25 (see Figure 14.1). While Table 14.1 shows that chronic offenders are significantly less likely to enter into ex-post good marriages than were desisters, some did enter into good marriages. The regression results for the combined Groups 1 and 2 suggest that even for these individuals, ex-post good marriages hasten the decline in offending. By the third period after an ex-post good marriage, the offense rate of these chronic offenders is 61 percent smaller than it would have been had their marriage not been good. This finding is compatible with the analyses of the criminal careers of convicted felons by Horney et al. (1995), who found that the behavior of even highly deviant actors is amenable to change. Some criminals *do* marry, and some of these marriages reduce propensities to offend.

In another test of our hypotheses we not only divided the sample by group but also included only individuals who entered into ex-post good marriages. This sample division creates homogeneity at age 32 in both the degree of

Table 14.5 Coefficients from Poisson Regressions of Arrest Rate on the Timing and Quality of Marriage, by Group Membership

Independent Variable	Groups 1 and 2		Group 3		Group 4	
	Estimate	t-Ratio	Estimate	t-Ratio	Estimate	t-Ratio
Marriage Period − 2	.141	(1.52)	−.110	(−.86)	.014	(.04)
Marriage Period − 1	.020	(.23)	−.205	(−1.50)	−.054	(−.13)
Marriage Period 0	−.081	(−.80)	−.508***	(−3.29)	−.074	(−.14)
Marriage Period + 1	−.011	(−.12)	−.099	(−.73)	−.509	(−.69)
Marriage Period + 2	.084	(.82)	.153	(1.11)	.290	(.54)
Marriage Period + 3	.358***	(3.74)	.403**	(2.82)	.226	(.37)
Good-Marriage Period − 2	−1.066*	(−2.34)	.013	(.08)	.095	(.22)
Good-Marriage Period − 1	−.393	(−1.14)	−.182	(−.90)	−.321	(−.65)
Good-Marriage Period 0	.035	(.13)	.559**	(2.93)	.542	(.99)
Good-Marriage Period + 1	.263	(1.23)	−.238	(−1.18)	.004	(.01)
Good-Marriage Period + 2	−.686*	(−2.08)	−.693***	(−2.90)	−1.437	(−1.88)
Good-Marriage Period + 3	−.939**	(−2.87)	−1.029***	(−3.56)	−.721	(−.98)
Age at Marriage						
17 to 18	.135	(1.35)	1.351***	(9.60)	1.760***	(4.97)
19 to 20	.108	(1.04)	1.069***	(7.34)	.653	(1.62)
21 to 22	.161	(1.48)	1.074***	(7.15)	.657	(1.59)
23 to 24	.105	(1.02)	1.154***	(7.79)	.362	(.81)
25 to 26	.106	(1.03)	.850***	(5.56)	.441	(.99)
27 to 28	.227*	(2.28)	.279	(1.67)	−.255	(−.51)
29 to 30	.102	(.98)	.216	(1.27)	.357	(.85)
Juvenile Arrest	−.049	(−.46)	.099	(.89)	.047	(.12)
Constant	.831***	(9.28)	−.874***	(−6.39)	−2.394***	(−6.83)
Number of Observations	627		1,261		914	

$*p < .05$ $**p < .01$ $***p < .001$ (two-tailed tests)

desistance *and* the quality of the marriage bond and offers a still more demanding test of whether a quality marital bond hastens desistance. For this regression, there is no evidence of a courtship effect for any of the subsamples, and for each subsample the good-marriage period and one period after good marriage effects are positive but not significant (results available on request). However, the effects two and three periods after a good marriage effect are negative for each subsample. Although not significant by conventional criteria, this lack of significance appears to be largely attributable to a loss of statistical power, because the magnitudes of the coefficients are reasonably large. In fact, for Group 4 and Groups 1 and 2, the results imply that their arrest rates were about 40 percent smaller than those for their counterparts who had not yet entered into the courtship phase of their ex-post good marriage. The estimate for Group 3 is 26 percent smaller. To be sure, the patterns are somewhat erratic, but we are encouraged to find even tentative support for our hypotheses about change in such a highly restricted sample with reduced variation.[9]

CONCLUSION AND IMPLICATIONS

Several conclusions flow from our analyses. First, there are distinct trajectories of individual offending that diverge markedly from the aggregate age-crime curve. Four offender groups characterize the delinquent sample from Glueck and Glueck (1950). Although two of these groups follow the conventional age-crime curve with sharp declines in offending in adulthood (Farrington, 1986; Hirschi & Gottfredson, 1983), two groups do not. In fact, at least one group and probably a (small) second group of men continue to offend at a fairly high and relatively flat rate even as they age into their thirties. These findings emerge from a group of high-rate juvenile offenders. The delinquents in the Gluecks' study were serious, persistent offenders, and consequently, they were remanded to juvenile institutions. Yet as they age, the heterogeneity in offending patterns becomes sharper, so that by age 32 the skewness of offending that we observe in general population samples is evident in this group too (albeit at a higher level of overall offending).

The second finding, implied but not compelled by the first, is that childhood and juvenile characteristics are insufficient for predicting the patterns of future offending in a high-rate group of juvenile offenders. The divergent pathways that unfold over time can be predicted by concurrent events in the transition to young adulthood. Recall that many of the staple variables of delinquency theory (e.g., being a difficult child, low IQ, living in poverty, poor parental supervision) were unable to differentiate offending trajectories into mid-adulthood. These findings suggest that many of the classic predictors of the onset and frequency of delinquency may not explain desistance.

The third major finding concerns the timing and quality of marriage: Early marriages characterized by social cohesiveness led to a growing preventive effect. Consistent with the informal social control theory of Sampson and Laub (1993) and Nagin and Paternoster (1994), the data support the investment-quality character of good marriages. The effect of a good marriage takes time to appear, and it grows slowly over time until it inhibits crime. Our findings accord well with studies using contemporary data. For example, Horney et al. (1995) showed that large *within-individual* variations in criminal offending for a sample of high-rate convicted felons were systematically associated with local life circumstances (e.g., employment and marriage). As they noted, *some* of the time, *some* high-rate offenders enter into circumstances like marriage that provide the

---

[9]We replicated the main analysis disaggregating crime into the two major crime types—violent crimes and property crimes. For both types of crime, good marriage has a significant lagged preventive effect on offending (two years out for violence and three years out for property crime), net of group membership, age, and juvenile arrests. Furthermore, marriage alone has no effect on desistance independent of its quality.

potential for informal social control. When they do, and in our case when marital unions are cohesive, the investment has a significant preventive effect on offending (Farrington & West, 1995). "Good" things sometimes happen to "bad" actors, and when they do desistance has a chance. Of course, our perspective suggests that outcomes are always in doubt, but that is even more reason not to give up hope based on negative returns from the early years alone.

REFERENCES

D'Unger, Amy, Kenneth Land, Patricia McCall, and Daniel Nagin. 1998. "How Many Latent Classes of Delinquent/Criminal Careers? Results from mixed Poisson Regression Analyses of the London, Philadelphia, and Racine Cohort Studies. *American Journal of Sociology* 103: 1593–1630.

Farrington, David P. 1986. "Age and Crime." Pp. 189–250 in *Crime and Justice,* vol. 7, edited by M. Tonry and N. Morris. Chicago, IL: University of Chicago Press.

Farrington, David P. and Donald J. West. 1995. "The Effects of Marriage, Separation, and Children on Offending by Adult Males." Pp. 249–81 in *Current Perspectives on Aging and Life Cycle,* vol. 4. *Delinquency and Disrepute in the Life Course,* edited by Z. Smith Blau and J. Hagan. Greenwich, CT: JAI Press.

Glueck, Sheldon and Eleanor Glueck. 1950. *Unraveling Juvenile Delinquency.* New York: Commonwealth Fund.

———. 1968. *Delinquents and Nondelinquents in Perspective.* Cambridge, MA: Harvard University Press.

Gottfredson, Michael R. and Travis Hirschi. 1990. *A General Theory of Crime.* Stanford, CA: Stanford University Press.

Hirschi, Travis and Michael Gottfredson. 1983. "Age and the Explanation of Crime." *American Journal of Sociology* 89:552–84

Horney, Julie, D. Wayne Osgood, and Ineke Haen Marshall. 1995. "Criminal Careers in the Short-Term: Intraindividual Variability in Crime and Its Relation to Local Life Circumstances." *American Sociological Review* 60: 655–73.

Land, Kenneth C., Patricia L. McCall, and Daniel S. Nagin. 1996. "Comparison of Poisson, Negative Binomial, and Semiparametric Mixed Poisson Regression Models with Empirical Applications to Criminal Careers Data." *Sociological Methods and Research* 24:387–441.

Laub, John H. and Robert J. Sampson. 1993. "Turning Points in the Life Course: Why Change Matters to the Study of Crime." *Criminology* 31: 301–25.

Loeber, Rolf and Magda Stouthamer-Loeber. 1986. "Family Factors as Correlates and Predictors of Juvenile Conduct Problems and Delinquency." Pp. 29–149 in *Crime and Justice,* vol. 7, edited by M. Tonry and N. Morris. Chicago, IL: University of Chicago Press.

Moffitt, Terrie E. 1993. "Adolescence-Limited and Life-Course Persistent Antisocial Behavior: A Developmental Taxonomy." *Psychological Review* 100: 674–701.

Nagin, Daniel S. and David P. Farrington. 1992. "The Stability of Criminal Potential from Childhood to Adulthood." *Criminology* 30: 235–60

Nagin, Daniel S. and Kenneth C. Land. 1993. "Age, Criminal Careers, and Population Heterogeneity: Specification and Estimation of a Nonparametric, Mixed Poisson Model." *Criminology* 31: 327–59.

Nagin, Daniel S. and Ray Paternoster. 1991. "On the Relationship of Past and Future Participation in Delin-quency." *Criminology* 29: 163–90.

———. 1994. "Personal Capital and Social Control: The Deterrence Impli-cations of Individual Differences in Criminal Offending." *Criminology* 32: 581–606.

Nagin, Daniel S., David P. Farrington, and Terrie E. Moffitt. 1995. "Life Course Trajectories of Different Types of Offenders." *Criminology* 33: 111–39.

Robins, Lee N. 1978. "Sturdy Childhood Predictors of Adult Behavior: Replica-tions from Longitudinal Studies." *Psy-chological Medicine* 8: 611–22.

Roeder, Kathryn, Kevin Lynch, and Daniel Nagin. "Modeling Uncertainty in Latent Class Membership: A Case Study from Criminology." *Journal of the American Statistical Association,* in press.

Sampson. Robert J. and John H. Laub. 1993. *Crime in the Making: Pathways and Turning Points through Life.* Cam-bridge. MA: Harvard University Press.

———. 1994. "Urban Poverty and the Family Context of Delinquency: A New Look at Structure and Process in a Classic Study." *Child Development* 65: 523–40.

Interventions to Reduce Crime over the Life Course

Life-course theories and research provide rich insight into the nature of offending behavior. At the same time, the life-course perspective presents numerous opportunities for developing and implementing age appropriate interventions for preventing and reducing criminal and antisocial behavior. In this final section, two papers provide concrete examples of how developmentally appropriate programs can reduce crime and antisocial behavior over the life course.

In the first article, Richard Tremblay and his colleagues describe results from a comprehensive parent/child training program designed to prevent early onset to delinquency. Some of the key aspects of the program include: providing a literacy component for parents, training parents to successfully monitor their children's behavior, training parents to offer positive reinforcement for their child's prosocial behavior, and training parents to punish their children's antisocial behavior in an effective yet nonabusive manner. Results from a three-year follow-up of program participants reveal that disruptive boys whose parents receive the "treatment" are less physically aggressive in school, have less serious school adjustment problems, and report fewer delinquent behaviors.

The second article from David Olds and his colleagues reports on a quasi-experimental assessment of the long-term effects of nurse–home visitation on children's future criminal and antisocial behavior. In theory, nurse–home visitation programs should increase fetal health through the stages of childhood development. This study, which uses data from New York State, compares families receiving an increased number of home visitations during pregnancy and until their child's second birthday to a control group of families who receive standard prenatal and well-child care.

Fifteen-year follow-up results reveal that adolescents born to unmarried, low socioeconomic status women receiving increased nurse–home visits report fewer instances of running away; fewer arrests, convictions, and violations of probation; and fewer tobacco and alcohol usage relative to comparison groups. This program illustrates the benefits that can accrue from investing, on the front end, in public health programs specifically targeted to the conditions that can foster crime, delinquency, and other negative life outcomes.

These two articles provide examples of evaluations of interventions grounded in the life-course approach to studying human behavior. It is clear from the results of these articles that some developmentally appropriate programs are indeed effective in reducing crime and antisocial behavior over the life course.

SUGGESTED READINGS

McCord, J. (1979). A thirty-year follow-up of treatment effects. *American Psychologist, 33,* 284–289.

Kellam, S. G., Rebok, G. W., Ialongo, N., & Mayer, L. S. (1994). The course and malleability of aggressive behavior from early first grade into middle school: Results of a developmental epidemiologically-based preventive trial. *Journal of Child Psychology and Psychiatry, 35*(2), 259–281.

Tremblay, R., McCord, J., Boileau, H., Charlebois, P., Gagnon, C., LeBlanc, M., & Larivee, S. (1991). Can disrup-tive boys be helped to become competent? *Psychiatry, 54,* 148–161.

Gottfredson, D. C., & Gottfredson, G. D. (1992). Theory-guided investigation: Three field experiments. In J. McCord, & R. E. Tremblay (Eds.). *Preventing antisocial behavior: Interventions from birth through adolescence.* New York: Guilford.

Tremblay, R. E. & Craig, W. M. (1995). Developmental Crime Prevention. In M. Tonry, & D. P. Farrington (Eds.). *Building a safer society: Crime and justice, an annual review of research.* Chicago: University of Chicago Press.

15

Parent and Child Training to Prevent Early Onset of Delinquency

The Montréal Longitudinal–Experimental Study

RICHARD E. TREMBLAY HÉLÈNE BEAUCHESNE
FRANK VITARO HÉLÈNE BOILEAU
LUCIE BERTRAND LUCILLE DAVID
MARC LEBLANC

The power of longitudinal studies to test causal hypotheses is relatively weak, especially when the onset of causal factors cannot be clearly identified in time. Experimental studies will reveal causal effects only if the subjects are followed until the effects are manifested. If a preschool intervention aims at preventing delinquency, the impact of the intervention must obviously be measured when delinquent behavior usually appears, that is, no earlier than preadolescence. Clearly, we must expect interventions that aim to change the course of human development will have long-term effects. In fact, there may be more long-term effects than short-term effects (McCord, 1978). Unfortunately, most experimental studies concerned with changing children's or parents' behavior have had very short follow-ups. By nesting an experimental study in a longitudinal study, the long-term effects of the experiment can become part of the routine assessments of the longitudinal study. The latter gives a broader perspective to the experimental study by showing how the experimental group develops compared to the whole cohort. The experimental study also permits the test of causal hypotheses that the longitudinal study itself cannot test (Farrington, Ohlin, & Wilson, 1986; Tonry et al., 1991).

The results from longitudinal studies of large samples from childhood to adolescence and adulthood suggest that poor parenting may lead to disruptive and antisocial behavior (Loeber & Stouthamer-Loeber, 1986). It must be noted, however, that parents' poor parenting has been shown to be antecedent to delinquent behavior only because a distinction has been made between

SOURCE: In Joan McCord and Richard Tremblay (Eds.). *Preventing antisocial behavior: Interventions from birth through adolescence*, pp. 117–138. Reprinted by permission of The Guilford Press.

disruptive behavior and *delinquent* behavior. Longitudinal studies that have measured both parenting skills and disruptive behavior in childhood have shown that they are highly concurrently correlated (Campbell, 1990; Eron, Huesmann, & Zelli, 1991). Because disruptive behavior in childhood is also highly correlated with later delinquent behavior, it has been suggested that they are both the expression of an underlying continuum (Rowe & Osgood, 1990). Thus, poor parenting may be antecedent to delinquent behavior, but it may not be antecedent to disruptive behavior (Bates, Bayles, Bennett, Ridge, & Brown, 1991).

In a review of research on parent and child effects leading to boys' conduct disorder, Lytton (1990) has argued that the boys' characteristics are generally more important as a cause of conduct disorder than their parents' parenting behavior. Indeed, some evidence indicates that genetic and/or perinatal factors can lead to disruptive behaviors (Cloninger & Gottesman, 1987; Mednick, Gabrielli, & Hutchings, 1987), and that children's disruptive behavior has an impact on the quality of parenting behaviors (Bell & Chapman, 1986). However, both parenting skills and the child's inherited behavioral dispositions are related to the parents' behavioral characteristics before the birth of the child (Huesmann, Eron, Lefkowitz, & Walder, 1984; Plomin, DeFries, & Fulker, 1988). Thus, the search for "The" cause of antisocial behavior can lead to a neverending search for antecedents to the antecedents.

These genetic-intergenerational-developmental studies do make sense if we want to understand the ontogenesis as well as the intergenerational basis of deviant behavior. However, the problem of causation can be addressed from a more circumscribed perspective. For example, if we start with a group of disruptive 6 year olds, we can ask the question "Will the future quality of parenting behavior have an effect on their social development?" A longitudinal study would enable us to monitor the variation in disruptive behavior and parenting behavior to verify the extent to which they covary over time. If amelioration in parenting behavior is followed by less disruptive behavior and lower levels of delinquent behavior, these results would be an indication that parenting has a causal effect on deviant behavior. If, conversely, decreasing disruptive behavior is followed by better parenting, this would indicate that children's behavior has an effect on parenting.

However, we know that disruptive behavior is quite stable, and we expect that parenting behavior will also be relatively stable. In such a stable world we will observe high correlations between variables both cross-sectionally and longitudinally. This argument has been used by Gottfredson and Hirschi (1987) to justify cross-sectional studies and to criticize longitudinal studies. Experimental studies are probably the only way to solve these causal questions (Farrington et al., 1986; Gottfredson & Hirschi, 1987). *If* good parenting can prevent antisocial behavior in boys who are disruptive, and *if* we can change parenting behavior from inadequate to adequate, *then* we should observe the causal effect of better parenting behavior on antisocial behavior.

A number of parent-management training programs have been devised in the past 20 years, based on the hypothesis that parenting skills have an impact on children's disruptive behaviors. Dumas (1989) and Kazdin (1987) reviewed studies of the effects of these programs and both concluded that they were the most promising forms of intervention. If we are interested in verifying the hypothesis that parenting has an effect on the social development of disruptive boys, we must continue to ameliorate parent-management training programs so that they will be more successful in changing the parents' behavior, and then verify if a change in the child's behavior will occur.

But we are asking a lot from these training programs and from parents. Since the boys are already disruptive, training programs for parents appear to be based on the idea that parenting skills should succeed independently from the child's behavior. The child effect studies (Bell & Chapman, 1986) have shown that adults' behaviors toward children are strongly affected by the children's behaviors. If children's behavior could be changed *at the same time* as parents' behavior, we would expect that such concurrent changes would have a greater impact on preventing delinquency than if change occurred only in the parents' behavior. Such a strategy for intervention, from a theory-based, causal perspective, confounds parents' and child behavior as "The" cause for future antisocial behavior. But it replaces the single-cause model by an interactive model that can be formulated as follows: the social development of a child is dependent on the interaction of his or her parents' parenting skills and the behavioral dispositions of the child himself or herself. Most studies of mother–infant interactions have indeed shown that they form an interactive system in which both partners are constantly affecting each other (Trevarthen, 1980; Tronick, Ricks, & Cohn, 1982). It would be surprising if this were not also the case when the infants have grown up to become cognitively and behaviorally more sophisticated. This truth appears to have been recognized for a number of centuries. Gouge (1627), in a volume on "domestical duties," outlines in detail the duties of the child toward his parents as well as the duties of the parents toward the child. There is no reason to believe that a one-sided approach, in a situation which is interactional, would change these interactions.

Evidence shows that poor peer relations are preceded by poor parent-child relationships (Putallaz & Heflin, 1990). One would not expect a child with significant behavior problems to have positive peer relations. The basics of positive communication between parent and child must be closely related to the basics of positive communication with other adults and peers. Thus, one would expect that social skills learned to interact with parents would generalize to peer relationships. Inversely, learning of interpersonal skills through social skills training would improve peer and parent relationships. Together, parent training and social skills training could prove successful in reducing disruptive behaviors and improving parent child interaction, whereas only one component could prove insufficient.

We have conducted a longitudinal–experimental study to describe the social interactions of disruptive boys during the primary school years, and also to verify the effects of both parent training and children's social skills training for the prevention of delinquent behavior. The aim of the experimental intervention was clearly pragmatic (see Schwartz, Flamant, &

Lellouch, 1981). We were interested in the preventive impact of the intervention, but both forms of interventions were aimed at variables that have been postulated to be causes of delinquent behavior; poor parenting skills and poor social skills. Thus, if a change in these behaviors leads to lower delinquency involvement, these results could be interpreted as confirming the hypothesis that parenting skills *and* social skills are causally related to delinquent behavior. We did not have control groups that received *only* parent training or *only* social skills training. Thus the design did not enable us to see the extent to which both types of interventions are needed to prevent delinquent behavior. However, there are enough studies of each type of intervention to indicate the low level of their effectiveness when used individually (Dumas, 1989; Kazdin, 1987).

SUBJECTS AND RANDOMIZATION PROCEDURE

The study's population consisted of kindergarten boys from low socioeconomic areas of Montréal, a large metropolitan city with a 70% French population. To control for cultural effects, boys were included in the study only if both their biological parents were born in Canada and the parents' mother tongue was French. These criteria created a culturally homogeneous, white, francophone sample. To ensure that the sample would consist of boys from families of low socioeconomic background, we also eliminated each family in which either of the parents had more than 14 years of schooling. This criterion eliminated families in which a parent had completed postsecondary technical training (a 3-year program after high school), or had completed more than 2 years of college education.

Boys were assessed by their kindergarten teachers at the end of the school year, in May. Two questionnaires, the Preschool Behavior Questionnaire (Behar & Stringfield, 1974; Tremblay, Desmarais-Gervais, Gagnon, & Charlebois, 1987) and the Prosocial Behavior Questionnaire (Weir & Duveen, 1981), were mixed to form one containing 38 items. The resulting Social Behavior Questionnaire yields four components: disruptive (13 items), anxious (5 items), inattentive (4 items), and prosocial (10 items) (Tremblay, Loeber, Gagnon, Charlebois, Larivée, & LeBlanc, 1991). The disruptive factor was subdivided into three a priori categories of behavior (Loeber, Tremblay, Gagnon, & Charlebois, 1989): fighting (3 items), oppositional behavior (5 items), and hyperactivity (2 items). We obtained an 87% response rate from the kindergarten teachers. Questionnaires were received from 53 schools and 1161 boys were evaluated. After having eliminated subjects who did not meet the ethnic criteria or could not be reached to obtain the information, 1034 subjects were retained for the longitudinal study. This total sample has been followed yearly from age 10 onward (Tremblay, 1992). For example, teachers rated 96% of the boys at age 9, 90% at age 11, and 85% at age 12.

A random subsample ($n = 118$) of the 1161 boys was first created to obtain a small normative sample. For purposes of comparison with the disruptive boys, 43 nondisruptive boys were identified from among the randomly selected normative sample. All boys who had a disruptive score above the 70th percentile were considered to be "at risk." These disruptive boys ($n = 319$) were randomly allocated to three groups. For each boy selected, a brief telephone interview with the mother verified whether the family met the criteria for ethnicity and education. If the family did not meet the criteria, or if it could not be found or refused to answer the relevant questions, the boy was excluded from the study. Altogether, 248 (78%) of the disruptive boys met the selection criteria.

The first of the at–risk groups was created for the experimental study of prevention. This treatment group, originally composed of 96 subjects, was reduced to 68 (71%) through the criterial screening. Among these, 46 families (68%) agreed to participate in the treatment program. The second of the three at-risk groups is called the observation group. This group is providing information for a longitudinal observational study of disruptive boys' social interactions (Tremblay, Gagnon, Vitaro, Boileau, & Charlebois, 1991). This group is equivalent to a no-treatment contact control group. In all, 152 boys were allocated to this group. After elimination of cases that failed to meet criteria and cases lost because the family had moved to an unknown address or could not be reached by telephone, 123 families (81%) remained. Each of these families was invited to participate in the study and 84 (68%) accepted. The last group of at-risk boys was created to act as a no-treatment, no-contact control group for assessing effects of the prevention experiment, and also for evaluating effects of the longitudinal follow-up. The control group consisted of 71 subjects when it was created and was reduced to 58 (80%) after considering the qualifying variables described above. In order to ensure that the control group was equivalent to the other two groups, each of which required consent, those assigned to the control group were asked if they would participate in the activities required for the observational group if the research team was able to include them. Among the control group, 42 families (72.4%) agreed to participate in the study. Consent from the control group not only contributed to making the three groups equivalent but also permitted the outcome assessments.

We compared the groups on kindergarten teacher ratings (evaluating disruptiveness, oppositional behavior, hyperactivity, fighting, anxiety, prosocial behavior, and inattentiveness) to see whether the randomization process had successfully created equivalent groups on the outcome variables we intended to measure, and whether the consent requirement had operated differently among the groups. No main effect was found for consent, but an interaction effect indicated that more families of boys who were frequent fighters consented among the treatment group than among the control or observation groups. A post hoc comparison of the consenters among the three groups showed that in no case did the treatment group differ significantly from the other two (Tremblay, McCord, Boileau, Charlebois, Gagnon, LeBlanc, & Larivée, 1991). The same type of analysis was done for family characteristics. There were no significant differences in number of children in the families, for family structure (intact, single-mother, other), for number of years mothers and fathers went to school, or for age of parents at birth of first child. The socioeconomic status of the treatment group mothers, based on last occupation, was significantly lower than that of the other two groups, but no significant differences were observed for the fathers' SES. There was also a significant difference in ages of parents at birth of subject. Mothers of the observational group were younger than the control group mothers, while fathers of the observational group were younger than fathers of the treated group.

TREATMENT

During the planning phase of the study in 1982–83, the Oregon Social Learning Center's work with parents (Patterson, 1982; Patterson, Reid, Jones, & Conger, 1975) appeared to us to be one of the most innovative training programs for parents with aggressive children. It was decided that techniques developed at the Oregon Social Learning Center would be a major component of the treatment program. Accordingly, the program coordinator was trained at the Center. In brief, the procedure involved: (1) giving parents a reading program; (2) training parents to monitor their children's behavior; (3) training parents to give positive reinforcement for prosocial behavior; (4) training parents to punish effectively without being abusive; (5) training parents to manage family crises; and (6) helping parents to generalize what they have learned. The parent training component was supplemented by eliciting cooperation from the teacher. Work with parents and teachers was carried out by two university-trained child-care workers, one psychologist, and one social worker, all working full-time. Each of these professionals had a caseload of 12 families. The team was coordinated by a fifth professional who worked on the project half-time. Work with the parents was planned to last for 2 school years with one session every 2 weeks. The professionals were, however, free to decide that a given family needed more or fewer sessions at any given time. The maximum number of sessions given to any family was 46 and the mean number of sessions over the 2 years was 17.4, counting families that refused to continue.

For the social skills training component of our intervention, two types of training were given to the disruptive boys within a small group of prosocial peers in school. During the first year a prosocial skills program was devised based on other programs (Cartledge & Milburn, 1980; Michelson, Sugai, Wood, & Kazdin, 1983; Schneider & Byrne, 1987). Nine sessions were given on themes such as "How to make contact," "How to help," "How to ask 'why?'," and "How to invite someone in a group." Coaching, peer modeling, role playing and reinforcement contingencies were used during these sessions. During the second year the program aimed at self-control. Using material from previous studies (Camp, Blom, Hebert, & Van Doorminck, 1977; Goldstein, Sprafkin, Gershaw, & Klein, 1980; Kettlewell & Kausch, 1983; Meichenbaum, 1977), 10 sessions were developed on themes such as "Look and listen," "Following rules," "What to do when I am angry," "What to do when they do not want me to play with them," and "How to react to teasing." Coaching, peer modeling, self-instructions, behavior rehearsal, and reinforcement contingencies were also used during these sessions. This treatment too was offered by the professionals who provided parental training, although different workers assisted the parents and the child.

We also experimented with stimulating fantasy play and teaching the boys to be critical of television. However, because of lack of funds, only half the treated group ($n = 25$) received the fantasy play training and one fifth ($n = 9$) received the television intervention.

FOLLOW-UP ASSESSMENTS

After an assessment period of 4 months, the treatment lasted 2 school years (September 1985 to June 1987). The boys were in treatment from an average age of 7 to an average age of 9. Behavior ratings were obtained from teachers, peers, mothers, and subjects themselves each year since the spring of 1987.

Teacher and mother ratings were obtained with the Social Behavior Questionnaire that had been used for the original assessments in kindergarten. This questionnaire yielded main factor scores for disruptive behavior, anxiety, inattentiveness, and prosocial behavior. Additionally, the disruptive factor was subdivided into fighting, oppositional behavior, and hyperactivity.

Subject and peer assessments were obtained with the Pupil Evaluation Inventory (PEI; Pekarik, Prinz, Liebert, Weintraub, & Neale, 1976). The PEI contains 34 short behavior descriptors. Each child in the class of at least one of our subjects was asked to identify four children in his class who were best described by each of the items. Children responded to the PEI in a group format. The PEI yields three factors: disruptive behavior,[1] containing 20 items (e.g., Those who can't sit still; Those who start a fight over nothing; Those who are rude to the teacher); withdrawal, with 9 items (e.g., Those who are too shy to make friends easily; Those whose feelings are easily hurt; Those who are unhappy or sad); and likability, with 5 items (e.g., Those who are liked by everyone; Those who help others; Those who are especially nice). Each rater can nominate himself for each item, so the instrument provides both a self-rating and a peer rating for each scale.

At age 10 (spring 1988), the boys answered a 27–item self-report antisocial behavior questionnaire asking them to report if they had ever been involved in antisocial behavior (LeBlanc & Fréchette, 1989). The questions enabled measurement both of frequency and of range of involvement. The questions asked about misbehavior in the home (including fighting, theft, and vandalism)

---

[1]This factor was originally labeled "Aggression," but it contains only two clear physical aggression items. The content is similar to the disruptive factor of the SBQ.

and outside the home (including fighting, theft, vandalism, and trespassing), and about drinking alcohol and using illegal drugs. In the following years the same questions were modified to obtain answers about involvement in antisocial behavior during the past 12 months.

To measure achievement in school, grade point average in mathematics and French were obtained from the files of the schoolboard. However, grade point average is related to the school level, so a boy who was held back could have a relatively high grade point average compared to another at his age-appropriate level. We thus decided that being in a regular classroom appropriate for their age provided a better measure of school achievement.

To provide a *global assessment of adjustment,* children were classified as *well adjusted* if they were in a regular classroom at the appropriate level for their age were also rated by teachers and peers below the 70th percentile in disruptive behavior. Children were classified as having *few difficulties* if they were in a regular classroom appropriate for their age but were rated above the 70th percentile by peers or teachers; or were not disruptive (i.e., were rated below the 70th percentile in disruptive behavior by peers and teachers), and were in a regular classroom but not at the level appropriate for their age. Children classified as having *serious difficulties* were both not in a regular classroom at the level appropriate for their age and rated by peers or teachers above the 70th percentile on disruptive behavior. Children who were placed in a special environment because of their adjustment problems in school (special class, special school, residential institution) were automatically classified as having serious difficulties.

RESULTS

Achievement in School

To obtain a general estimate of achievement in school we charted the percentage of boys who were in an age-appropriate regular grade. That is, at age 7 they should have been in grade 1, at age 9 they should have been in grade 3, and so on. Results are presented in Figure 15.1. It can be seen that at age 12 only 62% of the whole sample were in a regular sixth grade. This is a good indication that our original sample was taken from a population that is at high risk for psychosocial adjustment problems. We can observe that there were no significant differences at age 6, before treatment.[2] During treatment, at age 8 and 9 the treated group started to differentiate itself from the control and observational group. The year after the end of treatment the difference was significant. There was some form of relapse at age 11. But at age 12, the last year of primary school, we still had a significant difference between the treated and not treated high-risk boys.

---

[2]The χ^2 compares the treatment group to the combined observational and control groups. There were no significant differences between the observational and control groups at any age.

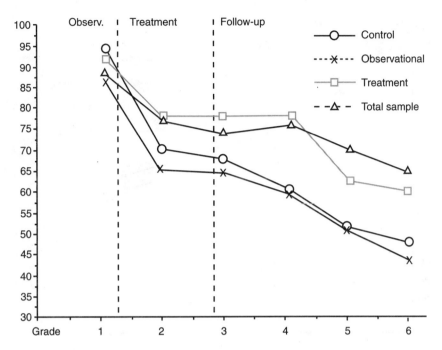

FIGURE 15.1 Percent in age-appropriate regular grade from grade 1 to 6. For grade 1: age = 7, χ^2 = 0.36, p = .55. For grade 2: age = 8, χ^2 = 1.87, p = .17. For grade 3: age = 9, χ^2 = 2.14, p = .14. For grade 4: age = 10, χ^2 = 4.15, p = .04. For grade 5: age = 11, χ^2 = 1.43, p = .23. For grade 6: age = 12, χ^2 = 3.95, p = .05. χ^2 compares the treatment group to both the observational and control groups.

Teacher-Rated Fighting

One of the major aims of our treatment was to reduce the boys' aggressive behavior. Teacher ratings of the boys' fighting behavior from the end of kindergarten at age 6 to the end of primary school at age 12 are presented in Figure 15.2. These results show that the treatment achieved its aim to a certain extent. We can see that at age 6, in kindergarten, the treatment group had the highest fighting score. At age 9, when treatment ended, the treated group mean fighting score was lower than the control and observational group. At age 12, three years after treatment, the treatment group had a mean fighting score identical to the mean of the total sample, whereas the control and observational group had a significantly higher mean fighting score. Note that the scores from age 9 to age 12 were adjusted with a covariance procedure, using age 6 fighting scores in order to correct for differences among the groups before treatment started. The difference at age 12 remained significant when the groups were compared without the introduction of the covariate (t = 2.02, p = .04).

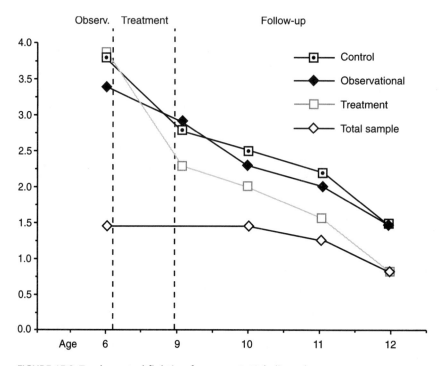

FIGURE 15.2 Teacher-rated fighting from age 6–12 (adjusted scores at age 9–12). For age 6: $F = 1.67$; $p = .19$. For age 9: $F = 3.33$; $p = .07$. For age 10: $F = 1.06$; $p = .31$. For age 11: $F = 1.55$; $p = .22$. For age 12: $F = 4.69$; $p = .03$. F is based on a comparison of the treatment group with the observational and control groups combined.

Global School Adjustment

We created an index to take into account both school behavior problems and school performance. To be classified as having serious school adjustment problems, a boy needed to be rated among the 30% most disruptive by his teacher or his peers and not be in his age-appropriate regular grade or be placed in a special environment. We first computed this index at the end of treatment, when the boys were age 9. The treatment group tended to have fewer boys with serious adjustment problems than the nontreatment groups, although the difference was not significant. We computed the same index 3 years later, when the boys were age 12. The mean disruptive scores at ages 11 and 12 was used with the grade status at age 12. Mean scores of 2 school years for behavior problems are probably a better reflection of the subjects' age level, since it captures ratings from two different teachers and two somewhat different sets of peers over 2 years. Results presented in Figure 15.3 clearly show that the treated group had proportionally more well-adjusted boys (29% vs. 19%), and fewer boys with serious difficulties. There were twice as many boys with serious difficulties in the nontreatment groups (44%) as there were in the treatment group (22%). When the comparison

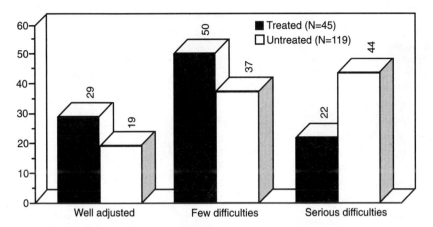

FIGURE 15.3 Percent of treated and untreated boys in different school adjustment groups at age 11–12. $\chi^2 = 6.49$; $p = .04$; $df = 2$.

between the treated and not-treated boys was made using the dichotomy "serious difficulties versus others," the chi-square test indicated that there was only 1% chance of making an error in rejecting the null hypothesis ($\chi^2 = 6.40$, $df = 1$) concerning the interaction between treatment status and adjustment.

In order to test if these differences could be due to differences already present in kindergarten, we did a discriminant function analysis, where the two groups to be predicted were the boys with serious difficulties and those without these serious difficulties, as defined in the previous analysis. It should be noted here that the groups were created without reference to the fact that they were treated or not. Treatment, in this analysis, was considered a predictor that would discriminate between the groups created on the basis of their adjustment level at age 11–12. The predictors where (1) the kindergarten behaviors: fighting, hyperactivity, inattentiveness, anxiety, prosociality; (2) an index of family adversity, created with family structure, parents' education, parents' age at birth of first child, and parents occupational status (Tremblay, Loeber, Gagnon, Charlebois, Larivée, & LeBlanc, 1991); (3) having received the treatment or not. It was expected that if treatment had an effect on adjustment level at age 11–12, over and above behavioral problems and family adversity, which were present before treatment started, it would be a significant predictor in the discriminant function analysis.

Table 15.1 shows the results of the discriminant function analysis. Family adversity in kindergarten had the highest standardized canonical discriminant function coefficient (.70), followed by the presence or absence of treatment (.54), disruptive behavior in kindergarten (.49), and anxiety in kindergarten (.33). From these results it is clear that treatment explains part of the outcome in adjustment problems at the end of primary school after the level of family adversity before treatment has been taken into account. Treatment is also a better predictor of outcome than differences in behavior before the treatment

Table 15.1 Results of Discriminant Function Analysis to Predict Boys with Serious School Adjustment Problems at Age 11–12

Predictors	SCDF Coefficients	Wilks Lambda
Family Adversity in Kindergarten	.70	.91
Treatment (Y-N)	.54	.85
Disruptive in Kindergarten	.49	.84
Anxiety in Kindergarten	−.33	.83
Hyperactivity in Kindergarten	−.28	.82
Inattentiveness in Kindergarten	.21	.82
Total Cases Correctly Classified	69% (112/162)	
True Positives Cases	69% (42/61)	
True negatives cases	69% (70/101)	

Note. Canonical correlations = .43; p = .000

started. The discriminant function correctly classified 69% of the subjects, including 69% of the true positives and 69% of the true negatives.

Onset of Delinquent Behavior

One of the important aims of our intervention was to prevent delinquent behavior. The boys in our study have not yet reached the age of intense delinquency involvement, but early onset of delinquent behavior is a predictor of later serious delinquency (Farrington et al., 1990). We have data on self-reported delinquent behavior from age 10 to age 12. Results indicating the preventive effects of the experiment on early onset of self-reported delinquency are presented in Table 15.2. At age 10 (1 year after treatment) the boys were given a list of 27 delinquent acts and asked how often they had ever been involved in such acts. Then at ages 11 and 12 they were given the same list and asked how often they were involved in the acts during the past 12 months. The percentage of boys from the treated and not-treated groups who reported to have ever been involved in a given delinquent behavior up to age 12 are reported for each item for which there was a significant difference. It can be observed that for all four behaviors where there was a significant difference, a smaller percentage of the treated group were involved: fewer treated boys reported trespassing, stealing objects worth less and more than $10, and stealing bicycles.

Mothers' Perception of Antisocial Behavior

All the results presented above indicate that the treatment has had beneficial effects. These results were based on teacher and peer ratings as well as self-reports. Our intervention was focused on parent training and social skills training. We expected that both parent training and social skills

**Table 15.2 Percentage of Boys Ever Involved
in Selected Delinquent Behaviors Up to Age 12**

	Treated ($n = 42$)	Untreated ($n = 118$)	χ^2
Trespassing	40%	62%	5.76**
Taking Objects Worth < $10	19%	45%	9.01***
Taking Objects Worth > $10	7%	20%	3.85*
Stealing Bicycles	5%	19%	5.10**

*p < .05
**p < .03
***p < .003

training would have an impact on the boys' social adjustment. This appears to have been the case with regard to school adjustment and general delinquency. How about home adjustment? One would expect that if parent training has had an impact on school adjustment and general delinquency, it would also have an impact on social adjustment at home. Mothers rated the behavior of their sons each year in the spring at the same time as did teachers and peers.

Results from mother ratings indicate that treatment had a short-term paradoxical effect on mother's perceptions, but no long-term effects were observed. Indeed, at the end of treatment, when the boys were age 9, the treated boys' mothers reported that their sons were more disruptive compared to mothers of the nontreated boys ($M_1 = 13.11$; $M_2 = 10.87$; $t = 2.48$, $p = .02$), fought more ($M_1 = 2.78$; $M_2 = 1.85$; $t = 3.08$; $p = .003$), and were more inattentive ($M_1 = 5.19$, $M_2 = 4.52$; $t = 1.99$, $p = .05$). These significant differences had disappeared by age 10 and were not observed again at age 11 or 12. Since part of the parent training program was focused on helping parents monitor their boys' behavior, mothers of the treated group could be expected to report more accurately their child's behavior. If this were the case, we would have to conclude that mothers who did not receive the parent training underreport their sons' disruptive behavior. There was an indication that this was indeed the case when we compared mothers' report of their sons' stealing to the sons' self-report of stealing. Table 15.2 indicates that 45% of the untreated boys reported having stolen objects worth less than $10, compared to 19% of the treated boys. Mothers were asked if their son ever steals, and how often. The percentage of mothers, from both treated and untreated groups, who reported their son between ages 9 and 12 to "sometime or often" steal varied between 20% and 25%; there was never more than a 4% difference between the two groups in any given year. Thus, the reports of the mothers from the treated group appears to be close to their sons' reports, while mothers from the nontreated groups clearly underestimated their sons' stealing behavior.

Parent Behavior

If parent training had an impact on a boys' behavior, we expect that this will be because it modified parents' behaviors meant to be changed by the training. Our research program did not include direct observation of parenting behaviors for the treated group during or after treatment. This is clearly a necessary procedure it we want to establish a causal link between changes in parent behavior and changes in the child's behavior. But there is an indirect way to measure changes in parents' behavior: through the sons' perceptions of their parents behavior. There is a possibility that the changes in a parent's behavior that have the greatest impact on a boy's behavior would be those that the boy himself has perceived. This idea is somewhat speculative since one could argue that children are far from being conscious of parent behaviors having an effect on them. But, since part of our knowledge of the relationship between parenting behavior and antisocial behavior comes from the child's report of his parent's behavior (Hirschi, 1969), the former should help understand the causal links between parent training and antisocial behavior.

Each year, from age 10 onward, the boys were asked a series of questions on their relationship with their fathers and their mothers. Some of these questions referred to parental monitoring and discipline, the basis of the parent training program. Of 15 questions asked each year for 3 years, such as "Do your parents physically punish you," "Do your parents praise you when you have behaved well," "Is there a rule about how late you can stay out at night," "Do your parents know where you are when you are out of the house," "Do your parents know with whom you are when you are out of the house," there was only one significant difference between the treated and untreated groups: at age 12 the boys from the untreated group reported more often than those from the treated group that there was a rule at home concerning the friends with whom they could play ($M_1 = 21\%$; $M_2 = 38\%$; $\chi^2 = 3.95$, $df = 1$, $p = .05$).[3] Clearly, there was no indication from the boys' perception of their parents' behavior that the treatment had an effect on the parents monitoring and disciplining behavior. One could argue that the lack of significant differences between the treated and untreated subjects could be due to a lack of sensitivity of the measures. However, developmental changes within groups appears to rule out this hypothesis. For example, reports of physical punishment by parents were made by 70% of the boys at age 10 and only 42% at age 12.

DISCUSSION

The aim of our experimental study was to help prevent the antisocial behavior of boys who were disruptive in kindergarten. Although this aim was clearly pragmatic, it offered the opportunity to test the hypothesis that poor parental management of disruptive boys contributes to the development of antisocial behavior.

---

[3]No significant differences when the items were grouped into scales for monitoring and disciplining.

The results from 3 years of follow-up (from ages 9 to 12), after 2 years of treatment (at ages 7 and 8) indicated that the treated disruptive boys were less physically aggressive in school, that they were more often in an age-appropriate regular classroom, that they had less serious school adjustment problems, and that they reported fewer delinquent behaviors. A discriminant function analysis indicated that treatment helped discriminate between the well-adjusted and not-well-adjusted boys, after having controlled for family adversity.

Thus, there are relatively strong indications that the intervention was successful in helping some of the kindergarten disruptive boys. It is still too early to confirm that treatment has helped prevent juvenile delinquency. Although the treated group was better adjusted on a number of important indicators, there were no significant differences on other indicators (e.g., hyperactivity, prosociality, vandalism). If fighting, stealing, and poor school adjustment between age 9 and 12 are important precursors of later delinquency (Farrington et al., 1990), there is a chance that our intervention succeeded in breaking the path between childhood disruptive behavior and juvenile delinquency (Tremblay, 1992). Eron (1990) has suggested that aggressive antisocial behavior crystallizes around age 8. Our intervention between age 7 and age 9 may have hit a sensitive period in some of these boys' social development. Other experiments will have to show if these results can be replicated. Still others should aim at younger boys to see if the effects can be greater at an earlier age. There is a possibility that in the worst of cases antisocial behavior crystallizes much before age 8.

Although our treatment program, which included parent management training and social skills training, appears to have had an impact on the course of disruptive boys' development, we need further evidence to attribute the changes in the boys' behavior to changes in parent management, and thus confirm the theory that parent management is an important cause of antisocial behavior. An attempt was made to obtain such evidence by analyzing the boys' perceptions of their parents' monitoring and disciplining strategies. We did not observe any differences between the treated and untreated group that would indicate that the group of parents who received training had better management strategies. Although these results do not prove that parent training did not change parent monitoring and disciplining techniques in the long run, they do show that disruptive boys' behavior can be changed without changing their perception of their parents' monitoring and disciplining techniques. This is an indication that we should not attribute a causal effect to the correlation between self-reported delinquency and perceptions of parental management. Parent training may have indirect effects on their children's disruptive behavior. For example, parent training may have a general impact on parents' attitudes toward child rearing without changing their "style" of interaction with the child. They may, for instance, meet teachers more often, be more receptive to teachers' comments, and thus change teachers' attitudes toward the parents and the child. In turn, parents may adopt more positive attitudes toward school and foster positive expectancies towards school for their son. In this way parent training would have an effect on the type of environment parents create for their child, without necessarily changing their behavioral style with the child.

Few investigators disagree with the statement that experimental studies are better than longitudinal studies to verify causal effects. However, causal effects are extremely hard to clearly demonstrate in the field of human development. A large number of experimental studies with long-term follow-ups will have to be undertaken before we start really understanding the complexity of child rearing and child development. This could be a discouraging statement for those who want to help at-risk children *now*. They should find comfort in the results from this experiment and others presented in this book. Experiments are useful not only to test theories but also to show that a given intervention achieves its aim. In most of these cases we cannot demonstrate that the cause-effect mechanism works exactly the way it was planned. We still do not know exactly how aspirin relieves pain or how certain drugs reduce hallucinations. But we know that a particular medication for a particular syndrome generally has a beneficial effect. We are starting to obtain evidence that particular deviant behaviors can be prevented by a particular set of interventions. What we urgently need are experimental replications that will show that these positive effects are not the product of a unique set of circumstances.

ACKNOWLEDGMENTS

This study was funded by the following agencies: National Welfare Grants Program of the Canadian Ministry of Health and Welfare, Conseil Québécois de la Recherche Sociale, Conseil de la Santé et des Services Sociaux Régional du Montréal Métropolitain, Fondation Cité des Prairies, Fonds FCAR-Centre et Équipes, Institut de la Recherche en Psycho-Éducation de Monréal, and Centre d'Accueil le Mainbourg. Lucie Bertrand, Rita Béland, Michel Bouillon, Raymond Labelle, Hélène O'Reilly, and Daniel Reclus-Prince performed the intervention. Pierre Charlebois, Claude Gagnon, and Serge Larivée collaborated on the planning and execution of the longitudinal study. Danièle Royal and Minh T. Trinh provided the documentation, and Chantal Bruneau typed the manuscript.

REFERENCES

Bates, J. E., Bayles, K., Bennett, D. S., Ridge, B., & Brown, M. M. (1991). Origins of externalizing behavior problems at eight years of age. In D. J. Pepler & K. H. Rubin (Eds.), *The development and treatment of childhood aggression* (pp. 93–120). Hillsdale, NJ: Erlbaum.

Behar, L. B., & Stringfield, S. (1974). A behavior rating scale for the preschool child. *Developmental Psychology, 10,* 601–610.

Bell, R. O., & Chapman, M. (1986). Child effects in studies using experimental or brief longitudinal approaches to socialization. *Developmental Psychology, 22,* 595–603.

Camp, B. W., Blom, G. E., Hebert, F., & Van Doorminck, W. J. (1977). Think Aloud: A program for developing self-control in young aggressive boys. *Journal of Abnormal Child Psychology, 5*(2), 157–169.

Campbell, S. B. (1990). The socialization and social development of hyperactive children. In M. Lewis & S. M. Miller (Eds.), *Handbook of developmental psychopathology* (pp. 77–91). New York: Plenum Press.

Cartledge, G., & Milburn, J. F. (1980). *Teaching social skills to children. Innovative approaches* (pp. 92–109). New York: Pergamon Press.

Cloninger, C. R., & Gottesman, I. I. (1987). Genetic and environmental factors in antisocial behavior disorders. In S. A. Mednick, T. E. Moffitt, & S. A. Stack (Eds.), *The causes of crime: New biological approaches* (pp. 92–109). New York: Cambridge University Press.

Dumas, J. E. (1989). Treating antisocial behavior in children: Child and family approaches. *Clinical Psychology Review, 9,* 197–222.

Eron, L. D. (1990). Understanding aggression. *Bulletin of the International Society for Research on Aggression, 12,* 5–9.

Eron, L. D., Huesmann. L. R., & Zelli A. (1991). The role of parental variables in the learning of aggression. In D. J. Pepler & K. H. Rubin (Eds.), *The development and treatment of childhood aggression* (pp. 169–188). Hillsdale, NJ: Erlbaum.

Farrington, D. P., Loeber, R., Elliott, D. S., Hawkins, J. D., Kandel, D. B., Klein, M. W., McCord, J., Rowe, D. C., & Tremblay, R. E. (1990). Advancing knowledge about the onset of delinquency and crime. In B. B. Lahey & A. E. Kazdin (Eds.), *Advances in clinical child psychology* (pp. 283–342). New York: Plenum Press.

Farrington, D. P., Ohlin, L. E., & Wilson, J. Q. (1986). *Understanding and controlling crime: Towards a new research strategy.* New York: Springer-Verlag.

Goldstein, A. P., Sprafkin, R. P., Gershaw, N. J., & Klein, P. (1980). The adolescent: Social skills training through structured learning. In G. Cartledge & J. F. Milburn, (Eds.), *Teaching social skills to children: Innovative approaches* (pp. 249–277). New York: Pergamon Press.

Gottfredson, M., & Hirschi, T. (1987). The methodological adequacy of longitudinal research on crime. *Criminology, 25,* 581–614.

Gouge, W. (1627). *The workes of William Gouge: Vol. 1. Domesticall duties.* London.

Hirschi, T. (1969). *Causes of delinquency.* Berkeley: University of California Press.

Huesmann, L. R., Eron, L. D., Lefkowitz, M. M., & Walder, L. O. (1984). Stability of aggression over time and generations. *Developmental Psychology, 20,* 1120–1134.

Kazdin, A. E. (1987). Treatment of antisocial behavior in children: Current status and future directions. *Psychological Bulletin, 102,* 187–203.

Kettlewell, P. W., & Kausch, D. F. (1983). The generalization of the effects of a cognitive behavioral treatment program for aggressive children. *Journal of Abnormal Child Psychology, 11,* 101–114.

LeBlanc, M., & Fréchette, M. (1989). *Male criminal activity from childhood through youth.* New York: Springer-Verlag.

Loeber, R., & Stouthamer-Loeber, M. (1986). Family factors as correlates and predictors of juvenile conduct problems and delinquency. In M. Tonry & N. Morris (Eds.), *Crime and justice: An annual review* (pp. 29–149). Chicago: University of Chicago Press.

Loeber, R., Tremblay, R. E., Gagnon, C., & Charlebois, P. (1989). Continuity and desistance in boys' early fighting at school. *Development and Psychopathology, 1,* 39–50.

Lytton, H. (1990). Child and parent effects in boys' conduct disorder: A reinterpretation. *Developmental Psychology, 26,* 683–697.

McCord, J. (1978). A thirty-year follow-up of treatment effects. *American Psychologist, 33,* 284–289.

Mednick, S. A., Gabrielli, W. F., & Hutchings, B. (1987). Genetic factors in the etiology of criminal behavior. In S. A. Mednick, T. E. Moffitt, & S. A. Stack (Eds.), *The causes of crime: New biological approaches* (pp. 74–91). New York: Cambridge University Press.

Meichenbaum, D. (1977). *Cognitive-behavior modification: An integrative approach.* New York: Plenum Press.

Michelson, L., Sugai, D., Wood, R., & Kazdin, A. E. (1983). *Social skills assessment and training with children.* New York: Plenum Press.

Patterson, G. R. (1982). *Coercive family process.* Eugene, OR: Castalia.

Patterson, G. R., Reid, J. B., Jones, R. R., & Conger, R. E. (1975) *A social learning approach to family intervention: Vol. 1. Families with aggressive children.* Eugene, OR: Castalia.

Pekarik, E. G., Prinz, R. J., Liehert, D. E., Weintraub, S., & Neale, J. M. (1976). The Pupil Evaluation Inventory: A sociometric technique for assessing children's social behavior. *Journal of Abnormal Child Psychology, 4,* 83–97.

Plomin, R., DeFries, J. C., & Fulker, D. W. (1988) *Nature and nurture during infancy and early childhood.* New York: Cambridge University Press.

Putallaz, M., & Heflin, A. H. (1990). Parent-child interaction. In S. R. Asher & J. D. Coie (Eds.), *Peer rejection in childhood* (pp. 189–216). New York: Cambridge University Press.

Rowe, D., & Osgood, D. W. (1990). A latent trait approach to unifying criminal careers. *Criminology, 28,* 237–270.

Schwartz, D., Flamant, R., & Lellouch, J. (1981). *Clinical trials.* New York: Academic Press.

Schneider, B. H., & Byrne, B. M. (1987). Individualizing social skills training for behavior-disordered children. *Journal of Consulting and Clinic Psychology, 55*(3), 444–445.

Tonry, M., Ohlin, L. E., Farrington, D. P., Adams, K., Earls, F., Rowe, D. C., Sampson, R. J., & Tremblay, R. E. (1991). *Human development and criminal behavior: New ways of advancing knowledge.* New York: Springer-Verlag.

Tremblay R. E. (1992). The prediction of delinquent behavior from childhood behavior: Personality theory revisited. In J. McCord (Ed.), *Advances in criminological theory: Vol. 3. Facts, frameworks, and forecasts* (pp. 193–230). New Brunswick, NJ: Transactions.

Tremblay, R. E., Desmarais-Gervais, L., Gagnon, C., & Charlebois, P. (1987). The Preschool Behavior Questionnaire: Stability of its factor structure between cultures, sexes, ages and socioeconomic classes. *International Journal of Behavioral Development, 10,* 467–484.

Tremblay, R. E., Gagnon, C., Vitaro, F., Boileau, H., & Charlebois, P. (1991). *The prediction of conduct disorder in early adolescence from childhood laboratory observations of parent–child interactions.* Paper presented at the Third Annual Meeting of the Society for Research in Child and Adolescent Psychopathology, Zandvoort, The Netherlands.

Tremblay, R. E., Loeber, R., Gagnon, C., Charlebois, P., Larivée, S., & LeBlanc, M. (1991). Disruptive boys with stable and unstable high fighting behavior patterns during junior elementary school. *Journal of Abnormal Child Psychology, 19,* 285–300.

Tremblay, R. E., McCord, J., Boileau, H., Charlebois, P., Gagnon, C., LeBlanc, M., & Larivée, S. (1991). Can disruptive boys be helped to become competent? *Psychiatry, 54,* 148–161.

Trevarthen, C. (1980). The foundations of intersubjectivity: Development of interpersonal and cooperative understanding in infants. In D. R. Olson

(Eds.), *The foundations of language and thought* (pp 316–342). New York: Norton.

Tronick, E. Z., Ricks, M., & Cohn, J. F. (1982). Maternal and infant affective exchange: Patterns of adaptation. In T. Field & A. Fogel (Eds.), *Emotion and early interaction* (pp. 83–100). Hillsdale, NJ: Erlbaum.

Weir, K., & Duveen, G. (1981). Further development and validation of the prosocial behaviour questionnaire for use by teachers. *Journal of Child Psychology and Psychiatry, 22*(4), 357–374.

16

Long-term Effects of Nurse Home Visitation on Children's Criminal and Antisocial Behavior

15-Year Follow-up of a Randomized Controlled Trial

DAVID OLDS, PhD

CHARLES R. HENDERSON, JR.

ROBERT COLE, PhD

JOHN ECKENRODE, PhD

HARRIET KITZMAN, RN, PhD

DENNIS LUCKEY, PhD

LISA PETTITT, PhD

KIMBERLY SIDORA, MPH

PAMELA MORRIS

JANE POWERS, PhD

Context—A program of home visitation by nurses has been shown to affect the rates of maternal welfare dependence, criminality, problems due to use of substances, and child abuse and neglect. However, the long-term effects of this program on children's antisocial behavior have not been examined.

Objective—To examine the long-term effects of a program of prenatal and early childhood home visitation by nurses on children's antisocial behavior.

Design—Fifteen-year follow-up of a randomized trial. Interviews were conducted with the adolescents and their biological mothers or custodial parents.

Setting—Semirural community in New York.

Participants—Between April 1978 and September 1980, 500 consecutive pregnant women with no previous live births were recruited, and 400 were enrolled. A total of 315 adolescent offspring participated in a follow-up study when they were 15 years old; 280 (89%) were born to white mothers, 195 (62%) to unmarried mothers, 151 (48%) to mothers

SOURCE: *JAMA*, Vol. 280, No. 14, pp. 1238–1244. Reprinted by permission of the American Medical Assn.

From the University of Colorado Health Sciences Center, Denver (Drs. Olds and Luckey); Cornell University, Ithaca, NY (Mr. Henderson, Drs. Eckenrode and Powers, and Ms. Morris); the University of Rochester, Rochester, NY (Drs. Cole and Kitzman and Ms. Sidora); and the University of Denver (Dr. Pettitt).

younger than 19 years, and 186 (59%) to mothers from households of low socioeconomic status at the time of registration during pregnancy.

Intervention—Families in the groups that received home visits had an average of 9 (range, 0-16) home visits during pregnancy and 23 (range, 0-59) home visits from birth through the child's second birthday. The control groups received standard prenatal and well-child care in a clinic.

Main Outcome Measures—Children's self-reports of running away, arrests, convictions, being sentenced to youth corrections, initiation of sexual intercourse, number of sex partners, and use of illegal substances; school records of suspensions; teachers' reports of children's disruptive behavior in school; and parents' reports of the children's arrests and behavioral problems related to the children's use of alcohol and other drugs.

Results—Adolescents born to women who received nurse visits during pregnancy and postnatally and who were unmarried and from households of low socioeconomic status (risk factors for antisocial behavior), in contrast with those in the comparison groups, reported fewer instances (incidence) of running away (0.24 vs 0.60; $P = .003$), fewer arrests (0.20 vs 0.45; $P = .03$), fewer convictions and violations of probation (0.09 vs 0.47; $P < .001$), fewer lifetime sex partners (0.92 vs 2.48; $P = .003$), fewer cigarettes smoked per day (1.50 vs 2.50; $P = .10$), and fewer days having consumed alcohol in the last 6 months (1.09 vs 2.49; $P = .03$). Parents of nurse-visited children reported that their children had fewer behavioral problems related to use of alcohol and other drugs (0.15 vs 0.34; $P = .08$). There were no program effects on other behavioral problems.

Conclusions—This program of prenatal and early childhood home visitation by nurses can reduce reported serious antisocial behavior and emergent use of substances on the part of adolescents born into high-risk families.

J UVENILE CRIME is a significant problem in the United States. In 1996, law enforcement agencies made 2.9 million arrests of juveniles (children < 18 years). Moreover, 19% of all arrests and 19% of all violent crime arrests were accounted for by juveniles. Although the number of juvenile Violent Crime Index arrests (i.e., for murder, forcible rape, robbery, and aggravated assault) declined in both 1995 and 1996, the rate in 1996 was still 60% higher than the 1987 level.[1]

Antisocial behavior can be classified according to its time of onset: prior to puberty (childhood onset) vs after puberty (adolescent onset).[2,3] Childhood onset is characterized by more serious behavioral disruption, such as violent behavior toward classmates and cruelty toward animals beginning as early as age 3 years, but occurs less frequently. The adolescent-onset variety, although sometimes expressed as aggression toward peers, is generally less serious (e.g., shoplifting, lying to teachers and parents) and occurs so frequently that some consider it normative.[3] Childhood-onset antisocial behavior is associated with neuropsychological deficits (e.g., impaired language and intellectual functioning, attention–deficits/hyperactivity disorder) and harsh, rejecting parenting early in the child's life.[4,5] The adolescent-onset type has been hypothesized to be a reaction to the limited number of responsible roles for adolescents in Western societies.[3]

In earlier articles, we have shown that a program of prenatal and infancy home visitation by nurses improved women's prenatal health-related behavior[6] and reduced the rates of child abuse and neglect,[7,8] maternal welfare dependence, closely spaced successive pregnancies, maternal criminal behavior and behavioral problems due to use of alcohol and other drugs,[8] and children's intellectual impairment associated with prenatal exposure to tobacco.[9,10] These aspects of maternal and child functioning represent significant risks for early-onset antisocial behavior.[11]

This article examines the extent to which this program produced a reduction in children's criminal and antisocial behavior. We expected that the program would reduce antisocial behaviors indicative of the early-onset type but did not expect it to have as dramatic an effect on adolescent-onset antisocial behavior.[11] We expected that program effects would be concentrated on children born to women who were unmarried and from low-income families at registration during pregnancy. One of the treatment conditions used in this study consisted of prenatal home visitation with no postpartum follow-up. We expected that the group receiving only prenatal home visitation would function better than the comparison group but not as well as the group that received prenatal and postnatal home visitation.

METHODS

The details of this study's design can be found in an earlier article.[8] A summary of the design is given herein.

Setting, Participants, and Randomization

Pregnant women were recruited from a free antepartum clinic sponsored by the Chemung County, New York, health department and the offices of private obstetricians in Elmira, NY. We actively recruited women with no previous live births who were less than 25 weeks pregnant and who were young (aged < 19 years at registration), unmarried, or of low socioeconomic status (SES). Women without these sociodemographic risk characteristics were permitted to enroll if they had no previous live births. From April 1978 through September 1980, 500 women were invited to participate and 400 enrolled. Eighty-five percent were young, unmarried, or from low-SES households (August Hollingshead, PhD, unpublished manuscript, 1976). After completing informed consent and baseline interviews, women were stratified by sociodemographic characteristics and randomized to 1 of 4 treatment conditions. Persons involved in data gathering were blinded to the women's treatment conditions.

Treatment Conditions

Families in treatment group 1 (n = 94) were provided sensory and developmental screening for the child at 12 and 24 months of age. Based on these screenings, the children were referred for further clinical evaluation and treatment when needed. Families in treatment group 2 (n = 90) were provided the screening services offered those in treatment group 1 in addition to free transportation (using a taxicab voucher system) for prenatal and well-child care through the child's second birthday. There were no differences between treatment groups 1 and 2 in their use of prenatal and well-child care (both groups had high rates of completed appointments). Therefore, these 2 groups were combined to form a single comparison group as in earlier articles. Families in treatment group 3 (n = 100) were provided the screening and transportation services offered to treatment group 2 and in addition were provided a nurse who visited them at home during pregnancy. Families in treatment group 4 (n = 116) were provided the same services as those in treatment group 3 except that the nurse continued to visit through the child's second birthday.

Program Plan and Implementation

In the home visits, the nurses promoted 3 aspects of maternal functioning: (1) positive health-related behaviors during pregnancy and the early years of the child's life, (2) competent care of their children, and (3) maternal personal development (family planning, educational achievement, and participation in the workforce). In the service of these 3 goals, the nurses linked families with needed health care and human services and attempted to involve other family members and friends in the pregnancy, birth, and early care of the child. The nurses completed an average of 9 visits during pregnancy (range, 0–16) and 23 visits from birth to the child's second birthday (range, 0-59). Details of the program can be found elsewhere.[12,13]

Overview of Follow-up Study

The current phase of the study consists of a longitudinal follow-up of the 400 families who were randomized to treatment and control conditions and in which the mother and child were still alive and the family had not refused participation at earlier phases. The flow of patients from recruitment through the 15-year follow-up is presented in Table 16.1. Interviews were conducted with the adolescents, their biological mothers, and their custodial parents if the biological mother no longer had custody. Assessments using parent reports used interview data from the parent who was judged to have had the greatest amount of recent experience with the child.

Assessments and Definitions of Variables

Assessments conducted at earlier phases are specified in previous articles.[7,8] At the 15-year follow-up assessment, adolescents completed interviews that measured whether they had been adjudicated a person in need of supervision (PINS) resulting from incorrigible behavior such as recurrent truancy or

Table 16.1 Flow of Patients from Recruitment During Pregnancy Until 15 Years After Delivery of First Child

	TREATMENT GROUPS*		
	1 and 2 (n = 184)	3 (n = 100)	4 (n = 116)
Program Implementation			
No. of Completed Prenatal Home Visits, Average (Range)	. . .†	8.6 (0–16)	8.6 (0–16)
No. of Completed Postnatal Home Visits, Average (Range)	. . .	. . .	22.8 (0–59)
Intervening Years			
No. of Fetal, Infant, or Child Deaths	10	7	9
No. of Children Adopted‡	7	6	2
No. of Maternal Deaths§	1	1	0
15-Year Follow-up Study			
No. of Missing Biological Mothers	12	1	4
No. Who Refused to Participate‖			
Mothers	6	5	4
Adolescents	10	8	7
No. of Completed Interviews			
Parents (Biological or Custodial)	152	81	97
Adolescents	144	77	94
No. of Cases with School Data (Grades 7–9)	139	68	84
No. of Cases with Teacher Report Data¶	117	66	79
No. of Cases with Probation or Family Court Data#	60	27	29

*Treatment groups 1 and 2 are the comparison; treatment group 3 was nurse-visited during pregnancy; and treatment group 4 was nurse-visited during pregnancy and infancy. Of 500 eligible persons invited to participate, 100 refused and 400 were randomized to the various treatment groups.

†Ellipses indicate data not available.

‡There were 2 adoptions in which interviews were conducted with the child but not the mother. They are not shown.

§For both cases in which the mother died, the adolescents were interviewed.

‖Refusals include 8 mothers who refused to participate during earlier phases and were not approached for the 15-year follow-up.

¶Data are for cases with at least 1 mathematics or English teacher report of classroom behavior.

#Data are for subsample of children who resided in original community for their entire lives.

destroying parents' property; their frequency of running away from home; and the number of times they had been stopped by the police, arrested, convicted of a crime or of probation violations, and sent to youth correctional facilities.[14] They also reported on their disruptive behavior in school; number of school suspensions; delinquent and aggressive behavior outside school; experience of sexual intercourse; rates of pregnancy; lifetime number of sexual partners; and frequency of using cigarettes, alcohol, and illegal drugs during the 6-month period prior to the 15-year interview.[15]

Variables were created to summarize the number of occurrences of being stopped by the police, arrested, convicted (adjudicated) of the original crime or of probation violations, and sent to a youth correctional facility. Although we asked the children to report their number of school suspensions and disruptive behaviors in school, we used archived school data and teacher reports to measure these outcomes because they are less subject to reporting bias than are self-report data.

A variable was constructed to characterize the total number of cigarettes currently smoked per day. Separate variables were constructed to count the number of days the children had consumed alcohol or used illegal drugs during the 6-month period prior to the interview. The adolescents were asked questions regarding the effect of alcohol on 5 domains of their lives (trouble with parents, trouble at school, problems with friends, problems with someone they were dating, trouble with police).[16] These data were summarized in an alcohol-use behavioral problem scale (range, 0-5). Corresponding questions regarding use of illegal drugs were omitted because of clerical error.

The self-reports of antisocial and delinquent acts were factor analyzed and found to produce 2 factors, major delinquent acts and minor antisocial acts, with Cronbach α coefficients of .82 and .68, respectively. The adolescents also completed the Achenbach Youth Self-Report of Problem Behaviors, which produces 2 broadband scales: internalizing (anxiety/depression, social withdrawal and somatic complaints) and externalizing (delinquency and aggression) behavior problems.[17]

Parents were asked questions about their children's behavioral problems (the Achenbach scale); school suspensions; arrests; and use of cigarettes, alcohol, and illegal drugs, including the effect of alcohol and other drugs on their children's lives. Variables were constructed to coincide with those based on the child's self-report of behavior. Parents' reports of their children's behavioral problems caused by substance use included children's use of illegal drugs (range, 0–10).

The number of short-term and long-term suspensions were counted from an abstraction of the children's school records for grades 7 through 9. In New York State, long-term suspensions require a hearing and usually are for serious infractions such as assaulting a student or teacher. Records were analyzed when there were complete school data for 2 of the 3 years. The students' current teachers in English and mathematics completed an "acting out" scale that rated children's disruptive behavior in the classroom (e.g., disruptive in class, defiant, obstinate, stubborn).[18]

Finally, the records of 116 children who lived in Chemung County for their entire lives were reviewed by the Chemung County Probation Department and the Chemung County Family Court. Identifying information on the adolescents (name, birth date, sex, Social Security number) was provided to these departments for purposes of matching their records with the participants in this study. The department staff summarized the counts of arrest and PINS records within treatment and risk-status groups. Individual identifiers were not returned in the abstraction of these data, although the children's treatment group, sex, and risk status (i.e., whether they were born to an unmarried mother from low SES) were returned.

Statistical Models and Methods

The study was conducted with an intention-to-treat approach. A core statistical model was derived that was consistent with the one used in the earlier phases of this research. It consisted of a $3 \times 2 \times 2 \times 2$ factorial structure and 6 covariates. The classification factors were treatment groups (1 and 2 vs 3 vs 4), maternal marital status (married vs unmarried at registration), social class (Hollingshead I and II vs III and IV at registration), and sex of child. All interactions among the first 3 factors were included.

Interactions with sex of the child also were examined. Although sex was a significant predictor of the antisocial behavior outcomes, it did not interact in a fully interpretable way with other terms in the model for some outcomes, so it was included without interactions. Where program effects were moderated by the child's sex in a coherent way, we have noted this in the presentation of the findings, in which case the model includes SES as a covariate rather than a classification factor and includes all interactions among treatment, marital status, and sex. This model was preferable to a 4-factor classification structure with all interactions because of the low incidence of some outcomes for certain subclasses, compromising the stability of the Poisson log-linear models used in the analysis. In addition, for 2 variables, the core log-linear model produced unstable variance estimates for the tests of treatment main effects. In these cases, SES and marital status were included without interactions for that test.

Race of the mother was among a number of additional classification factors examined in deriving the core model but was not included because it was not a significant predictor of outcomes once other terms were included.

The 6 covariates included in the final models were maternal age, maternal education, locus of control,[18] support from husband or boyfriend, maternal employment status, and paternal public assistance status. All covariates were measured at registration and tested for homogeneity of regressions for the hypothesized contrasts.[19]

Dependent variables with normal distributions were analyzed in the general linear model and low-frequency count data (e.g., number of arrests) in the log-linear model (assuming a Poisson distribution). In the log-linear model, the analysis was carried out and estimates were obtained in terms of the logs of the incidence. We use the term *incidence* to refer to the actual count or mean of counts during specific periods of measurement. A careful examination of the distributions of each of the dependent variables was carried out. Low-incidence count variables with values higher than 20 were analyzed in a log-linear model, correcting for overdispersion.

For outcomes reported by more than 1 respondent (e.g., child and parent or teachers), we carried out repeated-measures analyses, adding to the basic model fixed factors for respondent and a random factor for individuals. The focus of interpretation was on the average of the 2 sources of information.

All treatment contrasts focused on the comparison of the combination of treatment groups 1 and 2 (the comparison group) with treatment group 4 (the pregnancy and infancy nurse-visited group) because we hypothesized that the greatest treatment effect would be exerted by the combination of prenatal and postnatal home visitation, as found in earlier evaluations.[7,8] The results for the group that received prenatal home visitation only (treatment group 3) are included to report whether that group had intermediate levels of functioning. To address our primary hypotheses, treatment effects also are shown for adolescents whose mothers were unmarried and from low-SES households at registration during pregnancy. All estimates of treatment main effects and effects for the unmarried, low-SES group are derived from a common statistical model.

RESULTS

Equivalence of Treatment Groups
on Background Characteristics

As indicated in Table 16.2, for those families for which 15-year assessments were completed, the treatment groups were essentially equivalent on background characteristics for both the sample as a whole and for women who were unmarried and from low-SES households. Small differences on some background variables (such as paternal receipt of public assistance) led us to include them as covariates.

Encounters With the Criminal Justice System

Table 16.3 shows that adolescents born to nurse-visited women (treatment group 4) reported more frequent stops by police ($P < .001$) but fewer arrests and convictions and violations of probation ($P = .005$ and .001, respectively); the arrest and convictions and probation violation effects were concentrated among children born to women who were unmarried and from low-SES families ($P = .03$ and $< .001$, respectively). For the subsample of children who lived in Chemung County for their entire lives, nurse-visited children (treatment group 4) had fewer official PINS records ($P = .007$). Nurse-visited children whose mothers were unmarried and from low-SES families were reported by their parents to have been arrested less frequently than were their counterparts in the comparison group ($P = .05$). In addition, among adolescents born to unmarried women from low-SES households, those in treatment group 4 reported fewer instances of running away ($P = .003$). As indicated in Table 16.3, with the exception of parent report of child arrests, most of these effects were present for children whose mothers were visited only during pregnancy (treatment group 3).

The effect of the treatment group 4 program on the children's reports of running away was concentrated in girls, whereas the effect on parents' reports of the children's arrests and children's reports of convictions and probation

Table 16.2 Equivalence of Treatment Conditions on Maternal Background Characteristics Measured at Registration for Children Assessed at 15-Year Follow-up*

Dependent Variables	Total Sample of Treatment Groups			Low SES, Unmarried Sample of Treatment Groups		
	1 and 2 (n = 148)	3 (n = 79)	4 (n = 97)	1 and 2 (n = 62)	3 (n = 30)	4 (n = 38)
Unmarried, %	62	59	64	100	100	100
Low-SES Household, %	64	70	61	100	100	100
White, %	90	91	86	87	87	77
Smoker (> 4 Cigarettes/Day)	47	46	58	51	60	59
Male Children, %	55	44	55	44	53	49
Mother Working, %	39	36	31	24	20	20
Mother Receiving Public Assistance, %	9	10	13	23	20	20
Father Working, %	70	70	67	42	50	52
Father Receiving Public Assistance, %	4	3	3	10	6	2
Husband or Boyfriend in House, %	58	76	60	21	47	22
Maternal Age, Mean (SD), y	19.3 (2.9)	19.5 (3.1)	19.4 (3.7)	18.6 (2.5)	19.0 (2.8)	18.2 (3.3)
Maternal Education, Mean (SD), y Completed	11.2 (1.5)	11.6 (1.5)	11.1 (1.6)	10.7 (1.4)	10.9 (1.4)	10.3 (1.5)
Husband or Boyfriend Education Competed, Mean (SD), y	11.4 (1.4)	11.7 (1.7)	11.5 (1.6)	11.1 (1.4)	11.0 (1.8)	10.8 (1.5)
Grandmother Support, Mean (SD)†‡	100.4 (10.1)	97.7 (9.2)	101.3 (10.3)	101.6 (10.9)	98.1 (10.3)	104.1 (11.2)
Husband or Boyfriend Support†‡	99.6 (10.5)	102.0 (9.0)	99.0 (9.9)	94.2 (10.6)	98.6 (9.4)	96.8 (9.3)
Locus of Control, Mean (SD)†	99.3 (10.1)	100.6 (9.5)	100.6 (10.2)	97.5 (10.2)	99.2 (10.3)	99.1 (9.9)
Incidence of Maternal Arrests in New York State Prior to Randomization§	0.09	0.13	0.06	0.13	0.13	0.18

*Treatment groups 1 and 2 are the comparison; treatment group 3 was nurse-visited during pregnancy; and treatment group 4 was nurse-visited during pregnancy and infancy. SES indicates socioeconomic status.

†Standardized to mean (100) and SD (10).

‡Locally developed scale that assesses degree to which individual provides emotional and material support to mother.

§Incidence indicates the mean number of infrequently occurring events within the stated period. Individual cases may have values greater than 1.

Table 16.3 Adjusted Rates of Children's Encounters with Criminal Justice System from Birth to 15 Years of Age*

Dependent Variables	Total Sample					Low-SES, Unmarried Sample				
	Treatment Group			P Value†		Treatment Group			P Value†	
	1 and 2	3	4	T1 & T2 vs T3	T1 & T2 vs T4	1 and 2	3	4	T1 & T2 vs T3	T1 & T2 vs T4
Ever PINS, %	13	11	8	.75	.33	14	10	5	.63	.14
Incidence of Times Ran Away‡	0.29	0.23	0.34	.83	.07	0.60	0.14	0.24	<.002	.003
Incidence of Times Stopped by Police	0.80	0.53	2.25	.24	<.001	1.16	0.78	1.46	.34	.46
Incidence of Arrests	0.36	0.16	0.17	.005§	.005§	0.45	0.15	0.20	.02	.03
Incidence or Convictions and Probation Violations	0.27	0.06	0.10	<.001§	<.001§	0.47	0.07	0.09	<.001	<.001
Incidence of Times Sent to Youth Corrections	0.05	0.05	0.04	.98	.98	0.06	0.03	0.02	.32	.12
Incidence of Arrests (Mother Report)	0.12	0.11	0.08	.73	.37	0.19	0.16	0.04	.79	.05
Incidence of PINS Records (Subsample, Archived Data)‖	0.31	0.17	0.03	.06	.007	0.35	0.33	0.00	.94	.07
Incidence of Arrests (Subsample, Archived Data)‖	0.35	0.14	0.32	.15	.94	0.55	0.22	0.44	.24	.74

*Treatment group 1 and 2 (T1 and T2) are the comparison; treatment group 3 (T3) was nurse-visited during pregnancy; and treatment group 4 (T4) was nurse-visited during pregnancy and infancy. Data are adjusted for socioeconomic status (SES), maternal marital status, age, education, locus of control, support from husband or boyfriend, and working status; husband or boyfriend use of public assistance at registration; and sex of child. PINS indicates person in need of supervision.

†Test of treatment effect performed on odds ratios for percentage outcomes and difference of logs of incidence for incidence outcomes.

‡Incidence indicates the mean number of infrequently occurring events within the stated period. Individual cases may have values greater than 1.

§Test conducted without interactions for SES and marital status.

‖No covariates were included in the analysis of this outcome.

violations was greater for boys (data not shown). The effect of the program on arrests was not limited to any specific type of crime, although property crimes were more frequent and, therefore, accounted for a larger portion of the program effect on arrests overall.

School Suspensions, Behavior Problems, and Use of Substances

Table 16.4 shows that children born to nurse-visited (treatment group 4) women who were unmarried and from low-SES households reported having fewer sexual partners ($P = .003$), smoking fewer cigarettes per day ($P = .10$). and consuming alcohol fewer days during the 6-month period prior to the 15-year interview ($P = .03$). Parents of children born to nurse-visited, unmarried women from low-SES families reported that their children had fewer behavioral problems related to their use of alcohol and other drugs ($P = .08$). For these outcomes, there was some indication that the group visited by nurses only during pregnancy (treatment group 3) did not do as well. Although adolescents in the unmarried, low SES group reported smoking fewer cigarettes, they also reported higher levels of illegal drug use and their parents reported more behavioral problems due to the use of alcohol and other drugs than did their counterparts in the comparison group. There were no treatment differences in teachers' reports of the adolescents' acting out in school; short-term or long-term suspensions; the adolescents' initiation of sexual intercourse; or the parents' or children's reports of major delinquent acts, minor antisocial acts, or other behavioral problems.

COMMENT

Adolescents born to nurse-visited (treatment group 4) women who were unmarried and from low-SES families had fewer episodes of running away from home, arrests, and convictions and violations of probation than did their counterparts in the comparison group. They also had fewer sexual partners and engaged in cigarette smoking and alcohol consumption less frequently. Their parents reported that they had fewer behavioral problems related to the use of drugs and alcohol. There were no program effects on less serious forms of antisocial behavior, initiation of sexual intercourse, or use of illegal drugs. Children in treatment group 4, irrespective of risk, reported being stopped by police more frequently, but they reported fewer arrests and convictions and violations of probation, and the official PINS records corroborated this pattern. The higher rates of being stopped by police is an anomalous finding that has no coherence with any other effects and is likely to be either a sampling or reporting artifact.

The concentration of beneficial effects among children born to unmarried women of low SES is consistent with the results of other preventive interventions that have shown greater effects for children of families at greater social

Table 16.4 Adjusted Reports of Problem Behavior, Sexual Activity, Pregnancy, and Use of Substances at 15-Year Follow-up*

| | TOTAL SAMPLE | | | | | LOW-SES, UNMARRIED SAMPLE | | | | |
| | TREATMENT GROUP | | | P VALUE[†] | | TREATMENT GROUP | | | P VALUE[†] | |
Dependent Variables	1 and 2	3	4	T1 & T2 vs T3	T1 & T2 vs T4	1 and 2	3	4	T1 & T2 vs T3	T1 & T2 vs T4
No. of Minor Antisocial Acts, Mean[‡]	2.99	2.54	2.88	.50	.86	4.06	3.25	3.38	.42	.47
No. of Major Delinquent Acts, Mean[§]	3.02	2.79	3.57	.93	.48	4.09	3.45	3.99	.60	.77
No. of Externalizing Problems, Mean[‖]	13.73	13.65	13.88	.95	.89	14.18	15.63	11.85	.42	.17
No. of Internalizing Problems, Mean[‖]	10.58	11.19	11.66	.46	.19	10.82	11.15	9.85	.80	.44
No. of Acting Out Problems, Mean[¶]	9.61	8.97	9.47	.41	.85	10.36	9.79	10.58	.62	.85
Ever Had Sexual Intercourse, %	35	35	42	1.00	.32	45	55	46	.44	1.00
Ever Pregnant or Made Someone Pregnant, %	3	2	4	.97	1.00	8	9	7	.90	.74
Incidence of Sex Partners[#]	1.56	1.10	1.16	.48	.90	2.48	2.23	0.92	.73	.003
Incidence of Short-Term School Suspensions	0.28	0.11	0.27	.96	.97	0.32	0.16	0.38	.11	.63

Table 16.4 continued

Dependent Variables	Total Sample					Low-SES, Unmarried Sample				
	Treatment Group			P Value[†]		Treatment Group			P Value[†]	
	1 and 2	3	4	T1 & T2 vs T3	T1 & T2 vs T4	1 and 2	3	4	T1 & T2 vs T3	T1 & T2 vs T4
Incidence of Long-Term School Suspensions	0.04	0.00	0.01	1.00	1.00	0.15	0.01	0.04	.97	.25
Incidence of Cigarettes Smoked per Day	1.30	0.91	1.28	.49	.76	2.50	1.32	1.50	.07	.10
Incidence of Days Drank Alcohol	1.57	1.81	1.87	.97	.96	2.49	1.84	1.09	.41	.03
Incidence of Days Used Drugs	2.28	3.55	2.04	.49	.54	4.04	9.38	2.50	.01	.24
Alcohol Impairment, Self-Report	0.52	0.50	0.47	.95	.35	0.49	0.38	0.55	.36	.60
Alcohol and Drug Impairment, Parent's Report	0.18	0.20	0.28	.96	.68	0.34	0.62	0.15	.05	.08

*Treatment groups 1 and 2 (T1 and T2) are the comparison; treatment group 3 (T3) was nurse-visited during pregnancy; and treatment group 4 (T4) was nurse-visited during pregnancy and infancy. Data are adjusted for maternal socioeconomic status, marital status, education, locus of control, support from husband/boyfriend, and working status; husband/boyfriend use of public assistance at registration; and sex of child.

†Test of treatment effect based on mean differences for means, odds ratios for percentages, and difference of logs of incidence for count data outcomes.

‡Minor antisocial acts included lied to parents, lied to teacher, took car without permission, stayed out all night without permission, been passenger in car where driven drunk, and used fake identification to enter bar.

§Major delinquent acts included hurt someone who needed bandages, stole something worth more than $50, stole something worth less than $50, trespassed, damaged property on purpose, hit someone because did not like what he or she said, carried weapon, set fire on purpose, and been in fight with gang members.

‖Average of parent and child reports of behavioral problem (analyzed with repeated measures).

¶Average of mathematics and English teachers' reports of students' disruptive behavior in school (analyzed with repeated measures).

#Incidence indicates mean number of infrequently occurring events within the stated period. Individual cases may have values greater than 1.

risk.[20] This suggests that these kinds of services ought to be focused on families in greater need by virtue of the mothers' being unmarried and poor.

In general, these findings are consistent with program effects on early-onset antisocial behavior rather than on the more common and less serious antisocial behavior that emerges with puberty.[3] The mere presence of arrests, convictions, and probation violations by the time the children were 15 years old suggests that these children started offending early and that they may be on life-course trajectories that portend recurrent and more serious offenses in the future. Given that early-onset antisocial behavior is associated with (1) subtle neurological impairment, (2) harsh, punitive, and neglectful parenting, and (3) family contexts characterized by substance abuse and criminal behavior,[2–5] it is important to note that this program has affected these aspects of maternal, child, and family functioning at earlier phases in the child's development.[6–11] Moreover, genetic vulnerability to impulsivity and aggression is expressed much more frequently when vulnerable rhesus monkeys experience aberrant rearing[21] (also Allyson J. Bennett, PhD, K. Peter Lesch, Armin Heils, et al., unpublished data, 1998), adding to the plausibility of the findings reported here.

The prenatal phase of the program reduced fetal exposure to tobacco, improved the qualities of women's prenatal diets, reduced rates of pyelonephritis, improved levels of informal social support, and reduced intellectual impairment and irritable behavioral styles associated with fetal exposure to tobacco.[6,10,11,22] Prenatal exposure to tobacco is a risk factor for easily behavioral dysregulation, problems with attention, and later crime and delinquency.[22] Moreover, the combination of birth complications (and, by implication, neurological impairment) and rejecting parenting substantially increases the likelihood of violent offenses by the time children are 18 years old.[5]

We did not expect prenatal home visitation (treatment group 3) by itself to be as effective as it was in preventing criminal behavior among children born to low-SES, unmarried women. This occurred even though these children's mothers showed almost none of the postnatal benefits observed for those visited during pregnancy and infancy (such as reduced welfare dependence, substance abuse, criminal behavior, and child abuse and neglect).[8] The mechanisms through which these beneficial effects occurred will be examined in future reports, with a focus on the alteration of maternal prenatal health and the children's corresponding neuropsychological functioning,[22,23] as well as prenatal stress, given that stress during pregnancy affects the social and neuromotor development of nonhuman primates.[24,25]

The impact of the full program (prenatal and infancy home visitation) on children's use of alcohol and number of sexual partners is important because recent evidence indicates that alcohol use prior to age 15 years multiplies the risk of alcoholism in adulthood[26] and multiple partners increase the risk for sexually transmitted diseases, including human immunodeficiency virus infection.[27,28] The effect of the program on alcohol use is consistent with greater alcohol consumption observed among adult rhesus monkeys who experienced aberrant rearing.[29] These findings must be tempered, however, with an acknowledgment of their limitations.

The first limitation is that most of the positive results were concentrated among children born to women who were unmarried and from low-SES households. Although we hypothesized originally that the effects would be greater for women who experienced higher levels of stress and who had fewer personal resources, we did not fully operationalize the stress and resource variables prior to the beginning of the trial. We chose to use characteristics used for sample recruitment as indicators of long-term stress (e.g., coming from a low-SES household) and having few personal resources (e.g., being unmarried), 2 factors associated with a host of adverse outcomes. However, positive early results from a large urban replication of this study focusing almost exclusively on unmarried, low-income women support our interpretation that the effects observed in the current study are due to the program.[30]

The second limitation is that the arrest and conviction data were based primarily on the children's and parents' reports, which may be subject to treatment-related reporting bias. To validate the children's and parents' reports of undesirable behavior, we compared the rates of school suspensions derived from the school records with the parents' and children's reports of suspensions and found no treatment differences in accuracy. We also regressed the English and mathematics teachers' averaged reports of the adolescents acting out in school on the adolescents' self-reports of their acting out in school separately for the nurse-visited and comparison group children and found no treatment differences in the slopes of these regressions.

Importantly, the pattern of mean differences for treatment groups 1 and 2 vs treatment group 4 for PINS records on the subsample of children who lived in Chemung County for their entire lives corroborated the pattern of the children's reported arrests. The PINS finding increases our confidence that the treatment differences in the adolescents' reported involvement with the criminal justice system are not the result of the nurse-visited children and their parents simply underreporting their actual levels of involvement. The absence of program effect with the official arrest data may be explained by a significant, 9-fold higher rate of official arrest records prior to randomization (0.44 vs 0.05) found for treatment group 4 mothers who were unmarried and of low SES and whose children remained in Chemung County compared with their treatment group 1 and 2 counterparts.

Finally, we note that the adolescents' self-reports of delinquent and antisocial behavior are not completely consistent with the data on reports of arrests and convictions. A survey that used follow-up questions to the assault questions asked in the current study showed that the answers to the questions we used produced responses that frequently were trivial (e.g., 33% of the serious violent responses and 64% of the self-reported minor assaults were too insignificant to lead to arrests).[31] This suggests that the particular questions used in this study regarding delinquent behavior did not adequately assess the severity of delinquency. Thus, the treatment differences found in reports of arrests and convictions are likely to be indications of underlying treatment differences in the severity of antisocial behavior that were not assessed adequately by the set of questions asked about particular antisocial behaviors.

This program prevented only the more serious forms of antisocial behavior leading to arrests and convictions. Other types of prevention programs may be necessary to reduce more normative types of disruptive behavior among young adolescents.[32] In light of the impact of this program on maternal and youth crime and corresponding government expenditures,[8,33] the US Department of Justice is now supporting an effort to make this program available to a larger number of high-crime communities.[34]

REFERENCES

* This research was supported by Senior Research Scientist Award 1-K05-MH01382-01 (Dr. Olds) and grants from the Prevention Research and Behavioral Medicine Branch of the National Institute of Mental Health (R01-MH49381) and the Assistant Secretary for Planning and Evaluation, Department of Health and Human Services (grant 96ASPE278A). Earlier phases of this work were supported by the Bureau of Maternal and Child Health, Department of Health and Human Services, Washington, DC; the Robert Wood Johnson Foundation, Princeton, NJ; the W. T. Grant Foundation, New York, NY; the Ford Foundation, New York; and the Commonwealth Fund, New York.

We thank John Shannon for his support of the program and data gathering through Comprehensive Interdisciplinary Developmental Services, Elmira, NY; Alise Mahr, Darlene Batroney, Karen Hughes, Barbara Lee, Sherry Mandel, and Barbara Ganzel for tracing and interviewing the families; Kathleen Buckwell, Sondra Thomas, and Sharon Holmberg for coding the data; Robert Chamberlin, MD, MPH, and Robert Tatelbaum, MD, for their contributions to earlier phases of this research; the Chemung County Probation Department (John Sutton, director) and the Chemung County Family Court (Marie Brewer, chief clerk) for their assistance with extraction and coding of the criminal justice data; Del Elliott, PhD, Zorika Henderson, Dave Huizinga, and John Reid for their comments on the manuscript; Jackie Roberts, Liz Chilson, Lyn Scazafabo, George McGrady, and Diane Farr for their home visitation work with the families; and the families who participated in the research.

1. Snyder H. *Juvenile Arrests 1996*. Washington, DC: US Dept of Justice; 1997:1–12. Office of Juvenile Justice and Delinquency Prevention, Juvenile Justice Bulletin.

2. Patterson G. R., DeBaryshe B. D., Ramsey E. A. developmental perspective of antisocial behavior. *Am Psychol.* 1989;44:329–334.

3. Moffitt T. E. Adolescence-limited and life-course-persistent antisocial behavior: a developmental taxonomy. *Psychol Rev.* 1993;100:674–701.

4. Moffitt T. E. The neuropsychology of conduct disorder. *Dev. Psychopathol.* 1993;5:135–151.

5. Raine A., Brennan P., Mednick S. A. Birth complications combined with maternal rejection at age 1 year predispose to violent crime at age 18 years. *Arch Gen Psychiatry.* 1994;51:984–988.

6. Olds D., Henderson C., Tatelbaum R., Chamberlin R. Improving the delivery of prenatal care and outcomes of pregnancy: a randomized trial of nurse home visitation. *Pediatrics.* 1986;77:16–28.

7. Olds D., Henderson C., Chamberlin R., Tatelbaum R. Preventing child abuse and neglect: a randomized trial of nurse home visitation. *Pediatrics.* 1986;78:65–78.

8. Olds D., Eckenrode J., Henderson C., et al. Long-term effects of home visitation on maternal life course and child abuse and neglect: 15-year follow-up of a randomized trial. *JAMA.* 1997;278:637–643.

9. Olds D., Henderson C., Tatelbaum R. Intellectual impairment in children of women who smoke cigarettes during pregnancy. *Pediatrics.* 1994;93:221–227.

10. Olds D., Henderson C., Tatelbaum R. Prevention of intellectual impairment in children of women who smoke cigarettes during pregnancy. *Pediatrics.* 1994;93:228–233.

11. Olds D., Pettitt L. M., Robinson J., et al. Reducing risks for antisocial behavior with a program of prenatal and early childhood home visitation. *J. Community Psychol.* 1998;26:65–83.

12. Olds K., Kitzman H., Cole R., Robinson J. Theoretical and empirical foundations of a program of home visitation for pregnant women and parents of young children. *J. Community Psychol.* 1997;25:9–25.

13. Olds D., Korfmacher J. *Journal of Community Psychology Special Issue: Home Visitation I.* 1997; 25.

14. Baker P., Mott F. *NLSY Youth Handbook 1989.* Columbus: Center for Human Resources Research, Ohio State University; 1989.

15. Jessor R., Donovan J., Costa F. *Health Behavior Questionnaire.* Denver: Institute of Behavioral Science, University of Colorado; 1992.

16. Kessler R. The National Comorbidity Survey: preliminary results and future directions. *Int. Rev Psychiatry.* 1994;6:365–376.

17. Achenbach T. M., Edelbrock C. S. Behavioral problems and competencies reported by parents of normal and disturbed children aged 4–16. *Monogr Soc Res Child Dev.* 1981;46. Serial No. 188.

18. Hightower A. D., Spinell A., Lotyczewski B. S. Teacher-Child Rating Scale (T-CRS) guidelines. *Sch Psychol Rev.* 1986.

19. Henderson C. Analysis of covariance in the mixed model: higher level, non-homogeneous, and random regressions. *Biometrics.* 1982;38:623–640.

20. Brooks-Gunn J., Gross R. T., Kraemer H., Spiker D., Shapiro S. Enhancing the cognitive outcomes of low birth weight, premature infants: for whom is the intervention most effective? *Pediatrics.* 1992;89:1209–1215.

21. Higley J., King S. Jr., Hasert M., Champoux M., Suomi S., Linnoila M. Stability of interindividual differences in serotonin function and its relationship to severe aggression and competent social behavior in rhesus macaque females. *Neuropsychopharmacology.* 1996;14:67–76.

22. Olds D. Tobacco exposure and impaired development: a review of the evidence. *Ment Retard Dev Disabilities Res Rev.* 1997;3:257–269.

23. Pennington B., Bennetto L. Main effects or transactions in the neuropsychology of conduct disorder? commentary on "the neuropsychology of conduct disorder." *Dev Psycholpathol.* 1993;5:153–164.

24. Clarke A. S, Soto A., Bergholz T., Schneider M. Maternal Gestational stress alters adaptive and social behavior in adolescent rhesus monkey offspring. *Infant Behav Dev.* 1996;19:453–463.

25. Schneider M. L., Coe C. L. Repeated social stress during pregnancy impairs neuromotor development of the primate infant. *J Dev Behav Pediatr.* 1993;14:81–87.

26. Grant B., Dawson D. Age at onset of alcohol use and its association with *DSM-IV* alcohol abuse and dependence: results from the national Longitudinal Alcohol Epidemiologic Survey. *Natl J Subst Abuse.* 1998;9:103–110.

27. Shafer M. A, Hilton J. F., Ekstrand M., et al. Relationship between drug use and sexual behaviors and the occurrence of sexually transmitted diseases among high-risk male youth. *Sex Transm Dis.* 1993;20:307–313.

28. Joffe G. P., Foxman B., Schmidt A. J., et al. Multiple partners and partner choice as risk factors for sexually transmitted disease among female college students. *Sex Transm. Dis.* 1992;19:22–278.

29. Higley J. D., Hasert M. F., Soumi, S. J., Linnoila M. Nonhuman primate model of alcohol abuse: effects of early experience, personality, and stress on alcohol consumption. *Proc Natl Acad Sci.* 1991;88:7261–7265.

30. Kitzman H., Olds D., Henderson C., et al. Effects of home visitation by nurses on pregnancy outcomes, childhood injuries, and repeated childbearing: a randomized controlled trial. *JAMA.* 1997;278:644–652.

31. Huizinga D. Assessing violent behavior with self reports. In: Milner J. S., ed. *Neuropsychology of Aggression.* Boston, Mass: Kluwer Academic Publishers; 1991.

32. Hawkins J. D., Von Cleve E., Catalano R. F. Reducing early childhood aggression: results of a primary prevention pro-gram. *J Am Acad Child Adolesc Psychiatry.* 1991;30:208–217.

33. Karoly L. A., Greenwood P. W., Everingham S. S., et al. *Investing in Our Children: What We Know and Don't Know About the Costs and Benefits of Early Childhood Interventions.* Santa Monica, Calif: RAND; 1998.

34. Elliott D. S. *Blueprints for Violence Prevention.* Boulder: Center for the Study and Prevention of Violence, Institute of Behavioral Science, University of Colorado at Boulder, 1997.

Index